W9-BIW-371

A LIBRARY OF LITERARY CRITICISM

*A Library*

# MODERN

*Volume I*

## A-F

*Fourth enlarged edition*

*of Literary Criticism*

# AMERICAN LITERATURE

*Compiled and edited by*

**DOROTHY NYREN CURLEY**

*Coordinator of Adult Services*
*Brooklyn Public Library*

**MAURICE KRAMER**

*Assistant Professor of English*
*Brooklyn College, The City University of New York*

**ELAINE FIALKA KRAMER**

*Frederick Ungar Publishing Co., New York*

Copyright © 1960, 1961, 1964, 1969 by Frederick Ungar Publishing Co., Inc.
Printed in the United States of America
Library of Congress Catalog Card No. 76-76599
ISBN 0-8044-3046-2 Set
0-8044-3047-0 Vol. I
0-8044-3048-9 Vol. II
0-8044-3049-7 Vol. III

Second Printing, 1970

# FOREWORD TO THE FOURTH EDITION

The fourth edition of *Modern American Literature* is a major enlargement of Dorothy Nyren's representation of the "critical accomplishment" to twentieth-century American literature. One hundred and fifteen authors have been added to the roll, while more recent excerpts have also been added on two-thirds of the authors in the third edition; none of the excerpts previously included has been omitted. Thus, this new edition continues the endeavor of its predecessors: to indicate critical attitudes—sometimes remarkably stable, sometimes mercurial—toward now close to three hundred American authors of the twentieth century.

The new authors added here vary from a few overlooked elders to some of the younger writers who have very definitely established themselves in the Sixties.* Some minor but mighty playwrights of the early part of the century (Belasco, MacKaye) have been recognized for their places in the not-too-brave history of American drama. Some outstanding essayists, philosophical and social as well as literary (William James, Reinhold Niebuhr), have now been included. The novelists of black humor (Hawkes, Barth), of the pastoral-allegorical-comical-tragical romance, make their appearance here to a very mixed reception. Among the new are several young middle-aged poets (Duncan, Merwin et al.), a few barely read figures out of the Twenties and Thirties whose reputations refuse to disappear (Bourne, Frank, Fuchs), and even some mystery writers who have risen above their generally stereotyped genre (Hammett, Chandler, Macdonald). There are also a few "phenomena"—writers of questionable quality who have been sufficiently a part of the American literary scene to warrant being a part also of the record being tallied here.

For keeping a record is certainly a major function of this book. It is, however, a record with two sides to it. First of all it is a record of reputations. Though an attempt has been made to keep out comments that are merely either blurbs or blasts, the sense of a writer's quality will communicate itself in almost anything that is said about his work, no matter

---

* The elders include Kate Chopin and Harold Frederic, who published in the 1890's, but whose work has been most highly praised in recent years.

how balanced. It is also to the point here to note that the number of selections for each author bears some connection to reputation.

A wide-ranging look at this record of reputation would seem to justify a frequent assertion about American writers, that they fail to develop. So many of these authors make a grand critical entrance, often with a first or second, sometimes a third book, only barely to sustain themselves thereafter or to burn out altogether. Often enough, reputations established by early books wither and then grow strong again as the early books are rediscovered and a later generation decides that the test of time has been passed.

The other side of the record presented in this book is the change in criticism itself. The Fifties and Sixties saw an increase in published criticism, especially of a scholarly nature. We have tried to include representative examples of all types. The narrowing of differences among the various kinds of criticism—from the first book review to elaborate studies —is perhaps the greatest change. The influence of the *New York Review of Books* may be largely responsible for this shift; in any case, one often finds weekly reviews now weighted with scholarship, large critical statements, and even with detailed exegesis. But one continues to look, in all kinds of criticism, for illuminating insights, and the editors have tried to include many of them along with the evaluative comments.

A note on style: Except for the regular italicizing of titles of books, the correction of some obvious typographical errors, and a few grammatical changes requested by the authors themselves, the selections quoted in this work have not been stylistically altered. Accuracy of quotation has been considered a primary good.

In this fourth edition the excerpts have been drawn from criticism published through 1967; the bibliographies, a new addition to the work, have been completed through 1968.

In acknowledging the debts incurred in compiling this material, we wish, first of all, to name Dorothy Nyren Curley, whose imaginative lead we have only had to follow. We wish also to thank, less formally than in the attributions in the text and the acknowledgment pages, the many authors, editors, and publishers who granted permission to reprint these excerpts—with a special word of thanks to those whose cordiality and cooperation made the entire task a little easier. The compiling was done almost entirely at two libraries: the Ingersoll branch of the Brooklyn Public Library and the library of Brooklyn College of the City University of New York; to the Humanities Division of the latter library, and to its chairman, Professor Alex Preminger, we owe a special debt.

M. K.<br>E. F. K.

February, 1969

# FOREWORD TO THE FIRST EDITION

When Charles Wells Moulton completed in 1905 the last of the eight volumes of his *Library of Literary Criticism of English and American Authors,* English literature was undeniably more important than its American counterpart. Quite sensibly he decided to devote most of his useful compendium to commentaries on English authors.

America had already had some important writers: Cooper, Whitman, Poe, Melville, Hawthorne, Emerson and Thoreau, but our great stylists were few in comparison with those of England and even the names of those few were not widely known. It has happened, fortunately, that this is no longer the case. During the past half century American literature has grown greatly in quantity and in importance. Henry James and Mark Twain have become major figures since Moulton edited his serviceable volumes. We have had generations of writers from "Bitter Bierce" and Jack London to the Beatniks on the West Coast, from Dreiser to James Jones and Saul Bellow in the Middle West, from Cabell to Faulkner and Penn Warren in the South, and from the comfortable gentility of Edith Wharton to the uncomfortable acerbity of James Gould Cozzens in the East. It is time indeed that "American Authors" be brought up to date.

Following Moulton's idea (but not in all details his method), the editor has systematically reviewed the critical accompaniment to the major literary performances of the past half century and more, going through the literature of criticism as it appeared in the popular and scholarly journals and in books, and choosing excerpts which reflected the sweep and variety of the literary taste, critical standards, and attitudes of the period. The over-all result is, it is hoped, a fairly definitive critical key to twentieth-century American writing through the 1950's.

One hundred and seventy American authors who wrote or became prominent after 1904 are included in this survey of significant criticism. Most of the authors in this volume may be found in Stanley Kunitz's *Twentieth-Century Authors* and its *First Supplement,* which should be consulted for biographical information.

*A Library of Literary Criticism: Modern American Literature* is intended primarily as a reference tool for school, library, or home, for the use of scholars and students as well as browsers. Each citation is accompanied by full bibliographical information indicating its source. A highly selective list of books by the author being considered is also appended to each group of citations as suggestions for first readings in the author himself. It must be remembered, above all, that a guide of this sort becomes valuable only when used in connection with a careful reading of the books under discussion.

The editor expresses her gratitude to the numerous publishers who made this book possible by granting permission to use quotations from their publications. While it has not always been possible to obtain permission to use desired quotations, cooperation from those owning copyrighted material has been, with few exceptions, generous and helpful.

D. N.

# CONTENTS

# AUTHORS INCLUDED

*Authors added in the fourth edition are marked* (†)

## VOLUME I

Adams, Henry
Adams, Leonie†
Agee, James
Aiken, Conrad
Albee, Edward†
Alfred, William†
Algren, Nelson
Anderson, Maxwell
Anderson, Robert†
Anderson, Sherwood
Auchincloss, Louis
Auden, W. H.
Axelrod, George†
Babbitt, Irving
Baldwin, James
Barnes, Djuna
Barry, Philip
Barth, John†
Behrman, S. N.
Belasco, David†
Bellow, Saul
Benchley, Robert†
Benét, Stephen Vincent
Berryman, John†
Bierce, Ambrose
Bishop, Elizabeth
Bishop, John Peale
Blackmur, Richard
Bodenheim, Maxwell
Bogan, Louise

Bourjaily, Vance†
Bourne, Randolph†
Bowles, Jane†
Bowles, Paul
Boyle, Kay
Brooks, Cleanth
Brooks, Gwendolyn†
Brooks, Van Wyck
Buck, Pearl
Buechner, Frederick†
Burke, Kenneth
Burns, John Horne
Burroughs, William†
Cabell, James Branch
Cahan, Abraham†
Cain, James†
Caldwell, Erskine
Capote, Truman
Cather, Willa
Chandler, Raymond†
Cheever, John†
Chopin, Kate†
Ciardi, John
Clark, Walter Van Tilburg
Condon, Richard†
Connelly, Marc†
Cowley, Malcolm
Cozzens, James Gould
Crane, Hart
Crane, Stephen

**VOLUME II**

**VOLUME III**

Reed, John†
Rexroth, Kenneth
Rice, Elmer
Rich, Adrienne†
Richter, Conrad
Roberts, Elizabeth Madox
Roberts, Kenneth
Robinson, Edwin Arlington
Roethke, Theodore
Rölvaag, Ole†
Roth, Henry†
Roth, Philip
Rourke, Constance†
Rukeyser, Muriel
Runyon, Damon†
Salinger, J. D.
Sandburg, Carl
Santayana, George
Saroyan, William
Sarton, May
Schisgal, Murray†
Schulberg, Budd
Schwartz, Delmore
Scott, Winfield Townley
Sexton, Anne†
Shapiro, Karl
Shaw, Irwin
Sherwood, Robert
Simon, Neil†
Simpson, Louis†
Sinclair, Upton
Snodgrass, W. D.†
Sontag, Susan†
Stafford, Jean
Steele, Wilbur Daniel†
Steffens, Lincoln†
Stegner, Wallace
Stein, Gertrude
Steinbeck, John

Stevens, Wallace
Stickney, Trumbull†
Styron, William
Swados, Harvey†
Tarkington, Booth†
Tate, Allen
Taylor, Peter
Thomas, Augustus†
Thurber, James
Torrence, Ridgely†
Trilling, Lionel
Twain, Mark
Updike, John
Van Doren, Mark
Van Druten, John
Veblen, Thorstein†
Viereck, Peter
Wallant, Edward Lewis†
Warren, Robert Penn
Welty, Eudora
Wescott, Glenway
West, Nathanael
Wharton, Edith
Wheelock, John Hall
Wheelwright, John Brooks
White, E. B.†
Whittemore, Reed†
Wilbur, Richard
Wilder, Thornton
Williams, Tennessee
Williams, William Carlos
Wilson, Edmund
Winters, Yvor
Wolfe, Thomas
Wouk, Herman†
Wright, James†
Wright, Richard
Wylie, Elinor†
Young, Stark†

# PERIODICALS USED

Where no abbreviation is indicated, the magazine references are listed in full.

|        | Accent                                     |
|--------|--------------------------------------------|
| *AHR*  | American Historical Review                 |
| *AJHQ* | American Jewish Historical Quarterly       |
| *AJS*  | American Journal of Sociology              |
| *AL*   | American Literature                        |
| *Am*   | America                                    |
| *AM*   | American Mercury                           |
| *AmQ*  | American Quarterly                         |
| *AnR*  | Antioch Review                             |
|        | Arizona and the West                       |
| *AS*   | American Scholar                           |
| *ASR*  | American Sociological Review               |
| *At*   | Atlantic Monthly                           |
| *Bkm*  | Bookman                                    |
| *BkmL* | Bookman (London)                           |
|        | Book World                                 |
| *BNYPL*| Bulletin of the New York Public Library    |
|        | Carleton Miscellany                        |
|        | Century                                    |
|        | Chimera                                    |
| *CC*   | Christian Century                          |
| *CE*   | College English                            |
| *CF*   | Canadian Forum                             |
|        | Christian Scholar                          |
| *Cmty* | Commentary                                 |
|        | Columbia University Forum                  |
| *Com*  | Commonweal                                 |
| *CR*   | Chicago Review                             |
| *Crit* | Criterion                                  |
|        | **Critic**                                 |

|  | Criticism |
|  | Critique |
| *CS* | Chicago Sun Book Week |
| *CSM* | Christian Science Monitor |
| *CW* | Catholic World |
|  | Denver Quarterly |
|  | Dial |
| *DR* | Dublin Review |
| *DS* | Drama Survey |
| *EJ* | English Journal |
| *ELH* | English Literary History |
|  | Encounter |
|  | English Studies |
| *ER* | Evergreen Review |
| *ETJ* | Educational Theatre Journal |
|  | Forum |
| *Fm* | Freeman |
|  | Griffin |
|  | Georgia Review |
| *Harper* | Harper's Magazine |
| *HdR* | Hudson Review |
| *HR* | Hopkins Review |
|  | Horizon |
| *IJE* | International Journal of Ethics |
|  | Independent |
| *IW* | Independent Woman |
| *JEGP* | Journal of English and Germanic Philology |
| *JF* | Jewish Frontier |
| *JHI* | Journal of the History of Ideas |
| *JP* | Journal of Philosophy |
| *JSS* | Jewish Social Studies |
|  | Judaism |
| *KR* | Kenyon Review |
|  | Library Chronicle |
|  | Life |
| *LJ* | Library Journal |
| *LM* | London Mercury |
| *Lon* | London Magazine |
| *LR* | Literary Review |
| *LtR* | Little Review |
| *MD* | Modern Drama |
| *MFS* | Modern Fiction Studies |
| *MinnR* | Minnesota Review |

| | |
|---|---|
| *MLQ* | Modern Language Quarterly |
| | Midstream |
| | Modern Age |
| *MP* | Modern Philology |
| *MR* | Massachusetts Review |
| *NAR* | North American Review |
| | Nation |
| | National Review |
| *NC* | Nineteenth Century |
| | Nineteenth Century Fiction |
| *NDQ* | North Dakota Quarterly |
| *NEQ* | New England Quarterly |
| *NL* | New Leader |
| *NMQ* | New Mexico Quarterly |
| *NR* | New Republic |
| *NSN* | New Statesman and Nation, later Statesman and Nation |
| *Nwk* | Newsweek |
| *NWW* | New World Writing |
| *NY* | New Yorker |
| *NYEP* | New York Evening Post Book Section |
| *NYHT* | New York Herald Tribune Book Section |
| *NYHTts* | New York Herald Tribune Theater Section |
| *NYR* | New York Review of Books |
| *NYT* | New York Times Book Section |
| *NYTd* | New York Times Daily Newspaper |
| *NYT mag* | New York Times Magazine Section |
| *NYTts* | New York Times Theater Section |
| *OM* | Overland Monthly |
| | Outlook |
| *Per* | Perspectives U. S. A. |
| | Phylon |
| *PMLA* | Publications of the Modern Language Association |
| | Poetry |
| *PR* | Partisan Review |
| *PS* | Pacific Spectator |
| *QJS* | Quarterly Journal of Speech |
| *Ren* | Renascence |
| | Reporter |
| | Salmagundi |
| *SAQ* | South Atlantic Quarterly |
| | Science |
| *Scy* | Scrutiny |
| *SLM* | Southern Literary Messenger |

| | |
|---|---|
| *SoR* | Southern Review |
| | Southern Folklore Quarterly |
| *Spec* | Spectator |
| *SR* | Saturday Review of Literature, later Saturday Review |
| | Survey |
| *SwR* | Sewanee Review |
| *SWR* | Southwest Review |
| *TA* | Theatre Arts |
| *TC* | Twentieth Century |
| *TCL* | Twentieth Century Literature |
| *TDR* | Tulane Drama Review, later The Drama Review |
| | Theatre Magazine |
| | Time |
| | Tri-Quarterly |
| *TSL* | Tennessee Studies in Literature |
| *UKCR* | University of Kansas City Review, later University Review |
| *UR* | University Review |
| *UTQ* | University of Toronto Quarterly |
| *VQR* | Virginia Quarterly Review |
| *WHR* | Western Humanities Review |
| *WLB* | Wilson Library Bulletin |
| | Works |
| *WSCL* | Wisconsin Studies in Contemporary Literature, later Contemporary Literature |
| *YR* | Yale Review |

# ADAMS, HENRY (1838–1918)

The value of the work of Henry Adams is that he was a scholar who saw the difference between knowledge and ignorance, an historian who studied the sequence of cause and effect, and a mystic who entered at times into the world of the "other reality," where there is neither cause and effect, nor object and subject.

Like all mystics it was the "other" reality which he prized most, although—like all intelligent mystics—he also valued highly the world in which we live.

Kirsopp Lake. At. April, 1924. p. 529

This gentleman from the House of Adams is preeminently a modern American scholar. He had a singular capacity for original research and polished presentation. He was both a student of history and a literary artist and in all his work he combined his abilities in the one with his powers in the other. To match his breadth and depth of knowledge he had a keen critical sense and a clear judicial mind. He had creative imagination, a sensitive appreciation of significant form, and a remarkable skill in removing the clutter of details and depicting essentials. He was a master of facts, pursuing his ideas with minute research and solid reasoning. He was a superb maker of phrases, but he sketched with accuracy and precision, coloring his narrative with his own personality and toning his portraits with insight and understanding.

Marian D. Irish. AS. March, 1932. pp.223–4

Henry Adams recapitulated on American soil the romantic tradition of Europe. This tradition included aesthetic pessimism, in which framework he built up a personality-image which he came to enjoy artistically. The image was that of the failure, the heroic failure. He came to enjoy the spectacle doubly: on the stage as an actor, from the wings as an onlooker who revels in the gaping audiences. . . . Adams's failure was only a pen and paper failure. He wrote "a terribly ironic estimate of himself" because it pleased his artistic fancy to do so.

Max I. Baym. AS. Winter, 1945. pp. 87–8

Pessimism was both a pose and a habit of mind with Henry Adams. Only fools and great statesmen were paid to be optimists. Furthermore, as

1

Adams remarked, "no one can afford to pose as an optimist, short of an income of a hundred thousand a year." Adams had about twenty-five thousand and considered himself to be neither a great statesman nor a fool; thus, pessimism was for him the only dignified pose. And dignity was important, as well as required. However, something of his pessimism was genuine because his scientific and metaphysical speculations had convinced him that the cherished assumptions of his culture and tradition were totally wrong, and worse than useless; because by stubbornly defending the old notions of order, unity, the unique value of the individual, freedom of the will, one would only hasten the acceleration towards the inevitable catastrophe of all civilization.

Gerrit H. Roelofs. *ELH*. Sept., 1950. p. 231

It is dangerously easy to overstress the near-tragic quality of the aging scholar, caught as never before in the impingement of beauty but knowing, too, the final ineffectuality of its comfort for one whose mind insisted on discovering monstrosity and chaos on every side. He still was one to relish good food and drink, to enjoy the company of handsome women and vigorous men and stimulate them by questions and banter. He was by no means the bitter, broken prophet that many critics, gullibly misreading his own account, have pronounced him to be. . . . One comprehends Adams most clearly as a man who to the last felt and not quite successfully defied the personal and universal disorder encroaching upon a sensitive dweller in the nineteenth and twentieth centuries. His dilemma was at once individual and typical.

Robert A. Hume. *Runaway Star* (Cornell). 1951.

pp. 35–6

He was very shy of self-revelation. Some of it came out, disguised, in the novels, biographies, and *History*. He could be more naked, for instance in *Esther* than in the first-person books, *Mont-St.-Michel* and *The Education*. *Democracy* is his political ordeal; *Esther,* his own, as well as his wife's religious plight. And where one might least expect to find it, in the heavily documented, nine-volume *History of the United States,* there are passages of lyrical intensity which tell us as much about the subjective Henry Adams as any of (his) letters.

Elizabeth Stevenson. *Nation*. Jan. 26, 1952. p. 87

Adams was not a likeable man; he was an important man. Like the intellectuals who would model themselves on his legend, he cultivated his snobbism too lovingly; he was something of what the Germans call *ein Besserwisser;* and his attitudes always seem a bit disassociated from his individual experience. In his own life he suffered the destructive split between literary and political vocations which has since become so prevalent. . . . But it was greatly to his credit that even as he submitted to this split, he did not approve of it; he knew that for the intellectual, health is possible only through a unity of the two parts, even if a unity in tension.

Irving Howe. *NR*. Sept. 22, 1952. p. 26

The greatness of the mind of Adams himself is in the imaginative reach of the effort to solve the problem of the meaning, the use, or the value of its own energy. The greatness is in the effort itself, in variety of response deliberately made to every possible level of experience. It is in the acceptance, with all piety, of ignorance as the humbled form of knowledge; in the pursuit of divers shapes of knowledge—the scientific, the religious, the political, the social and trivial—to the point where they add to ignorance, when the best response is silence itself. That is the greatness of Adams as a type of mind. As it is a condition of life to die, it is a condition of thought, in the end, to fail. Death is the expense of life and failure is the expense of greatness.

R. P. Blackmur. *The Lion and the Honeycomb*
(Harcourt). 1955. p. 95

To agree that after his wife's death Adams devoted his talent to indicting the universe that had produced her and destroyed her is, of course, to oversimplify. Yet, once the *History* is finished, everything else of import seems to turn upon the theme of conflict between tranquillity and force. . . . This gifted man was in some sense the child of Byron and Voltaire. There was something in him elementary as well as ironical. A hostile critic might plausibly demonstate that, because it was outrageous of the universe to deal with Mr. and Mrs. Henry Adams as the universe had done, the scholar would condemn the universe. The rebelliousness, the self-incrimination, the irony of the mature Byron are paralleled by Adams, the principal difference being that in the American these qualities were held in restraint as judgments, not hurled at the target as weapons.

Howard Mumford Jones. *Nation*. Dec. 24, 1955.
pp. 558–9

Henry Adams had a rich and sensitive mind and was, behind his misanthropic exterior, a deeply humane individual. He had been formed rather rigidly in the heavy heritage of his Presidential ancestry and of New England dogma; and by the most subtle and delicate process he achieved, within his sensibility, a system of feathery balances, so that the discharge of his emotions might be propped by flying buttresses and filtered through his stained-glass windows. His mind was like the cathedrals he came to study; it was no accident that he turned to them.

Leon Edel. *SR*. Dec. 10, 1955. p. 15

Yet Adams's quest had led beyond the limits of either intellectual curiosity or the hope of fame (for he could satisfy neither) to bring him at last to that vantage point where the world of past and present took on that comprehensible form which gave him emotional and intellectual peace. If the journey from nineteenth-century Boston to twelfth-century Chartres had any meaning, it was expressed in the last subjective works, in the acceptance of the relativity of all historical interpretation, the tentativeness of all understanding. It was a conclusion, he must have known, no more valid than any other, a point of view for the time being useful and necessary. It made sense of what for Henry Adams was otherwise chaos. It explained, if it did not justify. One might wonder whether a study of history could ever do more than that.

(K)                    John C. Cairns. *SAQ*. Spring, 1958. pp. 192–3

. . . he stands alone among all the thinkers of his generation, in having made a timely effort to understand the forces of science, technology, and politics that have brought us to the verge of a gigantic and irretrievable disaster. His eminence as a historian only emphasizes his loneliness as a social diagnostician. Adams' contemporaries, in the words of John Bigelow in 1899, regarded Adams as either "an inspired prophet or crazy," but they were no more disposed to heed his inspiration than to believe that his madness would, fifty years later, become the very criterion of sanity.

(K)                    Lewis Mumford. *VQR*. Spring, 1962. p. 197

For [Adams], value or meaning is only conceivable as originating in final, impersonal ends. He cannot think of life as having meaning apart from a goal that is outside of and larger than the individual. This is the most fundamental and omnipresent manifestation of his Puritanism; it is a mental habit shaped by an obsessive need of his conscience to relate every event, every moral act, and every individual self to some ultimate and all-embracing unity. . . . [I]n reaching the end of his quest, he arrived at a colossal irony. For what Adams discovered was that life had no meaning; . . . Always pressing for certainty, for nothing less than an absolute certainty, he found it in universal death, an event no less meaningless than certain.

(K)          George Hochfield. *Henry Adams: An Introduction and Interpretation* (Barnes and Noble). 1962. pp. 32, 139

He did aim very high. If he could not be a universal man, he did never-theless deal in universals. Historians before his time often spoke of "universal" history. What it might amount to none could precisely ex-plain. Even so, the idea persisted as a grand if indistinct challenge. Adams attempted to combine this earlier search for the philosopher's stone with the newer passion for "scientific" history, so as to arrive at universal scientific history. The product would have to be on the scale of Marx or Comte, Darwin or Spencer, but still more intellectually exact than these. Adams could not have labored so long and hard if he had not in his inmost being clung to the vision of winning immortality as one of the great system-builders of his time. . . . The compromise of his later days, when he devised *Mont St. Michel* and the *Education* as private entertainments, was in literary terms brilliantly right. Here, as in his private correspondence, he hit upon just the appropriate form in which to disport the *persona* of one whom friends dubbed the Angelic Porcupine. By his standards it was a minuscule achievement; yet it has been the principal guarantor of im-mortality for Henry Adams.

(K)                                        Marcus Cunliffe. *Cmty.* June, 1965. p. 70

Only temperamentally and, in the narrow sense, biographically, did Adams seek out those avenues of silence where he could imagine the medieval world unified. But he knew more and better than this. He was not going to deny either the enthusiasm with which he and his friends had begun life in a "race for power" or the fact that they had miserably lost. . . . He knew he had had his historical neck broken. He grasped multiplicity not just as a term defining the inevitable movement of gold-bug capitalism to socialism and communism, not just as something scientists were beginning to define, not just as an antonym to twelfth century unity brought about by society's obedience to the laws of acceleration, not just as the chaos that would transform democracy into a form of totalitarianism, but as a master that simultaneously rendered impossible his personal scene of education and forced upon him definitions of education broader than himself or the teachings of his heritage. . . . The accelerated speed of forces has guaran-teed that only ideas of education as subtle and flexible as Adams' can survive for as long as two generations; the problem now is not, as it once might have been, one of choosing the pot in which to be melted, but of learning how to swim in the big pot that is the only one large enough to contain all the forces at work.

(K)                                        Roger Sale. *HdR*. Autumn, 1965. pp. 430–2

He wanted an honest American polity, but, more or less despairing of that, he wanted at any event to know the 'behind the scenes' mechanism of Federal polity—of which he presents a bitter picture in his novel,

*Democracy.* He was never content with slogans, pious commonplaces, unsupported and unexamined generalizations. If he spent seven years 'teaching "history" ' and wrote a nine-volume history of two early nineteenth-century American administrations, he wanted, with equal accuracy and relentlessness, to know his own time. But that did not content him. 'History' is a loose concept; but, if it is to be other, one must seek to make himself a philosopher of history. What, precisely, do you mean by 'history'?

I see the intellectual conscience of Adams as beginning, where it should begin, with one's private history—with the Adams family and Quincy and Boston and New England, then moving on and outward to the ever-larger questions—which are, indeed, really involved even when one deals with the seemingly nearest and most particular concerns. The dialectic relation between the smallest 'fact' and the most grandiose generalization can never be overcome.

(K)                          Austin Warren. *The New England Conscience*
(Michigan). 1966. p. 180

## Mont-Saint-Michel and Chartres

Scenery, psychology, history, literature, poetry, art—all these are materials for the story he relates. But the controlling purpose of the narrative is to show, in its own form as in its subject, how vast a world can be found by the senses and how great a work the intellect may do when it serves the highest vision of the imagination and defies, knowingly, the terrors of fact which always beset that vision. Because the pilgrim-artist has discovered the realm of tragedy, the tourist-historian of *Mont-Saint-Michel and Chartres* works in a realm beyond that which can be marked out by any particular theory of history. The naïvete of the Romanesque, the refinement of the Transition, the scientific modernity of the Gothic all had their appeal to him because he saw them as phases of life which he had experienced in his role of human being as well as in his capacity as scholar. His aspiration expressed itself in the very shape of his composition, but the anguish of his doubt was also there, almost buried out of sight, in the continual presence of time that foreshadowed the end of love.

J. C. Levenson. *The Mind and Art of Henry Adams*
(Houghton). 1957. p. 288

. . . in the New Jerusalem, faintly envisaged within the pages of the *Chartres,* rational science would yield the final authority to the mystical intuitions of vital instinct. All the ransacking of the literature of science was a prodigious effort to justify this thesis. From the side of feeling, instinct, art, romantic aspiration, Adams unequivocably leagued himself with the counter-revolution against materialistic science. In the *Chartres* he took his stand with Nietzsche and their fellow instinctualists for the claims of Dionysiac man.

(K)                    Ernest Samuels. *Henry Adams: The Major Phase* (Harvard). 1964. p. 305

## The Education of Henry Adams

*The Education of Henry Adams,* conceived as a study of the philosophy of history, turns out in fact to be an *apologia pro vita sua,* one of the most self-centered and self-revealing books in the language.

The revelation is not indeed of the direct sort that springs from frank and insouciant spontaneity. Since the revelation was not intended, the process is tortuous in the extreme. It is a revelation that comes by the way, made manifest in the effort to conceal it, overlaid by all sorts of cryptic sentences and self-deprecatory phrases, half hidden by the protective coloring taken on by a sensitive mind commonly employing paradox and delighting in perverse and teasing mystification. . . . The *Education* is in fact the record, tragic and pathetic underneath its genial irony, of the defeat of fine aspirations and laudable ambitions. It is the story of a life which the man himself, in his old age, looked back upon as a broken arch.

Carl Becker. *AHR*. April, 1919. pp. 4245–6

In a manner he was a microcosm of American history, for what of history his family had not actually made, he had written or had watched. America knew him not, but he had known America; and his autobiography stands in a class with that of Benjamin Franklin. He described it as "the education of Henry Adams," a process he seems to have abandoned in despair; but the reading of the book will give an American a European education, and a European an American one.

Shane Leslie. *DR*. June, 1919. p. 218

Henry Adams, very early, became too pessimistic and cynical to go on being a participant. He chose, instead, a place on the sidelines, and from there set about recording the minutes of all the unsavory transactions of America's public life. The picture of such proceedings which Adams drew, or at least suggested, in the *Education* is a final one. For not only were its revelations damning, but its sources were unimpeachable. It was the indictment of a supremely placed worldling who had listened at the most private keyholes, who had been told—or allowed to guess—the secrets of those who worked behind the scenes. Scarcely anyone else who did so little knew so much. Adams's indictment stands: the great documentary merit of the *Education* is its demonstration of what nineteenth-century America had become, and by what process, and on what terms.

Louis Kronenberger. NR. March 15, 1939. p. 156

Read as a novel of spiritual quest, an initiation romance of Adams's alter ego, the *Education* exhibits a structure of extraordinary complexity, moving simultaneously on many levels of meaning. The "Henry Adams" of the narrative is as protean as Whitman's "I" and contains its own multitudes. . . . The "air of reality" with which Adams invested the tragic hero of his autobiographical-philosophical romance is the product of a masterfully sustained illusion. Not that the author really undervalued his manikin; no theme is more often reiterated than that if he was wrong his fellows were even more mistaken. . . . Within his exacting inner world his pose of ignorance was no affectation, but in the world of his miserable fellow insects it was little more than the ironic condescension of the resolute schoolmaster setting traps for the complacent.

(K)    Ernest Samuels. *Henry Adams: The Major Phase*
(Harvard). 1964. pp. 353, 359

See *The Henry Adams Reader;* also *The Education of Henry Adams* (autobiography) and *Mont-Saint-Michel and Chartres* (long essay).

## ADAMS, LÉONIE (1899–    )

Hers is an accent which is as sensitive as it is strange, a register that seems to tremble with certain Elizabethan echoes but which vibrates with a lyric passion that proceeds from no other century but our own. Miss Adams is, as even the simplest of her poems reveals, a metaphysical poet; her most candidly declared descriptions blossom suddenly in an unearthly and intensified air. . . . One waits, with something greater than curiosity, for the successor to *Those Not Elect*. Meanwhile, it is almost enough to say that even where Miss Adams is least successful, she fails on a high plane and that, among the "emerging" lyricists none lead us to expect—and demand—more.

Louis Untermeyer. NR. Nov. 25, 1925. p. 23

Leonie Adams takes us palpably into a world of her own. . . . All the poems in her book have the stillness, the faint lighting, the introspection and retrospection of an awakening at dawn when our labor is yet a dream and our dream has the burthen of labor. . . . But perhaps *High Falcon* is lacking in a quality that would fill up the measure of our admiration for a fine book of poetry. That quality is fulness. The moods that the poems come out of are real and poignant, but again and again we wish they had been given a fuller body. Too often, the poet gives us the trees stripped bare. We want her sometimes to give us the tree with its leaves and fruits and a bird singing in the leaves. . . .

These poems do not clamorously tell us an emotional history; they are in undertones; they are for those who prefer cold airs and bare lands to noontide brilliancy and crowds and colors. They are not poems that can be taken in by a quick perusal; the reading of them must be accompanied by a certain meditation. They are poems of tragic life.

Padraic Colum. *NR*. Dec. 18, 1929. p. 113

*Those Not Elect,* 1925, is an unusual first volume, though it owes a bit of its inspiration to classic metaphysicians. The Brooklyn mystic is a comparatively difficult poet by virtue of her devotion to the reflections of the mind over matter. Her exquisite psyche, aware of the inconsequence of man in eternity, ventures among problems abstruse to the average mind; but she molds her thought into concrete images. She rarely relaxes the high tension of her inquiry; there are no banal, and few colloquial lines along the way.

Alfred Kreymborg. *Our Singing Strength* (Coward-McCann). 1929. p. 554

Her observations are on the whole free from remote astronomical and supernatural references, adhering instead to the city, the countryside of farms, the intimate landscape with many of its conventional properties retained, or of the pages of books. . . .

Natural sympathy has given Miss Adams' observations a rare opulence. She has explored the details of rural landscape and weather almost to the point of specialty. . . . The world is static, as the metaphysical observer requires it to be. In no poem may be found the impulsive capture of impression (together with the accompanying swell in phrase). . . . Miss Adams' virtue is of another order. She displays the persistent curiosity which pushes an analysis forward until it has achieved a perfect distillation of the essence of a perception. This is a clue to her spiritual bravery. It may be delayed by physical reticence, but it attains to freedom in the end.

Morton Dauwen Zabel. *Poetry*. Feb., 1930. pp. 334–6

. . . certainly, Leonie Adams' re-creation of her world had a closer kinship to the revivals of a Gothic imagination in the poetry of the early and late nineteenth century than it had to metaphysical poetry. . . . The frequent use of the word "sweet," the "so sweet pain," and the adjective "cold," even the sound of her "airy shell" spoke of her mingled debt to and careful, attentive readings in the poetry of [Walter] de la Mare and Gerard Manley Hopkins.

Horace Gregory and Marya Zaturenska. *A History of American Poetry* (Harcourt). 1946. pp. 297–8

Miss Adams's poetry is a difficult labor. Intensely compact, intensely intellectualized, and rigorously ascetic, it comes true, but it does not come easy. The matter, as she writes in "Sundown," is sanctified, "dipped in a gold stain." It seems doubtful that there can be a wide audience for Miss Adams's gold stain, but that there will always be a group of discerning and enthusiastic readers seems certain.

John Ciardi. *Nation.* May 22, 1954. p. 445

The world of Leonie Adams is one of forms and pure relationships. Her gaze . . . is never intercepted by dreams, never blurred by mistiness. It is clairvoyant. She sees the formal rigor of all the things she looks at. And the emotion which these things generate, no matter how subtle or delicate it is, finds the exact word with which to express itself. Her poems . . . testify to a very real world of nature, and at the same time to a willful abstraction which isolates all the objects considered. . . . She is a watcher at the extreme edge of love and gentleness. . . . But she should be called the poet who has undertaken a metaphysical reintegration in a century when many poets, the surrealists especially, have been engaged in just the opposite process, that of disintegrating the cosmos.

Wallace Fowlie. *Com.* Nov. 26, 1954. pp. 224–6

The present volume [*Poems: A Selection*] opens with 24 poems written since [1929], continues by reprinting nearly the whole of *High Falcon* (37 poems), and concludes by selecting 24 poems out of nearly 40 in her first volume, *Those Not Elect* (1925). The proportion is right: *High Falcon* shows her work consistently at its best, as in the famous "Country Summer"; though a few of her later poems, chiefly the shorter ones, display the same mysterious evocation of moods from piled-up images of green, sun, wind, and light. . . . Some of the longer pieces in the first section seem to suffer from incoherence and turgidity: they are too "poetic," too full of terms like "else-wending," "rime-bedabbled," "empery," "en-duskings," and "ambient."

Louis Martz. *YR.* Winter, 1955. p. 305

See *Those Not Elect, High Falcon and Other Poems, Poems: A Selection*

# AGEE, JAMES (1909–1955)

Mr. Agee's delight has been in literature. He has no simple and direct view of a real scene, no sensuous world of experience save books. . . . Mr. Agee is, I take it, Anglo-Catholic, scholarly, classical in his desire to be in the stream of literary tradition. . . . There is little perception in his work except for words and their values. Nevertheless his music, his exquisite choice of phrase and word, will gain him recognition.

Eda Lou Walton. NLHT. Dec. 9, 1934. p. 19

Fortunately for the general reader, Mr. Agee is not only a poet but a corking good journalist when he needs to be. . . . With the combined sensitive perception of a poet, the exact, almost microscopic recording of a scientist, and the generic sharpness of observation making a good reporter, Agee shows us places and things, camera-eye plain. . . . Mr. Agee's main literary weaknesses (as well as his virtues) stem mostly from his influence by and allegiance to such writers as Joyce, Kafka and Céline.

Ruth Lechlitner. NYHT. Aug. 24, 1941. p. 10

Mr. Agee does a good deal to antagonize the reader. There are too many tongues, too many attitudes, too many awarenesses on the subjective side (perhaps defenses would be more precise); even the sincerity is too much, is too prostrate. And yet, visible through all this, are some unmistakable virtues: Mr. Agee, at times, writes brilliantly . . . ; he is extraordinarily sensitive and aware and, above all, concerned with that deeper honesty that assembles before itself all those minute rationalizations and nuances of feeling that are always a kind of havoc inside ourselves.

Harvey Breit. NR. Sept. 15, 1941. p. 348

James Agee was born in the South and retains the pride and piety and love of language of the Southern writer. . . . Genius he surely had; the trouble perhaps lay in his trying to read that genius into things not of his own making. In a vague way his instinct resembled that of Proust, whose genius was of a kind that could only portray genius, nothing but genius, whether in painters, duchesses, or elevator boys. Yet where Proust actually recreated his powers, Agee was content to delegate his.

F. W. Dupee. Nation. April 28, 1951. p. 400

James Agee . . . was a writer who gave all of himself . . . to every medium that he worked in—poetry, fiction, reportage, criticism, movies, television. He was not only one of the most gifted writers in the United States, but such a natural as a writer that he found a creative opportunity in every place where drearier people pitied themselves for pot-boiling. . . . Agee was a writer who actually did better in popular and journalistic media—where certain objective technical requirements gave him a chance to create something out of his immense tenderness and his high sense of comedy than when he let himself go in purely speculative lyricism. He was a natural literary craftsman, not a literary intellectual, and it was only *avant-garde* associations that ever misled him. His most beautiful poems—like the title poem of his first book, *Permit Me Voyage*—are those which are most traditional in form.

Alfred Kazin. *NYT*. Nov. 17, 1957. p. 5

Agee was a very gifted and versatile writer; his best-known work is *Let Us Now Praise Famous Men,* an account of sharecroppers in the depression, with photographs by Walker Evans. He wrote for motion pictures and was the finest critic of films this country has produced. . . . The most remarkable thing about Agee's new book—*A Death in the Family*—is that it is exactly the kind of novel that a great many people have tried to write and have not been able to bring off, at least not the way Agee does. The subject is extremely simple: a man dies. There is no plot or story, just an account of the reactions of his relatives and one friend. But the writing is brilliant, because it manages to be so sensitive to every nuance of emotion without ever going soft.

Paul Pickrel. *Harper*. Dec., 1957. p. 88

The posthumously published *A Death in the Family* is Agee's final item of his career in letters, a novel on which he had been at work for eight years. It does not give him any new importance as an American writer, but it does bring to a delicate and satisfactory flowering his very great ability to create the qualities and nuances of private feeling. . . . There are moments of grief and loss in everyone's life which one cannot live with, but can only recover from. And they are, oddly, the moments when one recognizes one's feelings to have been most alive. The success of *A Death in the Family* is that it brings to the surface of the reader's consciousness these forgotten, rejected moments—his own tender, unusable anguish.

David L. Stevenson. *Nation*. Dec. 14, 1957. pp. 460–1

The late James Agee was a writer at the opposite end of the literary spectrum to James Jones. He had a poet's sensitivity to and mastery of language; a depth of awareness which rescued ordinary happenings from banality and drew out of them their universal significance; the capacity to be tender without being mawkish, to celebrate life without sententiousness.

Charles Rolo. *At.* Jan., 1958. p. 79

The sternest criticism that can be made of these collected articles [*Agee on Film*] is that, from them, emerges not so much a critical intelligence or a Promethean appreciator of an art as a lovable and admirable man. Sometimes his lines soar; sometimes they merely gush. Sometimes his rhapsodic stabs penetrate to the heart; sometimes they flounder. He is given to meaningless distinctions. . . . But he had what is missing from most criticism today—of films and all arts: fierce intensity. The bitter image he leaves is not of a facile, corrosive cynic but of a blazing pessimist.

(K)                        Stanley Kauffmann. *NR.* Dec. 1, 1958. p. 19

Throughout [*Agee on Film*], in which the best criticism by the late James Agee has been collected, there runs the assumption that the film is an art as well as a business—without, fortunately, any of the coterie cuteness about "art cinema." This assumption is apparent in the casual, unselfconscious way he uses the word "poem" to describe a film in which realism is lifted beyond itself into the aesthetic, in his use of other arts—music most often—in comparing effects, not means, and in his persistent discussion of superior films in terms of content *and* form, avoiding the ordinary preoccupation with content alone. . . . His descriptions of the photographic texture of films and his recognition of the ways the textures were used or misused are easily the most perceptive accounts of pure "seeing" that film criticism offers. . . . On the whole, *Agee on Film* is a long, literate, loving collection of one intelligent, sharp-eyed critic's very personal comments; it is also America's most important contribution to film criticism.

(K)                        Gerald Weales. *Reporter.* Dec. 25, 1958. pp. 38–9

When he finally quit *Time* he wrote one first-rate novella, *The Morning Watch,* and left one unfinished full-length novel, *A Death in the Family,* that for all its excellences must be described as pathetic rather than tragic. It has been over-praised, primarily, it seems, because those who give prizes felt that Jim ought to have some of the trappings of greatness he had wanted so badly. He wrote almost no poetry after that first promising volume. The "really great writer" never appeared. Agee had feared as much right from the beginning. . . . The real waste in the life of James Agee is not that he never became "a really great writer" but that this foolish fantasy kept both Agee and his friends from accepting and being comfortable with the minor but extremely valuable writer he certainly was. . . .

And in one field he was beyond all rivalry. He craved superlatives, so let us give them to him: he was the best film critic there ever was. . . . Agee wrote with a wit that never became smart-alecky and a sophistication that never corrupted his profound common sense.

(K)                              Robert Bingham. *Reporter*. Oct. 25, 1962. pp. 56–7

[*A Death in the Family*] shows that Agee had the technical, intellectual, and moral equipment to do major writing. By "moral," which has a terribly old-fashioned ring, I mean that he believed in and—what is rarer—was interested in good and evil. Lots of writers are fascinated by evil and write copiously about it, but they are bored by virtue; this not only limits their scope but also prevents them from giving a satisfactory account of evil. In the novel, Jay Follett is a good husband and father, Mary is a good wife and mother, and their goodness is expressed in concrete actions. . . . The theme is the confrontation of love, that is carried to its highest possible reach, and death, as the negation of life and yet a necessary part of it. Only a major writer could rise to such a theme.

(K)                              Dwight Macdonald. *Encounter*. Dec., 1962. p. 75

Agee in the rootlessness and disorder of Northern urban life sought always for order, definition, discipline, but he found there no firm tradition, no community of writers or intellectuals with whom he could ally himself. Though his career was lived during the Depression and World War II and the immediate postwar years, a time of strident political movements and intense ideological argument, he refused to assume an ideological "position." . . .

To all of his writing, whether journalism, movie scripts, or fiction, he brought the same sort of moral earnestness and what one critic has called "an almost religious sense of commitment to the truth." These qualities, it is clear enough, were stimulated and nurtured at that small church school in rural Tennessee and by the wise moral and spiritual guidance of a dedicated Episcopal priest, "my oldest and dearest friend," as Agee calls him in his letters. It is the moral and religious aspect of the Southern story that forever haunted Agee, that he was forever telling, no matter what the subject.

(K)                              Nash K. Burger. *SAQ*. Winter, 1964. pp. 36–7

See *Permit Me Voyage* (poetry), *Let Us Now Praise Famous Men* (documentary), *The Morning Watch* and *A Death in the Family* (novels), and *Agee on Film* (criticism).

# AIKEN, CONRAD (1889–    )

He was master of a smooth limpid flow of verse narrative from the beginning. He did not have to learn and unlearn his technique. It was an authentic gift. Such a poet is rare enough even in England, still rarer in America. . . . Now it seems to me that, apart from his incontestable gifts as a prosodist and word-controller, Conrad Aiken's mind has up to the present worked on somewhat too narrow a basis. His poems, in short, are variations of but one idea—the idea of sexual disillusionment.

John Gould Fletcher. Dial. March 28, 1918. pp 291–2

Apparently he believes in poetry as a craft, a sport, a profession—like boxing or magic—which must be thoroughly studied before it can be improved. He examines other poets accordingly, not to imitate them, but to learn their tricks. He never echoes. Sometimes he uses the devices of other poets as a vehicle for his own expression, but in any case he mingles them with devices of his own discovery so that he does not merely live in a tradition; he aids with his proper hands in building it.

Malcom Cowley. Dial. Nov., 1922. p. 564

He has gone as far as possible in the direction of spiritual disorder, without plunging into madness. He has made the case for sensitive living today as bad as possible. His disillusion is fearful and complete, his melancholy incurable. He always manages to disclose the worst side of things, to use his knowledge to increase confusion. And yet this later poetry of Aiken's is so honest, extravagant and inspired, that it is actually invigorating. It is so much richer than pale moderation. It carries us triumphantly to the metaphysical bottom. Now we can say that the bitterest songs have been sung.

Houston Peterson. The Melody of Chaos<br>(Longmans). 1931. p. 280

His has been a stubborn and, in many ways, heroic journey inward, following the Freudian stream. The political and social forces of our time have failed to touch him at his creative centers, though I do not doubt his intellectual awareness of them. What needs to be kept in mind is that the seemingly inexhaustible fertility of his imagination would seem to indicate that the course he has chosen may be, for him, the proper course. . . . His vision is of the shadows in the cave, and the cave itself impalpable as fog, of the swirling of phantoms, the dance of atoms, the blind gusts of desire. . . . What holds the dissolving cloudrack together is memory, the persistence of mind.

Stanley J. Kunitz. Poetry. May, 1937. pp. 103–4

Conrad Aiken's early association with the Imagists obscures rather than clarifies the basic movement of his spirit. He was never in any real sense an Imagist, although certain early poems have a harsh reality that made them seem fresh and novel. But he turned quickly away from such external realism to a solitary devotion to the creation of poetry that should come as close as possible to the art of music. To this end, he cultivated the flowing repetitious movement of symphonic music, the emphases on emotion and feeling at the expense of thought, and the substitution of emotional coherence for the logical coherence conventional in poetry.

Fred B. Millett. *Contemporary American Authors* (Harcourt). 1940. p. 144

Probably no poet has been more concerned with music than Conrad Aiken, or has used it more fruitfully. The interest is visible even in the titles of his poems, where we find nocturnes, tone-poems, variations, dissonants, and symphonies. . . . The formal arrangement of a good deal of his poetry is based on musical principles rather than on the more widely accepted poetic ones. His symbols are developed and combined in ways analogous to the composer's handling of themes. He has given us, here and there, enough information about the theoretical basis of his work to make it clear that the musical analogues are deliberately and skilfully cultivated. And, finally, this poetry based on music is alive with musical references which reinforce both the implications of its structure and a philosophy in which music is that epitome of the individual and the universe which it was to Schopenhauer.

Calvin S. Brown. *Music and Literature* (Georgia). 1948. p. 195

The voice of Mr. Aiken—in his prose as in his poetry—has never been a loud one. His work is melodically beguiling rather than demandingly active. Quietly it reveals to us hidden facets of our behavior, recalls old and lost desires. The range is perhaps too narrow, the characters have too cultivated a sensibility, the disillusionment is too complete, the defeat is too Calvinistically inevitable. Gehenna is the recurrent symbol, *Feldeinsamkeit* the persistent mood. But within his range Mr. Aiken works with precision and persuasiveness.

E. J. Fitzgerald. *SR*. Sept. 16, 1950. p. 16

As long ago as the First World War, Conrad Aiken was writing of the poet as being "a curious blending of the psychoanalyst and patient." In novels, short stories, and a prolific poetry, all Aiken's work has exemplified the doctrine. He very early grafted upon traditional romanticism the golden bough of Freud. And somehow the undeviating process

has made him one of the most distinguished unassessed writers of our era
—perhaps the most distinguished.

Winfield Townley Scott. SR. Oct. 11, 1952. p. 26

Where other modern poets take the modern image of the cosmos as, at
most, a point of departure, or a background irrelevant to human concerns
and values, in Aiken's work it is always present as an inevitable awareness, as a kind of cold night which surrounds all things, like the sky itself.
. . . But no matter how great the darkness, one cannot live by darkness.
One must confront the darkness of existence—the silence of the stars,
the depths of the atom, the gulf between each conscious being with all the
attitudes which the imagination makes possible. This is the essential center
of Aiken's poetry.

Delmore Schwartz. NR. Nov. 2, 1953. pp. 24–5

Aiken has sought his style in many directions, his experiments ranging
from the diffuse allusiveness of Senlin to the archaic slam-bang theatrics
of John Deth. Through every change, however, his devotion has been to
the idea of the symphonic tone-poem, to a dissolving watery music, to a
rain-swept and fog-abstracted landscape of the psyche. He has sought, in
his own phrase, an "absolute poetry."

The weakness of that poetry seems to have centered from the beginning
in its excess of melody and in the indefinitiveness of tone. . . . There is not
much of the "real world"—whatever that is—in Aiken, but certainly one
is persuaded that he had found music for everything that dreams.

John Ciardi. Nation. Nov. 14, 1953. p. 410

He is in the tradition of Romantic poets from Shelley to Swinburne but
with the manners and sensibility of one who knows London's twentieth-
century Bloomsbury as well as Boston Common. If one thinks or speaks
of such a thing as "poetic talent," there is more of that almost inde-
finable quality in a half dozen pages of Mr. Aiken's book (Collected
Poems) than can be unearthed in whole volumes written by hundreds of
his younger contemporaries. . . . As poet Mr. Aiken's gifts are rich and
obvious, but the flaw among his gifts is not a superficial one. His deep
lapses into flabby diction indicate that somewhere below the surface of
his poems a flabby moral attitude exists.

Horace Gregory. NYT. Dec. 20, 1953. p. 5

How does the bard sing? In the easiest external forms of any modern poet
of stature. He sings by nature and training out of the general body of
poetry in English. He writes from the cumulus of cliché in the language,
always, for him, freshly felt, as if the existing language were the only

reality outside himself there were. There is hardly ever in his work the stinging twist of new idiom, and the sometimes high polish of his phrasing comes only from the pressure and friction of his mind upon his metres. . . . Aiken depends on the force of his own mind and the force of metrical form to refresh his language. The cumulus upon which he really works is the cumulus of repetition, modulation by arrangement, pattern, and overtone. He writes as if the words were spoken to let the mind under the words sing. He writes as if it were the song of the mind that puts meaning in the words.

R. P. Blackmur. *At.* Dec., 1953. p. 82

Whatever stature the work of Conrad Aiken may ultimately assume in the long run of criticism, we can affirm now, that he is one of the supreme technicians of modern English poetry. There are few writers, either in prose or in verse, who can challenge his mastery of language, who give us anything comparable to his assurance in controlling the most powerful and varied and nervous resources of expression. His writing has the inevitability of the highest art; it is, rhetorically, definitive.

Dudley Fitts. *NR.* Dec. 26, 1955. p. 19

Aiken is a kind of Midas: everything he touches turns to verse. Reading his poems is like listening to Delius—one is experiencing an unending undifferentiating wash of fairly beautiful sounds—or like watching a fairly boring, because almost entirely predictable kaleidoscope; a kaleidoscope all of whose transmutations are veiled, misty, watered-down. These are the metamorphoses of a world where everything *blurs* into everything else, where the easy, automatic, lyric, elegiac, nostalgic tone of the verse turns everything into itself, as the diffused, Salon photography of the first part of this century turned everything into Salon photographs.

Randall Jarrell. *YR.* Spring, 1956. pp. 479–80

An alternation between dramatic and lyrical themes and styles is manifest from the very beginning of his career. We may define his two modes of investigation in this way: In the dramatic, the ego of the poet as poet explores itself by seeing what kind of characters it can create. In the lyric, this ego confronts and explores itself directly. . . . I take it that there is a definable tradition in American poetry—dominant in the nineteenth, but continuing into the twentieth century—in which the poet is concerned with exploring and defining himself as poet. To this tradition Aiken belongs; in some senses, it culminates in his work.

(K)                    Jay Martin. *Conrad Aiken: A Life of His Art*
(Princeton). 1962. p. 14

All the same, I think, once you have the *feel* of Aiken, his gamut becomes peculiarly consistent. He has always been like the slightly neurasthenic talker who needs a wall at his back, the room carefully arranged, the fire just so, and can then begin to give his all, ranging over everything from minutiae to vast abstractions, from "I, who drink Vermouth" to "I who rode the air." . . . This is not to say—as many have done—that Aiken has not developed; he has; but he has done it by ebbing and flowing, by coming back to the same shore with the same footprint. He has been coming and going for so long that he has become something of the unspectacular letter carrier, regularly bringing the emotional mail in. Too regular to be much noticed.

(K)                                        Paul West. *KR*. Winter, 1963. p. 189

Conrad Aiken has always had the nebulous quality of the admitted, congratulated poet who has never written Poems; that is, the poems do not *stick,* as poems; a general impression of excellence remains, of competence and skill. Lines come out and fix themselves, but can you fasten upon a poem of his, put it in your mind, and keep it there? It all flows away, beyond the margins; it ebbs, it is lost there. You look back again in the memory, and you have nothing left. . . .

There has always been about Aiken more of the literary figure, more of the distinguished man of letters of brilliant intellect, than of the poet. He is wordy and diffuse; the words and ideas spill on and on: . . . There is no drama, no story: the endless buzz, buzz, buzz of an Aiken poem. Yet suddenly we come up against the brilliance of an image so sharp, that we fall back breathless from contact with it; so fine, so enormous a mind, so dynamic and bitter an *intelligence:* . . .

(K)                                  Joseph Bennett. *HdR*. Winter, 1963–4. p. 630

### Fiction

A neurologist tells us that, given the present rate of increase in nervous diseases, the civilized world will be insane in a couple of centuries. Mr. Aiken's work is a prophecy of that grim failure. His detachment, his underemphasis, his humor are in a way deceptive, and conceal from us the fact that many of his characters, even those who are so like ourselves that we exclaim, "There but for the grace of God go I," are on, or beyond, the verge. There is no heaviness or melodrama in their tragedy; they may even amuse us. But they are lost people in a sense more real than figurative, lost to the world, sometimes even lost to themselves.

R. M. Lovett. *NR*. May 30, 1934. p. 80

In contrast to most of his contemporaries in fiction, he peoples his books with civilized, educated, extraordinarily alert and sensitive human beings. They live in the modern world. When they are abnormal it is not the abnormality of degeneracy, but of the hypersensitive personality. Though in general they are characters untouched by the social, political and economic conflicts of contemporary life, they are vitally alive, and are depicted with a realism that is rendered palatable by the author's flawless prose.

Clayton Hoagland. *SLM*. April, 1940. p. 260

A story by Conrad Aiken is a horror wrapped in actuality, a fantasy all rooted and real, all rooted in a real detail. . . . Just as the structure of these stories characteristically develops in the effort of the material to assert a reality beyond or below its mundane shape, so their drama struggles to break over the edge of its own limitations. . . . We have, I think, no other body of contemporary fiction like this—so centrally coherent, its very coherence derived from a contemplation of the intransigence of that incoherence that lies scattered on all sides of us, and above and below.

Mark Schorer. *NR*. March 31, 1952. pp. 19–20

. . . I want to show very briefly that . . . Aiken's fiction often issues from his own experience. I should first make it clear that Aiken drew details from his own life not as an easy way to fill in his narrative, but that he might relive (and so understand) the inner experience associated with those details. . . . Aiken would enrich not simply his awareness of himself, but also his ability to articulate that understanding with greater intensity. What experience he would use had, for the most part, been already stored up. He had now to explore and perfect by art what he would call in *Ushant* this "gold-mine of consciousness." He would make a myth out of himself. . . . Such novels as *Blue Voyage* and *Conversation,* and stories like "The Last Visit" and "The Night Before Prohibition"—indeed nearly all of his fiction—explore the ego to reveal failures of honesty, kindness, and integrity.

(K)                     Jay Martin. *Conrad Aiken: A Life of His Art*
(Princeton). 1962. pp. 80–1, 86

*Blue Voyage* seems to me the best of the novels, but that may be because I remember so well my first reading of it. At any rate it has considerable historical importance, for in it Aiken combined techniques that had been influenced by Joyce with insights that had been fostered by Freud. Countless novels have appeared in the past three decades that are indebted in one way or another to *Blue Voyage*. . . . The best parts of the novels are very much like the poems, but, as I have tried to point out, Aiken has many of the specific attributes of a writer of fiction—skill in dialogue, narrative force, a way of making his people recognizable even when they are mysterious. It is good to have his novels in print.

(K)                              Granville Hicks. *SR*. Jan. 11, 1964. pp. 53–4

It is because Aiken has been so versatile and protean, has tried so many forms, and created so many verbal palaces, that he has lagged behind his sometimes less-endowed contemporaries. They were more single-minded. Aiken's houses are houses of words but also of cards, and somehow the internal monologues, in their endless clutter, do not give shape to people, only shadowy personages who talk too much. The conversations pyramid; they are often brilliant; but there are limitations even to good talk and Aiken errs by excess.

His novels therefore remain distinguished failures; they are object-lessons in the shortcomings of the internal monologue, and in the danger of using psychological theory to replace the lived experience—from which theory derives. Within the saturated literary qualities of Aiken's discipline there is the flaw of "everything"—there is the failure to capture the "epiphany" as Joyce did, or "the moment" as Virginia Woolf did.

(K)                              Leon Edel. *NYHT*. Jan. 19, 1964. p. 8

Not that he ever tried to kill his own active, generous and excitable con-science—who more scornful of the conscience-killers than he?—but rather that this thin mentalistic word "consciousness," for better or for worse, was to be his sign of everything generous, adventurous, dramatically, vigorously, and cleansingly outrageous. I think you must admit this to "get" Aiken, the man who successfully crossed the abyss between Santa-yana and Freud. . . . The younger novelists are catching up to Aiken and acting a lot more solemnly about it. Aiken is deeply, soul-stirringly *amusing*. . . . His "vaudeville of the psyche" enlists, in spurts and flashes, every kind of gusto that fiction has known.

(K)                              R. W. Flint. *NYR*. Feb. 6, 1964. p. 13

The five novels that Conrad Aiken wrote between 1925 and 1940 were not much noticed at the time and one of them, [*A Heart for the Gods of Mexico*], was not even published in the United States, although in many respects it stands as his best. Now that they are available in one volume, we see not only that Aiken was one of the best American novelists of the period between the two World Wars, but that he still, a quarter of a century later, speaks to us with charm, vivacity and great acuity. . . . [The novels] have practically no plots, either in the conventional sense of a story or in the more highly developed sense of a structure of interacting moods, ideas and images. Nevertheless, they give the impression of being complete and integrated; the reader is never left with a feeling that the novels have failed to fulfill their inner necessity. . . . Aiken has confined himself to the simplest possible "verity": the conflict between the urgency and the obscenity of sex.

(K)                        Hayden Carruth. *Nation*. Feb. 17, 1964. pp. 171–2

See *Selected Poems; Ushant* (autobiography); *Short Stories; Collected Novels.*

## ALBEE, EDWARD (1928–     )

. . . Edward Albee . . . comes into the category of the Theatre of the Absurd precisely because his work attacks the very foundations of American optimism. . . . Albee has produced a play that clearly takes up the style and subject matter of the Theatre of the Absurd and translates it into a genuine American idiom. *The American Dream* . . . fairly and squarely attacks the ideals of progress, optimism, and faith in the national mission, and pours scorn on the sentimental ideals of family life, togetherness, and physical fitness; the euphemistic language and unwillingness to face the ultimate facts of the human condition that in America, even more than in Europe, represents the essence of bourgeois assumptions and attitudes.

Martin Esslin. *The Theatre of the Absurd* (Doubleday
Anchor). 1961. pp. 225–6

Strangely enough, though there is no question of his sincerity, it is Albee's skill which at this point most troubles me. It is as if his already practiced hand had learned too soon to make an artful package of venom. For the overriding passion of the play is venomous. There is no reason why anger should not be dramatized. I do not object to Albee's being "morbid," for as the conspicuously healthy William James once said, "morbid-mindedness ranges over a wider scale of experience than healthy-mindedness." What I do object to in his play is that its disease has become something of a brilliant formula, as slick and automatic as a happy entertainment for the trade. The right to pessimism has to be earned within the artistic terms one sets up; the pessimism and rage of *Who's Afraid of Virginia Woolf?* are immature. Immaturity coupled with a commanding deftness is dangerous. . . . Vividly as each personage is drawn, they all nevertheless remain flat—caricatures rather than people. Each stroke of dazzling color is superimposed on another, but no further substance accumulates. We do not actually identify with anyone, except editorially. Even the non-naturalistic figures of Beckett's plays have more extension and therefore more stature and meaning. The characters in Albee's *The Zoo Story* and *Bessie Smith* are more particularized.

Harold Clurman. *Nation*. Oct. 27, 1962. p. 274

With *Who's Afraid of Virginia Woolf?* the Broadway season at last comes into possession of a play. . . . Following in the footsteps of [Eugene] O'Neill and [Tennessee] Williams, Albee looks unflinchingly at the putrescent cadaver, or near-cadaver, of our collective decency. But, with Albee, there is a catch. . . . The trouble with Mr. Albee's play is that, instead of being motivated by stern impartiality or a fierce muckraking fervor, it seems mostly to be getting nasty little kicks from kicking society in the groin.

John Simon. *HdR*. Winter, 1962–1963. pp. 571–2

The dramaturgy is simple naturalism, and the image on the stage has no philosophical or religious scope. The play is political out-and-out, remaining on the level of social criticism from beginning to end. What is striking about it is that for two long acts Albee alienates the audience to the point where it considers *him* vulgar, petty, sadistic, over-sexed and desexed, or perhaps just hopelessly middlebrow. In the last act, however, he pulls everything out of the fire with some old-fashioned emotional dynamics that are as electric as they are only because of what has come before. There is no pretentiousness, and so the honesty of the play comes home.

L. E. Chabrowe. *KR*. Winter, 1963. p. 146

Albee has a sense of character and drama that isn't ordinary. He can put two people on the stage and make them immediately lifelike: they respond to each other at once, which is exciting, especially since the response is usually revulsion. He handles demotic and clichéd speech in such a way that it seems fresh. He has a sense of humor which, though it is practically always exerted at the expense of his characters, can often make you laugh out loud. And best of all, he isn't afraid of corny theatricalism—in this of course he has the blessings and the precedent of contemporary French playwrights—and possesses an energy that never seems to flag.

Alfred Chester. *Cmty*. April, 1963. p. 297

As a maker of plots, Albee hardly exists. Both *The Zoo Story,* his first play performed in New York, and *Who's Afraid of Virginia Woolf?,* his most successful, are built upon an unbelievable situation—namely, that a sane, average-type person would be a passive spectator in the presence of behavior obviously headed toward destructive violence. . . . Whatever may be said against Albee . . . one must also say that his best is wholly theatrical. All his mistakes are theatrical mistakes. . . . I expect this instinct for the theatrical is what people really have in mind when they refer to Albee's talent. "Talent" is the wrong word, for the nature of a talent is to grow, and Albee shows no signs of that. He does show a theatrical instinct. . . . In his badly written plays he jabs away at life with blunt instruments. If his jabbing hit the mark, that would be another matter. But it doesn't, no more than does a child in the nursery when he tears up his toys. That is why Albee is the pet of the audience, this little man who looks as if he dreamed of evil but is actually mild as a dove and wants to be loved. In him America has found its very own playwright. He's a dream.

Tom F. Driver. *Reporter*. Jan. 2, 1964. pp. 38–9

The hardest thing to determine about "camp" literature, movies, and painting is the extent of the author's sincerity. A hoax is being perpetrated, no doubt of that, but is this intentional or not? Is the contriver inside or outside his own fraudulent creation? Does Andy Warhol really believe in the artistic validity of his Brillo boxes? *Tiny Alice* is a much more ambitious work than the usual variety of "camp," but it shares the same ambiguity of motive. For while some of Albee's obscurity is pure playfulness, designed to con the spectator into looking for non-existent meanings, some is obviously there for the sake of a sham profundity in which the author apparently believes.

Robert Brustein. *NR*. Jan. 23, 1965. pp. 33–4

His first play, indeed, is not only within its limits a good and effective play; it is virtually an epitome, for good and for ill, of all his later original drama. . . . Since *The Zoo Story* does argue—not only through Jerry but through the action the play presents—that in mid-twentieth-century America the possibility of genuine intellectual understanding is lost beyond recall, consistency compels Albee to take great care that the events of his play be no more intellectually understandable to his audience than they are to Jerry and Peter; and I believe that his care has on the whole been rewarded: many of Albee's admirers have seemed to feel deeply for Jerry and Peter, but no one has claimed to know them. . . . Albee's comprehensive denial of intellect establishes a theatre incapable of resolution—a theatre suitable to fantasy, perhaps, but a theatre in which Albee's realism cannot help being inconclusive.

Melvin L. Plotinsky. *DS*. Winter, 1965. pp. 220–3

Probably the only way to save the play [*A Delicate Balance*] would be to dump all the harangues, and explanations, and most of the ideas, and to replace them with scenes. But scenes take longer to write. Those two people who are afraid of their own house are worth a play, and for the few minutes that they are treated comically (a la his own *American Dream*) Albee shows us what he might have done.

But he seems to have lost faith, or patience, in his own gift. Treated comically, these people are terrifying; treated seriously, they are nothing. Enough scraps and bits of bone can be found in the play to form the nucleus of a good surreal comedy: but they are kept rigidly apart by lead-weights of preachment and unearned poetry.

Wilfred Sheed. Com. Oct. 14, 1966. p. 56

Considering the thoughtful nature of Albee's plays, why have they aroused so much resentment? Why do his attackers seem to spend less effort trying to understand his plays than simply documenting their own distaste?

The causes are complex, and both the playwright and his critics have reasons for complaint. A lot of the discomfort has to do with Albee's use of abstract symbols and ideas. Nameless fears or, as in *Virginia Woolf,* mythical sons can be not only puzzling but exasperating. We are more at home with facts than ideas, and Albee's plays are very short on facts. Only the crackle and swing of his dialogue compensate us for the fact that his plays are practically plotless and his characters are not always fully fleshed out. What he offers as compensation is a new kind of theatricality: a continuous interplay of ideas and subtle implications.

Tom Prideaux. Life. Oct. 28, 1966. p. 120

Albee is progressing. *Who's Afraid of Virginia Woolf?* was about the emptiness that surrounds and threatens to swallow our relationships; *Tiny Alice* was about the void lurking behind our deepest beliefs; now, *A Delicate Balance* is about the nothingness, the bare nothingness of it all—it is a play about nothing. . . . What, one wonders, was the real motive behind *A Delicate Balance?* I, for one, still believe in Albee's perceptiveness and even in his talent (he did, after all, write *The Zoo Story* and *Virginia Woolf*); why would he hurtle into such utter pointlessness? It occurs to me that at least since *Virginia Woolf,* Albee's plays and adaptations have been viewed by many as dealing overtly or covertly with homosexual matters; Albee may have resolved here to write a play reeking with heterosexuality.

John Simon. HdR. Winter, 1966–1967. pp. 627–9

This is probably going to be a difficult review to write and to read, so let me clear the decks with a deliberately unclear statement. Edward Albee's *Everything in the Garden* . . . is both extraordinarily flawed and extraordinarily engrossing. The latter remark the producers will doubtless quote, and the former will be remembered in my favor by at least my friends.

Mr. Albee is not merely our most hopeful playwright, our most promising playwright, our most interesting playwright—he is, quite simply, our best playwright. This is a position he won by virtue of *A Zoo Story* and *The Death of Bessie Smith.* Since then everything he has done has had to be regarded with seriousness and respect. . . .

Yet, in the final account this is a monstrously heavy handed account by

Mr. Albee of a stealthily subtle play. If Mr. Albee wishes to sing us a song of social significance he should not choose such a shrill and hysterical falsetto.

Clive Barnes. *NYTd.* Nov. 30, 1967. p. 60

Albee's version of *Everything in the Garden,* in short, is without interest, and I'm not concealing very well my reluctance to write about it. What continues to remain somewhat interesting, because unresolved, is the author's ambiguous relationship to his audience. As I have had occasion to remark somewhat too often, Albee's identity as a dramatist is highly uncertain. Lacking his own vision, he turns to adaptation; lacking his own voice, he borrows the voice of others. What has remained constant through his every change of style—through the progression of his influences from Genet to Strindberg to Pirandello to Williams to Ionesco to Eliot—is his peculiar love-hatred for those who attend his plays. Albee's desire to undermine the audience and be applauded for it is now leading him into the most extraordinary strategems and subterfuges, just as his desire to be simultaneously successful and significant has managed by now to freeze his artistic imagination. He has two choices, I think, if he is ever to create interesting work again: either to resolve this conflict, or to write about it. But both alternatives oblige him to become a great deal less masked, a great deal more daring, a great deal more open than he now chooses to be.

Robert Brustein. *NR.* Dec. 16, 1967. p. 27

See *The Zoo Story, The Death of Bessie Smith, The American Dream, Who's Afraid of Virginia Woolf?, Tiny Alice, A Delicate Balance, Everything in the Garden.*


# ALFRED, WILLIAM (1923–    )

William Alfred's purpose in writing this verse play in four acts [*Agamemnon*] is not to make an adaptation of Aeschylus; he wishes to penetrate the myth itself, that "ambush of reality," that familiar place (he goes on to say in his preface) we might find in no matter how foreign a city. Thus he would work where Aeschylus worked, and where the imaginations of his "private" readers work, whether consciously or not; and he would make his play directly from—or in?—the life of that myth, and not from its literature. . . . What is sure is that he has done a fine play, with a few moments of really high distinction.

Henry Rago. *Com.* Dec. 3, 1954. p. 259

The prime virtue of William Alfred's verse-drama, *Hogan's Goat,* is its absolute lack of shrewdness. It embodies none of the fashionable attitudes of the contemporary stage, whether commercial or avant-garde, and it is written with an ingratiating naïveté, as if the author had just emerged, play in hand, from a time capsule entered many decades before. . . . and while the blank verse is a little excessive in its use of simile, and a little unfamiliar in the mouths of Irish wardheelers, it is generally a serviceable dramatic instrument, especially as a source of invective.

For all its charm, however, the play is decidedly minor, mainly because it fails its own intentions. In the conflict between a young ambitious insurgent who wants to be mayor and the cynical, corrupt old incumbent who will use any device to keep his cherished office, Mr. Alfred has the opportunity to examine what has recently become an extremely important subject in America—the rise of Irish political power; but the author unfortunately gets sidetracked into writing pseudo-tragedy about his hubristic hero, concluding not with social-political insights but rather with a moral lesson about pride and selfishness. . . .

Robert Brustein. NR. Nov. 27, 1965. p. 46

To begin with, the . . . intention [of *Hogan's Goat*] is implied in such lines as "There are some things in life you can't take back"—the plot consequence of which is that not only the sinner but also the innocent are destroyed. Concomitant with this thought is the idea that in the quest for power lie the seeds of crime.

Further, the author wished to recreate the Irish Brooklyn of old with its mixture of religiosity, ignorance, provincial charm, fecklessness and brutality—the sweetly rancid festering of our ghettos in their growth and in their dissolution. Finally there is the purely literary striving . . . to envelop and elevate all this material through the use of modern verse forms, language which makes poetic patterns of the vernacular.

Harold Clurman. Nation. Nov. 29, 1965. p. 427

I remember William Alfred reading, some dozen years ago in Harvard's Sanders Theatre, from his verse play, *Hogan's Goat*. I recall being impressed by his reading and unimpressed by his writing. The American Place Theatre has now given *Hogan's Goat* a compact and tidy production, but the play continues to be sprawling, sentimental melodrama decked out with verse that smacks of a Christopher Fry hopped up on Sean O'Casey. Oh, the heart is in the right place in this tale of an 1890 scandal that cost an eagerly aspiring immigrant-Irish publican the mayoralty of Brooklyn; and his passionate young spouse, her life. But plays do not live by heart and vaulting metaphors alone. . . . Nevertheless, this is not really an offensive play, merely a benighted one. It does, in any case, attempt to create plot and characters, and even if these Irish priests, politicos, ward-heelers, floozies, biddies, and bibbers have worn their

garments of lovable local color hopelessly threadbare, and even if the
romantic and political intrigues, clashes, and lightning revelations are
smudged with the thumbprints of countless popular dramatists, there is
here an old-fashioned love of old-fashioned theatre for which one may
heave a sympathetic sigh.

John Simon. *HdR*. Spring, 1966. pp. 114–5

See *Agamemnon, Hogan's Goat*.


## ALGREN, NELSON (1909–    )

Nelson Algren is one of God's angry and gifted men, a Chicagoman—and
maybe a Chicago-firster—to the bitter end. As his admirers know, his
fiction is a heady, curious blend of skidrow Chicago talk and poetic
insight. He writes like no one else in America today.

Budd Schulberg. *NYT*. Oct. 21, 1951. p. 3


The point is that Algren's topical figures are failures even at vice. They
are the underdogs of sin, the small souls of corruption, the fools of poverty,
not of wealth and power. Even the murders they commit, out of blind rage
or through sheer accident—or through another ironic twist of their impoverished destiny—are not important. . . . Thus Algren's work represents
an extreme phase of the native American realism which opened in the
1900's. . . . And there are obvious limitations and aesthetic dangers in the
social area and the kind of human material that Algren has made his own.

Maxwell Geismar. *EJ*. March, 1953. pp. 124–5


It might be said that Algren's novels are weak in structure, and that they
evince a lack of good constructive sense and an inability to maintain a
narrative pace. Algren writes all around a character and gradually you
realize that his character is real. He is atmospheric and impressionistic.

James Farrell. *NR*. May 21, 1956. p. 19


Algren's is a world of exotics—the last jungle inhabited by the last of
the Noble Savages, the final goal of literary tourism.

It is, then, as an exotic, a romantic purveyor of escape literature that
Algren must be read—this apparent "realist" whose fictional world is
at the ultimate remove from any reality his readers know. Beyond Tahiti
and Samoa, there exists the last unexplored island: Ultima Skid Row, on
which nothing is merely dull, grimy, and without savor, but all grotesque
and titillating in the lurid light of Algren's "poetic" prose.

Leslie A. Fiedler. *Reporter*. July 12, 1956. p. 44

The notion that prostitutes have hearts of gold is of course a literary cliché, and you will find it in much of the slumming fiction of the past, but nowhere in Algren's books is there any prostitute with a heart of gold. *Time's* reviewer would find himself hard put to find a single line in *A Walk on the Wild Side,* or *Never Come Morning,* where prostitution is part of Algren's theme, that could be quoted or twisted to support the notion. Algren's prostitutes are people, good, bad, and indifferent, like any other women. If they perform a good deed or an unselfish act their motives are as mixed as those of any wife or sweetheart—or any businessman on the make for a buck. As for the bums, the charge of idleness is itself a cliché. It was always leveled against itinerant workers, "tramps," "hoboes," who followed the harvest or preferred pick-up jobs to punching a time-clock. For Dove Linkhorn in *Wild Side* it is work or starve from start to finish, and he is seldom idle. Far from being a bum in the *Time* reviewer's sense of the word (as distinguished from "people who work"), Dove is clearly intended to be a parody of the young man on the make for money and success. . . .

(K)                        Lawrence Lipton. *CR.* Winter, 1957. pp. 6–7

Nelson Algren . . . has been fretfully silent, the fret manifested by occasional reviews, interviews, magazine pieces, comments, groans and gripes. A born writer, for one reason or another stalled in his vocation, may back and fill in this way. *Who Lost an American?* is the distillation of this fret, a collection of memories, notes, burlesques and prejudices in a book that is part fact, part fiction. . . .

The best thing in the book is Algren's personal rhythm—irreverent, funny, surreal, as if he has blended the lyricism of his early writing, "within a rain that light rains regret," with a tough meander and wail like that of funky jazz. Algren is a writer, the authentic poetic article; a fresh haircut strikes his eye as vividly as the murder of a Chicago poker player on a backstairs. It would be fine to discover him working once again on people whom he could feel in his blood and within an action that might carry his special melody.

(K)                        Herbert Gold. *NYT.* June 2, 1963. p. 23

There is something fundamentally dispiriting about *Who Lost an American?,* not because its inner feeling is irrelevant to life today—I do not believe it is—but because Algren, who is after all an accomplished writer, is so utterly helpless to turn this feeling into anything but a commonplace buffoonery. Caught between his own past, in which a deep identification with the social outcast and the working class was all but inseparable from his sense of literary vocation, and the present, in which money seems to brutalize equally those who have too much and those who have too little,

Algren seems to have lost all sense of what useful literary tasks might remain open to him. His detestation of the prevailing moral atmosphere, not only of society at large but of the literary pretensions to which it has given rise, seems to have deprived him of his own seriousness as a writer. (K)                    Hilton Kramer. *Reporter*. June 30, 1963. p. 47

This arch, arbitrary tone is all that binds the two sets of fragments that, spliced together, form *Notes From a Sea Diary*—short declamations on Hemingway and his critics, and long anecdotes of life on board ship and in the ports. . . .

In the anecdotes, as in the criticism, there are moments of real emotion and power, but they are brief. What his book might have been shows in the chapters describing the caged whores of Bombay. Despite sometimes shoddy writing ("She was the eldest child and had eleven siblings, all younger than herself."), Algren is moving because he concentrates not on his performance but on his subject.

Then quickly it is over, and we are back in the romance of the hard-boiled, the soggy mess behind the hard exterior, the male counterpart of the myth of the golden-hearted whore. In all his talk of junkies and hoods, the violent and violated, Algren never talks about the central facts of their lives: anxiety and boredom. Instead he creates a noble savagery—a literary cult of the antisocial, as little connected with life as the literary communism of the thirties was with *realpolitik*.

What began years ago as a small but unique gift became a habit, and finally a tic, a machine clanking out a self-intoxicating gabble of Algrenisms.
(K)                        Arno Karlen. *NYT*. Aug. 22, 1965. p. 4

### Never Come Morning

It is a novel about depressed people by a depressed man, and it is most convincing in its complete unity of action, mood, and form. . . . The whole narrative is pervaded by a feeling of loss rather than of bitterness or horror. And Algren's realism is so paced as to avoid the tedium of the naturalistic stereotype, of the literal copying of surfaces. He knows how to select, how to employ factual details without letting himself be swamped by them, and finally, how to put the slang his characters speak to creative uses so that it ceases to be an element of mere documentation and turns into an element of style.

Philip Rahv. *Nation*. April 18, 1942. pp. 466–7

The scene in *Never Come Morning* that most people will remember is the rape of Bruno's girl in the cellar. . . . There are other scenes as brutal.

. . . But the really good scenes are quieter; they are still lifes and genre pictures instead of being sensational films—the girls sitting around the juke box in Mama Topak's flat, the boys playing under the El, the look of Chicago streets in the rain, the tall corn growing between the slag heaps down by the river. It is this poetry of familiar things that is missing in the other Chicago novels and that shows the direction of Algren's talent. In spite of the violent story he tells—and tells convincingly—he is not by instinct a novelist. He is a poet of the Chicago slums, and he might well be Sandburg's successor.

Malcolm Cowley. NR. May 4, 1942. pp. 613–4

## The Man with the Golden Arm

*The Man with the Golden Arm* . . . seems to declare that admirable human qualities have little—or perhaps a negative bearing on social status and that the poetry of human relationships appears most richly where people are stripped down to the core of survival and have not strength or use for complicated emotions. Living on the barest edge of physical survival, his people simply have no use for vanity, sanctimoniousness, or prestige; being free and pure, their loves and affections are beautiful. . . . Society has become a jungle of viciousness and injustice beyond reclamation; only the waifs and strays merit attention because only they are capable of tender and beautiful feelings. One may be deeply moved by *The Man with the Golden Arm* but must, I believe, finally regard it as irresponsible and inaccurate—a sentimental contrivance that has little to do with reality but rather explores a cul-de-sac in the author's imagination.

Charles Child Walcutt. American Literary Naturalism<br>(Minnesota). 1956. 298–9

## A Walk on the Wild Side

Algren's narrative . . . flickers to life only intermittently among the lay sermons and the miscellaneous information about jails and whorehouses. *A Walk on the Wild Side* is . . . documented, out of the same sense, I suppose, which compels popular magazine fiction, the notion that "truth" resides in avoiding inaccuracies; in knowing, for instance, exactly what equipment a New Orleans prostitute of the '30's would have had on her table. It is all part of the long retreat of the imagination before science, or our surrender to information.

Leslie A. Fiedler. PR. June, 1956. p. 361

*A Walk on the Wild Side* is in an American tradition of emotional giant-ism: its comedy is farce, its joys are orgies, the feats of its characters

Bunyanesque, the sexuality is prodigious, their sorrow a wild keening almost too high for ordinary ears. Dove Linkhorn is pioneer stock gone bad, grown up and gone to seed, caught in a neon-lit jungle in a time of break-down. The picture of Dove burning out his dammed up, useless energies in a bonfire of lust and violence is one of the most extraordinary in contemporary fiction.

Milton Rugoff. *NYHT*. May 20, 1956. p. 4

The Chicago School of Realism has a new headmaster who frames his materials in back-country balladry and earthy lyricism. Enveloping pornography, as bluntly couched as ever, has now become incidental to the journalist's desire to get the facts and the historian's need to relate them to human affairs. To complete the effect, one could only ask for Toulouse-Lautrec illustrations and Louis Armstrong music. . . . *A Walk on the Wild Side* will be too rough for frail sightseers, but a participant's backward look at a wild 1931 landscape with figures seems worth the effort.

James Kelly. *SR*. May 26, 1956. p. 16

See *Somebody in Boots, Never Come Morning, The Man with the Golden Arm, A Walk on the Wild Side* (novels); *The Neon Wilderness* (stories); *Who Lost an American?, Notes from a Sea Diary* (essays).

# ANDERSON, MAXWELL (1888–1959)

Mr. Anderson's uncommon virtues and regrettable shortcomings are once more visible (in *The Wingless Victory* and *High Tor*). Both contain much lovely song. Both . . . disclose a mind and a point of view infinitely superior to the playwrighting general. And the second combines with its other qualities a sound originality and a small measure of that precious after-image, a small measure of the day-after recollective warmth, which in its full is the stamp and mark of important drama. But both the superior second as well as the inferior first, lack the strong, taut, purple cords to tie up and bind closely into a whole their isolatedly commendable elements and their periodic stirring notes of dramatic music.

George Jean Nathan. *SR*. Jan. 30, 1937. p. 19

Mr. Anderson, it seems to me, in his own plays has given the most striking confirmation of the obsolescence of verse technique. He is capable of writing well—in prose, and when he is close to real American speech. But in these recent plays he writes badly. I do not mean that he is technically incompetent; but he writes badly because English blank verse no longer has any relation whatsoever to the language or tempo of our lives, and because, as soon as he tries to use it, he has no resources but a flavorless imagery which was growing trite in our grandfathers' time.

Edmund Wilson. *NR*. June 23, 1937. p. 194

Maxwell Anderson has been at his best, in recent years, when he was angry. But because his language lacks any basis for hope, for a constructive point of view towards what disgusts him, it must in the end turn back upon itself, and render him peevish and despairing. Fine words and despair are not enough on which to nurture a dramatic talent; Anderson's latest plays show a marked decline. Yet his great gift is apparent whenever he permits himself to write immediately and simply about human beings.

Eleanor Flexner. *American Playwrights* (Simon).
1938. pp. 128–9

In eleven plays "poetic" from beginning to end, Maxwell Anderson, America's chief verse writer for the theatre, has produced very little poetry. . . . Consciously or otherwise, Mr. Anderson seems more interested in arguing for his philosophy of life than in any particular happening, past or present. Each of the full-length plays turns upon a love story, essentially the same in all. A potentially perfect romance is frustrated by another need, political (the crown in *Elizabeth, Mary,* etc.), social (*Wingless Victory, Winterset*), or private ( *High Tor, Key Largo*). While an assortment of contemporary topics are touched upon—the decay of aristocracy, race prejudice, class injustice, revolution, and absolution—the mechanism of the play is always the love affair, and the issue always a certain omnipresent danger of "dying within."

Harold Rosenberg. *Poetry*. Jan. 1941. pp. 258–60

Maxwell Anderson's independence set him apart from his time. Not only as a literary craftsman—since he alone was writing poetic and romantic tragedies—but in other respects, he was an alien voice. In an age of increasing collectivism this voice could be heard praising individualism, independence, and the frontier spirit. In an age of increasing governmentalism he could still maintain that the best government was that which governed least. As the last champion of what almost amounts to a laissez-faire and rugged individualism, he is an isolated figure, almost an anachronism.

Vincent Wall. *SwR*. July, 1941. p. 339

I am sure of this: the Anderson plays are declining in theatrical effectiveness but rising steadily in intellectual significance. If he is not an original thinker, Mr. Anderson has at least dug his teeth into a great subject; he has gradually moved beyond the crudely American conception of freedom as license to buy and sell anything at a profit to an Emersonian vision of the "infinitude of the private man." And always one feels—here is the peculiar appeal of the dramas—that he has achieved insight by staring hard at facts. Only Sean O'Casey among his contemporaries can hammer as much of the crude stuff of living into poetry for the stage.

Edward Foster. SwR. Jan., 1942. p. 100

As Mr. Anderson's art matured . . . he evolved at the end of the first decade a working group of principles which were later stated as explicit theory. . . . This theory conceives of drama as having a high destiny, not only in its obligation to reflect a moral universe, but also in its function as inspirer of man's faith and as prophet of his future. The dramas Mr. Anderson wrote during his first decade did not fulfill these high purposes; nor did some of those he wrote during the second decade. But there are half a dozen plays from the later period which come close to his ideal and three or four which realize it fully; among the latter are *Mary of Scotland, Winterset,* and *Key Largo.*

Allan H. Halline. AL. May, 1944. p. 81

Mr. Anderson really discovered himself, I think, in the historical plays. Here he developed his characteristic verse-form—a rather rough blank verse with a sort of tumbling, hurrying rhythm, like that of a tossing sea —a verse that can be used in colloquial realistic scenes, but that is capable of rising to high levels of imaginative beauty. Here also, through the study of historical figures and the attempt to recreate and interpret them, he gained a firmer grasp on character than he had shown in his earlier plays —a more penetrating insight, and greater skill in revealing character through speech. And here, too, I think he learned to simplify and clarify his story, just because the material with which he was dealing was so complex that severe simplification was necessary.

Homer E. Woodbridge. SAQ. Jan., 1945. p. 60

Many persons who do not count themselves among his most enthusiastic admirers would probably be willing to admit that he has succeeded more fully than any of our other dramatists in persuading a large popular audience to follow him gladly beyond the rather narrow circle of subjects, attitudes, and methods within which it has grown accustomed to remain confined. . . . Something of the same sort may be said of his verse which found ready comprehension in part because it did not, like so much modern poetry, require for its comprehension a familiarity with a modern tradition of which four-fifths of the theater-going public is completely ignorant. It has at least the primary virtue of dramatic verse inasmuch as it is easily speakable and easily understood when spoken.

Joseph Wood Krutch. *American Drama since 1918* (Braziller). 1957. p. 305

See *What Price Glory?*, *Winterset*, *Mary of Scotland*, *Elizabeth the Queen*, *High Tor*, and *Key Largo* (plays).

# ANDERSON, ROBERT (1917–    )

The main theme . . . [of *Tea and Sympathy*] is a defense of the special person in a society which tends to look askance at the "odd" individual, even the unpremeditated non-conformist. If the play has a message, it is to the effect that a boy like its protagonist may be more truly a man than those falsely rugged folk who oppress him.

The play also cautions us against prejudice, slander and false accusation —in a word, is a plea for tolerance. Naturally, we are all for it: every contribution in this direction is more than welcome. Yet in this regard I cannot help thinking that we have arrived today at a peculiar brand of tolerance. We tolerate the innocent! . . . Though now easily acceptable, a play like *Tea and Sympathy* is probably still regarded by many as adventurous and advanced, though it is actually primitive in its theme, characterization, and story development. It is, in fact, a very young play.

This is no adverse comment on it. It is the work of a young playwright, Robert Anderson, whose approach is honorably craftsmanlike and humane.

Harold Clurman. *Nation*. Oct. 17, 1953. p. 318

*Tea and Sympathy* is a highly superior specimen of the theatre of "realist" escape. Superior in craftsmanship, superior in its isolation, combination, and manipulation of the relevant impulses and motifs. Its organization of the folklore of current fashion is so skillful, it brings us to the frontier where this sort of theatre ends. But not beyond it. So that one does not ask the questions one would ask of a wholly serious play. . . . Instead, one drinks the tea of sentiment and eats the opium of sympathy. . . . At every moment in the evening, one can say: this *has* to be a hit, or men are not feckless dreamers, the theatre is not a fantasy factory, and this is not the age of anxiety. . . . Anyway, it is a play for everyone in the family. The script is far better than most; folklore and daydream are not less interesting than drama. . . .

Eric Bentley. *NR*. Oct. 19, 1953. pp.20–1

Among the season's most interesting offerings is Robert Anderson's *Tea and Sympathy*. Though Mr. Anderson (no relation of Maxwell Anderson) has had three plays produced, this study of a boy unjustly accused of homosexuality is his first hit. I can't pretend to believe completely in Mr. Anderson's play. I doubt if any boy of eighteen in these post-Kinsey days would reach his final year at boarding school without knowing the facts of life. I am confident that masters, worthy of being employed by such a school, would not accept the flimsy charge brought by a filthy-minded student or behave as these masters do after the charge is brought. And I am well aware that, if it were not a matter of saving a change of scenery, the final episode in all likelihood would not take place in the boy's dormitory room. I do know, however, that Mr. Anderson has a genuine flair for the theatre, that he can write fine individual scenes, and that he can hold an audience as I have seldom seen an audience held.

John Mason Brown. *SR*. Dec. 12, 1953. p. 45

This slender and touching drama [*Silent Night, Lonely Night*] about two lonely people in a New England inn at Christmas time unaccountably failed on Broadway. It is, perhaps, Robert Anderson's best play, and will be widely produced throughout the country.

George Freedley. *LJ*. Oct. 1, 1960. p. 3459

Robert Anderson has not had a real success on Broadway since *Tea and Sympathy*. In *You Know I Can't Hear You When the Water's Running*, he deliberately set out to lower his insights and write something brightly commercial, something that people would like to see on Saturday nights. On their own terms—as lightweight sex plays—the four one-acts that comprise the package are successful at least half of the time.

Mel Gussow. *Newsweek*. March 27, 1967. p. 110

. . . Robert Anderson's *You Know I Can't Hear You When the Water's Running* begins with a very funny idea. . . . [O]ne is delightfully surprised to discover the sober author of *Tea and Sympathy* and a number of other anguished plays, has a flair for comedy.

However, the three playlets that follow are less pure comedy than the opening one. For while Anderson continues his comic invention, he permits it to become adulterated with his serious concern for problems of marital adjustment. . . . The playwright refuses to write a pure comic exercise and mixes in a certain naturalistic pathos.

It is probably inevitable that Mr. Anderson's work express his responsible recognition of the American scene. And if it strikes us as less enter-

taining than his free-swinging fun, it at least gives the evening character.
Henry Hewes. *SR*. April 1, 1967. p. 42

See *Tea and Sympathy, All Summer Long, Silent Night, Lonely Night, You Know I Can't Hear You When the Water's Running* (plays).

# ANDERSON, SHERWOOD (1876–1941)

He sits across the table from you as you read. You can almost hear him breathe. It is all so real. This is the way people feel and the way they think, the way a story of this kind must be told. And though this may not be all the world, the world of flowers and ships at sea, it is the frustrated world of the artist, driven back upon himself, and the repressed world of youth. And between the lines there is something—call it symbolism, atmosphere, the mystery of being, what you will—that is in all of Anderson's stories. . . . To him the world is—close-knit, throbbing, pulsating with one life, men and animals, trees, clouds, earth, the whole of nature. And it is this throb, the pulse of creation, that makes the rhythm of his prose.
Charles C. Baldwin. *The Men Who Make Our Novels*
(Dodd). 1919. p. 27

Out of . . . fallen creatures, Sherwood Anderson has made the pure poetry of his tales. He has taken the words surely, has set them fiercely end to end, and underneath his hand there has come to be a surface as clean and fragrant as that of joyously made things in a fresh young country. The vocabulary of the simplest folk; words of a primer, a copybook quotidianness, form a surface as hard as that of pungent fresh-placed boards of pine and oak. Into the ordered prose of Anderson the delicacy and sweetness of growing corn, the grittiness and firmness of black earth sifted by the fingers, the broad-breasted power of great laboring horses, has wavered again. The writing pleases the eye. It pleases the nostrils. It is moist and adhesive to the touch, like milk.
Paul Rosenfeld. *Port of New York* (Harcourt). 1924.
p. 176

The thing which captures me and will not let me go is the profound sincerity, the note of serious, baffled, tragic questioning which I hear above its laughter and tears. It is, all through, an asking of the question which American literature has hardly as yet begun to ask. "What for?" . . . It is that spirit of profound and unresisting questioning which has made Russian literature what it is. "Why? why? why?" echoes insistently through all their pages. . . . It echoes, too, in this book, like a great bell pealing its tremendous question to an unanswering sky, and awakening dangerously within one's self something that one has carefully laid to sleep—perhaps one's soul, who knows?

Floyd Dell. *Looking at Life* (Knopf). 1924. pp. 83–4

Sherwood Anderson is something of an anomaly. He has been more daring than any of his contemporaries in his attempts to get to the basic facts about people. He has tried to explore deeper into human emotions and reactions than they. He has tried to seize on the important, significant moments in the dull and drab lives that go on about him. In his search for the until recently disguised facts about modern life, and in his statement of human problems he stands shoulder to shoulder with the best of his contemporaries the world over. But if he has attempted much, he has often failed. In his disposal of these facts and in his interpretation of these problems he often goes as far off the track as did the writers of the Pollyanna school. His work contains more sentimental alloy than that of any other "serious" modern writer.

Cleveland B. Chase. *Sherwood Anderson* (McBride).
1927. pp. 4–5

To the student of human nature under the conditions of provincial neo-Puritanism there must always belong a high interest to these documents with their toneless murmur as of one who has exhausted eloquence and passion and found them of no avail, with their tortured sense of life as a thing immitigably ugly and mean, with their delineation of dull misery so ground into the bone that it no longer knows itself for what it is. Nowhere in all these pages of Anderson will this student find a breath of freedom or of joy—never the record of an hour of either passion or serenity. Life is walled in; it is imprisoned from itself, from the sources without which it withers and dies. Who will knock down the walls? There is no one, least of all the author himself.

Ludwig Lewisohn. *Expression in America* (Harper).
1932. p. 484

(Hemingway and Gertrude Stein) disagreed about Sherwood Anderson. Gertrude Stein contended that Sherwood Anderson had a genius for using the sentence to convey a direct emotion, this was in the great American tradition, and that really except Sherwood there was no one in America who could write a clear and passionate sentence. Hemingway did not believe this, he did not like Sherwood's taste. Taste has nothing to do with sentences, contended Gertrude Stein.

Gertrude Stein. *The Autobiography of Alice B. Toklas*
(Harcourt). 1933. p. 268

Anderson turned fiction into a substitute for poetry and religion, and never ceased to wonder at what he had wrought. He had more intensity than a revival meeting and more tenderness than God; he wept, he chanted, he loved indescribably. There was freedom in the air, and he would summon all Americans to share it; there was confusion and mystery on the earth, and he would summon all Americans to wonder at it. He was clumsy and sentimental; he could even write at times as if he were finger-painting; but at the moment it seemed as if he had sounded the depths of common American experience as no one else could.

There was always an image in Anderson's books—an image of life as a house of doors, of human beings knocking at them and stealing through one door only to be stopped short before another as if in a dream. Life was a dream to him, and he and his characters seemed always to be walking along its corridors. Who owned the house of life? How did one escape after all? No one in his books ever knew, Anderson least of all. Yet slowly and fumblingly he tried to make others believe, as he thought he had learned for himself, that it was possible to escape if only one laughed at necessity.

Alfred Kazin. On Native Grounds (Reynal). 1942.<br>pp. 210–1

Read for moral explication as a guide to life, his work must seem un-satisfactory; it simply does not tell us enough. But there is another, more fruitful way of reading his work: as an expression of a sensitive witness to the national experience and as the achievement of a story teller who created a small body of fiction unique in American writing for the lyrical purity of its feeling. So regarded his best work becomes a durable part of the American literary structure. . . . While Steinbeck and Saroyan could enlarge on his occasional sentimentalism and Hemingway could tighten and rigidify his style, no American writer has yet been able to realize that strain of lyrical and nostalgic feeling which in Anderson's best work reminds one of another and greater poet of tenderness, Turgenev. At his best Anderson creates a world of authentic sentiment, and while part of the meaning of his career is that sentiment is not enough for a writer, the careers of those that follow him—those who swerve to Steinbeck's senti-mentalism or Hemingway's toughness—illustrate how rare a genius sen-timent still is in our literature.

Irving Howe. Sherwood Anderson (Sloane). 1951<br>pp. 249, 255

The exactitude of purity, or the purity of exactitude: whichever you like. He was a sentimentalist in his attitude toward people, and quite often incorrect about them. He believed in people, but it was as though only in theory. He expected the worst from them, even while each time he was prepared again to be disappointed or even hurt, as if it had never happened before, as though the only people he could really trust, let himself go with, were the ones of his own invention, the figments and symbols of his own fumbling dream. And he was sometimes a sentimentalist in his writing (so was Shakespeare sometimes) but he was never impure in it. He never scanted it, cheapened it, took the easy way; never failed to approach writing except with humility and an almost religious, almost abject faith and patience and willingness to surrender, relinquish himself to and into it. He hated glibness; if it were quick, he believed it was false too.

(K)                                    William Faulkner. *At.* June, 1953. p. 28

Anderson's new approach to the Midwest drew its strength from humility and love. There was also the unabashed lyricism which, though it was to be transmuted in the later work by sympathy, here cut loose from the clogs of realistic convention. But particularly, the [*Mid-American*] *Chants* revealed a concentrated effort to make poetry out of Anderson's own language. This was simple and limited, frequently not sufficient to the demands he put upon it. In the *Chants,* for the first time, he came down upon his language, not to prune and order, but to let come from it whatever was, in nature, there. This was a part of his acceptance. He had felt in Gertrude Stein the achievement of poetry in the aggressively simple. And that, in a literary way, was where his own work must begin and end.

(K)                    Bernard Duffey. *The Chicago Renaissance in American*
*Letters* (Michigan State). 1954. p. 205

What Anderson did for younger writers was to open vistas by finding new depths or breadths of feeling in everyday American life. Again with Whitman he might have boasted that he led each of them to a knoll, from which he pointed to "landscapes of continents, and a plain public road." He gave them each a moment of vision, and then the younger writer trudged off toward his separate destiny, often without looking back. Re-reading Anderson's work after many years, one is happy to find that its moments of vision are as fresh and moving as ever. They are what James Joyce called "epiphanies"; that is, they are moments at which a character, a landscape, or a personal relation stands forth in its essential nature or "whatness," with its past and future revealed as if by a flash of lightning. For Anderson each of the moments was a story in itself. The problem he almost never solved was how to link one moment to another in a pattern of causality, or how to indicate the passage of time.

(K)                                    Malcolm Cowley. *NR.* Feb. 15, 1960. p. 16

Anderson's attitudes after 1912 remained basically unchanged. His heart lay in the rural simplicity of his youth, but it was the ideals rather than the facts, the feelings and the sentient newness of his Midwestern youth, that he wanted all his life to recapture. Armed with little more than a deep nostalgia for a way of life that could never be called back into being, he found in writing the sense of communion and sentient vitality he believed had been lost with the disappearance of the yeoman farmer and the trades- man. But his own regeneration could scarcely serve as a universal model; and, when he tried to prescribe sex and collectivism as workable popular alternatives to art, he invariably oversimplified both the nature and the problems of urban industrial society.

His thesis, to the end of his life, was that only a spiritual rebirth could save modern men from the machine; but he was never able to present his primitivistic modes of regeneration in convincing narrative terms. . . .

But Anderson's discouragingly long list of failures by no means diminishes the brilliance of his successes. If he failed as a sophisticated novelist, this failure was at least partly because he himself was not sophisticated, because he was a deeply involved purveyor of impressions and a man who suffered with his hurt and puzzled grotesques, and because he was not an intellectual or a detached observer and recorder of manners.

(K)                    Rex Burbank. *Sherwood Anderson* (Twayne). 1964.
pp. 139, 141

Anderson's abandonment of pure naturalism involved him in a movement away from structures dependent upon sequential action or gradually in- creased intensity and toward an arrangement of events which would better dramatize the centrifugal, diffused, resonant effect his materials called for. The halting, tentative, digressive style, and the circular, hovering or "Chinese box" approach to "what happened" thus do not so much demon- strate Anderson's affectation of the manner of oral tale-telling as they illustrate his understanding that the "epic" base of the story must be manipulated in such a way that weight is thrown upon the significance of the happenings as it reveals itself to the central consciousness and to the reader, rather than upon the events themselves. This is, of course, es- sentially a "poetic" strategy.

(K)                    Sister M. Joselyn in *The Twenties,* edited by Richard
E. Langford and William E. Taylor (Everett Edwards).
1966. p. 71

## Winesburg, Ohio

*Winesburg, Ohio* is a primer of the heart and mind, the emotions and the method of Sherwood Anderson. It is the most compact, the most unified, the most revealing of all his books. It is his most successful effort tech- nically, for in it he has told the story of one community in terms of isolated short stories. . . . The author presents the impression that he is discovering for the first time the situations that he reveals to the reader, consequently he leads up to them as haltingly, as slowly as a child opening a door and entering an old, unused room. In the end the effect is cumulative and powerful.

Harry Hansen. *Midwest Portraits* (Harcourt). 1923.

pp. 147–8

*Winesburg, Ohio* is a psychological document of the first importance; no matter that it is an incomplete picture of modern American life, it is an honest and penetrating one done with bold and simple strokes. These pictures represent the finest combination Anderson has yet achieved of imagination, intuition and observation welded into a dramatic unity by painstaking craftsmanship. They are one of the important products of the American literary renascence and have probably influenced writing in America more than any other book published within the last decade. They made and they sustain Anderson's reputation as an author worthy of comparison with the great short story writers.

Cleveland B. Chase. *Sherwood Anderson* (McBride).

1927. pp. 51–2

We must enter the realm of myth if we are to penetrate deeply into the form of *Winesburg*. . . . The myth of *Winesburg* concerns the legendary American small town, the town represented in the popular tradition as the lazy, gentle village of the Christian virtues. . . . The author's intention is to replace the myth of the small town Christian virtues with the myth of the "grotesques." It is important to remember that the "grotesques" are not merely small town characters. They are universal people, defeated by their false ideas and dreams. . . . The "grotesque" is neither misshapen nor abnormal. He is an unintegrated personality, cut off from society and adrift in his own mind.

James Schevill. *Sherwood Anderson* (Denver). 1951.

pp. 100–103

If we approach the novel from the direction of George Willard, the young reporter presumably on the threshold of his career as a writer, instead of from that of the *subjects* of the sketches, *Winesburg* composes as a *Bildungsroman* of a rather familiar type the "portrait of the artist as a young man" in the period immediately preceding his final discovery of *métier*. In order to arrive at the rare excellence of *Winesburg*, we must first see that it is a book of this kind; and then we must go on to see in what ways it is not typical of the *genre*, for it is in the differences that Anderson's merits are revealed. An initial formulation of this difference would mainly call attention to Anderson's almost faultless holding of the balances between his two terms, artist and society, a delicacy that was perhaps made easier for him by the genuine uncertainty of his feelings. To put it bluntly, there are few works of modern fiction in which the artist's relations with ordinary men are seen with such a happy blend of acuity and charity, few works of any age in which the artist and ordinary men are seen so well *as fitting together* in a complementary union that permits us to make distinctions of relative value while at the same time retaining a universally diffused sense of equal dignity. We need look no further for the cause of the remarkable serenity of tone of *Winesburg.*

(K)                                      Edwin Fussell. *MFS.* Summer, 1960. pp. 108–9

## Poor White

*Poor White* belongs among the few books that have restored with memorable vitality the life of an era, its hopes and despairs, its conflicts between material prosperity and ethics, and its disillusionments, in a manner that stimulates the historical imagination. . . . No novel of the American small town in the Middle West evokes in the minds of its readers so much of the cultural heritage of its milieu as does *Poor White;* nor does Anderson in his later novels ever recapture the same richness of association, the ability to make memorable each scene in the transition from an agrarian way of living to a twentieth-century spectacle of industrial conflict with its outward display of physical comfort and wealth.

Horace Gregory. Introduction to *The Portable Sherwood Anderson* (Viking). 1949. pp. 16, 22

In *Poor White* Anderson has given untainted expression to the persistent American myth of isolation: the society that has made money its dominant objective indicates its self-doubt and guilt by stubbornly insisting that the wealthy are unhappy; the society that believes, as no other, in success yet feels a need to brand it with disapproval. Hugh McVey, combining two main constituents of American character, Ford's mindless inventiveness and Lincoln's lonely brooding, has been driven to his work largely by the barrenness of his life; which is to say that the rise of American industrial society is the culmination of previous failure in sociality and that in such a society work is intimately related to the absence of creative activity. The central symbol of the book, through which it gains a quality of muted pathos, is the basket woven in desperation: the basket that is neither produce nor commodity but token of despair.

Irving Howe. *Sherwood Anderson* (Sloane). 1951.
p. 129

See *Winesburg, Ohio* and *The Triumph of the Egg* (short stories); also *Poor White, Many Marriages,* and *Dark Laughter* (novels).

# AUCHINCLOSS, LOUIS (1917–    )

He is wonderfully adept at showing the conflicts between personalities; at exposing the tyrannies, the dominations, the iron fingers in the velvet gloves of courtesy and social convention and family relationships. . . . His style is fluent, cultivated, urbane. . . . He has wit and irony; he has also a real understanding of and pity for the seekers of their own hurt.

Sara Henderson Hay. *SR*. Oct. 14, 1950. pp. 37–8

In this novel (*Sybil*), his first, Mr. Auchincloss shows many faults. His style is rather flat, and at times even clumsy; he has a sharp eye, but seldom describes what he observes with quite enough flair or wit. His heroine, furthermore, is a little too sensitive to ring true, a little too much the faithful recorder of her creator's feelings and ideas.

In spite of its limitations, however, *Sybil* is one of the most promising American novels in a long time. This is because Mr. Auchincloss succeeds in giving us vivid portraits of nearly every one of the people in his story. . . . Mr. Auchincloss shows them no mercy, spares them none of their faults, and yet manages to give a little twist of tenderness, an unexpectedly sympathetic turn, to each of them.

James Yaffe. *YR*. Spring, 1952. p. vi

With his four previous books, Louis Auchincloss has won a solid reputation as a polished and eminently civilized writer with a cool, discerning eye and a quietly satiric sense of humor. *The Romantic Egoists,* in addition to these qualities, has a somewhat higher voltage than Mr. Auchincloss has hitherto succeeded in generating. The writing is more pointed; some of the characterizations are stronger; the storytelling has more pull and it achieves a sharper impact.

Charles J. Rolo. *At.* July, 1954. p. 83

*The Romantic Egoists* is a book of quite remarkable distinction and solidity. The method is rather like Anthony Powell's—there is a similar dry reticence, a similar quiet building up of surprises from everyday incidents. But where Mr. Powell sticks out his legs and beams at you, Mr. Auchincloss, being a *New Yorker* writer, screws the pressure up till something explodes—and in his case that something is not just another taut nerve, it is a new idea. Not all the sketches are equally thought-provoking; one or two are a trifle self-satisfied. But most of them are brilliant essays in that most difficult theme, change of character. Butterflies turn into caterpillars, stones into bread, faces into stone. Hardly anyone has the nerve to contemplate these things. Mr. Auchincloss, cucumber-cool, can watch them happening to himself.

> Mary Scutton. *NSN*. Oct. 9, 1954. p. 449

Apart from his knowledge of the law, Mr. Auchincloss probably knows more about traditional New York City society than any other good novelist now working. Furthermore, he seems to believe in the continuing importance of what is left of such society, and the values it attempts to preserve and hand down. It is precisely the background of such belief that makes his satirical jibes so entertaining, and makes the rather neat, foursquare world of his books so comfortable to read about. *The Great World and Timothy Colt* appeals in part, perhaps unintentionally, to the escapist impulse; but it also shows how traditional writing methods and social attitudes can throw a refreshing light on parts of the contemporary scene.

> John Brooks. *NYT*. Oct. 21, 1956. p. 50

Louis Auchincloss . . . has a direct acquaintance with investment banking and . . . has made himself a skilful craftsman. In several novels and a couple of collections of short stories he has written authoritatively and persuasively about a small but important segment of American business. . . . Auchincloss is a deft prober, and he shows us how a sense of inadequacy and guilt can be created and how it can shape a life. To me the psychological problem to which he addresses himself in *Venus in Sparta* is less interesting than the ethical problem with which he was concerned in his preceding novel, *The Great World and Timothy Colt*. In its portrayal of a particular milieu, however, of a world in which there not only is money but has been money for several generations, the novel demonstrates that Auchincloss knows his stuff and knows how to use it to literary advantage.

> Granville Hicks. *SR*. Sept. 20, 1958. p. 18

It is obviously high time someone pointed out that he is one of our very best young novelists. This is far more than a matter of his knowledge of "the highest stratum of American society" or his alleged resemblance to Edith Wharton. It is true that Mr. Auchincloss knows a good deal about the successful and indifferent children of the earth . . . these people he represents with such complete and quiet understanding that it is easy to overlook their horror and their ultimate pathos.

What moves Mr. Auchincloss is the miracle of the developing heart flourishing incongruously in the great world. . . . Their honesty in his comedy.

> Arthur Mizener. *NYT*. Sept. 21, 1958. p. 4

Auchincloss has tried less for dramatic effect in this [*The House of Five Talents*] than in some of his books. His choice of an old lady as narrator is a happy one, because there is something old-fashioned in his writing, some sympathy with the past, that makes him more at ease in looking at the world through the eyes of an older character. Then too he is at his best not so much when he is trying for the big scenes as when his work is more essayistic—a brooding description of a family portrait by Sargent or the list of an old aunt's favorite topics of conversation. In some of his novels his presentation of characters is so much better than their actions that a reader who believes in them hardly believes in what they do, but in *The House of the Five Talents* they do not have to do very much.

Auchincloss has wit and intelligence and good taste, not necessary attributes of a novelist but nevertheless helpful. He is not overimpressed by the rich; I would guess that he knows people who have money and how they behave a good deal better than most writers who tackle the subject.
(K)                                     Paul Pickrel. *Harper*. Oct., 1960. p. 102

It should be pointed out, I think, that when Louis Auchincloss calls attention to the novelist's duty to entertain he is not offering comfort to those who say, with their own little air of superiority, that they read to be amused but who really mean that they read to be put to sleep. Like the master himself [Henry James], Auchincloss asks these things of a good reader: a scrupulous attention to the page, a ready responsiveness to passion and to effects of power, an awareness of design, an appreciation of subtle wit, and, above all, a cooperative resourcefulness in using fiction to expand the panorama of society into one more stimulating than meets the sluggish eye. It is to this level of entertainment that he invites an audience and to it I hope that his witty and satisfying book [*Reflections of a Jacobite*] may guide many.
(K)                                     James Gray. *SR*. June 3, 1961. p. 38

As for *Portrait in Brownstone,* one may say that this is good standard Auchincloss. It moves in that well-heeled world of New York lawyers and financiers which is his particular hunting-ground—the world of Edith Wharton, I suppose, two or three generations later—and part of the satisfaction which it gives comes from the confidence it instils. This writer, you feel, really *knows* the people he writes about. Knows them, gets on well with them, but is quite independent enough to judge them: indeed, the picture he draws of intricate networks of selfishness and domination, deceptions and self-deceptions, is rather horrifying. It reminds me of early Galsworthy—not a comparison which will be taken nowadays as a compliment, but in fact Galsworthy before he went soggy, the Galsworthy of

*The Man of Property* and *In Chancery,* was a much better novelist than his present obscurity would suggest.

(K)                          Patrick Cruttwell. *HdR*. Winter, 1962–63. p. 594

Though Auchincloss indicts fashionable society harshly (perhaps a bit too harshly), still his acid description of the social aquarium provides amusing as well as sober moments for the reader, for he, like so many novelists of manners, wields the weapon of satire most skillfully. Striking in an urbanely lethal way, he makes his "fish" wiggle before our eyes. . . . Fortunately, Auchincloss has the style—a fastidious and polished one— to complement his generally derisive attitude toward the aristocratic set. In the first place, his figures of speech, particularly the similes, possess sparkle and wit as well as appropriateness to the context. His description of the process of handling the closing papers—checks, bonds, mortgages, assignments, affidavits, guarantees, etc.—in a legal deal captures the ritualistic and elaborate nature of the performance by likening the shuffling of the papers across the long table to the "labored solemnity of a Japanese dance."

(K)                          W. Gordon Milne. *UKCR*. Spring, 1963. p. 183

He knows the people who work in downtown New York, how they make their money and how they spend it. He is, indeed, an authority on whatever survives as an upper class in America, and he is one of the few contemporary writers who can be described as a novelist of manners. . . . Auchincloss entitled a collection of his essays *Reflections of a Jacobite,* and it is true that he is something of a conservative, in the sense that he accepts the world as he finds it, believing that, though it has its evils, any change would probably be for the worse. He has the kind of irony that often accompanies a mild conservatism.

(K)                          Granville Hicks. *SR*. Aug. 17, 1963. pp. 15–16

Mr. Auchincloss always writes with urbanity. He knows the moods of New England and depicts them well; he knows the rivalries and pettiness of faculty life and the resentment and loneliness of boys who cannot be pushed. I think the older women in the book [*The Rector of Justin*], notably Mrs. Prescott, are more believable than the younger, such as Eliza Dean. But my deeper misgivings have to do with the form of the narration; the story begins in Brian's journal, then we have excerpts from a book by Horace Havistock, Dr. Prescott's oldest friend, who has come down to the school expressly to tell him that he must resign. Then we have a series of notes by David Griscam, followed by the memoir of Jules Griscam, his grandson and a black sheep of Justin. This shift from writer to writer is not contrived with enough individual divergence. I am not convinced that they would all take to paper this way; nor when they come to writing dialogue, that they would do it with the skill of an experienced novelist. (K)                                                    Edward Weeks. *At*. 1964. p. 133

In effect, Mr. Auchincloss writes, like a latter-day Trollope, a pseudo-critique of commercialism which collapses docilely as soon as one perceives it is being launched from a platform provided by commercialism itself. Like Mr. Auchincloss's blunted little semi-ethical studies of legal mores, the present novel [*The Rector of Justin*] is fake criticism, moral calisthenics for the already-palpitating. It is a shame, too, for the man has intelligence; but really good novels can't be written by men who are afraid to ask the questions that hurt. As for the book's picture of life in our better prep schools, well, perhaps someone better qualified can report if living, breathing people ever spoke the way Brian Aspinwall and Frank Prescott —with their repeated solicitation of the Deity's help to solve small, severely practical problems—are made to speak in this novel. (K)                                          Robert M. Adams. *NYR*. July 9, 1964. p. 15

Mr. Auchincloss loves novels, to read as well as to write. He becomes involved with plot, takes a personal interest in character, indulges a curiosity (and displays an expertise) about the subject of manners that place him in the company of such unabashedly Philistine critics (fellow novelists) as E. M. Forster and Mary McCarthy herself. His tone, even when critical, oscillates between the admiring and the deferential. . . . Mr. Auchincloss's slender study [*Pioneers and Caretakers*] opens up a more interesting question than that of the presumed limitations of women as writers of fiction: what have been their special gifts and strengths? What have women brought to fiction from their own unquestionably other, female experience, what have they done well that men have not? Mr. Auchincloss suggests—it is a very Victorian idea—that they have shown a persistent if not uncritical attachment to a regional homeland ennobled by childhood and ancestral associations. Against the dominant (in America) masculine fiction of rootlessness and rejection, he implies, women's fiction has provided a saving, a "more affirmative note" of conservatism. (K)                                          Ellen Moers. *NYT*. July 25, 1965. p. 1

The immediate setting of *The Embezzler* is as familiar as the story. It is Auchincloss' endlessly revisited Eastern urban, almost exclusively WASP-ish, upper-middle-class society, from about 1900 onward. . . . It is a world . . . of well-conducted adulteries and a slow drying-up of moral resolve, a world that has its troubles and tremors, but is by no means on the brink of disaster—no apocalyptics here. It is solid, recognizable and something to be reckoned with, and has at least as valid a claim on our interest as the Brooklyn waterfront or a pad in California. If it is not deep enough to be explored in great depth, Auchincloss has been exploring it to the depth and width it possesses. . . . He does not dispute literary traditions; he revels in them, is nourished by them and seeks to perpetuate them. He has as fruitful a consciousness as Trollope about the particular tradition he is himself working in: the now darkening comedy of manners, with its established conventions and rhythms of action—and especially as practiced by a series of gifted Americans.

(K)                                    R.W.B. Lewis. *NYHT*. Feb. 20, 1966. p. 1

Aside from its inventive ironies, Auchincloss's prose is all polish and no spit. It glitters a bit too brightly, like the over-varnished canvases of an adroit and expensive portraitist. He is a good hand with a haughty witticism. . . . The needle-pointed aphorisms and genteel clubman tradition go down easily enough in these deftly drawn stories [*Tales of Manhattan*], but an aura of armchair diversion lingers in the end, the yawning sensation of having been charmingly entertained.

(K)                                    S. K. Oberbeck. *Nwk*. March 27, 1967. p. 106

See *The Great World and Timothy Colt, Venus in Sparta, Pursuit of the Prodigal, The Rector of Justin, The Embezzler* (novels); *The Romantic Egoists, Powers of Attorney* (stories); *Reflections of a Jacobite, Pioneers and Caretakers* (essays).

# AUDEN, W. H. (1907–    )

Mr. W. H. Auden is a courageous poet. He is trying to find some way of living and expressing himself that is not cluttered with stale conventions and that is at once intellectually valid and emotionally satisfying. In order to do so he is obliged to hack his way in zigzag fashion through a stifling jungle of outworn notions which obstruct progress. . . . The only difficulty in following him is that he seems to be perpetually mixing up two levels of experience, private and public. Publicly he tries to persuade us that the world is a farce, privately we feel that he regards it largely as a tragedy.

John Gould Fletcher. *Poetry*. May, 1933. pp. 110–1

Auden is a stylist of great resourcefulness. He has undoubtedly drawn heavily on the experimenters of the past decade, Eliot, Pound, Graves, and Riding in verse, and Joyce and Woolf (especially *The Waves*) in prose. But he is not an imitator, for very rarely has he failed to assimilate completely what the model had to give. He is not a writer of one style.

The lyrics written in short lines display an aptitude for economy of state-ment that is almost ultimate; he has sometimes paid for this by an insoluble crabbedness or a grammatical perversity in the unsuccessful pieces, but a few of this type are among his best poems. On the whole, he is most effec-tive in the poems using a long line, poems where the difficulty his verse offers is more often legitimate, that is, derives from an actual subtlety of thought and effect rather than from a failure in technical mastery.

Robert Penn Warren. *AR*. May, 1934. p. 226

Mr. Auden's ideas are not so important as the way in which he expresses them. In his early work he is frequently obscure, not only because of the presence of private jokes which only a few intimates may understand, but because he oversimplifies the communication of complex experiences. He has used the imagery of psychoanalysis for the illumination of the sub-conscious mind and has left the uninitiated bewildered. . . . It is, of course, still too early to prophesy Mr. Auden's ultimate position. . . . But there can be no doubt that the corpus of his good work, already large enough to merit serious attention, communicates the truth as he has seen it.

James G. Southworth. *SwR*. April, 1938. p. 205

As a technical virtuoso, W. H. Auden has no equal in contemporary English or American poetry; and no equal in French, if we except Louis Aragon. There has been no one since Swinburne or Hugo who rhymed and chanted with the same workmanlike delight in his own skill. . . . He combines a maximum of virtuosity with . . . you could hardly say a max-imum, but still a considerable density of meaning. . . . Whether you ap-proach his work through his theology or his virtuosity, he is one of the most important living poets.

Malcolm Cowley. *Poetry*. Jan., 1945. pp. 202–9

In the poems written since Auden came to America the effects are clarified, the ambiguities have all but disappeared. The music hall im-provisations which he favors—the purposeful blend of casual horror and baleful doggerel—sometimes make him seem the Freudian's Noel Coward; but the combination of acridity and banality is unsurpassably his own. No living poet has succeeded so notably in the fashioning of metropolitan eclogues. . . . The virtuoso has extended his range, and cleverness is no longer the dominant note. Versatile but no longer special, elaborate with-out being finicky. Auden has become not only the most eloquent and influential but the most impressive poet of his generation.

Louis Untermeyer. *SR*. Apr. 28, 1945. p. 10

When we compare the Auden of the *Collected Poetry* with the Eliot of *The Waste Land,* we find in Auden more vigor, more scope, greater tension, but less fulfillment. This is natural enough, for Auden is in the middle of the arena riding a wildly bucking horse, whereas Eliot, on the sidelines, has just completed the examination of his horse's broken leg and has shot the horse neatly through the head.

Dan S. Norton. *VQR.* Summer, 1945. pp. 435–6

The best poet of the Auden generation is Auden. His *Poems* (1930) reveal a new social consciousness in original rhymes, conversational or jazz techniques, and unlimited sensitivity. By these rhymes, and by suitable images of deserted factories, frontiers, invalid chairs, glaciers, and schoolboy games, Auden suggests the death of his class. Ideas for improvement, resembling those of D. H. Lawrence, stop short of Marx, who had little use for the individual change of heart that Auden prescribes.

William York Tindall. *Forces in Modern British Literature* (Knopf). 1947. pp. 56–7

He has a brain nimble, alert, never-resting; perception, alive and darting; an imagination which sweeps over his world of perceived things with bewildering brilliance; he has humour which turns to satire; passion, which often consumes itself in scorn. In poetry he may be intensely serious or he may be playing a game in the use of words. His play is grim and his seriousness playful, and you can never be sure where the fireworks will lead you. In much of his work scorn is the predominant note—scorn of shallow emotion, philanthropic pretension, plutocratic display, slickness, trite phrases, borrowed metaphors, sentimentality, secret vice—and these are things which distract his attention when pure beauty is ready to move him.

R. A. Scott-James. *Fifty Years of English Literature* (Longmans). 1951. p. 216

We may sometimes feel that his view is distorted, that, for example, he thinks more are frustrated today than are in fact frustrated, or that he does not give sufficient weight, especially at present, to the surrounding evidence of human goodness as against the evidence of human sin. . . . Nevertheless, he is a significant figure, and in nothing more than in his sensitivity to the tensions of the age . . . Auden is at one of the frontiers of this anxiety-torn world; he is one of those who play out in themselves, with unusual and revealing clarity, struggles to which, whether we recognize it or not, we are all committed.

Richard Hoggart. *Auden* (Chatto and Windus). 1951. pp. 218–9

Auden's ideas have changed as strikingly as his way of life has remained the same. There is a dualistic idea running through all his work which encloses it like the sides of a box. This idea is Symptom and Cure. . . . The symptoms have to be diagnosed, brought into the open, made to weep and confess. . . . They may be related to the central need of love. . . . It is his conception of the Cure which has changed. At one time Love, in the sense of Freudian release from inhibition; at another time a vaguer and more exalted idea of loving; at still another the Social Revolution; and at yet a later stage, Christianity. Essentially the direction of Auden's poetry has been towards the defining of the concept of Love.

Stephen Spender. *At.* July, 1953. p. 75

Perhaps Auden has always made such impossibly exacting moral demands on himself and everybody else partly because it kept him from having to worry about more ordinary, moderate demands; perhaps he had preached so loudly, made such extraordinary sweeping gestures, in order to hide himself from himself in the commotion. But he seems, finally, to have got tired of the whole affair, to have become willing to look at himself *without doing anything about it,* not even shutting his eyes or turning his head away. In some of the best of his later poems he accepts himself for whatever he is, the world for whatever it is, with experienced calm; much in these poems is accurate just as observed, relevant, inescapable fact, not as the journalistic, local-color, in-the-know substitute that used to tempt Auden almost as it did Kipling. The poet is a man of the world, and his religion is of so high an order, his mortality so decidedly a meta-morality, that they are more a way of understanding everybody than of making specific demands on anybody.

Randall Jarrell. *YR.* Summer, 1955. p. 607

Mr. Auden . . . identifies himself with the humanity of suffering, neurosis, and fear. He is a tragic poet who does not particularly care about the dignity of tragedy. His poetry, by turns rhetorical and colloquial, is always about to slip into bathos. Like its creator it is not concerned with correct attitudes. I hope I shall not be misunderstood if I say that it is Mr. Auden's readiness to risk a thoroughly bad poem that makes him a far greater poet than Mr. Empson, the most original English poet, in fact, to appear during the last thirty years.

Anthony Hartley. *Spec.* Dec. 9, 1955. p. 816

As our undoubted master of poetic resources, Auden has experimented with every device that would flat the poem into a true statement of the human position as he sees it. Meter, diction, imagery—every device of Auden's great skill (even his flippancy) is a speaking way of refusing to

belie the truth with false compare. . . . In the native motion of his genius
. . . Auden implicitly warns us away from the stereotyped affirmation of
the good, the true, and the beautiful. He is not against the good, the true,
and the beautiful, as some foolish critics have argued. Rather, he asks
us to weigh these values in mortal fear of smudging them with prettiness,
and with an instinctive recognition of the fact that, being human, our
feelings are subtle, various, and often conflicting.

John Ciardi. SR. Feb. 18, 1956. p. 48

In a work of art, as in a man, we are best satisfied when we are confidently
aware of a wholeness, or integrality, that underlies all the diverse and even
conflicting elements. And we are most satisfied when there is a consistent
thread running through the whole course of a man's life or the whole body
of an artist's work.

In the case of Auden, it is our doubt on this point that makes us hesitant
to class him with writers in whom we have this sense of wholeness or
integrity. We do not take in his work the confident satisfaction that we do
in the work of a Voltaire, a Swift, a Molière, a Wordsworth, a Keats, or a
Browning. Or to take examples from the poets of our own time, we do not
feel in his work the integrity that we feel in poets of lesser gifts—in
Spender, or Marianne Moore, or in Robinson Jeffers; or in poets of comparable or greater gifts—Wallace Stevens, or Dylan Thomas, or Frost, or
Eliot. Through a man's work we are reaching out to the man. And if it is
true that the style is the man, we feel with these that we are making
contact with at least as much of the man as shows in his work, and that we
know sufficiently with whom we are dealing. With Auden we are not
sure of this.

We know that he is a very gifted actor and mimic; and he has beguiled
many an hour with his impersonations. But we cannot give ourselves up
to him without certain reservations.

(K)                    Joseph Warren Beach. The Making of the Auden
Canon (Minnesota). 1957. p. 253

He can almost never do without this third element: the impersonal point
of reference to which he directs the reader. It does not much matter
whether this is society, literature, mythology or politics, or whether it is
the subtle and elaborate game of serious light verse. Once he has an
impersonal framework his real gifts come into action: his technical inventiveness, his striking but scrappy ideas, his great range of reading, his
wit and, above all, his suberb command of language.

These are rare gifts, stimulating and admirable. Yet somehow I can't,
in the real sense, agree with Auden as I agree with Lawrence and Yeats.
What he has positively to offer does not seem to matter much. I cannot,

that is, get much from his work beyond the extraordinary ability and cleverness. He has caught one tone of his period, but it is a cocktail party tone, as though most of his work were written off the cuff for the amusement of his friends.

(K)                                    A. Alvarez. *Stewards of Excellence* (Scribner).
                                                                    1958. pp. 104–5

It is remarkable that in *The Dyer's Hand* Auden is constantly able to do two things at once: to develop an argument about a literary subject which casts light on it and on literature in general, and simultaneously to develop a general moral or religious argument, with a particular relevance to the contemporary world. This is plainest in the section on Shakespeare, but I hope that my inadequate summary has indicated that it is characteristic of the whole book. In addition to their intrinsic interest and value, these larger themes and moral arguments supply the context within which various of Auden's aphorisms and statements that have been puzzling or curious in some earlier form now are thoroughly intelligible. It becomes clear that he does not divorce poetry from truth and seriousness, as he has sometimes been accused of doing, and his emphasis on play, frivolity, the comic, and the fantastic takes on its full significance. The book offers a magnificent example of a mature and powerful intelligence, aware of its nature and limitations, casting fresh light upon individual works and writers, upon the perennial problems of criticism, and upon the nature of man. . . .

He is more like Dryden . . . than like most modern poets: he is a kind of maverick and extremely unofficial Anglo-American laureate, and, appropriately, writes much occasional verse. Like Dryden, he was much reproached for changes of faith and allegiance, and like him outmoded such reproaches by the tenacity and obvious sincerity of his convictions. Auden, too, has genuine modesty with regard to his own gifts, developing them with conscious craftsmanship but employing them prodigally and hence unevenly, so that high-minded critics accuse him of insufficient respect for his art.

(K)                            Monroe K. Spears. *The Poetry of W. H. Auden: The
                            Disenchanted Island* (Oxford). 1963. pp. 308, 337–8

Auden, wrote Orwell, is "the kind of person who is always somewhere else when the trigger is pulled." When that was said (in 1940), the implication was insincerity. That implication is one which no literary critic should ever make; you can make it against someone you know as a person, but when you are judging a writer, the accusation to be made, if any, is not: "You are insincere," but: "You are playing the wrong part, you are trying a style you can't manage." (This accusation may be kinder to the person;

it is far, far deadlier to the writer.) And this is what I feel about Auden. I could never accept him in the part for which Orwell flayed him, that of Marxist revolutionary; nor can I now, in the part he plays today, that of Christian sage. Not for five minutes could I take either role with the smallest seriousness; I am naively astonished when others do take them seriously, and I have to fight hard against the temptation of doubting if Auden himself does.

(K)                          Patrick Cruttwell. *HdR*. Summer, 1963. pp. 316–17

Auden is pre-eminently the poet of civilization. He loves landscapes, to be sure, and confesses that his favorite is the rather austere landscape of the north of England, but over and over he has told us that the prime task of our time is to rebuild the *city,* to restore community, to help re-establish the just society. Even a cursory glance over his poetry confirms this view. Who else would have written on Voltaire, E. M. Forster, Matthew Arnold, Pascal, Montaigne, Henry James, Melville, and Sigmund Freud? On any one of them, yes, any poet might. But only a poet of civilization would write poems about them all. If one looks through the reviews and the criticism that he has published during the last thirty years, the case for calling Auden the poet of civilization becomes abundantly clear.

A great deal of this criticism is non-literary or only partially literary. Characteristically, it has to do with the problems of modern man seen in an economic or sociological or psychological context. Auden is everywhere interested in the relation of the individual to society, of the metaphysical assumptions implied by the various societies that have existed in history, and of the claims of history and of nature as they exert themselves upon the human being.

(K)                          Cleanth Brooks. *KR*. Winter, 1964. p. 173

He wants to try out what every poetic resource and every possible combination of poetic resources can mold out of the life of the present. As a deeply traditional poet, he can never be satisfied with a single style or a single kind of poem. Auden wants to compose every kind of poem, and he very nearly has. Even among the relatively few works this study has singled out for special consideration, his range of poetic strategy is imposing. A truer sense of his scope can be gained by reading seriatim through *The Collected Poetry,* limited though it is to works written by 1945. Auden's has been a sustained examination of our world through a complex series of prisms drawn from past poetries. As a result, not only can we now appreciate unsuspected beauties that he has drawn from familiar poetic elements, but we can measure our surroundings against a broader perspective that is as directly artistic as it is philosophic or religious. Auden has been the more effective for having long ago ceased to worry about stating profound or final truths in poetry. Instead he has concentrated on the ultimately more fruitful goal of perfecting each new amalgamation of poetic resources with experience.

(K)                              John G. Blair. *The Poetic Art of W. H. Auden*
(Princeton). 1965. pp. 186–7

I think I am the third poet the editor of this magazine has tried to get to review *The Dyer's Hand,* a major poet's assay of literary criticism, and it has taken me a year and a half to muster the bad judgment to try it. The gates of the book are defended by gargoyles of the superfluous critic. It is a work intended to reprove unnecessary criticism, and it does this both explicitly and by the performance of feats of insight and sensibility that I have come to feel (and the book has been around for almost three years now) are in fact *necessary* to modern thinking and feeling. . . . The last and highest opportunity a critic has to serve, Auden says, is to "Throw light upon the relation of art to life, to science, economics, ethics, religion, etc." The book does this, I feel, in the way only a complete and unique human personality can do.

(K)                              William Meredith. *Poetry.* Nov., 1965. pp. 118, 120

All through the 'thirties Auden had scorned transcendental escapists of all kinds (religious as well as psychological). His emphasis had been on the world of making and doing, and this never disappears. He does not write of the wish for, the delight in, or even the desirability of permanently transcending worldly secular existence. In fact he is always suspicious of such an effort. On the other hand . . . Auden's interest in changing the secular world almost completely disappears in the 'forties. In fact soon he begins to satirize those who believe change to be possible. What position is left, then, if he favors neither religious transcendence nor secular reform? Acceptance of life as it is. Always a strong underlying inclination, now given philosophical sanction by the Kierkegaardian dialectic, this becomes henceforth Auden's dominant impulse.

(K)                              Justin Replogle. *WSCL.* Winter-Spring, 1966. p. 64

From the beginning, Auden's poetry has devoted itself to the idea of the human. It has sought, in a most difficult time, to define the unique nature and terms of human existence and to recommend, in the face of powerful discouragements, modes of human conduct that would nurture the potentialities and implications of that existence. This preoccupation and this end impel his much-discussed, wide-ranging searches and researches among the enterprises, dangers, and possibilities of modern life, so many of which, as we all helplessly agree, are largely inhuman. As poet, Auden has sought to use poetry to establish and preserve our humanity in an age

more than half in love with dehumanization. It is a large and noble work, this delineation of a life wish, and a large and noble talent has gone into it.
(K)                            Robert Bloom. *VQR*. Spring, 1966. p. 208

W. H. Auden began to write poetry when he was very young. In some respects the boyishness that was natural at the time has persisted with him ever since, as one's first habits almost always do. Then, he was impudent and appealing by turns; damning us at one moment, requisitioning our love the next; with really tremendous displays of variety and virtuosity to keep us attentive. His politics were Marxist, but of the clever rather than the deep-dyed kind, and his travels were exotic: the Orient, the Far North, the dives of Berlin. There followed a time of withdrawal and real exile; anxiety; shabby Ischia and nerveless New York. For a while we thought he might actually become an American. He was trying, however futilely. He loved us, that much was evident, even our wealth, even our vulgarity; but he could not learn to speak our language. He moved then, ever gentler and more restrained, into a religious phase; hurt, tentative, masked. He wrote, finally, in a language moving to long, sorrowful measures yet still with upcroppings here and there of the old insuppressible zeal, a sequence called *Horae Canonicae,* poems too ashamed to be devotional, too bitter to be ceremonious, though they had a shot at both; poems close, peculiarly close, to the puckered spirituality of the age. And now, a decade later, a new phase has opened. . . . Recently Auden has been living in Austria in a house that has become his refuge; but more than that—a sanctuary, a center, a resort. As he moves about the house, from room to room, from poem to poem, he writes about the house: its qualities, its place, its people; and hence about all people to whom the qualities of houses are important.
(K)                            Hayden Carruth. *Poetry*. May, 1966. p. 119

See *The Collected Poetry, The Age of Anxiety, Nones, The Shield of Achilles, Homage to Clio, About the House* (poems); *The Enchafèd Flood, The Dyer's Hand* (essays).

# AXELROD, GEORGE (1922–    )

*The Seven Year Itch* is funny, somewhat erotic, and in English. The sum of these virtues seems to be a smash hit, and a safe play to recommend to almost anyone who is looking for a pleasant evening's entertainment. What George Axelrod's romantic comedy amounts to is a series of *New Yorker* jokes attached to what (I am told) is a very true and rather ordinary situation—namely the light-hearted adultery of a happily married man while his wife and child are out of town for the summer. . . .
Henry Hewes. *SR*. Oct. 13, 1952. p. 25

*. . . The Seven Year Itch . . .* is an ingenious, knowing, and very amusing sketch of a husband whose wife has gone to the country and has left him wide open to summer temptations in the city. The model upstairs comes down, the husband succumbs, and is thereupon beset by rosy daydreams in which the model throws herself at his feet, by counter nightmares in which his wife throws him out of the house, and by another set of fantasies in which his wife leaves him for another man who is paying her attentions in the country. It all ends happily as he rushes off for a connubial week-end. The piece is cleverly written. . . .

Margaret Marshall. *Nation.* Dec. 13, 1952. p. 563.

*Will Success Spoil Rock Hunter?* by George Axelrod . . . is a fantasy disguised as an ordinary farce. All farces are essentially fantastic, but in this case there is almost no pretense that the story is even fictitiously real: the central character is the Devil in the familiar form of a movie agent.

I believe I should have liked the play more if it had been presented as a fantasy—an entertainment which took even greater liberties with reality than farce permits. . . .

Some of the jokes are funny and there is . . . a bit of rancid ribaldry about many of them. I am a poor audience for these jokes because I consider most of the quips about Hollywood to be based on a lie. The joke about Hollywood's stupidity, madness, and immorality was effective as long as we believed that the people who made the joke had values which were not those of Hollywood—but this is no longer true. Motion pictures are a great industry at which many able people are hard at work, and the product of which most of us patronize. We now realize—if we never did before—that the majority of the people who scoff at Hollywood are extremely eager to become and remain part of its corruption, madness, etc.

Harold Clurman. *Nation.* Nov. 5, 1955. p. 405

See *The Seven Year Itch, Will Success Spoil Rock Hunter?* (plays).

# BABBITT, IRVING (1865–1933)

The distinction of Professor Irving Babbitt is that he endeavours to acquire the now unfashionable but not outworn Socratic virtues: he works for an attitude toward letters and the life of which letters are symptomatic that shall be comprehensive, cohesive and based upon perceptions of wholes.

This direction and this effort enables him to outrank almost all his colleagues in American literary criticism. . . . It is Professor Babbitt's Socratic merit that he has succeeded in charting the contemporary chaos and in construcing for himself a unifying attitude.

> Gorham B. Munson. *Crit.* June, 1926. pp. 494–6

It is an unpleasant task to profess skepticism about the value of a group of writers who are aiming at the betterment of conduct. The philosophical difficulties that may inhere in Mr. Babbitt's particular defense of sane conduct, I do not feel myself competent to discuss. . . . The ethical code of the Humanists is probably sound enough, but, however sound these abstractions may be, they are of no use to the Humanists or to us so long as they retain the status of pure abstractions; the abstractions remain what Mr. Tate has called wisdom in a vacuum. The arbitrary and mechanical application of these principles to organic experience, whether the experience be literary or non-literary, does not constitute a discipline but rather a pedantic habit.

> Yvor Winters. *The Critique of Humanism,* edited by
> C. Hartley Grattan (Brewer). 1930. pp. 329–32

Professor Babbitt's doctrine is a compound of snobbery of the kind I find most irritating. Yet it has some elements in it of sense, even if these elements happen to be platitudes which my iceman, cigar dealer, grocer, butcher, bootlegger, garbage man and dentist already know; i.e., that it is best to keep temperate and thrifty, not to let your temper run away with you, not to make a nuisance of yourself, not to get up in the air over trifles, to see that your family gets properly fed and clothed, to pay your bills and not violate the laws. But what is new or Humanistic about that? Not a single person among my personal acquaintance has ever abandoned a child, although quite a few of them have read Rousseau.

> Burton Rascoe. *The Critique of Humanism,* edited by
> C. Hartley Grattan (Brewer). 1930. p. 123

There is no doubt that his aim is the same as that of Brunetière. He attacks the same multiform manifestations of naturalistic relativity. He agrees with him that "there is needed a principle of restraint in human nature (*un principe refrénant*)," that something must be opposed to "the mobility of our impressions, the unruliness of our individual sense, and the vagrancy of our thought." Brunetière, however, finally came to seek this principle of restraint in revealed religion. Babbitt does not deny that it may be found there, but the conversion of Brunetière is for him an occasion for insisting that the immediate data of consciousness reveal such a principle of restraint at work within the individual, whether or not he believes in revealed religion. Thus Babbitt finds a way to ground his humanism purely on individualism.

Louis J. A. Mercier. *The Challenge of Humanism*
(Oxford). 1933. pp. 60–1

How perfectly he knew each of those great, queer but powerful beasts, the modernist ideas, how convincingly he set forth the origin, growth, and present shape of each. How admirably he described their skill in concealing themselves, or in appearing innocent while stalking their prey. And how he dissected them all, showing their powerful muscles, their great fangs, and their sacks of poison. . . . To hear him was to understand the modern world.

In his astonishing power of understanding and analysing his enemy, his skill in diagnosing the modernist disease, lies his unique importance.

Hoffman Nickerson. *Crit.* Jan., 1934. p. 194

The astonishing fact, as I look back over the years, is that he seems to have sprung up, like Minerva, fully grown and armed. No doubt he made vast additions to his knowledge and acquired by practice a deadly dexterity in wielding it, but there is something almost inhuman in the immobility of his central ideas. He has been criticized for this and ridiculed for harping everlastingly on the same thoughts, as if he lacked the faculty of assimilation and growth. On the contrary, I am inclined to believe that the weight of his influence can be attributed in large measure to just this tenacity of mind. In a world visibly shifting from opinion to opinion and, as it were, rocking on its foundation, here was one who never changed or faltered in his grasp of principles, whose latest words can be set beside his earliest with no apology for inconsistency, who could always be depended on.

Paul Elmer More. *UTQ.* Jan., 1934. pp. 132–3

His own manner of speech was of the substantial order, straight forward, unadorned, unimaged, owing its flashes of color either to quotations artfully interwoven or to the antics of a playful humor, which in lighter vein regaled itself by caricaturing and distorting any illogical statement or any lapse from good sense in one's hurried interjections. He had, in dialoguing, a mischievous fondness for playing out the game of argument to a finish and inflicting a sudden and disastrous checkmate on any unwary advances of his opponent—a process not always relished by those whose sense of humor was less active than his own.

William F. Giese. *AR*. Nov., 1935. p. 78

Though Babbitt became identified in the public mind with one cause, that which bore the never fully elucidated name humanism, it was recognized in the academic world that he was also the proponent of a cause in one sense larger and more catholic—the cause of the humane study and teaching of literature. At Harvard he fought, in behalf of every American professor who believes that his function comprehends interpretation and criticism, against all who would restrict the academic office to fact-finding, fact-compilation, fact-reporting. Frequently viewed as a reactionary, he defended an academic freedom precious and perishable—the freedom to judge.

Austin Warren. *Com*. June 26, 1936. p. 236

In exposing an idea he would often use a peculiar and significant gesture. His right hand, rising beside its shoulder with spread fingers and outward palm, would make short lateral pushes in the air. There was not the slightest volitant or undulatory motion of the arm—no concession to flying, no fluent gracefulness. Those shoves of the open hand into space—into the spaces of thought—were rigid and impersonal. They insisted that the principle on which he talked was patently universal, belonging to everyone and no one. As for wrong opposing notions, his fingers would sweep them down and away, one after another, while his tongue attacked them.

G. R. Elliott. *AR*. Nov., 1936. p. 41

His opinions were hard-set, his statements clean-cut and definitive. There was no budging him from his positions. This is what made him a precious friend for me, though I did not share in all his principles or judgments. He was the touchstone on which to assay your own thoughts, when you wanted the stimulus of contradiction—always based on deep reflection, fortified by vast learning, ordered by nimble didacticism. His militant spirit (equal to his athletic strength), and his dogmatic preemptoriness (marked on his deep-set features), displeased some. I felt always attracted to his decided personality. . . . The geniality of his smile and wink took away the sharp edge of his obstinacy.

C. Cestre. *Irving Babbitt,* edited by Frederick Manchester (Putnam). 1941. p. 55

The humanistic point of view is auxiliary to and dependent upon the religious point of view. For us, religion is Christianity; and Christianity implies, I think, the conception of the Church. It would be not only interesting but invaluable if Professor Babbitt, with his learning, his great ability, his influence, and his interest in the most important questions of the time, could reach this point. . . . Such a consummation is impossible. Professor Babbitt knows too much; and by that I do not mean erudition or information or scholarship. I mean that he knows too many religions and philosophies, has assimilated their spirit too thoroughly (there is probably no one in England or America who understands early Buddhism better than he) to be able to give himself to any.

T. S. Eliot. *Selected Essays* (Harcourt). 1950.
pp. 427–8

See *The New Laocoon, Rousseau and Romanticism,* and *On Being Creative* (criticism).

## BALDWIN, JAMES (1924–    )

*Go Tell It on the Mountain*'s beauty is the beauty of sincerity and of the courageous facing of hard, subjective truth. This is not to say that there is nothing derivative—of what first novel can this be said?—but James Baldwin's critical judgments are perspicacious and his esthetic instincts sound, and he has read Faulkner and Richard Wright and, very possibly, Dostoevski to advantage. A little of each is here—Faulkner in the style, Wright in the narrative, and the Russian in the theme. And yet style, story, and theme are Baldwin's own, made so by the operation of the strange chemistry of talent which no one fully understands.

J. Saunders Redding. *NYHT*. May 17, 1953. p. 5

There are many strong and powerful scenes in this work (*Go Tell It on the Mountain*). Mr. Baldwin has his eye clearly on the full values that his sincere characters possess, though these values often are tossed aside and trampled. His people have an enormous capacity for sin, but their capacity for suffering and repentance is even greater. I think that is the outstanding quality of this work, a sometimes majestic sense of the failings of men and their ability to work through their misery to some kind of peaceful salvation. Certainly the spark of the holy fire flashes even through their numerous external misfortunes.

T. E. Cassidy. *Com.* May 22, 1953. p. 186

*Go Tell It on the Mountain* is an attempt by a Negro to write a novel about Negroes which is yet not a Negro novel. "I wanted," he says, "my people to be people first, Negroes almost incidentally." In this he is eminently successful, yet, paradoxically, he at the same time manages to convey more of the essential story of the American Negro than do most avowedly hortatory books on the subject. . . . *Go Tell It on the Mountain* is impressive not only for its psychology or saga, but for its construction, which employs a skillful timeshift, and for a style rich in metaphor and in a sad eloquence.

John Henry Raleigh. *NR*. June 22, 1953. p. 21

*Go Tell It on the Mountain* may be the most important novel written about the American Negro. . . . Although *Go Tell It on the Mountain* is meticulously planned, and every episode is organic to the governing conception, it is not primarily a novel of delicate relations, subtle qualifications, and minutely discriminated personalities. There is instead a force above the characters and their relations—adequately realized though they are—which creates an impression of terrible uniformity and strangeness. One of the best things this novel does is capture all the uniqueness, foreignness, and exoticism of Negro life. Like an anthropologist, Mr. Baldwin shows us these people under the aspect of homogeneity; their individual lives represent their collective fate. . . . Mr. Baldwin shows the basic separateness of his people without making them depersonalized savages.

Steven Marcus. *Cmty*. Nov., 1953. pp. 459–61

Mr. Baldwin has been enraged into a style; the harshness of his lot, his racial sensitivity, and the sense of alienation and displacement that is frequently the fate of intellectuals in this country has moved him to portray in lyrical, passionate, sometimes violent prose the complex, oblique, endless outrages by which a man, particularly a black man, can be made to feel outside the established social order.

Dachine Rainer. *Com*. Jan. 13, 1956. p. 385

Few American writers handle words more effectively in the essay form than James Baldwin. To my way of thinking, he is much better at provoking thought in an essay than he is at arousing emotion in fiction. I much prefer *Notes of a Native Son* to his novel *Go Tell It on the Mountain,* where the surface excellence and poetry of his writing did not seem to me to suit the earthiness of his subject matter. In his essays, words and material suit each other. The thought becomes poetry, and the poetry illuminates the thought.

Langston Hughes. *NYT*. Feb. 26, 1956. p. 26

His most conspicuous gift is his ability to find words that astonish the reader with their boldness even as they overwhelm him with their rightness.

The theme of *Giovanni's Room* is delicate enough to make strong demands on all of Mr. Baldwin's resourcefulness and subtlety. . . . Much of the novel is laid in scenes of squalor, with a background of characters as grotesque and repulsive as any that can be found in Proust's *Cities of the Plain,* but even as one is dismayed by Mr. Baldwin's materials, one rejoices in the skill with which he renders them. . . . Mr. Baldwin's subject (is) the rareness and difficulty of love, and, in his rather startling way, he does a great deal with it.

Granville Hicks. *NYT.* Oct. 14, 1956. p. 5

James Baldwin, the young American writer whose first novel *Go Tell It on the Mountain* received wide critical praise, has chosen the special, tortured world of the homosexual as the subject of his second (*Giovanni's Room*). . . . Mr. Baldwin has taken a very special theme and treated it with great artistry and restraint. While he is franker about the physical aspects of male love than other writers who have written on the subject, he manages to retain a very delicate sense of good taste so that his characters never really offend us even when they appear most loathesome, most detestable. This truly remarkable achievement is possible because of Mr. Baldwin's intense sincerity and genuine ability to understand and pity the wretches involved.

David Karp. *SR.* Dec. 1, 1956. p. 34

*Giovanni's Room* is the best American novel dealing with homosexuality I have read. . . . James Baldwin successfully avoids the cliché literary attitudes: over-emphasis on the grotesque and the use of homosexuality as a facile symbol for the estrangement which makes possible otherwise unavailable insights into the workings of "normal" society. . . . Baldwin insists on the painful, baffling complexity of things. . . . The complexities are of course most numerous in the treatment of the relationship between David and Giovanni. The void of mutual lovelessness . . . is the central pain of homosexual relationships.

William Esty. *NR.* Dec. 17, 1956, p. 26

Though Baldwin has abandoned the primitive Calvinism on which he was reared, its dogma still has him in thrall. Everything he has written is filled with a sense of human depravity, a deterministic view of the universe, a hopeless search for salvation, and a conviction that unregenerate, alienated modern man is doomed. . . . Baldwin's style is, perhaps, his greatest strength; he is never obvious, banal, or trite. And the determinism and outraged horror with which he views life crops up in a hundred images and ironies. . . . In Baldwin the culminating effect is one of damnation;

wretched man is dragged before the bar and condemned to endless fires of guilt and fear. It is the New Calvinism dramatized.

Charles H. Nichols. Cmty. Jan., 1957. pp. 94–5

Baldwin is a man possessed by the necessity of coming to grips with himself and his country. He is also concerned with forcing our nation—with which he has had a turbulent love affair—to come to grips with itself. Because he is a gifted black man in an environment controlled by whites, his view of life is especially illuminating. He is, as he has said in a recent radio discussion, "the maid" in the American house. He is the outsider within, the agonized repository of the family's most intimate secrets.

Julian Mayfield. NR. Aug. 7, 1961. p. 25

I'm sure that Baldwin doesn't like to hear his essays praised at the expense (seemingly) of his fiction. And I'm equally sure that if Baldwin were not so talented a novelist he would not be so remarkable an essayist. But the great thing about his essays is that the form allows him to work out from all the conflicts raging in *him,* so that finally the "I," the "James Baldwin" who is so sassy and despairing and bright, manages, without losing his authority as the central speaker, to show us all the different people hidden in him, all the voices for whom the "I" alone can speak. . . . To be James Baldwin is to touch on so many hidden places in Europe, America, the Negro, the white man—to be forced to understand so much.

Alfred Kazin. Contemporaries (Little). 1962. pp. 255–6

While any evaluation of Baldwin as writer must consider both his essays and his novels, it is, hopefully, for the latter that he will be remembered. Since the essays, for the most part, deal with contemporary problems, they will become historical; that is, again hopefully, they will cease to apply to current situations. Yet it is partly on the basis of the essays that one has faith in his value as a novelist, for some of the resources on which he must draw are revealed most sharply in the essays. What seems to be the case is that Baldwin has yet to find the artistic form that will reveal the mystery, that will uncover the truth he knows is there. If he does, if his intention and accomplishment become one, if his intellectual grasp is matched by his imaginative, he will be a writer whose measure it will be difficult to take.

James Finn. Com. Oct. 26, 1962. p. 116

James Baldwin has written, in *Another Country,* the big novel everyone has thought for years he had in him. It is a work of great integrity and great occasional power; but I am afraid I can do no more than the damned compact liberal majority has done, and pronounce it an impressive failure. Spiritually, it's a pure and noble novel; though it's largely populated by perverts, bums, queers, and tramps, with only an occasional contemptible square interspersed, I wasn't much distressed by their comings, couplings, and goings. They are looking for love in some fairly unlikely ways and places, but the commodity is a rare one, and we can't afford to overlook possibilities. No, the book's faults are mainly technical. One of them has to do with the difficult question of dialect. Most of Mr. Baldwin's characters are of the hipster persuasion, or at least on the near fringe of hipsterism, and the patois he makes them talk has most of the faults of artifice and few of the merits of originality. In effect, their argot is dull and uninventive. We are supposed to feel about many of these characters that they're proud, sensitive, suffering souls; it is thoroughly depressing to find, when they open their lips flecked with anguish, that, man, they talk like trite. They're always mouthing about "making it" and if they could break the shackles of their degenerate dialect, it's indeed conceivable that they might make a phrase or an image or something.

Robert M. Adams. *PR.* Spring, 1963. pp. 131–2

When Baldwin records, with finest notation, his exacerbated sense of what it is like to be a Negro; when he renders, with furious conviction, the indignities and humiliations which attend his every step, the stiffening and perpetual pressure which closes in upon a Negro simply because he is one; when he conveys his sense of the social climate by which the Negro comes despairingly to know, from earliest childhood, the atmosphere in which desperation is bred, that he is a pariah, a little more than animal, but less than human—then, I have no doubt, there can scarcely be a Negro who does not listen to him with full assent. But when we listen to any of Baldwin's voices—his passionately exhoratory warning or his pleading—it is not the voice, nor is it the tone of reason we are hearing, for Baldwin is not a "reasonable" man; it is a lamentation and a curse and a prayer.

Saul Maloff. *Nation.* March 2, 1963. p. 181

The largeness of purpose and gentleness of intention which Baldwin voices have brought a new climate, a new element, a new season, to our country in our time. That season, that climate, that element which are James Baldwin, they are now in the foreground of America's awareness. There is no way now that anyone can fail to recognize them, and to endure them, and to contend with them. They cannot be dismissed. It may even be that crops will have to be planted differently out of a consideration of this new season, or that quite new crops will have to be found which will flourish in the new climate, and that all the old fences and defences will be levelled by the fury of that new element. In his essays, his novels, his

short stories, Baldwin has levelled the ground so that we may start anew.
(K)               Kay Boyle in *Contemporary American Novelists,*
                  edited by Harry T. Moore (Southern Illinois). 1964.
                                                              p. 156

We should note that the title "Another Country" is lively with irony, for the novel presents a world as we know it but as it has not before been put in fiction to be seen, "other" by its ominous distance from what it ought to be and from real human needs, and then "other" as some private land where a handful of people have honored and renewed themselves. This tension epitomizes the book's role in Baldwin's vision. It does not cry out with the so bold and explicit warnings of "Letter from a Region in My Mind," but the prophet's tones there are really based in *Another Country.* An analogy is the way the self-reliance of "Civil Disobedience" is founded on the renewal and independence of vision Thoreau established at Walden. Baldwin had to discover his "distant land"—to use Thoreau's term—from which to see the essential unreality of New York. In this respect this third novel might be called the greatest of his liberal educations, just as it is the most informative for his audience. It is only from the distant land of *Another Country* that he can criticize the false land both toughly and compassionately, and the simultaneous violent content and delicate style in other work depends on this distance.
(K)               Robert F. Sayre in *Contemporary American Novelists,*
                  edited by Harry T. Moore (Southern Illinois). 1964.
                                                              p. 167

To solve our national problem of racial tensions we must think clearly and plan soundly because we are in a delicate moment, when the anger of many Negroes is naked and the sorrows and guilts of whites more exposed. For Mr. Baldwin, regardless of *what* we say or try to do, Western civilization seems suspect and faltering. He allows the Negro scant susceptibility to the many problems which afflict whites—of identity, of religion, of survival, of intimacy and sexuality. The Negro is an outcast, plundered so long that his fate becomes an almost total historical judgment upon the white, Western world, a world which, according to Mr. Baldwin, knows very little about itself, because as he points out, it cannot understand the Negro. Yet, apparently the Negro can understand the white man, and can save him from his impending doom. The Negro, having given love to inadequate whites, is the crucial factor in finally enabling the white man to solve his problems of identity. There is a cynical medical and psychiatric core in me which must reject such an argument. The problems of "identity" and sexuality are simply too complicated for rhetoric of Baldwin's kind.
(K)                         Robert Coles. *PR.* Summer, 1964. p. 414

A "protest play," unfortunately, always has a hard time of it artistically, and even more so if, like Baldwin, the playwright doth protest too much. And not only too much but too much, too soon. Right at the outset [of *Blues for Mister Charlie*] we are clobbered with a tirade which is an inflammatory inventory of all the injustices toward the Negro, and, justified as these grievances are, they strike a false note: you do not paint a picture that is to be a work of art with air brush and poster paint—unless, that is, you are a pop artist—and Baldwin would shudder at the thought of having written a pop-art play. But that is what it is: agit-prop art.

Baldwin is undoubtedly one of our ablest essayists and literary journalists—terms I use with respect—but as a novelist he has always struck me as a failure, and a progressively worse one, at that. Somewhere hedged in by fact and opinion lies the domain of fiction, which is neither brute reality nor the spinning out of speculation, however profound or piercing. In fiction—and in drama, too—certain moods, experiences, states of being and insights achieve a solidity of texture through psychological exactness, tasteful selection of detail, architectural structuring, and (most important, though least definable) a poetic sensitivity to words. In these things, Baldwin is more or less deficient, and his assumption of the mantle of embattled prophethood and the consequent thickening of his voice have made matters worse.

(K)                                    John Simon. *HdR*. Autumn. 1964. p. 421

It is pleasant to be able to report that *Going to Meet the Man,* Baldwin's first collection of short stories, is closer in spirit, tone, and achievement to his best critical work than it is to his "sensational" fiction. These are stories beautifully made to frame genuine experiences in a lyrical language. They are, for the most part, free from the intellectual sin of confusing the Negro's (and/or the white man's) tragedy with the homosexual's psychic deformity. They sing with truth dug out from pain.

(K)                                    Daniel Stern. *SR*. Nov. 6, 1965. p. 32

Baldwin's writing, depending so much on the straightforward humane statement rather than on irony, wit, or the savage comic imagination of a Ralph Ellison, occasionally falls into platitude; but Baldwin is intuitive and courageous enough to know that this is where his chief strength lies— common experience uncommonly probed—so that while he occasionally expects the flat statement to do more literary work than it humanly can, I am still impressed by his maturity and understanding as a man. He knows life in a way that I can only call enlightened by Negro wisdom; it is the same older, deeper, seamier, finally larger grasp of suffering and reality that I have heard in the great Negro singers and have observed in certain subtly seasoned Negro acquaintances.

(K)                                    Seymour Krim. *NYHT*. Nov. 7, 1965. p. 5

The lives of the characters in these stories seem to possess an extra dimension of emptiness, because he sees them against the possibility of a very different kind of life: a life of ceremonies and mysteries touching the absolute. He is searching for another city and another country. Like the great moralizing novelists, he is a preacher; he writes to bear witness. It would be ridiculous, as well as rude, to tell him he should take another tack. My complaint is simply that the total hunger aching inside him has driven him on to invest certain aspects of secular life—notably sex—with a blasphemous grace, and, alas, the grace is artistically unconvincing. The beauty of the language in *Go Tell It On the Mountain* brought the hero's experience of salvation to life; and, faithful to the spirit of the blues, Baldwin left much of the book's anguish unresolved. But in recent works he has made larger and larger claims for his various instruments of salvation, while the instruments themselves have become less and less convincing. When, in *Another Country,* Baldwin gives us the word about the redeeming majesty of the orgasm—multiracial, heterosexual, or homosexual— you sense a lack of artistic control, to say nothing of a loss of common sense.

(K)                    Joseph Featherstone. *NR.* Nov. 27, 1965. pp. 34–5

When he is not playing the role of the militant Negro intellectual or proving his social relevance, and especially when he is not writing about the United States, James Baldwin is willing to recognize the importance of status and place and of a reasonable degree of hierarchy in an orderly and civilized society. He remarks approvingly that Europeans have lived with the idea of status for a long time. . . . But when he speaks of America, he insists that the past has no relevance, that the heritage of Western civilization is of questionable value, that what we have in this country must be unrelated to any past scheme of social order. . . . He is, as we might expect, suspicious or even resentful of Faulkner's identification with the place Mississippi— which makes it all the more interesting and ironic that Mr. Baldwin's own best work is the result of his marked (if unwilling) identification with Harlem.

(K)                    M. E. Bradford. *Georgia Review.* Winter, 1966. p. 439

See *Go Tell It on the Mountain, Giovanni's Room, Another Country* (novels); *Going To Meet the Man* (stories); *Blues for Mr. Charlie* (play); *Notes of a Native Son, Nobody Knows My Name, The Fire Next Time* (essays).

# BARNES, DJUNA (1900–    )

A facetious commentator has said of Miss Barnes that she has a white pine mind with a mahogany finish, which for all its disrespect, is a fairly accurate description of the surface brilliance which glosses the simple, soft, and human intimations of beauty, truth, and pathos in Miss Barnes's work. Her prose is firm, vibrant, and rhythmical and her poetry ambiguous but melodious. Her stories, playlets, and dialogues are for the most part no more than a succession of brilliant, unrelated, ironic comments in an unintegrated design. . . . In escaping the commonplace, the platitude, the cliché and the formula she has retreated so far into ironic and disillusioned disdain that she has seemingly nothing left but a will for acrid observation and grim absurdities.

Burton Rascoe. *NYHT*. Oct. 14, 1923. p. 25

In the details of Djuna Barnes's stories there is a great deal of fine observation, clearly as well as beautifully phrased. It is the larger outlines of her stories that are obscure. This is perhaps because she sees in detail what the rest of us see, but feels about life as a whole differently from the rest of us. . . . The whole book (*A Book*), when one has ceased to ponder its unintelligibilities, leaves a sense of the writer's deep temperamental sympathy with the simple and mindless lives of the beasts: it is in dealing with their lives, and with the lives of men and women in moods which approach such simplicity and mindlessness, that she attains a momentary but genuine power.

Floyd Dell. *Nation*. Jan. 2, 1924. pp. 14–15

No one need be entirely unhappy this fall with such a book as *Ryder* newly come into the world—no one, at least, with a clear head and a stout stomach. Here are nimble wit, gay humor, trenchant satire, and, above all, a grandiose imagination creating a robustious world of loose-tongued, free-living characters such as have hardly ventured on paper for a century. . . . *Ryder* is certainly the most amazing book ever written by a woman. That much abused word "Rabelaisian" . . . is here perfectly in place. In fact, *Ryder* is more "Rabelaisian" than Rabelais himself.

Ernest Sutherland Bates. *SR*. Nov. 17, 1928. p. 376

(In *Nightwood*) the web of entanglement is naturally and inevitably woven, and the action progresses powerfully to its horrible conclusion. Though the characters are plainly and obtrusively psychopaths, the quality of the book does not derive from that particular, which is simply the mechanism of the tragedy, but from the force and distinction of Miss Barnes's writing. Her style is richly poetic; sometimes it becomes oppressive from a too conscious refinement of perception and language, but for the most part her wit and passion rescue it from its faults. In some passages the intensity of pity and terror effects something akin to genuine catharsis; in others, where the scope of implication contracts to the particular dilemma of the characters, a kind of hysteria results that leaves the reader merely horrified.

Philip Horton. *NR*. March 31, 1937. p. 247

If genius is perfection wrought out of anguish and pain and intellectual flagellation, then Djuna Barnes's novel *Nightwood* is a book of genius. In language, in philosophy, in the story it unfolds, she has woven a dark tapestry of spiritual and emotional disintegration whose threads never outrage each other in clashing disharmony. No gayety and no light falls upon her pattern, which is not to say that her pages are devoid of laughter or humor. For humor she has in abundance but it runs deep in hidden places and the laughter it evokes is tragic. If she has been ruthless and cruel to herself in writing this book out of the rich essence of her knowledge and her thinking and her experience, she has the compensating reward of compelling the thoughtful reader into attention to what she has to say and her manner of saying it. Her prose is lyrical to a degree where it seems of another age and another world but at the same time it does not lose kinship with the earthiness of humans.

Rose C. Feld. *NYHT*. March 7, 1937. p. 4

In her novel (*Nightwood*) poetry is the bloodstream of the universal organism, a poetry that derives its coherence from the meeting of kindred spirits. The "alien and external" are, more than ever, props; they form the hard rock on which Miss Barnes's metaphysically minded characters stand and let their words soar. The story of the novel is like the biological routine of the body; it is the pattern of life, something that cannot be avoided, but it has the function of a spring, and nothing more. It is in their release from mere sensation, or rather the expression of such an attempted release, that Miss Barnes's characters have their being.

Alfred Kazin. *NYT*. March 7, 1937. p. 6

This (writer) stares away from her in a rigor of horror, probing distance with fixed eyes in the hope that it will yield a niche where the contemporary mind, trained on distrust and disgust, can lose itself in stretches of time beyond our time. . . . For brilliance and formal beauty few novels of any age can compare with it (*Nightwood*). But one must also say how desperate it is.

Mark Van Doren. *Nation*. April 3, 1937. pp. 382–3

In *Nightwood,* as in the work of Braque and the later abstract painters, the naturalistic principle is totally abandoned: no attempt is made to convince us that the characters are actual flesh-and-blood human beings. We are asked only to accept their world as we accept an abstract painting . . .

as an autonomous pattern giving us an individual vision of reality, rather than what we might consider its exact reflection. . . . The eight chapters of *Nightwood* are like searchlights, probing the darkness each from a different direction, yet ultimately focusing on and illuminating the same entanglement of the human spirit. . . . (*Nightwood*) combines the simple majesty of a medieval morality play with the verbal subtlety and refinement of a symbolist poem.

Joseph Frank, *SwR*. Summer, 1945. pp. 435, 438, 455–6

*The Antiphon* is unmistakably the work of a mind of distinction and stature. I was not so much moved as shaken by the spectres it raises. But is it, as a work of art, successful? Is it really comparable with Webster, or is the style a sham Jacobean, or a sham Eliot-Jacobean make. . . . The speeches of the characters are never, in the true sense, dramatic, shaped by a living emotion. For all the sombre violence of imagery, they are aggregates of fancy, not imaginative expression proceeding from an inner unity of condition and thought.

Kathleen Raine. *NSN*. Feb. 8, 1958. p. 174

In *Nightwood,* published in 1936, Djuna Barnes gave us a novel of extraordinary and appalling force, a study of moral degeneration recited in a rhetoric so intensely wrought, so violent and so artificial, that it discouraged all but the hardiest readers and became a kind of symbol of sinister magnificence. *The Antiphon,* a verse play in three acts, repeats the oratorical modes of the novel, though with less obscurity and with some reduction of queerness. It is still difficult, perversely wayward; but it does make concessions to ordinary humanity, and there are in it moments of poetry and true excitement. It is scarcely a play: one cannot imagine it on any stage this side of Chaos and Old Night; but it is dramatic poetry of a curious and sometimes high order.

Dudley Fitts. *NYT*. April 20, 1958. p. 22

Some of Miss Barnes' profundities are pseudo-profundities, and her rhetoric occasionally falls into bathos. The end is not an adequate catharsis for the pity and terror that the book evokes; no more than Dr. O'Connor can Miss Barnes grant absolution. *Nightwood* is not a fully achieved tragedy like Nathanael West's *Miss Lonelyhearts,* but *Miss Lonelyhearts* is the only comparable work of our time. In the years since the '30's we have had nothing to equal those two great cries of pain, in their combination of emotional power and formal artistry. The writers who have copied Djuna Barnes—Truman Capote, William Goyen, and so many others—

have her surface without her depths. In *Nightwood,* at least, she produced a masterpiece.

(K)                        Stanley Edgar Hyman. *New Leader.* April 16, 1962. p. 23

In *Nightwood* the sentences are as heavy and intricate, as finely sewn as an old brocade, but their very grandeur serves only to muffle and disguise the human events they ostensibly depict. The whole tone and atmosphere of the novel are redolent of scandal, sin, and wayward confidence; everything about its language and setting promises extravagant revelations of the soul. Yet it remains curiously reticent and evasive, its characters fixed in a kind of verbal frieze. Reading it through again in this collection [*Selected Works*], I am reminded of how much more its author owes to Mr. Eliot than just a preface. The bogus aristocrats, the half-world of ambiguous sexuality, the self-conscious symbolism and mythic allusions as well as its fragmented shape, plainly remind us of the world of *The Waste Land.*

(K)                              Hilton Kramer. *Reporter.* July 5, 1962. p. 39

It is virtually impossible to speak of an ethic in Djuna Barnes' view of human situations, because that view rests on a total psychological determinism. Man is subject to the dictates of his unconscious nature even in his revolt against that nature itself. The courses of all the relationships in *Nightwood* are inevitable once chance has initially brought the characters together at certain particular places at certain particular times. . . . No ethical principle can aid the hero who enters the world of the night through love or disorientation; the only dictum which can be directed to the ordinary person who is spared this suffering is a warning to pay homage to the dark gods for continued preservation from a destruction which it is finally beyond the individual's power to prevent. . . .

Safety is the reward of moderation; but for man in his highest state of consciousness, which comes only in aspiration and revolt, destruction is inevitable. Pain increases in direct proportion to consciousness. Thus conscious life seems to be a mere freak of nature, or at most a register through whose tormented search for unity and permanence the inhuman universe is made aware of its own disorder and flux. Yet in this situation Djuna Barnes finds a basis for attaching a tragic value, which extends beyond stoicism, to human aspiration and suffering. Love, in that it seeks to heal fragmentation, to overcome solitude, and to deny mortality, is man's most perfect act of revolt; and in love man himself, by the force of his own suffering, of love as spiritual death, invests the loved object's existence with a value which it, as a meaningless freak of creation, did not possess before it was loved.

(K)                        Alan Williamson. *Critique.* Spring, 1964. pp. 64–5

*Nightwood* aims at another mode of transcendence, a kind of "transcendence downward," if I may give further application to a term I worked with in my *Attitudes Toward History*. The terministic basis of the development is indicated in the titles of the first and seventh chapters: "Bow Down" and "Go Down, Matthew." The process is completed by stylistic devices and an enigmatic conclusion designed to make the plot seem absolute, and to present the Lamentations much as though this were the "primal" story of all mankind.

(K)                                        Kenneth Burke. *SoR*. Spring, 1966. p. 335

See *The Selected Works of Djuna Barnes*.


# BARRY, PHILIP (1896–1949)

Mr. Barry has had the best preparation that America can give. He has been educated by our professors and theorists and has built upon the foundation thus attained with experience in the hard school of Broadway. If he allows nothing to turn him aside from it, he may yet write a great play. . . . His knowledge of the technique, his ability to write sincere and moving dialogue, his poetic sensitivity, the acting quality of his work, his varied experience, all forecast an achievement of which America may be proud.

Carl Carmer. *TA*. Nov., 1929. p. 826


The characteristic cleverness and brightness of Philip Barry's dialogue have tended to obscure the similarity of pattern of his plays. He deals for the most part with the individual's revolt against conventional pressure for social conformity and attempts to force him into a pattern of behavior to which he is inimical. Most frequently his antagonist is "business" and everything it stands for: its goal, way of life, its hostility to originality and individuality. To Barry "big business" represents everything he abhors in modern life.

Eleanor Flexner. *American Playwrights* (Simon).
1938. p. 249


Before the emergence of S. N. Behrman, Mr. Barry was our best writer of polite comedy. The true gift was his, but he valued it so little that he was said to have only contempt for *Paris Bound,* one of the earliest as well as one of the best of his pieces, and he gradually sacrificed success to two tendencies incompatible not only with the spirit of comedy but also, it would seem, with each other. Increasingly Mr. Barry became a snob and a mystic. His later plays were full of yearning elegants who seemed equally concerned with the meaning of the universe and with what the well-dressed man will wear—in his head as well as on it.

Joseph Wood Krutch. *Nation*. Dec. 24, 1938. p. 700

I carefully reread what Mr. John Anderson, Mr. John Mason Brown, and Mr. Brooks Atkinson had in their various columns seen fit to record (about *Here Come the Clowns*). . . . I was compelled to admire the diffused and sociable precision with which they expressed their respect for the playwright's intentions, past achievements, forward-looking subject matter and approach, and the equally exact conveyance of the tedium they felt at his present effort. Each of these reviews of theirs conveyed also the sense we get of fine intervals as such, of genuine and thrilling inventions now and then. . . . That the critics wished the author well was clear, and wished his play well, and clearly too they could not find their way in it. Which . . . is pretty much the way I feel about it.

Stark Young. *NR*. Dec. 28, 1938. p. 230

On the whole Mr. Barry has written an interesting play (*The Philadelphia Story*), with shrewd touches of character, and much humour. Moreover, Mr. Barry's heart and brain are both on the side of the angels, which is something in this day of inverted values in the theatre. . . . Also Mr. Barry can write admirable dialogue, though at times his tendency to preciosity is evident. In fact this latter tendency is his greatest artistic sin. But despite this fault Mr. Barry has written his best comedy since *Holiday*, though not his finest play—that is *Here Come the Clowns*.

Grenville Vernon. *Com*. April 14, 1939. p. 692

Phil was as serious at heart as he was gay on the surface. He was at once a conformist and a non-conformist, a sophisticate and a romantic. He was a good American from Rochester who never ceased to be Irish. The accent of his spirit, regardless of the accent of his speech, remained Gaelic. The fey quality was there, the ability to see the moon at midday. He had the Irish gift for both anger and sweetness, and the Irish ferment in his soul. He was a Catholic whose thinking was unorthodox and restless. Even in his comedies, when apparently he was being audacious, he employed the means of Congreve to preach sermons against divorce which would have won a Cardinal's approval.

John Mason Brown. *SR*. Dec. 24, 1949. p. 26

Barry was essentially a writer of comedy, and repartee was his stock in trade. He did however aspire to a greater seriousness, and there are passages in *Hotel Universe* and *Here Come the Clowns* which indicate ability in that direction. The difficulty, whenever he attempted heavier fare, was that he seemed to walk on tiptoe, perhaps in fear that he would be laughed at, and his work always seems to be trying to anticipate that possibility by getting in the first laugh. It moves gingerly among the more disturbing moral problems, darting and feinting, always ready to withdraw into the security of a smart remark, as though to indicate that the author has not lost his sense of humor or got himself out of his depth.

Walter Kerr. Com. Jan. 26, 1951. p. 398

Barry's was a healing art at a time when dramatic art was mostly dissonance. Perhaps Barry felt the need for healing too greatly himself to add to the dissonance and to widen the rifts in the topography of the modern, specifically contemporary American, scene. Whatever the reason, and regardless of the risk of indecisiveness, Barry sought balm in Gilead, found it somehow, and dispensed it liberally—and with gentlemanly tact. . . . It was not the least of Barry's merits, a mark of both his breeding and manliness, that his manner was generally bright and brisk and that the hand he stretched out to others, as if to himself, was as firm as it was open.

John Gassner. TA. Dec., 1951. p. 89

Certainly it falls far short to dismiss Barry as a witty writer of high comedy of manners, bantering, facile, and superficial. He was that and more. Beneath his flippancy and "chit-chat" was a sensitive and deeply spiritual writer coming to grips with the psychology of his times and expressing a yearning for maturity and emotional wholeness. No other American playwright was able to transmute the raw elements of unconscious life into a work of art so delicate, so subtly ingratiating, and so fresh in form, as did Philip Barry. If these are the criteria of greatness, *Hotel Universe* belongs among the great plays.

W. David Sievers. Freud on Broadway (Heritage).<br>1955. p. 211

See *Holiday, The Philadelphia Story, Here Come the Clowns,* and *Hotel Universe* (plays).

# BARTH, JOHN (1930–    )

To say that Mr. Barth's second novel [*The End of the Road*] concerns a neurotic suffering from "immobility" makes it sound deadly; but in fact, it is interesting and witty, if a bit puzzling in its implications. . . . The plot sounds absurd, but beneath the comic surface, questions are being raised regarding choice and meaning in life. The writing is very good, but may occasionally shock some readers.

Paul C. Wermouth. LJ. Sept. 1, 1958. pp. 2319–20

The recent monstrous novel of John Barth, . . . *The Sot-Weed Factor,* could scarcely have been written by a European, because it involves a *new* concept rather than a variation on an existing one. . . . It presents itself as a "historical novel," or again, as a "joke on historical novels," and each guise is strong enough that the work may be, and is, read as either. It is also, like *Finnegans Wake,* a proof of what cannot be done, or else the reason for no longer doing it; theoretically at least, the existence of *The Sot-Weed Factor* precludes any further possibility for the "historical novel." This does not mean that the book is one to be especially recommended; readers familiar with the extraordinary art of Mr. Barth's earlier novel, *The End of the Road,* will probably find *The Sot-Weed Factor* prolix and overwhelmingly tedious. This is, of course, an integral part of the book's destructive function . . . ; Mr. Barth's sense of humor, in short, is an extremely advanced one.

Terry Southern. Nation. Nov. 19, 1960. p. 381

The mark of style in [*The Sot-Weed Factor*] is untiring exuberance, limitless fertility of imagination (fancy, if you prefer), a breathless pace of narrative that never lets the reader rest or want to rest. Superficially one might say that our author "imitates" seventeenth century style, but he doesn't really; he only makes us think he does. He thereby avoids the stiffness of pedantry and at the same time gets a flavor of the antique. The aim . . . is burlesque—even the apparently inordinate size of the book is a joke. It was a dangerous joke, but he gets away with it. He burlesques the aged conventions of fiction—mistaken identity, "the search for a father," true love, and all the rest—with merciless ingenuity. No moral purpose is discoverable, no arcane "significance," simply fun.

Denham Sutcliffe. KR. Winter, 1961. p. 184

Primarily, John Barth is a novelist of ideas. The situations in his comic works are always directed toward establishing his twin themes of the individual's quests for value and identity in a world of gratuitous events. Clearly aligned with existentialist conceptions, Barth, nevertheless, denies a formal knowledge of philosophy and prefers to describe himself as "reinventing" ideas to cope with his view of the modern world. . . .

*The Sot-Weed Factor* is Barth's most complete and satisfactory treatment of his themes of value and identity. Here his approach is primarily a negative one. Through the destruction of a false ideal of innocence, Barth establishes his picture of man as a complex, emotional and sexual being and stresses the value of sympathetic ties between men.

Part of Barth's success in *The Sot-Weed Factor* comes from the book's form. As opposed to his first two novels which are realistic treatments of bizarre situations, the third novel is purposely artificial.

John C. Stubbs. Critique. Winter, 1965–66. pp. 101, 108

If we can measure literary achievement at all, we can measure the value of a novel by the extent to which it succeeds in the impossible task of getting the sloppy richness of life into the satisfying neatness of artistic shape.

By any such standard, *Giles Goat-Boy* is a great novel. Its greatness is most readily apparent in its striking originality of structure and language, an originality that depends upon a superb command of literary and linguistic tradition rather than an eccentric manipulation of the "modern." . . . Barth employs the traditional patterns of myth, epic and romance to generate a narrative of extraordinary vigor and drive. At the same time, he freights this narrative with ideas and attitudes in combinations so varied and striking that the reader is torn between stopping to explore the book's philosophical riches and abandoning himself to the pleasure of immersion in a story. . . .

Robert Scholes. NYT. Aug. 7, 1966. pp. 1, 22

Barth had the unfashionable audacity to take on the historical novel in *The Sot-Weed Factor,* and in *Giles Goat-Boy* he deliberately chooses the kind of romance most often considered flimsy or trivial—science fiction. . . . The world of *Giles Goat-Boy* is the end product of the ideas of Marx, Freud, Ford, Sartre, Einstein, and perhaps the Marquis de Sade, but George [the novel's hero] goes on echoing the adventures of Ulysses, Sinbad, Oedipus, Jesus and Huck Finn. As mythic parallels clash with modern ideology, Barth works the parallels both ways to suggest that traditional heroism may be futile or even wildly comic in action, but that it remains somehow noble in spirit.

Scott Byrd. Critique. Autumn, 1966. p. 111

Barth's *Giles Goat-Boy* is not so much science fiction as undergraduate humor-magazine fiction. . . . Plato and his followers regretted that the mind had a body; D. H. Lawrence and his followers regretted that the body had a mind; Rabelais regretted neither; Barth regrets both. His celebrated change of direction turns out to be no change at all. He still thinks sex is dirty, he still likes it dirty, and he is still a relativist. His values, that is to say, are still those of a tame goat.

J. Mitchell Morse. HdR. Autumn, 1966. p. 512

See *The Floating Opera, The End of the Road, The Sot-Weed Factor, Giles Goat-Boy* (novels).

# BEHRMAN, S. N. (1893–    )

In this American play (*The Second Man*) the talk is fresh, the epigrams are not machine made but seem spontaneous and in keeping with the character, and there is a merry note of satirical burlesque in the melodramatic episodes introduced into the story. . . . This play may owe much to *The Importance of Being Earnest* (as it owes something, also, to *Man and Superman*), but it is no mere rehash of ancient styles. It is much more ironic Yankee burlesque-comedy of Hoyt and Cohan touched with literary distinction and a hint—just a pleasant hint—of thoughtfulness.

Walter Prichard Eaton. NYHT. June 26, 1927. p. 12

Mr. Behrman . . . remains one of the few playwrights that we have ever had in America who does not cause embarrassment to dramatist, actors, and audience, when he indulges in brains or sophisticated statement. . . . He is one of those rare authors in the theatre who do not mistrust civilized society and do not think that Times Square must understand or no tickets will be sold. He has sensed the fact that in our theatre there is a genuine opening for such dramatists as might leave the mass of theatre-goers confounded or displeased; for him the French proverb, "Pour les sots acteurs Dieu créa les sots spectateurs," extends to audiences and plays, and he has taken the bold risk of failing in his own way instead of failing in somebody else's.

Stark Young. NR. Dec. 28, 1932. p. 188

The remarkable thing about Mr. Behrman is . . . the clarity with which he realizes that we must ultimately make our choice between judging men by their heroism or judging them by their intelligence, and the unfailing articulateness with which he defends his determination to choose the second alternative. . . . Mr. Behrman's plays are obviously "artificial"—both in the sense that they deal with an artificial and privileged section of society and in the sense that the characters themselves are less real persons than idealized embodiments of intelligence and wit. . . . No drawing room ever existed in which people talked so well or acted so sensibly at last, but this idealization is the final business of comedy.

Joseph Wood Krutch. Nation. July 19, 1933.<br>pp. 74–6

You must grant S. N. Behrman the privilege of writing plays on his own terms, if you want to enjoy them in the theatre. His dramas have little plot and less action. People come and go as often as they do in other men's plays; they meet and part and meet again, but they do so because the conversation—which is the alpha and omega of Behrman's playwriting—needs a shift in emphasis or in attack, rather than because of any change in the aspect of the situation. You cannot fairly say that his plays are "not about anything," for they fairly bristle with the contemporary, social, economic, controversial things they are about. But his drama is in his talk, and it would be well for people who think they do not like "talky" plays to consider carefully what Behrman can do with talk, before they decide too definitely that many words never made a play.

Edith J. R. Isaacs. *TA*. April, 1936. p. 258

Behrman is a man of rather emotional, almost lyrical and, if you will, sentimental nature, embarrassed by a sense that this nature is not quite smart enough for the society in which he finds himself and in which he would like to occupy a favored place. Thinking of himself—and he is preoccupied with the subject—he is ready to weep, but society, he believes, would consider such behavior unseemly. Looking at the world, he is almost ready to cry out or at least to heave so profound a sigh that the sound might be construed as a protest, so he suppresses his impulse and flicks our consciousness with a soft wit that contains as much self-depreciation as mockery. He tries to chide his world with a voice that might be thought to belong to someone else—a person far more brittle, debonair, urbane than he knows himself to be.

Harold Clurman. *NR*. Feb. 18, 1952. pp. 22–3

Something deeper than style alone distinguishes him from our many purveyors of light entertainment, including those who have at one time or another made a specialty of skepticism and debunking. That something is his habit of balancing the score. It makes him not merely a judicious but an acute playwright rather than a merely congenial one. He always remains *two* men; one man makes the positive observations, the second proposes the negative ones. . . . Behrman's art of comedy, including his so-called comic detachment, consists of an ambivalence of attitudes that has its sources in the simultaneous possession of a nimble mind and a mellow temperament.

John Gassner. *TA*. May, 1952. pp. 96–7

Providence Street, the background for most of (*The Worcester Account*), is the scene of Mr. Behrman's early life. . . To one who comes, as I do, from a similar place, the half-ghetto of the American city, these people are immediately familiar. I recognize them in Mr. Behrman's skillful reproduction and wonder why they often appear shortened, flattened, and lacking in vigor and primitive idiosyncrasy. They have been written of with charm and in the process have emerged somewhat tamed and weakened. Somehow the charm does not seem to belong to them; it is not their native charm but one which the author has lent them, returning to them after long separation. The air of nostalgia which pervades the book is often appealing but many times emphasizes the quaintness of Providence Street rather than its difficulty and poverty.

Saul Bellow. *SR*. Nov. 20, 1954. p. 41

. . . Behrman has never been seriously considered as a comedian of ideas. One reason may be that he sets his plays in drawing rooms. His drama moves in that international half-world in which art and intellect meet money, in which celebrity, notoriety, or wealth is a necessary entree. Invariably, the dramatic situation against which the conflict of ideas is played is one that involves the discovery or dissolution of love, and there is always a central female character, who could be and often was played by Ina Claire. When an elegantly dressed play, with articulate and often amusing lines, is centered on a character who is played by an extremely sophisticated actress, it is not surprising that substance is ignored for surface.

There is another, and probably more important, reason why the ideas in Behrman's plays have been passed over. The bulk of his plays were written in the 30's and his objectivity, if taken seriously, would have been completely unacceptable in that decade. Basically conservative, Behrman stood on middle ground, trying to hold on to the area, once staked out by humanists, in which tolerance of ideas and of human weakness could flourish. His plays show a fascination and a distaste for the man who becomes completely absorbed in himself or his beliefs—the complete egoist or the convinced idealist.

(K)                    Gerald Weales. *Cmty*. March, 1959. p. 256

Here, then, is Mr. Behrman, during the last three years of Max's life, assiduously visiting Rapallo, armed with what I take to have been an invisible notebook. He has constructed his portrait [of Max Beerbohm] round these visits, and with the cleverness of a superlative photographer he has timed his shots so that he can, at will, step into the picture himself. The final chapter is headed "The Last Civilized Voice." But Max's voice was not the last. Mr. Behrman has a voice of his own, and its pitch is exactly right for the matter in hand. He catches Max's inflexions to the life, and he adds his own very personal wit. Nothing in the world is harder than to be both amusing and affectionate throughout 300 pages; but that is precisely what Mr. Behrman has accomplished.

(K)                    Alan Pryce-Jones. *NYHT*. Oct. 2, 1960, p. 1

S. N. Behrman's *Lord Pengo,* based loosely on Mr. Behrman's study of Duveen, is based equally loosely on the requirements of the stage. . . .

The true picaresque hero is a psychologist as well as a rascal: Lazarillo de Tormes, as a mere child, realizes that "there are many people in the world who run away from other folks only because they don't know themselves." It is on similar psychological perceptions that Pengo operates, but the trouble is that suave, persistent, slow-working wiles are not the stuff dramas are made on. Epics and novels, yes; but not plays, which need conflict. So Mr. Behrman drags it in in the shape of a rebellious son complete with appropriate platitudes ("I don't seem to get a chance to talk to you, Father!"). Out of love for Pengo, Mr. Behrman, moreover, neglects the other characters, and clients, in any case, are not ideal dramatic fare. Devoted but tough female secretaries, for that matter, have long since had their day.

Despite urbane dialogue and some bubbles of iridescent fun, *Lord Pengo* is weighed down with *longueurs* and fillers and a general feeling of fatigue.

(K)                                                    John Simon. *HdR*. Spring, 1963. pp. 83–4

Already famed as a dramatist and author of the highly successful *Portrait of Max,* Mr. Behrman here [*The Suspended Drawing Room*] brings together a collection of short pieces originally done for the *New Yorker.* Included are two essay-impressions of London during, and just following, the last war. The remainder of the volume is devoted to seven character sketches. . . . Mr. Behrman, through deft skills, removes the reader from shackling reality and introduces him to other times and unforgettable characters. . . . The really satisfying feature is the clever selection of the perfect detail. Finding London during the war too large a vista for his small canvas, he chooses to describe only the bomb shelters and in doing so, he captures the horror and senselessness of the bombings, while also clearly revealing the indomitable spirit of the English.

(K)                                                    Richard K. Burns. *LJ*. Aug., 1965. p. 3290

See *Four Plays; The Worcester Account* (autobiography); *Portrait of Max* (biography).

# BELASCO, DAVID (1859–1931)

Belasco's contribution to the American drama is that of a producer and stage director rather than that of an author. His plays—mostly melodramas —have little permanent value, but as a creator of stage-effects, in elaboration of detail, in arrangement of action and stage pictures, he is recognized to be without a master in the modern theatre.

Arthur Hornblow. *A History of the Theatre
in America* (Lippincott). 1919. p. 340

David Belasco, with his passion for thoroughness, was particularly instrumental in giving a certain substantial illusion to the box-set interior, and eliminating the most grossly artificial features from exteriors. But this revolt was solely in the direction of naturalism. It did not start with the desire to bring the setting into closer harmony with the spirit of the play, but only with the object of making the scene more natural. It removed the worst absurdities of Nineteenth Century staging; but in its later elaboration it provided distractions quite as foreign to the substance of the drama. In the pursuit of the natural, Belasco and others began to build scenes so finely imitative, so true to the surface appearances of life, that the audience often forgot the play in wonder at the photographic perfection of the setting.

Sheldon Cheney. The Art Theatre (Knopf). 1925.<br>pp. 189–90

Beginning 1893 with his first great success, *The Girl I Left Behind Me* (by Belasco and Franklin Fyles), he won a national reputation for colorful plays produced with meticulous Naturalism. . . . It is impossible not to see in Belasco the return of that cycle which would bring back Naturalism to the bathos of Romanticism from which it had once emerged. . . . Belasco's melodramas had an admixture of sweetness and light in a blend to which, it is likely, he had a unique claim. If any social criticism remained, it was reduced to a whisper. . . .

Belasco used an idiom newer than that of his Romantic predecessors. The acting was believable in comparison with nature; the settings were infinitely more lifelike than in the past. But underneath both the Romantic stereotype was there for any alert observer to see. By the time Naturalism received its American expression at the hands of Belasco, it was no longer a life-storming technique.

Mordecai Gorelik. New Theatres for Old<br>(Samuel French). 1941. pp. 160–3

The [Henry C.] De Mille-Belasco collaborations were playwrought before they were playwritten. Except for experimental snatches, dialogue was held in abeyance until character had been conceived and developed and situations devised and arranged in elaborate detail. Most of the actual writing was done by De Mille, most of the planning and dramatic construction by Belasco. The preliminary discussions over and the development of the action clear in their minds, the two men repaired to the theater and staged the play. De Mille sat at a table in the front row of the orchestra; Belasco on the stage impersonated all the characters in the situations which had been plotted. Such dialogue as had been written down was primarily a point of departure, a means by which the situations were set in motion. The dialogue which emerged in final form sprang less from the preliminary speeches than from the situations in action; the determining factor was stage effectiveness. De Mille would read a few lines; Belasco would set them in motion, suggest alterations, omissions, and enlargements to fit stage business.

Robert H. Ball. Introduction to America's Lost Plays,<br>vol. 17 (Princeton). 1941. p. xii

As a playwright Belasco had his training in a rough-and-ready school, where action and strong, simple motives were dominant. Although in the course of his life he passed through many phases, and although he adapted himself somewhat to changing styles and points of view, he never relinquished his fundamental belief in simplicity of motive and strength of situation as the basic factors in drama. A direct approach to the human heart was his chosen path, and from that path he never strayed. Many of his plays disclosed a love of the morbid, but his morbidity was natural, not decadent. Even his sensuousness escaped the charge of perversion.

Realistic effect was his forte. Knowing that, he could indulge his fancy, for to a showman like Belasco the theater is primarily a place where the implausible is made plausible. In print many of his plays seem today too implausible, but plausibility in the theater is a variable thing, and in their day, presented by the hand of the master, they were plausible. History is consistent on that point.

Glenn Hughes and George Savage. Introduction to
*America's Lost Plays,* vol. 18 (Princeton). 1941.
pp. x–xi

A consideration of the plays written, rewritten, adapted, arranged and produced by David Belasco . . . might lead one to believe that the work of this extraordinary man was more closely related to the development of modern American drama than it actually was, but it is impossible to determine the precise extent of his cooperation with other writers in all the plays to which his name is attached, either as sole author or collaborator; and even where his share as playwright is relatively clear, what he added as director and stage manager rather obscures his role as writer. . . . Even such picturesque and more or less "original" plays as *The Girl of the Golden West* . . . and *The Return of Peter Grimm* . . . , are little more than local-color pastiches written largely to exhibit his own virtuosity as director and the special talents of his actors.

Barrett H. Clark. *A History of Modern Drama*
(Appleton-Century). 1947. p. 652

Working with highly theatrical, sentimental plays (mostly of his own authorship), he directed and set them with consummate "naturalism." He exactly reproduced a Child's restaurant down to a cook flapping pancakes in the window; he cluttered the setting of *The Return of Peter Grimm* with hundreds of theatrically extraneous properties "because that was the way the room would be" . . . ; he erected complete rooms beyond the entrances of a setting in order to help the actors acquire a strong sense of illusion as they traversed these extra rooms on their way to the stage; he expected actors to "engross themselves in their parts"; and he kept his electricians busy developing lighting equipment that would more nearly reproduce natural light.

Like the painted actuality of Romanticism, this extreme Naturalism defeated its purpose because it drew attention to the setting instead of providing an environment that strengthened the believability of the dramatic action.

> H. D. Albright, William P. Halstead, Lee Mitchell.
> *Principles of Theatre Art* (Houghton). 1955. p. 162

For this Belasco was a clever man—the cleverest, and by all odds, in the native theatre—and, doubtless chuckling up his sleeve, for it is impossible to imagine him deceived by his own tin-pantaloonery, he witnessed the canonization of his simple humbug and through that simple humbug the canonization of himself by the absorbent rhapsodists. But this was yesterday. . . . Mr. Belasco has contributed one—only one—thing for judicious praise to the American theatre. He has brought to that theatre a standard of tidiness in production and maturation of manuscript, a standard that has discouraged to no little extent that theatre's erstwhile not uncommon frowsy hustle and slipshod manner of presentation.

> George Jean Nathan. *The Magic Mirror* (Knopf).
> 1960. pp. 59, 62

In the days of Belasco realism, every effort was made to produce the effect of reality on the stage. For this the late David Belasco should be praised rather than condemned, for he came into the theatre as an innovator at the turn of this century, and at a time when lighting and scenery were in the age of innocence. However, he ultimately made realism an end in itself, which defeated his original purpose.

> Lawrence Langner. *The Play's the Thing* (Putnam).
> 1960. p. 160

See *La Belle Russe, The Heart of Maryland, Madame Butterfly, The Girl of the Golden West, The Return of Peter Grimm* (plays).

# BELLOW, SAUL (1915–    )

It was of Dostoevsky that André Gide once said all factions could find something in him to support their claims but no one faction could claim him exclusively. Some of this holds true for Saul Bellow. He came up as a writer out of the tough, tight literary magazines, established his beachhead, as it were, and is now successfully fanning out into the broader and brighter domains; his talents, valued from the start by the severer literary critics, have gradually begun to be noticed by greater numbers of the ordinary, intelligent vintage. Mr. Bellow's work contains innumerable diverse elements, it has variousness and is against the grain. His readers, therefore, are to be found anywhere and everywhere and they can be any-one at all.

Harvey Breit. *The Writer Observed* (World). 1956.

p. 271

Saul Bellow views the past in an almost anthropological way. He finds no moral in it, but rather senses the shaping force of heredity and social circumstances upon man, the isolation and burden of human life, the natural ruins of time, and the continuity of human history. Like James Joyce, a chronicler of the city, Bellow attempts to discover pattern and meaning in the hidden fantasies of man living in a mechanized urban world where the daily routine obscures private realities and where normal human reactions are expected to be proper, abstractions systematized by a code of social behavior, not deeply felt, emotional or genuine. . . . Although Bellow seems more suited by temperament and ability than any writer of his generation to create for America "the uncreated conscience" of mod-ern man.

Edward Schwartz. *NR*. Dec. 3, 1956. pp. 20–1

The suffering, the humility, the moral goodness in his books, the honest and ironic realization of human weakness: these are the traits that appeal to us. But this note of resignation, of acceptance does not appear in Bel-low's work after the violence and passions of life, as it commonly does in the work of major artists. It appears in Bellow's fiction *instead* of the emotional storm and stress it should transcend. The central image of the hero in his novels and stories is not indeed that of the rebellious son, but of the suffering, the tormented, and the conforming son.

To use the phraseology of Salinger, this hero is the good boy, the sad sack; or to use the terms of depth psychology, he is the castrated son. . . . There is something in Bellow's accent that may remind us of the innocent and childlike spirit of a Stephen Crane, consumed as the earlier writer was also by the flames of his oedipal and religious conflict.

Maxwell Geismar. *American Moderns* (Hill and
Wang). 1958. pp. 221–4

It appears that although Bellow's insistence on being free is not a com-plete view of human destiny, neither is it simply a piece of naïvety or moral irresponsibility, as has sometimes been suggested. He believes that if we ever define our character and our fate it will be because we have caught up with our own legend, realized our own imagination. Bellow's fertile sense of the ever-possible conversion of reality and imagination, fact and legend, into each other is the source of the richness and significance of his writing. He differs in this respect from the traditional practice of American prose romance, which forces the real and imaginary far apart and finds that there is no circuit of life between them. Bellow differs, too, from the pure realist, who describes human growth as a simple progress away from legend and toward fact.

Richard Chase. Cmty. April, 1959. p. 327

Bellow's artistic progress reveals itself in the stages his heroes mark. . . . The movement . . . is towards a resolution of the conflict between self and world; the movement is from acid defeat to acceptance, and from acceptance to celebration. All these heroes are in some way or other outsiders to the world they inhabit; all are on intimate terms with pain; and all affirm the sense of human life. The affirmation has an ironic knowledge of its limits. For if Joseph (of *Dangling Man*) is the eternal victim, he is victim to his own lack of resolution; and if Henderson is the eternal savior, he is at the same time a bungling and grotesque redeemer. Thus does the progress of Bellow's hero maintain a sense both of hope and humility. And thus does it disclose to us a *form* of human courage.

Ihab H. Hassan. Critique. Summer, 1960. pp. 35–6

The matter has become more and more apparent, but since the beginning all Bellow's heroes have started in a gesture of escape from burdens, an extreme romantic gesture. It is a gesture which in its extremity brings Bellow into touch with one of the defining impulses of American character, into touch with at least all the classic Redskins of American letters, from Leatherstocking to Whitman to Mark Twain to Hemingway, all those who light off for the woods, the open road, the Territory, and into touch perhaps with the Palefaces, too. (The extreme need to escape burdens, to be free of all the clutter, is certainly as well a distinction of Hawthorne and Henry James.) Bellow's hero is tempted frequently to epiphanies of love for mankind in general, though never for things, and his motion is brought to various thematic significances, but he is in the first instance activated by the need to rid himself of the weight of the chaos.

Marcus Klein. KR. Spring, 1962, p. 211

Let me, then, put down what I will not discuss: a few rejected theses which may find themselves the center of despair in an otherwise capable Master's Essay. Let me reject: (a) that Bellow probes the meaningful questions of our times; (b) that his Jewishness is crucial to his success as a writer; (c) that his heroes help us see ourselves as we really are; (d) that his imagination and inventiveness give pleasure by themselves; and (e) that he is to be identified closely with his own heroes. Any of these propositions is capable of being maintained; any is perhaps true. The only difficulty is that they are irrelevant to discussing Bellow *as a novelist*. They can change our feeling or commitment to the novels, but they cannot change our judgment of the novels. *Herzog* is not a vehicle for philosophical speculations nor an embodiment of the mores of particular subcultures nor an attempt toward mass therapy in the guise of education nor an object of entertainment and titillation nor a wheelbarrow for the burden of autobiography. Or, of course, it may be all these things; but what makes *Herzog* a novel is, simply, that its form gives it a unique significance.

(K)                                        James Dean Young. *Critique*. Spring-
                                                          Summer, 1965. p. 8

The evocation of the reality of intellectual anguish, never more powerful than in *Herzog,* is the major achievement of Bellow's work as a whole. Though his other heroes are not professional intellectuals, their crises are of intellectual and philosophical nature and origin. Bellow's fiction is the richest and deepest view of these problems in contemporary American literature. . . . But the passionate intellectual concern of Bellow's fiction can also become a limitation. His most recent work has become increasingly pedagogic. It is often a view of ideas rather than of life, and human experience is used as a gloss on Bellow's theories about it.

(K)                                     Howard M. Harper. *Desperate Faith* (North
                                                     Carolina). 1967. p. 62

### The Victim

What Mr. Bellow attempts is to compress into an arena the size of two human souls the agony of mind which has ravaged millions of Jews in our century. *The Victim* rates as a subtle and thoughtful contribution to the literature of 20th century anti-Semitism.

                                        Richard Match. *NYHT*. Nov. 23, 1947. p. 10

*The Victim* . . . is hard to match in recent fiction, for brilliance, skill, and originality. . . . *The Victim* is solidly built of fine, important ideas; it also generates fine and important, if uncomfortable, emotions.

                                        Diana Trilling. *Nation*. Jan. 3, 1948. pp. 24–5

*The Victim* depended much on intensification of effect, by limitations on time, by rigid economy in structure of scene, by placement and juxtaposition of scenes, by the unsaid and the withheld, by a muting of action, by a scrupulously reserved style. The novel proved that the author had a masterful control of the method, not merely fictional good manners,

the meticulous good breeding which we ordinarily damn by the praise
"intelligent."

Robert Penn Warren. NR. Nov. 2, 1953. p. 22

This leads us to the central moral dilemma of the novel [*The Victim*]:
How far can a man be held responsible for the unintentional consequences
of his acts? Bellow never wholly resolves the question, but he suggests that
the intention and the act are not ethically separable, that morality relies on
each man's existential responsibility for his acts. Yet Bellow is aware that
absolute responsibility is an impossible ideal, a saint's ideal, and that, in a
practical, moral sense, an intentional evil is more egregious than an unconscious one.

(K)                     Jonathan Baumbach. *The Landscape of Nightmare*
(NYU). 1965. pp. 50–1

### The Adventures of Augie March

Reading *The Adventures of Augie March* in 1953 must be a good deal
like reading *Ulysses* in 1920. . . . Tentatively: Saul Bellow is perhaps a
great novelist, *The Adventures of Augie March* perhaps a great novel. If
*The Adventures of Augie March* is great, it is great because of its comprehensive, non-naturalistic survey of the modern world, its wisely inconclusive presentation of its problems; because its author dares to let go
(as so many very good and very neat modern writers do not); because
the style of its telling makes the sequence of events seem real even when
one knows they couldn't be; because the novel is intelligently and am-
bitiously conceived as a whole that esthetically comprehends its parts;
because it is an achievement in and a promise of the development of a
novelist who deserves comparison only with the best, even at this early
stage of his development.

Harvey Curtis Webster. SR. Sept. 19, 1953. pp. 13–4

Augie introduces the most startling extremes of realism with cheerful
casualness. He does not hold them against life itself. There is a great deal
of vigorous love-making, explicitly described, but with a joy and attrac-
tiveness very rare in recent fiction. . . . Not since Dos Passos's *U.S.A.* has
there been in a novel such an enormous range of discriminating reporting
as in this one. . . . The crowding of descriptive epithets and hyphenizations
recalls Hopkins.

Robert Gorham Davis. NYT. Sept. 20, 1953.<br>pp. 1, 36

If such a novel is to be fully effective the sense of dramatic improvisation
must be a dramatic illusion, the last sophistication of the writer, and . . .

the improvisation is really a pseudo-improvisation, and . . . the random scene or casual character that imitates the accidental quality of life must really have a relevance, and . . . the discovery, usually belated, of this relevance, is the characteristic excitement of the genre. That is, in this genre the relevance is deeper and more obscure and there is, in the finest examples of the genre, a greater tension between the random life force of the materials and the shaping intuition of the writer.

It is the final distinction, I think, of *The Adventures of Augie March* that we do feel this tension, and that it is a meaningful fact.

Robert Penn Warren. *NR*. Nov. 2, 1953. p. 22

Saul Bellow's new novel is a new kind of book. The only other American novels to which it can be compared with any profit are *Huckleberry Finn* and *U.S.A.*, and it is superior to the first by virtue of the complexity of its subject matter and to the second by virtue of a realized unity of composition. In all three books, the real theme is America, a fact which is not as clear in this new book as it is in its predecessors, perhaps because of its very newness. . . . *The Adventures of Augie March* is a new kind of book first of all because Augie March possesses a new attitude toward experience in America: instead of the blindness of affirmation and the poverty of rejection, Augie March rises from the streets of the modern city to encounter the reality of experience with an attitude of satirical acceptance, ironic affirmation, and comic transcendence of affirmation and rejection.

Delmore Schwartz. *PR*. Jan. 1954. pp. 112–3

Mr. Saul Bellow's *The Adventures of Augie March* is (a) study in the spiritual picaresque, a later form of the traditional *bildungsroman* in which the *picaro* or hero is consciousness rather than swashbuckling rogue, and so is required, as the rogue is not, to develop, deepen, strike through its first illusion to the truth which, at the end of the road, it discovers to be its fate. But *Augie March* begins with the aphorism, "Man's character is his fate," and ends with the aphorism, "Man's fate is his character." The learning is in the transposition. Man's fate is that he shall inherit, be stuck with, his character. The movement which the transposition represents is the movement from the naturalist to the existentialist, from what is determined to what is accepted or chosen.

John W. Aldridge. *In Search of Heresy* (McGraw).
1956. pp. 131–2

### Henderson the Rain King

*Henderson the Rain King* differs from *Augie March* in many interesting ways. In the earlier novel Bellow uses a loose structure to illustrate, through a long series of essentially realistic episodes, the vast possibilities of contemporary life. Beginning in poverty and illegitimacy, Augie ranges far, horizontally and vertically, to end in uncertainty. Henderson, on the other hand, born to every advantage, has lived fifty-one years of unquiet desperation. Of Augie's kind of patient pilgrimage he has never been capable. He is driven by the voice that cries, "I want, I want," and the story of his search is both romantic and dramatic. I cannot say that *Henderson the Rain King* is a better book than *Augie March:* the denseness of the experience in the earlier novel is something almost unparalleled in contemporary literature. But it is a wonderful book for Bellow to have written after writing *Augie March*. It is a book that should be read again and again, and each reading, I believe, will yield further evidence of Bellow's wisdom and power.

Granville Hicks. *SR*. Feb. 21, 1959. p. 20

Anyone unfamiliar with Mr. Bellow's earlier work would, I think, immediately recognize from a reading of *Henderson* why so many of our best critics consider him the most important American novelist of the postwar period. For one thing, it contains a wealth of comic passages that bear comparison with the wild, grotesque humor we find in some of Faulkner's stories, and for another it is endlessly fertile in invention and idea. Beyond that, however, this is by all odds the most brilliantly written novel to have come along in years. Mr. Bellow has finally been able to discipline the virtuosity that ran away with *Augie March,* and the result is a prose charged with all the vigor and vitality of colloquial speech and yet capable of the range, precision, and delicacy of a heightened, formal rhetoric.

Norman Podhoretz. *NYHT*. Feb. 22, 1959. p. 3

For Bellow, as for Malamud and some of the other fine novelists of the time, personality is back in the middle of the novel, not where their great predecessors—Proust, Joyce, and to somewhat lesser extent, Mann—put it, as part of the thematic scheme which apportions the size and intensity of every element. *Henderson* is a kind of bridge between *Augie, Seize the Day,* and these thematic novels; the difficulty is that the bridge must bear the weight of constant invention, invention which can draw hardly at all on the home detail in which the other novels luxuriate. . . . Bellow readers, used to commodity markets, Mexican resorts, Evanston haberdasheries, and Machiavellians and con-men who in vintage Bellow load the pages, must go into another gear. They will be helped by the fact that *Henderson* is a stylistic masterpiece.

Richard G. Stern. *KR*. Autumn, 1959. p. 660

### Seize the Day

*Seize the Day* is Bellow's one exercise in pure naturalism. He takes a character ill-equipped for life, whose mistakes become more and more unredeemable as he grows older, and lets him sink under their weight. But is this really the end for Tommy? . . . Is the consummation referred to in the last sentence some kind of new beginning spiritually? What is the "heart's ultimate need" referred to so cryptically?

(K)                          Robert Gorham Davis in *The Creative Process*, edited
                             by Nona Balakian and Charles Simmons (Doubleday).
                             1963. pp. 126–7

### Herzog

For some time now the critical consensus has been, expressed not so much formally in writing as in the talk of literary circles, that *Seize the Day,* published some eight years ago, was his best single performance. *Herzog* is superior to it, I think, even if not so tightly organized and in fact a bit loose on the structural side. For one thing, it is a much longer and fuller narrative than *Seize the Day,* which is hardly more than a novella. For another, it is richer in content, in the effective disposition of tone and language, as well as in intellectual resonance and insight of a high order into the make-up of modern life—insight into what is really new and perhaps all too hazardous about it in its strange, almost inconceivable, mixture of greater freedom and maddening constriction.

Above all, this novel positively radiates intelligence—not mere brightness or shrewdness or that kind of sensitiveness which sometimes passes for mind among us. It is a coherent, securely founded intelligence—a real endowment—of genuine intellectual quality which, marvelously escaping the perils of abstraction, is neither recondite nor esoteric. It is directed towards imaginative ends by a true and sharp sense of the pain that rends the human world of its ills, both curable and incurable, and equally by a bracing, unfailing sense of irony and humor serving to counteract such chronic vulnerabilities of intelligence as over-solemnity of mind on the one hand and perversity of sensibility on the other.

(K)                          Philip Rahv. *NYHT*. Sept. 20, 1964. p. 1

Willy nilly, then, all these later heroes of Bellow are gluttons for suffering —for what suffers is still alive and still has the possibility of renewal. They are all also trying to reach the deeper sources of grief and impulse, to reconstitute the past in order to shed it, to clear away the cultural conditioning that has deflected them from a simple understanding of their desires. Herzog's case, however, is a much more complicated one. He has so many roles and images and is so divided among them that simplicity is impossible. A child of the immigrant ghetto, to which his heart is still tied, he has written his first and only book on *Romanticism and Christianity*. A bookish, urban type, he has tried to turn himself into a New England country squire. A scholar, a foot-loose intellectual, a lover of fancy women, he is also a dutiful man around the house and a patient caretaker of his wife's neurosis. No wonder he has problems of identity. He is a Romantic who sets great store by "the heart"—a term that is constantly on his mind —but he is also a Rationalist who has more principles of ethics than Spinoza.

(K)                          Theodore Solotaroff. *Cmty*. Dec., 1964. p. 63

In both *Augie March* and *Henderson* Bellow has run down well before the end: Augie, after the trip to Mexico, only sits around and has others tell him who Augie March is; Henderson, save for the great scene with the frogs, barely survives the trip to Africa. Technically Bellow has solved this problem by cheating, for in *Herzog* he does not really begin his story until half way through. Herzog's life is slowly gathered, then he has it snapped in a terrifying courtroom scene, and this propels him from New York to Chicago and enables Bellow to march home to a stunning triumph in the last third of the book. But this solution is not just a technical one and is not really cheating at all. For Augie and Henderson the only way to see right side up is via primitivism, and Bellow seems to have realized or discovered that primitivism was for him more theoretically than actually valid. The answer in *Herzog* is quite different: a novel of ideas and a hero who feels his having come to the end of the line so well that the touters of the Void can be sneered at if only because they cannot reckon with Herzog's narcissism and buoyancy.

The result is the first or at least the largest step taken beyond Lawrence and the romanticism that is bought at the terrifying expense of fear and loathing of human kind. Dignity must go and without any accompanying comic reassurance—Herzog must scurry like a rat from his will and need to be kept in shelter, and he must end in silence. But the gains are great: a repeated and convincing insistence that the equation of reality with evil is sentimental and a demonstration that existentialism is only the most recent attempt of the romantic to be respectable and aristocratic.

(K)                          Roger Sale. *HdR*. Winter, 1964–65. pp. 617–18

To a considerable degree the novel [*Herzog*] does work as a rather conventional drama of alienation, though this is precisely what Bellow doesn't want it to be. It is about the failure of all available terms for interpretation and summary, about the intellectual junk heap of language by which Herzog-Bellow propose dignities to the hero's life and then as quickly watch these proposals dissolve into cliché. A similar process goes on in

*Augie,* against the competition of an anxious and often phony exuberance, and it was there that Bellow began to fashion a comic prose which could bear the simultaneous weight of cultural, historical, mythological evocations and also sustain the exposure of their irrelevance. His comedy always has in it the penultimate question before the final one, faced in *Seize the Day,* of life or death—the question of what can be taken seriously and how seriously it can possibly be taken. The result, however, is a kind of stalemate achieved simply by not looking beyond the play of humor into its constituents, at the person from whom it issues, at the psychological implications both of anyone's asking such questions and of the *way* in which he asks them. It seems to me that Bellow cannot break the stalemate with alienation implicit in his comedy without surrendering to the Waste Land outlook and foregoing the mostly unconvincing rhetoric which he offers as an alternative. That is why his comic style in *Herzog,* even more than in *Henderson* or *Augie,* is less like Nathanael West's than like that of West's brother-in-law, S. J. Perelman.

(K)                                    Richard Poirier. *PR.* Spring, 1965. pp. 270–1

### The Last Analysis

If there is one thing the American theatre cannot afford to throw away, it is a play. And yet after twenty-eight painfully eked-out performances, Saul Bellow's *The Last Analysis* had to close, as though it were another confection, another soufflé that did not quite rise to the occasion. The truth is that the production was frightful, but no amount of superimposed opacity could obscure the underlying translucence and purity; what was here being rejected was rarer than a pearl in an oyster; a play in a Broadway playhouse.

I am not saying that Bellow's farcical fantasy about a once hugely successful comedian restaging his life as a closed-circuit TV show for an audience of psychiatrists at the Waldorf-Astoria, in order to shed light on the terrible disease Success, is a flawless dramatic creation. But there are things in it that we must hold dear. There is, first of all, the intense rhetoric that makes the word become flesh before our very ears and eyes: such throbbing flesh that it scarcely matters if the personages uttering it are somewhat less than people. Nor does it matter all that much (though it does matter) that this galaxy of galvanic words does not compose itself into a well-shaped entity; this, at least, is a case where the sum of the parts is greater than most other wholes.

(K)                                    John Simon. *HdR.* Winter, 1964–65. p. 556

See *Dangling Man, The Victim, The Adventures of Augie March, Henderson the Rain King, Herzog* (novels); *Seize the Day* (stories); *The Last Analysis* (play).

# BENCHLEY, ROBERT (1889–1945)

Mr. Benchley has a genuine sense of the ridiculous; he passes through the semi-intelligent world of the business office, the city room, the theatre, with an amused appreciation of its vanities; he takes an absurd pleasure in his grimaces and horseplay not so much because they make others laugh but because they are required of him by the pompous stupidities of civilized existence. Unhappily he has had to fill two hundred and fifty pages with this sort of thing. In half that number he could have published all of his parodies, including the "Christmas Afternoon," which is very good, "From Nine to Five," "Football," a few of his little farces, and all of the pages between the flyleaf and the contents page. He would have succeeded in omitting all of the distressing bits quoted by his friends as the best things in the book.

Gilbert Seldes. *Dial.* Jan., 1922. p. 95

Here . . . is Robert C. Benchley, perhaps the most finished master of the technique of literary fun in America. Benchley's work is pure humor, one might almost say sheer nonsense. There is no moral teaching, no reflection of life, no tears. What Benchley pursues is the higher art of nonsense and he has shown in it a quite exceptional power for tricks of word and phrase.

Stephen Leacock. *The Greatest Pages of American Humor* (Doubleday). 1936. p. 233

Along comes Robert Benchley like those hardy perennials, [P. G.] Wodehouse and [E. Phillips] Oppenheim. When I was still in college in 1921 . . . I read *Of All Things,* which I still consider his best and freshest book. . . . He is popular now, and I believe that he syndicates his articles. At any rate, they are seriously the work of the serious humorist; still funny, but too much of the same thing to make one laugh anew. Yet those who do not know Mr. Benchley and his illuminator, Mr. Gluyas Williams (never better than in this role), have missed something unduplicated in American humor. He can write on anything, and does. Falling flat, Mr. Benchley is sharper than all his imitators. . . . He is a rare and natural wit who . . . writes too much and too often.

David McCord. *YR.* Autumn, 1936. p. 81

The man seems to be a humorist, and yet the Pagliacci undertones are seldom absent. . . . Generalizations about Benchley are dangerous. . . . But surely spontaneity is the key to his particular form of mental disorder. The man is spontaneously cuckoo. . . . Still, he says some pretty acute things. . . . I have said that Benchley seems to be a humorist, and right now, in order to give Bob a break, I want to retract that "seems." Maybe "humorist" isn't the right word either. All I know is, he makes you laugh.

William Rose Benét. *SR*. Jan. 8, 1938. p. 7

"Is Robert Benchley a solar myth?" That is the question little knots of curious people, as well as curious knots of little people, have been asking ever since Mr. Benchley traded in his quill for an Actor's Equity card and abandoned the craft of writing. It has often been said—and it is being said again right at this minute—that the Ice Age of American humor began the moment he stopped practicing letters. For the sad fact is that when Benchley went out of business he forgot to appoint a successor. He just locked up the store and threw away the key. . . .

In this, his latest garland [*Benchley Beside Himself*], Mr. Benchley proves again what needs no confirmation, that for sheer guile and sprightliness he leaves his competitors, imitators and apostles tied to a tree. Whether you begin with "Polyp With a Past," or the masterly inquiry into Negro folksong . . . or any one of twenty others, it is a dead cert you will wind up clawing at your collar and emitting a series of strangled little yelps.

S. J. Perelman. *NYT*. June 13, 1943. p. 2

. . . in past years I was probably afraid to read him for fear of finding out how many of my own humorous bits had already been written by the Master. I think that most humorists today must humbly admit to the same indebtedness.

Benchley *was* humor. His writings were only one of the outward and visible evidences of the inner grace, the divine essence. . . . Benchley *did* give out a radiant glow; his friends and his millions of readers *did* warm themselves and feel better because of his presence. But he was not one to be operated by a switch; he was a flame, capable of leaping out of the fireplace and bitterly searching the hypocrite, the pretentious, the inhuman.

Donald Ogden Stewart. *Nation*. Oct. 16, 1954. p. 343

To read *The Benchley Roundup* . . . is to reread some of the most laughable prose of the past thirty years and to be reminded of how much we still miss Bob Benchley. He had the most ingenious way of submitting himself to exasperation. The causes of his annoyance he would describe with wonderful accuracy, and with a slow burn. . . . [But] the worm always turns, in a Benchley essay; the moment comes when the gentle sufferer can stand no more, and this is the fun of the thing—to see him rise in his wrath and impale the nuisance with the deftest of phrases.

Edward Weeks. *At.* Nov., 1954. p. 88

Benchley was a highly subjective writer, and most of what he wrote was conditioned by his feelings about himself. Among his gifts was the ability to set these feelings down neatly and precisely. . . . He was willing, even eager, to make fun of himself, provided he was reasonably sure that others would know what he was talking about, but he was reluctant to do anything that appeared to be straining to make the point.

Nathaniel Benchley. Robert Benchley (McGraw-<br>Hill). 1955. p. 2

It's pretty hard to find anything dated in his gallery of cheerful incompetents failing calamitously to adapt themselves to modern man's living habits, and his genial, bumbling authorities lecturing on how to figure income-taxes, raise babies, sub-let apartments, control crime, take vacations, vote, train dogs, and other subjects susceptible to hilarious exploitation. . . . Very properly "kindliness" has been used more than any other word to describe the basic quality of Benchley fun-making. . . . He could also express a cold, virtuous anger in his writing. A lot of unscrupulous reporters and editors felt the bite of Robert Benchley's contempt in the acid comments on current journalism which *The New Yorker* frequently published above the sobriquet of Guy Fawkes.

Marc Connelly. NYHT. Nov. 13, 1955. pp. 1, 13

Benchley's Little Man has an integrity that can be strained but never quite broken; it gleams sullenly through his foggiest notions. In *The Neurotic Personality of Our Time,* Karen Horney says that one refuge of the intellectual sort of neurotic is a detachment in which he refuses to take anything seriously, including himself. The self-mockery of Benchley's fictive double is never carried to the point where he loses his wholesome awareness that man's environment was made for man, not he for it, and if things don't seem that way (here the reformer speaks)—well, things had better be changed. Miss Horney also states that the neurotic feels a compulsion to be liked. Benchley's double is less concerned with being liked than with preserving his integrity and his ethical vision.

Norris W. Yates. The American Humorist (Iowa<br>State). 1964. p. 246

See *The Benchley Roundup.*

# BENÉT, STEPHEN VINCENT (1898–1943)

*John Brown's Body* . . . is as good as knowledge, sincere personal feeling, and Mr. Benét's particular literary expertness, could make it. To argue that it is more than this, would be quite specially unjust. It is a popular patriotic epic of essentially the same order as Noyes's Elizabethan Odyssey; regarded as a grand historical poem like *The Dynasts,* it would be a heavy disappointment. All the virtues of readability, romantic charm, reminiscent pathos, it has in abundance; the higher virtues that one might expect of such a performance, it very definitely lacks. It lacks these partly because it is not organized and controlled, as such a poem would be, by a clear and sweeping philosophic vision; partly because it is not directed for all its competence, by a rigorous and corrective artistic purpose.

Newton Arvin. *NYHT.* Aug. 12, 1928. p. 2

*John Brown's Body* has been called among other things an epic and it has been compared, not unfavorably, to the *Iliad.* Mr. Benét himself has no such pretensions. . . . The poem is not in any sense an epic; neither is it a philosophical vision of the Civil War; it is a loose episodic narrative which unfolds a number of unrelated themes in motion picture flashes. In spite of some literary incompetence in the author and the lack of a controlling imagination, the story gathers suspense as it goes and often attains to power.

Allen Tate. *Nation.* Sept. 19, 1928. p. 274

Epic is too heroic a word, no doubt, to stand alone as descriptive of this poem (*John Brown's Body*); a word associated too loftily with Homer and Virgil, with Dante and Milton; suggestive of masterpieces of the past, whose royal rhythms carry mythical gods and heroes through magical exploits. Mr. Benét's poem is a kind of cinema epic, brilliantly flashing a hundred different aspects of American character and history on the silver screen of an unobstrusively fluent and responsive style.

Harriet Monroe. *Poetry.* Nov., 1928. p. 91

Stephen Benét has the true gift of poetry, and he has a scope and energy of ambition that is rare among poets in this practical age. . . . Even where Benét's poetry is not so fine, it is sustained by a fine sincerity—by the poet's own heart honestly feeling all that is felt—and it is adorned with interruptions of excellent lyrical song. All these virtues compel one to judge *John Brown's Body* by the standards of great art. And as a great work of art, I think the book fails. . . . It is a sophisticated book, an intellectual book, full of complicated, diverse and extremely up-to-date ideas. Only as a whole it lacks idea. It lacks attitude. It lacks the unity that is imparted by an intention.

Max Eastman. *Bkm.* Nov., 1928. p. 362

Mr. Benét keeps to the middle of the road in his verse as in his thinking. Neither an innovator nor an imitator, he is an able craftsman who draws upon sources both old and recent. With some lapses his poetry is interesting, perceptive, and in good taste. . . . He is the critical historian who shrinks from the half-truths and savageries of prophecy and partisanship; lacking the evidence for a final judgement, he is content to chronicle. As such he has his place and a not undistinguished one; for an honest chronicler who is also a skilful poet is better than a score of false prophets without art.

Philip Blair Rice. *Nation*. July 18, 1936. pp. 81–2

His verse is a survival of an abundant native line; it has become a virtual guide-book of native myth and folklore, their place-names, heroes, humours, and reverences. . . . Mr. Benét derived, through Lindsay, from the bardic romantics who held sway in American poetry for over a century. . . . In America this tradition, in its homeliest form, was the living authority of text-books and family anthologies all the way from Neihardt, Riley, and Markham, back through Hay, Harte, and Miller, to the bearded dynasties of Longfellow and Bryant—a succession hostile to eccentric talent or refined taste, scornful of modernity or exotic influence, once the pride of the burgeoning Republic, and now chiefly a source of cheerful embarrassment to teachers and blushing incredulity to their students. Mr. Benét has aspired from his school-days to a place in this old American line.

Morton Dauwen Zabel. *Poetry*. Aug., 1936. pp. 276

Mr. Benét, when not writing hundreds of pages of flat free verse, can be a poet, and can tell a first-rate story when not wrestling with attitudes towards history. I think posterity will treat him much like Stevenson. Some will ignore him; the young will treasure his adventure tales, especially *Spanish Bayonet;* and most people will like his ballads, love poems, and prose fantasies. At his unpretentious best he is a writer of sure skill and simple charm. But his efforts as interpreter of the American scene and the world crisis will be tactfully forgotten. No matter how fertile their imagination, little of worth results when writers who do not feel *prophetically* the power of ideas attempt to express social and historical truths.

Frank Jones. *Nation*. Sept. 12, 1942. p. 218

He was in sheer fact the poet so urgently called for by our last national poet, the first to chant songs for and of all America, Walt Whitman. And unlike Walt Whitman, whose prophetic symbolism could be read by the people only in single poems and passages, he broke through the ivory wall and was read (as Whitman prophesied some American would be) by the population at large. It seems probable that no writer of poetry in English has ever been read by so many in his lifetime—not even Longfellow—as was Stephen Benét. And while he was popular, he never wrote down to his public. He gave them his best, and it was good.

Henry Seidel Canby. *SR*. March 27, 1943. p. 14

His life was a model, I think, of what a poet's life should be—a model upon which young men of later generations might well form themselves. He was altogether without envy or vanity. He never considered appearance, or tried to present himself as anything but what he was, or paid the least attention to the prevalent notions of what a poet ought to be. Also, and more important, he was truly generous. . . . Moreover, his generosity was not a moral quality alone. It was an intellectual quality as well. . . . It was this warm and human concern with things seen, things felt beyond himself, which gave him his quality as a poet.

Archibald MacLeish. *SR*. March 27, 1943. p. 7

Stephen Vincent Benét's death was a particular loss because he added to the variety of American poetry. His contribution of the historical narrative was unique, since few practiced it and no other approached his success. It is important to define his effort. He was not interested in mouthing the word "America." . . . Benét's deep regard for the United States of America was based not on a feeling of blood and earth, but on an honest belief in this country as remarkably permitting human freedom. He knew the misery and corruption, and you'll find them in his books. But, stronger than any other motive, you will find Benét's fascination with the effort of these states to be a place where that reckless and distorted word "liberty" actually means individual right and intellectual exemption.

Paul Engle. *Poetry*. Dec., 1943. p. 160

Whatever may be the eventual position of Benét's work in the ranks of American letters, one suspects that it will persist, in a quiet way, pretty far forward, despite the cyclical clamor as advance guards change. . . . Stephen Vincent Benét had a faith and a delight in people and a belief that they could come to good ends. And it is precisely this faith and delight and belief that distinguish his work from that of most of his noisier contemporaries, that make his storied people stand out. . . . Benét's people exist in an older context . . . a context of accomplishment; of reaffirmation of the ancient and necessary faith that man not only can defeat his devils but can act with decency toward his fellows.

Robeson Bailey. *SR*. Jan. 4, 1947. p. 16

See *The Selected Works of Stephen Vincent Benét*.

# BERRYMAN, JOHN (1914–    )

In terms of what he is doing he has considerably more control than [Randall] Jarrell, but it is possible that the control is premature. For example, too many of his poems go off into the fixed direction of the meditative convention of Yeats: at his comparatively early age he seems to have got set in the tone of pronouncement and prophecy, with the result that his powers of observation are used chiefly for incidental shock. Yet his line has more firmness and structure than Jarrell's, and there is a sense in which he is more mature: he is not afraid to commit himself to systematic and even solemn elaborations of metaphor.

Allen Tate. *PR*. May–June, 1941. p. 243

John Berryman . . . is a complicated, nervous, and intelligent writer whose poetry has steadily improved. At first he was possessed by a slavishly Yeatsish grandiloquence which at its best resulted in a sort of posed, planetary melodrama, and which at its worst resulted in monumental bathos. . . . [His] latest poetry, in spite of its occasional echoes, is as determinedly individual as one could wish. Doing things in a style all its own sometimes seems the primary object of the poem, and its subject gets a rather spasmodic and fragmentary treatment. The style—conscious, dissonant, darting; allusive, always over- or under-satisfying the expectations which it is intelligently exploiting—seems to fit Mr. Berryman's knowledge and sensibility surprisingly well, and ought in the end to produce poetry better than the best of the poems he has so far written in it, which have raw or overdone lines side by side with imaginative and satisfying ones.

Randall Jarrell. *Nation*. July 17, 1948. pp. 80–1

John Berryman has at least in a limited degree the gift for language . . . , but it is frustrated by his inability to define his theme and his disinclination to understand and discipline his emotions. Most of his poems appear to deal with a single all-inclusive topic: the desperate chaos, social, religious, philosophical, and psychological, of modern life, and the corresponding chaos and desperation of John Berryman. No matter what the ostensible subject, this is commonly what emerges, and most of the poems are merely random assortments of half-realized images illustrating this theme.

Yvor Winters. *HdR*. Autumn, 1948. p. 404

[*Homage to Mistress Bradstreet*] is a sort of miniature "Wasteland" and will fascinate the intellectuals; the allusions, the style, the several voices, even the notes and the account of spiritual travail, will be talked about. . . . The whole power of the poem can be understood only by much rereading.

The poet by concealing transitions helps make the difficulty, yet this, too, is part of the likeness. Anne Bradstreet's mind and imagination worked furiously, and neither her outer nor her inner life gave her ease. The poem carries us in a storm of her memories, responsibilities, pains and perceptions, and we suffer all she suffers. It is her agony we re-enact; to call the poem homage is to name the after-effect of coming so close to her, admiration for the stout heart of this extraordinary colonial.

John Holmes. *NYT*. Sept. 30, 1956. p. 18

*Homage to Mistress Bradstreet* is a long poem written in fifty-seven stanzas —except for two they are of eight lines each—on the subject of Anne Bradstreet, 1612-1672, wife to Simon Bradstreet (colonial governor of Massachusetts after her death), and perhaps America's—almost surely Massachusetts'—first poet. . . . Its triumph, what makes it so very interesting, is the curious diction employed, a truly personal speech which without seeming archaic neither seems quite contemporary: it is a strange, and touching, going-out from oneself, a feeling-back into our common past. The tensions of the present poem exist in the unfolding of a double mystery: that of life and death, of the past and present. . . . The poem is somewhat uneven. But at its best the mystery is embodied in lines that (if one might presume a little) ought to have pleased George Herbert.

Ambrose Gordon, Jr. *YR*. Winter, 1957. pp. 299–300

The poems [in *77 Dream Songs*] that strike me as being best . . . I read as marvelous play by a passionate, despairing, cracked, erudite, utterly poetic genius. Moreover, though they are called dream songs, and though they are apparently supposed to be the dreams of a character "Henry" (who, in 17 of the poems, is joined by "Mr. Bones"), I do not read the poems as songs, nor can I read many of them as dreams; and I read Henry and Mr. Bones as being no more than playful half-masks for John Berryman, Halloween masks covering only the eyes and part of the cheeks. In a strange way, the poems do not mean anything much; that is, their value comes not from any ideas or emotions or experiences or things they refer to and derive from; it comes from the virtuosity of the poet. They are pure poets' poems: even one with few devices and disguises is still so contrived (in the best sense) that the anguish which the poem may be about affects the reader less than the poet's artifice.

George P. Elliott. *HdR*. Autumn, 1964. p. 458

Dream Songs: eccentricity may be implicit in having the second word with the first. Berryman's prefatory note issues what amounts to a warning to this effect, and the Songs do prank and bash away in babytalk, in dialect, in comical, boozy private language. Perhaps the modern world has been so nightmarish that a writer can feel required to use disguising and enhancing techniques analogous to those used in dreamwork—perhaps a truly accurate naturalism must show a dreamworld America of repetitive, sudden, wish-fulfilling shifts of scene; of familiar objects that gleam with horror, with absurd humor; an America of abortive, seemingly unconnected vignettes which illustrate vengeance, humiliation, thwarted this and that. But I think it is just that Berryman found he prospered with a style that allowed him such concentration of material and such freedom, and allowed him humor.

Frederick Seidel. Poetry. Jan., 1965. p. 257

Basically both *Mistress Bradstreet* and *Dream Songs* are memory pieces, historical complements. In the first Berryman simultaneously affirms and denies the faith of our fathers; in the second he stumbles about the shards. *Mistress Bradstreet* is the old America, the puritan symmetry, ritual, and worldly disgust, reset with the Songs of Solomon. *Dream Songs* is where we are now: a finky sophistication, unexpiated guilt, those collision-course thrills the American dream assumes. The dream itself is a tyrannical cliché, a vaudeville for Fort Knox. Again and again, interpreting the American scene, past or present, Berryman, even with all his highly individualized tics, takes on its contrary pulls, its mocking lawlessness and hidebound creeds. There is throughout all of Berryman a double movement, a wrenched, wistful backing away and sticking close: Berryman, the artful dodger, in love with the enemy, the pop world's loony pursuits; and Berryman, the shut-in scholar, accumulating the saving remnants. . . .

Robert Mazzocco. NYR. June 29, 1967. p. 14

A case could be made, I think, for the thesis that sexual curiosity and the writer's need to find a self outside his own skin are the driving force behind this poem [*Homage to Mistress Bradstreet*]. It rises to its highest points when his imagination is entirely released toward the satisfaction of his curiosity—that is, when he not only envisions Anne's physical experience but identifies with it and, as it were, finds her language for her. The passionate climax at the center of the poem, in which the two poets are imagined in a transport of discovery of each other, through speech and through love, creates Anne as in a frenzy of desire and guilt. The naive fantasy in which the poem begins has now become a vision of the torment of religious conscience in conflict with sexual need. . . . The physical ardor and stormy melancholy of Anne, and her death-horror that makes itself felt more and more forcibly, are a means for Berryman to objectify his feelings more simply than he does through the several voices of the *Dream*

*Songs*—which are, after all, only private voices despite his attempt to keep them distinct.

M. L. Rosenthal. *The New Poets: American and British Poetry Since World War II* (Oxford). 1967. pp. 129–30

See *The Dispossessed, Homage to Mistress Bradstreet, 77 Dream Songs, Berryman's Sonnets* (poetry); *Stephen Crane* (biography).


# BIERCE, AMBROSE (1842–1914?)

His stories are their own justification. We may not agree with the method that he has chosen to use, but we cannot escape the strange, haunting power of them, the grim, boding sense of their having happened—even the most weird, most supernatural, most grotesquely impossible of them—in precisely the way that he has told them. . . . Mr. Ambrose Bierce as a story teller can never achieve a wide popularity, at least among the Anglo-Saxon race. His writings have too much the flavour of the hospital and the morgue. There is a stale odour of mouldy cerements about them. But to the connoisseur of what is rare, unique, and very perfect in any branch of fiction he must appeal strongly as one entitled to hearty recognition as an enduring figure in American letters.

Frederic Taber Cooper. *Bkm.* July, 1911. pp. 478–80

He was as great a satirist as we have record of, and in his hands satire became a keen and terrible weapon. It has been deplored that he used his vast equipment of offense on small fry, but all the folk with whom he concerned himself satirically shared, in his estimation, a common insignificance, and he saw the great and famous of London and New York condemned in time to a like oblivion. . . . He was rich in anecdotes of lethal horrors, and neither the visible nor the unseen appanages of death seemed to hold any terrors for him. . . . For his exceeding power in invoking images and emotions of the uncanny and supernatural, we had dubbed him the Shadow Maker.

George Sterling. *AM.* Sept., 1925. pp. 15–8

Bierce was of imperial bearing, and cavalier beauty. His friends still speak of his deep blue steel-like eyes, his curly crown of tawny hair, his voice of haughty taciturnity. Almost six feet in height, his compact, well-knit figure gave the impression of clean-cut strength and restrained power. This appearance of rugged manhood Bierce never lost; when at the age of seventy-two he crossed the Rio Grande, he was as well preserved as an English country squire.

Leroy J. Nations. *SAQ*. July, 1926. p. 255

There was nothing of the milk of human kindness in old Ambrose; he did not get the nickname of Bitter Bierce for nothing. What delighted him most in life was the spectacle of human cowardice and folly. He put man, intellectually, somewhere between the sheep and the horned cattle, and as a hero somewhere below the rats. His war stories, even when they deal with the heroic, do not depict soldiers as heroes; they depict them as bewildered fools, doing things without sense, submitting to torture and outrage without resistance, dying at last like hogs in Chicago, the former literary capital of the United States. So far in this life, indeed, I have encountered no more thorough-going cynic than Bierce was.

H. L. Mencken. *Prejudices: Sixth Series* (Knopf).
1927. p. 261

With his air of a somewhat dandified Strindberg he combined what might be described as a temperament of the eighteenth century. It was natural to him to write in the manner of Pope: lucidity, precision, "correctness" were the qualities he adored. He was full of the pride of individuality; and the same man who spent so much of his energy "exploring the ways of hate" was, in his personal life, the serenest of stoics. The son of an Ohio farmer, he had no formal education. How did he acquire such firmness and clarity of mind? He was a natural aristocrat and he developed a rudimentary philosophy of aristocracy which, under happier circumstances, might have made him a great figure in the world of American thought. But the America of his day was too chaotic.

Van Wyck Brooks. *Emerson and Others* (Dutton).
1927. p. 152

In his stories . . . the events are narrated with restraint, the descriptions have no excessive details, for the various details are "constituents" of the atmosphere and nearly every word is necessary for the realization of the detail. As a rule, Bierce aims to obtain the total and enduring effect by means of atmosphere, and in many stories it would be unsafe to say that the narrative has greater importance than the impression or the conviction that he wishes to "flow" from the stories; in some instances, he allows us to view an action from several points of vantage. He has a delicate sense of the shades of meaning and of strength in words; therefore, he puts the right word in the right place. The style, in brief, is excellent.

Eric Partridge. *LM*. Oct., 1927, p. 637

Sense was in the balance with sensibility, for Bierce was in the very nature of the case a man of feeling. So on the aesthetic side he added the delicate perception of the portrait painter to the caustic judgements of the cartoonist. The attitude and utterance of the two are in complete contrast. The intellectual Bierce was always on the offensive; always ready to express himself in brilliant brevities. But the Bierce who wrote of the mysteries and the thrills of individual experience was receptive, deliberate, and deliberative, ready to surrender to a mood in a wise passiveness; willing to court in the shadows the shy thoughts that would not come out in the sunlight.

Percy H. Boynton. *More Contemporary Americans* (Chicago). 1927. p. 89

The force which resided in Bierce and wrought through him was wit. The wit was coupled with, actuated by, a perversity which made it recoil even from itself, to the redoublement of both movements. And action and reaction, wit and recoil, coming into play as one impulse in one instant, as a lightning-stroke and a thunder-clap so near that no interval is detected— these determined the odd pattern of Bierce's thought and of his personal literary idiom.

Wilson Follett. *Bkm.* Nov., 1928. p. 284

If his name lives, it is within the range of probabilities that it will be as a tradition of wit, courage and decency. Whatever judgement may be passed on his work, it does not affect the important fact that Bierce was one of the most provocative figures of his generation. One cannot reflect on the facts of his life without coming to entertain an admiration for his splendid courage and indomitable spirit. To those of us in the West who have watched the fate of his reputation with a peculiar and personal interest, it has always been a source of satisfaction to realize that dead, absent or unknown, he has survived his critics and that he has even bettered his enemies who pursued him into Mexico, "to feast on his bones."

Carey McWilliams. *Ambrose Bierce* (Boni). 1929.

p. 335

The fame of Ambrose Bierce ultimately will rest upon his literary work as a whole. That his distinction as an author is not confined to his short-stories alone is apparent, for his fame as a writer was firmly established before any of them were written; they but extended his renown. To be sure, I hold these stories to be the greatest ever published in any language. . . . But Bierce was a great artist in all that he wrote; he was no better in one branch of literature than he was in another, poetry excepted—and his verse that was not poetry was yet the best of verse. So numerous were

his literary activities, embracing so many classifications of literature—
more classifications well done than any other author in all time achieved—
that I find it impossible to isolate any one classification and say that his
fame will endure mainly because of his contributions to that particular
field.

Walter Neale. Life of Ambrose Bierce (Neale). 1929.<br>pp. 453–4

Rejecting violently the novel, realism, dialect, and all use of slang, humorous or otherwise, Bierce stood firmly for the short story, romance, and
pure English produced through intense, self-conscious discipline. Bierce
was first and foremost a disciplinarian. He placed great emphasis on the
technique of fiction and verse. He was constantly eager to be correct, and
to see that others were correct even in the details of punctuation. . . . He
sought, like Poe, to make a single vivid impression upon the reader. To
that end he eliminated all extraneous references. Furthermore, each story
is a complete world in itself, controlled by the writer's logic, not by the
illogicality of life. Since Bierce saw no point in reproducing the flat tones of
ordinary life, he found an interesting topic only in the impingement of the
extraordinary or the unreal on the normal course of events.

C. Hartley Grattan. Bitter Bierce (Doubleday). 1929.<br>pp. 118, 121–2

His stark simplicity, uniting beauty of diction with truth of presentation,
arouses wonder, apprehension, curiosity and thrill, and the climax arrives
with the reader pent-up with emotion. Then comes the startling <i>dénoue-
ment,</i> subtly simple, extremely plausible and pregnant with power. Bierce,
the soldier, had lived dangerously. His stories of the American Civil War
are among his best, realistic to a high degree, provocative of deep thought.

Clifford Bower-Shore. BkmL. August, 1930. p. 283

If it be objected that Poe's characters seldom seem lifelike, what must
be our objection to Bierce? They have absolutely no relevant characteristics that strike us as human, save their outward description; it is never
for the character's sake but always for the plot's sake that a Bierce story
exists. Bierce was interested, even more than Brown, Poe, or Melville, in
the <i>idea</i> of the story—seldom in the human significance of it. In fact some
of the stories exist essentially for the whiplash ending, which in Bierce's
handling antedated O. Henry. But the Bierce story can be reread with
some profit for there is real evidence of a technician's hand.

George Snell. AQ. Summer, 1945. p. 51

It is fitting that someone should be born and live and die dedicated to
the expression of bitterness. For bitterness is a mood that comes to all

intelligent men, though, as they are intelligent, only intermittently. It is proper that there be at least one man able to give penetrating expression to that mood. Bierce is such a man—limited, wrong-headed, unbalanced, but in his own constricted way, an artist. He will remain one of the most interesting and eccentric figures in our literature, one of our great wits, one of our most uncompromising satirists, the perfecter of two or three new, if minor genres: a writer one cannot casually pass by.

Clifton Fadiman. SR .Oct. 12, 1946. p. 62

Along with Poe, Bierce was one of those rare birds in American literature —a Dandy in Baudelaire's sense of the term. The Dandy opposes to society, and to the human world generally, not some principles but himself, his temperament, his dreamed-of depths, his talent for shocking, hoaxing, and dizzying his readers. An aesthetic Enemy of the People, Bierce exploited whatever was most questionable in his personality, dramatizing his sense of guilt and perdition in theatrical horrors and a costume of malice. . . . Out there in his West Coast newspaper office Bierce was somehow seized by the hypnosis of evil and defiance that has inspired so much of modern literature from symbolism to Dada and Surrealism.

Harold Rosenberg. Nation. March 15, 1947. p. 312

There was never any danger that Bierce's stories would be forgotten. Now they are old-fashioned, creaky, melodramatic, but they are also art. . . . Throughout the writings runs a kind of fierce, disillusioned democracy, negative rather than positive—a warfare on all injustice and impiety. In Bierce's bitterness there is never a whine or whimper. You feel he had a relish for it. Or say he had a relish for the world, and finding it bitter he hated it with a whole heart.

Walter Havighurst. SR. Jan. 25, 1947. p. 16

Like Swift he was driven by a passion for clarity; he simply could not write a muddy sentence. Like Swift, too, he was obsessed by a fierce determination to be precise and was, so to speak, a lexicographer by instinct. Not only does the *Dictionary* contain the best of Bierce's satire but it also reveals some of his underlying preoccupations.

Most readers of *The Devil's Dictionary* are so entertained by Bierce's wit that they fail to notice the recurrent themes. Politics, for example, was high on the list of subjects that most frequently engaged his attention. Bierce lived and wrote in a period when American politics were turgid, fatuous, and corrupt—the period from "the bloody shirt" through "rum, romanism and rebellion" to "Remember the Maine!" An idealist by temperament, he had recoiled violently from the bombast and corruption of the post-Civil-War decades. He liked to convey the impression that he regarded practical politics with complete disdain. But almost single-handedly he defeated the attempt of the Southern Pacific Railroad to make a final raid on the federal treasury—in the fight over the so-called Funding Bill in 1896—and in doing so had a strong case made for the public ownership of railroads.

(K)          Carey McWilliams. Introduction to *The Devil's Dictionary* by Ambrose Bierce (Hill and Wang). 1957. p. vii. [1952]

Bierce wrote in the tradition of Swift, attacking the corrupt social institutions of his time and addressing his work to those "enlightened souls who prefer dry wines to sweet, sense to sentiment, wit to humor, and clean English to slang." While many persons were stung by his trenchant comments on mankind, few could deny the clarity of observation behind them. . . . The fact that the same pomposities and hypocrisies exist today in much the same form makes these verses and prose sketches especially pertinent today.

(K)          George Barkin. Preface to *The Sardonic Humor of Ambrose Bierce* (Dover). 1963. pp. v–vi

If Bierce has proved a protean figure, his fiction, at least, has a curiously homogeneous quality which originates in his obsessive vision. Specifically, Bierce's fiction takes its form from a series of violent oscillations between art and life, idealism and cynicism, and a richly romantic imagination and a rational awareness of life as a diminished thing. It was the pressure of the warring impulses Bierce could never manage in his own life that determined the controlling conception of his short stories. The conception itself severely restricted the range of his ideas and finally destroyed him as a serious writer. But in a handful of his war tales, it also enabled him to do what time may judge to be his finest writing.

(K)          Stuart C. Woodruff. *The Short Stories of Ambrose Bierce* (Pittsburgh). 1964. pp. 2–3

While Bierce was read and admired by many another writer, it is difficult to see his work as a direct influence on the journalistic style of later practitioners, few of whom possessed his skill. The same factors which formed his techniques—the cynicism which allowed him to live with conditions he felt himself powerless to affect; his fascination with words and their syntactic combinations as opposed to straight reporting styles—could have led others to imitate him unconsciously. But the imitations, conscious or unconscious, lacked Bierce's distinguishing mark, the tone of arrow-like contempt, because they were assumed as an artificial way of dismissing the troubles of the world. Bierce's tone was a natural outgrowth of a personality so shocked by war that it held itself together only by the compulsive demonstration that meaningless slaughter contained all the meaning there was.

(K)                                       Larzer Ziff. *The American 1890s* (Viking). 1966.

p. 170

It was his precise recollection of atmosphere, the limpid clarity of his description of physical setting that gave his Civil War stories such a startling air of realism. Mencken considered him the "first writer of fiction ever to treat war realistically." Certainly he was the first to show that heroism had no place in the scientific slaughter which war had become even in his time. Both in his short stories and in his nonfictional sketches he conveyed the reality of Shiloh, Stones River, Chickamauga, Kenesaw Mountain and Franklin as no other writer has. . . .

If he is rediscovered in the near future, it will likely be as the first notable exponent of black humor in America. Prudish as he was in anything written for publication, he would be offended at inclusion in such raffish company. Anything bordering on the pornographic evoked an outcry for rigid censorship and harsh penalties from Bierce. Today's black humorists could, however, meet him with profit. He is their natural father.

(K)                                       Richard O'Connor. *Ambrose Bierce* (Little).

1967. pp. 5, 7

See *The Collected Writings* (1947 edition).

# BISHOP, ELIZABETH (1911–      )

Elizabeth Bishop is spectacular in being unspectacular. Why has no one ever thought of this, one asks oneself; why not be accurate and modest? Miss Bishop's mechanics of presentation with its underlying knowledge, moreover, reduce critical cold blood to cautious self-inquiry. . . . With poetry as with homiletics tentativeness can be more positive than positiveness; and in *North and South* a much instructed persuasiveness is emphasized by uninsistence. . . . At last we have someone who knows, who is not didactic.

Marianne Moore. *Nation*. Sept. 28, 1946. p. 354

The publication of Elizabeth Bishop's *North and South* . . . is a distinct literary event.

"The Map" introduces us to her strongly delineated, subtly colored world. Following it south, from "The Imaginary Iceberg" to "the state with the prettiest name" (Florida), we are exploring a style supple, versatile and idiomatic, brilliant without being shallow, profound without trying. . . . Without striving for novelty Elizabeth Bishop's poems make their appeal to the senses, the mind, the heart, and what goes beyond classification since it is, as in all original poetry, the reflection of a "light that never was, on sea or land."

Lloyd Frankenberg. SR. Oct. 12, 1946. p. 46

If the author of the thirty-two remarkable poems in this book used paint she would undoubtedly paint "abstractions." Yet so sure is her feeling for poetry that in building up her over-all water-color arrangements she never strays far from the concrete and the particular.

"The Fish" is a case in point. There has not been a poem like it, I think, since Richard Eberhart's "The Groundhog," But Miss Bishop approaches her symbol more impersonally and the diction is less mannered.

Selden Rodman. NYT. Oct. 27, 1946. p. 18

I find the same detached, deliberate, unmoved qualities in the new work as in her old. She is unhurried. The new poems represent two a year for the past nine years. . . . Miss Bishop is not interested in changing the language of poetry. She conserves good means. She is devoted to honest announcements of what she knows, to purity of the poem, to subtle changes in scope and intention. . . . Her work is as steady as prose, but it has its own poetic luminosity.

Richard Eberhart. NYT. July 17, 1955. p. 4

The augury of Miss Bishop's early poems has been fulfilled in a small body of work which is personal, possessed of wit and sensibility, technically expert and often moving.

The first collection of her poems brought together thirty poems and established Miss Bishop's reputation more soundly than is often achieved by a first book. One or another of a half dozen of the poems . . . have already become almost indispensable items in any anthology of modern poetry. . . . The poems of *A Cold Spring* offer not a further range but new poems which, at their best, have the same qualities which distinguish the most memorable of her previous work.

Coleman Rosenberger. NYHT. Sept. 4, 1955. p. 2

The distinction of the poetry . . . has been most often its insistence on the opacity and impenetrable presence of the object, whose surfaces will yield, to a pure attention, not sermons, but details. . . . The happiest consequence of this kind of work will be the refreshment it affords the language (which becomes impoverished by the moralizing of descriptive words) and the sense it gives of immense possibility opening; as if from playing checkers we now come to chess, we delightedly may foresee combinations endlessly intricate, and the happier for going beyond the range of conscious intention a good deal of the time. But there are consequences less cheerful as well: one of them is triviality, or you may call it the want of action, where the poem never becomes so much as the sum of its details and so, in two senses, fails to move; another closely related, is the inspired tendency to believe all things possible to a clever precision and a dry tone.

Howard Nemerov. *Poetry*. Dec., 1955. pp. 181–2

Miss Bishop's world is opulent, but in the most unexpected and most humble ways. As a poet, she gives order to this opulence. She enumerates it. She stabilizes the shudder, the nerve, the reflection, the pleasure and the irradiation. . . . In this poetic world there is nothing merely invented. There is no fantasy and no delirium. There are embellishments, in the best tradition, but what is embellished is always true. What is sanctioned is what has been found to be authentic. . . . Elizabeth Bishop is a partisan in the world.

Wallace Fowlie. *Com*. Feb. 15, 1957. p. 514

She never moralizes. She is not interested in the abstract truth at the end of the road, but in the concrete truths that lie along the way—the shape of a tree, the look of gently broken water in the morning sunlight, or the appearance of an old fish half-in half-out the boat. Her truths are the truths of a bowl of peaches by Cézanne, a wheat field by Van Gogh, a lady playing the lute by Ter Borch. The reader must therefore be interested in the manner in which she selects or "filters" her subject, in the tonality she achieves, in her massing of the details into significant form. Her best poems do reveal moments of vision, but she inserts them so unpretentiously amid carefully and skillfully selected objective details that a careless reader easily misses them. Her vocabulary, too, is so utterly free from pomposity that its accuracy and suitability to the occasion is not at first apparent. Only rarely is she obscure, but on these rare occasions it is an obscurity arising from reticence rather than from a desire to mystify or to conceal lack of thought. She never forces a poem beyond its limits, nor herself to assume a pose that is unnatural. In this lies her strength, a strength with limitations.

(K)                    James G. Southworth. *CE*. Feb., 1959. p. 214

Elizabeth Bishop is one of those poets of rare sensitivity, meticulous craftsmanship, and limited production whose work is of such a high caliber that she must be set apart from many of her more prolific rivals. Miss Bishop has, so far, published only two collections of verse, with a third one recently announced but not yet published at the time of this writing. . . . Miss Bishop more than compensates for her limited canon by her impeccable artistic judgment; even the slightest piece of her work is finished to perfection, glows with an unchangeable completeness. The poetic universe created within this framework of formal excellence, a universe translated by language into something unmistakably hers, as if she had dreamed it up just for her own contemplation, stands out with marvelous fullness and with an admirable exactitude.

(K)                                    Ralph J. Mills. *Contemporary American Poetry*
                                                   (Random). 1965. p. 72

Elizabeth Bishop is modest, and she is dignified. Because she is modest, she has not presumed to assign to her artistic sensibilities an importance incommensurate with their value. Hers may be a minor voice among the poets of history, but it is scarcely ever a false one. We listen to it as one might listen to a friend whose exceptional wisdom and honesty we gratefully revere.

Because Elizabeth Bishop is dignified she has been reluctant to fling her troubles at the world; she prefers always to see herself with a certain wry detachment. As a result, her poems are occasionally artificial; there is sometimes a coy archness which undermines the strength of her deeper perceptions. On the other hand, her tone savors more good manners than of mannerism. She would not insult us as she tells us the often unflattering truth. . . .

Elizabeth Bishop is a realist, but she sees miracles all the time. In her poems it is as if she were turning again and again to say to us: "If man, who cannot live by bread alone, is spiritually to survive in the future, he must be made to see that the stuff of bread is also the stuff of the infinite." The crumb which becomes a mansion in "A Miracle for Breakfast" is more than a clever poetical conceit. It is a symbol of hope in a world which can be bearable—for some mysterious reason—in spite of its evils.

(K)                                    Anne Stevenson. *Elizabeth Bishop* (Twayne).
                                                   1966. pp. 126–7

Already, when her first book, *North and South,* was published in 1946, she was the tourist, the curious, sympathetic and delighted observer of place and custom, animal, and person, and the interaction between them which gave them identity and character. Now, twenty years later, she still has the eye for detail, the capacity for detachment, the sense for the right word and the uncanny image, and the mental habit that imposes order, balance, and clarity on everything she sees. But this third book [*Questions of Travel*] holds more yet: a greater richness of language, a grasp of proportion and progression that makes every poem appear flawless, and an increased involvement between the "I" of the traveler and the "it" and "thou" of landscape and stranger. As the sense of place becomes ever more insistent, the questions of travel are asked more openly and urgently, including the final, inevitable one: where is home? Miss Bishop does not provide answers. Her eagerness to discover, examine, and celebrate "the sun the other way around" exists for its own sake: her answers are the poems themselves.

(K)                                    Lisel Mueller. *Poetry*. Aug., 1966. p. 336

*Questions of Travel* is her first collection since 1955, and it shows her at the full maturity of her powers. There are 19 poems, many of them first-rate—it's not a term that comes easily—and there is a long prose story of childhood, "In the Village," whose wide-eyed lucidity charges details with emotions and meanings.

Miss Bishop's method astonishes with its flexibility; within plain wrappers, it registers an extraordinary range of experience. It can deal with Trollope's journal, or the life of the slums of Rio; it can face death in Nova Scotia, control the rainy season in a metaphor, take a close look at virtually anything, and tell the fantastic story of the Amazonian villager who decides to become a witch. The method—since it is a vision—suits itself to a variety of forms, to the ballad or the sestina, to the quatrain and to the stanza built of rhythms that refine and elaborate those of casual speech. In short, Miss Bishop can entertain artificialities without losing her directness; her genius is for seeing clearly. This book is a formidable achievement.

(K)                                    Gene Baro. *NYT*. March 26, 1967. p. 5

See *Poems: North and South and A Cold Spring, Questions of Travel* (poems).

# BISHOP, JOHN PEALE (1892–1944)

His tradition is quite evidently aristocratic. He prefers the fine, the delicate, the rare in character or in performance. Several of the poems have to do with the aristocracy of the South. I do not think, however, that one can accuse Mr. Bishop of snobbery. Through the poems runs the realization that, regardless of preference, the time has come when the fine flower of aristocracy is decadent, that terrible though this process may be, aristocracy must now be reinvigorated by contact with more primitive and ignorant classes. . . . He shrinks a little from the common herd, but he does not entirely deny them.

Eda Lou Walton. *Nation*. Feb. 7, 1934. pp. 162–3

There is, then, the contemporary preoccupation with styles (not simply style), with metrical forms, and with the structure of the line. But Bishop, of all the modern poets who take this approach, feels the least uneasiness about a proper subject matter. There is no one subject, no one scene, nor a single kind of imagery coming from a single subject or scene: every poem, as I say, is a new problem. And Bishop feels no inhibition in the presence of any kind of material.

Allen Tate. *NR.* Feb. 21, 1934. p. 52

One would surmise, even without the specific information, that his acquaintance with French poetry of the later nineteenth century is immediate, and not second-hand through Eliot and Pound. But it seems that Eliot, Pound, and Yeats have done something to define the precise use Bishop has made of these and other models. And it is not that Bishop has merely re-adapted current techniques; it is that he has written with the same attitudes from which those techniques were developed. The principle of unification to be detected in the attitudes behind the present poems is not so much the unification of a single personality or a philosophy or a fundamental theme, as it is the unification that a period affords its various fashions.

Robert Penn Warren. *Poetry.* March, 1934. p. 345

Mr. Bishop is one of the school of Eliot and Pound; he has the sense of an individual poem as being something as separately well made as a vase or a candlestick, a sense hardly to be found in Jeffers or Sandburg. . . . The range of Mr. Bishop's achievement is not great: a few detached observations sensitively recorded over a number of years; but he understands the meaning of craftsmanship. He knows that for words to take on the illusion of life there must be the precarious marriage between content and form.

F. O. Matthiessen. *YR.* Spring, 1934. p. 613

I believe that John Peale Bishop has written one of the few memorable novels of this decade (*Act of Darkness*). . . . Mr. Bishop has chosen his material with the same care that he devotes to the writing of a poem; and since he is a poet of unusual sensibility, one finds in his prose an admirable restraint in the use of the so-called "poetic" image and vocabulary. There is fine economy of words in his paragraphs; and by effective inversion of adjectives his prose cadence is of highly individual (but not spectacular) quality. I believe these matters were of concern to Mr. Bishop in the writing of his novel—and not whatever social implications it may contain. He had, however, something to say which was a record of experience, and the fact that he has said it well produced a narrative of continuously exciting revelation.

Horace Gregory. *NYHT.* March 10, 1935. p. 7

This sensitive re-creation of adolescence (*Act of Darkness*), poetic, obviously autobiographical, Proustian in conception although not in style, introduces a new Southern novelist. . . . If I have read the novel aright, it is this: That body and spirit are not one but two that move along parallel lines, supplementing each other to form a track. . . . *Act of Darkness* must by all means be set down as a superior book. There is power behind its sensitivity. And in its best passages this first novel achieves distinction.

Fred T. Marsh. *NYT*. March 17, 1935. p. 6

Mr. Bishop is one of the few men now writing in America or elsewhere who recognize the privileges, tests, and ordeals of the aesthetic discipline. . . . The unity in (his) poems derives from his effort to return, after widely eclectic experiences in art and the sophistication of New York and Paris, to his native roots and loyalties, his moral plight as an individual, and to the recovery of his local habitation and a name. . . . Mr. Bishop still respects the impersonal discipline and objective moral sense of his symbolist teachers. His work asks to be considered as poetry before it makes its appeal as a private history or an American document. . . . His work has everything that taste, finish, and conscience can give it.

Morton Dauwen Zabel. *Nation*. April 12, 1941.

pp. 447–8

It is difficult enough to describe Mr. Bishop's essential talent. It is a rather unusual combination of the scholar and the sensualist. The intellectual today likes his learning and the lyricist, of course, loves his love poems. There is a bad separation. Mr. Bishop thinks what he feels, he experiences actually what ideally he knows as a scholar, he can be at the same time serenely intellectual and terribly sensual. . . . He combines one's feeling with one's thinking.

Peter Monro Jack. *NYT*. Jan. 4, 1942. p. 5

Bishop's basic theme is the loss of form, the loss of myth, the loss of a pattern. . . . It is true that Bishop's poetry is often poetry about poetry, but then Bishop's conception of poetry is more profound than the man-in-the-street's essentially "literary" conception. The problems of writing poetry and the problems of a formless and chaotic age become at many points identical. . . . Certainly none of Mr. Bishop's problems would be solved by his abandoning his theme. . . . Or by giving up a concern for "form." Indeed, the most successful of Bishop's poems are precisely those which exploit his theme most thoroughly and which are most precisely "formal."

Cleanth Brooks. *KR*. Spring, 1942. pp. 244–5

One of Bishop's great merits was to have realized his limitations and, unlike so many other American writers, to have preferred perfect minor achievement to over-ambitious failure. In this way he turned a defect of destiny into an aesthetic virtue. He was that rare thing in American literature, a true type of the second-order writer who, though incapable of supreme creative achievement, keeps alive a sense for the highest values. It is this type of writer whom the French delight to honor, recognizing their importance for the continuance of a vital cultural tradition; and this is perhaps one reason why Bishop felt so powerful an attraction for French culture.

Joseph Frank. SwR. Winter, 1947. pp. 106–7

We have been used to hearing the West Virginian dismissed as *too* typical, i.e., too derivative on the one hand, too immersed in class consciousness (upper level) on the other; yet his essays and poems in their progress . . . amply display an original mind and reveal the generous, passionate, humane personality finally emerging from beneath the successive masks of the "provincial," the dandy, the snob, the ironist. . . . Toward the end, the romantic exile came home to his own idiom, and achieved in his poetry a density of meaning projected with classic purity of tone.

Gerard Previn Meyer. SR. Oct. 2, 1948. p. 24

As a poet he is, perhaps, not obscure; his life was outwardly serene but it conceals a sensiblity that was courageously tortured; conditions that look identical seem simultaneously to have hamstrung his talents and set him free. He is infinitely discussable, for he raises (how forcibly I was not aware) the crucial problems of writing now, in America, as well as the adequacy of available solutions. He is more pertinent, both in achievement and mechanism, than, say, Kafka. The achievement matters but the torture is instructive, for it is the torture of the creative will, persistently willing to will, but the will being again and again dissipated, and reviving, being frittered or smashed, but always returning.

William Arrowsmith. HdR. Spring, 1949. p. 118

See *Collected Poems, Collected Essays,* and *Act of Darkness* (novel).

# BLACKMUR, RICHARD (1904–1965)

**Poetry**

Blackmur is preoccupied with pure poetry. . . . His metrics have the individuality of the classic composers of chamber music. . . . The joints of his moods with everyday are thin at times, and one must be alert with utter inner poise to hear or to heed him. A whole page of print, which yesterday opened vistas, today will seem blank until tomorrow it opens wider. Always the subject matter . . . illustrates human subterfuge from oblivion and ruse against the unavoidable futility of existence. . . . Even as he finds home Way Down East and in the Hub where landscape and men exhausted smile and move and speak with grace unknown to their past times of strength, so does he universally at once express and comment upon a cultural decadence.

John Brooks Wheelwright. NR. July 21, 1937. p. 316

The writing . . . is nervous, extraordinarily complex in texture, and urgent with a kind of religious New England cantankerousness that one has scarcely heard in contemporary verse since the too early death of John Wheelwright—not that I mean to imply that Mr. Blackmur derives from Wheelwright (the debt, if it exists, must surely be reckoned the other way around), but that the vibrant originality of the one stirs memories of the other, *discordes concordantes*. . . . I am saying, in short, that Mr. Blackmur, extraordinarily difficult though he can be, is a poet *sui generis;* and the *genus* is rare and important.

Dudley Fitts. SR. March 20, 1948. p. 28

The poems . . . are nakedly of and about the human spirit, seriously concerned with the state of the individual caught in the enormous trap of a universe of things and theories.

It isn't easy to write poetry of a high metaphysical order. Blackmur avoids rhetorical bombast, occult mystification, overmodernized trimmings. . . . The fault of Blackmur is his deadly seriousness unlightened by even the grim humor of irony.

Oscar Williams. Nation. Oct. 10, 1942. p. 354

These are poems of the most extreme situations possible, of a constricted, turned-in-upon-itself, contorted, almost tetanic agony: the poet not only works against the grain of things, but the grain is all knots. . . . Sometimes the pain is too pure to be art at all, and one is watching the nightmare of a man sitting in the midst of his own entrails, knitting them all night into the tapestry which he unknits all day. But there is in the poems, none of that horrible relishing complacency with which so many existential thinkers insist upon the worst; the poems try desperately for any way out, either for the Comforter—*some* sort of comforter—or else for that coldest comfort, understanding.

Randall Jarrell. Nation. Apr. 24, 1948. p. 447

**Criticism**

Specifically and primarily, the method can be described as that of taking hold of the words of the poem and asking two very important questions:

(1) Do these words represent a genuine fact, condition, or feeling? (2) Does the combining of these words result in "an access of knowledge"? Knowledge in the full sense, one must add, for something must be made known "publicly," "objectively," in terms which any intelligent reader, with the proper effort, can grasp; as distinct from terms and language used "privately," "personally," "subjectively." Now of the two questions, it is the first that Blackmur emphasizes and the second which he often neglects. The discrete parts—sentences, phrases, single words (which are sometimes counted)—are the main object of his attention. The way in which they combine is sometimes an afterthought (though this is less so in the more recent essays).

Delmore Schwartz. *Poetry*. Oct., 1938. p. 30

With a critic like Richard P. Blackmur, who tends to use on each work the special technique it seems to call for, and who at one time or another has used almost every type of criticism, the difficulty of placing any single way of operating as his "method" is obvious. What he has is not so much a unique method as a unique habit of mind, a capacity for painstaking investigation which is essential for contemporary criticism, and which might properly be isolated as his major contribution to the brew. . . . Blackmur is almost unique in his assumption that no demand for knowledge the poet makes on the serious reader (that is, the critic) is unreasonable, and that if he doesn't have the information he had better go and get it.

Stanley Edgar Hyman. *Poetry*. Feb., 1948.
pp. 259, 262

For Mr. Blackmur poetry is the supreme mode of the imagination and in his quest for the genuine in the mode he is nearly fanatical. He likes nothing better than breaking butterflies of poetry on the wheel of criticism, although it must be noted that almost every poet thus broken . . . emerges whole again and illuminated. What Blackmur does is focus attention and heighten awareness.

Milton Rugoff. *NYHT*. Dec. 28, 1952. p. 5

Again and again, until it touches a note of hysteria and one wonders at such insistence, Mr. Blackmur speaks out against his anathema—expressive language. He makes constantly an appeal to reason, which in poetry is objective form. . . . The fact is, Mr. Blackmur has been attempting as difficult a critical job as was ever conceived. . . . Perhaps Mr. Blackmur's fearful note is near to the cry of those who push analysis to the limit of reason. And perhaps, as I think, he has been pushed himself into statements that exceed his purpose, as when he says, for instance, that poetry is "language so twisted and posed in a form that it not only expresses the matter in hand but adds to the stock of reality." . . . Mr. Blackmur arrives, by way of the back stairs, at a sort of higher romanticism, where we children of his prior, or downstairs enlightenment are likely to feel timid or ill at ease.

Hayden Carruth. *Nation*. Jan. 10, 1953. p. 35

In recent years as a Professor of English at Princeton he has become the fountainhead of a distinctly personal and highly original school of criticism. His standards are high, his language fluent, though sparse, and on occasion recondite, and he pays extraordinary attention to minute detail; his work represents a constant searching of the mind for the highest amount of intellectual pressure and insight it will yield.

During these years Mr. Blackmur has, in reality, gone to the school of his own bold intelligence and allowed himself that free and full "response to experience" he deems to be the first duty of a critic.

Leon Edel. *NYT*. April 17, 1955. p. 4

The alienated artist is . . . ordinarily forced into one of two possible roles: that of the lonely prisoner in a personal "ivory tower," or that of a prophet without honor, a rather owlish Cassandra.

To some extent, perhaps, R. P. Blackmur fills both these roles. . . . While he has not abandoned the technique of "criticism of criticism" which is often regarded as a kind of hallmark of modern ivory-towerism, he is essentially engaged in a work of public persuasion, evangelical, almost apocalyptic. . . . Criticism should turn, Mr. Blackmur, believes, from poetry, which, as poetry, seems to him to have declined in value for us, to the novel, which he regards as the most significant literary form now and in the future. The ideal which he sets before the critic is thus a synthesis of Coleridge and Aristotle.

John F. Sullivan. *Com*. May 13, 1955. p. 159

Mr Blackmur is all these things: poet, rhetorician, evangelist, university teacher, a lover of words, master of a weighted vocabulary. It is surely the poet in him and equally the rhetorician which makes one, reading this book, hate the things Mr Blackmur hates: formula, methodology, prejudgement, slogan. And love the things he loves; the acts behind such words as imaginative, plastic, symbolic, responsive, actual, form. It is also the poet in Mr Blackmur which makes him use, quite freely and without quotation marks, phrases which he has remembered from such writers as Henry James, Melville, Thomas Mann, Ransom, and Santayana: sacred rage; compositional centre; operative consciousness; the sense of life; the shock of recognition; the outsider; a poet nearly anonymous; a philosopher almost a poet. There are other phrases, including

'disconsolate chimera', which appear to be quotations from Mr Blackmur himself.

(K)                              Denis Donoghue. *TC*. June, 1957. pp. 540–1

In criticizing poetry, his concern is not with pattern but with language. He
knows what words or groups of words affect him, and he wants to know
why they affect him. He is aesthetic about words and carries them back
into the poet's mind and forth into his own with a relished complexity that
is as obscure and seemingly chaotic as anything in modern poetry.

Basically Blackmur is an impressionistic critic rapturizing over words
and images. However, his raptures do cling to a theory that is worked out
precisely as his impressions develop into speculations (which they often
do). It is quite possible, to be sure, that the complicated verbiage of his
essays fools one into suspecting more precision than is actually present,
and sometimes one is startled by a dangerous overemphasis or even a
contradiction, but the theory is there and can be described.

(K)                              Maurice Kramer. *CE*. May, 1961. p. 553

Blackmur has tried to recreate in his own way Arnold's vision of the
"future of poetry," first by encouraging against the current of modern
pragmatization and secularization a passion and a reverence for sensed
mysteries; and second by discovering works of literature, whether for
audience or artist, as experiences which put that passion and reverence
into formal relation with the sense of the mysteries, with this discovered
relation perhaps finally to be considered a kind of "knowledge." It was
something as ambitious and esoteric as this that Blackmur had in mind
when in "The Lion and the Honeycomb" he wrote, with a rather irrelevant
metaphoric humility for one who is nothing if not virtuoso, that the critic
as "go-between" ought to disappear "when the couple are gotten
together."

Blackmur's first task, to cultivate the mysteries, is very materially aided
by his style. Rhythmic incantation, allegorical indirection, the mystical
rhetoric of pun and paradox—these are the sorts of techniques creating
in his criticism its distinctive aura of priestly and prophetic power.

(K)                              Richard Foster. *The New Romantics* (Indiana).
                                                                    1962. p. 98

Beside him, [Allen] Tate and [John Crowe] Ransom are boring indeed, and
their styles, compared to his, are never capable of the resonance and sug-
gestiveness that finally is essential to the literary essayist who is only incidentally a critic. From the early pieces on modern poets and the magnificent omnibus reviews now in *The Expense of Greatness* to the
Byzantine labyrinths of the later essays on James and Eliot, Blackmur has

shown that he can elevate the characteristic gestures of the New Criticism to a self-sustaining art. There is, furthermore, a wit in him which is quite uncharacteristic of the others.

(K)                                    Roger Sale. *HdR*. Autumn, 1962. pp. 478, 480

Blackmur's theory, roughly, is this: the poet, by varied preparation, builds up to a climactic moment, but, once reached, it makes no difference what words he uses. Fortunately, before twenty pages have passed, Blackmur has his theory safely tucked away and once more shows himself to be among the best of our practical critics.

(K)                                    Lee T. Lemon. *The Partial Critics* (Oxford).
1965. p. 136

See *From Jordan's Delight, The Second World, The Good European* (poetry); *Language as Gesture, The Lion and the Honeycomb, The Expense of Greatness, A Primer of Ignorance* (criticism).

# BODENHEIM, MAXWELL (1893–1954)

He has humiliated nouns and adjectives, stripped them of their old despotisms and loyalties, and of the importance which ages of power as vehicles of broad emotions had given them over the minds of poets and men. He has given them the roles of impersonal figures tracing his mathematics of the soul. His words are sharp, neatly strung, with tapping consonants and brief unemotional vowels, like the chip of a fatal chisel. . . . Metaphysics is a man's choice of his own *mise en scene*—in Bodenheim's poems it is an arctic light in which his brilliant images accept their own insignificance as finalities, yet are animated by the macabre elation which has thrown them into relief.

Louis Grudin. *Poetry*. Nov., 1922. pp. 102–4

His verse is Chinese. It does not resemble Chinese poetry; it is not a direct and unfigured commentary on nature; quite the contrary. It is Chinese in etiquette rather, being stilted, conventional to its own conventions, and formally bandaged in red tape. It is a social gathering of words; they have ancestries and are over-bred; they know the precepts of the Law and take delight in breaking them. Meeting together they bow too deeply, make stiff patterns on paper or silk, relate their adventures in twisted metaphor and under an alias, sometimes jest pompously behind a fan. They discovered irony late in life.

Bodenheim is a master of their ceremony and arranges it with an agile fantasy which takes the place of imagination.

Malcolm Cowley. *Dial*. Oct., 1922. p. 446

Here is a ferocious anti-sentimentalist. I am not sure how much of a poet Mr. Bodenheim is. What I am sure of is that his work is honest—honest to the point of mocking at its own honesty—and that it never mistakes a state of sentiment for one of intense feeling. . . . Mr. Bodenheim is, as the stinging acidity of his style betrays, less concerned anyway with feeling than with thought. Life is to him a boundless paradox, an irony of defeat, a bitter act of treachery. Alike in his method of writing, his attitude to society at large, and his defiant individualism, he reveals the poet pre-occupied with moral, rather than aesthetic values.

John Gould Fletcher. *Fm.* Jan. 30, 1924. p. 502

One has a picture of Bodenheim as ring master, cracking his savage whip over the heads of cowering adjectives and recalcitrant nouns, compelling them to leap in grotesque and unwilling pairs over the fantastically piled barriers of his imagination. It is a good show—particularly for those who have not seen it too often. . . . He is still—if I may take my metaphor out of the circus—the sardonic euphuist; his irony leaps, with fascinating transilience, from one image to another. . . . But, for all his intellectual alertness, the total effect is an acrobatic monotony: what started as a manner is degenerating into a mannerism.

Louis Untermeyer. *Bkm.* April, 1924. pp. 220–1

Though his sensitive feeling for words betrays him sometimes into pre-ciosity, mostly he makes it serve his purpose. For his is an art of veiled and egoistic emotions, in which the immediate subject, be it a lady or a buttercup or the rear porch of an apartment building reflects, like an actor's practice-mirror, the poet's swiftly changing expressions and atti-tudes. . . . With Mr. Bodenheim it is the one all-engrossing phenomenon of the universe. Standing before the mirror, he is kindled to frozen fires of passion over the ever-changing aspects of his thought in its mortal sheath; he is intrigued—nay, moved to the white heat of ice by the subtle workings of his mind, trailing off from the central unreal reality there visible out to nebulous remote circumferences of an ego-starred philosophy.

Harriet Monroe. *Poetry.* March, 1925. pp. 322–3

His poems frequently testify to the fact that he has had, and that he is capable of emotion; but they are almost never a direct expression of emotions. Rather, they are an analytic recollection of such states of mind; and the effect, in the hands of the curious word-lover that Mr. Bodenheim is, is odd and individual and not infrequently pleasing. In his simpler and less pretentious things, when he merely indulges his fancy, as in "Chinese Gifts," he can be charming. Here the verbalist and the cerebralist momen-tarily surrender, the colder processes are in abeyance, and the result is a poetry slight but fragrant. But for the rest, one finds Mr. Bodenheim a little bit wordy and prosy. One feels that he works too hard and plays too little; or that when he plays, he plays too solemnly and heavily.

Conrad Aiken. *NR*. June 1, 1927. p. 53

To consider Mr. Bodenheim at all is very much like considering a prickly pear; one never knows when he is going to get a thorn run through his finger. Still, like the prickly pear, once the combative surface is pierced an edible and tasty (albeit faintly acidulous) fruit is to be discovered. In other words, Mr. Bodenheim has his values, his poetical accomplishments (of no mean order, either), his impalpable connotations, and his savage satirical zest that is quite often salty enough to delight the victim. Together with his value he has drawbacks. Now these drawbacks are mainly on the surface, as the thorns of the prickly pear are. They are evidenced mainly in an undue suspiciousness of the world at large, in an instinctive gesture of defense that reveals itself in a consistent offensive, in an emphatic disgust for the commonplaces and courtesies of polite living and in a passion for cerebralism that sometimes goes to such lengths as to defeat its objective.

Herbert Gorman. *SR*. June 18, 1927. p. 912

Maxwell Bodenheim's book of poems (*Bringing Jazz*) might well be used as a starting point for a definition of jazz esthetics. First of all, it provides a particular kind of superlative entertainment that depends almost entirely upon the titillations of jazz rhythm and the impact of a brilliant, quickly assimilated image. . . . Next we see that Bodenheim's specific brand of irony which he has employed throughout his work, including the discovery of the American underworld in his novels, is converted into a jazz medium. . . . In spite of the many attempts to capture jazz rhythm with all its essentials intact and at the same time to create actual poetry, we have but two successful examples of this style, both significant because they display a like precision in technique: T. S. Eliot's "Fragments of an Agon: Wanna Go Home, Baby?" and a selection of three or four poems from *Bringing Jazz*.

Horace Gregory. *NR*. March 12, 1930. p. 107

Mr. Bodenheim is all personality. He has become a legendary figure of Bohemianism, a vague mixture of Greenwich Village orgies and soapbox oratory. Of course he is neither one nor the other. He is a poet entirely writing about himself and when he seems to be writing about the injustice of the world and the wretched social system of the world he is still writing about himself, as one might almost say, a willing and masochistic victim. He takes upon himself the whole burden of the worker's complaint against the capitalist's way of making his life. . . . His poems are largely a set of grievances, and they have their value. . . . Their value, in so far as it is a value, is in personality, not at all in communism or in religion but in one's self. . . . It is the quick, involved and rude life that Mr. Bodenheim writes of, his own life, not necessarily correlated with the life of our time.

Peter Monro Jack. *NYT*. March 29, 1942. p. 4

See *Selected Poems;* also *Blackguard, Georgie May, Crazy Man,* and *Sixty Seconds* (novels).

# BOGAN, LOUISE (1897–1970)

Under a diversity of forms Miss Bogan has expressed herself with an almost awful singleness. . . . One can be certain that experience of some ultimate sort is behind this writing, that something has been gone through with entirely and intensely, leaving the desolation of a field swept once for all by fire. But the desolation is not vacancy or lassitude. The charred grass is brilliantly black, and the scarred ground is fascinating in its deformity. There still is life, hidden and bitterly urgent.

Mark Van Doren. *Nation*. Oct. 31, 1923. p. 494

Miss Bogan's themes are the reasons of the heart that reason does not know, the eternal strangeness of time in its period and its passage, the curious power of art. Her mood is oftenest a sombre one, relieved not by gaiety but by a sardonic wit. She is primarily a lyricist. . . . It is the spirit's song that Louise Bogan sings, even when her subject is the body. The texture of her verse is strong and fine, her images, though few, are fit, her cadences well-managed. . . . Implicit in her work is the opposition between a savage chaos and the world that the ordering imagination, whether directed by the intellect or the heart, controls.

Babette Deutsch. *Poetry in Our Time* (Holt). 1932.
pp. 238–9

There are bitter words. But they are not harassingly bitter. . . . There are paralleled series of antithetical thoughts, but the antithesis is never exaggerated. . . . There are passages that are just beautiful words rendering objects of beauty. . . . And there are passages of thought as static and as tranquil as a solitary candle-shaped flame of the black yew tree that you see against Italian skies. . . . There is, in fact, everything that goes to the making of one of those more pensive seventeenth century, usually ecclesiastical English poets who are the real glory of our two-fold lyre. Miss Bogan may—and probably will—stand somewhere in a quiet landscape that contains George Herbert, and Donne and Vaughan, and why not even Herrick?

Ford Madox Ford. Poetry. June, 1937. pp. 160–1

I hope she now decides to make some change in her theory and practice of the poet's art. Together they have been confining her to a somewhat narrow range of expression. Her new poems—meditative, witty, and sometimes really wise—suggest that she has more to say than can be crowded into any group of lyrics, and that perhaps she should give herself more space and less time. Most American poets write too much and too easily; Miss Bogan ought to write more, and more quickly, and even more carelessly. There are poems, sometimes very good ones, that have to be jotted down quickly or lost forever.

Malcolm Cowley. NR. Nov. 10, 1941. p. 625

Miss (Leonie) Adams and Miss Bogan were surely sisters in the same aesthetic current; and while I must confess that I have often wondered why that sisterhood insisted on wearing its chastity belt on the outside, poetry nevertheless remains wherever the spirit finds it.

But—speaking as one reader—if I admire objectively the poems of the first three (the earlier) sections of Miss Bogan's collection, with the poems of section four, I find myself forgetting the thee and me of it. . . . Miss Bogan began in beauty, but she has aged to magnificence, and I find myself thinking that the patina outshines the gold stain. . . . Miss Bogan sees into herself in the late poems—and not only into herself, but deeply enough into herself to find within her that jungle—call it the Jungian unconscious if you must—that everyone has in himself.

John Ciardi. Nation. May 22, 1954. pp. 445–6

Louise Bogan has always seemed to me a considerable problem. . . . At first you can see only the special hyperesthesia, the trance state so common in the poetesses of the first quarter of the century. . . . As you read on, you discover a fundamental, all-important difference. Louise Bogan really means what she says. . . . You have an honest, yet piercing awareness of life as fundamentally tragic. The hyperesthesia is there, but it is embroiled in life, it handles and judges life in real terms.

Kenneth Rexroth. NYHT. July 4, 1954. p. 5

The virtues of her writing which have been most often spoken of are, I should suppose, firmness of outline, prosodic accomplishment, chiefly in traditional metrics, purity of diction and tone, concision of phrase, and, what results in craft from all these, and at bottom from a way of seizing experience, concentrated singleness of effect. . . . A large part of their moral force derives from the refusal to be deluded or to be overborne. The learning of the unwanted lesson, the admission of the hard fact, a kind of exhilaration of rejection, whether of the scorned or the merely implausible, the theme appears in the earliest work. . . . It is an art of limits, the limit of the inner occasion and of the recognized mode.

> Leonie Adams. *Poetry*. Dec., 1954. pp. 166–9

Women are not noted for terseness, but Louise Bogan's art is compactness compacted. Emotion with her, as she has said of certain fiction, is "itself form, the kernel which builds outward from inward intensity." She uses a kind of forged rhetoric that nevertheless seems inevitable. . . . One is struck by her restraint—an unusual courtesy in this day of bombast.

> Marianne Moore. *Predilections* (Viking). 1955. p. 130

Miss Bogan's volume . . . is not the volume of a poet for whom verse is merely a pastime, a diversion; the care with which the details have been selected and ordered . . . is the care of devotion. . . . All this is fine and dandy, and it may properly lead—as it has led—to observations about the importance of cultivating a poetry of care in a careless world. . . . (Yet) some of the critics . . . have noted a coldness here, an overscrupulousness there, and a general absence of the warm rhetoric of persuasion in poems so strenuously dedicated to the "verbal discipline."

> Reed Whittemore. *SwR*. Winter, 1955. p. 163

See *Collected Poems* and *Selected Criticism*.

# BOURJAILY, VANCE (1922–    )

There are tenderness and violence in Mr. Bourjaily's story, the genuine, not the movie-advertisement kind, and there is much more than that. There is a lot about a generation that is without much hope, that has never known stability, that found, even in [World War II], not much to inspire a thinking man. I hope a lot of people will read *The End of My Life;* I'm sure almost everybody will enjoy it, despite its faults, which are numerous and obvious, and I'm equally certain that Bourjaily is going to write other and better novels. He has done an almost first-rate job with this one.

> Merle Miller. *SR*. Aug. 30, 1947. pp. 17–8

In literary terms, *The End of My Life* stands as a transitional novel squarely between the two generations. Its early lyricism that is so much in the spirit of the old war writing gives way to the dead futility at its end that anticipates the spirit of the new war writing. The development of

Skinner through the novel, from the confident cynicism of his prewar attitude to the self-destructive horror induced in him by the reality of war, sets the pattern of the new writing as surely as if he had written it himself. It shows how the discovery of war's truth carried this generation beyond the narrow but highly effective literary frame of simple disillusion and left them with an acute but essentially inexpressible awareness of the complex ills of their time.

John W. Aldridge. *After the Lost Generation* (McGraw). 1951. pp. 131–2

He has surrounded his main character [in *The Hound of Earth*] with a variety of co-workers and acquaintances (some of them brilliantly characterized) designed to show the more outrageous aspects of American life. . . . But the book attempts too much; it is indiscriminate; its tone is too uniformly shrill. Mr. Bourjaily is the old-fashioned voice of protest whose passing from the literary scene has sometimes been lamented.

Paul Pickrel. *YR*. Spring, 1955. p. 479

Vance Bourjaily's first novel, *The End of My Life,* had a slightly anachronistic flavor. It told of a second world war that was something of a lark, with ironic sad young men going to Africa to make funny conversation and die. With its extreme youthfulness it constituted a poignant memorial to the wide-eyed college intellectual of the last days of the New Deal.

*The Hound of Earth* reveals a writer purified of most of the postures of extreme youth. The mocking bright-boy melancholy . . . has been succeeded by a frighteningly immediate, perversely humorous perspective upon contemporary American problems of conscience. . . .

This novel is sometimes arch, as in the romance of its moral suicide; it is frankly sentimental at times and then abandons itself to whimsey. . . . But for the most part it holds in balance its humor and its pathos—this tension is the special note of Bourjaily's style—and endures past a first reading as an effective drama about how difficult it is to be both responsible and an individual in contemporary America.

Herbert Gold. *Nation*. July 23, 1955. p. 79

All the characters in Vance Bourjaily's novel *The Violated* . . . pursue contemptible ideals insofar as they pursue anything other than love affairs. This enormously long, soggily earnest book is the more exasperating because it contains enough brilliant flashes to keep the reader hoping for better things.

According to Mr. Bourjaily, his novel is about a group of people who are "violated . . . by their inability to communicate, to love, to comprehend, to create—violated by neurotic commitments to preposterous goals or, more tragically, to no goals at all." This is a perfectly accurate description of the three men whose dreary careers are followed over some thirty years, and also of everyone connected with them, and this is the book's weakness. . . . The nervous, inquisitive rootlessness of late adolescence is well conveyed, but the disabilities that prevent these characters from attaching themselves to the world as they grow older are nebulous. . . . They seem to be people congenitally incapable of coming to grips with anything. . . .

While it is possible to admire the skill with which Mr. Bourjaily writes, and respect his concern for the unhappy people he writes about, it is difficult to share his assumption that the plight of these unaccountable cripples is worth 599 pages.

Phoebe Adams. At. Oct., 1958. pp. 90–1

*The Violated* seems to me a failure, but an interesting one, if only because of the way in which Mr. Bourjaily's courage and ambition lead him to repeated troubles. He has chosen to write one of those full-scale, lavishly detailed narratives composed of parallel and intersecting levels. Such a technique, borrowed from the social novel of the early years of the century, assumes that society is distinctly, even rigidly stratified; that its component classes are intrinsically interesting and worth observing; that a novelist can arrange a conflict between members of these classes which will be dramatic in its own right and representative of larger issues; and that thereby the narrative can finally be brought to a coherent climax.

But for the material Mr. Bourjaily has chosen—the lives of pitiful and bewildered drifters during the past two decades—these assumptions do not operate with sufficient force. His central characters are not distinctive enough, either in social or personal qualities, to warrant separate strands of narrative. As they collapse into each other's lives, the successes of one indistinguishable from the failures of the other, they create a smudge of sadness at the very point where the novel demands tension and clarity. Like the post-war society they reflect, these characters are too much of a sameness, so that one wearies of their presence almost as quickly as one credits their reality.

Irving Howe. NR. Nov. 10, 1958. p. 17

Bourjaily's first two novels were . . . "symbolic." The main character in *The End of My Life* . . . is made to stand for an entire generation. As he gradually comes to lose all his feeling for other people, and thus all his desire for life, he represents in extreme . . . the effects of the war. . . . But Bourjaily's last two books have made every attempt to eschew these metaphorical devices, and for this reason they stand apart from most

American fiction. . . . The characters, events, and ideas in *Confessions of a Spent Youth* are held together by a tone of detached yet committed inquiry and by a conversational style that moves easily from quiet humor to unobtrusive lyricism.

Harris Dienstfrey. Cmty. April, 1961. pp. 360–2

Vance Bourjaily in *The Man Who Knew Kennedy* . . . is examining the meaning of the event [the assassination of Kennedy] for the generation to which Kennedy belonged, and his novel is the story of a part of that generation. . . . In an earlier novel, *The Hound of Earth,* one I have always liked, Bourjaily also made a historic event his center—the explosion of the atom bomb over Hiroshima. . . . Bourjaily's most recent novel, on the other hand, *Confessions of a Spent Life,* seems to grow almost entirely and directly out of his own experience. His strength, whether his approach to a novel is subjective or objective, is his familiarity with American manners in the postwar world. It is really, of course, only a small segment of American experience that he presents in *The Man Who Knew Kennedy;* but such as it is, he gives it life.

The book is extremely readable, and in part, despite its solemn theme, it is charming. . . . What mildly bothers me about the book is that parts of it seem to me a little slick in a way that Bourjaily's earlier novels haven't been.

Granville Hicks. SR. Feb. 4, 1967. pp. 35–6

See *The End of My Life, The Hound of Earth, The Violated, Confessions of a Spent Youth, The Man Who Knew Kennedy* (novels).

# BOURNE, RANDOLPH (1886–1918)

Here was no anonymous reviewer, no mere brilliant satellite of the radical movement losing himself in his immediate reactions: one finds everywhere, interwoven in the fabric of his work, the silver thread of a personal philosophy, the singing line of an intense and beautiful desire.

What was that desire? It was for a new fellowship in the youth of America as the principle of a great and revolutionary departure in our life, a league of youth, one might call it, consciously framed with the purpose of creating, out of the blind chaos of American society, a fine, free, articulate cultural order. That, as it seems to me, was the dominant theme of all his effort, the positive theme to which he always returned from his thrilling forays into the fields of education and politics, philosophy and sociology. . . . Here was Emerson's "American scholar" at last, but radiating an infinitely warmer, profaner, more companionable influence than

Emerson had ever dreamed of, an influence that savored rather of Whitman and William James. He was the new America incarnate, with that stamp of a sort of permanent youthfulness on his queer, twisted, appealing face.

> Van Wyck Brooks. Introduction to *The History of a Literary Radical and Other Papers* by Randolph Bourne (S. A. Russell). 1956. [1919]. pp. 3–4

He discovered new educational experiments; new pathfindings in philosophy and literature; new flights in politics and musical art. To the problems of each field he seemed to bring the whole sum of his former experience, his deep intuition and sure sense of fact, sharp comprehension, quick imaginativeness, and pleasure in the sensuous. And through this liberal delivery, the reports of his discoveries, whether they assumed the shape of a description of the schools in Gary or of a review of a novel, of a whimsical account of friends, children, teachers, or a serious discussion of the future of American culture, became, almost always, experiments in themselves, new theories of facts, new keen images of reality. Bourne could speak with equal sureness, humanity, lightness on a dozen different topics; and his talk itself, like his book-reviewing, was a sort of adventure.

> Paul Rosenfeld. *Dial*. Dec., 1923. p. 552

Already he is more or less a legend to many persons who have not even opened his books and do not know that they contain all the germs of the new spirit. But even a casual examination will prove that those germs are there. Touchingly prophetic, Bourne felt the coming struggle before it had become evident to less subtle observers. During his brief, vivid life he managed to utter some significant reflection upon almost every topic which vitally concerns the age. He wrote of religion, the state, property, the arts, education.

> Carl and Mark Van Doren. *American and British Literature Since 1890* (Century). 1925. p. 123

All of this work [of Bourne] represented the very first quality in the journalism of ideas, but for the most part, it was still journalism. His view of life was maturing, deepening, not yet ready for rounded expression, it was still a promise. . . . Randolph Bourne was precious to us because of what he was, rather than because of what he had actually written. . . . He will never occupy the place of a great teacher, but one feels that potentially he had exactly that office, and that in ten years, in twenty years, he would have distilled out of such pain and frustration as only a crippled man can know, a new image of beauty and perfection.

> Lewis Mumford. *NR*. Sept. 24, 1930. pp. 151–2

He was very deformed. Not alone was he dwarfed and hunchbacked: his face was twisted, he had a tortured ear, his color was sallow and his breathing was audible and hard. He walked in a cape that hid him. He took a chair for the first time in your presence, let fall the black shroud about him, and revealed a form so mangled that you despaired ever to find sufficient ease for the sort of conversation his immediately brilliant mind demanded.

But the magic of Randolph Bourne was not separate from his poor body, and at once you knew this. This is why, in writing of this splendid spirit, it is meet to dwell upon his misery. Within half an hour, your discomfort was gone—so miraculously gone that your mind was prone to look about for it. But whenever, in the future, awareness did return of the grotesque shape in which this spirit was imprisoned and was doomed to walk, it was intellectual altogether: the mind needed to stir the senses with the thought of it, while the senses moved in full ease within his presence.

Waldo Frank. In the American Jungle (Farrar and<br>Rinehart). 1937. pp. 59–60

His book-reviews tended always to be critical essays on the social roots of a man's thinking. They were radical in the sense that they were unsparing in the application of the critical canons they chose. Not that Bourne lacked a breadth of sympathy: his essay on Cardinal Newman had in it generosity and enjoyment. But the main direction of his mind was more exacting. . . . His attacks on the Philistines among novelists and critics . . . had a joyful abandon. He was, in a sense, an American Matthew Arnold, with a touch of Nietzsche's "gay science," who had studied Veblen and delighted in him. His writing, like Veblen's, was ironic: and I am using the term here in Bourne's sense of irony—as flowing from a democracy of the literary realm in which no idea can plead privilege or immunity from a drastic deflation. . . . His attack on the liberal intellectuals of his day and on their role in bringing America into the war was one of the most scathing in American political literature. Bourne was pacifist in his deepest convictions; he was also a democrat in the truest cultural sense. The war crossed his grain on both counts.

Max Lerner. Twice A Year. 1940–1941. pp. 65, 68

Above all Bourne was the perfect child of the prewar Enlightenment; when its light went out in 1918, he died with it. Afterward his story seemed so much the martyrology of his generation that the writer was lost in the victim. Yet even when one goes back to Bourne's books—not merely his bitter and posthumously published collections of essays, but his early studies of contemporary youth, education, and politics—it is not hard to see why Bourne must always seem less a writer than the incarnation of his time. For from his first book, *Youth and Life,* to the *Impressions of Europe* which he wrote on a fellowship abroad and his books on education and the Gary schools, Bourne proved himself so inexpressibly confident of a future established on the evangelicisms of his period, so radiant in his championship of pragmatism, art, reason, European social democracy, and the experimental school, that he now seems a seismograph on which were recorded the greatest hopes and fiercest despairs of his time.

Alfred Kazin. On Native Grounds (Reynal). 1942.<br>pp. 183–4

The key to the bewildering variety of essays and book-reviews which Bourne poured out in the short space of his career lay in their literary quality. He drew strength from the forces which were rapidly transforming the country; he was eager to assist that transformation. But his articles dealing with city and town planning, feminism, Americanization, and college reform—though keen and even startling, although based on solid studies in education, sociology, and political science—were essentially fragments. They served to show the impact of new social developments on a sensitive mind. Bourne's literary essays, on the other hand, were not only thought through, but made up a collection of work which could bear examination years later.

Louis Filler. Randolph Bourne (American Council on<br>Public Affairs). 1943. p. 79

From a pragmatic standpoint Randolph Bourne was a tragic failure. In possession of all the intellectual qualifications for leadership, well on his way towards a position of power and influence, he deliberately rejected the world at a time of crisis and assumed the role of an outcast crying in the wilderness. With the Kaiser's military might let loose over Europe, with democratic society in grave danger, he quixotically expounded a pacifistic anarchism. It might even be argued that the poison of perversity had early entered his spirit and embittered his entire life's experience. From his first passionate attacks on the folkways and activities of the older generation he proceeded in a contrary direction which logically ended in his uncompromising opposition to a war which the best minds accepted as the lesser of the dire alternatives confronting the country. For all his native gifts, he was only a negative and fanatical eccentric.

History, however, will deal more fairly with him. For he belongs not with the politicians but with the prophets. What matters in his case was not his reaction to daily events nor his judgment of temporal affairs but his energetic stimulation of minds and his vision of the good life. Few Americans possessed his enthusiasm for the deepening and enrichment of our indigenous culture. He early sought to remove the layer of rust and rot which crusted the minds of many Americans.

Charles Madison. *Critics and Crusaders* (Holt). 1947.
pp. 440–1

Like Socrates he was a creative critic who placed his faith in the education of youth, education built around a fresh, intense, and on-going examination of society. Bourne's life was all of a piece. Consistency was its badge. One can refer, as we shall see, to any part of his career without worry of finding contradictions in thought or method. He called continually for social progress through social enrichment.

Contrary to the misreading of critics, the core of Bourne's philosophy was neither the relation between political power and cultural creation nor a naïve faith in a revolutionary mass movement of youth against the older generation. The root of Bourne's thinking was the conviction that modern times need a modern religion, a reestablishment of values and methods.

A. F. Beringause. *JHI*. Oct., 1957. p. 598

The only public issues that engaged Bourne's imagination for very long were questions, not of politics, but of culture: education, feminism, the rebellion of youth. . . . [A]ll his works came back in one way or another to the fact which from childhood had burned itself into Bourne's consciousness, the gap between the generations. . . . Bourne thought he was repudiating politics, and he attacked other progressives as having subordinated everything else to political concerns; and yet his own conception of politics as a "means to life" represented an extension of the political into the most intimate areas of existence. To say that politics was of no use unless it could improve the very tone and quality of people's private lives was to argue in effect that every aspect of existence was ultimately a question for political decision.

Christopher Lasch. *The New Radicalism in America*
(Knopf). 1965. pp. 83, 90

Bourne had also begun to make literary experiments. Half a dozen of his "portraits," some satiric, some almost poetic, were published in *The New Republic*. Like Henry Adams, he was captivated by the feminine mystique, and felt keenly the energy and the vitality and the attraction of women. He wrote of the suffragettes with a tartness. . . . But he wrote also of their longings and of their loneliness. He wrote of young men who played the violin, who spent long hours reading in the cavernous halls of the Forty-second Street Library. His portraits were not "grotesques," as Sherwood Anderson would call his sketches of *Winesburg, Ohio;* they were wistful and lonely. Bourne's people were not yet adrift in Dos Passos' pulsating world; they were not yet "lost" in Paris cafes. They were at once gay and sad. Bourne was a poet of solitaries, of the ironic, idealistic young people who had not yet had the war cross their lives.

Lillian Schlissel. Introduction to *The World of Randolph Bourne* (Dutton). 1965. xxviii–xxix

See *Youth and Life, The Gary Schools, Education and Living, The History of a Radical and Other Papers, The World of Randolph Bourne* (essays).


# BOWLES, JANE (1917–    )

My feeling is that Mrs. Bowles has developed—and exploited—her own brand of lunacy and that she is, perhaps fortunately, unique. . . . To attempt to unravel the plot of *Two Serious Ladies* would be to risk, I feel sure, one's own sanity. . . . What does, however, link both the "Two Serious Ladies" and the other characters in the book is their mad, their wayward, their bizarre aberrations, in which they indulge with so reasonable an air. . . . *Two Serious Ladies* is intermittently funny and certainly original, but I also felt that it strains too hard to startle and to shock and that it all too often is just merely silly.

Edith H. Walton. *NYT*. May 9, 1943. p. 14

There is nothing propagandistic or topical in Jane Bowles's *In the Summer House*, . . . which is not the only reason I prefer it to most of the plays I have seen this season. Its author has an original writing talent and a not at all stock sensibility. It may even be deemed a paradox that I like the earlier or wackier part of the play better than the last part, in which the characters are resolved with the aid of a little off-the-cuff psychoanalysis. . . . The aimless dialogue, the sadly abstract atmosphere of the first part of *In the Summer House*, is lovely, colorful and strangely evocative: it spins a melody of the trivial and "pointless" which emanates from the semiconsciousness of rather ordinary folk with a primitive directness that is essentially poetic.

Harold Clurman. *Nation*. Jan. 16, 1954. p. 58

. . . Mrs. Bowles has fashioned a work of intricate and seductive beauty, harmonious and subtle in its impact on the sensibility as a musical composition. And like a piece of music, it is accessible to criticism largely in terms of its modulation and coloring, its sensuous texture and expressive content. . . . It is Mrs. Bowles' special distinction to have rendered as faithful a justice to the external reality of her characters as she has to their interior substance: she is not in collusion with their psychic discomfort:

one never feels of *In the Summer House* that it is but another gratuitous portrait of the debilitated sensibility.

Richard Hayes. *Com*. Feb. 5, 1954. pp. 449–50

Surrounding Mrs. Bowles's art is an effluvium of chic despair which will alienate many readers. On the other hand, her work can easily be over-valued since it combines proud idiosyncrasy with a rather startling pre-science (her novel, *Two Serious Ladies*, . . . forecast the current vogue of comic gothicism). When that book first appeared here, reviewers could damn it with a clear conscience: modernism had not yet become an oblig-atory mass fashion. . . . Today in the United States, where the cultivated reader feels duty-bound to be affronted, Mrs. Bowles's controlled derision is likely to seem the definitive force of civilized disgust.

Surely her indictments have an easy inclusiveness. Like her husband Paul, Mrs. Bowles writes tight little anecdotes about the pull of bestiality, an unexpected form of self-fulfillment. Like her husband's stories, hers pit the weak against the strong, the righteous against the sensual, only to record a general rout. Though her tales lack his intellectual clarity, they have greater charm.

Charles Thomas Samuels. *NYR*. Dec. 15, 1966. p. 38

. . . I saw *In the Summer House* three times . . . because it had a thorny wit, the flavor of a newly tasted, refreshingly bitter beverage—the same qualities that had initially attracted me to Mrs. Bowles's novel, *Two Serious Ladies*. . . . And yet, though the tragic view is central to her vision, Jane Bowles is a very funny writer, a humorist of sorts—but *not,* by the way, of the Black School. Black Comedy, as its perpetrators label it, is, when successful, all lovely artifice and lacking any hint of compassion. Her subtle comprehension of eccentricity and human apartness as re-vealed in her work require us to accord Jane Bowles high esteem as an artist.

Truman Capote. Introduction to *The Collected Works of Jane Bowles* (Farrar). 1966. pp. viii–ix

But Mrs. Bowles makes what might seem just strange into something wonderful—both haunting and witty—by her unsentimental feeling for these lost creatures, and the odd elegance of her writing. The atmos-phere of almost all the works is overwrought or overheated, at times reminiscent of Tennessee Williams or even Ronald Firbank; but through all this miasma, the characters tend to speak to each other (and them-selves) with the clarity and decision of people in Lewis Carroll. As you can imagine, this effect alone is extraordinary. Her writing is funny or sad or sharp or mysterious, but always arresting.

Roderick Cook. *Harper*. Jan., 1967. p. 98

It is to be hoped that she will now be recognized for what she is: one of the finest modern writers of fiction, in any language. . . . Mrs. Bowles's seemingly casual, colloquial prose is a constant miracle; every line rings as true as a line of poetry, though there is certainly nothing "poetic" about it, except insofar as the awkwardness of our everyday attempts at communication is poetic. This awkwardness can rise to comic heights, and in doing so evoke visions of a nutty America that we have to recognize as ours. . . .

In her later stories Mrs. Bowles has played down the picaresque local color she used to such effect in the novel. . . . As in all her work, it is impossible to deduce the end of a sentence from its beginning, or a paragraph from the one that preceded it, or how one of the characters will reply to another. And yet the whole flows marvelously and inexorably to its cruel, lucid end; it becomes itself as we watch it. No other contemporary writer can consistently produce surprise of this quality, the surprise that is the one essential ingredient of great art. Jane Bowles deals almost exclusively in this rare commodity.

John Ashbery. NYT. Jan. 29, 1967. pp. 5, 30

See *The Collected Works of Jane Bowles* (*Two Serious Ladies* (novel); *In the Summer House* (play); also stories).

# BOWLES, PAUL (1910–    )

Much of this almost Gothic violence arises from the clash of the civilized with the primitive, but more basically it stems from the fact that Mr. Bowles's characters (both enlightened and native) are warped and morbid beings. They are all, if not mad, severely neurotic, hugging to themselves some quietly terrible frustration, some taint, some malevolent perverseness that finally can be no longer controlled and explodes with twisted fury.

John J. Maloney. NYHT. Dec. 3, 1950. p. 4

Paul Bowles is a man and author of exceptional latitude but he has, like nearly all serious artists, a dominant theme. That theme is the fearful isolation of the individual being. He is as preoccupied with this isolation as the collectivist writers of ten years ago were concerned with group membership and purposes. . . . Bowles is apparently the only American writer whose work reflects the extreme spiritual dislocation (and a philosophical adjustment to it) of our immediate times. He has "an organic continuity" with the present in a way that is commensurate with the great French trio of Camus, Gênet, and Sartre.

Tennessee Williams. SR. Dec. 23, 1950. p. 19

Mr. Bowles is one of the very few writers to depict the part Arab, part colonial-cosmopolitan life of North Africa without any trace of romanticization. He has a remarkable gift for evoking its atmosphere with graphic authenticity; and, at the same time, he externalizes in that atmosphere the inner drama he is unfolding—the drama of the Hollow Man, the man things are done to. . . . The weakness of both Bowles's novels is that a man as hollow as Nelson Dyar (and previously Port Moresby)—a man without purpose or will; a cipher—is not a hero whose fate can stir us deeply. If fiction is to have life it must see something more in life than a dreamlike drift from nullity to nothingness.

Charles J. Rolo. *At.* March, 1952. pp. 84–5

Paul Bowles stages his impressive novels in a climate of violence and pervading sentient awareness. The atmosphere in which his characters move and have their being is arid and parched, nourished by no springs of feeling or sentiment, relentless and neutral as the shifting yet eneluctable sands always just beyond the city. . . . The fruit of which Paul Bowles has eaten is, unfortunately, that which confers knowledge only of evil, not of good. But a writer with no awareness of this essential duality can never fully explore the country of horror into which he has ventured.

Richard Hayes. *Com.* March 7, 1952. p. 547

Mr. Bowles's stories and novels are the work of an exposed nerve. The pain is felt before the experience. There is a perennial dryness and irony in American literature of which Bowles is the latest and most sophisticated exponent; it has the air of premature cynicism, prolongs the moment when civilisation itself becomes entirely anxiety and disgust. . . . Bowles has been properly compared with D. H. Lawrence, for he has a marvelous eye for the foreign scene as it comes to the eye of the rich, rootless wanderer. He is also a brilliant collector of items of human isolation in its varying degrees of madness, and he is intellectually disapproving of both the isolated man and the man who has merely the apparent solidarity and gregariousness of the urban creature. . . . Where Bowles fails is that in reducing the Lawrence situations . . . to a kind of existentialist dimension, he has made them merely *chic*. The moral passion has vanished; even passion has gone.

V. S. Pritchett. *NSN.* July 12, 1952. p. 44

Bowles is an obsessionist, and his obsession may be simply stated: that psychological well-being is in inverse ratio to what is commonly known as progress, and that a highly evolved culture enjoys less peace of mind than one which is less highly evolved. . . . It is no accident that the three novels and that fifteen of the seventeen stories in *The Delicate Prey* have a foreign setting. Nor is it true, as has sometimes been charged, that Bowles is merely indulging in a pointless exoticism, for not only are the settings foreign, they are usually primitive as well. For this reason he chooses such remote locales as a small town in the Sahara, a Columbian jungle, a river boat winding painfully through the interior of an unidentified Latin-American country. And in nearly all of his work the tension arises from a contrast between alien cultures: in a typical Bowles story, a civilized individual comes in contact with an alien environment and is defeated by it.

(K)                              Oliver Evans. *Critique.* Spring–Fall, 1959. p. 44

Paul Bowles's universe (and it is a mark of distinction that there *is* a Bowlesian universe) is made up of primitive but wise natives and effete children of the West searching for escape from the self—that self that supposedly hangs like an albatross around the neck of modern literature, from Hemingway to Herzog, feeding thought and stifling feeling.

These clichés of the romantic genre are the dangers he lives with; his victories over them are the signposts of his artistry. They are to be seen scattered through his new volume of short stories, *The Time of Friendship,* his first such collection since that excellent book, *The Delicate Prey.*

(K)                              Daniel Stern. *NYT.* Aug. 6, 1967. p. 4

The abysses and furies of the human psyche; the fragile, provisional nature of the civilized instincts; the lure of the primitive and the inhuman; the sadness of deracinated people; the underground warfare of marriage and friendship; the lonely divisions between desire and behavior, between having and holding, between one hand and the other hand; the modern world's contagions of angst, dread, deadness: all these strains of the existentialist vision are dramatically presented in Bowles' earlier work and come to a classic statement in his novel, *The Sheltering Sky,* one of the most beautifully written novels of the past twenty years and one of the most shattering. . . .

. . . *The Time of Friendship* brings together his first collection of stories in more than twenty years. Most of them are effective, several are memorable, but only one seems to me to break fresh ground. This is the long title story in which Bowles abandons his rather static view of primitivism, and moves beyond his somewhat fatigued fascination with its timeless mysteries and perversities, to write about post-colonial Algeria. . . .

The story is as complex in the telling as any Bowles has written; what is so strange and moving is its benignity. What it portends for his future work, I don't profess to know. But it's good to find him writing a tender story and one which strengthens his grip on contemporary experience. Perhaps the world is moving too fast for even his nihilism to have the last word. It's nice to think so.

(K)                                       Theodore Solotaroff. *NR*. Sept. 2, 1967. pp. 29–31

## The Sheltering Sky

There is a curiously double level to this novel. The surface is enthralling as narrative. It is impressive as writing. . . . In its interior aspect, *The Sheltering Sky* is an allegory of the spiritual adventure of the fully conscious person into modern experience. . . . Actually this superior motive does not intrude in explicit form upon the story, certainly not in any form that will need to distract you from the great pleasure of being told a first-rate story of adventure by a really first-rate writer.

Tennessee Williams. *NYT*. Dec. 4, 1949. pp. 7, 38

It has been a number of years since a first novel by an American has contained as much literary persuasion and original interest as *The Sheltering Sky*. . . . It is also the first time to my knowledge that an American novelist has met the French Existentialists on their ground and held them to a draw. . . . His characters are profoundly contemporary, out of a world that has neither God nor ethics. . . . Unlike other records of the same moral dilemma, this is not history, nor argument, nor description of moral paralysis. The cataclysm has occurred; the land is waste yet there are mirages; the water holes beckon. This is a carefully devised piece of fiction of unfaltering interest about some of those "ridiculous" mirages.

Florence Codman. *Com*. Dec. 30, 1949. p. 346

## Let It Come Down

The metaphysical and imaginative dimensions of the pathological visions are impressive as created by Paul Bowles. They are quite unaccountable in the lay figure Dyar to whom they are attributed and who is totally uninteresting when he is not under narcosis. Yet it is clear that the action of the novel is intended to be taken as a philosophical and even spiritual quest for "reality" on Dyar's part. There is an uncomfortable suggestion that Dyar's murderous hashish dreams are the only possible equivalents in our time for the Platonic delight in beauty, even for the beatific vision, and that a masochistic torture dance is the only equivalent for the redeeming sacrifice of love. . . . The evidence is insufficient, especially when we have only the blank eyes of a Dyar to see it through.

What *Let It Come Down* does demonstrate is Paul Bowles's talent for dealing with the macabre, the dreamlike, the cruel and the perverse in a genuinely imaginative way.

Robert Gorham Davis. *NYT*. March 2, 1952. pp. 1, 17

Once again, Mr. Bowles has written a frightening book. Only now there is an important difference. The *shock* is present, but is no longer a device. It is a conclusion justified by the hashish delirium that is the one possible resolution of Dyar's existentialist pilgrimage into the unknown interior of himself. If Mr. Bowles takes the chance of losing the *voyeurs* in his audience by this new discipline, he asks of others that he be judged more specifically on his merits.

These merits are considerable, but of a technical and exterior sort. Mr. Bowles, who is an accomplished composer, presents his characters contrapuntally. What each is doing at a particular moment is artfully disclosed. The theme of one is offered first and then followed by his antiphonal response to another whose theme has already been given. But only sensibility joins them, and a terrible rootlessness.

Leonard Amster. SR. March 15, 1952. p. 21

### The Spider's House

The world and the people created by Mr. Bowles are completely convincing. *The Spider's House* is not a pleasant book, and its uncompromising portrayal of individual, group, and national wrongdoing will disturb the romantic or the squeamish reader. But this is the story of a mature writer who has freed himself from the excesses and eccentricities of his earlier fiction, who has something significant to say and who says it with authority, power, and frequently with beauty.

William Peden. SR. Nov. 5, 1955. p. 18

*The Spider's House* is richer than *The Sheltering Sky,* full of compassion and perceptive both intellectually and intuitively. As writing, it is powerful and moving. As reporting, it goes far beyond what the correspondents see or write. Few Americans have understood the forces at conflict in Morocco as well as Paul Bowles has done . . . or conveyed the spirit of the Arab world with such delicate nuance.

Ralph de Toledano. NYHT. Nov. 6, 1955. p. 4

See *The Sheltering Sky, Let It Come Down, The Spider's House* (novels); *The Delicate Prey, The Time of Friendship* (stories).

# BOYLE, KAY (1903–     )

Anyone . . . whose standards of the short story are not the standards of the correspondence school will appreciate that the work of Miss Boyle, for simple craftsmanship, is superior to most of that which is crowned

annually by our anthologies. Anyone with an ear for new verbal har-
monies will appreciate that Miss Boyle is a stylist of unusual taste and
sensibility. It is time, therefore, to cease to regard her as a mere lower
case révoltée and to begin to accept her for what she is: more enterprising, more scrupulous, potentially more valuable than nine-tenths of our
best-known authors.

Gerald Sykes. Nation. Dec. 24, 1930. p. 711

Gertrude Stein and James Joyce were and are the glories of their time
and some very portentous talents have emerged from their shadows. Miss
Boyle, one of the newest, I believe to be among the strongest. . . . She
sums up the salient qualities of that movement: a fighting spirit, freshness of feeling, curiosity, the courage of her own attitude and idiom, a
violently dedicated search for the meanings and methods of art. . . . There
are further positive virtues of the individual temperament: health of mind,
wit and the sense of glory.

Katherine Anne Porter. NR. April 22, 1931. p. 279

Her short stories and her novels deal with the distress of human beings
reaching for love and for each other, under the cloud of disease, or the
foreknowledge of death. Her daring lies in an extravagance of metaphor,
in roguishness, in ellipses. The short stories particularly revive for us the
painful brilliance of living. Here is poison—in the small doses in which
arsenic is prescribed for anaemia. . . . The author has a deep distrust of the
false clarities which destroy overtones and mystery, since actions are the
solid but not too significant residues of what goes on in heads and hearts.

Evelyn Harter. Bkm. June, 1932. pp. 250–3

Imagistic prose, stemming from the stream-of-consciousness, is a natural
mode to people highly keyed to sensuous perception. But it varies in kind.
In Virginia Woolf, where the approach is intellectual as well as sensuous,
it is derived, an imagism of what the mind knows, a subtle and sophisticated play. If the balance is decidedly in the other direction, as in Waldo
Frank, we have a feverish, almost physiological imagery. In Kay Boyle,
at her best, the balance is nice—emotional, but with the perception swift
and right. Where others clothe feeling in a bright array of words, she
gives it the exquisite body in which it lives.

Myra Marini. NR. July 13, 1932. p. 242

Somewhere on the church at Gisors there is a wanton efflorescence of the
latest Gothic which reaches its most intricate virtuosity only a stone's
length from the pure and simple lines of the earliest Renaissance. In the
tangle of the exquisite carving, figures of a brilliant precision are half

hidden in a lush overgrowth of tortured stone wreathing into meaningless shapes. The grace of a detail catches the breath, the whole is a nullity, a confusion of motives eluding form.

Kay Boyle's writing is like that. . . . The carving hides the design, the figures are blurred by it.

Henry Seidel Canby. *SR*. Nov. 4, 1933. p. 233

She is one of the most eloquent and one of the most prolific writers among the expatriates; her work is always finished in the sense that her phrases are nicely cadenced and her imagery often striking and apt; her characters are almost always highly sensitized individuals who are marooned or in flight in some foreign country, banded together in small groups in which the antagonisms often seem intense beyond their recognizable causes. . . . It is noteworthy how much Kay Boyle gets out of the casual coming together of her people, what untold dangers and mysterious excitement she finds in their first impressions of each other—out of the tormented relationships and the eventual flight.

Robert Cantwell. *NR*. Dec. 13, 1933. p. 136

Kay Boyle is Hemingway's successor, though she has not that piercing if patternless emotion which is what we remember of Hemingway at his best. It is significant that both writers received their literary training in Paris, as did Henry James, that they are familiar with deracinates and those casual sojourners in Paris whose search is for the exciting and the momentary. Each has the observational facility of the newspaperman, with the poet's power of meditating on life; their work stands out from any other type of fiction written in any other country, in both content and technique.

Mary M. Colum. *Forum*. Oct. 1938. p. 166

To my mind, the chief defect in Miss Boyle's equipment as an artist is to be traced to her lack of a subject which is organically her own; and by an organic subject I mean something more tangible than a fixed interest in certain abstract patterns of emotion and behavior. Being in possession of an elaborate technique and having developed disciplined habits of observation, Miss Boyle seems to be able to turn her hand to almost anything. As a result one feels all too often that she is not really involved with her themes, that she has not conceived but merely used them.

Philip Rahv. *Nation*. March 23, 1940. p. 396

Never in my life have I come across such descriptions of mountains. Never. . . . And I say this as a mountain-man. Her sentences about mountains go up and up to snow-peaked beauty almost unbearable, just as great mountains do, or swoop down like glaciers and snowfields, or are close and warming and exciting like snow in a village. Never have there been such descriptions of mountains.

Struthers Burt. SR. Jan. 15, 1944. p. 6

Kay Boyle . . . is one of the shrewdest stylists in the language and something of a mystic no matter what material she makes momentary use of. . . . The best thing she does is to transform the mundane detail and wring some spiritual essence from it; quite literally she can make (at her best) silk purses out of sows' ears, and you watch her writing as you would some marvelously deft machine performing this miracle, holding some scene or some person still while she outlines in space the nature of its, or his, meaning. And even when the miracle doesn't come off . . . even when the gears turn and the music soars, yet nothing is revealed but the fine hands of the operator, still the process is an exciting thing to behold. Miss Boyle can so compel us with symbols that we are lulled almost into accepting them as the stuff of life.

Nathan L. Rothman. SR. April 9, 1949. p. 13

She has written of love in all of its possible phases. . . . She has written of all people and of their virtues, their sins, their crimes, their loves. There is also a deep love of nature, of mountains, snow, and forests. Even in stories the theme of which may be marital maladjustment, the devotion to the country in which the drama is played exceeds the author's concern with the drama itself. A preponderant part of her writing is descriptive, although she does not conceive of scenery merely as background. In her character portrayals a kind of compassion permits Miss Boyle to enter into the life of others with an intensity as violent as if the life were her own. This compassion gives a moving quality to her skillful portrayals of the blight of Nazism and fascism in Europe.

Harry R. Warfel. American Novelists of Today<br>(ABC). 1951. p. 45

Miss Boyle achieves her characteristic force by showing us a vision of humanity in need of pity and understanding, a central idea that does not make for light reading but one which accounts for the realism and effectiveness we inescapably feel as we read through her work. While probably not the end result of a reasonable philosophy, it is a telling and significant attitude toward life that makes of her writing much more than a pretty toy or a tract. Miss Boyle is not simply *interested* in people; she is vitally *concerned* with people and profoundly moved to write about their struggle with themselves and with their dreams.

Richard C. Carpenter. EJ. Nov. 1953. p. 427

In her best work, it seems to me, her style is never noticeably brilliant; it is always subdued, always subservient to the creation of scenes and characters. One seldom feels, either, that Miss Boyle's stories or novels have been carpentered to fit a carefully worked out thesis. The best of her fiction is convincing and lifelike; the "meaning," seldom forced or imposed, rises—or seems to rise—naturally out of characters and actions, as though the author had actually observed the people and events just as she writes about them. . . . [S]he appears to be deeply committed to some ideal of social equality, personal freedom, universal tenderness or love—it is difficult to label what is usually subtle and complex—and she sees in the world about her the brutal violation of those who embody these ideals. Again and again in her fiction we are shown sensitive individuals, who respond to life feelingly rather than conventionally, attacked and defeated by tough, well-insulated barbarians flying the banners of custom and tradition.

(K)                    William Stuckey, *MinnR*. Fall, 1960. p. 118

Kay Boyle has added eighteen poems from the last ten years to her earlier work in verse that culminated in the long 1944 poem *American Citizen;* these *Collected Poems* are elusive but—as always in the poetry of a writer whose characteristic achievement is in prose—they offer a reliable thematic index to Miss Boyle's preoccupations over the years: she aspires to be, doubtless is, a good European, the kind of person who knows the right café to sit in front of, the interesting wine to order, a hard ski slope to descend, an easy man to love. Her landscapes, both American and European, are made into emblems of the wild heart, the behavior of her animals likened to the actions of men. It is not entirely fair, by the way, to refer to her "earlier work in verse," since so many of these difficult pieces are experiments in mixing verse with extended prose passages; indeed, however obscure it may be, such prose is always firmer and, if not more deeply felt, then more dramatically honed than the verse, which in even the very latest poems is without much spine or spring, though Miss Boyle has spirit and to spare.

(K)                    Richard Howard. *Poetry*. July, 1963. pp. 253–4

Put simply, Kay Boyle's theme is nearly always the perennial human need for love; her design is woven from the many forms the frustration and misdirection of love may take. Her style and the care with which she limns a setting are, as they inevitably must be with a creative artist, but vehicle and adjunct for her central meaning. Although on occasion she may have forgotten the artistic obligation in exchange for sheer virtuosity (always a danger for the virtuoso), using her style to bedazzle rather than to aid vision, or letting exotic setting obscure the human situation with

which she is dealing, in her better fiction, style, setting, and theme form a seamless web in which all the threads are held under a precise tension. (K)                                     Richard C. Carpenter. *Critique.*
Winter, 1964–65. p. 65

She is the author of 13 novels, some of them very good, but she is not quite a major novelist. Her major medium has always been the short story and the novelette. (And it is typical of this aristocrat, whose earlier work lay in the tradition of Edith Wharton and Henry James, not to use the fashionable word, novella.) But even here, she was in the early thirties, a writer of superior sensibility—or so I thought—using a foreign scene more successfully than her native one, and belonging, in essence, both to the expatriate line of James and Wharton and to that later "lost generation" of the 1920's.

What this new collection of Miss Boyle's short stories and novelettes does prove is that while all of the speculation above is somewhat true, none of it is really true, or profoundly true. She has all these elements in this new collection of her mature work. But, as in the case of every first-rank writer, she rises above the disparate elements in her work or in her temperament, to become something else. What *Nothing Ever Breaks Except The Heart* proves, in short, is that Kay Boyle has at last become a major short-story writer, or a major writer in contemporary American fiction, after three decades of elusiveness, sometimes of anonymity, almost of literary "classlessness," while she has pursued and has finally discovered her true metier. . . . To her earlier vision of sensibility, she has added what every first-rate writer must have, a standard of human morality— and the fact that human morality is usually, if not always, related to a specific social or historical context.

It is this familiar concept, missing in so much current and "new" American fiction, that is embodied in the magnificent stories of her maturity. (K)                          Maxwell Geismar. *NYT.* July 10, 1966. pp. 4, 16

See *Plagued by the Nightingale, Year Before Last, Her Human Majesty, Death of a Man, Monday Night* (novels); *Thirty Stories, Nothing Ever Breaks Except the Heart* (stories); *Collected Poems.*

# BROOKS, CLEANTH (1906–    )

*Modern Poetry and the Tradition* is sound without being sententious; it is suggestive yet precise; it avoids the temptation of sensationalism and the opposite extreme of stodginess. Mr. Brooks writes lucidly rather than brilliantly about the reach of the image . . . and goes to some length to explain the "difficulty" of modern poetry and the reader's resistance to it. . . . All in all, this is the work of a scholar who is sensitive to every nuance of feeling and every change of pitch. Mr. Brooks is a probing analyst, but he is not a pedant. His work, reflecting his subject, is allusive rather than simple and straightforward, complex but clear.

Louis Untermeyer, SR. Jan. 13, 1940. p. 17

One test of a critical theory is its range of enlightenment. Mr. Brooks is illuminating about Eliot and Yeats, but neglects certain poets altogether— D. H. Lawrence, for example, who is certainly witty, or Laura Riding who is certainly intellectual. He may say that they are not good poets— though I should disagree with him—but it is up to him to show why, and their omission makes me doubt if his theory is equipped with the necessary critical tools. . . . Admirable as far as it goes, his criticism of the propagandist view of art fails to account for its success not only among hack critics but quite good artists. In my opinion the social-significance heresy is a distortion of a true perception, namely, that the *Weltanschauung* of a poet is of importance in assessing his work, and that there is, after all, a relation, however obscure and misunderstood, between art and goodness.

W. H. Auden. NR. Feb. 5, 1940. p. 187

Poetry is assumed to rest within a sacred circle, from which historical and psychological considerations on the critic's part are exorcised as profane. To this illiberal outlook Brooks gives the name "humanism." A core of vigorous understanding is thus surrounded with inhibitions by no means always free from intellectual morbidity. Order becomes for Brooks almost an obsession. . . . Brooks is imprisoned in a cage. He suffers from the familiar limitations of narrow and dogmatic doctrines; yet within these limits he frequently writes with admirable discernment.

Henry W. Wells. SR. April 12, 1947. p. 50

Mr. Brooks suggests that poetry is great in proportion to its power to contain and reconcile whole systems of conflicting values. Truth in poetry is dramatic, determined by a right relation to its context. By studying the interior structure of poems it should be possible for criticism to discriminate the greatest poems from the less great and so to prepare the way for a new history of poetry based not on extraneous considerations but on solid observations of poems as poems.

Mr. Brooks's studies in the structure of poetry are masterly exercises in the kind of close critical explication that enriches our appreciation of the poems examined and confers a new dignity on the work of the poet.

George F. Whicher. NYHT. Apr. 20, 1947. p. 2

There was developed in the quarter-century between the wars both a system of criticism and a sensibility of poetry, the one fitting and predicting the other, which when they wanted a sanction invoked Donne and when they wanted a justification exhibited Eliot or Yeats. It is not surprising, therefore, that this criticism and this sensibility should bend backwards and try a testing hand on all the poetry that lay between Donne and Eliot. This is what Mr. Brooks tries for. . . . He reads the poems as if their problems were the same as those found in a new quartet by Eliot or a late poem of Yeats; and for his readings he uses the weapons of paradox, irony, ambiguity, attitude, tone, and belief.

R. P. Blackmur. *NYT*. June 8, 1947. p. 6

Either I imperfectly understand Mr. Brooks's theory of poetry . . . or there is nothing very new about it. A poem, I take it, cannot contain one thing only: out of several things it makes its single effect. Some of these, we learn, are *different* from others. In the laboring of this, "paradox" behaves like an acrobat. I share Mr. Brooks's interest in the history of English poetry and his resistance to the critical relativists, but to pinch the diversity of observable phenomena into a single set of terms or insist on anything resembling a unanimity of style seems to me to be indiscreet, or worse. Worse, because it will blind you.

John Berryman. *Nation*. June 28, 1947. p. 776

If there is one formulation which seems to him more suitable than others, for it recurs oftenest, it is that which asserts that the unity of poetic language has the form and status of a verbal paradox. He has always liked to stand and marvel at paradox—"with its twin concomitants of irony and wonder"—while I think it is the sense of the sober community that paradox is less valid rather than more valid than another figure of speech, and that its status in logical discourse is that of a provisional way of speaking, therefore precarious. We do not rest in a paradox; we resolve it. . . . As a literary critic he has a hollow scorn for the procedures of logic, which he generally refers to as the procedures of "science"; and he advises the scientists in effect that they cannot understand poetry and had better leave it alone. But this is to underestimate the force of logic in our time and, for that matter, the great weight of the rational idea in western civilization.

John Crowe Ransom. *KR*. Summer, 1947. pp. 437–8

I do not question . . . that "irony," in Brooks's sense of the term, is a constant trait of all good poets, and I should have no quarrel with him had he been content to say so and to offer his analyses of texts as illustrations of one point, among others, in poetic theory. What troubles me is that, for Brooks, there are no other points. Irony, or paradox, is poetry, *tout simplement,* its form no less than its matter; or rather, in the critical system which he has constructed, there is no principle save that denoted by the words "irony" or "paradox" from which significant propositions concerning poems can be derived. It is the One in which the Many in his theory—and there are but few of these—are included as parts, the single source of all his predicates, the unique cause from which he generates all effect.

R. S. Crane. *MP*. May, 1948. pp. 226–7

It may be making virtues of natural limitations, but Brooks's style seems a deliberately plain, steady, utilitarian style. The critical commentary does not emulate but only serves the poem, assists it in the performance of its "miracle of communication," like the disciples distributing the bread and fish. . . . If one can avoid thinking of a critical essay as properly either a contest or an amorous exercise between the author and the reader, Brooks is perhaps simply trying very earnestly to be precise about what he is saying, and again, not saying. Further, he makes no pretensions. One perfectly good reason for putting it plainly might be that he thinks it is a plain thing he has to say.

John Edward Hardy. *HR*. Spring, 1953. pp. 160–1

There have even been objections from within the ranks to intrusions of "personality" into the critical labor. Cleanth Brooks, a New Critic whose style has always been efficient and spare, and who—aside from a catchword or two—has contributed nothing to the poetry of New Criticism, once defended to Alfred Kazin the supposed "impersonality" of the New Critic (a supposition not easily supported outside Brooks' own work) and indicated his opposition to criticism that attempts "rivalry with the work of art."

(K)                          Richard Foster. *The New Romantics*
(Indiana). 1962. pp. 186–7

*For whom, then, has Mr. Brooks caused his book [The Hidden God] to be published in hardback?*

For a hypothetical "Christian looking at modern literature," who, he says, ought to find in that literature "a great deal that is heartening and helpful." . . .

*Is it Mr. Brooks' assumption, then, that his Christian reader has special difficulties with such a writer as Yeats?*

It is: and with most other great modern writers; for many who are aware that a great modern literature exists "continue to dismiss it as merely sensational, violent, meaningless, or nihilistic." It is his hope that he can

induce such readers to approach and perhaps digest this literature. . . .
*Is Mr. Brooks' effort then wasted?*

No effort of so skilful a propagandist for literacy is ever wholly wasted.
Ultimately those who must read will read, and will find out what they
must read; and if Mr. Brooks can do no more with a segment of the rest,
he will at least inhibit their too ready prattle about what they have not
read or read imperfectly, and hence reduce their power to drive dedicated
readers into rebellion against what is represented to them as Christianity.
So at least one may pray.

(K)                                          Hugh Kenner. *National Review*. Aug. 13,
                                                            1963. pp. 109–10

. . . in *The Hidden God* Mr. Brooks, who is one of modern criticism's
most distinguished practitioners of exacting verbal analysis, has chosen
the broad view, and he offers us a series of essays on five major twentieth-
century writers. These pieces, enclosed between an introductory and a
concluding chapter, make up a little book that forsakes stringent inspec-
tion of the single text for a general reassessment of what is centrally definitive in the work of Hemingway, Faulkner, Yeats, Eliot, and Robert
Penn Warren. . . . Mr. Brooks wants most cautiously to forego any claim
that we are confronted with some sort of crypto-Christianity in the fiction
of Hemingway and Faulkner or in the poetry of Yeats and Warren. He
claims only that many of the great writers of our time are engaged by
the essential problems of Christianity, that their work can be significantly
illumined by reference to Christian premises—and this is brilliantly demonstrated by a sensitive marshaling of a solid body of evidence.

(K)                                          Nathan A. Scott. *SR*. Sept. 28, 1963. p. 60

. . . Mr. Brooks's study [*William Faulkner*] gives the impression of striving
to do nothing less than to set the entire world of Faulkner scholarship,
criticism, and appreciation in order. Since I have nothing like the space
necessary to discuss his thesis in detail, suffice it to say that he is arguing
principally that Faulkner is a writer whose Southern quality has been
ignored to the detriment of accurate critical understanding. More specifically, Mr. Brooks places the community at the center of both Faulkner's
life and work where it provides simultaneously a moral impetus and touchstone. In working out his thesis Mr. Brooks uses a multifaceted method.
Thus, he attacks technical questions in a scholarly manner, as when he
works out the time sequence of *Sanctuary*. He also devotes considerable
space to correcting earlier critics guilty of either factual or interpretative
errors. And, finally, he employs both the impressionistic and what might
loosely be called the history of ideas approaches. . . . [T]hough he has many
astute things to say—he is particularly rewarding on *The Unvanquished*—

the general impression is one of a very uneven critical performance, one whose dominant trait seems to be that of extreme nervousness. It is this that seems to be back of the testy and selective treatment of critics, the hesitant and yet insistent reference to authors and concepts only tenuously related to Faulkner, and the largely unnecessary (in a scholarly work) stress on the immediacy of Faulkner's power as a writer. From all of this, one is led to conclude that Mr. Brooks has no real critical rationale for the study of fiction, or at least none of the order of coherence he has so ably demonstrated in the past with regard to poetry.

(K)                 Olga W. Vickery. *AL*. Nov., 1964. pp. 380–1

Cleanth Brooks's work is significant not only because it is extremely influential, but also because it has, until recently, persistently advanced a single, coherent theory despite the author's awareness of its limitations. Much literary criticism since the 1920's has been theoretically irresponsible; it has tossed out theories and terminologies, then immediately denied or ignored them. Brooks's work, on the other hand, illustrates the virtues and vices of theoretical consistency. Most of his criticism develops from three sets of terms: irony (and its near equivalents, paradox and wit), drama, and metaphor (or one of its variants). Irony creates unity in variety and helps to establish aesthetic distance; drama achieves both variety and distance; metaphor fuses meanings and removes the object from reality. Brooks has, then, two criteria for aesthetic value—structure (the combination of unity and complexity) and aesthetic distance. His varied but related critical machines are built to show that if a poem has a certain kind of complex structure and achieves a certain distance, it is a good poem.

(K)                 Lee T. Lemon. *The Partial Critics* (Oxford).
1965. p. 139

See *Modern Poetry and the Tradition, The Well Wrought Urn, The Hidden God, William Faulkner: The Yoknapatawpha Country* (criticism).

# BROOKS, GWENDOLYN (1917–    )

All in all, despite the fact that this first book [*A Street in Bronzeville*] has its share of unexciting verse, there are considerable resources evidenced for future work. Miss Brooks, to use one of her own phrases, "scrapes life with a fine-tooth comb." And she shows a capacity to marry the special quality of her racial experience with the best attainment of our contemporary poetry tradition. Such compounding of resources out of varied stocks and traditions is the great hope of American art as it is of American life generally.

Amos N. Wilder. *Poetry*. Dec., 1945. p. 166

This little book of poems [*A Street in Bronzeville*] is both a work of art and a poignant social document. It is doubly effective on both scores because it seems such delightfully artless art and (in spite of its razor edges) so innocent of deliberation in its social comment. Simply out of curiosity, let us say, the reader begins a stroll down that unnamed Street. Almost immediately, and with no coercion on the part of the author, we abandon our present identity and become one of the denizens of Bronzeville. . . . Oddly enough, we never feel sorry for these neighbors as we move among them. We know them instead. What we feel is not pity but sympathy—an extension of our capacity for aliveness and awareness of being.

Starr Nelson. *SR*. Jan. 19, 1946. p. 15

The work of this young Chicago poet never fails to be warmly and generously human. In a surly and distempered age one is genuinely grateful to Miss Brooks for the lively and attractive spirit that sallies forth from her poems. In contrast to most of her contemporaries, she is neither ridden by anxiety nor self-consumed with guilt. There is in her work a becoming modesty. Though the materials of her art are largely derived from the conditions of life in a Negro urban milieu, she uses these incendiary materials naturally, for their intrinsic value, without straining for shock or for depth, without pretending to speak for a people. In reading this second volume [*Annie Allen*] by the author of *A Street in Bronzeville* I have been impressed by how little of the energy that should go into the building of the work has been diverted to the defence of the life.

Stanley Kunitz. *Poetry*. April, 1950. p. 52

With a few exceptions when straightforward narrative takes over, [*Maud Martha*] is presented in flashes, almost gasps, of sensitive lightness—distillations of the significance of each incident—and reminds of Imagist poems or clusters of ideograms from which one recreates connected experience. Miss Brooks' prose style here embodies the finer qualities of insight and rhythm that were notable in her two earlier books of poetry (her *Annie Allen* received the Pulitzer Prize), and gives a freshness, a warm cheerfulness as well as a depth of implication to her first novel. In technique and impression it stands virtually alone of its kind.

Hubert Creekmore. *NYT*. Oct. 4, 1953. p. 4

Nothing vague here [in *The Bean Eaters*], nothing European, nothing mystical. These poems, generous and full of humanity, rattle with verbs and jangle with action. Their images are everyday; their subjects are poor people (often Negroes), the dreams of the downtrodden, the frustrations of the meek.

Yet, for all the worthiness of their themes and their aims, you will probably find them incomplete as poems. Miss Brooks appears more concerned to condemn social injustice and to draw sympathetic character portraits than to write poems that echo on every level, and as a result she repeats the same kind of statement too often for poetic truth.

Peter Davison. At. Sept., 1960. p. 93

She has a warm heart, a cool head and practices the art of poetry with professional naturalness. Her ability to distinguish between what is sad and what is silly is unfailing, and she deals with race, love, war and other matters with uncommon common sense and a mellow humor that is as much a rarity as it is a relief. Sometimes she is overly sentimental or gets too involved with furniture and ephemera, but on the whole this selected volume [*Selected Poems*] . . . is a pleasure to read.

Carl Morse. NYT. Oct. 6, 1963. p. 28

Gwendolyn Brooks' *Selected Poems* contain some lively pictures of Negro life. I am not sure it is possible for a Negro to write well without making us aware he is a Negro; on the other hand, if being a Negro is the only subject, the writing is not important. Unfortunately, Miss Brooks too often says the obvious, in the easiest way. . . . Miss Brooks must have had a devil of a time trying to write poetry in the United States, where there has been practically no Negro poetry worth talking about. She deserves to be praised for her seriousness, and to be criticized into writing more poems on the order of her "The Bean Eaters."

Louis Simpson. NYHT. Oct. 27, 1963. p. 25

Gwendolyn Brooks does the thing that so few poets anywhere can do, and that is to take a really spoken language and make it work for her. Most everyone writes a "writing" language, but in her work, there are all the familiar cadences and sounds of speech, right down to the bone-hard rhetoric of the 1960s. . . . I say that her technique is really useful to her because in addition there is visible a whole person behind her poems, and you always feel that she "writes committed." She is one of the very best poets.

Bruce Cutler. Poetry. March, 1964. pp. 388–9

See *Selected Poems;* also *Maud Martha* (novel).

# BROOKS, VAN WYCK (1886–1963)

He seems to wake up every morning and regard America, and everybody who ever wrote in America, or who signified anything in American life, with fresh, eager, and ever-interested eyes. His mind perpetually revolves around the idea of a national culture in America, and he pursues all sides of the subject with such a vividness of interest and vividness of language, that when you have read three or four of his books, you begin to believe that the creation of such a culture is one of the few causes left worthy of the devotion and self-sacrifice of men.

Mary M. Colum. *Dial*. Jan., 1924. p. 33

He, more than any one else, more even than Mr. H. L. Mencken, has created a certain prevalent taste in letters, a certain way of thinking about literature.

This eminence, though I feel it has been won through default, has been graced by estimable qualities of Mr. Brooks. He has scholarship which becomes imposing when applied to the waste land of American letters. . . . Happily, Mr. Brooks has a style at the service of his erudition and historical consciousness. . . . What is wrong with Mr. Brooks and what is wrong with nine-tenths of American critical writing is no less than a deficiency in the sense of proportion. . . . It lacks a standpoint which is high enough for the vision of contributory elements melting into a major and vital organism.

Gorham B. Munson. *Dial*. Jan., 1925. pp. 28–9, 42

He has been the most influential critic of the past twenty years. His early work was the principal factor in the erection of the lofty cultural standards that have encouraged the rise of a mature, serious, philosophical criticism. The effect of his later work was not so praiseworthy, for it led to the embittered subjectivity of Lewis Mumford's *Melville* and Matthew Josephson's *Portrait of the Artist as American*. . . . In any event, for good or bad, something of Brooks has seeped into almost every American critic under fifty (including even the Marxist, Granville Hicks). There is no better testimony to his fine mind, his exquisite taste, his integrity and unselfishness.

Bernard Smith. *NR*. Aug. 26, 1936. p. 72

When all is said and done, Mr. Brooks's achievement remains a prodigious one, conceived with audacity and carried out with extraordinary skill. In reading his literary history, one has a sense that Mr. Brooks has repeopled the American continent. On his benign Judgment Day, the dead arise from their graves, throw off their shrouds and become flesh and blood again, ready to take their place in eternity. The writer who in his youth called for a usable American past has, in the full tide of maturity, created that past for us; and has shown us that it was far richer, far sweeter, far more significant than we could, in our rebellious, dissident, adolescent days have dreamed of. To the writer who has accomplished this great feat, we owe unending admiration and gratitude.

Lewis Mumford. *SR*. Nov. 8, 1947. p. 13

Brooks has made so many switches in his forty years of writing and his nineteen books that it is difficult to perceive any consistent pattern. He has been an aesthete, a socialist, a Freudian, a manifesto-writer, a Jungian, a Tolstoyan book-burner, and finally a compiler of literary pastiche and travelogue for the Book-of-the-Month Club. He has moved from total arty rejection of America and its culture to total uncritical acceptance. He has occupied almost every political and philosophic position of our time, and called them all "socialism." Nevertheless, there is a consistent pattern to his work, from his first book to his last, but it is a method rather than a viewpoint, the method of biographical criticism.

Stanley Edgar Hyman. *The Armed Vision* (Knopf).
1948. pp. 106–7

It is always said that Mr. Brooks is "readable." This means that his style is pleasant and his anecdotes are delightful. Now Mr. Brooks's prose does have very agreeable manners, it has the air of well-tempered conversation. And his little stories are often charming. . . . We could wish for so civilized a "desire to please" in the writers of the humorless, perspiring little essays in some of American literary journals. But the chit-chat is too often without edge, where edge is needed: good form does not demand such a sacrifice. And the anecdotes come too close to being the whole of the book; so much so that for me they cease to be "readable," they are too dense on the page, they are so many acres of underbrush.

Henry Rago. *Com*. March 28, 1952. p. 619

It is a complex personality, that of a cosmopolitan bent at all costs on being a glorious provincial. We can discuss all the high qualities, those that make him our genuine "man of letters"—in the old-fashioned sense of the term—since the death of Howells. He has a style and manner, a sense of picturesque, a feeling for the anecdote as a work of art. He has a genuine relish for the idiosyncrasies and the *bizarréries* of literary bohemia and a tendency to suffuse with a pastel optimism even the dark moments in the lives of our great writers.

Leon Edel. *NR*. March 22, 1954. p. 20

By his own account of childhood and youth Brooks is the heir of culture and breeding; in this sense he is perhaps the last great disciple of the genteel tradition in our letters. But what is heroic and admirable in all this is the rejection of his own tradition in favor of the new forces which have appeared in our society since the 1850's. And his affirmation of our central "Western" line of progressive or radical thought extends even to his praise of the "vulgarian immigrant" Dreiser. We know this vein of American thought is at present in eclipse, with both our literary critics and our politicians. When—or perhaps, in more desperate moments, *if*— our mood changes, Brooks will be seen as a major spokesman for our literature who is indifferent to leadership but who has never relinquished his "position." How could he? It is inside himself.

Maxwell Geismar. *Nation*. Apr. 3, 1954. p. 283

After *The Ordeal of Mark Twain*—and after "America's Coming-of-Age" and "Letters and Leadership," essays that Brooks wrote in the same pe- riod—there was a second renaissance, not so rich as the first in great personalities, perhaps not so rich in great works, but still vastly produc- tive; it was a period when American writers once again were able to survive and flourish in their own country. The *Ordeal* and the essays had helped to make it possible. How much they had helped it would be hard to decide; one would have to know all the apprentice writers of the time who read them, and what the writers told their friends, and how the *Ordeal* in particular affected their ideals of the literary vocation. I can testify from experience, however, that the climate of literature seemed different after Brooks had spoken. He had given courage to at least a few writers, and courage is hardly less contagious than fear.

Malcolm Cowley. *NR*. June 20, 1955. p. 18

As anyone would expect who has read Van Wyck Brooks's definitive vol- umes about the writer in America from 1800 to 1915 or his *John Sloan*— or, for that matter, any of his books—the chief trouble with *The Dream of Arcadia* is the embarrassment of riches it contains. Like all of his books, his account of American writers and artists in Italy from 1760 to 1915 is packed with detail, full of quotable quotations, wealthy in insights dropped casually even in footnotes. Before one begins to read, he wonders whether the subject is enough for a full-length book; before he finishes he realizes that here compressed is material for several volumes—the history of what Italy has meant to the American artist and, through him, to American culture as a whole.

(K)                                            Harvey Curtis Webster. *SR*.
                                                    Sept. 27, 1958. p. 19

*The Ordeal of Mark Twain* is one of the earliest books in which a prom- inent American critic makes use of psychoanalytic ideas, although they furnish him neither the central theme of the book nor its chief method. . . .

The foundation of the book, however, does not seem to me to be wholly psychological, since it gives at least as much stress to social factors in the America of the Gilded Age and to Mark Twain's relationships with friends and business associates as it does to the primary bases of these in the family constellation. The book, consequently, may be characterized as a combination of criticism and biography using a method which is a combination of sociology and psychology. Its intention is to show the stultifying effect of psychic trauma, maladjustment, and frustration induced by adverse social conditions upon Mark Twain's latent artistic ability. This it does by tracing the ineffectual struggle which he waged against their combined power.

(K)                              Louis Fraiberg. *Psychoanalysis and American Literary Criticism* (Wayne State). 1960. pp. 120–1


Even though Brooks did not know [William Dean] Howells as Howells knew Clemens, he has imparted to this volume something of the tone that Howells imparted to *My Mark Twain*. In its special fashion, Brooks's *Howells* is a masterpiece by one who has actually experienced a part of Howell's world and has vicariously lived in all of it as an indefatigable reader and writer.

But with a reminiscence done by a friend and contemporary we only ask on the factual level whether the author has remembered right or not. With the quasi-reminiscence that Brooks has done we are entitled to know something of his sources. Of these he tells us only a little in his prefatory note, asking readers to trust him rather than oblige him to fill another volume with "the usual scholarly apparatus."

(K)                              George Arms. *AL*. Jan., 1961. pp. 478–9


As a biographer, Van Wyck Brooks believes that there is a fundamental relationship between the lives men lead and the things they do. He is primarily a chronicler and an *evoker;* he likes an atmosphere and a background. And he works, as biographers must, in mosaic, putting together bits and pieces of information as best he can to demonstrate human accomplishment. To be sure, we are sometimes too aware of the separate pieces; and sometimes a piece is fitted the wrong way, or is out of place. But Brooks' studies, compared with our giant biographies, exemplify the art of concision.

The shortcomings of Van Wyck Brooks' portraits stem from his reluctance to probe into the why and how of human endeavor. This seems to reflect his eternal optimism and faith in man's will to struggle and to succeed—and a particular faith in America's "coming of age."

(K)                              Leon Edel. *NR*. Sept. 17, 1962. p. 14

As a critic, a single dissenting voice, he realized that he couldn't do much "to change the whole texture of life at home." He might, however, do something to change our conception of the writer in America, and the writer's conception of his own task, always with the aim of encouraging himself and others to do better work, the best that was in them. To this aim he devoted himself with admirable consistency and—let it be recorded— with an amazing degree of success.

There is one field in which the success can be measured. When we think of the contempt for American authors, mixed with ignorance about them, that prevailed in universities during the reign of Barrett Wendell; when we contrast it with the reverence for many of the same authors that is now being proclaimed in hundreds of scholarly monographs each year, as well as being revealed statistically by the multiplication of courses in American literature—while living writers share in the glory reflected from the past by being invited to the campus as novelists or poets in residence— we might also remember that Brooks had more to do with creating the new attitude than anyone else in the country.

(K)                                Malcolm Cowley. *SR*. May 25, 1963. p. 18

Brooks was not the critical Pollyanna that those New Critics who have read little by him maintain. Nobody in all our critical writings so far has been so perceptive about the faults of our writings and, indeed, of our whole literary tradition. Read *The Wine of the Puritans* (1908) and read *America's Coming-of-Age* (1915), and see what intelligent, well-informed, well-mannered criticism of our literary products can be. Brooks loved, but he also knew. Brooks searched for things to praise, but he was not blind to things not worthy of praise. Sometimes, indeed, he was so disappointed in many of the things he found that he overstated his disappointment—to take it back years later in his massive and magnificent five volumes about the *Makers and Finders* of our literary culture.

(K)                                Charles Angoff. *LR*. Autumn, 1963. p. 31

It has become the fashion today to regard the earlier work of Van Wyck Brooks as his main achievement. It is as the author of *America's Coming of Age, Letters and Leadership,* and the studies of Mark Twain, Henry James and Emerson, books of protest and of criticism, that he makes his chief appeal to the younger generation. And it is true that these are the books that cleared the air for a more wholesome creative life in America and tilled the ground in which many vigorous talents were able to take root. In his emphasis on our native note, as opposed to the then prevalent literary provincialism, his courageous holding up of the mirror to our spiritual life, his insistence upon the cultural communion out of which great literature arises, and his early discernment of the deep cleft, in the American soul, between idea and practice, Van Wyck Brooks was a forerunner, a voice crying in the wilderness. But this was only one part of his achievement. He had been a pioneer. Now he saw his vision coming true, and turned to the other and essential task that lay ahead: to bring to life for us our entire literary heritage, to exhibit the pageant of genius in our country, and give us, in his own phrase, "a usable past." . . . This was the second and greater part of the achievement of Van Wyck Brooks, a man in quest of the truth; truly, a man driven by the furies.

(K.)                              John Hall Wheelock. *Library Chronicle.*
                                              Winter, 1965. p. 4

The clue to Brooks' way of thinking may be found in his remark that "Allston liked to contemplate extremes and try to fill, imaginatively, the space between." So, for example, he gives us "highbrow" and "lowbrow," and the mediating term, "middlebrow." More often, however, there is no mediation but only opposition, as in the "creative life" *vs.* the "acquisitive life." Here, Brooks, a master polemicist, has followed his own advice to critics to find the deep, irreconcilable "opposed catchwords"; and in what follows we realize that his melodramatic way of seeing is supported by an equally melodramatic way of feeling.

(K)                              Sherman Paul. *NL.* Feb. 15, 1965. p. 20

It may be said that after *America's Coming-of-Age, Letters and Leadership* (1918), and *The Literary Life in America* (1927), his three deservedly famous manifestoes, he never wrote a whole book in his own person, but always masked himself in the identities of those about whom he wrote, or invented an alter ego, as in *Oliver Allston* (1941). This is also true of *An Autobiography* which in part reads like left-over notes from his literary chronicle. Yet he is capable for short stretches of an ordered amplitude and downrightness which puts us to shame.

                                  Quentin Anderson. *NR.* April 17, 1965. p. 15

See *Three Essays on America, The Ordeal of Mark Twain, Makers and Finders, The Dream of Arcadia, Fenellosa and His Circle, John Sloan: A Painter's Life, Howells* (criticism and biography); *An Autobiography.*

# BUCK, PEARL (1892–    )

There is a firm unity in her work which makes its component parts not easily distinguishable, . . . an identification with one's characters so complete and so well sustained is rare in fiction. . . . The language in which Mrs. Buck presents this material . . . is English—very plain, clear English;

yet it gives the impression that one is reading the language native to the characters. . . . Mrs. Buck never, I think, uses a word for which a literal translation into Chinese could not be found. . . . Whether any novelist can be in the very first flight who depicts a civilization other than his own, I do not know. . . . But we may say at least that for the interest of her chosen material, the sustained high level of her technical skill and the frequent universality of her conceptions, Mrs. Buck is entitled to take rank as a considerable artist.

                    Phyllis Bentley. *EJ*. Dec., 1935. pp. 791–800

Throughout her writing life, Pearl Buck has been building bridges of understanding between an old and a new civilization, between one generation and another, between differing attitudes toward God and nationality and parenthood and love. Not all Miss Buck's bridges have withstood the weight of problems they were designed to bear. But *The Good Earth* will surely continue to span the abyss that divides East from West, so long as there are people to read it.

                    Virgilia Peterson. *NYT*. July 7, 1957. p. 4

Mrs. Pearl Buck has been enveloped in a kind of critical and popular literary personality which has very little to do with what she actually writes. To the professional critic, she is suspiciously prolific and somewhat single-minded. To the political extremists, she is subversive just because she has been so prescient on Asian affairs. Her sense of Asian politics and society results in such accurate predictions that it is, by the logic of the extremist, a clear-cut evidence of her advocacy of what has happened.

   *The Living Reed* will confirm both the critic and the extremist in their views. To a wide public, it will be the most powerful and informative book Mrs. Buck has written in some years. *The Living Reed* retains Mrs. Buck's sense of tradition, her deep commitment to the family scanned over several generations as a microcosm of larger social configurations, and her almost visceral feel for how the civil Leviathan can crush the bones of mere mortals.

(K)                    Eugene Burdick. *NYHT*. Sept. 15, 1963. p. 5

The reason Miss Buck has refused to keep pace with modern techniques is not far to seek. She is following the old-fashioned Chinese story practice of emphasizing event and characterization. And yet there is a dichotomy even here. In the 1930's her best fiction was objective, and the didactic element was usually muted or subordinated. When written in this vein, her work takes on force and meaning. After 1939, however, she breaks away from objectivity; didacticism becomes a dominant feature, and the quality of her work declines. If she had followed the same form of imitation of the Chinese novel type in her post-Nobel Prize writing, her work after 1939 might have reached the significance of her earlier productions. Increasing humanitarian interests brought a lack of *vraisemblance* and demonstrated the inadvisability of distorting what Thomas Hardy calls "natural truth" for the purpose of stressing didactic points. A growing sentimentalism also makes itself felt more and more in her later writing, and this attitude is detrimental to the highest artistry.

(K)                    Paul A. Doyle. *Pearl S. Buck* (Twayne). 1965. p. 151

Written about a quarter century ago, around the time when Pearl Buck's *The Good Earth* was winning a Pulitzer, and, with her other work, a Nobel award, this novel [*The Time Is Noon*] was once set in type, only to have publication canceled with her approval—because, supposedly, it was "too personal." . . .

The parts that ordinary novelists do well stump this author, unfortunately; the parts that stump the others she handles wonderfully. Her villains are completely unbelieveable—as if, in fact, she never really knew one. The minister father who steals the money hoarded by his wife, the farmer-husband and his doltish family, the scoundrel of a church organist are right out of dime novels. But her good people, customarily skimped or short-changed in fiction, often come touchingly, dramatically alive. . . .

(K)                    W. G. Rogers. *NYT*. Feb. 19, 1967. p. 44

### The Good Earth

She is entitled to be counted as a first-rate novelist, without qualification for the exotic and unique material in which she works. . . . This is the elemental struggle of men with the soil.

The design is filled out with richness of detail and lyric beauty. If now and then there is a straining for effects of biblical poetry, more often there is poignancy in the simple narrative of simple, rude events. . . . Most of all there is verity.

Nathaniel Peffer. *NYHT*. March 1, 1931. p. 1

Such a novel as *The Good Earth* calls at once for comparison with other novels of the same general design—novels of the soil on the one hand and novels concerning Oriental life on the other. Any such comparison brings out the fact that despite Mrs. Buck's very good narrative style, despite her familiarity with her material, her work has a certain flatness of emotional tone. . . . Mrs. Buck is undoubtedly one of the best Occidental writers to treat of Chinese life, but *The Good Earth* lacks the imaginative intensity, the lyrical quality, which someone who had actually farmed Chinese soil might have been able to give it.

Eda Lou Walton. *Nation.* May 13, 1931. p. 534

It ought to be very moving to a Western reader. There is only one difficulty. Romantic love is a fake center of psychology to ascribe to the typical Oriental man or woman, reared in the traditional bondage to quite different ideals. Although romantic love is second nature to the Western woman, trained to it by the traditions of a thousand years, it would not even be understood by an old-fashioned Chinese wife. By placing the emphasis on romantic love, all Confucian society is reduced to a laughable pandemonium. . . . *The Good Earth,* though it has no humor or profound lyric passion, shows good technique and much artistic sincerity. Thus, it is discouraging to find that the novel works toward confusion, not clarification. . . . Mrs. Buck, the daughter of a missionary, refuses from the start of her book to admit that there is such a culture as Confucianism.

Younghill Kang. *NR.* July 1, 1931. p. 185

Mrs. Buck is clearly not the destined subject of a chapter in literary history, and would be the last to say so herself. . . . (But) *The Good Earth,* the first volume bearing that name, not the trilogy, is a unique book, and in all probability belongs among the permanent contributions to world literature of our times. . . . It is a document in human nature, in which questions of style—so long as the style was adequate, and of depth—so long as the surfaces were true and significant—were not important. It did not have to be as well written as it was, in order to be distinguished. . . . We do not wish to be unjust to Mrs. Buck. Her total achievement is remarkable even though it contains only one masterpiece.

Henry Seidel Canby. *SR.* Nov. 19, 1938. p. 8

Although *The Good Earth* was among the most popular books of the 1930's—ranking just after *Gone with the Wind* and *Anthony Adverse*— and although it has received more prizes and official honors than any other novel in our history, there are still literary circles in which it continues to be jeered at or neglected. . . . It is the story of Wang Lu, a poor farmer who becomes a wealthy landlord, but it is also a parable of the life of man, in his relation to the soil that sustains him. The plot, deliberately commonplace, is given a sort of legendary weight and dignity by being placed in an unfamiliar setting. The biblical style is appropriate to the subject and the characters.

Malcolm Cowley. *NR.* May 10, 1939. p. 24

It is a quarter of a century since Pearl Buck wrote a novel which, perhaps more than all earlier books combined, made the outside world China-conscious. In *The Good Earth* millions of Westerners first met the Chinese people as they really feel and think and behave. . . . Before 1930 many Americans pictured the Chinese as queer laundrymen, or clever merchants like Fu Manchu, or heathens sitting in outer darkness; few believed they could greatly influence our own fate. Since then historical events have taught us otherwise—and among those "events" Pearl Buck's book might well be included. Her more than two dozen novels, translations, and non-fiction books interpreting traditional and revolutionary Asia have fully justified the early award to her of the Nobel prize in literature.

Edgar Snow. *Nation.* Nov. 13, 1954. p. 426

See *The Good Earth, The Patriot, Dragon Seed, The Living Reed* (novels).


# BUECHNER, FREDERICK (1926–     )

There is a quality of civilized perception [in *A Long Day's Dying*], a sensitive and plastic handling of English prose and an ability to penetrate to the evanescent core of a human situation, all proclaiming major talent. . . .

The author's main objective seems to be to explore the implications of sensibilities which operate without a clearly perceived moral base. This is, of course, one of the central themes of modern fiction: it is, in a sense, the sole theme of such a novelist as Virginia Woolf. But Mr. Buechner goes at it in his own way, probing into each incident until he has presented it in all its delicate significance, using background and setting to develop a tone in the light of which action and even dialogue take on new and richer meanings.

Yet this is not a fussy or a pretentious novel. The line of action moves clearly and steadily ahead, and modulations of the emotional pattern are achieved deftly and without any discursive speculation or brooding prose.

David Daiches. *NYT.* Jan. 8, 1950. p. 4

And yet, in spite of these cavils, and of passages where the ghost of Henry James for no good reason haunts the diction, Mr. Buechner's novel [*A Long Day's Dying*] sticks in the memory with a certain impressiveness. Perhaps his tale is more of a caricature of life than he intended; and yet the dominant key of his imaginings, in spite of a lapse here and there, is on the whole sustained to the book's ending. Or, another way of putting it, Mr. Buechner seems to have considered his material and the phrasing of it with a more patient attentiveness than is common among young writers. He has noticed both what he has seen and what he has read. His comments frequently verge on wit, and need only a larger view of life to attain it.

F. Cudworth Flint. *SwR.* Winter, 1951. p. 149

It is truly as if Buechner had written [*A Long Day's Dying*] to fulfill an assignment in a Creative Writing course. Not only does he seem to have memorized a list of the exact ingredients that must go into a "significant" modern novel, but he seems to have gone to the library and set out consciously to collect them. He appears, furthermore, to have been exceedingly careful to choose only those which are in particularly special favor at the moment and of which his instructor would be absolutely certain to approve.

John W. Aldridge. After the Lost Generation (McGraw).<br>1951. p. 222

There is a deceptive air of ease about [*The Return of Ansel Gibbs*]. There are pages of witty and urbane conversation which are a pleasure to read, but every passage serves to advance the plot, to develop characters that live and feel and interact. Mr. Buechner is an abundant writer: epigrams, aphorisms, skilful and original imagery enliven his prose.

There is a quality of distinction about Frederick Buechner's writing which might best be compared to the gleam of hand-polished old silver— as opposed to the chromium gloss of much of the "sophisticated" writing being done today.

A. C. Spectorsky. SR. Feb. 15, 1958. p. 21

. . . Buechner's very interesting, perhaps over-subtle attempt is evidently to show how the springs of Gibbs' decisions flow and function, how underneath the perplexing movements of the mind of a "rational man" the deep currents of emotion and intuition may carry him to his real destiny. . . . Buechner's style, as others have remarked of his earlier books, is often noticeably "Jamesian." Sometimes it echoes James's arch manipulations of phrases and attitudes, sometimes his comma-laden, packed attempts at precision. Occasionally it is overwrought. . . . In this novel there is less of the seemingly deliberate attempt to create bizarre situations than in *A Long Day's Dying* . . . or *The Season's Difference*. . . . Despite faults in both conception and execution, the maturity of tone and the skill with which it is constructed make *The Return of Ansel Gibbs* the firmest and clearest of his works.

Edwin Kennebeck. Com. April 11, 1958. pp. 53–6

[*The Return of Ansel Gibbs*] is a dialectical novel of ideas . . . a readable, upstanding and ambitious member of the school. Mr. Buechner gained a somewhat unfair reputation for "Jamesian" preciosity in 1950 with *A Long Day's Dying* which he is now, and successfully on the whole, trying to shake off. As a job of intellectual and emotional plotting, in which events are arranged to force the characters to reveal themselves as candidly and concisely as they know how, it is very well done.

Mr. Buechner once again locates us in the mainstream between Wall Street and the East sixties, with climactic sidetrips to Washington, Harlem and big-time TV. But the real axis of the novel is that which ran, and may still run, between Stevensonian liberalism and a tragic (or "pessimistic") view of life derived from, or resembling, [Reinhold Niebuhr's] analysis of history and morals. . . . We are still in the familiar Buechner atmosphere of rather chic good living, good eating and genteelly toughminded conversation. . . . But a novel of ideas as well-conceived can survive such things.

R. W. Flint. NR. June 23, 1958. p. 29

. . . the tone of The Final Beast . . . is religious and moral throughout—so much so at times that he seems almost to be moralizing. Yet it is a fine and moving novel, deeply and quietly felt, even though Mr. Buechner has unnecessarily complicated an essentially simple story. . . . The ironic moralities here are patent: the gossips of a New England town have been more destructive than the German concentration camps that the old woman had been able to survive; and the destroying instrument is a child who thought he was befriending the man of God.

William Barrett. At. Feb., 1965. pp. 140–1

He is like Salinger and Updike: all three are deft, charming and sensitive writers, but they all tend to suppose that those virtues automatically confer value on the people and situations they are writing about. Since that is not necessarily so, their work often turns into a merely narcissistic display of deftness, charm and sensitivity. They are all good at depicting wayward and vulnerable characters, but since they are all tempted to suppose that waywardness and vulnerability are in themselves manifestations of moral sanctity, we are constantly being called on to admire their characters, no matter how seedy they may otherwise be and no matter how much harm they do to themselves or to others.

Howard Green. HdR. Summer, 1965. pp. 285–6

For a clergyman to become a novelist is one thing, but for a presumably decadent novelist to become a clergyman (and a Presbyterian at that) is less easy to encompass. Still, it is a fact of life like martyrdom and malnutrition, and if we are to read Buechner's novels with the respect they deserve, we have to accept that there is a very definite connection between his two vocations. . . . His references are often literary or mythic, although he began in the second novel to make remarkable use of ordinary events infused with new meaning, as in the fine scene in The Season's Difference in which the dotty old clergyman, playing Statues with the children, re-enacts the Fall. In *A Long Day's Dying,* the symbols are either literary or bizarre, and they are usually overexplained. The style, once considered a virtue of the book, seems now one of its weaknesses. The novel is still absorbing in its own right, but in retrospect it is primarily interesting as a starting point for Buechner's later work. If the end of the book is a little ambiguous, if the birds that abound are symbols of grace as well as of sex, it may be pointing beyond life as a long day's dying. In general, however, it is a picture of the world after the Fall.

In all three of the later novels, Buechner is concerned with the possibility of being born again. . . . The inspiriting power in *The Season's Difference* and *Ansel Gibbs* becomes explicitly Pentecostal in *The Final Beast.*

Gerald Weales. *Reporter.* Sept. 9, 1965. p. 46

See *A Long Day's Dying, The Season's Difference, The Return of Ansel Gibbs, The Final Beast* (novels).


# BURKE, KENNETH (1897–        )

Kenneth Burke is one of the few Americans who know what a success of good writing means—and some of the difficulties in the way of its achievement. . . . *The White Oxen* is a varied study, as any book where writing is the matter, must be. American beginnings—in the sense of the work of Gertrude Stein, difficult to understand, as against, say, the continuities of a De Maupassant. It is a group of short accounts, stories, more or less. They vary from true short stories to the ridiculousness of all short stories dissected out in readable pieces: writing gets the best of him, in the best of the book: "The Death of Tragedy" and "My Dear Mrs. Wurtlebach."

William Carlos Williams. *Dial.* Jan., 1929. pp. 6–7

Mr. Burke has a quick, assimilative, complicated mind, one not devoted to trivialities but not above them—the kind of mind which we stand to profit most from but which we do most to cramp in colleges. It is essentially a creative mind. Though devoted to criticism it is not less creative than the minds of most of the so-called "creative writers." It is especially creative in its ability to perceive connections between disparate entities. By choice he has worked mainly outside universities, as a critic among writers rather than as a literary historian or philosopher among dead or classical writers.

Arthur E. DuBois, *SwR.* July, 1937. p. 345

Burke's approach to symbolism is not susceptible of verification, and depends for its convincing force on his ability to make the reader perceive immediately the author's intuitions. This is to say that the method is essentially a-scientific if not unscientific. A generation of readers brought up on the facile technique of popularized psychoanalysis will no doubt find this method acceptable. But even those who look with suspicion on the explosions of an imagination uncontrolled by a scientific governor must frequently adjudge Burke's intuitions to be happy hits indeed, often throwing a burst of light on the dark pockets of our social scene.

Eliseo Vivas. Nation. Dec. 25, 1937. p. 723

If he suffers from a restraint, I should think it a constitutional distaste against regarding poetic problems as philosophic ones. I suppose his feeling would be that poetry is something bright and dangerous, and philosophy is something laborious and arid, and you cannot talk about the one in terms of the other without a disproportion and breach of taste. . . . He has a whole arsenal of strategies, like the German general staff, who are said to have whistling bombs if they like, and whose campaigns rest upon a highly technical and sustained opportunism. . . . He is perspicuous and brilliantly original, and I would venture to quarrel with no positive finding that he makes, but only with his proportions, or his perspective.

John Crowe Ransom. KR. Spring, 1942. pp. 219, 237

Mr. Burke's distinction as a critic is twofold. First, he is a man of amazing learning, who knows how to use his learning unpedantically and, if necessary, with a dose of irony. Second, he is that very rare thing among critics: a man who examines creative manifestations without parti pris, who does not put his own intention before the intention of the poet but carefully scrutinizes the mind of the agent as embodied in the act. His erudition aids him in treating literature universally, i.e. each particular literary instance is brought into relation with the whole body of Weltliteratur; while his patient ingenuity manages to disengage the hidden cross-references and ambiguities of each work.

Francis C. Golffing. Poetry. March, 1946. p. 339

Fortunately, Mr. Burke's arduous argument and idiosyncratic use of key terms are made somewhat easier by a generous use of ranging illustrations. His focus fans out so extensively that only careful study can comprehend his system. He seeks to impose a pattern on all historical consciousness. He is more sympathetic to social thinkers than to rhetoricians, to anthropologists than to philologians. In essence, Mr. Burke writes a study on human relations. The psychological as well as the sociological cast leads the reader at last to suspect all motives, and to feel that in Mr. Burke's mind most idealisms are outmoded and should be treated as myths to be analyzed and dissected.

Donald A. Stauffer. NYT. June 11, 1950. p. 30

Mr. Burke's courage is not purely of the theoretical kind. He dares to translate his doctrines into very definite instances, although his purpose is not indoctrination. He is fighting for free thought and free speech at a time when these are denounced as un-American activities. . . . It is a great comfort to find one who, ignoring the stampede, dares to say: "So help me God, I cannot otherwise." There are enough clear-sighted and vigorous pronouncements in this book (*A Rhetoric of Motives*) to insure the wrath of Senator McCarthy; if the Senator could understand them.

Albert Guerard. *NYHT*. July 23, 1950. p. 8

He started from literary criticism (after writing two books of fiction); he has provided us with many brilliant examples of the critic's art; and yet the most brilliant of all the examples is possibly his essay on *Mein Kampf,* in which he explains Hitler's strategies of persuasion. In other words the quality of his intention does not depend on the literary greatness of his subject; and when his literary subject happens to be a great one, as in another brilliant essay, on *Venus and Adonis,* he may not even discuss the qualities that make it a masterpiece. He is more interested in mechanisms of appeal, as in the Hitler essay, and in the disguises of social attitudes, as in the *Venus and Adonis*. We could, however, go further and say that his real subject is man as a symbol-using animal.

Malcolm Cowley. *NR*. Sept. 14, 1953. p. 17

Is it unfair to suggest that Burke may be the prime example of the sophisticated mind ready, even eager, to embrace the naïve for its value as renewal? . . . This culture type continues, long after the Industrial Revolution, to be repelled by the city's artifacts. . . . This jump from sophistication to naïveté, coupled with a deeply-felt experience of the Depression, would account for a view of society that echoes the old socialist diatribes. . . . But truly, if his social protests posit any sort of political alignment, it's more a Thoreau-going party of one than the one-party state. . . . Burke is more the Old Bohemian than the Old Bolshevik—the last of the Bohemians, possibly, with a humor wry enough to go with his awry feeling.

Gerald Previn Meyer. *SR*. Sept. 3, 1955. p. 28

Burke's gift as a poet is . . . real. His word play is true mortal-fun, and his ear for a rhythm is rich and right. He does especially well in ending a poem on a kind of dissolving rhythm. Not with a bang but a whimper, prehaps, but the whimper sings. Above all, the poems, when put together, generate the sense of a real person—learned, bourbony, getting on to mortality as a bit of a hard case but still, and always, sweet on life. I like both the cantankerousness and the sweetness; one flavors the other. No one should have trouble believing that Kenneth Burke's despairs are humanly real.

John Ciardi. *Nation*. Oct. 8, 1955. pp. 307–8

Throughout his writings Burke seems to have effected a neat "conversion downwards" of phenomena into terms. His system is, it seems to me, essentially a verbal one which treats words at what is often a great distance from the reality of things and people. It would be interesting . . . to study Burke semantically and to examine, among other things, the fluctuations in verbal level which he employs. His theory of poetic performance leads through the ascending order: poetry, act, motive, power, reality. This scale might well be applied to his critical system. Were this to be done, I have the impression that we would find it to be as much a poetic as a critical performance.

(K)                    Louis Fraiberg. *Psychoanalysis and American Literary*
                              *Criticism* (Wayne State). 1960. p. 200


Kenneth Burke . . . combines the methods of Marxism, psychoanalysis, and anthropology with semantics in order to devise a system of human behavior and motivation which uses literature only as a document or illustration. The early Burke was a good literary critic, but his work in recent decades must rather be described as aiming at a philosophy of meaning, human behavior, and action whose center is not in literature at all. All distinctions between life and literature, language and action disappear in Burke's theory. He seems to have lost all sense of evidence in his recent analyses of poetic texts. Thus he interprets Coleridge's "Ancient Mariner" as "ritual for the redemption of his drug," and Keats's "Ode on a Grecian Urn" he reads in terms of the identity of love and death, of capitalist individualism and Keats's tubercular fever, in almost complete disregard of the text. A system which plans to embrace all life ends as a baffling phantasmagoria of bloodless categories, "strategies," "charts," and "situations."

(K)                    Rene Wellek. *YR*. Autumn, 1961. p. 109


It would be a mistake not to see Burke's work in its historical context, not to realize that all of his books are verbal acts upon a historical scene, and that the dramatistic system as a whole is a humanist's counter-statement offered to the public at large as a reaffirmation of *human* purpose and as a means of "purifying war" (man's greatest rational lunacy) so that each person, in his own way, may *peacefully* and intelligently pursue the better life.

Since 1945, Burke has worked with missionary zeal to spread the good word (dramatism) that came to him upon completing the work started in the 1930's when he first began his study of communication and dedicated himself to the attainment of peace through knowledge. . . . As a theory of language, dramatism attempts to isolate and study the essence of language and, by systematically examining the uses to which man puts it, to isolate and study the essence of man and the drama of human relations. One of the main conclusions reached is that man's views of himself, other men, nature, society, and God are language-ridden—that man necessarily views everything through a "fog of symbols."

(K)                         W. H. Rueckert. *Kenneth Burke and the Drama of Human Relations* (Minnesota). 1963. p. 161

. . . because Miss [Marianne] Moore was a person with roots in the American resurgence, in those lyric years when poets sought to revive and rephrase Whitman's messianic spirit, during her turn as editor [of *The Dial*] she achieved one splendid feat. She recognized Kenneth Burke as the critic who might well map a path along a middle road to the heavenly kingdom. Deciding that *The Dial*'s Award should go to Burke, she did not celebrate Burke's arrival there. Rather she hoped to dramatize the ways in which Burke exercised the highest care and accuracy and diligence . . . in pursuit of the life of letters. In her view, he was the one American critic who possessed technique and sensibility enough to reconcile letters and culture, science and imagination in a single theory of literary value which is simultaneously a theory of human virtue in a comprehensive but probably not final sense of that bloody word.

(K)                         William Wasserstrom. *WHR*. Summer, 1963. p. 262

Kenneth Burke's *The Rhetoric of Religion,* like everything else that Mr. Burke has written, is highly original, brilliantly stimulating, infinitely suggestive, and ultimately baffling. Mr. Burke is so thoroughly *sui generis* that it is difficult to fit him into any contemporary philosophical pigeon-hole; but if he belongs anywhere, it is certainly with those who have restored the symbolic imagination to a central place in modern thought. Mr. Burke's attention has always centered on the emotive, psychic, and ethical-moral needs of the human spirit, and on the "symbolic actions" by which these needs are expressed. Much of the paradoxical originality of his thinking comes from applying concepts taken from the study of magic or religion and employing them to characterize completely secular historical and cultural phenomena. If a good deal of modern thought has been engaged in debunking, or, to be more formal, in "demythification"—that is, the interpretation of one or another "sacred" ideology in terms of "profane" categories—then Kenneth Burke might be said to have adopted the opposite tack of "remythification."

(K)                         Joseph Frank. *SwR*. Summer, 1964. p. 484

As Burke's general philosophy developed, the notion that literature can transform life because it begins in the life of the poet and ends in the life of the reader became more important. Although this sounds like personality theory, it is not. In the first place, Burke's theory is too broadly conceived to be so easily classified; and secondly, he is willing to give more attention to technique and form than personality theory would permit.

(K)                              Lee T. Lemon. *The Partial Critics* (Oxford).
1965. p. 190

Like Freud, Burke looks forward to a modification in our experience of guilt. Unlike Freud, however, he does not trace the origins of suppressed guilt-feelings to events in prehistory, recapitulated during the first few years of life; nor does he look upon religion precisely as a mass-neurosis, no better at promoting an ideal inner strength than the individual neuroses of secular men. For Burke, on the contrary, guilt is endemic to *any* human condition: it is virtually identical with the unacknowledged self-hatred that must accompany man's conflict with himself, nature, his fellowmen. . . . Man's life comprises not only physical motion but also symbolical action; one can quarrel with one's father or, like Hume, write a book denying the real, substantial power of antecedent causes. Burke doesn't mean to challenge the autonomy of philosophic effort by such interpretations; he means rather to argue the presence of poetic motives in metaphysical thought—means, that is, to underwrite poetry as the archetype of symbolic action generally, because it offers not only symbolical experiences but also appropriate symbolical expiations.

(K)                              Alvin C. Kibel. *AS*. Spring, 1965. pp. 304–5

For Burke, meaning itself is bound up essentially with programmes of action and seems in fact to be defined in terms of them. The reading of a given meaning will then depend for its sensitivity on the comprehensiveness of the programme to which the critic is dedicated. . . . Burke, it may be said, though he sometimes knows the right questions to ask, has not sufficient faith in literature to let it give its own answers. His understanding of the *general* situation in which poetry finds itself today is, I think, sound enough. But in almost every statement of this theme come expressions which reveal the strong arm of the politician who has already made up his mind.

(K)                              Andor Gomme. *Attitudes to Criticism* (Southern
Illinois). 1966. pp. 40, 43

A book [*Towards a Better Life*] so absorbed with style and stylization had better be well-written. Mr. Burke's prose, which has been known to develop opacities, displays here a translucent elegance and humor, but the novel isn't just fine writing. It is, in addition, beautifully expressive writing, with a vein of mockery at work under the formal turns of phrase. . . . *Towards a Better Life* is likely to count more, in future histories of American literature, than any given dozen of its soggier contemporaries.

A word here, in celebration of Mr. Kenneth Burke. He has been among us so long in so many capacities, and to such pervasive effect, that it is easy to lose track of how much the literary temper of our time owes to him. In whatever genre, his work has always carried the strong stamp of his individuality; he has never dissolved it into pap for the multitude or codified it into tablets for quick absorption by graduate students. He has never made it with a book club; he has never seemed ashamed of being learned. The subtlety of his critical work has challenged, its perversity has provoked, its original insights have opened up immense corridors of thought.

(K)                              Robert M. Adams. *NYR*. Oct. 20, 1966. p. 33

See *The Philosophy of Literary Form, A Grammar of Motives, A Rhetoric of Motives, The Rhetoric of Religion, Perspectives by Incongruity & Terms for Order, Language as Symbolic Action* (essays); *Towards a Better Life* (novel); *White Oxen and Other Stories; Collected Poems, 1915–1967*.


# BURNS, JOHN HORNE (1916–1953)

Each of (his) three books owes its degree of power to the author's ability to write exquisitely observed *mot*-filled prose which lends a stylish quality to every incident, even ones which might better have been omitted for reasons of taste. And common weaknesses stem mostly from the fact that Mr. Burns, the angry moralist, appears to be in conflict with Mr. Burns, the detached artist.

James Kelly. *NYT*. Sept. 7, 1952. p. 4


## The Gallery

Mr. Burns writes unevenly, perhaps deliberately so, sometimes using the shock technique of photographic realism, sometimes employing a kind of stylized symbology, but always with telling effect. In this, his first novel, Mr. Burns shows a brilliant understanding of people, a compassion for their frailities and an urge to discover what inner strength or weaknesses may lie beneath the surface.

J. D. Ross. *NYHT*. June 8, 1947. p. 5


The appreciation of the Italian people grows occasionally into something like a sentimental idolatry. The bitterness against American crudity comes close in places to a youthful intolerance. And the steady stress upon sex . . . grows into what looks like an inadvertent concentration upon one aspect of human experience as if it were the sole aspect. The genuine love and understanding which marks much of this work are, indeed, in a real way, vitiated by what appears a far too simple, far too easy falling back upon both sexual activity and a kind of vague, wistful brotherliness.

Richard Sullivan. *NYT*. June 8, 1947. p. 25

In *The Gallery* John Horne Burns absorbs the soldier's idiom into a spacious narrative prose that modifies but does not dominate the language. It is an appropriate device, as the matter of the book is the mental confusion and emotional disruption of our American soldiers abroad. . . . On the one hand (Burns) is uneasy and guilty about the smug, provincial, materialist life in America, and shocked by the conduct of many American soldiers. . . . On the other hand, his sympathy with the Neapolitans is generous and ingratiating, and his affection for them is too specific and imaginative to be merely sentimental. . . . One regrets that he didn't employ his human insight and talent for social analysis to go beyond a just indignation and consider whether even American boorishness and immaturity couldn't be the reverse of certain substantial national virtues.

John Farrelly. *NR*. July 7, 1947. p. 28

It is not a book for little boys in any school, but for adults who recognize the truth and know good writing when they see it, and who do not object to blatant four-letter words. The author's place in American war fiction seems certain. Compared with *The Gallery* . . . *Three Soldiers,* the novel that started off the realistic fiction of the First World War, was a fragrant and tender lily.

Harrison Smith. *SR*. Feb. 14, 1948. p. 7

*The Gallery* is a hybrid book, made up of two kinds of material set in two different literary devices that are never fused. The affirmation of values in the "Promenades" is consistently thwarted by the negation of values in the "Portraits"; and the non-dramatic treatment of the one is in the end completely overcome by the tensely dramatic treatment of the other. There is one step that Burns might have taken to ensure his point. He might have disregarded altogether the innate potentialities of the material he put into the "Portraits" and twisted the action in such a way that the book would have been forced to end on an affirmative note . . . but it would have meant a deliberate falsification of the truth as he saw it, and Burns was too scrupulous an artist for that.

John W. Aldridge. *After the Lost Generation*
(McGraw). 1951. pp. 145–6

### Lucifer with a Book

Mr. Burns was not far enough removed from his experiences to be capable of relating them without an excess acidity. Consequently his attack is not pointed as directly as it might have been. His book is too long, and a few of his most acute and penetrating observations are obscured by paragraphs of unleashed fury which become rather tedious.

Virginia Vaughn. Com. Apr. 29, 1949. p. 76

The central love affair of the novel, through which Guy Hudson finally realized the difference between sex and love, is not altogether convincing. What is apparent, however, just as in the English sophisticates, is the dominant sexuality of the novel, and a sexuality that finds expression in harsh and even violent terms. There is an inverted Puritanism in Mr. Burn's work, and a remarkably sophisticated sense of evil and malice.

Maxwell Geismar. SR. Apr. 2, 1949. p. 16.

John Horne Burns is one of those American writers who believe in shock treatment. To judge by *Lucifer with a Book* he is a satirical moralist rather than a novelist. He has much of Henry Miller's rich comic gift, a fluency which amounts at times to lallomania, a passion for scatological images and a strong tendency to preach. It is not always easy to discover, in this whirlwind of words, just what Mr. Burns is preaching about, but one thing seems to emerge clearly; nothing is so dangerous and destructive as virginity of mind and body and, until this impediment has been removed, preferably by rape, no one can begin to live.

Antonia White. NSN. Nov. 5, 1949. p. 520

See *The Gallery, Lucifer with a Book,* and *A Cry of Children* (novels).


# BURROUGHS, WILLIAM (1914–    )

The ten episodes from William S. Burroughs' *Naked Lunch* [which had appeared in *Big Table,* a magazine], on the other hand, is writing of an order that may be clearly defended not only as a masterpiece of its own genre, but as a monumentally moral descent into the hell of narcotic addiction. . . . [The] writing does, to be sure, contain a number of four-letter words, but the simple fact is that such obscenities—if obscenities they are—are inseparable from the total fabric and effect of the moral message. . . .

What Burroughs has written is a many-leveled vision of horror. . . . And only after the first shock does one realize that what Burroughs is writing about is not only the destruction of depraved men by their drug lust, but the destruction of all men by their consuming addictions, whether the addiction be drugs or over-righteous propriety. . . . Burroughs is not only serious in his intent, but he is a writer of great power and artistic integrity engaged in a profoundly meaningful search for true values.

John Ciardi. SR. June 27, 1959. p. 30

*Naked Lunch* belongs to that very large category of books . . . whose interest lies not in their own qualities, but in the reception given to them in their own time. In itself, *Naked Lunch* is of very small significance. . . . From the literary point of view, it is the merest trash, not worth a second glance. What is worth a glance, however, is the respectful attitude that some well-known writers and critics have shown towards it. . . .

The only writer of any talent of whom Burroughs occasionally manages to remind one is the Marquis de Sade; but if one turns to the pages of Sade after *Naked Lunch* the resemblance soon fades, since Sade, however degenerate he can be at times, has always some saving wit and irony. Burroughs takes himself with a complete, owlish seriousness; indeed, in his opening section he seems, as far as one can make out through the pea-soup fog of his prose, to be offering the book as some kind of tract against drug addiction. . . . Altogether, *Naked Lunch* offers a very interesting field for speculation, both pathological and sociological. No lover of medical textbooks on deformity should miss it.

John Wain. *NR*. Dec. 1, 1962. pp. 21–3

In its theme and techniques, the novel is open to misunderstanding by the highbrow Philistine (an animal possessed of a highbrow sophistication and a lowbrow taste). It is finally concerned with the extremes of horror in human life; and, therefore, it takes its place in that literary tradition pre-occupied with the possibilities of emotional experience. . . . The effect of the book is Kafkaesque—a simultaneous sense of stark terror and reeling comedy. . . . In short, *Naked Lunch* is one of the more truly original and exciting pieces of prose to emerge from the fifties. It is precisely these elements that [John] Wain, in his youthful senility, is incapable of seeing.

Richard C. Kostelanetz. *NR*. Dec. 15, 1962. p. 30

According to literary legend, Allen Ginsberg, while visiting Burroughs in his Paris apartment sometime during the 1950's, found the floors littered with hundreds of sheets of paper that Burroughs had scrawled on while high on heroin. Ginsberg, it is said, gathered the papers together, read them with reverence, and put them into the form, or rather sequence, they now have. He needn't have bothered to sort them, since the book would have almost the same effect if he had shuffled the manuscript like a deck of cards. . . . It is all somehow a work of spite, a work of revenge—revenge against beer bottles and God, against matchsticks and love, against war and peace and Tolstoy and fingertips and sealing wax. Some of it is funny and some of it marvelously dirty, but it just goes on and on; it begins to sound like the whine of a girl who's been stood up. It begins to sound like a tantrum.

Alfred Chester. *Cmty*. Jan., 1963. pp. 90–1

The best comparison for the book, with its aerial sex acts performed on a high trapeze, its con men and barkers, its arena-like form, is in fact to a circus. A circus travels but it is always the same, and this is Burroughs' sardonic image of modern life. The Barnum of the show is the mass-manipulator, who appears in a series of disguises. *Control,* as Burroughs says, underlining it, *can never be a means to anything but more control— like drugs,* and the vicious circle of addiction is re-enacted, worldwide, with sideshows in the political and "social" sphere—the "social" here has vanished, except in quotation marks, like the historical, for everything has become automatized. . . .

The phenomenon of repetition, of course, gives rise to boredom; many readers complain that they cannot get through *The Naked Lunch.* And/or that they find it disgusting. It *is* disgusting and sometimes tiresome, often in the same places. . . . Yet what saves *The Naked Lunch* is not a literary ancestor but humour. Burroughs' humour is peculiarly American, at once broad and sly.

Mary McCarthy. *Encounter.* April, 1963. pp. 94–6

It is easy enough to treat such a book [*The Ticket that Exploded*] as pathology, or to take the fact that Burroughs exists and is widely read and part of a literary movement as warning that some sort of counter-action is necessary. But this is not a literary judgment, and may be, as Sartre argued in the case of Jean Genet's early work, an inhumane one. We cannot know what the vision means unless we experience it totally, giving ourselves up to it as we do to other works of art, with suspension of dis-belief and—in this instance—of distaste. We must confront Burroughs as a free being who in some sense chose to have his kind of life and write his kind of book. Our solemn, almost religious duty is to reach the bottom of his experience, take on the burden of it, see ourselves in it, temporarily *be* Burroughs. There may even be hyprocrisy in pretending it is a burden. Some of the violence and filth is an expression of Swiftian disgust at the way things are. But obviously, as was true of Swift, the author delights in such imaginings. If we read the book properly we can feel the pleasure also—or learn to.

Robert Gorham Davis. *HdR.* Summer, 1963. p. 281

The element of humor in *Nova Express,* as in *Naked Lunch* and his two other novels, has moral strength of historic proportions, whereby the existentialist sense of the *absurd* is taken to an informal conclusion. It is an absolutely devastating ridicule of all that is false, primitive, and vicious in current American life: the abuses of power, hero worship, aimless vio-lence, materialistic obsession, intolerance, and every form of hypocrisy. . . .

His attunement to contemporary language is probably unequalled in

American writing. Anyone with a feeling for English phrase at its most balanced, concise, and arresting cannot fail to see this excellence. . . . Compared to Burroughs' grasp of modern idiom in almost every form of English . . . the similar efforts of Ring Lardner and of Hemingway must be seen as amateurish and groping.

Terry Southern. NYHT. Nov. 8, 1964. p. 5

Naked Lunch records private strategies of culture in the electric age. Nova Express indicates some of the "corporate" responses and adventures of the Subliminal Kid who is living in a universe which seems to be someone else's insides. Both books are a kind of engineer's report of the terrain hazards and mandatory processes which exist in the new electric environment.

Burroughs uses what he calls "Brion Gysin's cut-up method which I call the fold-in method." To read the daily newspaper in its entirety is to encounter the method in all its purity. Similarly, an evening watching television programs is an experience in a corporate form—an endless succession of impressions and snatches of narrative. Burroughs is unique only in that he is attempting to reproduce in prose what we accommodate every day as a commonplace aspect of life in the electric age. If the corporate life is to be rendered on paper, the method of discontinuous non-story must be employed.

Marshall McLuhan. Nation. Dec. 28, 1964. p. 517

William Burroughs' popular reputation dates back only about two years. At that time Mary McCarthy and Norman Mailer proclaimed his talent in a moment of intemperate enthusiasm and Burroughs' most famous book, Naked Lunch, was subsequently published in this country in the general lapse of censorship restrictions. Burroughs' first book had appeared some ten years earlier under the pseudonym William Lee. This was entitled Junk and is now available in a paperback edition called Junkie under Burroughs' own name.

Junk is a more or less journalistic account of the experiences of a drug addict. It rises, however, considerably above the general literary level of sensational exposé. It is an authentically macabre vision of Hell and the flat literalism of the writing makes it more appalling in some ways than Burroughs' later accounts of the same material. . . .

Naked Lunch is the Revelation of an irreligious world. Its apocalyptic vision is more than the raving of a mind distraught by drugs. It is a terrible book in the true sense of the word. Even its humor and its pornography are streaked with blood and terror. . . . But it is not possible to dismiss it as mere pathology. It is a "serious" book for all its surface wise-cracking and toughness; it is serious in that it is a total vision of man in the universe, an existentialist attempt to extract meaning from total horror. . . . Unfortunately, the independent talent which expressed itself so powerfully in *Naked Lunch* has become, in *Nova Express,* the silliness of extreme hipsterism.

William James Smith. *Com.* Jan. 8, 1965. pp. 491–2

The "color" [in *Nova Express*] changes from time to time as Burroughs feeds into his verbal kaleidoscope the major forms of science fiction: space mercenaries, time distortion, exotic symbiosis, galactic catastrophe, supergadgetry, and lost worlds. For all I know, he may have used existing texts; certainly he cribs (quite honestly, it should be said) from Kafka, T. S. Eliot and others, mixing their phrases into the plastic phantasmagoria. The effect after a time is pleasantly hypnotic. . . . At intervals, timed to check complete blackout, sense pops out of the amalgam; sometimes it is funny, more typically it is outrageous along the lines of Burroughs's well-established scatology. . . .

I'll accept his premise that we're being flummoxed out of our honest animal senses by high powered manipulators, and I think he is right to be sore about it. The trouble is that in his zeal to conjure with words he has produced what looks more like an abstract decoration than a terrible warning.

Robert Hatch. *Harper.* Jan., 1965. p. 91

Burroughs is clearly writing, as does any novelist, his spiritual autobiography. Some novelists tell it through controlled fantasy, using the objective resources of action and invented character. Others disguise their own lives and write romanticized autobiographies, punishing their enemies and rewarding their friends (or sometimes the reverse). And a few, like Kafka and Burroughs, use neither plot nor personal career to carry the essential burden, but fly into fantasy, nightmare, persuaded dream. In *The Soft Machine* it is as if Burroughs does not trust the power of his nightmares. He jiggles and toys with them; he repeats naggingly; he eliminates the degree of sanity which makes the irony cut.

Herbert Gold. *NYT.* March 20, 1966. p. 4

Admittedly, there is more variety in *The Soft Machine* than in *Naked Lunch*—a journey backward in time, some flecks of social satire, an ingenious method of construction that has the book rotating around a single axis; but as a window on reality it strikes me as too resolutely boarded up. How much can you see through a knot-hole?

John Wain. *NYR.* April 28, 1966. p. 19

I know that it seems odd to compare a writer to Lenny Bruce and T. S. Eliot in one and the same review. But such are the extremes of experience from which the writing of William Burroughs derives and draws its energies. He is one of the small group of American novelists today who are both vital and complex, and though his last three books seem to me to reach a brilliantly lit dead end they also possess the kind of genuine innovation that keeps the novel alive and the literary enterprise going.

Theodore Solotaroff. *NR.* Aug. 5, 1967. p. 34

See *Junkie, Naked Lunch, Nova Express, The Soft Machine, The Ticket that Exploded* (novels).

# CABELL, JAMES BRANCH (1879–1958)

That he says impeccably his say is indisputable; that he says it for only a few is undebatable. . . . He is . . . enjoyed only by those who possess a certain scholarship plus a but slightly secondary interest in fiction plus a mental kinship that recognizes the aptness of his means.

Blanche Williams. Our Short Story Writers (Moffat).<br>1920. p. 23

Mr. Cabell, by questioning the reality of reality, has been naturalized in the world of dreams till he moves about there without the scruples lasting over from another allegiance. Thus the beauty of his Poictesme is double-distilled. Those lovers of beauty who must now and then come down to earth for renewal will occasionally gasp in Poictesme, wishing the atmosphere would thicken and brilliant colors change. But always Poictesme hangs above the mortal clouds, suspended from the eternal sky, in the region where wit and beauty are joined in an everlasting kiss.

Carl Van Doren. James Branch Cabell (McBridge).<br>1925. p. 83

Here at last is an American novelist with a culture and style of his own, a conscious artist and a man of letters. . . . Cabell . . . is an adept at artistic writing, the only prose writer in American fiction who cultivates style for its own sake. . . . He likes to call himself a classic, classic in style, though romantic in inspiration. . . . Cabell's ideal is harmony, clearness and grace. He moves within fiction as if it were a natural element and not as in a quarry where he is painfully hewing out stones.

Régis Michaud. The American Novel Today (Little).<br>1928. pp. 202–3

The high repute of the works of Mr. Cabell has not been attacked by critics, partly out of a faint snobbishness; partly for the amusing reason that those who were fit to criticize him found him almost impossible to read, and lastly because scholarship and love of good prose seemed too rare in America to be discredited on other grounds without a pang. His prose is, indeed, not only correct but constantly graceful in diction and liquid in rhythm. The trouble is that there is nothing in all these romances for the mind to grasp; one fumbles in a sunny mist; one hopes from page to page to come upon something either sharp or solid; that hope is soon abandoned and next it becomes clear that even the grace of this style is often falsely arch and knowing or effeminate and teasing. The style, in brief, is married to the matter and both are *articles de luxe,* like gorgeously enameled cigarette étuis diamond and ruby-studded, or riding crops with jeweled handles.

Ludwig Lewisohn. Expression in America (Harper). 1932. p. 531

This Virginian gentleman and genealogist could hardly be expected either to approve of life in the United States or to feel that he was under any obligation to improve it. Instead he has converted his petulant disgust into a melodramatic pessimism. . . . The artist has a function in this mad world, Mr. Cabell argues; it is to create beautiful illusions, which alone make life endurable. But, far from occupying himself with the dissemination of dynamic lies, Mr. Cabell has devoted all his talents to attacking man's illusions. He is, then, a fraud, for neither his romanticism nor his pessimism is genuine. He is a sleek, smug egoist, whose desire to be a gentleman of the old school breeds dissatisfaction with the existing order, but who has not enough imaginative vigor to create a robust world in which deeds of chivalry and gallantry are performed. Instead he has written mild little fantasies, carefully baited with delicate obscenities.

Granville Hicks. The Great Tradition (Macmillan). 1933. p. 221

His own style is indubitably established, consciously dependent on archaism, but dependent for relief on marked and homely modernisms. On the whole it is attractive, and sometimes it is charming. But it is pedantic in phrasing and in dispensable detail. Knowing that fancy is more important than fact in the tales, the reader is annoyed and distracted by circumstantial matters of chronology and genealogy that delay action and throw no light on motivation.

The notable fact about Cabell in the modern pageant has been his persistence in playing his own role until through ability and cooperation of the censors he achieved a wide hearing. He ought to be taken as seriously as he takes himself, which is not very seriously, for his tongue as a rule is ostentatiously in his cheek.

Percy H. Boynton. Literature and American Life (Ginn). 1936. pp. 799–800

Critics have persisted in putting Cabell into the wrong category. They have repeatedly called him a romanticist, bent upon escape. They refuse to see that his extravanganzas of Poictesme are all allegories. He is as close to the modern pulse as the most intense realist, and as alarmed over it. He is a humorist, a wit, a satirist, an intellectual, a classicist. And he is a characteristic twentieth-century pessimist. He is right in the thick of life, and he is so disgusted with it that he can see nothing sensible to do except laugh. If he is a romanticist bent upon escape, then so were Aristophanes, Rabelais, Ben Jonson, Congreve, Voltaire, Mark Twain, and Anatole France.

Vernon Loggins. *I Hear America* (Crowell). 1937.
p. 287

Unlike that other artificer of the medieval. Thomas Chatterton, Cabell never persuaded himself; and he had no need to persuade his readers. They wanted just what he gave them: the touch of life bereft of life's prosaic sordidness; an easy road to wisdom; a masquerade of the soul in which, by mocking the daydreams of the great herd, one could liberate and enjoy one's own. Cabell did not pretend to be an "escapist"; he was a realist whose cynical appreciation of reality encouraged him to make it ridiculous. By dismissing the superficial world of the present, he illuminated its pathos lightly and fleetingly. . . . The critical Babbitts might think Cabell a satanic figure, but he was not even attempting to *épater le bourgeois;* he sought only to amuse him. Reading his books, good middle-class fathers and citizens, like good middle-class undergraduates, enjoyed the luxury of a depravity that was as synthetic as breakfast cereal, and as harmless.

Alfred Kazin. *On Native Grounds* (Reynal). 1942.
pp. 233–4

See *Domnei, Chivalry, The Rivet in Grandfather's Neck, The Cream of the Jest,* and *The Nightmare Has Triplets* (novels).

# CAHAN, ABRAHAM (1860–1951)

As Mr. Cahan is a Russian, and as romanticism is not considered literature in Russia, his story [*Yekl*] is, of course, intensely realistic. It could not be more so indeed than Mr. [Stephen] Crane's stories, and it is neither more nor less faithful than these. The artistic principle which moves both writers is the same; but the picturesque, outlandish material with which Mr. Cahan deals makes a stronger appeal to the reader's fancy. He has more humor than the American, too, whose spare laughter is apt to be grim, while the Russian cannot hide his relish of the comic incidents of his story. It is mainly not at all comic, however, but tragical as the divorce of the poor little Russian wife can make it, though the reader is promptly consoled by her marriage with a man worthier of her than Jake the Yankee. He goes away and weds the Americanized "Polish snope" whom he had flirted with before his wife came out to him. . . .

I had almost forgotten to speak of his English. In its simplicity and its purity, as the English of a man born to write Russian, it is simply marvelous.

William Dean Howells. New York World. July 26, 1896,<br>in Clara M. and Rudolf Kirk. AJHQ. Sept., 1962. p. 52

He is a humorist, and his humor does not spare the sordid and uncouth aspects of the character whose pathos he so tenderly reveals. Poor, work-worn, ambitious, blundering, grotesque lives they mostly are which he deals with, but they have often a noble aspiration, to which he does justice with no straining or vaunting. The rich Jew going home to his village in Poland to get a husband for his Americanized daughter, whose ideal is to marry an "up-town feller," and bringing back a dreamy young Talmudist, who turns agnostic on his hands; the prosperous pedlar who sends to his native place, where he has been the byword and laughing-stock, and demands the daughter of the wealthy distiller in marriage; the young Russian wife, whose heart goes from her work-dulled husband to the student they have taken for a lodger to eke out their pitiful fortunes; the Yiddish bride who imagines spending all her savings on a wedding supper in the vain hope that the guests will bring gifts enough to set her up in housekeeping—such are the materials which the author handles so skillfully that he holds the reader between a laugh and a heartache, and fashions into figures so lifelike that you would expect to meet them in any stroll through Hester-street. It will be interesting to see whether Mr. Cahan will pass beyond his present environment out into the larger American world, or will master our life as he has mastered our language. But of a Jew, who is also a Russian, what artistic triumph may not we expect?

William Dean Howells. Literature. Dec. 31, 1898, in<br>Clara M. and Rudolf Kirk. AJHQ. Sept., 1962. p. 41

And for a background that immense Russia, a country which has produced the greatest novelists and is the most illiterate of Europe, a nation of nations whose history is stained with the blood of conquered races and massacred sects. It is from this rich mine that Mr. Cahan has selected with an artist's care his material. But in *The White Terror and the Red* we have something far more interesting than a narrative of sensational episodes, or a gallery of interesting types, more valuable than a vivid picture of melodramatic history in the making. We have a work of art of the highest class.

It was reserved for a Russian realist to do full justice to the subject, and Mr. Cahan is a Russian and a realist. He is concerned with life. His literary god is the truth as he sees it, and because he is an artist and his theme throbs with passionate human interest, he has succeeded in writing a novel which bears out the bright promise of his earlier work.

Edwin Lefevre. *Bkm.* April, 1905. p. 187

*The White Terror and the Red* is, as far as I know, the first important novel which has applied the general spirit of Russian fiction to the literal facts of the revolution [of 1879–81]. Mr. Cahan has been enabled to do this by virtue of an exceptional position. He is a Russian, living in America, and writing in English. He is, therefore, not limited by the despotism of the Russian government, as the Russian writers are. He is one of the very few men not now in Russia who combine with genuine literary ability an inside knowledge of the facts leading to the assassination of the Czar. In his book the Russian realistic method and the Russian idealistic spirit have for the first time been applied to the direct and literal facts of the revolution.

This directness of approach Mr. Cahan has had. *The White Terror and the Red,* is, therefore, at once a genuine historical novel, dealing with the events which resulted in the assassination of the Czar, and a genuine realistic novel, a rare combination.

Hutchins Hapgood. *Critic.* June, 1905. p. 561

The portrait of David Levinsky is a portrait of society, not simply of the Jewish section of it, or of New York, but of American business. And business is business whether done by Jew or Gentile. If Levinsky is a triumphant failure, he is so because American business, which shaped him to its ends, is, viewed from any decent regard for humanity, a miserable monster of success. Not that Levinsky is an abstraction, or that the novelist is forcing a thesis. Far from it. . . . Mr. Cahan is an artist; he knows how to think through his characters, by letting them do the thinking, as if it were their affair and not his.

John Macy. *Dial.* Nov. 22, 1917. p. 522

Of this East Side world, with its thick vitality, and push against the city, Mr. Cahan has drawn a picture of incomparable vigor, richly documented, admirably proportioned. This, you say, is the very life which corresponds to what the outsider can only see in street and shop and through his imagination. You are immersed in the life of the family, the synagogue, the sweatshop, the cafe, the theatre, the socialists and intellectuals. And you witness it through the eyes of a man of vigor and intelligence, David Levinsky, who is engaged in mastering, appropriating, nourishing his senses and ambitions by means of that life. Consider Mr. Cahan's art in the light of his opportunity for propaganda. For he makes his hero not a socialist but an exploiter who has no sympathy with the helpless workers from whom he has come, who fights the unions, is afraid of socialism, and remains unregenerate to the last, justifying his "individualism" by the Darwin and Spencer he had read during the intellectual ferment of the sweatshop. . . . Mr. Cahan makes him tell the story in rich human detail, as an understandable human being. You are no more appalled at David's tyrannies and greeds than David is himself. Yet in David's unperceptive reactions to the women he desires, in his annoyance at the radicals and "intellectuals," Mr. Cahan makes a subtle back-fire of criticism more deadly than the most melodramatic socialist fiction.

R. B. NR. Feb. 2, 1918. pp. 31–2

There is no question whatever that the work of Abraham Cahan, Yiddish scholar, journalist, novelist, belongs to the American nation. As far back as the year in which Stephen Crane stirred many sensibilities with his *Maggie,* the story of an Irish slum in Manhattan, Mr. Cahan produced in *Yekl* a book of similar and practically equal merit concerning a Jewish slum in the same borough. But it and his later books *The Imported Bridegroom and Other Stories* and *The White Terror and the Red* have been overwhelmed by novels by more familiar men dealing with more familiar communities. The same has been true even of his masterpiece, the most important of all immigrant novels, *The Rise of David Levinsky.* It, too, records the making of an American, originally a reader of Talmud in a Russian village and eventually the principal figure in the cloak and suit trade in America. But it does more than trace the career of Levinsky through his personal adventures: it traces the evolution of a great industry and represents the transplanted Russian Jews with affectionate exactness in all their modes of work and play and love—another conquest of a larger Canaan. Here are fused American hope and Russian honesty. At the end David, with all his New World wealth, lacks the peace he might have had but for his sacrifice of Old World integrity and faith. And yet the novel is very quiet in its polemic. Its hero has gained in power; he is no dummy to hang maxims on. Moving through a varied scene, gradually shedding the outward qualities of his race, he remains always an individual, gnawed at by love in the midst of his ambitions, subject to frailties which test his strength.

The fact that Mr. Cahan wrote *David Levinsky* not in his mother-tongue but in the language of his adopted country may be taken as a sign that American literature no less than the American population is being enlarged by the influx of fresh materials and methods.

Carl Van Doren. Contemporary American Novelists,<br>1900–1920 (Macmillan). 1922. pp. 144–5

Cahan's absorbing interest in literature has been one of the reasons that the standard of literary criticism as well as the quality of fiction printed in the *Forward* has always been high. . . . Cahan has mellowed somewhat with the years, but in the old days he was considered a bit of a tyrant in the office. Writers often had what they considered their best copy mercilessly derided as "fancy," and were told that the editor didn't want "any Carusoes in the office." Reporters who lapsed into polysyllables or put style ahead of content had to stand by helplessly while Cahan called upon the elevator man, or some other representative of the paper's readers to judge the disputed passage. If the man was unable to understand the copy it was thrown away or rewritten.

J. C. Rich. AM. Aug., 1947. pp. 175–6

I have purposely refrained from treating David Levinsky as a fictional character and have spoken of the novel as though it were the actual memoir of an American Jew, in tribute to Cahan's power of characterization. Such immediacy of revelation is the novel's strongest quality, and Levinsky is made to talk about himself not only with an authentic accent, but with a motive in disclosure verging on something sly—precisely as such a man would talk. This well known and widely respected businessman tells the truth about himself, his love affairs, his efforts to outsmart the unions, the way other men tell lies—to see if he can get away with it! But as fiction, Cahan's writing lacks continuity: his transitions from subject to subject tend to be abrupt, with a perseveration in the linking of sex and economics. . . . Often the trains of thought collide within the single paragraph, business plowing into everything else. True, Levinsky's mind would work this way, and the habit would also serve him the purpose of saying, "I may not be doing so well with the girls—but think of the money I'm making." (Though business is meaningless to Levinsky, one of the most touching insights of the novel is provided by Cahan's showing how he succumbs to a businessman's vulgarity of tone and manner, and berates himself for the weakness.)

Isaac Rosenfeld. Cmty. Aug., 1952. p. 135

And if one had to select a single person to stand for East European Jews in America, it would be Abraham Cahan, the editor of the *Jewish Daily Forward*. . . . In one of his novels, the best yet written about American Jewish life, we are given a vivid and convincing picture of the helplessness and irrelevance of East European Judaism in the America of the early years of the mass immigration. We read in *The Rise of David Levinsky* of how a young Russian Jewish yeshiva student, learned and pious, emigrates to this country. On the boat he eats no forbidden food and prays daily. In America he seeks out and finds solace in the synagogue established by the people from his home town. But he also moves inevitably from one transgression to the next. First his earlocks are cut off, then he shaves, soon he abandons the synagogue in favor of night school and English studies. And soon nothing is left—and with practically no soul-searching.

Nathan Glazer. American Judaism (Chicago).<br>1957. pp. 68–9

This perceptive Russian intellectual shared in all the experiences of his fellow immigrants: he was factory hand, lecturer, teacher of English, labor organizer, law student, and socialist preacher. But from the outset he cultivated literary ambitions. In his first year Cahan mailed an article describing the coronation of Tsar Alexander III to the *New York World* and it was promptly published. By the mid-1880's Cahan's journalistic career encompassed the Russian, Yiddish, and English fields. . . . In 1896 his first novel, *Yekl, A Tale of the Ghetto,* was published by Appleton's. . . . His novel, despite the high praise of William Dean Howells, brought him no royalties. Women, who constituted the major market for novels, devoured knightly romances but had no interest in immigrant stories; furthermore, an unmoral love story that alluded to sex was taboo.

Moses Rischin. The Promised City: New York's Jews,<br>1870–1914 (Harvard). 1962. p. 124

See *Yekl: A Tale of the New York Ghetto, The White Terror and the Red, The Rise of David Levinsky* (novels); *The Imported Bridegroom and Other Stories of the New York Ghetto.*

# CAIN, JAMES M. (1892–    )

Every so often a writer turns up who forces us to revalue our notions of the realistic manner, for, no less than reality itself, it is relative and inconstant, depending on the period, the fashion, the point of view. There is the feeling of realism, of intense realism, in James M. Cain's work, and yet he cannot be compared to such diverse types of realists as Zola, Ibsen, Sandburg, Dreiser, or Hemingway. It is the hard-boiled manner that has been heralded for some time, and is now upon us. . . . Cain can get down to the primary impulses of greed and sex in fewer words than any writer we know of. He has exorcised all the inhibitions; there is a minimum of reason, of complexity, of what we commonly call civilization, between an impulse and its gratification. In the broadest sense he is no asset as yet to American literature, for he adds nothing in breadth, but only in intensity, to our consciousness of life.

Harold Strauss. NYT. Feb. 18, 1934. p. 8

*The Postman Always Rings Twice* . . . is a brutal story of adultery and murder whose appropriate setting is a wayside filling-station in California. Up to a certain point it rings horribly true: the bungled attempt at murder, the unsuccessful crime, the maggots of mutual suspicion that begin to prey on the guilty partners. But then Mr. Cain begins to make things up. He has almost succeeded in showing two triumphantly evil people—the reader is uncomfortable but can't let the story drop—when his intention falters: he converts his two villains into another Paolo and Francesca and rings down the curtain on a Hollywood-tragic ending. *The Postman Always Rings Twice* is a short, meretricious but exciting book; it does not pretend to tell the whole story, but it does pretend to tell nothing but the truth.

T. S. Matthews. NR. Feb. 28, 1934. p. 80

In the theatre they call it "pace." Mr. Cain had phenomenal pace in his story *The Postman Always Rings Twice,* and he demonstrates this gift again in *Serenade.* And another thing. There is no use being too nice about the fact that what gives Mr. Cain's novels their intensely readable quality is their deliberate and even brutal sexual honesty. . . . Mr. Cain is a real writer who can construct and tell an exciting story with dazzling swiftness—one of our hard-boiled novelists whose work has a fast rhythm that is art.

William Rose Benet. SR. Dec. 4, 1937. p. 5

Cain deals with ciphers, picturesque cardboard characters whom he cuts into attractive designs. He has certain specific knowledges that he draws on in all his novels: the workings of the law, the inside of the restaurant business and the world of music. . . . He has a few favorite themes: fate, the relationship of art and sex, and particularly the relationship of sex and violence. All his books give the sense of having been pieced together skillfully out of these shiny bits of glass, having no organic existence or internal necessity.

Stanley Edgar Hyman. NR. Oct. 6, 1941. p. 442

. . . in his work there is clearly a difference between sensationalism for its own sake and the effects sought by a writer obviously concerned with style and technique, even when the basic premise is violence. And it is truly an astonishing style, rippling and easy in a nervous sort of way, the people talking as such people would talk, the writing vivid and direct. . . . For when Mr. Cain's faults have all been pointed out—and the principal one is that character doesn't matter much in his writing—the pertinent fact remains: when he is at the top of his form it is all but impossible to put down the story he is telling.

John K. Hutchens. NYT. April 18, 1943. p. 7

In every story the central cast is the same, the Mug ("I"), the Victim, and the Dame; these stock figures are set up methodically and then knocked methodically down by Fate, who happens to be Mr. Cain's bellboy. The Cain women are a trim-ankled lot, varying only as to the colors of their sweaters, but good or bad they push the button for the catastrophe. Either Mr. Cain likes his women spiced with evil, or he was frightened once by the Lorelei; anyway it's the lady's fault every time. . . . Validity in art is recognized by the after-effect, and the after-effect of a Cain book is a half-angry feeling of having been gypped, of having picked up the April Fool pocketbook or having cried over "Mother Machree." This is not to say that Mr. Cain's art is not important in its own peculiar way, or that it is mere hammock reading.

Dawn Powell. *Nation.* May 22, 1943. p. 745

The elements of a Cain novel add up to a kind of bogus tragedy, in which ill luck takes the place of fate. Perhaps here is one reason why the illusion of life is so strong in *The Postman.* Luck has no place in tragedy, but it has ample scope in our daily lives. At any rate, the illusion of life is there, so strong that we accept any number of details which, in another book, would thoroughly spoil the reader's pleasure. . . . What we have in *The Postman* is a dose of unattenuated violence, describable in the jargon appropriate to the dignity of the book as possessing "terrific punch." If the book were one of greater dignity and higher seriousness, we would stop talking of punch and begin to discuss "impact" or "concentration of effect." Such suddenly delivered impact is commonly recognized as one of the essentials of tragedy. Cain's books do not strike a tragic note, however, because the violence in them is not endowed with any sort of moral significance. We are aware of his violence not as something which we must accept because it is a part of Man's Fate, but as something for a clever writer to play tricks with.

W. M. Frohock. *The Novel of Violence in America*
(Southern Methodist). 1950. pp. 97–9

It is most pertinent to look at Cain's technical devices. Cain discovered that the first person narrative in the Southern California argot suited his novels best. A native of Maryland whose early stories and plays were in dialect, Cain retains a certain Southern tone, pattern of speech and diction at times which leaven the coarseness of the speech he cultivates. Conscious as he is of style, he makes no conscious effort to be tough; he simply writes as he thinks the hero would speak. . . .

In most of Cain's novels, money is at the heart of the love affairs. A crime for money and freedom must be committed, the lovers feel, before the course of love can run smoothly. Usually the husband, the major obstacle, is impotent in a sense, and the highly charged wife desires a potent stranger to take over. In only a few of the novels do the lovers commit no crime, and only in three is there no desperate love situation from beginning to end. None of the lovers pay legally for the crimes they commit for love and money; most set in motion circumstances which bring about their own horrible destruction.

An atmosphere of evil, often pagan in mood and enhanced by superstition, overhangs the tales and broods over events.

David Madden. *UR*. Winter, 1963; Spring, 1964.
pp. 147, 238

Bemused by violence, Americans like to feel out, Cain says, all the nuances of the cliché "There but for the grace of God go I." To involve the reader more intimately in the social communion with violence, ritualized by mass media reportage, Cain deals with characters just removed from the gangster and private eye milieu. . . . Cain admires the clear, hard, cold mind, and thrusts his characters into actions in which their daring and know-how enable them to meet any challenge. His typical hero is an "educated roughneck": a meat packing executive, an insurance agent, a bank executive, an engineer. But even his boxers, farmers, and mechanics prove adroit. These men crave praise and are sometimes immobilized, momentarily, by condemnation. . . .

Tough optimism is clearly expressed in all of Cain's writing. At times he is cynical and satirical, but the American brand of masculine romanticism is also active, and occasionally even sentimentality intrudes. In Cain's world, chance, luck, coincidence, gamble and counter-gamble, risk, audacity, and the ability to improvise upon the given serve his characters, but usually end in defeating them. While he is capable of creating finely drawn moral dilemmas, as in *Mignon,* he is primarily interested in the *action* produced by them and their impact on character rather than in elaborating upon facets of the abstract issues.

David Madden in *The Thirties,* edited by Warren French
(Everett Edwards). 1967. pp. 68–9

See *The Postman Always Rings Twice, Serenade, Mildred Pierce, Three of a Kind, The Butterfly* (novels).

# CALDWELL, ERSKINE (1903–    )

It is as difficult for an outsider as it is for Mr. Caldwell to find in his work any systematic, even any conscious doctrine. He has not shaped himself by reasoning and he does not make up stories to prove abstract points.

. . . (His stories) somehow sound as if they had been invented a long time ago and cherished in the popular memory, waiting for the hand of art if it should chance upon them. Mr. Caldwell, handling these matters, partly goes back to a manner at least a hundred years old. Again and again he brings to mind the native humorists before Mark Twain, when American humor had not yet been sweetened but was still dry, blunt, and broad. . . . It is in Mr. Caldwell's choice of heroes and in the boldness with which he speaks of their love and religion that he goes beyond any of the older humorists.

Carl Van Doren. *Nation.* Oct. 18, 1933. p. 444

I have denied that Caldwell is a realist. In his tomfoolery he comes closer to the Dadaists; when his grotesqueness is serious, he is a Super-realist. We might compromise by calling him over all a Symbolist (if by Symbolist we mean a writer whose plots are more intelligible when interpreted as dreams). . . . I am not by any means satisfied by the psychoanalytic readings of such processes to date, though I do believe that in moralistic fantasies of the Caldwell type, where the dull characters become so strangely inspired at crucial moments, we are present at a poetic law court where judgements are passed upon kinds of transgression inaccessible to jurists, with such odd penalties as no *Code Napoléon* could ever schematize.

Kenneth Burke. *NR.* April 10, 1935. p. 234

Caldwell has lived among these Georgians, and has studied them with the enthusiastic attitude of young genius. He has a healthy masculine love for them. The record of his impressions of their way of living is fearlessly frank. Although brutal, his realism is genuine. These Georgia "Crackers" are as benighted as he makes them out to be. . . . He has decided where to lay the blame for the decadence of his chosen people. The cause of their plight is not a frowsy religion, nor false standards in education. It is poverty. These people were long ago downed in the economic fight. All initiative was ground out of them. So Caldwell sees them. He is passionate for the return of their initiative. He would kindle public feeling in their behalf. He would have them taught how to get up and begin fighting all over again. Not only is he one of the best of the contemporary regional writers; he is also the strongest of the proletarian writers.

Vernon Loggins. *I Hear America* (Crowell). 1937.
p. 222

Mr. Caldwell is said to think of himself as a realist with a sociological message to deliver. If that message exists I fail to find it very clearly expressed in the present play *(Journeyman)*. . . . But there is no point discussing what a work of art means or whether or not it is "true to life" unless one is convinced that the work "exists"—that it has the power to attract and hold attention, to create either that belief or that suspension of disbelief without which its "message" cannot be heard and without which its factual truth is of no importance. And to me the incontrovertible fact is that both Mr. Caldwell's novels and the plays made from them do in this sense "exist" with an uncommon solidarity, that his race of curiously depraved and curiously juicy human grotesques are alive in his plays whether or not they, or things like them, were ever alive anywhere else.

Joseph Wood Krutch. *Nation.* Feb. 12, 1938. p. 190

His intention . . . seems to be that of arousing sympathy for Southern tenant farmers, black and white. I believe this intention is good and that nothing effective will be done to correct the bad conditions now prevailing throughout the South until the sympathy of the nation is aroused. At the same time, I am convinced that sympathy is not enough. There must be some real understanding, and the ideas in people's minds must have some correspondence with actual conditions as they exist. If the picture of tenant farmers and of poor people in the South generally, as rendered in *God's Little Acre* and *Tobacco Road* are authentic, then there is little which can be done by landlord or tenant, by government or God, unless, of course, Mr. Caldwell's writings should so arouse the interest of the Deity that he would then proceed to make tenant, landlord, and land over again.

W. T. Couch. *VQR.* Spring, 1938. p. 309

The chief theme of Caldwell's writing is the agony of the impoverished land, which has now so nearly reached a state of complete exhaustion in large sections of the old South that it is only a matter of time (he thinks) when the dust storms will cross the Mississippi and extend the desert to the east. This is the material basis for the social conditions which he sets forth in his stories. But, of course, it is the people who interest him as a student of human nature; and with the people, it is not so much their material sufferings as the moral degradation which follows steadily on the decline of their material well-being. It is the illiteracy passed on from generation to generation of those who cannot find time to go to school or have not clothes to wear to school. . . . It is the shiftlessness and irresponsibility wrought by habitual want of hope.

Joseph Warren Beach. *American Fiction 1920–1940*
(Macmillan). 1941. p. 223

Erskine Caldwell is two writers, both good of their kind, and one a sort of genius in his own narrow field. They collaborate on most of his books, but with conflicting aims; and the result is that reading some of his novels

. . . is like a week-end visit to a bickering household. "I am a social nov-elist," says the first Caldwell. . . . The second Caldwell does not talk about his aims, and in fact he isn't completely conscious of them; but sometimes, pushing his twin brother away from the typewriter, he begins pounding out impossible fancies and wild humor.

Malcolm Cowley. NR. Nov. 6, 1944. p. 599

Where Faulkner's supreme dimension is time, Caldwell's is space, and the whole quality of their art lies distinguished in these separate dimensions. Plot, being essentially a matter of space, becomes of necessity Caldwell's sphere of operations, and though his characters are seldom nuanced and the range of his emotions remains pretty narrow, he handles incident and action and spatial movement with a skill that holds the reader to attention. . . .

Yet the exigencies and narrowness of space landlock Caldwell's writing, and make it, despite its clearer and firmer outlines, more limited and less important than Faulkner's. It demonstrates that a mastery of plot linked to a cargo of social significance is not enough to establish a great reputa-tion. Though Caldwell impresses his readers, he does not haunt them in the sense of lingering in their imaginations or compelling them to read him a second time.

Leo Gurko. The Angry Decade (Dodd). 1947.<br>pp. 138–9

There is . . . no completely satisfactory attitude for the reader to assume toward these books. When we read them as comedies, Caldwell carefully and disconcertingly knocks the props from under the comic element; we look then for serious, socially-conscious reporting, and the comic element spoils our view; we resort, unwillingly, to taking them as exhibits of the picturesque, only to realize that Caldwell deserves better from his reader. So we come finally to the conclusion—for which we have been searching all along—that Caldwell's novels suffer from a multiplicity of meanings which are incompatible with one another. This is another way of saying that Caldwell's own attitude toward his material is ambiguous.

W. M. Frohock. The Novel of Violence in America<br>(Southern Methodist). 1950. p. 143

Certainly the humor is gusty, uniquely gratifying, a largess, a bounty, for which one always thanks the giver. We cannot thank Caldwell too much or too often for giving us the robust and depraved and homely and vulgar tom-foolery as no one else has given us in our time. His literalities, equiva-lents, and approximations, particularly concerning the sex content in the lives of his people, come forth genuinely incorporated and derived from the traditional and popular mind-body of the rural South.

> Robert Hazel in *Southern Renascence,* edited by Louis Rubin, Jr. (Johns Hopkins). 1953. p. 321

It's a shame that Erskine Caldwell in his new novel, *Claudelle Inglish* . . . is still imitating Caldwell in this, his thirty-eighth book. Since *Tobacco Road* (1932) he has written a series of vivid if uneven accounts of life and lust in the backwoods South. The South has not liked its picture as taken by the Georgia-born novelist.

But neither the South nor Mr. Caldwell can maintain the same indignation in the same form for twenty-seven years. As long ago as 1940 Clifton Fadiman suggested Caldwell was "beginning to repeat himself," and the quality of repetition has ranged from pretty good to pretty bad. Lately it has been pretty bad. . . .

It is said Caldwell was bitter when Broadway received *Tobacco Road* as comedy, yet humor has always seasoned the raw taste of his plots and social commentary in an up-again, down-again career. Both are tried in the same way in *Claudelle Inglish* but the lesson is no longer about the South or a bad economic system. It is about the dullness of the same joke and the same cry of protest too often repeated in the same tone.

(K)    Doris Betts. *SR.* May 2, 1959. p. 25

Erskine Caldwell, never a writer to let a prominent social cause go begging, has now trained his typewriter upon the problem of segregation in the South. Lest Mr. Caldwell's many admirers feel alarm that he has sold himself out to serious and solemnly purposeful fiction, they can rest assured that he wears his social indignation lightly in *Close To Home* . . . and that though his wrath may be righteous, his manner is still easygoing. His Southern crackers have been tidied up a bit, but his story is spiced with enough randy touches to make us remember the old denizens of Tobacco Road.

(K)    William Barrett. *At.* July, 1962. p. 112

See *God's Little Acre, Trouble in July,* and *Tobacco Road* (novels).

# CAPOTE, TRUMAN (1924–    )

"Get Capote"—at this moment the words are resounding on many a sixtieth floor, and "get him" of course means make him and break him, smother him with laurels and then vent on him the obscure hatred which is inherent in the notion of another's superiority.

> Cyril Connolly. *Horizon.* Oct., 1947. p. 5

Capote's imagined world is as beautiful as a water moccasin, and as poisonous. A Freudian critic would call it a world of infantile regression; a sinister underwater universe populated by monstrous children, expressionistic automats, and zombie adults, all viewed obliquely through the bang-shaded eyes of a Louisiana Caligari-Hoffmann. . . . There can be no doubt of Capote's evocative magic. . . . Only it is invariably black magic.

Charles A. Brady. CW. May, 1949. p. 156

Capote seems determined . . . to do nothing ordinary and therefore be memorable. This determination, plus an original sense for the macabre (exploited for all the sensationalism it is worth), a certain all too fallible delicacy and sensitivity, excellent powers of description and evocation, a genuine but unselective sense of humor, and an occasional sense for, and (rarely) the discipline of, poetry, sums up both his values and his equipment as a writer.

Alexander Klein. NR. July 4, 1949. p. 18

One thing about Truman Capote . . . that one notices right off is that he looks a little like a toy. That's what some people *say,* anyway. If he is a toy, he nevertheless has a mind that would turn those big thinking cybernetic machines green with envy. As a matter of fact, his mind has enough good steel in it to turn too many human beings the same violent color— and it has, no doubt about it. Mr. Capote's appearance is lamblike but all intellectual bullies are warned not to be deceived.

Harvey Breit. NYT. Feb. 24, 1952. p. 29

"When the cannons are silent the Muses are heard" is a phrase the Russian hosts of the *Porgy and Bess* company were fond of reiterating. This account [*The Muses Are Heard*] of the company's trip to Russia just about a year ago is fascinating on any number of levels. It is a lively, dramatic report of Russian attitudes toward art, toward Americans, toward food, clothes, and life in general. It is full of vivid descriptions of the Russian countryside and cities. It is a gallery of sympathetic portraits of the *Porgy and Bess* cast and the large group of people who traveled with them. . . . And Mr. Capote has used his novelist's technique in creating real suspense while everyone waited for the opening night in Leningrad for which they had come so far.

(K)          Katherine Gauss Jackson. *Harper.* Feb., 1957. p. 97

The dichotomy of good and evil exists in each Capote character just as the dichotomy of daylight and nighttime exists in the aggregate of his stories. We might almost say that Capote's stories inhabit two worlds— that of the realistic, colloquial, often humorous daytime and that of the dreamlike, detached, and inverted nocturnal world. This double identity must be viewed with a double vision because Capote's stories can be interpreted either psychologically or as an expression of a spiritual or moral problem. In either case, whether the story be realistic or fantastic, the central focus is on the moment of initiation and the central character is either adolescent or innocent.

(K)                                              Paul Levine. *VQR*. Autumn, 1958. p. 602

If the art of Truman Capote may be defined succinctly, it is highly-detailed perception by all the senses, in which nothing, however small, personal or languid escapes due attention, and which, by the time his fine-grained literary style has given it shape and perspective, has become an engaging tissue of story-telling. . . . Since this little world receives a precise accounting which inevitably suggests the whole-souled concentration of a precocious child, it for the moment becomes a much bigger world and one full of surprises and beauty.

Cyrus Durgin. *Boston Globe*. Dec. 15, 1958. p. 8

Among the surprising qualities of Truman Capote's mercurial talent and a quality that is made very plain by such a selection from the entire body of his work as this [*Selected Writings*] is its range, the variety of its development over the nearly twenty years in which the author has been publishing. A prose of many moods, it is equally at ease in situations of black nightmarish horror and of high, often hilarious comedy, and perhaps its single constant quality is the unerring sense of style. By style one means, when speaking of Capote's work, not only the right words in the right places, but the body of detail precisely and freshly observed and the varieties of the speaking human voice accurately heard and quintessentially reported.

(K)                                 Mark Schorer. Introduction to *Selected Writings of*
*Truman Capote* (Random). 1963. p. vii

This [*Breakfast at Tiffany's*] novella's similarities to Isherwood's *Sally Bowles* have often been noted. The difference is more revealing. Isherwood's story is quintessential social-political history. This quite beyond Capote who, for all the war-time detail, delivers finally a relatively isolated portrait of a romantic figure in quest of the perennial romantic grail, utter happiness. . . .

. . . His concluding essay [in *Selected Writings*] on Brooklyn Heights—written for *Holiday* in a manner quite different from his own pointillist travel pieces—proves yet once more that he is a literary actor, good only when he gets the right part. Capote's writing depends on which magazine commissions him or which author he is imitating. There is no clear personal imprint. The only generalization possible is that, so far, he is at his best with humorous observation. . . . His fiction is strongest, most vital, when it resembles his best non-fiction. It is noteworthy that he is now at work on a long examination of a Kansas murder case. . . . Almost half of this collection is non-fiction; the book on which he has been engaged for some years is non-fiction. Perhaps he has recognized that his forte is in using his artistic abilities on factual material, and in that self-recognition may be the pleasant end of a search. For this collection is the record of a man trying out many voices in many rooms.

(K)                           Stanley Kauffmann. *NR*. Feb. 23, 1963. pp. 22, 24

## Other Voices, Other Rooms

*Other Voices, Other Rooms* abundantly justifies the critics and readers who first hailed Capote as a writer of exceptional gifts. . . . Capote's sensibility is as notable as his insight, and its range is impressive, for it enables him to describe elements of physical environment that would be scarcely perceptible to most of us; yet these elements, however unnoticed, are recognized by the reader as authentic, and indisputably present. But although his descriptive writing is masterly, it is his ability to create and interpret character—to increase both the scope and depth of our understanding of ourselves and others—that yields the major excellences of *Other Voices, Other Rooms*. . . . It is not only a work of unusual beauty, but a work of unusual intelligence. In it, readers will establish contact with one of the most accomplished American novelists to make his debut in many a season.

Lloyd Morris. *NYHT*. Jan. 16, 1948. p. 2

Even if Mr. Capote were ten or twenty years older than he is, his ability to bend language to his poetic moods, his ear for dialect and for the varied rhythms of speech would be remarkable. In one so young this much writing skill represents a kind of genius. On the other hand, I find myself deeply antipathetic to the whole artistic-moral purpose of Mr. Capote's novel. . . . For it seems to me to create a world of passive acceptance in which we are rendered incapable of thinking anybody responsible for his behavior in any department.

Diana Trilling. *Nation*. Jan. 31, 1948. pp. 133–4

Mr. Capote *does* have a remarkable facility with words; he can make perfectly normal horrors and shocks appear like enormities upon the senses. At times we can even hear a haunting funereal music behind Mr. Capote's wayward language. If he had selected his material more carefully, shown more restraint, and had been less concerned with terrifying us out of our wits, he might have easily made a real and tenderly appealing story out of the experiences of thirteen-year-old Joel Knox and the people he meets during that long and lonely summer of his approaching maturity.

Richard McLoughlin. *SR*. Feb. 14, 1948. p. 12

*Other Voices, Other Rooms* is easily the most exciting novel to come from America this year. Though one of its chief characters is what is customarily referred to by reviewers as "decadent," both he and the rest of the characters in this emotional story of the South make the average character in contemporary American fiction seem perverted by comparison. For the only moral standard that literature knows is the truth, and it is the truthful intensity of Mr. Capote's book that makes it so remarkable. . . . He has dared to write of life in all its complex splendor and to tell of the human heart, and yet he has triumphed without sinking into romanticism or departing from any of the desired standards of taste and maturity. . . . But what ensures its success is the quality of Mr. Capote's writing, which is very high indeed, and original without being exhibitionist or obscure.

Robert Kee. *Spec*. Nov. 19, 1948. pp. 674–6

## Tree of Night

Evidently concerned to a rare degree with the technique of writing itself, Mr. Capote in his style reveals a combination of eloquence and of simplicity. The perfectly apt, homely but unexpected adjective in a carefully limpid phrase: a familiar, plain, yet nowise banal vocabulary: a rare verb chosen rather than an elegant one—such are some of its more obvious characteristics. . . . Moreover, Mr. Capote's style serves, generally, as a flexible and vigorous instrument for the communication of truly remarkable gifts of observation, whether of gesture or atmosphere.

Iris Barry. *NYHT*. Feb. 27, 1949. p. 2

If the Mad Hatter and the Ugly Duchess had had a child, and the child had almost grown up, these are almost the kind of short stories he could be expected to write. . . . Who wants, really, to crawl back into the twilit cave and roll the papier-mâché stone over the doorway? Who would want to let Alice's wonderland serve as the myth around which he organized his adult life? . . . With these reservations, however, one must fairly assert for these stories a kind of triple power: a mind at times disciplined toward poetry, with a special skill at naming; a pleasant and only slightly grotesque humor, and an ability to suggest, as in the novel, the outlines of haunted personalities.

Carlos Baker. *NYT*. Feb. 27, 1949. p. 7

As a teller of tales he has a peculiar and remarkable talent. . . . In his hands the fairy tale and ghost story manage to assimilate the attitudes of twentieth-century psychology without losing their integrity, without demanding to be accepted as mere fantasy or explained as mere symbol. . . . In Capote's stories the fairy world, more serious than business or love, is forever closing in upon the skeptical secure world of grown-ups.

Leslie A. Fiedler. *Nation.* April 2, 1949. pp. 395–6

## The Grass Harp

Mr. Capote's second novel, *The Grass Harp,* remains within the extreme limits of what we call Gothic, but it is a sunlit Gothic, an aberrant form with a personality, an agreeable personality, entirely its own. . . . Mr. Capote keeps his story beautifully under control. His story has elements of allegory, it expounds a rather simple, basic statement concerning the nature of love. . . . In the beginning of the novel one does catch whiffs of the well-known Southern decay, but the book is not concerned with morbidity. It is a light, skilful, delightful story.

Oliver La Farge. *SR.* Oct. 20, 1951. pp. 19–20

Within the slim compass of this work, Truman Capote has achieved a masterpiece of passionate simplicity, of direct intuitive observation. Without any loss of intensity, he has purified the clotted prose of *Other Voices, Other Rooms,* producing a luminous reflector for his unique visual sensibility. . . . He still deals in eccentricities but his characters are not wrenched out of their human context; in them, eccentricity becomes an extension, not a distortion of personality. Compassion, too—that abused quality—takes on a new depth here.

Richard Hayes. *Com.* Oct. 26, 1951. p. 74

Mr. Capote creates a world in which it seems perfectly natural for people to lodge in treetops; and equally natural for a retired judge to propose marriage to a dotty spinster while the two of them are perched on a branch. . . . Within its own terms, *The Grass Harp* comes pretty close, I should say, to being a complete success. It charms you into sharing the author's feeling that there is a special poetry—a spontaneity and wonder and delight—in lives untarnished by conformity and common sense.

Charles J. Rolo. *At.* Nov., 1951. pp. 89–90

## Breakfast at Tiffany's

The form of *Breakfast at Tiffany's* approaches perfection. It has pace, narrative excitement, a firm and subtle hold on the sequence of events from the first backward glance to the final salutation. A novelette in scope, it still manages to treat a subject usually accorded the fuller scope of the picaresque novel with marvelous selectivity. The point of view, the tone, the style herald no technical discoveries in the field of fiction: they simply blend to make the subject spring to life.

(K)                                    Ihab Hassan. *Radical Innocence* (Princeton).
1961. p. 254

## In Cold Blood

It is to Mr. Capote's disadvantage that every book he writes turns into what our great grandmothers used to call "a pretty book." He knows that ours is a bloodstained planet but he knows also that it turns on its axis and moves round the sun with a dancer's grace, and his style defines the dancer as ballet-trained. For this reason Mr. Capote is often not taken as seriously as he should be, and it is possible that his new book, *In Cold Blood,* may be regarded simply as a literary *tour de force* instead of the formidable statement about reality which it is. . . . That Mr. Capote has invented nothing and recorded with a true ear and utter honesty is proved by the conversations in the book. The inhabitants of Holcomb, Kansas, do not on any page engage in the subtle and economical dialogue Mr. Capote ascribes to the characters in his novels. They speak the words which reporters hear when they interview the participants in prodigious events, and listen to with embarrassed ears. The stuff is corny, yet not just corny. The corn is celestial. Even the cleverest writer who tries to invent it achieves an obvious fakery, which is quite absent from this book.

(K)                          Rebecca West. *Harper.* Feb., 1966. p. 108

As the present writer has at times felt obliged to remark in print, a lot of what passes for sociological observation is only private fantasy, the pulse not to the patient but of the hypochondriac healer at the bedside. "Parajournalism" is Dwight Macdonald's perhaps too glamorous-sounding term for this "creative" reportage or social criticism. And parajournalism is detestable because, to the many real crises that now lurk and loom, it adds another and quite unnecessary one, a crisis of literary truthfulness.

I am myself convinced that *In Cold Blood* is not parajournalism. Its general authenticity is established, for me, by what I hope to show is a species of internal evidence. I do nevertheless wish that Mr. Capote had gone to the trouble of taking us into his confidence—perhaps by way of an appendix explaining his procedures—instead of covering his tracks as an interviewer and researcher, and of generally seeming to declaim, with Walt Whitman in one of his seizures of mystical clairvoyance, "I am there

. . . I witness the corpse with its dabbled hair, I note where the pistol has fallen." . . . In so far as the crime has a definable and possibly remedial cause, it lies in the nature of prisons, the kind of mentalities and associations apt to be fostered by prisons. For the rest the cause is something in the relationship of Smith and Hickock, a relationship so involuted and internal that it can be made believable, as Capote does make it, not through any of the usual formulas of partnership or palship, but solely in the shifting minutiae of their behavior from incident to incident.

(K)                                    F. W. Dupee. *NYR*. Feb. 3, 1966. pp. 3–4

The author [of *In Cold Blood*] is . . . deeply concerned with his people and the six lives that were lost. To this he adds an acute and sympathetic interpretation of their behavior. Indeed, one feels throughout the book that he is in the company of a highly perceptive, very civilized man who wants to understand but has no desire to instruct, judge, or condemn. The literary form may not be new, but, it must be conceded, this self-restraint assuredly is.

But the special brilliance of the achievement lies in the writing. This serves flawlessly and effortlessly the purposes of the narrative. . . . But the author's resources go far beyond narrative. The main actors are visible in all dimensions and precisely as they must be seen for the purposes of the history.

(K)                    John Kenneth Galbraith. *Reporter*. March 10, 1966.
                                                                    p. 58

Much has been made, in the unprecedented hullabaloo that surrounded the publication of *In Cold Blood,* of that book's inaugurating a "new literary genre." . . .

What Mr. Capote thinks he has discovered is already known to the world by a different name: history. History is the art of telling the truth, selectively (so that the reader may not strangle on vast accumulations of data) and gracefully (so that the reader will want to read in the first place). That is what Mr. Capote has done. If it is objected that history is usually concerned with larger issues, reflect what the similar ordeal of a 15th century family might be worth today to the historian, if he were lucky enough to find it written in such careful and well-authenticated detail. . . .

What Mr. Capote wants to do for his history, I take it, is what the novel can do for its subject matter: present it so compellingly that it escapes its relatively narrow base into universal significance. That is a commendable ambition in the historian, who is far more than the novelist committed to specifics. It is in terms of this problem that I apprehend Aristotle's dictum that poetry is truer than history. Even so, the best historians have always been able to present their facts so creatively and suggestively as to make small incidents serve great generalizations.

(K)                    Charles Alva Hoyt. *Columbia University Forum*. Winter, 1966. p. 53

See *The Selected Writings of Truman Capote; In Cold Blood* (reporting).

# CATHER, WILLA (1873–1947)

Willa Cather's best work is satisfying because it is sincere. In her books, there is none of the sweet reek that pervades the pages of so many "lady novelists." Love, to her, is "not a simple state, like measles." Her treatment of sex is without either squeamishness or sensuality. She loves the west, and the arts, particularly music, and she has sought to express feelings and convictions on these subjects. She tried, failed, and kept on trying until she succeeded.

Latrobe Carroll. *Bkm*. May, 1921. p. 215

Miss Cather's mind is basically static and retrospective, rich in images of fixed contours. . . . The characteristic quality of her mind . . . is not its puritanism or its idealism, but something deeper in which these are rooted. She is preeminently an artist dominated by her sense of the past, seeking constantly, through widely differing symbolisms, to recapture her childhood and youth. A sort of reverence for her own early years goes, hand in hand, with her Vergilian ancestor-worship; and out of this has flowered her finest work.

Clifton Fadiman. *Nation*. Dec. 7, 1932. pp. 564–5

It is idle to try to classify her neatly as a realist, or a "novelist of character," or as one who went "beyond naturalism," as a satirist or a romanticist. She is all of these things. She is Willa Cather, mobile, capable, sometimes great, always clear-cut, and most of the time interesting, a social commentator whose pen is never sharp enough to hurt anybody, and whose vision is frequently inspiring. In her court the human race is acquitted of the most serious charges against it and given a character. It is very grateful for it, being in sore need.

Harlan Hatcher. *Creating the Modern American Novel* (Farrar and Rinehart). 1935. p. 59

Miss Cather's turn to the ideals of a vanished time is the weary response to weariness, to that devitalization of spirit which she so brilliantly describes in the story of Professor St. Peter. It is a weariness which comes not merely from defeat but from an exacerbated sense of personal isolation and from the narrowing of all life to the individual's sensitivities, with the resulting loss of the objectivity that can draw strength from seeking the causes of things. But it is exactly Miss Cather's point that the Lucretian *rerum naturae* means little; an admirer of Virgil, she is content with the *lacrimae rerum,* the tears of things.

Lionel Trilling in After the Genteel Tradition, edited<br>by Malcolm Cowley (Norton). 1937. pp. 61–2

Miss Cather's style, grave, flexible, a little austere, wonderfully transparent, everywhere economical, is wonderfully apt for her purposes. There are certain things, to be sure, it cannot do. It cannot register wit or amusement or even humor, save rarely; it never rises to passionate indignation; it lacks earthiness, despite Miss Cather's profound belief in a normal relation with the earth. Dialogue, as she reports it, is seldom more than adequate. But within its boundaries it is beautiful writing, liquid to the ear, lucent to the eye. . . . There are few to whom the adjective "classic" can be more truly applied, for beneath the quick sympathy there is a Roman gravity, a sense of the dignity of life which contemporary fiction . . . has mainly lost.

Howard Mumford Jones. SR. Aug. 6, 1938. p. 16

Willa Cather's traditionalism was . . . anything but the arbitrary or patronizing opposition to contemporary ways which Irving Babbitt personified. It was a candid and philosophical nostalgia, a conviction and a standard possible only to a writer whose remembrance of the world of her childhood and the people in it was so overwhelming that everything after it seemed drab and more than a little cheap. Her distinction was not merely one of cultivation and sensibility; it was a kind of spiritual clarity possible only to those who suffer their loneliness as an act of the imagination and the will. . . . Later, as it seemed, she became merely sentimental, and her direct criticism of contemporary types and manners was often petulant and intolerant. But the very intensity of her nostalgia had from the first led her beyond nostalgia; it had given her the conviction that the values of the world she had lost were the primary values, and everything else merely their degradation.

Alfred Kazin. On Native Grounds (Reynal). 1942.<br>pp. 250–1

From beginning to end, the Cather novels are not stories of plot, but chronicles, given a depth and significance lacking in the merely historical chronicle by that "sympathy" which leads to a perfect interplay of environment and character.

Her art was essentially a representation of this reaction between the soul of man and its environment. That is why the best of her stories are told against the land. . . . Her own absorption in her people and her land creates the suspense that she herself has felt. . . . She is preservative, almost antiquarian, content with much space in little room—feminine in this, and in her passionate revelation of the values which conserve the life of the emotions.

Henry Seidel Canby. *SR*. May 10, 1947. pp. 23–4

From the whole range of Cather's values, standards, tastes, and prejudices, her tone is that of an inherent aristocrat in an equalitarian order, of an agrarian writer in an industrial order, of a defender of the spiritual graces in the midst of an increasingly materialistic culture. . . . Selecting and enhancing the most subtle effects of wealth, she has, rather like Sam Dodsworth's wife, either looked down upon or ignored the whole process of creating wealth. Writing so discreetly about the age when business was a personal adventure, she has neglected to mention the most typical forms of the adventure.

Maxwell Geismar. *The Last of the Provincials*
(Houghton). 1947. pp. 217–8

Mr. Maxwell Geismar wrote a book about her and some others called *The Last of the Provincials*. Not having read it I do not know his argument; but he has a case: she is a provincial; and I hope not the last. She was a good artist, and all true art is provincial in the most realistic sense: of the very time and place of its making, out of human beings who are so particularly limited by their situation, whose faces and names are real and whose lives begin each one at an individual unique center. Indeed, Willa Cather was a provincial as Hawthorne or Flaubert or Turgenev, as little concerned with aesthetics and as much with morals as Tolstoy, as obstinately reserved as Melville. In fact she always reminds me of very good literary company. . . . She is a curiously immovable shape, monumental, virtue itself in her work and a symbol of virtue—like certain churches, in fact, or exemplary women, revered and neglected.

Katherine Anne Porter. *The Days Before* (Harcourt).
1952. pp. 72–3

Her vision is of essences. In her earlier novels the essential subject, a state of mind or feelings, was enveloped in the massiveness of the conventional realistic novel. It was there but it was muffled. Then she saw that if she abandoned the devices of massive realism, if she depended on picture and symbol and style, she could disengage her essential subject and make it tell upon the reader with a greater directness and power, help it to remain uncluttered in his mind. The things that pass, the things that merely adhere to states of mind and feeling, she began to use with a severe and rigid economy. Her fiction became a kind of symbolism, with the depths and suggestions that belong to symbolist art, and with the devotion to a music of style and structure for which the great symbolists strove, Pater and Moore and the later Henry James.

E. K. Brown. *Willa Cather* (Knopf). 1953. p. 340

Miss Cather's central theme is that of people who pull themselves up by their bootstraps. . . . The inner voice of the early novels of Willa Cather suggests this fascination with, and need to describe, various forms of success—but also certain forms of failure. The drive to power in these books is overriding, with the result that the novels contain no complicated plots, no complexity of human relationships, no love affairs that we can take seriously. Her heroines, those women with feminized masculine names, Alexandra, Ántonia—and the name Alexandra itself reminds us of one of history's greatest conquerors—have tenacious wills and an extraordinary capacity for struggle.

(K) Leon Edel. *Willa Cather: The Paradox of Success*
(Library of Congress). 1960. p. 8

What she did not want to admit was that the heroic ideal is impossible in the age of the machine; this was the real source of her animus against science, technology, and the industrial revolution. . . . Willa Cather was unwilling to give up her belief in hero worship; when she saw it failing in the modern world, rather than adopt some other view she made a villain of life. . . . Because of Willa Cather's aversion to conflict and because the whole impulse of her being tended toward the expression of a single unified emotion or mood, I have regarded her novels as being not novels at all in the conventional sense but extended lyrics in prose.

(K) John H. Randall. *The Landscape and the Looking*
*Glass* (Houghton). 1960. p. 372

Willa Cather's principal symbol is the vast panorama of an untamed land. But it is a functionally complex symbol, accommodating several thematic levels, all inherently united. Note, for instance, that she sees the land as a meeting place for her idealistic pioneers, who find here both common cause and spiritual sanctuary. Yet she is impressed that the land or nature is an overwhelming force, often capable of exacting rigorous submission even while it may offer protection. But above all, she ever reminds us that the land is the manifestation of a divine, supersensible force.

(K) Edward A. Bloom and Lillian D. Bloom. *Willa Cather's*
*Gift of Sympathy* (Southern Illinois). 1962. p. 27

Although in her later years Willa Cather closed the door firmly on all but a fraction of the work that had preceded *O Pioneers!* and did her best to discourage inquiry concerning it, in interviews before she achieved world-wide fame as a novelist she made some illuminating statements concerning her literary beginnings. Her initial impulse to write, she told Latrobe Carroll in 1921, came from "an enthusiasm for a kind of country and a kind of people, rather than ambition."

(K)                    Mildred R. Bennett. Introduction to *Willa Cather's*
                       *Collected Short Fiction 1892–1912* (Nebraska). 1965.
                                                                    p. xxvi

The country has shrunk, and our sense of the weight and relevance of Willa Cather's observation of Nebraska has shrunk with it. Nebraska is no doubt still there, but as a distinct imaginative possibility it has for the moment simply disappeared. As in so many other cases we are left confronting the artist who has been abandoned by his ostensible subject. The artist we now see is one whose energies are largely lavished on defensive maneuver, on masquerade. The power she now exercises is a measure of the degree to which the masquerade is itself something American. It is a small power when compared with Whitman's, but it is, despite the shell-work of fictional convention, a power of the same kind which engages us in "Song of Myself": a delighted absorption in the capacity of the self to embrace the world. In Whitman this play is overt; in Willa Cather it is masked. . . . Whitman's acceptance of his role was not open to a woman; instead Willa Cather carried on a masquerade which made it appear that she was accepting the conditions of adulthood while actually rejecting them. It was a shrewd woman of 40 who published *O Pioneers!,* and discovered the terms of her disguise.

(K)                    Quentin Anderson. NR. Nov. 27, 1965. pp. 28, 31

The wonder is in that barren land that she ever existed, and some kind of homage must be paid to her success, such as it was. . . . Willa's case is classic, for she had every conceivable gift: an inborn genius, a unique life in a vital phase of history, the perfect education for writing, vigor of observation and depth of understanding, intellectual maturity, a passionate devotion to craft—and then some flaw defaced her every production such that even the most Nebraskan of critics is forced to qualify his praise.

(K)                    Robert Edson Lee. *From West to East* (Illinois).
                                                            1966. pp. 112–13

### My Antonia

In Antonia's contented domesticity Miss Cather offers a modern variation of an old theme. In the pages of Mrs. Stowe the latter stages of Antonia's career would have been treated as steps of abnegation, the surrender to a sense of duty in a home on earth which would be rewarded by a mansion prepared on high. By most contemporary novelists it would be treated as complete defeat, with no compensation here or hereafter. But Miss Cather with all her zest for studio life, has retained an imaginative regard for four walls and a hearthstone, and the vital experience of mothering a family.

Percy H. Boynton. *Some Contemporary Americans*
(Chicago). 1924. pp. 169–70

In *My Antonia,* Antonia Shimerda . . . became the symbol of emotional fulfillment in motherhood on a Western farm. The thesis was arresting, appearing as it did in 1918 at the very moment when farm and village life were coming under the critical eyes of the novelists intent upon exposing its pollution. Without satire or bitterness and with only a little sentimentalism, Willa Cather pictured a strong character developing under severe difficulties which would crush a less heroic soul, surviving the most primitive hardships in a sod hut, toiling like an ox in the field with the men, enduring want, cut off from ordinary pleasures, withstanding betrayal and the cheap life as a hired girl in a village, and emerging at last after such desperate conditions to a triumphant serenity as mother to a healthy group of shy, awkward but happy and laughing boys who are content with their life on the farm.

Harlan Hatcher. *Creating the Modern American
Novel* (Farrar and Rinehart). 1935. p. 66

## A Lost Lady

*A Lost Lady,* Miss Cather's most explicit treatment of the passing of the old order, is the central work of her career. Far from being the delicate minor book it is so often called, it is probably her most muscular story, for it derives its power from the grandeur of its theme. Miss Cather shares the American belief in the tonic moral quality of the pioneer's life; with the passing of the frontier she conceives that a great source of fortitude has been lost.

Lionel Trilling in *After the Genteel Tradition,* edited
by Malcolm Cowley (Norton). 1937. p. 55

*A Lost Lady* reflects a curious "sunset of the pioneer"—a prismatic sunset, an almost mythical pioneer. Admirable as the story is with reference to its human relationships and emotional values, and remarkable for its creation of an atmosphere, it is still a kind of touching fairy tale of the more beneficent robber barons, or their second or third cousins. It is a reflection not of a society but of a point of view that, increasingly narrow, selective, and fanciful, is actually retreating further and further from society.

Maxwell Geismar. *The Last of the Provincials*
(Houghton). 1947. p. 183

### Death Comes for the Archbishop

*Death Comes for the Archbishop* is a historical novel; it is also a regional novel and a deliberately picturesque novel, with natural description helping to set the emotional tone. . . . The ritual and beliefs of the Catholic Church, the heroic activity of missionary priests, and the vivid colors of the southwestern landscape combine to produce a new kind of warmth and vitality in her art. . . . Yet one wonders whether this lively creation of a golden world in which all ideals are realized is not fundamentally a "softer" piece of writing. . . . There is, it is true, a splendid sympathy in the treatment of the characters and a most genuine feeling for the period and natural setting in which the action is laid. But there is no indication here of an artist wrestling successfully with intractable material. The material is all too tractable, and the success, though it is real, seems too easy.

David Daiches. *Willa Cather* (Cornell). 1951. p. 105

See *O Pioneers!, My Antonia, A Lost Lady, The Professor's House, Death Comes for the Archbishop,* and *Shadows on the Rock* (novels).

# CHANDLER, RAYMOND (1888–1959)

Most of the characters in this story [*The Big Sleep*] are tough, many of them are nasty and some of them are both. . . . The language used in this book is often vile—at times so filthy that the publishers have been compelled to resort to the dash, a device seldom employed in these unsqueamish days. As a study in depravity, the story is excellent, with Marlowe standing out as almost the only fundamentally decent person in it.

Isaac Anderson. *NYT*. Feb. 12, 1939. p. 20

After a long and notable career in the pulp magazines, Raymond Chandler made his mark in books with four novels published between 1939 and 1943. Most critics and almost all readers recognized in him the legitimate successor of Dashiell Hammett. . . . His new novel, *The Little Sister,* has been awaited with as much eagerness as Hammett's ten-year promised novel—especially by those critics and readers who have felt that Hammett and Chandler are significant exponents not merely of the detective story, but of the American novel. It is partly, of course, the heightened expectation which makes *The Little Sister* seem unsatisfactory. But partly, too, dissatisfaction comes from the revelation of an abyss of emptiness.

Plot and characters are the stuff of any run-of-the-mill toughie. Chandler's treatment differs from the routine in his prose, which is still vigorous, clean, distinctive. . . . But the great distinction dividing this from all other detective stories is its scathing hatred of the human race. The characters, aside from the little sister, are reasonably well-painted cardboard, brought to life only by the sheer force of their viciousness.

Anthony Boucher. *NYT.* Sept. 25, 1949. p. 24

Mr. Chandler is a serious-minded man, and it would be unjust not to take him seriously. Few writers have been more mannered . . . or more uneven. His similes either succeed brilliantly or fall flat. He can write a scene with an almost suffocating vividness and sense of danger—if he does not add three words too many and make it funny. His virtues are all there. If, to some restraint, he could add the fatigue of construction and clues (the writer he most admires, Mr. Hammett, has never disdained clues and has always given them fairly)—then one day he may write a good novel.

John Dickson Carr. *NYT.* Sept. 24, 1950. p. 36

*The Long Goodbye* more than assuages the disappointment [over *The Little Sister*]. . . . On the whole, despite occasional outbursts of violence, it's a moody, brooding book, in which Marlowe is less a detective than a disturbed man of 42 on a quest for some evidence of truth and humanity. The dialogue is as vividly overheard as ever, the plot is clearly constructed and surprisingly resolved, and the book is rich in many sharp glimpses of minor characters and scenes. Perhaps the longest private-eye novel ever written . . . it is also one of the best—and may well attract readers who normally shun even the leaders in the field.

Anthony Boucher. *NYT.* April 25, 1954. p. 27

I pulled his leg about his plots, which always seem to me to go wildly astray. What holds the books together and makes them so compulsively readable, even to alpha minds who would not normally think of reading a thriller, is the dialogue. There is a throw-away, down-beat quality about Chandler's dialogue, whether wise-cracking or not, that takes one happily through chapter after chapter in which there is no more action than Philip Marlowe driving his car and talking to his girl, or a rich old woman consulting her lawyer on the sun porch. His aphorisms were always his own.

Ian Fleming. *Lon.* Dec., 1959. p. 50

The writer of mystery novels, if he takes his work seriously, must find his situation maddening. His books may be relished by highly cultivated people and his literary skills widely admired, but through all the praise there will run a streak of condescension. Even his most ardent fans will never take him quite seriously, and their loftiest compliment is only too likely to be the suggestion that he ought to be writing "real" novels.

The frustrations this situation can provoke are vividly demonstrated in the letters of Raymond Chandler which have now been published, together with some essays, notes on writing, and scraps of fiction [*Raymond Chandler Speaking*] three years after his death. . . . They differ from most letters in that they are as gripping as any novel. They are cantankerous, forthright, and often hilarious. . . . But what they reveal most clearly is the anguish of a man who considered himself an artist but knew that he was generally regarded as merely a brilliant hack. . . .

Sarel Eimerl. *Reporter*. May 10, 1962. pp. 54–5

Mr. Raymond Chandler has written that he intends to take the body out of the vicarage garden and give the murder back to those who are good at it. If he wishes to write detective stories, i.e., stories where the reader's principal interest is to learn who did it, he could not be more mistaken, for in a society of professional criminals, the only possible motives for desiring to identify the murderer are blackmail or revenge, which both apply to individuals, not to the group as a whole, and can equally well inspire murder. Actually, whatever he may say, I think Mr. Chandler is interested in writing, not detective stories, but serious studies of a criminal milieu, the Great Wrong Place, and his powerful but extremely depressing books should be read and judged, not as escape literature, but as works of art.

W. H. Auden. *The Dyer's Hand* (Random). 1962. p. 151

Chandler's hero is the all-American boy with whom the reader easily identifies himself, the rough man of action who would never harm a fly but would stamp out injustice with a vigorous passion. Thematically, Chandler's work is in one of the mainstreams of American literature, not the nineteenth-century New England one of concern for the brooding thoughts of the introvert, but the broad stream of frontier literature that moved from Georgia of the 1830's to the California of the 1950's— enveloping as it traveled westward the simple problems of the extrovert who, by knowing right from wrong, had only to exert a courageous amount of rugged individualism in order to end up a hardened but virtuous hero. This mainstream of American literature contributed thousands of modern morality plays, of which Chandler's are excellently written examples.

T. S. Eliot discovered his poetic home in England; Eugene O'Neill rarely strayed from the Atlantic or its seaboard; Raymond Chandler found

Los Angeles to be the natural milieu for his hero's efforts to untangle the messy web into which the American man had naively wandered.

Philip Durham. *Down These Mean Streets a Man Must Go: Raymond Chandler's Knight* (North Carolina). 1963. pp. 5–6

The obvious accomplishment of his thrillers is to generate a sort of nervous tension which is the literary analogue to the tension generated by being an American. . . . Chandler's attitude is to look at what's there in the expectation that good and evil are all mixed together. . . . It is a stoic vision. In his novels Chandler did not quite sustain it, being much too romantic and not quite courageous enough to bear the full bitterness of that vision. . . . If you say that all this provides somewhat meager fare for romance, I must agree. But if you say that this distorts life beyond recognition, I must object that you do not know that meager region, Southern California, as well as Chandler did. His chief accomplishment, it seems to me, is to create for the place a fictional image which corresponds to the actuality more vividly and more accurately than anything written by anyone else. . . . Still, Chandler's version is not *the* version of Southern California. He, rather more than is strategic in a writer, puts himself at the mercy of the place's notion of itself; for this notion is self-deceiving, somewhat inaccurate and confused.

George P. Elliott. *A Piece of Lettuce* (Random). 1964. pp. 54–5, 58, 63

See *The Big Sleep, Farewell, My Lovely, The Lady in the Lake, The Little Sister, The Long Goodbye* (novels); *The Simple Art of Murder* (essay); *Raymond Chandler Speaking* (letters and essays).

# CHEEVER, JOHN (1912–    )

As examples of fiction from *The New Yorker,* these stories of Mr. Cheever's [*The Way Some People Live*] are among the best that have appeared there recently, and this is particularly true of those which exploit a cool and narrow-eyed treatment of tensions arising from the war. Mr. Cheever's drunken draft-dodger and his young draftee are particularly well managed, and the sketches in which they appear are quite unblemished by the pieties and embarrassments which ordinarily mark war fiction published while a war is on. Many of the other stories—and if my count is right, all but six of the thirty included here are from *The New Yorker*—have not improved by their being collected in a book. As individual magazine stories they seemed better than they are; read one after another, there nearly identical lengths, similarities of tone and situation, and their somehow remote and unambitious style, produce an effect of sameness and eventually of tedium. The formula has been flourished too obviously and too often.

Weldon Kees. *NR*. April 19, 1943. p. 576

The sense of drama in ordinary events and people; the underlying and universal importance of the outwardly unimportant; a deep feeling for the perversities and contradictions, the worth and unexpected dignity of life, its ironies, comedies, and tragedies. All of this explained in a style of his own, brief, apparently casual, but carefully selected; unaccented until the accent is needed. . . .

John Cheever has only two things to fear; a hardening into an especial style that might become an affectation, and a deliberate casualness and simplicity that might become the same. Otherwise, the world is his.

Struthers Burt. *SR*. April 24, 1943. p. 9

It is niggardly to complain of Mr. Cheever, for he almost always writes very well, and with a kind of hinted eloquence which is hard to find these days; but looking back at "Of Love: A Testimony," one sees that he could write not only well, but wonderfully, and one begins to quarrel with him because he does not.

The reason is not far to seek. . . . [He] limits himself . . . to the conventions of magazine realism and the kind of statement that realism is capable of making.

Mark Schorer. *YR*. Summer, 1943. pp. xii–xiv

He does not so much imagine experience as have clever ideas for stories. There are [in *The Enormous Radio and Other Stories*] the ingenious camera-angles, the elevator operators (two of these) and the apartment-house superintendents, very cute and innocent and staring wide-eyed at quality folk. There are the neat discoveries of commonplace morals in sophisticated lives. When Mr. Cheever tries for the big idea, his stories waver toward a formally—and therefore morally—ambiguous melodrama. . . . These are the stories of a clever short-story manufacturer, a man who has ideas about experience but has never known these ideas in experience. Their language and technique are highly refined; their feeling is crude.

Arthur Mizener. *NR*. May 25, 1953. pp. 19–20

*The Wapshot Chronicle* is an antique bureau filled with everything and apparently everybody under the sun. . . .

Roughly the first third of the book is devoted to life in this charming old river town. Most of the rest is about the fortunes and misfortunes of the two sons, Moses and Coverly, in Washington, New York, San Francisco, Island 93 in the South Pacific, a rocket launching settlement in the West, and an imported castle inhabited by an ancient Wapshot cousin named Justina and her toothsome ward, Melissa.

As readers of Cheever's short stories know, he is a wonder with the limited scene, the separate episode, the overheard conversation, the crucial confrontation. *The Wapshot Chronicle* reflects these powers with immense vitality, largesse, and profusion. But it is held together largely by spit and wire. It shows that while John Cheever's fortes are many, amusing, touching, and admirable, one of them is not architectonics.

Carlos Baker. SR. March 23, 1957. p. 14

This is . . . a central theme in Mr. Cheever's work: the power of human love and desire, which turns out to be a shield for human loneliness and melancholy—along with a note of broad farce, or of downright burlesque at times, which accompanies the tragicomedy of sex. It is at this point that [*The Wapshot Chronicle*] breaks through the proper confines of "sensibility" in the typical *New Yorker* story. The depth of the narrative lies in the accent on human "unrequital" and in the lyrical apostrophes to the sea-born Venus, to love and women. The ironic twist lies in the antics of lovers. . . . The last half of the book is a picaresque of modern times set against the earlier, nostalgic background of the New England past. The two parts don't quite hang together, and the story as a whole becomes rather fragmentary and episodic. One has the final impression of a series of related "sketches," which do not quite achieve either the impact of the short story proper or the inner growth and development of a novel.

Maxwell Geismar. NYT. March 24, 1957. p. 5

John Cheever possesses the love of created things in abundance. . . . *The Wapshot Chronicle* abounds in lights and colors and smells, but especially in the lights, colors and smells of water—a bay, a trout lake—for "all things of the sea belong to Venus," and Venus with her son Eros are the true heroine and hero of Mr. Cheever's novel. . . . Fans of Mr. Cheever's short stories laid in Manhattan know how this bottomlessly sophisticated writer can use the device of an innocent eye to reveal the grotesqueries inherent in what we all see and live every day. That grotesquerie is present in *The Wapshot Chronicle,* and also Cheever's awareness of the loneliness and sense of defeat that visit most of us; but all is overlaid with the gently reassuring atmosphere of a fairy tale for grownups.

William Esty. Com. May 17, 1957. p. 187

For years every discussion of what constitutes a typical *New Yorker* short story has got around to Cheever, the common view being that he is quite representative and yet a good deal better than average. . . . He is one of the sharpest of observers, and some of his descriptions of suburban scenes are a pure joy. He has also developed an admirable technique for handling a complex series of incidents, so that such a story as "The Trouble of Marcie Flint" has a remarkable density. But his great gift is for entering into the minds of men and women at crucial moments. . . . Cheever knows where drama is to be found, and he has taught himself how to make the most of it.

Granville Hicks. SR. Sept. 13, 1958. pp. 33, 47

What Cheever's well-heeled admirers want is what, by an ultimate failure of sensibility he recedes into giving them: an exercise in sophisticated self-criticism, together with a way back into the situation as before. This isn't to say that he has nothing else to give; only that the extravagance of esteem for him has psychological, not esthetic origins. . . For Cheever, with all his wit and sophistication and his coldness of eye, is essentially a sentimentalist and usually contrives to let his fish off the hook. It is never clearer than when he is opposing something to the toreador pants and sterile parties and waspishness of suburban marriages. The land of deliverance he prays for is wholesome and American: "the trout streams of our youth," a lighthearted game of softball, bright welcoming lights behind the picture window. Or else it is romantic and "deep"—the "churches of Venice" or islands in the "purple autumn sea."

Richard Gilman. Com. Dec. 19, 1958. p. 320

His first novel and best book, <i>The Wapshot Chronicle</i> (1957), was decorated with lively quotations from an old New Englander's autobiography, but its hero was a rocket technician. His four volumes of short stories tell of marital agonies and failures of love not wholly unheard-of in the past, but invariably these agonies have a spot news quality. . . . Cheever is never angry, merely sad; his own range of feeling extends only to a generalizing pity for human helplessness; he neither claims nor possesses a massive power of intellect. And as should be added, unrelenting contemporaneousness is, in his fiction, a form of built-in obsolescence. (The march of events is already overtaking some of Cheever's newsy tales— "The Enormous Radio" for one.) But if this writer is what is called a minor figure, he is also an American original: witty, suggestive, intelligent, aware of the endless fascination of the junk with which his world and ours is furnished, and able almost at will to make his audience laugh out loud. There are fewer than half a dozen living American writers of fiction for whom more than this can be said.

Benjamin DeMott. Harper. Feb., 1964. pp. 111–12

It is the peculiar and original genius of Novelist John Cheever to see his chosen subject—the American middle class entering the second decade of the Affluent Society—as figures in an Ovidian netherworld of demons. Commuterland, derided by cartoonists and deplored by sociologists as the preserve of the dull-spirited status seeker, is given by Cheever's fables the dignity of the classical theater. . . .

Cheever's art deals less with what is called character and idiosyncrasy than with archetypes: father, son, brother, husband, wife, lover, seen in situations so intensely felt as to claim universality. His people move like characters in classic drama; the actors wear their fixed masks and are not expected to change one mask for another in the course of the action. Over the formal masks are fitted others modeled in the naturalistic detail required by the conventions of realism. He is able to give to the abstract personalia of this theater a local habitation and a name—a habitation so truly seen in detail that it becomes more real than the town's tax rolls. But the easygoing realism that accepts wife-swapping or any impiety of evaded obligation with a sociological shrug enrages him, for at bottom he is a New England moralist.

*Time*. March 27, 1964. p. 66

Most of John Cheever's people, even the wicked ones, are wistful secret angels—like seraphim they have their errands and burdens, only nobody notices. That nobody ever notices is the real scandal of *The Wapshot Scandal*. It is, also, in a way, Cheever's own scandal as a writer. . . . [In] the latest Wapshot novel the chief character is the 20th century, and now everything but Cheever's prose has deteriorated and grown corrupt. . . . Confronted by vulgarity and evil, Cheever takes a cautious step backward, shuts his eyes, waves his fastidious wand, and ping! vulgarity and evil are all at once redeemed by a secret beauty—"the abandoned buildings with the gantries above them had a nostalgic charm," he writes of the weapons site. Ping!

And exactly this sentimental disposition in the Wapshots and in his rendering of them is what Cheever himself seems not to have noticed. His ironic exposures add up only to a lightweight comic deceptiveness . . . The larger deception implicit in his novel—the victory of supermarket and hardware culture over our better hopes—is lost finally in Cheever's hesitancy to push his irony to the hurting point, and to push right through the shield of his fantasy.

Cynthia Ozick. *Cmty*. July, 1964. pp. 66–7

Cheever writes in a relaxed, seemingly casual but thoroughly disciplined manner; his general mood is a compound of skepticism, compassion, and wry humor; he is concerned with the complexities, tensions, and disappointments of life in a strictly contemporary world, a world of little men and women, non-heroic, non-spectacular, non-exceptional. . . . He is concerned with the loneliness which festers beneath the facade of apparently "happy" or "successful" individuals; he suggests the potential terror or violence inherent in the metropolitan apartment-dweller's condition. Beneath the often placid, impeccably depicted surfaces of his stories there is a reservoir of excitement or unrest which is capable or erupting into violence; his well-mannered characters walk a tightrope which at any moment may break; the vast, shining city masks cruelty, injustice, and evil.

William Peden. *The American Short Story* (Houghton).
1964. pp. 47–8

See *The Way Some People Live, The Enormous Radio and Other Stories, The Housebreaker of Shady Hill and Other Stories, Some People, Places and Things That Will Not Appear in My Next Novel, The Brigadier and the Golf Widow* (stories); *The Wapshot Chronicle, The Wapshot Scandal* (novels).


# CHOPIN, KATE (1851–1904)

No writer of the period was more spontaneously and inevitably a story teller. There is an ease and a naturalness about her work that comes from more than mere art. She seldom gave to a story more than a single sitting, and she rarely revised her work, yet in compression of style, in forebearance, in the massing of materials, and in artistry she ranks with even the masters of the period. . . . She was emotional, she was minutely realistic, and . . . used dialect sometimes in profusion; she was dramatic and even at times melodramatic, yet never was she commonplace or ineffective. She had command at times of a pervasive humor and a pathos that gripped the reader before he was aware, for behind all was the woman herself. She wrote as Dickens wrote, with abandonment, with her whole self. There is art in her work, but there is more than art.

Fred Lewis Pattee. *A History of American Literature
Since 1870* (Century). 1915. pp. 364–5

Kate Chopin belongs to the artistic realism of today, as well as to her own generation. This generation sees life, or reality, differently from any generation before it. The literary artist in his absorbing process is no longer a discoverer, no longer a refiner, still less a dictator, but an observer at best, with an impulse to state his impressions clearly. And if one were to ask in what way after all Kate Chopin differs from a pastmaster in the short story art, say, de Maupassant, the answer may be that she blesses while he bewailed the terrible clearsightedness which is the strength and the anguish of every good writer. . . .

*The Awakening* follows the current of erotic morbidity that flowed strongly through the literature of the last two decades of the nineteenth century. The end of the century became a momentary dizziness over an abyss of voluptuousness, and Kate Chopin in St. Louis experienced a partial attack of the prevailing artistic vertigo. The philosophy of Schopenhauer, the music of Wagner, the Russian novel, Maeterlinck's plays—all this she absorbed. *The Awakening* in her case is the result—an impression of life as a delicious agony of longing.

In *The Awakening* under her touch the Creole life of Louisiana glowed with a rich exotic beauty. The very atmosphere of the book is voluptuous, the atmosphere of the Gulf Coast, a place of strange and passionate moods.

Daniel Rankin. *Kate Chopin and Her Creole Stories*
(Pennsylvania). 1932. pp. 170, 175

In the work of Kate Chopin . . . , it is not the glamour of the Creole past but the emotional life of a passionate people with which she is concerned. Her work is significant indeed not in terms of quantity but of quality. Her output was not large, but she carried the art of the short story to a height which even [George Washington] Cable did not surpass. . . . Mrs. Chopin's last novel, *The Awakening* . . . , caused a storm of unfavorable criticism. . . . The reality of the book is striking, in its revelation of the shifting moods of a passionate woman, and it is told with admirable economy. But the basic fault lies in Edna's utter selfishness, which deprives her of sympathy. The standards are Continental rather than Creole, and the novel belongs rather among studies of morbid psychology than local color.

Arthur H. Quinn. *American Fiction* (Appleton-
Century). 1936. pp. 354–7

The works of Kate Chopin, who wrote largely as a pastime, include only two short novels and two thin volumes of stories. But a few of her tales, based on observations made during her stay of some fifteen years in Louisiana, are little masterpieces. Like Grace King, she is best at picturing women, but she shows greater variety in the classes from which her characters are drawn.

Arlin Turner. *SR*. April 30, 1938. p. 4

But there was one novel of the nineties in the South that should have been remembered, one small perfect book that mattered more than the whole life-work of many a prolific writer, a novel of Kate Chopin, who wrote Creole stories, like one or two others in New Orleans who carried on the vein of George W. Cable. *The Awakening* was more mature than even the best of Cable's work, so effortless it seemed, so composed in its naturalness and grace was this tragic tale of Grand Isle, the fashionable New Orleans summer resort where the richer merchants deposited their wives and children. There, with the carelessness and lightness of a boy, the young Creole idler Robert awakened, with sorrowful results, from the dull dream of her existence the charming young woman whose husband adored her while he made the sad mistake of leaving her alone with her reveries and vague desires.

Van Wyck Brooks. *The Confident Years: 1885–1915* (Dutton). 1952. p. 341

There is a good deal of marital instability in the fiction of Kate Chopin, whether she writes of Acadians or New Orleans Creoles. She was bilingual and translated Maupassant. The situations in her first novel [*At Fault*] were already rather uncomfortable from the point of view of conventional morality; but in the central one she followed the then standard procedure of getting rid of an undesirable wife by having her accidentally drowned so that the lovers might be finally united. In 1899, however, she published a novel, *The Awakening,* quite uninhibited and beautifully written, which anticipates D. H. Lawrence in its treatment of infidelity.

Edmund Wilson. *Patriotic Gore* (Oxford). 1962. p. 590

In detail, *The Awakening* has the easy candor and freedom appropriate to its theme. It admits that human beings are physical bodies as well as moral and social integers and that spirit acts not only by sublimation but directly through the body's life. Not many English or American novels of the period had come so far. And its successive scenes—of household, country place, cafe garden, dinner party, and race track—are vividly realized. Kate Chopin seems to have paid some attention to the recently translated *Anna Karenina* and its extraordinary clairvoyance of observation. (Her short stories . . . are less successful, relying excessively on Maupassantesque twists of ironic revelation on the last page. But the people in them are real physical presences; invariably they strike us as having actual body, breath, color and temperature.)

Warner Berthoff. *The Ferment of Realism: American Literature, 1884–1919* (Free). 1965. p. 89

. . . there are two respects in which Mrs. Chopin's novel [*The Awakening*] is *harder* than Flaubert's [*Madame Bovary*], more ruthless, more insistent on truth of inner and social life as sole motivation. Edna Pontellier has her first affair out of sexual hunger, without romantic furbelow. . . . And, second, Mrs. Chopin uses no equivalent of the complicated financial maneuvers with which Flaubert finally corners his heroine. Edna kills herself solely because of the foredoomed emptiness of life stretching ahead of her. It is purely a psychological motive, untouched by plot contrivance.

The patent theme is in its title (a remarkably simple one for its day): the awakening of a conventional young woman to what is missing in her marriage, and her refusal to be content. Below that theme is the still-pertinent theme of the disparity between woman's sexual being and the rules of marriage. And below *that* is the perennial theme of nature versus civilization.

Stanley Kauffmann. *NR*. Dec. 3, 1966. p. 38

See *At Fault, The Awakening* (novels); *Bayou Folk, A Night in Acadie* (stories).

# CIARDI, JOHN (1916–    )

Evidently of immigrant family, Ciardi searches out for himself the meaning of America for his own generation. Undoubtedly he is well acquainted with the English poet, Auden. His technique, at best, stems from Auden. Weaker passages hint MacLeish. But, more important, he proves that for the young American poets as for the English, the personal themes of love, friendship and family relationships cannot be divorced from the social theme. . . . He can write . . . the symbolic lyric—and beautifully. But for his purposes—the precise representation of the American scene without utopian thinking, and of the growing psychology of general apprehension —his poetry of statement rather more than that of song or of violent image is successful.

Eda Lou Walton. *NYT*. Feb. 25, 1940. p. 5

The poems have a youthful ring which it is pleasant to come upon, and it is a tone not obscured by echoes. That Ciardi seems fresher than most poets is probably due to the fact that he is content with getting a scene down on paper, sometimes sprawlingly, but with care for the truth of it. He is not yet concerned to any great extent with interpretation.

Coleman Rosenberger. *NR*. July, 1940. p. 36

Unlike Eliot, who is only one of his "ancestors," Ciardi likes humanity well enough to satirize with warm wit, rather than with cold distaste. There is throughout his work a personality that expands to encompass the experiences of his fellows.

His considerable wit shows itself not only in the surprising juxtaposition of images, ideas, and language . . . but also in the rhythms and stanzaic forms. . . . But make no mistake—he deals in serious matters. His sense of the ironic gives him that authority (only the humorous should be allowed to be serious).

Gerard Previn Meyer. *SR*. Dec. 6, 1947. p. 60

John Ciardi is a poet of genuine if unequal gifts, whose best poetry has wit, perception and humanity. His greatest fault is lack of poetic liveliness, which derives not from any dullness of imagery or conventionality of vision but from rhythmic monotony. . . . But this fault Mr. Ciardi shares with many distinguished modern poets, including, in some degree, Eliot himself. His virtues are more individual and more interesting. . . . Ciardi produc(es) poetry both intelligible and mature, poetry which draws upon all the resources which the modern tradition has made available to the poet without losing touch with the reader.

David Daiches. *NYHT*. Jan. 1, 1950. p. 6

Mr. Ciardi's poetry depends on the world of his imagination as much as it does on the world in which he is living, and, they are not discrete but interdependent essences. Therefore, he writes a poetry that is psychologically sound as he exercises his wit, satire, and compassion with precise control. He may be acidulous, but he is genuinely humane.

I. L. Salomon. *SR*. Jan. 28, 1956. p. 24

The most notable thing about John Ciardi's *As If* is a kind of crude power. The hesitations, reticences, and inabilities of the poetic nature—for to be able to say what it does say is to be unable to say everything else—are unknown to natures of such ready force, natures more akin to those of born executives, men ripe for running things. This writer uses Stevens's, or Shapiro's, or half a dozen other poets' tricks and techniques as easily, and with as much justification as a salesman would use a competitor's sales-talk —it works, doesn't it? But he doesn't use the styles as delicately and helplessly as these poets used them—after all, he *can* help himself, has helped himself. . . . He is much at his best as a translator where his native force can put on a more sensitive and individual mask—his translation of the *Inferno* has more narrative power, strength of action, than any other I know.

Randall Jarrell. *YR*. Spring, 1956. p. 479

The one theme which stands out above others which could be cited in Mr. Ciardi's variously paced poetry is a concern with time, a concern which shows itself in the birthday poems, the elegies, the family poems . . . and those poems in which the poet mediates on the history and meaning of man. . . . Several of these poems which explore history and childhood are, at bottom, the signs of the poet's encounter with the hard old fact of death. The transiency of human life and all human things is a theme as old as poetry but Mr. Ciardi's version is so modern as to be almost fashionable. He faces time, death and change under the contemporary shadow of man's existential nothingness. . . . Yet the sweat of the engagement is real and is his own.

Ernest Sandeen. *Poetry*. July, 1956. p. 267

The best thing about John Ciardi is his personality. He is singularly unlike most American poets with their narrow lives and feuds. He is more like a very literate, gently appetitive, Italo-American airplane pilot, fond of deep simple things like his wife and kids, his friends and students, Dante's verse and good food and wine. The next best thing about John Ciardi is his poetry. It is truly refreshing. It is singularly free from the vices that beset most American poets nowadays, with their provincial imitations of English-Baroque verse and their trivial ambiguities. . . . These are good poems—clear, intimate and living.

Kenneth Rexroth. *NYT*. Aug. 3, 1958. p. 6

His poems show the same lack of subterfuge, perhaps even of nuance, as his editorial deeds. Everything is stated as it arises, with a curbed vigor rather than with mystery or subtlety. This poetry is the spectrum of a whole man who, however antic he may be in life, feels in his art no need to strike literary poses. . . . He is at times as good a phrasemaker as Dylan Thomas, but more sparing in his effects. . . . His phrases are the body, often the naked body, and not the clothing of his thought.

Dilys Laing. *Nation*. Sept. 13, 1958. p. 138

Most of the pieces in this book [*Dialogue with an Audience*] will be familiar to librarians, having first appeared in *The Saturday Review* where the author has been poetry editor since 1955. The book is composed of five general sections: "Dialogues," "Controversies," "Robert Frost," "On Reading and Writing," and "The Situation of Poetry." Included is the celebrated review of Anne Morrow Lindbergh's *The Unicorn and Other Poems* which precipitated such a wrath of indignation on the poor poetry editor's head. As interesting as that article is, it is not nearly so interesting as the reaction it provoked. Here are the letters that constituted "the biggest storm of reader protest in the thirty-three-year history of *The Saturday Review*." If "Controversies" is the most sensational part of *Dialogue with an Audience* (is this what makes the book so heavy?), this reviewer preferred the quieter pieces on Dante, Robert Frost, and poetry in general. Although Mr. Ciardi's style is marred by repetition and the relentless underlining of the obvious (e.g., "On Writing and Bad Writing"), he is a passionate partisan of poetry, a veritable Roman candle who strikes sparks.

(K)                              John C. Pine. *LJ*. Jan. 1, 1964. p. 108

He has not God's loveliest gift to poets, the gift of breathing in impressions and letting them gather in silence into a perfect richness. He is a controversialist, a banger-together of arguments, an anecdotalist of sorts, full of memories of his childhood in an Italian immigrant family. He likes to make loud noises, sometimes to impress a political point, sometimes in wryly comic deference to the family life he remembers, sometimes out of sheer exuberance and a purely technical interest in being noisy like Ezra Pound's when he was writing "Sestina: Altaforte." . . . And yet the quieter sensitivity that links him at times with Mr. [Richard] Wilbur is never altogether absent. . . . It is precisely this felt sensitivity, present but neglected in so many poems that leap about and shout and run as fast as their impatient metric can carry them, that is irritating in his poetry.

(K)                          M. L. Rosenthal. *Reporter*. Feb. 15, 1962. p. 50

The pressure of imagination is very low. Sometimes he rises above the dead level, with tenderness or good humor, but never does he surprise us. Now and then he remembers that he is a poet, and uses a word that has poetic pretensions. . . . But poetry is not a matter of mechanics, it is a vision; and vision Mr. Ciardi has not got.

(K)                          Louis Simpson. *HdR*. Spring, 1963. p. 134

See *As If, I Marry You, In the Stoneworks, In Fact* (poetry); *How Does a Poem Mean?, Dialogue with an Audience* (criticism).

# CLARK, WALTER VAN TILBURG (1909–    )

The tendency to explain, to probe, to analyze, is certainly more characteristic of the people of the eastern half of this country than it is of Westerners. Though born in the East, Walter Van Tilburg Clark is a Westerner in sympathy and spirit. Like the large landscapes with which the book is filled, his style is ample and spacious rather than compact. The reader whose life is not leisurely may find himself skipping paragraphs. . . . The dialogue is never false but it lacks the impact of character, and there is no humor.

William Maxwell. *SR*. June 2, 1945. p. 13

He is a storyteller before he is a moralist, a writer before he is a philosopher. . . . What makes him a serious writer, to my mind, is that he can write with parables which are as absorbing for their telling as for their moral. . . . It may just be that Walter Van Tilburg Clark is a Young Lochinvar coming riding out of the West to the American novel's rescue.

Hilary H. Lyons. *Holiday*. Oct. 1949. p. 20

(*The Watchful Gods*) reinforces our awareness of that combination of personal integrity and artful concentration which, aside from his Western settings, is the trade-mark of Mr. Clark's talent. . . . The activities of the Western setting seem always to be under examination, as though the author recognized the challenge to investigate the relationship of the human being to an environment which has too often frustrated the attempts of the writer to subdue it.

Mr. Clark's nature is not the idyllic world of nineteenth-century romanticism; neither is it a world of irrational malevolence such as that portrayed by our literary naturalists. Nature represents, rather, a stage whereon man's actions of necessity become more clearly defined.

Ray B. West, Jr. *SR*. Sept. 30, 1950. pp. 17–8

The difficulty is not that Mr. Clark is too much preoccupied with man's relation to the forces of nature but rather that he is apparently so little interested in the relations that exist between men, except in those limited areas where people have differing conceptions of their connection with the natural world. . . . When in 306 pages of short stories (*The Watchful Gods*) perhaps only 15 contain any dialogue, aside from people talking to animals, one must inevitably consider the extent of their relevance to the human situation, and one must wonder whether the writer's horizons are not bounded on the one hand by the hawk and on the other by the boy with the twenty-two.

Harvey Swados. *Nation*. Oct. 7, 1950. p. 318

Clark's world is spiritually the world of the rural American, consisting of Nature, on the one hand, and Man on the other. . . . In all of Clark's fiction his exceptionally acute observations of outdoor sound, light, smell, mass, texture, and relationship are superior to his understanding of the human psyche in any but a decivilised area of operation. There is no living American writer of fiction who can type a richer page of landscape but no writer of equal talent is more endangered by the inability to enrich his human types.

Vernon Young. *AQ*. Summer, 1951. pp. 110–1

## The Track of the Cat

*The Track of the Cat* deals with a great theme in American fiction, perhaps the greatest: the pursuit of an enemy in nature. . . . Clark localizes his theme in the attempt by a family of brothers to track down a great black panther during a mountain blizzard. His story is continuously and wonderfully exciting. He is able to bring before the reader with extraordinary vividness the clash of stubborn wills in the snow-bound ranchhouse, the unpopulated mountain landscape, the snow and cold, and above all, the hunt itself.

Paul Pickrel. *YR.* Autumn, 1949. pp. 190–1

There is an artistic unity and simplicity in *The Track of the Cat,* but there is also some of the looseness and apparent capriciousness of events which are in life. The actions have implications that go far beyond their limited context. . . . You can take *The Track of the Cat* as a symbolic, universal drama of Man against an implacable Evil Principle, forever stalking him, and you can ponder its implied question: If humility and violence meet the same end, is it a stalemate? Or you may enjoy it, without mysticism, as a stark story of man struggling with elemental antagonists in nature.

Edmund Fuller. *SR.* June 4, 1949. pp. 9–10

*The Track of the Cat* is one of the great American novels of "place." Something of its nobility should be suggested by the fact that one cannot bring to mind a similar novel of its kind that is quite worthy of comparison. One thinks of the best in the genre, even of such work as Elisabeth Madox Roberts' *The Tree of Man* and Willa Cather's *My Antonia,* and they come to seem, by comparison, more than ever like miniature studies of special manners, more than graceful surely, yet without grandeur. Mr. Clark's new novel likewise transcends his own earlier books. . . . *The Track of the Cat* may well be the achievement that twentieth-century American regionalism has needed to justify itself.

Mark Schorer. *NYT.* June 5, 1949. p. 1

See *The Ox-Bow Incident, The City of Trembling Leaves,* and *The Track of the Cat* (novels); also *The Watchful Gods* (short stories).

# CONDON, RICHARD (1915–    )

Mr. Condon shows himself well able to construct an exciting tale of crime on traditional lines, with all the homey concomitants of violence, double-cross, and rubbings-out. . . . Mr. Condon has placed his story [*The Oldest Confession*] in a Spanish setting so wild as to interfere with this enjoyable reading. We are constantly breaking off to laugh aloud or to rub our eyes and wonder if we really see what we think we do. . . . Mr. Condon can also be funny when he means to be. But the unconscious efforts remain, for me, the best.

Honor Tracy. *SR.* June 14, 1958. pp. 39–40

Unlike most other first novels, Richard Condon's [*The Oldest Confession*] is a fully controlled job of writing rather than an ardent grope. Written throughout with painstaking grace, not one scene or description is ever thrown away or treated in a commonplace manner. . . .

And yet the one thing its author is unable to convey is any feeling of depth, of real mortality unfolding before the reader. The deterioration of James Bourne, ivy-league master criminal, is singularly unmoving even as one stunningly dramatic scene or ingenious plot turn follows another. . . . If, the next time out, he can manage to open up and write more personally without marring his exceedingly refined sense of literary form, then we shall really be seeing a book. As things are now, no apologies are necessary to anyone for this is quite an impressive debut.

Gerald Walker. *NYT*. June 22, 1958. p. 18

Richard Condon has found an original way of avoiding the second-novel problem. Last year he published his stimulating *The Oldest Confession*. Now in *The Manchurian Candidate* he comes up, simultaneously as it were, with his second, third, and fourth volumes. Within two covers he compresses (a) a breathlessly up-to-date thriller, gimmicked to the gills, from judo to narco-hypnosis; (b) a psychoanalytic horror tale about (what else?) a mother and a son; and (c) an irate socio-political satire that tries to flay our shibboleths alive.

Into all three stories Mr. Condon wades with the same brash, flat vim and with widely varying degrees of skill. . . . Mr. Condon is a fervently vivid, phrase-prone writer whose every sentence packs a compulsory punch. As soon as he becomes aware of an insight, he hits it home promptly with such might that the bang often drowns out the meaning. When it comes to the rendition of mental states his typewriter really stutters.

His verbal manner fits much more happily into the satirical portions of *The Manchurian Candidate*. . . . Here Mr. Condon brings into play his true gift: a villainous flair for the ribald anecdote. His account of the sexual misadventures of a Senator is a wonderfully mean little masterpiece. The ignition and confusion of Washington's publicity engines by a surly Medal winner makes a vignette of murderous hilarity. What Mr. Condon has done to political conventions has been done to them before by other writers, but not very much better.

Frederic Morton. *NYT*. April 26, 1959. p. 4

Richard Condon has concocted a smooth and palatable pousse-café of political satire, psychological speculation, pleasantly risqué antics a la Thorne Smith, and espionage maneuvering. His characters [in *The Manchurian Candidate*] are believable, if one-sided: Shaw remains an automaton, despite a rather dream-like love affair; his mother, the lovely and ambitious Mrs. Iselin, is by all odds the wickedest witch since Lady Macbeth, guilty of incest, adultery, pandering, betrayal and a host of other crimes, including nailing a puppy's paw to the floor; the Russian agents are superhumanly efficient; our own FBI and CIA only too fallible. Also, the basic assumptions of the plot do not withstand close examination. Happily, however, such examination is not necessary: this is a diversion, and a good one.

Talliaferro Boatright. *NYHT*. June 28, 1959. p. 8

Meanwhile, we have Mr. Condon's spectacular—a documentary novel that reads rather like a newsreel with action packed people scenes between. *An Infinity of Mirrors* also has what film people call a strong story line as well as plenty of hotsy scenes. In fact the basic plot, like too many TV salesmen's faces, could move any product. It fits a western as well as a thriller. In this case, it just happens to be intercut with the holocaust. . . .

All the same, it's only fair to add that *An Infinity of Mirrors* is very readable, fast-moving, and rich in romantic detail of the high life. In fact what Mr. Condon has succeeded in doing is to make the rise of Hitler seem glamorous and sexy. There is even a comic sub-plot about secret agents in the best British film tradition. My chief complaint, then, is not that Mr. Condon has written a bad novel, it is that he has written an immoral one.

Mordecai Richler. *NYHT*. Sept. 13, 1964. pp. 4, 19

See *The Oldest Confession, The Manchurian Candidate, Some Angry Angel* (novels).

# CONNELLY, MARC (1890–    )

George S. Kaufman and Marc Connelly, whose delectable comedies *Dulcy* and *To the Ladies* struck one more through their reserve than through any expression of ironic vision, have let themselves go at last. . . . I wish to praise the authors of *Beggar on Horseback* most heartily for this, that they laugh at fatuousness and gross materialism, at triviality of mind and soul, at stubborn stupidity and dishonor no longer conscious of itself, not as these qualities are contrasted with some specious moralistic idealism, but as they are contrasted with art, with the eternal creative spirit, with the quest of him who is driven despite himself to pursue that beauty which is also truth.

Ludwig Lewisohn. *Nation*. Feb. 27, 1924. pp. 238–9

What would make *Beggar on Horseback*, agreeable as it is all through, into a play of importance, would be a continuation of the exact comment on life, and especially on middle-class American life, that appears in the first act. This satire, tinged with love and with the purity that arises in the young man through his desire for beauty and creation, might move to a slightly darker note now and again, but the comic simile and the wit of it would in the end arrive only through this exactitude and this patient study with delight. . . . In sum *Beggar on Horseback* starts sharply toward something that, if it were achieved, would be gayer by reason of its subtlety, more biting for its reckless satire and crude truth, and more unforgettable because of its long thought and because of the wistful, frank reserve that underlies so much of American self-expression. It does not arrive at this something, though the promise is there often enough, and in the first act almost always.

Stark Young. *NR.* March 5, 1924. p. 45

. . . Mr. Connelly does not go far into social philosophy; his play [*The Wisdom Tooth*] has only implications of social satire, only little hints about business men and boarders, and not many hints and implications at that. His hero is a single case and we are to watch his fortunes more, I gather, for the sentiment involved, the fantasy and the homely romance, than for any sting or theory about our society, our national or local characteristics, our blurred uniformity. And yet there are elements in *The Wisdom Tooth,* as there were in *Dulcy* and *To the Ladies* and *Beggar on Horseback,* that stick in the mind and ramify.

Stark Young. *NR.* March 3, 1926. p. 45

Leading the play [*The Green Pastures*] thus, through numerous scenes and incidents that may sometimes appear merely casual and relaxed, on to a final summit, makes for the inclusion of many conceptions familiar in religious thought—that, for instance, of God needing man as man needs God—and by ending on that note of God's sacrifice through his own son, achieves a genuinely heroic and mystical level. And this is accomplished with no violation of the material in the book. . . . In Mr. Connelly's play, in Mr. [Roark] Bradford's book [*Ol' Man Adam an' His Chillun*] . . . this figure of God, with his kindness, his tricks, his patience, pleasures and human troubles and ups and downs, is a remarkable interpretation of the whole soul of the people in the play; it is, in the finest sense, a creation of an idea in dramatic terms.

Stark Young. *NR.* March 19, 1930. p. 129

Marc Connelly, to whom the play was suggested by a series of stories in Negro dialect—Roark Bradford's *Ol' Man Adam an' His Chillun*—is the person most immediately responsible for the extraordinary performance, but neither he, the original author, nor even the fine cast of black actors can claim the largest share of the credit, since the fundamental creative work was done by the anonymous geniuses who composed the spirituals upon which the whole is based. Mr. Connelly and the rest have cooperated with great skill and delicacy; they seem, one and all, to have been gifted with a remarkable imaginative insight into the mood of the materials at hand. . . .

Joseph Wood Krutch. *Nation*. March 26, 1930. p. 376

. . . *The Green Pastures* is not a dramatization. Distinctly this is an adaptation. The book of [Roark] Bradford's served as a springboard for the play of Connelly's. I am aware that there are a number of lines in the play which are taken literally from *Ol' Man Adam an' His Chillun,* but there is a vast change in mood. Mr. Bradford seems to have been interested almost exclusively in the humorous potentialities of Bible folklore told from a Negro point of view in Negro dialect. The agonizing, heartbreaking moments of the play are wholly Connelly.

I do not hold that pathos is of necessity a higher artistic expression than the merely comic, but Connelly's contribution is better rounded. He has taken black loam and breathed upon it. There is nothing in the book which lays hands upon my spine as does the march of the Children in the scene which pictures the road to *The Promised Land.*

But whether the play or the book is better makes a small difference for the purpose of this piece. It is enough to indicate that they are different.

Heywood Broun. *Nation*. April 9, 1930. p. 415

In a sense *The Farmer Takes a Wife* is robustious enough and enlivened by a great deal of very picturesque speech, but I am led to wonder whether or not anyone has ever noted the fact that Mr. Connelly is distinguished from other Broadway playwrights with whom one might tend to think of him by the fact that he is not in the least "hard-boiled." Somehow or other he has managed to escape from the tough tradition which rules our stage in so far as it is dominated by that Broadway with which he is more or less associated. His plays are never vulgar and never, like the typical product, somehow unpleasantly brassy. Below the surface of his sophistication is a delicate fancy, an essentially gentle spirit, something one would be inclined to call a kind of quaintness if it were not for the unfortunate associations of that word. It is that which in general makes the charm of his plays and that which contributes so much to *The Farmer Takes a Wife.* It is romantic with a romanticism which takes one unawares, charming with a charm which one does not resent because it is insidious without being obtrusive.

Joseph Wood Krutch. *Nation*. Nov. 14, 1934. pp. 573–4

"Gangway! Gangway for de Lawd God Jehovah!" The modern theatre has produced no entrance cue better known or more affectionately remembered. These are words which even when read make the heart stand still. Heard again in the theatre, heard in the world as it now is, their impact is, if anything, greater than when they were spoken twenty-one years ago in that other simpler and comparatively civilized world in which *The Green Pastures* was first produced.

When Marc Connelly finished his script, he had written a far, far larger play than perhaps he realized he was writing. . . . *The Green Pastures* is a masterpiece. I came to realize this early during its initial run and only wish I had had the sense to do so on the night of its opening. But then, to my shame, I missed the boat, which was quite a boat to miss considering it was the Ark. Though back in 1930 I saluted *The Green Pastures* as being brave and meritorious, I felt that, in spite of its charms and delights, it somehow fell short of its ultimate goal. . . . Whatever my reasons may have been, this much I know: I was wrong.

John Mason Brown. *SR*. April 7, 1951. pp. 28–30

*The Green Pastures* has always seemed to me a deft, picture-book sort of play for big-city people who are nostalgic about a quality they believe their parents or grandparents once possessed and which they can only recapture in the form of "clever" fun—gay pigment and self-consciously cute drawing. I find no trace of genuine moral sentiment here, only the pseudo-religiosity of the Easter pageant in the larger movie houses—far more skillful and entertaining, of course, but only a little less hypocritical.

Harold Clurman. *NR*. April 16, 1951. p. 30

He says he is attempting [in *The Green Pastures*] to translate the religious conceptions of thousands of untutored Negroes as they have adapted the Bible stories to suit the experiences of their lives. Yet . . . he admits that he has used certain characters in his dramatization which are not in the Bible at all. His only justification for using such counterfeit characters is his belief that "persons like them have figured in the meditations of some of the old Negro preachers."

However, let us not hold this inconsistency against Mr. Connelly. Let us see whether or not he has achieved his main purpose, which is to present a genuine representation of the religious beliefs of thousands of untutored Negroes in the deep South.

I charge that Mr. Connelly has utterly failed to accomplish this purpose, and that his representation is counterfeit.

Nick Aaron Ford. *Phylon*. Spring, 1959. p. 68

See *Beggar on Horseback* (with George S. Kaufman), *The Wisdom Tooth*, *The Green Pastures*, *The Farmer Takes a Wife* (with Frank B. Elser) (plays).

# COWLEY, MALCOLM (1898–    )

### Poetry

By an ill adjustment Malcolm Cowley is best known as a critic and trans-lator, whereas his verse is by far his most important contribution. . . . Cowley is not to be labeled the poet exclusively of this or that. But the one note which appears most often is a kind of indefinite regret. Though willingly accepting this as the only possible of worlds, to the contempo-rary he supplies a Baudelairean corrective of nostalgia prior to the facts, a nostalgia which would prevail regardless of the environment. There is the frequent meditation upon death and upon that stagnation of the mind which may precede death by many years. There is the constant suggestion of a vague return. . . . There is the hankering after something native.

Kenneth Burke. *NYHT*. Aug. 18, 1929. p. 2

It would be difficult to find a single book of poems more symptomatic of the experiences of the post-war writers of America than Malcolm Cow-ley's. . . . *Blue Juniata* is important not only because it gives us the assembled verse of a new and definitely interesting poet, but because it sets itself up as a self-confessed logbook of literary youth in America during the ten years which followed the war. . . . Unlike many poets who at the present moment are being read and quoted with high favor, Mr. Cowley is not devising his tunes with gymnastic agility on a single string. He has obviously submitted to the charms of many influences, and he has managed to go through a period of high excitement in our cultural ex-perience and yet realized a significance in the manifold distractions and vogues that crowded it.

Morton Dauwen Zabel. *Nation*. Aug. 21, 1929.
pp. 200–1

His mind is basically concrete and unspeculative; he brings to facts and observations an even emotional tone that is the mark of a genuine style; but in criticism Cowley's instinct for exact definition is not strong; and the necessity for a certain amount of abstraction only violates the even tone of his style. It is in poetry, at least for the present, that Mr. Cowley may be seen at his best.

And yet the long discipline of prose has given to his poetry much of its distinction of form. . . . There are no great moments in Cowley, and there are no disconcerting lapses. There is subdued emotion; there are exact feelings and images; and over all, a subtle vision of the startling qualities of common things.

Allen Tate. *NR*. Aug. 28, 1929. pp. 51–2

Mr. Cowley's consciousness is that of a young America which is both on terms of some familiarity with tradition in letters and with the life we see around us. . . . And if his poetry lacks something of traditional beauty and lyricism, it is because his mind has been formed under conditions only partly amenable to change through his own efforts. The poems of *Blue Juniata* are of an intellectual order, wholly disciplined, but the indigenous flavor has not been intellectualized, so to speak, out of them.

John Chamberlain. NYT. Sept. 8, 1929. p. 2

### Criticism

"It was an easy, quick, adventurous age, good to be young in," Mr. Cowley remarks of the 1920's. That is the way in which some of us who shared the adventure he chronicles remember the era. It is evoking a revival of interest today, and it is being reconstructed with scholarly enthusiasm by young writers who were in their cradles when it passed. They have the right to their interpretation. But should you wish to know what it felt like to us who lived through it, read *Exile's Return*. Mr. Cowley has painted the classic picture, and it is not likely to be surpassed in authenticity, eloquence or beauty.

Lloyd Morris. NYHT. July 8, 1951. p. 10

Cowley has the sense of a lyric poet (which he is) for the unique value of the individual. . . . Yet because he also has the social historian's sense that each life, besides having a pattern of its own, is a part of the pattern of the age, he can make you see how all these lives fitted the pattern of alienation which led a whole generation of intellectuals into exile. . . . *Exile's Return* is far and away the best book about this generation (of the 1920's) by a participant, and this is a generation that was crucial not only for American literature but for the whole of American culture.

Arthur Mizener. NYT. June 10, 1951. p. 9

Calmly ignoring those austere critics who claim it is the literary work that should concern us and not the private life of the creator, Malcolm Cowley has put together a fascinating account of the American writer as a human being (in *The Literary Situation*). A critic, editor, and poet who brings to his interest in writers' lives an *avant-garde* background, Mr. Cowley transforms literary anecdotage and journalism into a valuable analysis of what makes the American writer run. His approach is like that of the Lynds to Middletown, U.S.A., except that his conclusions are based on personal observation and inquiry rather than statistics and questionnaires, and that some of the best things in the book are purely—and maliciously—subjective.

Milton Rugoff. NYHT. Oct. 24, 1954. p. 6

His experience of active emotional participation in the literary life apparently came to an end with the period which he documented in *Exile's Return,* and of late years he has retreated more and more into seclusion; his point of view has grown increasingly elder statesmanish; and his tone has undergone a gradual change from the lyric to the avuncular. . . . After thinking back over Cowley's critical career and setting aside those fine and definitive essays on writers like Hemingway and Faulkner which he has occasionally been able to do, one is forced to conclude that he has suffered increasingly from the effect of trying to simplify his ideas for the benefit of what he obviously considers a simple-minded reading public.

John W. Aldridge. *Nation.* Feb. 19, 1955. pp. 162–4


. . . it is indisputable that *The Portable Faulkner* made much of his work easily available when it was otherwise unavailable, gave an indication of its range, and accelerated recognition of Faulkner's stature. And Cowley's long preface was a seminal essay in Faulkner criticism. The book also gave comfort when it was badly needed; and its making gave another friend to a man who needed friends, no matter how forbidding his mien.

Perhaps the most complimentary assessment came from the author himself. "The job is splendid," he wrote Cowley.

(K)                               Joseph Blotner. *NYT.* July 24, 1966. p. 5


No other critic was more engaged in the *Kulturkampf* of the times or more strategically placed to observe the sorties of the warring intellectual platoons—Humanist, Communist, Technocrat, Agrarian, Liberal. And few writers identified with the left during this period managed better than Cowley did to remain on speaking terms with literary acquaintances to the right and left of him.

For more than ten years, beginning in 1930, Cowley ran the book section of The New Republic. Almost every week, from 1934 until the early 1940's, he reviewed a book that challenged his interest or provided him with a text. Through a newly acquired "Marxist" perspective he was able to arrange such diverse items as Yeats, the Bonus Marchers, Thomas Mann, revolutionary China, the Lynds' *Middletown,* Cummings's verse, Russian films, Trotsky's history and Faulkner's novels, in one ideological panorama. Each article or essay-review, composed under pressure, also served (Cowley tells us) as "my blank verse meditations, my sonnet sequence, my letter to distant friends, my private journal." Some of the men and events he dealt with now seem pretty remote, yet *Think Back On Us* . . . conveys the intellectual excitement and moral fervor of the period. Illuminating simply as social history, it can also be read as the public soliloquy of a man in the process of acquiring and shedding certain

political convictions; the Cowley of 1940 is not the Cowley of 1930.
(K)                                    Daniel Aaron. *NYT*. Feb. 12, 1967. p. 4

"Think back on us"—on the thirties as they are starting to emerge now, after the first siftings of time, the first corrodings of new perspectives, or on the thirties as they were in their own conceit? The option, when one reprints verbatim contemporary journalism, seems clearly to be for the latter alternative. Yet even here there is blurring, confusion, and a major omission.

For in fact if the Marxist movement of the American thirties had any authenticity at all, it lay in a questioning of the impersonal, ahistorical voice, the specious good sense which conceals its real premises (material as well as spiritual) behind a camouflage of fairness, impartiality, and good will expressed as compromise. The attack on the liberal ethos was ungainly and extravagant in many ways; it often went hand in hand with hypocrisy and stupidity of various sorts; it was inherently self-destructive, and thus compromised *ab ovo* the dogmatism it pretended to serve. But the attack on the privileged voice was a distinctive quality of thought in the thirties, thought which is really to be understood only as an attempt to transcend bourgeois liberalism as it has existed since John Stuart Mill. And of this quality one will not find very much in Mr. Cowley's pages; it must be sought in Sam Sillen's *New Masses,* Jack Conroy's *New Anvil,* Dwight Macdonald's *Politics,* and a dozen other hairy magazines of the then-far-left. In other words, kiddies, don't think you've seen the full spectrum of the thirties when you've retrospected on it through this particular low-resolution lens.
(K)                            Robert Martin Adams. *NR*. March 11, 1967. p. 25

I wasn't altogether happy when I heard last fall that Henry Dan Piper of Southern Illinois University was publishing a selection of pieces that Cowley had written in the Thirties. I had read the pieces as they appeared, with great eagerness and usually with marked appreciation though sometimes with sharp disagreement; but I didn't look forward to rereading them thirty years later. In those three decades I had changed and Cowley had changed and the world had changed, and I thought that the pieces would be dated if not dead. In a sense they *are* dated, and that is why the book [*Think Back on Us . . .*] serves the purpose for which Professor Piper edited it—to give young people some idea of what the Thirties were like. But almost nothing seems merely old stuff, and the best of the pieces are alive today.
(K)                            Granville Hicks. *SR*. March 11, 1967. p. 31

See *Blue Juniata* (poems); *The Lost Generation, Exile's Return, The Literary Situation, Think Back on Us* (Criticism).

## COZZENS, JAMES GOULD (1903–     )

He wrote three rather tropical and violent stories of Cuba and other southern latitudes in *Confusion, Cockpit,* and *Son of Perdition,* in which he derived something from Joseph Hergesheimer and maybe something from Nick Carter. He wrote one atrocious Elizabethan yarn, *Michael Scarlett.* He followed Conrad profitably in *S. S. San Pedro;* the result did no discredit to the model. Perhaps he is not committed to the hardboiled school beyond the present offering *(The Last Adam).* It will be exceedingly interesting to see what he will do next. For it is more than likely he has something of his own to say.

Isabel Paterson. *NYHT.* Jan. 8, 1933. p. 6

There is no question but that Cozzens's work, except in regard to his larger dramatic frames, shows a steady progress toward greater mastery of his craft, increased consciousness of his effects, and constantly augmented scope. Except for *Castaway,* however, he has given us every ingredient of first-rate novels except the novels themselves. His faults, the prejudices and blockages that make his treatment of race and sex so unsatisfactory, and his constant dissipating of tragedy into irony and melodrama, seem to be the obverse of his virtues: his enormously representative quality and his uncompromising honesty. When Cozzens can write novels with the breadth and depth of *The Just and the Unjust* or *Guard of Honor* in as taut and satisfactory a dramatic frame as *Castaway* has, when he learns to combine the realism of his later work with the symbolism of his middle period and deepen both in the process, he should be a novelist to rank with the best America has produced.

Stanley Edgar Hyman. *NMQ.* Winter, 1949. p. 497

He is a professional. . . . The professional as novelist is a man who has subdued himself to what he works in, who holds himself humbly in relation to fiction but holds fiction to be the most important thing in the world, whose deepest shame it would be not to write his novel wholly in the terms which the novel itself sets. He is also a man who has mastered his job and substitutes skill for literary pretensions and affectations. In his novels form and content are so welded together that they have become inseparable; they are the same thing. Moreover, each of his novels is a handful of novels made one; it is packed tight with life; any of its parts or characters and many of its mere parentheses would make a novel for a smaller man.

Bernard DeVoto. *Harper.* Feb., 1949. p. 73

He has nothing less than a passion for detachment.

This passionate detachment of his is closely associated with his great technical skill. I do not mean that he has acquired that skill merely by virtue of being detached, for obviously he has worked hard for it, but the basis on which his craftsmanship has developed is his objectivity. Deliberately standing apart from his material, he strives to see clearly and to render with perfect accuracy what he sees. His writing is always careful and never more careful than in the avoidance of pretentiousness.

Granville Hicks. *EJ*. Jan., 1950. p. 4

Mr. Cozzens's grasp of American life is not based upon long familiarity with a single region, . . . but upon his wisdom in the ways of the upper middle class, which is very much the same all over the country. He has profound respect for the responsible citizens who actually make our civilization work. Ibsen called them "pillars of society," and made the very term imply hypocrisy. Mr. Cozzens, on the other hand, likes to portray this class from the point of view of a member of one of the great professions, Law, the Church, Medicine, and by that means he brings out the humane values he sees in *his* pillars of society.

Francis Fergusson. *Per*. Winter, 1954. pp. 36–7

I know of no modern novelist who commands such a range of idiom, allusion, cadence, rhetorical radiation and vocabulary. It is a muscular, virile style with certain strong affinities to seventeenth-century prose— Cozzens is fond of Bunyan, Milton, Defoe, among others. Yet one does not get the feeling of reading a literary novel. The ironic view alone prevents this. . . . In Cozzens's novels the world of types explored by Dickens and by Shaw and by Ben Jonson comes before us again in its unfamiliar shape—the shape of the local, urban, and workaday, qualities too trivial to most novelists in recent years to seem worthy of their attention. Cozzens forces our attention, concentrates it, makes us inescapably aware of the density of the lives we live.

Louis O. Coxe. *AL*. May, 1955. pp. 163, 168–9

Cozzens is not Thackeray. He is more judicial, less sentimental and he lacks Thackeray's magic. But he deals as Thackeray did with man in society, with related man. And it is impossible to believe that Cozzens did not remember Colonel Newcome's "Adsum," when he wrote Winner's "I am here" (in *By Love Possessed*). Thackeray's passage has been in the anthologies for a hundred years. Far more moving, because it is a way of living instead of dying, is Winner's "I am here."

Jessamyn West. *NYHT*. Aug. 25, 1957. p. 1

Cozzens would no more deform a character to meet the demands of his plot than he would steal from his Delaware Valley neighbors. Nevertheless, it *is* a pattern, almost a formula, and it has reappeared in one of his novels after another.

There is a lawyer, young or old, or a staff officer in the Air Force, or a clergyman deeply involved in the lives of his parishioners. There is a climax in his career, a period of two or three days during which hell breaks loose; men die in accidents, women commit suicide, friends of his family are charged with sexual crimes, his closest associates betray him through irresponsibility; and meanwhile the hero tries to do his best for everyone, succeeding in some cases, failing lamentably in others, yet somehow surviving by force of character.

Malcolm Cowley. *NYT.* Aug. 25, 1957. p. 1

The essential difference between Cozzens and his contemporaries lies in the character of his work. Here he is the complete nonconformist: a classic man, operating in a romantic period. This, I suspect, is the basic reason why he has missed both popular and critical appreciation. He puzzles ordinary readers whose palates have been dulled by the Gothic extravagance of most fiction; and he offends critics whose professional mission has been to exalt the romantic novel which has been in high fashion for the last thirty years. . . . Cozzens may, indeed, signal the turning of the tide. In his salad days, he too flirted with the romantic technique, but in his mature novels he has moved steadily away from it. Instead he has been attempting something far more difficult: to write an engrossing story about ordinary people, living ordinary lives, in ordinary circumstances.

John Fischer. *Harper.* Sept., 1957. pp. 15–8

Cozzens's heroes are becoming steadily richer and more Protestant, while his upstarts—Catholics, Jews, or reformers—are something like caricatures and invariably obnoxious. (His Negroes now, because of spotless subservience, fare somewhat better. They *like* to take communion last.) He has, of course, like any author, the right to choose the class he will deal with—Jane Austen did as much—but this kind of limitation is doubled because of Cozzens's obvious distaste for the people into whose minds he will not choose or deign to enter. . . . His sympathy is husbanded too narrowly, and he lacks what Henry James called "the sacred rage." He walks away from us cool, disenchanted, a little superior, pleased to have kept his distance.

Richard Ellmann. *Reporter.* Oct. 3, 1957. pp. 43–4

Like most of Mr. Cozzens's novels (making some exceptions for *Castaway*) *By Love Possessed* suffers from a want of essential drama: though all the great rites of tragedy are prepared and invoked, the demonstration remains at last unmade; as though the author had some reservations— possibly about "real life" and "the way things really work out"—which protect his major actors from their ends. I cannot help thinking that the book, in this respect, functions as a kind of secular apologetics, the defense of an image of life, much idealized, which is regarded with so much reverence and nostalgia that its exemplars may not and must not be brought down from their high places. . . . The mere acknowledgement of the possibility will do instead, so that in the end honor, wealth, position, are saved at the expense of honesty, on the stated ground that considerations higher than honesty (charity, compassion, expedience) are involved, a shift of justifications not without its Jesuitical quality.

Howard Nemerov. Nation. Nov. 2, 1957. p. 308

Cozzens's work is defined not by these technical devices, the compression of dramatic time and the interpenetration of various actions, but also by certain pervading themes, the need for experience and the discrepancy between the ideal and the actual. . . . Because Cozzens does not write about the man in the gray flannel suit many readers will miss the fact that Cozzens is a contemporary writer in the deepest sense of the term. His subject is the limited world in which man is enmeshed in a congerie of forces which radiates far beyond his personal control. Cozzens's heroes are professional men, themselves an instance of a specialized society, and his subjects are various; but his theme is the complex world in which man, in his already limited estate, is further limited.

John W. Ward. AS. Winter, 1957. pp. 93, 99

In his previous works there has always been a certain absence of primary feeling; he is a cold writer who has needed a recharge, say, of human sympathy. To a certain degree By Love Possessed is probably the attempt to get at just this issue in his own work and career—but an attempt which, rather than enlarging the writer's capacity to feel, simply confirms his prejudice against feeling. It is a treatise on the different kinds of love— parental, oedipal, sibling, self-love or vanity, religious, sexual. But why is it that all these types of love are only destructive and never even momentarily rewarding? . . . What Mr. Cozzens does not seem to understand for all his classical lore, is that the Goddess of Love, whatever her cruel demands on her afflicted subjects, is also the Goddess of Life.

Maxwell Geismar. American Moderns (Hill and<br>Wang). 1958. pp. 148–50

He should not be ignored because he is unfashionable nor should he be disparaged because John Fischer nominated him for the Nobel Prize. He has been writing for a long time now, and he has shown a greater capacity for growth than the majority of his contemporaries. He clings tenaciously to his own point of view, and it yields him a vision of human experience that the reader has to respect even when he doesn't like it. We don't have to belittle other writers to appreciate Cozzens, although some critics . . . act as if we did. We can never have too much excellence, and if it takes different forms, so much the better.

Granville Hicks. *SR*. Aug. 8, 1959. p. 12

He is writing about the individual in society, about the obligations, the hazards, the rebellious and painful accommodation of human beings to the way things—not *are* (this has been misunderstood)—but *work:* the way things work, the functioning of the world. His heroes are men who understand these functions, live with them, interpret them for others and in some part keep the machinery running. Able, responsible men, more burdened by duty than eager for power, learning in maturity that one never really knows enough, stoically bearing the weight of the world— these are the men Cozzens sets up as admirable. They are admirable. But they are also the Ruling Class, if only on the provincial level.

This being so, it is easy to see why he has been attacked for supporting the status quo and writing "Novels of Resignation."

Elizabeth Janeway. *NYT*. Aug. 9, 1959. p. 1

His style is essentially eighteenth-century, like that of Swift or Steele, both of whom he admires. It is good for saying that whatever is, is right (or wrong, as the case may be), but it is not so good for saying that whatever is, is continually changing. He does not use the symbolic structure of death and rebirth which many romantics from Wordsworth to Hemingway have used to formulate the essence of change, nor does he use the kind of symbolic imagery with which they commonly reinforce that structure and that theme. As a result, his heroes tend to give an impression of stuffiness or priggishness instead of the vision of heroic maturity arising out of heroic struggle which they seem to be intended to give. They and the works they live in are, to a degree, intellectually abstract and emotionally thin.

(K)                    R. P. Adams in *Essays in Modern American Literature,* edited by Richard E. Langford (Stetson). 1963.

p. 110

The peculiar excellences or distinctions of Cozzens' art, more than anything else, justify critical study, for these distinctions reveal a complicated and deliberate novelist at work. No other writer of our time has dared to make such an extreme commitment to reason; and this commitment has led Cozzens into an attitude toward man which dares to be condescending, anti-democratic, and altogether dispassionate. To the rational principle Cozzens has remained firmly loyal, although his growing mastery of the technical aspects of literature has allowed him to dramatize his vision of reality with more and more impact and meaning. At the same time, Cozzens has persisted in standing apart from the literary fashions of his time: he has worked consistently within the framework of the traditional English novel, and has (with one exception) rejected any attempt at experimentation. And appropriately enough, a large part of his current significance lies in his ability to expand beyond the capacity of anyone else in his generation the scope and quality of the traditional.

(K)                          Harry John Mooney. *James Gould Cozzens*
                                    (Pittsburgh). 1963. p. 3

Cozzens has been described by one critic as "a novelist of intellect." On the evidence of *Children and Others* this is surely wrong; for his mind confines itself entirely to the same received ideas most unreflecting Americans live by. He believes in the importance of being a mature person, in the "pathetic impracticality" of socialism, in the immaturity of conscientious objectors, and so forth. If you have a stock idea in your head or a stock response in your heart take it to Cozzens and he will rubber-stamp it for you.

(K)                          Julian Moynahan. *NYR*. Sept. 10, 1964. p. 14

The stories [*Children and Others*] . . . are building blocks. They are the short form Cozzens put away once he fully matured as a writer; and more importantly, they build toward what has come to be Cozzens's major theme: what it is to grow up and be a man. Except for young Francis Ellery in *Ask Me Tomorrow,* the Cozzens hero is generally an older man, one schooled in the complexity of experience who still retains the capacity and the courage to act. Colonel Ross, the old judge on wartime duty in *Guard of Honor,* is the best instance. That hero is here in these stories, but on the edge of them, usually in the figure of the father. In "Total Stranger," the prep-school boy who discovers how little he knows his father muses in retrospect: "My father had the habit, half stoical, half insensitive, of making the best of anything there was." But since the stories present the world of children, the insensitive half of adult wisdom constantly undercuts the admirable stoical half.

(K)                          John William Ward. *Reporter*. Sept. 10, 1964. p. 53

Cozzens' respect for life as it is gives him an exceptional interest in the actual world. This interest ranges all the way from his pleasure in the ingenious organization of things like department stores and air force bases to his almost anthropological curiosity about the customary life of social institutions like the small town or of professions like the law and medicine. He has a deep respect for men who can function effectively in the world, whether they are skilled mechanics or talented pilots, able generals or smart judges, and this respect, because it is not dictated by a theory, is without condescension. Both *The Just and the Unjust* (1942) and *By Love Possessed* (1957) are legally impeccable novels about the law; the hero of *The Last Adam* (1933) is a doctor and the hero of *Men and Brethren* (1936) is a priest. Three of these four novels show a fascinated intimacy with the social life of the American small town. *Guard of Honor* (1948) is a novel about life on an Army Air Force base during the war; no one has ever been able to find a flaw in its minutely detailed account of that life. . . .

Cozzens confronts squarely the rawness of the deal that drives the subjective novelists to a defiance of life itself. He knows, as well as Melville and Faulkner, how strong the passions of the heart are. But, since he never loses sight of the simple, obvious fact that life is what life is, he is always conscious that it is not what these passions so often convince men it is, or may be. To him, their effect on men is a kind of possession—in the sense of being influenced to the point of madness.

(K)                                      Arthur Mizener. *KR*. Nov., 1966. pp. 598–9

See *The Last Adam, Castaway, S.S. San Pedro, The Just and the Unjust, Men and Brethren, Guard of Honor, By Love Possessed* (novels); *Children and Others* (stories).

# CRANE, HART (1899–1932)

Mr. Crane has a most remarkable style, a style which is strikingly original—almost something like a great style, if there could be such a thing as a great style which was, not merely not applied to a great subject, but not, so far as one can see, applied to any subject at all. . . . One does not demand of poetry nowadays that it shall provide us with logical metaphors or with intelligible sequences of ideas. Rimbaud is inconsecutive and confused. Yet, with Rimbaud, whom Mr. Crane somewhat resembles, we experience intense emotional excitement and artistic satisfaction; we are dazzled by the eruption of his images, but we divine what it is that he is saying. But, with Mr. Crane, though he sometimes moves us, it is in a way curiously vague.

Edmund Wilson. *NR*. May 11, 1927. p. 320

What is divine about the poetry of Crane is the energy which fills it, that intense, dionysian, exalted energy that by sheer pressure lifts him to heights unattainable by less titanic poets. . . . One can say this: at six-teen he was writing at a level that Amy Lowell never rose from and at twenty-eight he is writing on a level that scarcely any other living Ameri-can poet ever reaches.

> Gorham Munson. *Destinations* (Sears). 1928.
> pp. 162–4

It is in single grand passages, rather than whole poems, that Crane re-veals the power and sweep of his concentric vision. One cannot condone the obscurities in toto, nor entirely subscribe to a style which is often more grandiose than a given occasion demands.

> Alfred Kreymborg. *Our Singing Strength* (Coward-
> McCann). 1929. p. 604

Crane labored to perfect both the strategy and the tactics of language so as to animate and maneuver his perceptions—and then fought the wrong war and against an enemy that displayed, to his weapons, no vulnerable target. He wrote in a language of which it was the virtue to accrete, mod-ify, and interrelate moments of emotional vision—moments at which the sense of being gains its greatest access—moments at which, by the felt nature of the knowledge, the revealed thing is its own meaning; and he attempted to apply his language, in his major effort, to a theme that re-quired a sweeping, discrete, indicative, anecdotal language, a language in which, by force of movement, mere cataloging can replace and often sur-pass representation. He used the private lyric to write the cultural epic.

> R. P. Blackmur. *The Double Agent* (Arrow). 1935.
> p. 126

His world has no center, and the compensatory action that he took is re-sponsible for the fragmentary quality of his most ambitious work. This action took two forms, the blind assertion of the will; and the blind desire for self-destruction. The poet did not face his first problem, which is to define the limits of his personality and to objectify its moral implications in an appropriate symbolism. Crane could only assert a quality of will against the world, and at each successive failure of the will he turned upon himself. . . . By attempting an extreme solution of the romantic problem, Crane proved that it cannot be solved.

> Allen Tate. *Reactionary Essays* (Scribner). 1936.
> pp. 40–3. Courtesy of Alan Swallow

Although Pound and Eliot had been largely responsible for reviving an interest in the poetry of the sixteenth and seventeenth centuries, they were themselves temperamentally incapable of doing more than adapting, imitating, and assimilating certain of its characteristics. . . . It remained for Crane, unschooled, unspoiled by scholastic nostalgia and self-consciousness, to use the medium in a completely modern way, easily and naturally combining in it rhetoric, conversation, and discursive thought, and sounding afresh the grand note so rarely heard in modern times. . . . In the process of renovating blank verse Crane also revivified the poetic language of his time. He was able to discover words, and use them, almost as things in themselves, prized their colors, sounds, and shapes as more meaningful than their strict definitions.

Philip Horton. *Hart Crane* (Norton). 1937.
pp. 309–10

Crane's poems often have a hypnotic power about them which marks them out as among the most extraordinary performances with language to be found in American poetry. One may call it genius or one may say that he had a wholly exceptional mediumistic power to set on paper the contents of the subconscious carrying with them still a kind of inhuman quality.

Amos N. Wilder. *The Spiritual Aspects of Poetry*
(Harper). 1940. p. 124

Crane was incapable of a sustained irony, which might have produced an inclusive attitude harmonizing his vision of actuality, his romantic transcendentalism and his personal neuroses. His natural power of poetic expression was prodigious, but its effectiveness was defeated by his uncertainty of technical control. This accounts for his essential "patchiness," his exasperating combination of the meritorious and the meretricious. . . . His most extraordinary stirring and kindling power with words is most manifest in scattered lines which shoot suddenly like a rocket from dark surroundings.

Elizabeth Drew. *Directions in Modern Poetry* (Holt).
1941. pp. 69–70

Crane . . . had the absolute seriousness that goes with genius and with sanctity; one might describe him as a saint of the wrong religion. He had not the critical intelligence to see what was wrong with his doctrine, but he had the courage of his convictions, the virtue of integrity, and he deserves our respect. He has the value of a thorough-going demonstration. He embodies perfectly the concepts which for nearly a century have been generating some of the most cherished principles of our literature, our education, our politics, and our personal morals. . . . We shall scarcely get anything better unless we change our principles.

Yvor Winters. *In Defense of Reason* (Morrow).
1947. pp. 602–3. Courtesy of Alan Swallow

His efforts to create an artistic "shorthand," to rid poetry of the rigidity of logical sequence and make his language the equivalent of a state of consciousness and immediate experience, led him to employ the methods of displacement familiar among contemporary artists in music and painting. . . . The unit was the word, and, like the spot of color in pointillism, that word could be altered in various ways by the other words placed around it.

Barbara Herman. *SwR*. Jan., 1950. p. 61

Essentially Crane was a poet of ecstasy or frenzy or intoxication; you can choose your own word depending on how much you like his work. Essentially he was using rhyme and meter and fantastic images to convey the emotional states that were induced in him by alcohol, jazz, machinery, laughter, intellectual stimulation, the shape and sound of words and the madness of New York in the late Coolidge era. At their worst his poems are ineffective unless read in something approximating the same atmosphere, with a drink at your elbow, the phonograph blaring and somebody shouting into your ear, "Isn't that great!" At their best, however, the poems do their work unaided except by their proper glitter and violence.

Malcolm Cowley. *Exile's Return* (Viking). 1951.
pp. 230–1

Crane referred to *The Bridge* as his *Aeneid,* and his critics have generally taken the genre of the poem for granted. Yet what happens when the romantic poet becomes a culture hero, when the reference of the myth is shifted from the usual epic hero, who embodies the positive ideals of his world and is in tune with it, to a figure who stands outside society? When Crane interpreted the death of the voyager as the death of Everyman, he was doing no less than re-creating Everyman in the voyager's image, fashioning society in the image of himself; and it is here that the distinction between lyric and epic is wholly obscured.

Yet in another sense, Crane himself *is* representative, for his dilemma, establishing an imaginative vision in a society that no longer can believe in visions, is the dilemma of the twentieth-century man who finds himself alone and unimportant in the universe and will not accept his fate. Perhaps, after all, Crane was a kind of culture hero, appropriate to the times and in a way he never imagined: uneducated, alcoholic, homosexual, paranoic, suicidal—victimized by himself and by the world—he still wrote optimistic, visionary poetry. Indeed, Allen Tate has actually called him a hero, and it seems to me that those who believe in heroes would have to agree.

(K)                    L. S. Dembo. *Hart Crane's Sanskrit Charge* (Cornell).
1960. pp. 132–3

We can now see that *The Bridge* was germinally contained in the earlier lyrics of Hart Crane; it was, so to speak, their destiny, just as his whole work constitutes an episode in the modern attempt to proceed from the "exclusive" to the "inclusive" mode of poetry. Despite its unevenness, *The Bridge* is a document of great aesthetic and spiritual importance in our time; and we would question the ultimate validity of the judgment passed on it by such a sensitive critic as R. P. Blackmur, who denies Crane a real epic disposition and regrets that he should have betrayed his native vein of Dickinsonian lyricism for the Whitmanic equivocation of his major effort. Emily should have been his Beatrice to the end, according to Blackmur; Whitman was an unfortunate seducer. Actually the inclusive gesture of Whitman was necessary to the fulfillment of Crane's genius as a complement to the "exclusive" inspiration of Emily Dickinson. . . .

(K)                    Glauco Cambon. *The Inclusive Flame* (Indiana).
1963. pp. 126–7

In "The Broken Tower" Crane has succeeded in dramatizing not only the mystery of poetic creation in the style and idiom of his best poetry, but he has also succeeded in dramatizing himself and what he considered to be his mission. If the tower symbolizes the poet, it cannot help but symbolize Crane. Out of the almost insane months of his Mexican degradations Crane rallied his genius for what was to be his final "word."

If Crane in his less impressive poems seems like a man intent on satirizing himself, he is in his best poems a poet intent on transcending himself. The transcendence of "The Broken Tower" does much to refute the claim of a decline of Crane's poetic power in those final years in New York and Mixcoac and Taxco before he leaped into the sargasso fields of the Caribbean eighteen miles off the Florida keys.

(K)                    Samuel Hazo. *Hart Crane* (Barnes and Noble).
1963. p. 132

Crane's poetry is important for several reasons. First, he possessed an extraordinary gift for metaphor. As stated earlier, the remembrance of single phrases or lines is the most widespread general response to Crane's work. His poems, of course, present a harmony embracing more than single images, but their greatest intensity—their brilliance—is located in particular phrases. His distinguishing trait is the pitch of eloquence that he often achieves several times in a single poem through the startling aptness of his imagery. . . .

His work is significant, too, because of its irresistibly moving theme: man's quest for enduring love and absolute beauty. He expresses moods varying from exultant trust that the fulfillment of his quest is imminent to a downcast premonition of continued failure, but his desire never deviates from the true north of his idealism. This preoccupation gives a dignity and a universality to his poetry.

(K)                    Vincent Quinn. *Hart Crane* (Twayne). 1963. p. 127

Hart Crane's six "Voyages" are one poem, the only one of his poems in which Crane manages to express a sense of being at peace with himself. "The Broken Tower" tries to do the same, but the experience is new and uncertain; the title belies the swelling tower of the last stanza. In "For the Marriage of Faustus and Helen" and *The Bridge,* the positive, transcendental conclusions are doctrinaire rather than personal; they are necessary responses to poems full of experienced despair. In other personal poems of the mid-Twenties, the aspiration toward transcendence is itself a desperate maneuver. Only in "Voyages" can the tone even remotely be called serene. . . .

In another, less finished poem, "Repose of Rivers," the sound of willows is made to represent what happiness Crane knew as a child. His adult search to rediscover that happiness culminates in hearing the sound of the sea. At the end of the "Voyages," however, the sound is hushed. The "imaged Word . . . unbetrayable reply" is completely apart from Crane's hello-and-goodbye adventures in real life. At the top of his power, Crane isolates the axle-pole of his best self, assured that his love has found poetry and that his poetry has found infinity.

(K)                    Maurice Kramer. *SwR.* Summer, 1965. pp. 410, 423

Finally, one must point to the fundamentally religious character of his outlook as another source of his comparative obscurity. By nature and nurture a transcendental idealist, he embraced no formal philosophy and no organized religion, despite his reading of Plato and Nietzsche and his exposure to Christian Science. His religion became the pursuit of the Absolute, conceived not as God but as the equivalent of God and experienced as a living ideal whose reality transcends space and time. His pursuit of this ideal is manifested in religious diction which may often appear Biblical or Neoplatonic yet has no specific traditional content, no reference to a text which would guide us to his meaning. It is not so much the confusion of his "vision" as the relative lack of a traditional vocabulary that leads to the charge of unintelligibility. In short, Crane is one of the many who, through no fault of their own, have been largely deprived of the common sources of the western tradition—the Bible and classical mythology and philosophy.

(K)                    Hilton Landry in *The Twenties,* edited by Richard E.
                    Langford and William E. Taylor (Everett Edwards).
                                                    1966. p. 24

Crane ends ["Passage"], characteristically, with questions rather than answers (when his poetry contains answers, they are usually silent ones, as in "At Melville's Tomb"). But it seems evident that the grasp of memory and everything associated with it—memory that is committed to the already written and established, memory escaped from, earlier, and then yielded to—has been broken; and that hearing, the ability to hear the voice of spirit, is about to be restored. The ceremonial action of "Passage"— its rhythm of gain, loss and potential recovery—is badly cramped in execution. But it is Crane's honest and accurate account of the continuing rhythm of his own poetic career.

(K)                                          R.W.B. Lewis. *MR*. Spring, 1966. p. 232

## The Bridge

The late Hart Crane was not a learned man; he was not trained in or given to nice distinctions. . . . Now life was too proddingly real for him to concede the impossibility of giving it meaning. He might be said to be the only modern poet sufficiently *blind* to give his concepts the force of convictions *felt,* not cerebrally, and perhaps timorously, posited. That (*The Bridge*) is the product of desire rather than of fulfillment must mitigate, in the eliminating process of time, its claims as a successful epic. Its convictions are frenziedly positive; one's reactions are mixedly negative.

Howard Blake. *SwR*. Spring, 1935. pp. 193–4

The fifteen parts of *The Bridge* taken as one poem suffer from the lack of a coherent structure, whether symbolistic or narrative: the coherence of the work consists in the personal quality of the writing—in mood, feeling, and tone. In the best passages Crane has a perfect mastery over the qualities of his style; but it lacks an objective pattern of ideas elaborate enough to carry it through an epic or heroic work. The single symbolistic image, in which the whole poem centers, is at one moment the actual Brooklyn Bridge; at another, it is any bridge or "connection"; at still another, it is a philosophical pun, and becomes the basis of a series of analogies. . . . Alternately he asserts the symbol of the bridge and abandons it, because fundamentally he does not understand it. The idea of bridgeship is an elaborate blur leaving the inner structure of the poem confused.

Yet some of the best poetry of our times is in *The Bridge*. Its inner confusion is a phase of the inner cross-purposes of the time. Crane was one of those men whom every age seems to select as the spokesmen of its spiritual life; they give the age away.

Allen Tate. *Reactionary Essays* (Scribner). 1936.
pp. 32–8. Courtesy of Alan Swallow

*The Bridge* is a noble and basically impersonal poem of epic vision fulfilling its author's boldest claims as a monument to America. In fits of drunkenness Crane declared that he was a reincarnation of Christopher Marlowe. In one sense there is sober justice in the vaunt. The youthful and ecstatic Crane is at least as successful a poetic spokesman for modern America as the youthful and ecstatic Marlowe for Elizabethan England. The American public has as yet scarcely appreciated the contribution of *The Bridge* to a distinctively national literature.

Henry W. Wells. *The American Way of Poetry*
(Twayne). 1943. p. 204

We may ask whether the bridge, the metaphorical strength of which, obviously, is its power to unite one part with another, is as powerful a symbol as Crane thought. The bridge, over and above its metaphor value, does have ready associations for an industrialized world. But a more basic consideration is this: Can any amount of arbitrary spanning or bridging on the part of the poet—Crane bridges the agrarian and industrial worlds; the Tunnel and the final vision of hopefulness—create a unity in the minds of a society that normally sees the parts in isolation or in opposition? It would seem that the bridge symbol, which would have been remarkably appropriate to the medieval world, is an ironic one for ours.

William Van O'Connor. *Sense and Sensibility in
Modern Poetry* (Chicago). 1948. p. 23

In the tension set up between an oversimplified vision and a tortured awareness of realistic circumstance, the poem demonstrates the very mood of experiment in the literature of the 1920's: its complexities, its untraditional modes of approach to the uses of poetry, its attempts to force a new idiom and to utilize a new range of subject matter, and above all, its moral concern over the special value and function of poetry itself. The poet of *The Bridge* is a man alienated from his community because of (and in the very act of) his search for an acceptable, believable synthesis of that community.

Frederick J. Hoffmann. *The Twenties* (Viking).
1955. p. 239

Many have justly criticized *The Bridge* as a "Myth of America" for its chaotic historical and chronological sense and for the apparent lack of continuity between several of its sections. Yet it is fair to look again at the poem with a little more of Crane's eye. In the first place, he considered his poem symphonic, a "mystical synthesis" of America in which history, fact, and location "all have to be transfigured into abstract form." It was not to be a narrative epic which would proceed in historical sequence but an evolution in which idea and motif would in recurrence construct the imaginative body of the poem as an "organic panorama." Thus one might dare to say that *The Bridge* is not the Myth of America in an historical sense at all, but a construction and ritual celebration of the spiritual consciousness and creative force possible to America. Because present and past are often simultaneous and chronology distorted (as in a Faulkner novel), *The Bridge* must rely on a psychological order that is more intuitive, emotional, and mystical than rational.

(K)                    Bernice Slote. *Start with the Sun* [with James E. Miller and Karl Shapiro] (Nebraska). 1960. p. 163

Mistakenly assuming that Crane's intention was oversimple—a total, indiscriminate affirmation—critics have then condemned it for its complex duality, its vacillation, its merely partial affirmation, its tension between "an over-simplified vision and a tortured awareness of realistic circumstance." In one breath Crane is charged with a mindless optimism or idealism; in the next he is charged with including ugly realities and negations that conflict with this idealism and "confuse" the poem.

A more consistent and, I believe, more accurate view will recognize that *the ugly realities are intended*. The tortured awareness of realistic circumstance is *an integral part of the vision*. The poem's vacillation, or dialectic (to give it an approved name), serves the clear purpose of keeping the vision from being oversimple—tempers it, ironically qualifies it, complicates it. In short, Crane is trying for a difficult rather than an easy beauty, a complex rather than a synthetic coherence.

(K)                    Gordon K. Grigsby. *CE*. April, 1963. pp. 518–19

If one approaches *The Bridge* without a precommitment to Crane's own statement of its theme, it is possible to find in it a theme which provides a high degree of organic unity. The poem is a search or quest for a mythic vision, rather than the fixed, symbolic expression of a vision firmly held in the poet's mind. The vision sought is one that will be based on a knowledge of a glorious past, and will provide a bridge from that past to the hopeful future, in spite of the dearth of hopeful signs in the actual present. The poem is highly subjective in language and content, and understandably so, because the quest is a personal quest, the search of the poet for a vision that will satisfy his *own* needs. But Crane also saw the problem of the poet as reflecting the central problem of the society in which he lived, and the poet's solution to the problem—if he could achieve one—as having consequences far beyond the poet's own private life.

(K)                    Thomas A. Vogler. *SwR*. Summer, 1965. pp. 381–2

See *The Bridge, Collected Poems,* and *Letters.*

# CRANE, STEPHEN (1871–1900)

He sang, but his voice erred up and down the scale, with occasional flashes of brilliant melody, which could not redeem the errors. New York was essentially his inspiration, the New York of suffering and baffled and beaten life, of inarticulate or blasphemous life; and away from it he was not at home, with any theme, or any sort of character. It was the pity of his fate that he must quit New York, first as a theme, and then as a habitat; for he rested nowhere else, and wrought with nothing else as with the lurid depths which he gave proof of knowing better than anyone else.

William Dean Howells. *NAR*. Dec., 1902. p. 771

In his art he is unique. Its certainty, its justness, its peculiar perfection of power arrived at its birth, or at least at that precise moment in its birth when other artists—and great artists too—were preparing themselves for the long and difficult conquest of their art. I cannot remember a parallel case in the literary history of fiction. . . . His art is just in itself, rhythmical, self-poising as is the art of a perfect dancer. There are no false steps, no excesses. And, of course, his art is strictly limited. We would define him by saying he is the perfect artist and interpreter of the surfaces of life. And that explains why he so swiftly attained his peculiar power and what is the realm his art commands and his limitations.

Edward Garnett. *Friday Nights* (Knopf). 1922. p. 205

He had a quiet smile that charmed and frightened one. It made you pause by something revelatory it cast over his whole physiognomy, not like a ray but like a shadow. . . . Contempt and indignation never broke the surface of his moderation simply because he had no surface. He was all through the same material, incapable of affectation of any kind, of any pitiful failure of generosity for the sake of personal advantage, or even from sheer exasperation which must find its relief. . . . Though the word is discredited now and may sound pretentious, I will say that there was in Crane a strain of chivalry which made him safe to trust with one's life.

Joseph Conrad. Introduction to Thomas Beer's
*Stephen Crane* (Knopf). 1923. pp. 5, 7, 9–10

He is American literature's "marvelous boy." Like the Bowery, he was elemental and vital. He would sleep in a flop house to taste the bitter of experience. He loved living. And adventure enough was crowded into his eight sick years of manhood. He looked at life clearly and boldly, knew its irony, felt its mystery and beauty, and wrote about it with a sincerity and confidence that spring only from genius.

Vernon Loggins. *I Hear America* (Crowell)
1937. p. 23

Crane left on me an impression of supernaturalness that I still have. It was perhaps the aura of that youth that never deserted him—perhaps because of his aspect of frailty. He seemed to shine—and perhaps the November sun really did come out and cast on his figure, in the gloom of my entry, a ray of light. At any rate, there he stands . . . radiating brightness. But it was perhaps more than anything the avenging quality of his brows and the resentful frown of his dark blue eyes. He saw, that is to say, the folly and malignity of humanity—not in the individual but in committees.

Ford Madox Ford. *Portraits from Life* (Houghton).
1937. p. 24

For all its beauty, Crane's best work was curiously thin and, in one sense, even corrupt. His desperation exhausted him too quickly; his unique sense of tragedy was a monotone. No one in America had written like him before; but though his books precipitately gave the whole aesthetic movement of the nineties a sudden direction and a fresher impulse, he could contribute no more than the intensity of his spirit. Half of him was a consummate workman; the other half was not a writer at all. . . . His gift was a furious one, but barren; writing much, he repeated himself so joylessly that in the end he seemed to be mocking himself with the same quiet viciousness with which, even as a boy, he had mocked the universe.

Alfred Kazin. *On Native Grounds* (Reynal).
1942. pp. 71–2

Crane was one of the first post-impressionists. . . . He began it before the French painters began it or at least as early as the first of them. He simply knew from the beginning how to handle detail. He estimated it at its true worth—made it serve his purposes and felt no further responsibility about it. I doubt whether he ever spent a laborious half-hour in doing his duty by detail—in enumerating, like an honest, grubby auctioneer. If he saw one thing that engaged him in a room, he mentioned it. If he saw one thing in a landscape that thrilled him, he put it on paper, but he never tried to make a faithful report of everything else within his field of vision, as if he were a conscientious salesman making out an expense account.

Willa Cather. *On Writing* (Knopf). 1949. pp. 69–70

The immense power of the tacit . . . gives his work kinship rather with Chekhov and Maupassant than Poe. "I like my art"—said Crane—

"straight"; and misquoted Emerson, "There should be a long logic beneath the story, but it should be carefully kept out of sight." How far Crane's effect of inevitability depends upon this *silence* it would be hard to say. Nowhere in "The Open Boat" is it mentioned that the situation of the men is symbolic, clear and awful though it is that this story opens into the universe. Poe in several great stories opens man's soul downwards, but his work has no relation with the natural and American world at all. If Crane's has, and is irreplaceable on this score, it is for an ironic inward and tragic vision outward that we value it most, when we can bear it. . . . Crane does really stand between us and something that we could not otherwise understand. It is not human; it is not either the waves and mountains who are among his major characters, but it acts in them, it acts in children and sometimes even in men, upon animals, upon boys above all, and men. Crane does not understand it fully. But he has been driven and has dragged himself nearer by much to it than we have, and he interprets for us.

(K)                      John Berryman. *Stephen Crane* (Wm. Sloane
                                 Associates). 1950. pp. 291–2

Jean Julius Christian Sibelius (born six years before Stephen Crane) may or may not slink down the cellar stairs whenever "Finlandia" is played, and Stephen Crane might have developed a comparable skin-crawl every time *The Red Badge of Courage* was mentioned. The fact that his other novels, all of them short for their day and rather shorter for ours, now go unread might not distress him, and toward his verse, with its conscious and even proclaimed echo of Emily Dickinson (an echo louder than the voice of origin), he might today be as patronizing and indulgent as the next man. (There is one great advantage to dying young—you can impute all your faults to your youth.) But he would, I am sure, take high pride in his competence with the short story, and it would be a proper pride. For Crane still has, and always will have, the capacity to teach by sterling example (as in "The Open Boat" and "The Blue Hotel") the fine art of narration.

(K)                          John T. Winterich. *SR*. Feb. 3, 1951. p. 43

Irony is Crane's chief technical instrument. It is the key to our understanding of the man and of his works. He wrote with the intensity of a poet's emotion, the compressed emotion that bursts into symbol and paradox. . . .

*Crane's style is prose pointillism*. It is composed of disconnected images, which coalesce like the blobs of color in French impressionist paintings, every word-group having a cross-reference relationship, every seemingly disconnected detail having interrelationship to the configurated whole. The intensity of a Crane work is owing to this patterned coalescence of disconnected things, everything at once fluid and precise. A striking analogy is established between Crane's use of colors and the method employed by the impressionists and neo-impressionists or divisionists, and it is as if he had known about their theory of contrasts and had composed his own prose paintings by the same principle.

(K)                         Robert W. Stallman. *Stephen Crane. An Omnibus*
                            (Knopf). 1952. pp. xxv, 185

. . . the Crane story again and again interprets the human situation in terms of the ironic tensions created in the contrast between man as he idealizes himself in his inner thought and emotion and man as he actualizes himself in the stress of experience. In the meaning evoked by the ironic projection of the deflated man against the inflated man lies Crane's essential theme: the consequence of false pride, vanity, and blinding delusion.

(K)                         James B. Colvert. *MFS*. Autumn, 1959. p. 200

Any student can recall that Stephen Crane has been termed realist, romantic, naturalist, imagist, existentialist, symbolist, impressionist, expressionist, and *pointilliste*. (I may have overlooked some). That roster becomes doubly formidable when one remembers that somebody has taken the trouble to deny the validity of almost every one of those labels— if only to make room for pasting on his own red wafer. Common sense suggests, therefore, that we are dealing with a vivid and significant writer who cannot be categorized simply—perhaps not at all. . . .

One conclusion suggested by these facts is that Crane never outlived his apprenticeship. He did not live to become any sort of "ist." . . . Crane died a Seeker. . . .

His experience of sports brought Crane knowledge, and attitudes consequent on that knowledge, important to his point of view. It gave him the experience of testing his courage and thence personal knowledge of pain and fear, victory and defeat. From that vantage point he commanded the cosmic gambler's stoic outlook: despising the petty, safe and comfortable; prizing the chance-taking, the enterprising, the seeking, aggressive and tough. In this he was at one with the prophets of the strenuous life. But he went beyond them in the depth of his forceful but ambivalent compassion for losers. He was anxious that their courage or at least their agony be defended against and registered upon the smug and ignorant. But he would not defend them against the law, against the rules of the game of life.

(K)                         Edwin H. Cady. *ELH*. Dec., 1961. pp. 378, 381

Both Crane and Hemingway began with a sense of irony, a gift for understatement, an abhorrence of sentimentalism and a view of man that made war one of the important, inevitable metaphors for dramatizing their in-

sights. Man under stress, at the center of powerful, irrational forces, man forging and tempering an answerable courage and code is the repetitive situation at the center of both writers' works. They both assert that in heaven there is *nada,* that nature is indifferent, that the uninitiated, unwounded are ignorantly cruel and barbarously sentimental. Only the scarred can hope to offer even a tentative interpretation of man's dilemmas.
(K)                     Sy Kahn in *Essays in Modern American Literature,*
                        edited by Richard E. Langford (Stetson University).
                                                        1963. pp. 36–7

## Maggie

*Maggie* is not a story *about* people; it is primitive human nature itself set down with perfect spontaneity and grace of handling. For pure aesthetic beauty and truth no Russian, not Tchekhov himself, could have bettered this study which, as Howells remarks, has the quality of Greek tragedy.
                        Edward Garnett. *Friday Nights* (Knopf). 1922.
                                                        pp. 214–5

It is short, a novelette. Yet it suggests more life than any American contemporary of Crane could have depicted in a thousand pages. In its every crowded phrase and metaphor it is reality. The little book breaks all traditions of fiction. Crane has no model for it—except possibly the page or two he had read from Zola. But it is not Zolaesque. Critics like to call it the first specimen of genuine realism produced by an American. Perhaps it is that. But it should be judged as a thing unique—just a faithful and vivid projection of the grim degradation and sordid beauty of the Bowery.
                        Vernon Loggins. *I Hear America* (Crowell). 1937.
                                                        p. 25

## The Red Badge of Courage

The deep artistic unity of *The Red Badge of Courage* is fused in its flaming, spiritual intensity, in the fiery ardour with which the shock of the Federal and Confederate armies is imaged. The torrential force and impetus, the check, sullen recoil and reforming of shattered regiments, and the renewed onslaught and obstinate resistance of brigades and divisions are visualized with extraordinary force and color. If the sordid grimness of carnage is partially screened, the feeling of war's cumulative rapacity, of its breaking pressure and fluctuating tension is caught with wonderful fervour and freshness of style.
                        Edward Garnett. *Friday Nights* (Knopf). 1922.
                                                        pp. 212–3

Intense, brutal, bloody, *The Red Badge of Courage* vitalizes the smoke, noise, stench, dread, terror, agony, and death of the battlefield. Thrust into the horror, the reader identifies himself with Henry Fleming and feels with him the trepidation of fear and heroism. How a boy of twenty-two conceived the story and within a few days got it down on paper with such truthfulness to detail that no veteran soldier has ever been able to question its authenticity is one of the mysteries of artistic creation.

Vernon Loggins. *I Hear America* (Crowell). 1937.

p. 26

Suddenly there was *The Red Badge of Courage* showing us, to our absolute conviction, how the normal, absolutely undistinguished, essentially civilian man from the street had behaved in a terrible and prolonged war—without distinction, without military qualities, without special courage, without even any profound apprehension of, or passion as to, the causes of the struggle in which, almost without will, he was engaged. . . . With *The Red Badge of Courage* in the nineties, we were provided with a map showing us our own hearts. If before that date we had been asked how we should behave in a war, we should no doubt have answered that we should behave like demigods, with all the marmoreal attributes of war memorials. But, a minute after peeping into *The Red Badge* we knew that, at best, we should behave doggedly but with a weary non-comprehension, flinging away our chassepot rifles, our haversacks, and fleeing into the swamps of Shiloh.

Ford Madox Ford. *Portraits from Life* (Houghton).

1937. pp. 22–3

Crane's hero is Everyman, the symbol made flesh upon which war plays its havoc and it is the deliberation of that intention which explains why the novel is so extraordinarily lacking, as H. L. Mencken puts it, in small talk. Scene follows scene in an accelerating rhythm of excitement, the hero becomes the ubiquitous man to whom, as Wyndham Lewis once wrote of the Hemingway man, things happen. With that cold, stricken fury that was so characteristic of Crane—all through the self-conscious deliberation of his work one can almost hear his nerves quiver—he impaled his hero on the ultimate issue, the ultimate pain and humiliation of war, where the whole universe, leering through the blindness and smoke of battle, became the incarnation of pure agony. The foreground was a series of commonplaces; the background was cosmological.

Alfred Kazin. *On Native Grounds* (Reynal). 1942.

pp. 71–2

*The Red Badge of Courage* probes a state of mind under the incessant pin-pricks and bombardments of life. The theme is that man's salvation lies in change, in spiritual growth. It is only by immersion in the flux of experience that man becomes disciplined and develops in character, conscience, or soul. Potentialities for change are at their greatest in battle—a battle represents life at its most intense flux. Crane's book is not about the combat of armies; it is about the self-combat of a youth who fears and stubbornly resists change, and the actual battle is symbolic of this spiritual warfare against change and growth. Henry Fleming recognizes the necessity for change and development, but wars against it. The youth develops into the veteran: "So it came to pass . . . his soul changed." Significantly enough, in stating what the book is about Crane intones Biblical phrasing.

(K)                                 Robert W. Stallman. *Stephen Crane. An Omnibus* (Knopf). 1952. p. 193

The achievement of Crane in *The Red Badge of Courage* may be likened, it seems to me, to Chaucer's in *Troilus and Criseyde,* despite the lesser stature of the novel. Both works are infused with an irony which neatly balances two major views of human life—in *Troilus and Criseyde,* the value of courtly love versus heavenly love; in *The Red Badge of Courage,* ethical motivation and behavior versus deterministic and naturalistic actions. Both pose the problem, "Is there care in Heaven?" One is concerned with human values in a caring Universe, the other in an indifferent Universe. . . . Crane's magnum opus shows up the nature and value of courage. The heroic ideal is not what it has been claimed to be: so largely is it the product of instinctive responses to biological and traditional forces. But man does have will, and he has the ability to reflect, and though these do not guarantee that he can effect his own destiny, they do enable him to become responsible to some degree for the honesty of his personal vision. It is this duality of view, like Chaucer's, that is the secret of the unmistakable Crane's art.

(K)                          Stanley B. Greenfield. *PMLA.* Dec., 1958. pp. 571–2

Crane artistically rendered the raw experiences of war in a special, prismatic prose, in color-shot imagery and elegant impressions. It is a world where each sound is amplified by human terror, each color made brilliant and blaring by the frightened, wary eye, and the enemy invested with one's deepest, primitive fears. All this Crane instinctively knew in *The Red Badge of Courage.* In the fictional world of war, Crane's ironic vision, his talent for bizarre imagery, his curious religious and biblical diction (by which he inflates the egoistic actions and poses of his characters for later puncturing by pointed, ironic understatement), and his impressionistic descriptions could find their most ample expression. Crane's young soldier, Henry Fleming, like Hemingway's Nick Adams, finds himself thrust into a world that shocks him into new levels of feeling and perception; the two men are symbols of innocence blasted by violence, by what at worst seems an intelligent malevolence.

(K)                            Sy Kahn in *Essays in Modern American Literature*,
                               edited by Richard E. Langford (Stetson University).
                               1963. p. 36

## Poetry

The poems have an enigmatic air and yet they are desperately personal. The absence of the panoply of the Poet is striking. We remember that their author did not like to be called a poet nor did he call them poetry himself. How unusual this is, my readers will recognize: most writers of verse are merely dying to be called poets, tremblingly hopeful that what they write is real "poetry." There was no pose here in Crane. His reluctance was an inarticulate recognition of something strange in the pieces. They are not like literary compositions. They are like things just seen and said, *said for use*. . . . He has truths to tell. Everybody else in the 'nineties is chanting and reassuring and invoking the gods. So Crane just says, like a medicine man *before* chanting or poetry began. And what he says is savage: unprotected, forestlike.

(K)                            John Berryman. *Stephen Crane* (Wm. Sloane
                               Associates). 1950. pp. 272–3

Crane's best poems . . . present the bare outlines of a narrative situation in which there is a tension between two opposed forces. The tension may be expressed in terms of antithetical statements, dialogue, description, or the effect upon the observer of an action he witnesses. . . . By making his human figures faceless and nameless, by pitting them against elemental forces, by describing their ambitions and their plights in simple yet overwhelming metaphors, Crane created for his poetry a symbolical form which represented a great advance in subtlety and flexibility over its allegorical beginnings.

(K)                            Daniel Hoffman. *The Poetry of Stephen Crane*
                               (Columbia). 1956. pp. 263–4

See *Maggie, The Red Badge of Courage,* and *The Monster* (short novels); also *Twenty Stories* and *The Collected Poems.*

# CREELEY, ROBERT (1926–     )

Robert Creeley . . . is a hit-or-miss poet; and, if he is satisfied, then so must I be—for he is a good poet. Intransigent, "engaged," he can perceive the apocalypse in almost any moment he chooses. His method has been from the first poems in *Le Fou* staccato, elliptical. The dramatic situation—almost all the poems entail one or reactions to one—is made clear to the reader by shreds of rhetoric which are the involvement in it and act like images in a cluster. In this latter connection, Creeley's poems are one of our stronger links with other literatures—the Spanish and French especially—where writing from image to image is at least as important and frequent as protracting a single image into a rational conceit.

David Galler. *SwR*. Winter, 1961. p. 171

There is a good deal of emotion in Mr. Creeley's poetry; but it is not sullen, and if despair appears it is the kind which the poet confronts and faces down. His poems embody the imagination of a man who is not afraid of genuine feeling in his personal struggles to live day by day in the world, and who contends with feeling in a manner invariably marked by dignity and grace. He is able to create poems out of many feelings; but perhaps the one which is most noteworthy is the feeling of love. Mr. Creeley is one of the truest and most nourishing love poets alive.

James Wright. *MinnR*. Winter, 1961. p. 250

[William Carlos] Williams also presides behind the work of Robert Creeley. Most of the poems are short, and it is often the movement quite as much as the words that does the work, as for example in one of the best early poems, "The Innocence." At the same time his plainness of language may on occasion become a baldness, and the resulting poems are sometimes more similar to the notes for poems than to completed poems. . . .

His effect is at best one of purity and elegance; "care" is a favorite word in his early poems, and his care in suggesting minutiae is close to a moral care. There is a fragility, however, to most of his work, and it is only seldom (notably in "The Figures") that one feels his concerns are as fully explored as they deserve.

Thom Gunn. *YR*. Autumn, 1962. pp. 130–1

Creeley seems not to like pattern, really to be afraid of it, whether it is intellectual, structural (as in parallels or antitheses), metrical (when metric patterns are set up it is only so that they may be abandoned, thus defeating the expectation of recurrence), or a matter of rhyme (which is sometimes forced into a parody of itself that denies it value). Creeley seems not to like excitement either, at least in the forms of sound and image, for he persistently reduces poems to language that is prosaic. . . . What I hope is happening in Creeley's poetry is that the reticences are diminishing, and that the individual, direct and effective features of language which have been there all along—brevity of development, short lines, simple diction with considerable colloquialism and a little useful profanity—are now more willing to be united with an explicit situation.

William Dickey. Poetry. March, 1963. pp. 421, 423

Robert Creeley does a simple but rare thing. In each form he uses—up to now poetry, criticism, and a huge amount of letter writing—he insists on being "personal." That is, he allows his own mind to dominate, to dictate, formal procedure. He is the man who said it: "Form is only an extension of content"; and in his own work it is *consciously* so. He is, for instance, the only writer I know in whom I cannot find one rhetorical instance, i.e., "fitting" a sound: Creeley insists the opposite. And the forms themselves are of course changed by this, in the sense that they are "re-formed" each time to his personal measures. Also as a consequence, Creeley may maintain a consistency this way as "person" that is "trans-formal." He is one of the minority of poets who write good prose, and is even rarer for writing prose that is "like" his poetry.

Aram Saroyan. Poetry. April, 1964. pp. 45–6

The subject of [*The Gold Diggers and Other Stories*] is that kind of relation between people which is penetration, a locking or growing together in which the life becomes not what each one has alone but what is between them—all the inseparable pains and pleasures, terrors and joys of that kind of relation, in its presence, or at times in its absence. . . . In such an effort, the principled use of the conventional arts of fiction becomes a distraction. What takes their place, giving the stories the concrete texture of their substance and giving the reader his experience, are the kinesthetic rhythms of the utterance. These rhythms are the gestures of Creeley's apprehension of his characters, at the level where apprehension is itself response. . . .

It is because Creeley is so completely "in" these stories . . . that he has discarded conventional craft for utterance. It is for the same reason that in his poetry he has discarded the formal use of symbol and meter, again for utterance. He has minimized the differentia of poetry and fiction in his work, so that his stories take a position somewhere between the novel and the poems in a continuum, different not so much in kind from each other as in narrowness of focus. The stories are comparable in length to the chapters of the novel, but their intensity is much greater. The poems are at the other end of the range, straining articulation to its limits and approaching absolute intensity.

Samuel Moon. Poetry. August, 1966. pp. 341–2

If a last stand were necessary (it does not seem to be), one could say that this sort of poetry, like René Char's work in France during the Occupation and like some of the post-World War II poetry of England that makes a point of restraint and cool control, is the last stand of genuine sensibility against the violence and ruthlessness of twentieth-century civilization. But genuine sensibility cannot give up its passion quite so tamely; it all seems a little too confined to settle for just yet.—Perhaps after World War III? If so, Creeley is indeed ahead of his time.

> M. L. Rosenthal. *The New Poets: American and British Poetry Since World War II* (Oxford). 1967.
> p. 159

See *For Love* and *Words* (poetry); *The Island* (novel); *The Gold Diggers and Other Stories*.

# CULLEN, COUNTEE (1903–1946)

There are numerous things which Mr. Cullen as a poet has not yet begun to do, and there are some which he will never do, but in this first volume (*Color*) he makes it clear that he has mastered a tune. Few recent books of poems have been so tuneful—at least so tuneful in the execution of significant themes. . . . Mr. Cullen's skill appears in the clarity and the certainty of his song. . . . If Mr. Cullen faces any danger it is this—that he shall call facility a virtue rather than the aspect of a virtue.

> Mark Van Doren. *NYHT*. Jan. 10, 1926. p. 3

This first volume of musical verses (*Color*) offers promise of distinction for its author, shows him to be a young poet of uncommon earnestness and diligence. Serious purpose and careful work are apparent in all of his poems. One feels that he will cultivate his fine talent with intelligence, and reap its full harvest. He has already developed a lyric idiom which is not, perhaps, very unusual or striking in itself, but which he has learned to employ with considerable virtuosity.

> George H. Dillon. *Poetry*. April, 1926. p. 50

With Countee Cullen's *Color* we have the first volume of the most promising of the younger Negro poets. There is no point in measuring him merely beside Dunbar, Alberry A. Whitman, and other Negro poets of the past and present: he must stand or fall beside Shakespeare and Keats and Masefield, Whitman and Poe and Robinson. The volume has much promise, some achievement, and a long advertisement of its author's excessive youth and metrical conservatism. . . . That Cullen is a poet is clear; if he can attune himself to the negative merit of avoiding "the stock poetical touches," and build from that, he may grow to commanding stature.

> Clement Wood. *YR*. July, 1926. p. 824

Cullen is, it seems to me, just a little too much the product of our American colleges. His earlier work was more his own. This is true not only because his earlier poems had to do, often, with the emotions of the Negro race, but because they were more direct statements of the poet's own sensitivity. If the earlier poems were less perfect technically, they had more complete sincerity. Sincerity is not necessarily art, of course, but while a poet speaks his own language, however crudely, there is hope that he may develop the necessary skill of the true artist. When he speaks too often in literary phrase and image, he ceases to be significant. These last lyrics and sonnets of Cullen's have this defect.

Eda Lou Walton. *NYHT*. Sept. 15, 1935. p. 17

Where Oxford dons have so often failed, an American Negro writer has succeeded. Mr. Cullen has rendered Euripides's best known tragedy (*The Medea*) into living and utterable English. He has made little attempt to convey the poetry of the original, preferring to concentrate on dramatic situation and realistic portrayal of character. The result is a very forceful and poignant re-creation of the story of the barbarian sorcerer. . . . Mr. Cullen's version is admirably suited to the exigencies of the contemporary stage. For an adaptation which does not pretend to be a literal translation, it follows the original closely, giving English equivalents for all but a few of the speeches in the Greek.

Philip Blair Rice. *Nation*. Sept. 18, 1935. p. 336

One feels he is happiest in his sonnets to Keats and in his variations of the "made ballad." . . . At his best . . . Cullen shows a real gift for the neat, sensitive, and immediate lyric. When the observation contained in the poem is direct and personal, dealing immediately with people seen and events that really occurred, the poems emerge movingly.

Too often, however, the treatment is marred by a taint of "artiness" that is too obviously derivative. . . . It is for the one poem in ten that emerges whole that Countee Cullen will be remembered.

John Ciardi. *At*. March, 1946. p. 145

As one rereads Mr. Cullen's verses, deploring the pity that so real a talent should have been lost in early death, one is bothered by various doubts. Would his talent have matured if he had lived? Was it ever more than a skill at echoing, at assuming the poetic attitudes of the late Victorian and the Georgian past? Is not this verse pretty thoroughly undergraduate— smooth metric, pretty imagery, college Lit. diction? Mr. Cullen wrote like all of one's favorite poets of the traditional order.

Dudley Fitts. *NYT*. Feb. 23, 1947. p. 26

Cullen's verses skip; those by Hughes glide. But in life Hughes is the merry one. Cullen was a worrier. . . . Equally evident . . . was Cullen's tendency to get his inspiration, his rhythms and patterns as well as much of his substance from books and the world's lore of scholarship. . . . Cullen was in many ways an old-fashioned poet. . . . About half of his "best poems" were written while he was a student of New York University, and it was during these years that he first came up for consideration as an authentic American writer, the goal to which he aspired. . . . Cullen did not live to see another springtime resurgence of his own creative powers comparable with the impulse that produced his first three books of poetry, the books which give his selected poems most of their lilt and brightness.

Arna Bontemps. *SR*. March 22, 1947. pp. 12–3, 44

Probably no one can tell just how or why Cullen's promise faded into mediocre fulfillment, but it is possible to suggest some of the reasons. Cullen neither accepted nor developed a comprehensive world-view. As a consequence, his poems seem to result from occasional impulse rather than from direction by an integrated individual. . . . He was, in other words, an able and perplexed intelligence and a sensitive and confused heart.

Harvey Curtis Webster. *Poetry*. July, 1947. p. 222

As we read Cullen's racial poetry today, our feelings are mixed. Even though we understand and appreciate the larger implications of the alien-and-exile theme, we recognize its basic fallacy just as Cullen himself seemed to recognize it in *The Black Christ*. We also recognize that protest poetry of every type has lost much of its former popularity. We realize too that in the age of "new criticism" and intellectual verse, Cullen's style and general approach to poetry are dated; the Pre-Raphaelite delicacy of his lyrics is lost upon a generation which can find value only in "metaphysical" poetry. And yet in spite of these drawbacks, I believe that Cullen's racial poems will live. They will live first of all because they are a record of and a monument to the New Negro Movement, and as such they will always be important to the literary historian. Second, they will live for the social historian because they have made articulate the agony of racial oppression during a dark period in our continuing struggle for democracy. And most important of all, a few of them will live because they are good poems—good enough to survive the ravages of time and changing taste.

Arthur P. Davis. *Phylon*. Sept., 1953. p. 400

See *On These I Stand* (poetry).

# CUMMINGS, EDWARD ESTLIN (1894–1962)

The poet always seems to be having a glorious time with himself and his world even when the reader loses his breath in the effort to share it. He is as agile and outrageous as a faun, and as full of delight over the beauties and monstrosities of this brilliant and grimy old planet. There is a grand gusto in him.

Harriet Monroe. Poetry. Jan., 1924. pp. 213–4

Since the highbrows have taken to vaudeville, Cummings is their favorite Touchstone. At times, he overplays the clown; at others he has the instinct of the perfect comedian. When he is perfect, no poet is more dazzling; when he plays the bad boy too many times, one has an itch for spanking and shooing him to bed.

Alfred Kreymborg. Our Singing Strength<br>(Coward-McCann). 1929. p. 519

I have heard two personal friends of E. E. Cummings debating as to whether his prosodical and punctuational gymnastics have not been a joke at the expense of the critics of poetry. One of them thinks Cummings will some day come out and announce that he has been joking; the other insists with fervent and faithful admiration that he is really as crazy as he seems.

Max Eastman. The Literary Mind (Scribner). 1932.<br>p. 103

What Mr. Cummings likes or admires, what he holds dear in life, he very commonly calls flowers, or dolls, or candy—terms with which he is astonishingly generous; as if he thought by making his terms general enough their vagueness could not matter, and never noticed that the words so used enervate themselves in a kind of hardened instinct.

R. P. Blackmur. The Double Agent (Arrow). 1935.<br>p. 20

No American poet of the twentieth century has ever shown so much implied respect for the conventions of his milieu through conscious blasphemy as E. E. Cummings. If Cummings's verse seemed "revolutionary" and radical (which it was in the sense that its wit was concerned with the roots of syntax and grammar) it was because its life was and still is so completely surrounded by conventions. . . . The entire question of Cummings's maturity in the writing of his poetry has been and still remains a private matter. In the light of Cummings's accomplishments and in the recognition of the boundaries or limits that they have circumscribed, it is very nearly an impertinence for anyone to tell him to "grow up," for one must not forget that he is one of the finest lyric poets of all time.

Horace Gregory and Marya Zaturenska. History of<br>
American Poetry (Harcourt). 1947. pp. 337–47

If Cummings is undistinguished as a thinker, he is always surprising as a creative craftsman. He is simultaneously the skillful draftsman, the leg-pulling clown, the sensitive commentator and the ornery boy. The nose-thumbing satirist is continually interrupted by the singer of brazenly tender lyrics. A modern of the moderns, he displays a seventeenth century obsession with desire and death; part Cavalier, part metaphysician, he is a shrewd manipulator of language, and his style—gracefully erotic or downright indecent—is strictly his own.

Louis Untermeyer. Modern American Poetry<br>
(Harcourt). 1950. p. 509

In an age when language tends to become platitudinous and anemic, it is a splendid thing to have a poet take the most colourless words of all—the necessary anonymous neuter robots that ordinarily do their jobs without asking for wages of recognition—and suddenly give them character and responsibility. It's as if an albino sparrow were suddenly to grow red and blue feathers, or the little switch engine in the roundhouse were shown that it could draw the Sante Fe Chief.

Theodore Spencer in Modern American Poetry, edited<br>
by B. Rajan (Roy). 1952. p. 122

Some of Cummings's early lyrics have an Elizabethan decorativeness. His later poems make words as abstract as "am," "if," "because," do duty for seemingly more solid nouns. By this very process, however, he restores life to dying concepts. "Am" implies being at its most responsive, "if" generally means the creeping timidity that kills responsiveness, and "because" the logic of the categorizing mind that destroys what it dissects. Here is a new vocabulary, a kind of imageless metaphor.

Babette Deutsch. Poetry in Our Time (Holt). 1952.<br>
p. 113

At his worst, Cummings can achieve an almost Guestian bathos. At his best, he creates a pure poetry in which a venerable tradition meets the modern idioms. In these latter poems, e. e. resembles some of Lyonel Feininger's paintings: at first you see only non-representation, cubes and cones, but then, behind the very contemporary style, the shapes of familiar cities come before you.

Michael Harrington. Com. Dec. 10, 1954. p. 295

Are briskly vibrating sound and verbal paradox enough? . . . He is still a poet who is considerably more talked about than he deserves to be, a man who has made his vogue out of a large amount of—at best—casually semi-private writing.

Carl Bode. Poetry. Sept., 1955. pp. 362–3

(Cummings's poetry) has come . . . to assert, remonstrate, and define rather than simply to present, as it once predominantly did. Cummings's gift of impressionistic evocation, though it could not be said to have departed entirely . . . is sinking into desuetude together with his impulse toward typographical experimenting. . . . Regardless of the quality of change, one thing does not change: the unique Cummings voice. Or if it might be said to change, it is only in the direction of a still profounder individuality.

Rudolph Von Abele. PMLA. Dec., 1955. pp. 932–3

We see him ever as an individual, liking and respecting other individuals, but hating the masses as masses, hating governments, hating war, hating propaganda (ours or anybody else's), hating machinery, hating science. Willing to settle for nothing less than perfection, he is a great hater, although he is also a great lover, perhaps the most ardent or at any rate the most convincing poet of love in our day. Whom and what he loves he loves deeply, but for him the existence of love demands the expression of anger, contempt, disgust for what is unworthy of love. That is what he is and what he has been since coming of age, though practice has refined him in the art of being nobody-but-himself.

Granville Hicks. SR. Nov. 22, 1958. p. 14

Cummings' view of life is nonrational, and he sometimes sees himself as the Fool, the Outcast, the Clown, and so on, vis-à-vis ordinary society. He is more interested, as Walter Pater was, in experiencing life than in theorizing about it, but for a rather different reason—Pater's moments of crystallization were precious because nature is always dying, while Cummings' are precious because nature is always just being born. He is interested in what is alive and growing, in what is therefore immeasurable and mysterious.

(K)    Norman Friedman. e.e. cummings: The Growth of a Writer (Southern Illinois). 1964. p. 18

If life was not always black and white in Cummings' created universe, if the poet was sometimes "maturely" aware of complexity and of apparently ineradicable darkness, it is nevertheless true that he nowhere evidenced the developing vision that has characterized the work of, say, T. S. Eliot.

Cummings did not have to struggle through the Valley of Despond to the Celestial City. He was born there. He did not pass through a series of clearly demarked periods of technical development.

(K)                          Barry Marks. *E. E. Cummings* (Twayne). 1964. p. 141

Shoulders squared, the handsome and arrogant head sculptured by Gaston Lachaise held proudly, Cummings in his sixties was not much different from the young blond poet who had appeared so spectacularly with his poems and drawings in *The Dial* a generation before. He had remained an individual in the age of conformity, and the *enfant terrible* (and magic-maker) of the twenties had stayed young doing so. For he was still the same solitary and dedicated man he had always been, not so much aloof, as supposed, as keeping himself to himself, painting by day, writing at night, dreading company, and then entertaining the company that came with tireless, exuberant talk.

(K)                          Charles Norman. *E. E. Cummings: The Magic-Maker*
(Duell). 1965. p. 6

Cummings' concept of the individual did not emerge fully developed at the beginning of his career to be reaffirmed through successive volumes of poetry without any perceptible change or increase in significance, as has too often been stated. Rather, the early volumes primarily celebrate the simple joy of living through the senses, though they also contain some of Cummings' best satiric pieces.

The middle volumes, beginning approximately with *is 5* in 1926, reaching a culmination with *no thanks* in 1935, and showing evidence of a changing emphasis with *50 Poems* in 1940, reveal a heightened and defensively sensitive awareness of the individual in relation to his social environment. . . .

With the publication of *50 Poems* another important dimension becomes evident in Cummings' poetry. Beginning approximately with this volume and extending through *95 Poems* in 1958 and *73 Poems* in 1963, we find Cummings examining the positive impact that the individual exerts upon his fellow men. As we have seen, what the individual has to offer, what the pattern of his life illustrates, is love. He is a practitioner of love for life, for others, and for one particular beloved. In the latest poems the individual emerges as the only true exponent of love.

(K)                          Robert E. Wegner. *The Poetry and Prose of E. E.*
*Cummings* (Harcourt). 1965. pp. 80–1

. . . cummings' free style is exemplary in the sense that he seems never to imply, "Exactly imitate me!" but rather, "Here is what one of us can do with the conventions and still communicate effectively (at least on a par with most attempts); so why not go and see what you can do in *your* way? Each of us is valuable to others chiefly as he is honestly himself." Together, the love-poems and the satires, the many pages of vital, maturing poetry from *Tulips and Chimneys* (1923) to *73 Poems* (1963), present a broad spectrum, from brutal irony against what he felt unworthy of human beings to pure lyricism, celebrating the love which he found inseparable from truth and beauty, and the best, even the noblest, human experience. If he shocks, it is not to lower standards but to raise them—invariably in the direction of valuing and respecting individual worth and freedom, toward realizing and cherishing the dignity in each created soul.

(K)                         Robert G. Tucker in *The Twenties,* edited by Richard
                            E. Langford and William E. Taylor (Everett Ed-
                            wards). 1966. p. 26

Although in so frankly a primitivistic ethos as Cummings', ideal perception and response are not really a matter of exotic vision, Cummings is inclined to make the same kind of distinctions that one would find in objectivist theory. There are the deluded rationalists (bourgeois society) and the enlightened irrationalists (poets). . . . Similarly, Cummings' ideas concerning the "self" and its relation to the external world, nature, follow a logic not remote from the objectivist's. To begin with, identity with "Life" means "self-transcendence" and what would be called by "mostpeople" nonidentity, since to be "most truly alive" means to transcend the social self and to acquire the natural one (selflessness) that comes with response to the universe.

(K)                         L. S. Dembo. *Conceptions of Reality in Modern
                            American Poetry* (California). 1966. p. 119

### Love Lyrics

Cummings's Paganism is as much a reaction against New England Puritanism as it is a passionate embrace of the earth and its ladies. Behind his beautiful gamboling, one hears the heartbeats, subtle and exquisite, of a poet steeped in sentiment. He is the love poet of the radical era.

                            Alfred Kreymborg. *Our Singing Strength* (Coward-
                            McCann). 1929. p. 516

Cummings wrote excellent love lyrics, lyrics which contained all the compliments that a young woman would like to hear, and such compliments also enhanced the figure of a perennially youthful lover who would go to war against any and all of the conventions that were outside of or that threatened to impede or divert the course of courtly love. . . . All these were written (so it seems) in the same spirit that graced the songs and speeches of the *commedia dell'arte,* which traveled up from Italy in the sixteenth century to entertain the peoples of the rest of Europe.

Horace Gregory and Marya Zaturenska. *History of American Poetry* (Harcourt). 1947. pp. 338–45

This is courtly love, full of *thee's* and *thou's* and ballads to "my lady," and elaborate conceits which would be cloying were it not for the freshness of Cummings's rhetoric. These tender songs, delicate in grace, ethereal in mood, are founded on emotion, the realness of the feeling of this man for this woman. For all their delicacy they are resilient and durable; he is a love-lyricist of timeless appeal.

David Burns. *SR.* Dec. 18, 1954. p. 11

### Satiric Poems

Leave him alone, and he will play in a corner for hours, with his fragilities, his colors, and his delight in the bright shapes of all the things he sees. . . . The important point about E. E. Cummings is, however, that he was not left alone. He was dumped out into the uninnocent and unlyrical world. . . . His lyricism, shy enough at best, ran completely for cover, and he turned upon the nightmare worlds of reality, partly with the assumed callousness and defensive self-mockery of the very sensitive, and partly with the white and terrible anger of the excessively shy.

S. I. Hayakawa. *Poetry.* Aug., 1938. pp. 285–6

He has a nose for decay wherever it shows itself. It may be in verse that caters to the stock responses of flyspecked sensibilities. It may be in "the Cambridge ladies who live in furnished souls," those afflicted with the occupational diseases of gentility: blindness and deafness to the natural world. It may be the "notalive undead" who make up a "peopleshaped toomany-ness." He recognizes the fixed grin of death in the insane cheerfulness of the brotherhood of advertisers and high-pressure salesmen. His sales resistance to them is complete, whether their products be red shirts, brown shirts, white shirts with Arrow collars, or shrouds.

Babette Deutsch. *Poetry in Our Time* (Holt). 1952. p. 115

He challenges in a lyric version of civil disobedience the entire framework of our *soi-disant* civilization till the whole structure and its inhabitants threaten to fall down about his head.

Cummings has satirized . . . extinction of personality in some of the most virulent philippics to grace literature since mad Dean Swift.

David Burns, *SR.* Dec. 18, 1954. p. 11

**The Enormous Room**

The book has few dead phrases in it—it lives, if somewhat with the horrible life of a centipede. It has fire, now smoldering, now for a bit blazing into unhealthy violet and mustard-colored flame. There is precious metal in it, but Mr. Cummings has brought up from his agonized and subterranean digging along with some nuggets of character and description all manner of sweepings, cobwebs, and twisted iron.

Robert Littell. *NR*. May 10, 1922. p. 321

Butt of a great white joke, Cummings observed with awe and fascination the perfectly unreasonable geometry of cosmic antics. . . . A new, crisp, brindled style had presented itself for birth. The prose forming Cummings's vision of the illogical will of things and the unsuspected affinities between pain and delight, leads one out among advertising, skyscrapers, and movies. The verbal integument affirms utimate values, since it remains organic and subtle; and still it does not contradict the style of life existing in American streets and assembly places. . . . And shrilly pitched, caricatural, even more in tempo than in tendency, taut of rhythm, Cummings's prose relates rebellious matters, never before associated, with exquisite smoothness of modulation. It juxtaposes ancient elegances and brutalities of expression, sensitively employed traditional idiom and gamiest crudities of the vernacular.

Paul Rosenfeld. *Men Seen* (Dial). 1925. pp. 192–5

*The Enormous Room* has the effect of making all but a very few comparable books that came out of the War look shoddy and worn. It has been possible to re-read it, as I have done . . . and always to find it undiminished. . . . Cummings . . . encountered, in that huge barracks at La Ferté-Macé which he calls the Enormous Room, a sad assortment of men. They from being his companions in misery become, whether they speak or not—and the most eloquent are those who have the smallest command of words—his counsellors in compassion. . . . The mind provides no answer to the problem of suffering. . . . The answer, even for a poet, is not in words. . . . For what can oppose the poverty of the spirit, but the pride of the body? . . . And in Cummings there is from now on, in all he writes, an exaltation of the lowly and lively. He is himself, and he accepts his common lot.

John Peale Bishop. *Collected Essays* (Scribner). 1948.
pp. 89–91

See *Poems, 1923–1954;* also *i: six nonlectures* (memoirs), *him* (play), and *The Enormous Room* (novel).

# DAHLBERG, EDWARD (1900–    )

The author of *Bottom Dogs* is . . . very close to us—he is closer to us, indeed, than we quite care to have literature be. *Bottom Dogs* is the back-streets of all our American cities and towns. . . . The prose of *Bottom Dogs* is derived partly from the American vernacular, but to say this may give a misleading impression—Dahlberg's prose is primarily a literary medium, hard, vivid, racy, exact, and with an odd kind of street-light glamor. I do not agree with D. H. Lawrence . . . that the dominating feeling of the book is repulsion—it would be quite easy for a writer of the harsh or satirical kind to make Dahlberg's material repulsive, but I do not feel that Dahlberg has done so: the temperament through which he has strained the barber-shops, the orphan homes, the bakeries and the dance-halls of his story is, though realistic and precise, rather a gentle and unassertive, and consequently an unembittered, one.

Edmund Wilson. NR. March 26, 1930. p. 157

Dahlberg's second novel [*From Flushing to Calvary*] emerges from his first —*Bottom Dogs*. Having laid his foundations there, he here uses cinematic photography of the life of Lorry and his mother, Lizzie, in their new environment, the suburban slums of Long Island. . . . Dahlberg's gift lies in his ability to re-create actuality, either by a process of building up detail; as in his story of the orphan days in *Bottom Dogs,* or swiftly, sharply, as in this novel. There is no character study here. There is neither psychology nor ideas nor meaning nor interpretation. When he gives the thoughts of his people, it is their immediate conscious thoughts which interest him. The thinking is merely a phase of the realism. And his people are moths that flit in and out of the path of an intense light until, singed and defeated, they fall away into darkness. But during the intervals of light he sets them forth with remarkable accuracy, and in the same way he sets forth their background with definitive sureness.

F. T. Marsh. Nation. Nov. 16, 1932. pp. 483–4

Dahlberg is adept at taking grotesque, harried and abysmal characters, and prodding them to become more and more themselves. The persons of his books whom he has selected for particular dislike, he pursues with a corrosive brand of comment which constantly crashes through their own concepts of their lives, like a heckler who breaks a debater's sequence at every point by shouting out unwieldy questions. Dahlberg's style is highly

mannered, with a distinctiveness that can readily alienate whenever it
ceases to attract. . . . Dahlberg has obviously been under great strain in
this ailing society, and in his writing he is settling a score.

Kenneth Burke. *NR*. Nov. 21, 1934. p. 53


The author is mainly concerned [in *Do These Bones Live*] to apply his
principles to American literature, though he touches on other literature,
and civilization in general. Accepting the Freudian theory that all motives
reduce to the libido, he discovers in the works of Thoreau, Whitman,
Melville, Poe—who yet are the best of our writers—vast cloudy symbols
of sexual inhibition. . . . This "renunciation of the carnal heart and flesh"
in American literature has led to its ugly opposite, naturalism. Moreover,
by depriving us of "earth wisdom," it has produced the shallow regionalism, and the dreary sociological fiction, which in America are substitutes for a literature of deep consciousness. . . . Luckily the author's style
will prevent a popular resurrection of his unhealthy ideas. There is controlled beauty in a few passages. . . . But as a rule the style is overloaded
with exclamations, italics and capitals, and obscured by ellipsis, the use
of odd or invented words, a profusion of metaphors too often slightly inaccurate, and mere want of order.

Albert J. Steiss. *Com.* May 16, 1941. p. 89


Dahlberg and other writers of his ilk, together with their raving readers
and other less studious camp-followers, are but the pseudo-intellectual
auxiliaries, in our decadent civilization that they rightly revile, of the
"garage proletariat" that they unjustifiably despise. Their claims to an intuitional omniscience are thus another expression of the unlettered "know-
all" faith that also characterizes the modern gadget-maniac. The Dahlbergs
and those whom they attack thus represent, together, the two elements of
disruption that threaten our civilization most gravely: practical reason and
intuitional reason that both pose as pure reason.

Edouard Roditi. *Poetry*. Jan., 1951. p. 238


In the relatively few novels concerned with the "bottom dogs" of society,
the message tends, again with exceptions, to be implicit only. For the
most part refusing the assistance of slogans, resolutions, and other revolutionary gestures, these novelists ambush the reader from behind a relentlessly objective description of life in the lower depths. Here is the
vast area of failure, of have-not, of down-and-out. In *Bottom Dogs*,
Edward Dahlberg created a name for the genre when he described Lorry
Lewis's life at an orphanage, his careless drift from job to job, his hobo-

ing experiences while riding the freights, and his viciously directionless life in Los Angeles.

Walter Rideout. *The Radical Novel in the United States*
(Harvard). 1956. p. 185

Not surprisingly, the best depression novels are those which were least mindful of the party line as this was being laid down in the *New Masses* by Michael Gold and Granville Hicks, and proselytized locally over the country by the John Reed Clubs. Edward Dahlberg's *Bottom Dogs,* published in 1930 with a rather inappropriate introduction by D. H. Lawrence, has hardly any overt political feeling at all. But this mordantly whimsical and grotesque book, with its echoes of Mark Twain and Sherwood Anderson, makes very good reading, especially if one had shared the dim image of Dahlberg that came down into the 1940's as some sort of Lawrencian apocalypticist who had once said something important about Melville. The picaresque story has to do with the adventures of Lorry Lewis, who as a young boy is put in an orphanage by his mother, a lady barber with a horrible pair of pince-nez glasses that are always slipping awry, so that she can take up with a Mississippi river-boat captain. There is much sordid realism and much sharp observation in the chapters dealing with the boy's early days in Kansas City and the years in the orphanage with such brilliantly caricatured companions as Herman Mush Tate and Bonehead-Star-Wolfe. The later scenes, in which Lorry Lewis, now a tramp on the eve of the depression, winds up in Los Angeles and gets involved with a group of vegetarian intellectuals and homosexuals in the Y.M.C.A. are very funny. And the chapter about Solomon's Dancepalace is a memorable picture of the underside of the Fitzgerald era.

Richard Chase. *Cmty*. Jan., 1957. p. 69

The fine title *Sorrows of Priapus* is a monad mirroring the world of Edward Dahlberg as it shines from this book. It shows the concision, the music, the feeling and the ambivalent vision which we take as the properties of the poet, and this book is a poem in prose. . . . The book is filled with gorgeous images, with important false facts about animals and heroes, with richness of language and mythic material, not only of the Old World. In fact the sustained beauty of the chapters concerning pre-Columbian times in America easily rivals any long poem using American material. . . . The book is itself bizarre and beautiful. It is distracting, stimulating, disenchanting, and it is not conducive to love nor to interest in men and women rather than in the sexes. . . . The source of the deeper disturbance is the attitude toward love as it comes to one through the mixed glories.

John Logan. *CR*. Autumn, 1958. pp. 29–30

Mr. Edward Dahlberg's *Can These Bones Live* is an American classic, even if only a few people know it, but what kind of classic, it is difficult to say. Criticism as we write it at present has no place for it, and this means that I probably shall not be able to do justice to my own admiration. Mr. Dahlberg, like Thoreau whom he admires more than any other nineteenth-century American, eludes his contemporaries; he may have to wait for understanding until the historians of ideas of the next generation can place him historically. For we have at present neither literary nor historical standards which can guide us in to Mr. Dahlberg's books written since *Bottom Dogs,* which was published more than thirty years ago. It is significant that he has repudiated this early, naturalistic novel, in spite of the considerable admiration that it won and still retains among a few persons. *Can These Bones Live* may be seen as the summation of a three-part visionary and prophetic work which includes *The Flea of Sodom* and *The Sorrows of Priapus.*

We shall get nowhere with Mr. Dahlberg if we begin with an inquiry into his influences and his philosophy; this kind of thinking would inevitably be reductive. We must return repeatedly to the text to ponder the hundreds of aphorisms, epigrams, and paradoxes which add up to an intuitive synthesis of insights which defies logical exposition. . . . His tragic vision of the human condition redeems what might otherwise appear to be a kind of romantic anarchism. . . .

Allen Tate. SwR. Spring, 1961. pp. 314–16

. . . *Because I Was Flesh* in its way is a beautiful book in addition to being an extraordinary one; whereas *Bottom Dogs,* although powerful and disturbing, is not. What differentiates one from the other, I think, is not merely that Dahlberg is now looking at this mother and his environment from the inside out, but that he is also trying to understand his Ishmaelitish wanderings, to salvage some meaning from them, and to make tardy oblations to the Hagar toward whom he felt such shame and horror and love. Given the rhapsodic and often postured writing, his "impostumed" prose (to borrow one of the archaic or obsolescent words he seems fond of), one might be tempted to suspect the genuineness of Dahlberg's feelings. Yet to yield to such a temptation would be wrong. What keeps the confessional narration from becoming over-ripe and merely mannered is the distance he manages to place between his boyhood and his present self. His emotions are invariably tempered by reflection; the personal transmuted to the archetypal.

Daniel Aaron. HdR. Summer, 1964. p. 313

What appears at first to be no more than a rewrite of Dahlberg's *Bottom Dogs,* that expatriate log of a vernacular midwest childhood, a crapulous youth and a lady-barber mother, is in fact a performance of another order entirely—one of the rare examples in our letters of the self overtaken. For this new book [*Because I Was Flesh*] is the creative reflection (a reflexive as well as a reflective act) of a man upon his own life (autobiography and lyric) and his mother's (hagiography and demonology). By his metamorphosis of the first version of those lives, by what has happened to his prose since that version, we discover how *he* has been changed, what he has learned, lost, won. . . . It is only, at last, in this new book, a memorial instance "because a breath passeth away and cometh not again", that raw event is inspissated by myth and morality, transcending the limitations suggested by comparison with other great American autobiographies.

Richard Howard. *Poetry*. March, 1965. pp. 398–9

The fact is that in *Because I Was Flesh,* Dahlberg has given us a world of the kind we used to find in the great novels, and, that it casts a spell. One forgets that there were, and some still are, living people who walked the earth, for the book envelops us in so authentic an atmosphere that the actualities of time and space die down, and another existence, that of eternity, takes its place. Even the cobblestones of the old streets in Kansas City have their echoes, as does the very grass and sky, and the dinginess of the back-parlor,· where Lizzie heats soup in a battered kettle for her squeamish, delicate but remarkably enduring son, is no more than the mirrored light of countless scenes which most modern fiction would have us forget. The very image of a whole woman, sensual, pining, mistaken and utterly appealing in her unworldly attempts to battle with the world is, by this time, a novel event. One even forgets that the son, who flees the mother to find himself, and returns to the mother to beseech for the unknown father, and who must invoke the dream for revelation, is the author, and not the fable. For the fable takes over, as the dream enlightens the author, and the magic of an experience that sought the dark to find the light, casts its mighty spell.

*Because I Was Flesh* is a great achievement, and, as the culmination of a long, arduous, dedicated, creative venture during which the contraries, the irascible, the didactic were finally reconciled with the *Amor Fati* of acceptance, it is also a triumph.

Josephine Herbst. *SoR*. Spring, 1965. p. 351

Edward Dahlberg's imagination is rich in history and myth; his style is fresh in allusion and muscular with verbs. The best of his work, alive with incantatory rhythms and a prophetic tone, generates the power of psalm or prayer. In the title poem [*Cipango's Hinder Door*], celebrating the innocent antiquity of the western hemisphere, Mr. Dahlberg combines impeccably cadenced free verse with short prose paragraphs in a remarkably successful contrapuntal structure.

As these generalizations imply, this book transcends egocentricity. In a foreword, Allen Tate calls attention to the recurrent myth of Cain and Abel, which, he says, suggests "that the historical past (Abel) is dead and that it can live again only in the timeless intuition of the poet". That seems an oversimplification, partly because other mythological and historical symbols recur—Greek, Central American, North American Indian —and partly because Mr. Dahlberg invokes the past of the race for more specific reasons. Our slaughtered innocents lie there, but so does our lost innocence.

Donald W. Baker. Poetry. March, 1967. pp. 403–4

See *Bottom Dogs* (novel); *Can These Bones Live, The Sorrows of Priapus, Alms for Oblivion* (essays); *Because I Was Flesh* (autobiography); *Epitaphs of Our Times* (letters); *Cipango's Hinder Door* (poems).


# DELL, FLOYD (1887–1969)

*Moon-Calf,* by Floyd Dell . . . , will have a sequel and will certainly be compared with *Jean-Christophe,* but it has its private merits in moments of unexpected loveliness, in the occasional presentation of relevant and illuminating truth. These are chiefly in the story of Felix Fay's childhood, after which the author writes carefully until adolescence with all its terrors sets in. The author has surprised his enemies by not writing à *thèse* and delighted his friends by a masquerade, but *Moon-Calf,* as it stands, has the importance of showing how serious and how well-composed an American novel can be without losing caste. It is an effective compromise, in manner, between the school of observation and the school of technique.

Dial. Jan., 1921. p. 106

Sherwood Anderson's *Poor White* and Floyd Dell's *Moon-Calf* are the latest important recruits in the ranks of realistic reporting, but, to a certain extent, they march backward, backward toward the gods of an elder day. True, they maintain the Underwood and Underwood photographic standard of descriptive writing, and their atmosphere is that of the same unimportant middle class which pervades *Miss Lulu Bett* and *Main Street.* But in their heroes they forsake the commonplace. They are both unusual men, however usual their surroundings may be. . . . Felix Fay is not a successful inventor. In fact, he is not a successful anything. But he is not an ordinary boy by any means. He is a hyper-sensitive, nervous lad, whose confinement to the prosaic surroundings of his home town constitutes much more of a tragedy than the confinement of Carol Kennicott to Gopher Prairie in *Main Street,* for Felix's aloofness was born of a genuine distinction, whereas Carol was at heart a Gopher Prairieite herself with a Sears-Roebuck education.

And Felix Fay grows up to use his brain, which would disqualify him forever from competition with a hero of real life. It is true, he uses his brain to bad advantage and flounders about in a maze of socialism, atheism, and free-love, bungling them all very badly, especially the free-love. But he is a superman mentally compared to the people in *Miss Lulu Bett* and *Main Street,* and whoever heard of a superman in a novel which is strictly truthful?

Both *Moon-Calf* and *Poor White* have a certain vein of poetry running through them which distinguishes them from the rest of the realistic novels, and it is probably this poetic sense which would not allow their authors to have ordinary men for their heroes.

Robert C. Benchley. Bkm. Feb., 1921. pp. 559–60

The spirit of revolt and the passion of poetic protest infuse this book [*Intellectual Vagabondage*] with a beauty and an eloquence that are more reminiscent than real. The May Days of yesterday rather than of today and tomorrow afford its inspiration. The vagabondage is of a generation of youth that already has begun to age, already has begun the prosaic task of adjustment, marrying realities instead of dreams, forced to live life instead of changing it. . . . Mr. Dell is really an essayist and not a critic. He polishes a thought so neatly that its most radical import would never excite or offend.

V. F. Calverton. Nation. May 26, 1926. p. 585

The maladjustment of individuals to our modern society, so he tells us [in *Love in the Machine Age*], is caused by faults in their upbringing. These faults, in turn, are produced by lingering survivals of the patriarchal family system. Under this system, which was introduced by the aristocracy, but which spread through all classes of society, individuals were never permitted to become fully adult; especially they were prevented from making an adult choice of their life-mate. The results of this repression were public and private vices—prostitution, adultery, homosexuality, drunkenness—as well as celibacy, impotence, frigidity and neuroses of every sort. . . . Mr. Dell reveals the patent medicine he is vending. It is, in a word, liberty—the liberty of modern children to follow their own desires. He abandons other theories of education to preach the *laissez-faire* of the instincts.

Malcolm Cowley. NR. April 30, 1930. p. 304

Until now I have placed *Moon-Calf* well above Mr. Dell's other writings. My present judgment is that the autobiography belongs beside the autobiographical novel. Neither the one nor the other approaches greatness (even though I once called the earlier "a masterpiece of fiction"); and, as regards the probable life of either, we all know how oblivion scattereth her poppy. But *Moon-Calf* did reveal a character, and *Homecoming* confirms and extends the revelation. The first is an interesting novel of adolescence, and the second is an interesting record; more interesting, I am afraid, than has been indicated here, with its sexual and psychological data that could provoke comment and argument running far beyond this review or a dozen like it. But it is never a scandalous record. As the author said, he had no intention of telling other people's secrets.

Ben Ray Redman. *SR*. Sept. 30, 1933. p. 145

A large part of the work of Floyd Dell, including most of this autobiography [*Homecoming*], is amazingly intelligent and much of it is fine and sensitive. It is doubtful if any other writer has covered so expertly and broadly the mental world of the "intellectuals" of our time, and as a result the autobiography is constantly entertaining, the pages full of half and quarter-thoughts, perceptions, complex mental reactions and points of view. It is readable, surprisingly lucid and, particularly in the opening chapters, which deal with his childhood and family, rich in concrete detail presented with literary art. Yet, as in Floyd Dell's early work, there seems no personality behind his writing; the problems of his life, however vividly and entertainingly told, are reflections from the mental life of his environment.

Hutchins Hapgood. *NR*. Nov. 29, 1933. p. 80

Floyd Dell has the rare felicity of being able to remember and re-create the experiences of childhood and by a flawless selection of significant detail to bring out a "clear emotional pattern." The very nature of his materials in *Moon-Calf* permitted him to work in a realistic manner and at the same time introduce the poetry as well as the humiliations to which youth is subject. The book was so autobiographical that when he wrote his excellent *Homecoming* . . . he incorporated into it pages and paragraphs from *Moon-Calf* without change. . . . The novels came along through the twenties, amplifying with unequal power the themes defined in the first two. *Janet March* . . . moved directly into Greenwich Village in search of the ideal of joy, companionship, freedom, self-giving love, picnic excursions to the beach by moonlight or to the woods, and a carefree, irresponsible existence in an attic studio. Floyd Dell has written beautifully about it all in *Homecoming* in a fine chapter entitled "Greenwich Village." In fact, the autobiography is done so capably that, in a sense, it supersedes the novels.

Harlan Hatcher. Creating the Modern American Novel<br>(Farrar and Rinehart). 1935. pp. 77–8

If it was Francis Hackett who first brought the new light to Chicago, it was Dell who made plain the creative power of its rays, and his task by no means ended with its departure for New York in 1913. He moved on to Greenwich Village, the *Masses,* and a larger theater of operations, but the force he had acquired in Chicago and the Midwest remained fresh in his memory and operative in his life. In 1920 and 1921 he published two important novels, *The Moon Calf* [*sic*] and *The Briary Bush,* and wrote into them what must remain the classic account of the Chicago experience. The novels, written with the same lively and intelligent imagination Dell brought to all his work, caught up not only the details of his adventure but enlivened them with a high and dramatic sense of the whole movement.

Bernard Duffey. The Chicago Renaissance in American<br>Letters (Michigan State). 1954. p. 180

This "Spiritual Autobiography" [*Intellectual Vagabondage*] is a description of the literary and social influences which had produced in his time, he believed, a generation of intellectual vagabonds, a deracinate group pushed to the boundaries of society by its inability to find a place in or come to terms with a machine civilization. . . . In his excellent first novel, *Moon-Calf* . . . , he had drawn an autobiographical character sketch of a very young man who happens, as part only of his intellectual development, to join the Socialist Party. It was not a radical novel at all, in the usual sense, but a shrewd psychological study of an intellectual vagabond. His later novels were likewise psychological studies, for he had become deeply interested in Freudian theories.

Walter Rideout. The Radical Novel in the United<br>States (Harvard). 1956. pp. 125–6

The assault against Dell as the disagreeable anti-hero, the radical corrupted, was carried on by [Michael] Gold and the spiritual sons of John Reed with increasing bitterness after 1926. Gold and Dell had sparred with each other in *The Liberator* days when Dell repudiated his anarchistic notions about love and marriage and came out for monogamy and babies. He had also poked barbed fun at Gold's proletarian imago. Yet Dell had not given up his socialist convictions, and in such books as *Intellectual Vagabondage,* in his biography of Upton Sinclair, and in occasional reviews and articles, he continued to voice his radical opinions.

But to the young radicals, Dell was merely paying lip service to ideas he once believed in, and had retired from the class struggle.

Daniel Aaron. *Writers on the Left* (Harcourt). 1961. pp. 214–15

Few small-town lads ever had their high-school poems accepted by *Harper's* and *Century* and *McClure's,* as Floyd Dell's were. Nor had many been, like him, a card-carrying Socialist and religious freethinker at fifteen. Dell nevertheless fitted a certain pattern: the dreamy, sensitive boy or girl of impoverished family whose thoughts roamed to conquests of artistic worlds, the kind in whom a teacher or librarian saw the fire and felt the iron and urged, "Go try!"

Some time later Dell grew into the very picture of a gay, brave, poetically handsome city bohemian, indeed the acknowledged Prince of New York's Greenwich Village, lover of the haunting Edna St. Vincent Millay, his name a synonym for uninhibited, reckless love. He would sit nonchalantly in court as the Government sought his life for, so it claimed, treason in the first World War. He was to be, too, a well-known editor, a successful novelist, a Broadway playwright.

Yet his most important work was done in the first blush of young manhood, as a book critic on the one hand and on the other a personal leader among the young men and women of Chicago who were assaulting old traditions on their way to making a literary Renaissance.

Dale Kramer. *Chicago Renaissance* (Appleton-Century). 1966. p. 13

See *Moon-Calf, The Briary-Bush* (novels); *Intellectual Vagabondage, Love in the Machine Age* (essays); *Homecoming* (autobiography).

# D e V O T O ,   B E R N A R D   (1897–1955)

This book [*Mark Twain's America*] is a polemic, infused in many passages with the kind of exasperation which Mark Twain himself often exhibited; and its densely packed pages stir a crowd of responses. First of all, its importance as a "preface" for Mark Twain and also for an understanding of basic elements in American literature is unmistakeable. The book is not, strictly speaking, a biography; at the outset Mr. DeVoto declares that he has not tried to represent "the most engaging personality in American letters," and though he has not been able entirely to sustain this renunciation, the title is a true one. The major passages unroll Mark Twain's America, not with the obvious mileage of that great contemporary panorama which has sometimes been emulated by writers on the older

American scene, but with a highly knowledgeable sense of those influences that bore upon Mark Twain during his youth and early years as a writer. . . . For critics *Mark Twain's America* should provide life-giving provender for many a long day. It is, above all, in many of its passages an eloquent book, with the warm eloquence of partisanship, lavishly evoking a whole mind and an era.

Constance Rourke. *NYHT*. Sept. 11, 1932. p. 3

On certain aspects of life on the frontier and on its edge, in Mark Twain's early days, Mr. DeVoto is informed and eloquent; on the purely literary derivation of Mark Twain's humor (the tall tale, frontier burlesque, etc.), he makes a valuable contribution to criticism. But, taken as a whole and as a portrait of a complex character, his book [*Mark Twain's America*] is almost worthless. In his eagerness to adorn himself with the scalps of [Van Wyck] Brooks and his followers, Mr. DeVoto has overstated or misstated everything, and he leaves us with a false and superficial impression of his subject.

Newton Arvin. *NR*. Oct. 5, 1932. p. 211

Mr. DeVoto also belongs to the school of the gentlemanly essayist—though he might not like to be told so. "Tough guy's essays" might be his own term for these truculent and forthright papers, which range in subject from a study of the origin and evolution of the Mormon Utopia to appraisals of New England and culture and examinations of the theory of biography and criticism. In history, Mr. DeVoto wants us to remember—and very sensibly too—that we are dealing with a pluralistic world, about which it is dangerous to dogmatize on restricted evidence. In biography, he wants us to stick to facts, and nothing but facts—just the documents, no guesswork, no psychoanalytical reconstruction or re-creation or interpretation—which leaves just about nothing at all. . . . In criticism, he would like to see a sociological or functional check on esthetic and popular judgments, as on evolutions in taste or fashion—not an original idea, but worth saying often. In short, Mr. DeVoto *is* sensible, a lot of the time, but is inclined to be a little angry and repetitive about it, and a little too sure that nobody else is as sensible as himself.

Conrad Aiken. *NR*. Jan. 20, 1937. p. 364

This volume [*Mark Twain at Work*] contains the "Boy's manuscript," the *Huckleberry Finn* notes, and part of the most interesting manuscript preparatory for *The Mysterious Stranger*. It also contains three essays by Mr. DeVoto, one about the writing of each of the three books involved, in which he brilliantly records the results of his study of these and other relevant documents. He ponders all his evidence, reasons shrewdly, and unfolds the story of his deductions with skill comparable to that of a mystery novel writer. Consequently, this book sets forth information which hereafter will be indispensable to scholars, and sets it forth in such a way as to make it fascinating reading.

Walter Blair. *SR*. June 20, 1942. p. 11

On the whole I expect that Mr. DeVoto's conception of Mark Twain's development as a writer and of the partial disintegration of his talent after his bankruptcy and the deaths of his wife and daughter will gain more acceptance as time goes on. . . . Since Mr. DeVoto never forgets that he is dealing with an instinctive and great artist, his criticism of Mark Twain is the best that we are likely to have for some time to come.

George F. Whicher. *NYHT*. July 12, 1942. p. 7

When DeVoto is not attempting to defend any thesis, either about Twain or the frontier or himself, he gives us some of the ripened insights that can come only through years of devoted attention to an author. . . . We can be grateful for these insights, even though DeVoto seems determined to prove through his tub-thumping exaggerations that he possesses every temper except the critical temper.

F. O. Matthiessen. *NR*. Aug. 10, 1942. p. 179

Written in the tradition of vivid narrative history, this volume [*The Year of Decision: 1846*] is in many ways a prime example of its kind. Conceive of a latter-day poet of Manifest Destiny with a sense of humor and you have an idea of Mr. DeVoto's work. He has the first requisite of a good narrative historian: an imagination lusty enough to reach out for the full body of life, and yet disciplined enough to stay within range of his sources. He has done a capital job of research and he has a flair for getting a concrete image out of his documents. He has, moreover, a talent for cordial malice.

Richard Hofstadter. *NR*. May 3, 1943. p. 610

This complex narrative [*The Year of Decision: 1846*], managed with a firmness and vividness which can have proceeded only from an absolute steeping of the historian in his sources, is kept in perspective by constant reference to the endless political maneuvers in Washington . . . and by "Interludes" devoted to such aspects of mid-century American society as Stephen Foster's songs, the hints of the machine age in the National Fair of 1846, and William Morton's first public demonstration of anesthesia in Boston.

There can be no doubt that Mr. DeVoto has magnificently achieved his announced intention: "to realize the pre-Civil War, Far Western frontier as personal experience." This is, as he points out, a literary purpose, and he rather self-consciously adopts the fiction that he is only an amateur historian, half afraid to venture into the preserves of the professionals. It is a graceful pose; it would be less amusing and more convincing if Mr. DeVoto had not so resolutely disciplined himself to precisely those rigors of documentation, contempt for secondary sources, and thorough- ness in detail which make up four-fifths of the academic guild. If he com- ports himself in any ways unlike those of the professionals, it is in the liveliness of his style, his willingness to state conclusions even though they might be open to some question, and the frankness with which he avows his preferences among the characters who people his stage.

Henry Nash Smith. NEQ. Sept., 1943. pp. 499–500

When his *The Year of Decision* appeared last year and we found that if he would but gag his babbling ego he could still write remarkably sound and unhackneyed history, many of us believed, however, that he still had a soul to save, and that the salvation might require nothing beyond a couple of miracles and twenty years of patience. . . .

[*The Literary Fallacy*] certainly is not a complete account of the literary crimes of the 1920's. In fact, it is nothing at all but a long-winded con- fession of DeVoto's obsession about Van Wyck Brooks, plus a few en- vious references to other contemporaries, and two essays, one on the geologist John Wesley Powell and the other on the medical treatment of burns. These essays, which are as original and definitive as a high-school theme, are supposed to indicate how many things we others failed to know and write about in the 1920's and to show how our books would have been written if we had been so lucky as to have Mr. DeVoto write them for us.

Sinclair Lewis. SR. April 15, 1944. p. 10

The principal crime of which DeVoto accuses both generations together is that of indulging in what he calls "the literary fallacy." . . . There is also a critic's fallacy, however, and it is somewhat less innocent than the others we have mentioned. It consists in projecting an imaginary purpose for works of literature, quite different from the actual purposes of their au- thors, and then condemning the authors jointly and separately because they failed to achieve it. DeVoto writes as if to illustrate that fallacy. He takes for granted that the authors of the 1920's should all have been cultural historians and should all have depicted American civilization as DeVoto now sees it; then he charges them with offering only a false or fragmentary picture.

Malcolm Cowley. NR. April 24, 1944. p. 565

Bernard DeVoto's investigation of the origins and growth of what he calls the "continental mind" has been persistent and brilliant. *Mark Twain's America* displayed Manifest Destiny in its peak years, the period closed and symbolized by the meeting of the rails at Promontory. *The Year of Decision* went back in time to trace the complex lines of force that in 1846 made inevitable the pattern of western settlement, the war between the states, the eventual triumph of the continental idea. The present book *Across the Wide Missouri* goes still farther back, into the closing years of the mountain fur trade. In his next he will deal with Lewis and Clark, back in the years when the West was still Louisiana or Mexico, and the idea of a continental nation had just been born. . . . But because of its constant cross-references and its restless curiosity in a very wide context, it [*Across the Wide Missouri*] becomes something more: the kind of intelligent study of social dynamisms that not too many historians are capable of.

Wallace Stegner. At. Jan., 1948. p. 122

Mr. DeVoto makes a number of shrewd observations on the treatment of time, of character, of point of view ("means of perception" is the phrase he prefers), of conveying information, and of dramatizing ideas in novels. He returns again and again to the central truth that a novel is a story, a work of enchantment, a stay against boredom or confusion, whether it be by Margaret Mitchell or Marcel Proust. The novelist departs at his peril from the obligation to tell a story, and when new technical devices, new social sanctions, or new critical theory drive the novelist too far from this primitive but primary necessity, fiction reaches a dead end. The modern "revulsion against story" is, on the whole, a revulsion among a small group of persons who desire experience so far refined it cannot be recognized.

Howard Mumford Jones. SR. April 15, 1950. p. 46

The sustained poetic intensity of DeVoto's continental vision explains part of the success of *The Course of Empire*. Part lies too in his geographical intuition, which sharply indicates limitation and opportunity and places human striving in a specific background of land, water, forest and plain. And much of the success lies in his careful and exact knowledge and his inexhaustible curiosity—knowledge of the terrain, of the routes of trade, of the contemporary conditions of geographical understanding, curiosity about the human experience,—and in his style, a powerful weapon, more disciplined here, perhaps, than it has been before. . . .

Summary hardly does justice to this work. It brings the history of continental exploration into a new poetic perspective, and it founds its poetry on the hard substratum of provable fact. Mr. DeVoto's old and robust confidence has not waned; and occasionally he may utter judgments more definite than the facts permit; but on most points he argues his case fairly, temperately and convincingly. It is a book which will freshen the vision of the historian and renew his insights; and, for the lay reader of history, it will prove an exciting and rewarding experience.

Arthur Schlesinger, Jr. *NEQ.* June, 1953. pp. 259–60

. . . DeVoto spoke to his fellow Americans, off and on for twenty years. . . . He told them they needn't put up with either shoddy products or shoddy thinking, and, naming names, he attacked the purveyors of both with energy, zest, and skill. No doubt his responses . . . were somewhat disproportionate to the stimuli that evoked them. But considering the craven attitude of most of us in the face of the assorted impositions, shams, discomforts and uglinesses DeVoto denounced, we can only applaud his willingness to call for action against them in tones loud enough, frequently, to get it. . . .

DeVoto wanted the American past the way it was, not the way tendentious critics or historians thought it should have been, because he was deeply stirred by the drama and the greatness that it revealed to him and that he in turn revealed to an ever-growing number of readers. As for America today, he had a lover's quarrel with it. He could and did make frequent suggestions for its improvement, but that was because there was some practical point in doing so. He believed the improvements he advocated would enhance the American future, in which Bernard DeVoto never lost faith and in which, it seems both likely and fitting, he will be remembered for a long time to come.

L. H. Butterfield. *NEQ.* Dec., 1956. pp. 436, 442

DeVoto's histories are an extension of his fiction in that as he grew older his writing moved progressively back into the past, probing for the distinctive causative factors of the present, for one's inheritance. They are in a very small degree an escape from the present. . . . The intuitive understanding in DeVoto came from his own Western boyhood; the intellectual grasp of his subject is, of course, the product of his years in the East—and there is a kind of a tension between the two which is the source of literature.

Robert Edson Lee. *From West to East* (Illinois).
1966. pp. 146–8

See *The Crooked Mile, The Chariot of Fire, We Accept with Pleasure* (novels); *Mark Twain's America, The Literary Fallacy, Mark Twain at Work, The World of Fiction* (criticism); *The Year of Decision: 1846, Across the Wide Missouri, The Course of Empire* (history).

# DE VRIES, PETER (1910–    )

Mr. De Vries is a man with a scandalous addiction to wild puns and wilder rump-sprung aphorisms. In *The Tunnel of Love,* one of the funniest novels to come along in any season, he uses his puns and fantasies to mask a sometimes frighteningly keen observation of suburban and creative mores in one of those southern Connecticut communities populated by the Babbits of Bohemia. . . . Mr. De Vries is not a man who believes in letting his reader rest and he is also a man intoxicated completely by the fun one can have with words, juggling them himself, reporting with a sharp ear the monstrous and mirthful sentences one hears everywhere from the 5:15 to the rumpus room.

Al Hine. *SR*. May 15, 1954. p. 14

Set in the "psychosomatic belt" of Connecticut, Mr. De Vries's story is a comedy of "Eastern Commuting Culture" with a Sophoclean wind-up climaxed by a happy twist. The plot has to do with the efforts of the Pooles to adopt a baby and with the impudent misconduct of Augie Poole—a gentleman who has a flair for the fancier turns of life and no sense of the rudiments such as earning a dollar. *The Tunnel of Love* is an unqualified delight; and a shrewd sense of life's realities glints through the overtones of farce.

Charles J. Rolo. *At*. July, 1954. p. 85

In this, his fourth book [*The Mackerel Plaza*], Peter De Vries again makes hilarious sport of the problems confronting a man tossed about in the cross-currents set up by various devious and designing women who swim into his ken. . . . There's no denying that De Vries is a cheerful and bounteous humorist. His range is from Swiftian satire, through parody and burlesque, to schoolboy jokes—of which some fall flat and others are in dubious taste. . . . It might be correct to say, though, that *The Mackerel Plaza* is in intent more serious than its predecessors and somewhat less funny as a whole—possibly as a consequence of this preoccupation. . . . No, it would appear that he wanted (very much and very seriously), to expose pietistic sham and religious immaturity. . . . Apparently De Vries is so sick of it himself that he's risked giving offense—and losing some readers—with this wry and mocking manifesto of ministerial emancipation.

A. C. Spectorsky. *NYT*. March 9, 1958. p. 4

Like its predecessor, *The Tunnel of Love,* . . . *The Mackerel Plaza* makes a great deal of the antics of the predatory male, but it also, happily, makes some other noises too. For in the trumped-up ordeal of the Reverend Andrew Mackerel, novelist De Vries has written a meaningful and broad fable for our time.

E. P. Monroe. *SR*. April 5, 1957. p. 40

Peter De Vries has pitched *The Tents of Wickedness,* his most recent novel, in the small city of Decency, Connecticut, not far from the large indecent city of New York. Decency, as readers of *Comfort Me with Apples,* an earlier novel of Mr. De Vries, will remember, is lived in by the kinds of people who are picked upon and apart by sociologists and sociological-novelists as organization men, conformists, and most recently, "status seekers." Mr. De Vries, on the other hand, views them not as easily manipulated statistics but as uneasily struggling individuals trapped in a snare of clichés. . . .

But *The Tents of Wickedness* is only secondarily a novel; it is primarily a vehicle, a sort of circus wagon to transport and display Mr. De Vries's talents as a clown, a juggler, and a mimic. And very considerable talents they are. Mr. De Vries has an extraordinarily accurate ear for speech and for the nuances of literary style. His parodies of Marquand, Faulkner, Fitzgerald, Proust, James, and several other novelists are accurate to a fault. (The fault is that they are not always independently funny, which parody, I believe, should be.) But his verses . . . display not only acute understanding of the method and tone of voice of a variety of poets from Emily Dickinson to Dylan Thomas but the real comic spirit as well. His clowning is often pure boffola, but he also contrives comic situations that combine imaginative lunacy with considerable subtlety.

Russell Lynes. *SR*. July 18, 1959. p. 14

In recent years the Peter De Vries novel has become almost a sub-genre of our fiction. Its archetype is written in an antic spirit, savagely and broadly satirical. Generally it portrays exurbia. Its stock-in-trade includes a miscellany of tricks, japeries, buffooneries and parodies, the net effect of which—even including his addiction to comic names—he manages to make sophisticated. It varies in quality but is invariably fun to read.

*The Blood of the Lamb* is not that familiar Peter De Vries novel. This could be much to his credit as a demonstration of range and versatility. I wish I could call it an unqualified success but cannot do so. It does not seem to be all of a piece, to have assimilated its many elements and found its own nature. It shifts erratically, being now one kind of book and now another, its narrative sometimes interrupted simply to tell jokes. It does not have the effect of steady flow and progression, but lurches along.

On the other hand, the book is interesting and frequently funny. It keeps the reader's attention (partly hanging on unfulfilled hopes), and the closing section is painfully moving. . . . Questions of faith haunt the whole book.

Edmund Fuller. *NYT*. March 18, 1962. pp. 4, 37


Peter De Vries began as a *New Yorker* writer, a superior gagman whose comedy had an ambling and self-deprecating resemblance to the novel. His development has been steady and continuous; and in *Reuben, Reuben* . . . he is not only a very funny writer, but a serious novelist with very troubling themes behind all the laughter. . . . Mr. De Vries's title is taken from the old ballad in which Reuben and Rachel consider the prospect of transporting men and women as far from each other as they can get. Though sex is rampant all over the local landscape, men and women are unable to come to terms with each other. . . .

Mr. De Vries may have created a new genre of fiction, which could be labeled tragifarce. While he amuses us with his clowning, throwing away gags that a lesser writer would have to hoard, he is a disturbing moralist with a sharp and uncomfortable perception of things as they are.

William Barrett. *At*. March, 1964. pp. 180–2


Next to Peter De Vries most of our comic writers look like bumpkins. . . . Yet there are stretches in this [*Let Me Count the Ways*], as in his other recent novels, which suggest De Vries is wearying of a routine brought to perfection so long ago and has since had nowhere to go but down. He has, for one thing, neutralized some of the off-characters and off-scenes, so that every police sergeant, every waitress, is not one more daffy bearer of the De Vries point of view. The surface is inching closer to reality and De Vries is inching closer to a straight novel. . . . This final sequence of the book has a kind of somber charm, as the author's two muses, low farce and a sort of dandified melancholy, sing in sustained harmony for once. . . . But in the sickroom he really comes to the edge of great tragicomedy: and one wonders whether here, in the freakish disorder and the farcically helpless patient, this admirably restless writer may not find the key that he has been looking for to the serious novel. *Let Me Count the Ways* seems to mark a step in that direction, as well as being the most stylishly funny novel since Mr. De Vries' last one.

Wilfred Sheed. *NYHT*. July 25, 1965. pp. 3, 13

See *No, But I Saw the Movie* (stories); *The Tunnel of Love, Comfort Me With Apples, The Mackerel Plaza, The Tents of Wickedness, The Blood of the Lamb, Through the Fields of Clover, Reuben, Reuben, Let Me Count the Ways, The Vale of Laughter* (novels).

# DICKEY, JAMES (1923–    )

Close on the heels of an extraordinary first book, *Into the Stone,* James Dickey gives us his second, *Drowning With Others,* and we can no longer doubt that we are in the presence of a major talent, a true art. . . . his supreme contribution is the creation of a Dickey cosmos: a landscape into which breathe Dickey plants and in which are ensconced Dickey objects, through which race Dickey meters and metaphors overtaking the slower-moving Dickey animals and people under the gaze of emblematic Dickey-birds. . . . And always, whether a waterfall hurtles through the poet's eye or the dead are falling through time, everything is absorbed into a world consisting of pure fundamentals in all their plainness, intricacy, and intimate miraculousness. Dickey's poetry is cosmic; whether micro- or macrocosmic, it would be difficult—and needless—to say.

John Simon. HdR. Autumn, 1962. pp. 466–7

The poems in this book [*Helmets*] are written in the American grain on American soil; images of survival, in many cases, designed to hold out the continuing possibility of rising to local occasions, American occasions of insight. Mr. Dickey is devoted to the "spirit of the place," always mindful of its powers and ready to attend them in his own way which is not the same as William Carlos Williams' way. Many of his poems are experiments to see how gracefully the poet can proceed between clouds, grass, pools, horses, soldiers, dead bodies, reaching into the silence when justice has been done. The human sound of these poems arranges and enthralls and enchants the acres, otherwise wild, and prepares hopeless things for miracle.

But Mr. Dickey is never wide-eyed, his miracles are never cheap. He has one object: to do justice; to be faithful to human life.

Denis Donoghue. HdR. Summer, 1964. p. 275

Going into this book [*Helmets*] is like going into an experience in your own life that you know will change your mind. You either go in willing to let it happen, or you stay out. There are a lot of good poems here. . . . I realize to what an extent sympathy is the burden of this book, how much there is of seeing into the life of beings other than the poet. The reader is moved imaginatively and sympathetically into the minds of horses at nightfall, of farmer and animals divided and held together by fences, of a young girl scarred in a wreck, of bums waking up in places they never intended to come to. . . . But I think that Mr. Dickey is also capable of much less than his best. There are poems that seem to have been produced by the over-straining of method, ground out in accordance with what the poet has come to expect he'll do in a given situation. . . . But I want to end by turning back to the goodness of the book. There are poems here of such life that you don't believe they're possible until you read them the second time, and I've got no bone to pick with them.

Wendell Berry. *Poetry*. Nov., 1964. pp. 130–1

I have been drawn to the poetry of James Dickey by two poems, "The Being" and "Drinking from a Helmet," which tell of seizures or psychic invasions—"as if kissed in the brain"—where the erotic and the spectral seem to advance an initiation, as if he had passed a shadow-line that gave him a secret commission in poetry. . . . Wherever the thought of the dead, of animal, human or demonic hauntings—the theme of popular spiritism—comes to him, James Dickey's imagination is stirred. . . . I am moved by the suggestion throughout of the mysteries of Orpheus, the poet as hero who would charm the dead and the animal world with his music. . . . In these *Two Poems of the Air*—"The Firebombing" and "Reincarnation"— James Dickey continues in his fascination with the spectral, but he has shifted from the tense verse and concentrated stanza sequence, the direct mode of a poetic experience and commitment, towards a more casual verse following a set story line, allowing even clichés of the supernatural tale. . . .

Robert Duncan. *Poetry*. Nov., 1964. pp. 131–2

These brief reviews, many only a paragraph or two in length, no doubt were suitable to the space limits imposed by the publications in which they first appeared, but put together in book form [*The Suspect in Poetry*] they give the reader the impression, especially in the first half of the book, that Dickey's capacity for suspicion is enormous and that he likes nothing better than a quick, clean kill. On the few occasions in the book where Dickey does take the care and space to explain his positions, as in his pages on Randall Jarrell and E. E. Cummings, he can be very, very good. After he has given them their grades, Dickey dutifully gives the poets instructions on how they may improve themselves.

Robert Watson. *Poetry*. Feb., 1966. p. 332

James Dickey's fourth volume, *Buckdancer's Choice,* establishes him as one of the most important younger poets of our time. . . . The earlier volumes showed us the development of a style and an attitude, a purification of language; but in *Buckdancer's Choice* . . . his abilities are clearly focused. At last we get the definite and flawless statement, the controlled and exact utterance. The book has a passionate quality, an intense clarity, a lensing of the totality of being into a kind of carefully separated madness that makes it one of the remarkable books of the decade. . . . Dickey is not afraid of consistency, not afraid of eloquence; with them he gets emotion declaimed and public, pace and interest, timing and compression of detail. This is all for effect. The effect is unity: an organized, coherent whole. There is no place here for falsehood or prestige.

Joseph Bennett. *NYT*. Feb. 6, 1966. p. 10

This sense of motion, of engagement, is so strong in James Dickey's work that it largely dominates the book [*Buckdancer's Choice*]. Things exist here largely as parts of experiences, of something that is happening, that is verb-dominated, moving forward fast. The objects are often perfectly ordinary, not observed with special closeness. . . . Dickey is interested in exploring the possibility of dream worlds, situations in which the conventional patterns of relationship are replaced by others which may prove more meaningful. And to Dickey, memory too has something of the same comparing, releasing function that the dream may have: the worlds of past and present are regularly involved in a tensed relationship here. . . . The poet has done his work most completely when he has been able to show us the object not in one world but in two, when we sense not only the object, not only usual relationships, but the possibility of further extension, of further and more comprehensive relationships: "in all worlds the growing encounters."

William Dickey. *HdR*. Spring, 1966. pp. 154–5

Though Dickey will always retain, for strategic use, the rhythms he had early developed to be those in which he most naturally addresses himself, entrusts his consciousness to the language, it is evident that a formal metamorphosis must occur, after *Helmets,* to accommodate the other change, the transformation of ritual into romance, which Dickey has effected in his poetry. . . .

That metamorphosis has occurred in Dickey's latest book, *Buckdancer's Choice,* . . . and occurred with such a rush of impulse that the reader of the earlier collections, having come to expect the somnambulist forms of Dickey's imagination of recurrence, will be jarred by the immediacy, the brutality of disjunct actions, performed once and, however celebrated, done away with. . . . [F]or the most part, Dickey's universe, and the measures which accommodate and express his phenomenology of exchange, has ceased to be one of eternal return, of enchantment. Instead, once out of eternity, the poet confronts and laments (exults over) the outrage of individual death, of a linear movement within time—each event and each moment being unique, therefore lost. . . . Obsession, madness, excess: the burden of *Buckdancer's Choice* is altogether new in this poet, and crowned, or ballasted, by a pervasive terror of extinction.

Richard Howard. *PR*. Summer, 1966. pp. 480–1

An attempt to be guided by afflatus marks James Dickey's work. He is the most expansive and energetic of these poets, and his poetry is alive with fugitive notes of compassion, fantasy, empathy with personalities that sometimes hold, sometimes flicker in a poem and then disappear. He seems capable of great compression, of an economy that could hold within deliberately contrived limits diverse elements working together. But language for Dickey is a form of energetic action that does not necessarily allow him to work his materials into achieved formal shape and meaning. The poems tend to grow more than to be shaped; their expansion is a necessary aspect of his discovery of what he wishes to say and to release through them.

M. L. Rosenthal. *The New Poets* (Oxford). 1967.
pp. 325–6

The persona in James Dickey's new poems, those that appear in the final section ("Falling") of his new book [*Poems 1957–1967*], is a unique human personality. He is a worldly mystic. On the one hand, a joyous expansive personality—all candor, laughter and charm—in love with his fully conscious gestures, the grace and surety of moves of his body. An outgoing man. An extrovert. On the other hand, a chosen man. A man who has been picked by some mysterious intelligent agent in the universe to act out a secret destiny. . . . How does a man re-connect with common unchosen humanity when he has just returned from the abyss of non-human chosen otherness? That is the chief problem to which the final volume addresses itself. How to be a man who feels perfectly at home, and at his ease, in both worlds—the inner and outer. A man who can make of himself and his art a medium, a perfect conductor, through which the opposed worlds—both charged with intensity—can meet and connect, flow into each other. The worldly mystic. It is the vision of a man who for years has been just as committed to developing his potential for creative existence as for creative art. All discoveries and earnings, spiritual or worldly, must carry over from one universe to the other.

Laurence Lieberman. *HdR*. Autumn, 1967. p. 513

See *Poems 1957–1967; The Suspect in Poetry* (criticism).

# DICKINSON, EMILY (1830–1886)

I heard an extremely faint and pattering footstep like that of a child, in the hall, and in glided, almost noiselessly, a plain shy little person, the face without a single good feature, but with eyes, as she herself said, "like the sherry the guest leaves in the glass," and with smooth bands of reddish chestnut hair. She had a quaint and nun-like look, as if she might be a German canoness of some religious order, whose prescribed garb was white pique, with a blue net worsted shawl. She came toward me with two day-lilies, which she put in a child-like way into my hand, saying softly, under her breath, "These are my introduction," and adding, also under her breath, in child-like fashion, "Forgive me if I am frightened; I never see strangers, and hardly know what to say."

Thomas Wentworth Higginson. *Carlyle's Laugh*
(Houghton). 1909. p. 272

Emily Dickinson, New England spinster of the nineteenth century, was an unconscious and uncataloged *Imagiste*. She had the visual imagination, the love of economy of line and epithet, the rigorous austerity of style, and the individual subtlety of rhythm demanded by the code of the contemporary poets who group themselves under that title. Born a Puritan, her shy soul brooded upon the abstract, but her wildly pagan imagination at once transmuted the abstract into the concrete, gave it form and color.

Harriet Monroe. *Poetry*. Dec., 1914. pp. 138–9

The advance and retreat of her thought, her transition from arch to demure, from elfin to angelic, from soaring to drowning, her inescapable sense of tragedy, her inimitable perception of comedy, her breathless reverence and unabashed invasion upon the intimate affairs of Deity and hearsay of the Bible, made her a comrade to mettle inspiration and dazzle rivalry. . . . She revelled in the wings of her mind,—I had almost said the fins too,—so universal was her identification with every form of life and element of being.

Martha Dickinson Bianchi. Preface to Emily
Dickinson's *The Single Hound* (Little). 1914. p. xiv

Saint and imp sported in her, toying with the tricks of the Deity, taking them now with extreme profundity, then tossing them about like irresistible toys with an incomparable triviality. She has traced upon the page with celestial indelibility that fine line from her soul, which is like a fine prismatic light separating one bright sphere from another, one planet from another planet; and the edge of separation is but faintly perceptible. . . . Who has had her celestial attachedness—or must we call it detachedness?—and her sublime impertinent playfulness, which make her images dance before one like offspring of the great round sun?

Marsden Hartley. *Dial*. Aug. 15, 1918. p. 96

In her mode of life she carried the doctrine of self-sufficient individualism farther than Thoreau carried it, or the naïve zealots of Brook Farm. In her poetry she carried it, with its complement of passionate moral mysticism, farther than Emerson: which is to say that as a poet she had more genius than he. Like Emerson . . . she was from the outset, and remained all her life, a singular mixture of Puritan and free thinker. The problems of good and evil, of life and death, obsessed her.

Conrad Aiken. *Dial.* April, 1924. p. 305

Emily Dickinson is often abstract, sometimes even verbal, but she is always saved from the merely allusive cleverness of our cerebralists by the passion which runs through all her poetry like a consuming flame. . . . Her spiritual passion is all the more a thing of wonder because it so steadfastly refused to identify itself with any of our accepted faiths and symbols. . . . In short, Emily Dickinson's poetry leads straight to the conception of an intuitively felt spirit which can be subordinated neither to any of its experienced forms nor to any kind of absolute standing without.

Edward Sapir. *Poetry.* May, 1925. pp. 102–3

If the voice of heavenly vision alone had spoken in Emily, she would have been a mystic poet. She is not a mystic poet. She constantly corrects vision by another faculty. Vision is not her truth. What is her truth? She named it "fact"—the truth perceived and then anatomized. The real mystic's experience is an ecstasy, and his invariable report is that life is single and divine; he abhors a double. Against her primary impulse, which is something akin to the mystic intuition, Emily constantly placed her correcting fact.

Genevieve Taggard. *The Life and Mind of Emily Dickinson* (Knopf). 1930. p. 320

It is a tough and poetry-resisting soul which does not eventually succumb to her rhetoric, irregularities and all. Her vivacity covers self-consciousness and carries off her self-contradictions; her swift condensations—surpassed by no writer of any age—win the most reluctant. One gasps at the way she packs huge ideas into an explosive quatrain. . . . She may annoy us by her self-indulgent waywardness, but illumination is never far off; out of a smooth, even sentimental sky comes a crackling telegram from God.

Louis Untermeyer. *SR.* July 5, 1930. p. 1171

Emily Dickinson was reason's pupil but her technique was intuitive, and in that matter she was "wayward." Study which she bestowed on her poems related only to a choice of words that would sharpen the meaning, we are told. . . . A certain buoyancy that creates an effect of inconsequent bravado—a sense of drama with which we may not be quite at home— was for her a part of that expansion of breath necessary to existence, and unless it is conceited for the hummingbird or the osprey to not behave like a chicken, one does not find her conceited.

Marianne Moore. *Poetry.* Jan., 1933. pp. 223–5

I think it is a fact that the failure and success of Emily Dickinson's poetry were uniformly accidental largely because of the private and eccentric nature of her relation to the business of poetry. She was neither a professional poet nor an amateur; she was a private poet who wrote indefatigably as some women cook or knit. . . . She came, as Mr. Tate says, at the right time for one kind of poetry: the poetry of sophisticated, eccentric vision. That is what makes her good—in a few poems and many passages representatively great. But she never undertook the great profession of controlling the means of objective expression.

R. P. Blackmur. SoR. Autumn, 1937. pp. 346–7

The fragmentary nature of many of the poems, their irregularity of form, the grammatical aberrations which occur at times, the elaborate conceits and occasional mixed metaphors cannot dispel the unusual power of the imagery, the most salient characteristics of which are vividness, boldness of conception, interplay of the concrete and the abstract, variety of sense appeals, drama, freshness and surprise. On the other hand, the most abstruse and cryptic of her "versicles" and those most likely to be neglected are the ones lacking in imagery.

Ruth Flanders McNaughton. The Imagery of Emily Dickinson (Nebraska). 1949. pp. vii–viii

The most intelligible mode of relationship or tension within the poetry of Emily Dickinson is a relationship of the rococo and the sublime. There is hardly a poem in the whole canon which does not in some way exhibit both orders of experience. . . . In her best poems the rococo principle has been forced by the exigencies of the poem's structure to yield nothing but what is most admirable in it, its immediacy of pathos and its delicacy of form—the qualities with which, in these poems, the sublime must and does invest itself. This sustained imbalance constitutes the economy of Emily Dickinson's verse.

Richard Chase. Emily Dickinson (Sloane). 1951.<br>pp. 236–7

Feelings for her took the place of ideas, but feelings so clearly contemplated, so disciplined, and so wittily clear-cut, that they became the equivalent, in precision and in penetration of thought. . . . To read her letters is to be in a world that combines Kate Greenaway's elegant nostalgia, something of Beatrice Potter's innocent fantasy of a world of rabbits with blue jackets and housekeeping field-mice, and that American timor mortis that Emily Dickinson has in common with Edgar Allen Poe. What makes her a poet is her delicate precision of image, deliberately finite, as with Marianne Moore; and her wren's note of pure lyricism.

Kathleen Raine. NSN. April 19, 1952. p. 472

She has gone beyond all Christian orthodoxies by conferring upon the creature a partnership with the Creator. She insists that love is meaningless unless it is reciprocated, both in this life and in the life to come; and that God himself is not yet perfected, and perhaps never will be. Man of course is totally dependent upon God, but in some way, to some degree, God needs the love of man to keep the cycles wheeling and the stars in their course. To this extent Jehovah for her is not Zeus, all-sufficient, infallible, and arbitrary; but Prometheus, the friend of mankind, capable of suffering.

(K)                                Thomas H. Johnson. *Emily Dickinson: An Interpretive Biography* (Harvard). 1955. p. 255

Her great talents, to be sure, are those of a highly original sayer, not a seer. To set this emphasis right one more analogy will be cited in conclusion, the literary one used at the beginning of this book. If significance in literature can be measured by the quantity of metaphor thrown up, as Henry James believed, then her poems on death and immortality represent the summit of her achievement. The novelty and brilliance of her imagery in these last two chapters are memorable. Within the context of the individual poems, old and new symbols are maneuvered by the language of surprise so as to illuminate the two profoundest themes that challenged her poetic powers. This reveals her kinship with another article of James' esthetic faith: if the creative writer pushes far enough into language he finds himself in the embrace of thought. By slant and surprise, by wit and a novel reworking of traditional modes, she evolved a way with words that became her instrument of knowing. Committed to nothing but dedicated to a search for truth and beauty, hers was a free spirit for whom living was a succession of intense experiences and art an endless exploration of their meanings. A poet rather than a systematic thinker, she never came up with dogmatic answers. Indeed her most effective verbal strategy was to exploit ambiguity, as in the conflicting attitudes towards her flood subject Immortality.

(K)                                Charles R. Anderson. *Emily Dickinson's Poetry: Stairway of Surprise* (Holt). 1960. pp. 184–5

. . . the greatest interest lies in her progress as a writer, and as a person. We see the young poet moving away, by gradual degrees, from her early slight addiction to graveyardism, to an Emersonian belief in the largeness and harmony of nature. Step by step, she advances into the terror and anguish of her destiny; she is frightened, but she holds fast and describes her fright. She is driven to the verge of sanity, but manages to remain, in some fashion, the observer and recorder of her extremity. Nature is no longer a friend, but often an inimical presence. Nature is a haunted house. And—a truth even more terrible—the inmost self can be haunted.

(K)                    Louise Bogan. *Emily Dickinson: Three Views*
                       [with Archibald MacLeish and Richard Wilbur]
                                              (Amherst). 1960. p. 32

So superior did she feel, as a poet, to earthly circumstance, and so strong was her faith in words, that she more than once presumed to view this life from the vantage of the grave.

In a manner of speaking, she *was* dead. And yet her poetry, with its articulate faithfulness to inner and outer truth, its insistence on maximum consciousness, is not an avoidance of life but an eccentric mastery of it.

(K)                    Richard Wilbur. *Emily Dickinson: Three Views*
                       [with Louise Bogan and Archibald MacLeish]
                                              (Amherst). 1960. p. 46

Emily Dickinson always reported to the world her sense of herself and nature—in short, her sense of the world. The traditional editorial classification of her poems (Nature, Death, etc.) gives at best a too generalized plan by which to reconstruct her "world view." It seems more likely, especially in the light of the enormous variety in the 1,775 poems which we now have from her, that the matter of a coherent world-view is hardly material to the comprehension and appreciation of her poems. When the poems are arranged in classes and categories, the resulting structure of ideas is so general that it makes little or no sense unless referred back to the poems. This is not true of Poe, Emerson, and Whitman, whatever may be said against their aspirations toward a "philosophy." Their philosophies were nothing less than cosmic in intention. They felt drawn toward a philosophy as they came sharply up against the limitations which their poetic egocentrism set for them, and they strove increasingly to build "systems." Not so Emily Dickinson. Such generalizations as can be derived from her poems concern the egocentric predicament upon which they are postulated. It is exactly this predicament, forced upon the nineteenth-century American poet by the life-style of his culture, which made for the basic style of his poems. Emily Dickinson's situation, temperament, and genius made that style peculiarly and directly her own. As poet she was strong enough to need nothing else.

(K)                    Roy Harvey Pearce. *The Continuity of American
                       Poetry* (Princeton). 1961. p. 175

"Reeling—thro endless summer days" describes a condition that life does not long permit, and a conflict between such an ecstatic state of inflation and the world of fact could hardly be avoided. Something shattered the spell under which Emily was held. There came a point beyond which she could not go without carrying the emotion into a real relation with the person who had called it forth. Since many things point to an assumption that the loved one was a married man, the shock probably came when, by some word of his or a sudden revelation of her own intuition, she was forced to accept the reality of the situation. The miraculous condition of being in love fosters belief in infinite possibilities that bear no relation to fact, and in which the moral sense remains totally blind. If Emily suddenly became aware of what she had been wishing, her conscious attitude would have reinforced the inevitability of her fate. . . .

. . . It seems probable that at this point she seriously took up her role of poet, and began to work at her craft with full acceptance of her creative gift. Writing now to save her life, Emily was almost overwhelmed by the verses that poured from her pen. She knew now that, aside from its therapeutic value, the work for its own sake must go on.

(K)                    Theodora Ward. *The Capsule of the Mind* (Harvard).
                                                        1961. pp. 52, 56

Whatever the disadvantages of society-by-mail, there were rewards as well. Emily Dickinson lived deliberately and preferred to present herself to the world only by deliberate art. On the rare occasions when Emily met her friends, she made almost theatrical entrances, dressed completely in white and carrying flowers. Her conversations at such times are said to have been brilliant, but a conversation can have no second draft. Letters, however, can be deliberate creations from salutation to signature, and the letters of Emily Dickinson show a great deal of "stage presence."

Emily's creation of a letter might begin years before she mailed the final draft. Among her papers at the time of her death were hundreds of scraps and drafts of her writing. Some were torn corners of envelopes or backs of grocery lists; others were fair copies ready for mailing, or letters marred by corrections. The collection included poetry and prose in all stages of composition. It was the scrapbasket of Emily's workshop and she kept it as other New England women saved string and wrapping paper and ribbon, against a future need.

(K)                    David J. M. Higgins in *Emily Dickinson,* edited by
                        Richard B. Sewall (Prentice-Hall). 1963. p. 164

Though her vocabulary still includes such terms as *grace* and *redeem, election* and *salvation,* the terms turn up in human or natural contexts, never in connection with divine functions. But no more does she possess the private revelation. Though fully as convinced as Emerson or Whitman that the world is symbolic, she is never able to determine what nameless, unknowable quality it symbolizes. All hope of reconciling here with There becomes, in her case, the suspicion that since what can be seen is pervaded by misrule and disorder, the unseen There must be a place of pure bedlam—or, worse yet, an absolute inferno. What happens in Miss Dickinson's poetry is simply this: the unity, which was inherent in [Edward] Taylor's theology and which Emerson and Whitman wrested from experience by not looking too closely, collapses under a genuinely tragic gaze. Left with only the self, and unable to force the self to believe, Emily Dickinson, from poem to poem, explores a situation in which the older religious and philosophical orders, with the values they guaranteed, are dissolving into nothingness. Her vision is, basically, the vision of modern man, as, certainly, it is the vision recorded in a great deal of modern poetry.

(K)    Clark Griffith. *The Long Shadow* (Princeton). 1964.
pp. 268–9

. . . Emily Dickinson marked a turning point in the American poet's conception of his function. For all her experience of the blaze of noon and the lightning-flash, for all her knowledge of the flower's ecstasy and the bee's power, she had to reject the kind of "mysticism" which in Emerson became mistiness and in Whitman amorphousness. She wrote neither as a visionary nor as a genius but as a craftsman making order out of the fragments of mutability. The only question was how durable one's web was; and durability depended on how well one practiced one's "Trade." She could only trust with Thoreau and Keats that if the materials and the art were pure, the result could not be other than wonderful.

(K)    Albert J. Gelpi. *Emily Dickinson, The Mind of*
*the Poet* (Harvard). 1965. p. 152

The formal influence in all her poetry is the hymn. When music is considered along with hymn texts, that influence is seen as pervasive. Her poetry was written as Watts's was written, as most hymns are written, *par-odia,* to an existing tune.

If a hymn be defined as a lyric intended for congregational singing, she wrote none. Her poems were not so intended, have never been so used, would not be appropriate to such use. Yet she wrote no epic, drama, fiction, essay, sonnet, or villanelle, but only something she called hymns or psalms. Hymn meters set her meters. The range of the reading voice is restricted to hymn range. Vocabulary is impregnated with hymn vocabulary and strictly circumscribed by New England gentility. Questions are posed and answered with reference to religious thought.

(K)    Martha Winburn England. *BNYPL*. Feb., 1965. p. 88

See *Final Harvest* (selected poems), also Thomas H. Johnson's definitive editions of the poems and letters.

# DONLEAVY, J. P. (1926–    )

Mr. Donleavy doesn't care in the least why Sebastian [*The Ginger Man*] is what he is, what disorders in the world or, for that matter, what frustrations in the nursery have shaped him; he simply gives us Sebastian, and we may take him or leave him. If we take him, if we read about him with some pleasure, that can only be because we envy his arrogant self-indulgence even while we disapprove of it. We, of course, are far too civilized to behave in any such outrageous fashion, but perhaps we sometimes wish we weren't. . . . Mr. Donleavy's [writing] is distinguished by humor, often inelegant, even coarse, but explosive and irresistible. Humor and poetry are his weapons. The whole novel is a wild and unpredictable outburst. Yet Mr. Donleavy is anything but an artless writer. Observe, for instance, the adroitness with which he moves from outside Sebastian's mind to inside it, from writing in the third person to writing in the first, and you realize how much control has created this image of chaos. *The Ginger Man* is a disturbing book, not because of its occasional vulgarity but because of its fundamental nihilism; it is also a powerful and original one.

Granville Hicks. SR. May 10, 1958. p. 31

Portions of this book [*The Ginger Man*] are obscene and/or blasphemous; other portions may give offense to those who are Irish by birth or sentiment. . . . Mr. Donleavy, a New York Irishman now living in London, reads at first sight like Henry Miller turned loose in James Joyce's Dublin. Soon, however, we realize that he possesses what Miller lost long ago— a sense of humor. . . .

Mr. Donleavy has been classed with England's "Angry Young Men," and his hero's revolt-against-society-without-social-revolution attitude certainly resembles that of Lucky Jim and his successors. But right there all resemblance stops. Mr. Donleavy's Irish eloquence and American drive make him a Don Juan among the eunuchs. . . . Sebastian Dangerfield may not fully realize what a prize s.o.b. he is, but his creator does—and yet Donleavy finally makes us feel affection for him.

Vivian Mercier. Nation. May 24, 1958. p. 480

A novelist must not simply abandon himself to every mood and every crazy idea that occurs to him as he writes. This is exactly what Mr. Donleavy appears to have done. . . . There is a lot of Joyce in the style: indeed, the presentation of much of the story through the consciousness of the hero is done in short, jerky sentences, so that we begin to weary of them. The writing is, in fact, rather slovenly, with many sloppy sentences and some confused grammar which I don't think are meant to represent the hero's way of putting things but simply represent Mr. Donleavy's way of writing. They can be found in *The Ginger Man* too.

This is an amusing and intriguing novel [*A Singular Man*], and it lacks the aimless cruelty that I for one found offensive in *The Ginger Man*. Its exuberance, comic imagination and sheer inventiveness make it easy and pleasant reading. But it frustrates the reader at the same time as it amuses him. A writer who can do this can surely do more, we feel, if he would both deepen and discipline his imagination.

David Daiches. *NYHT*. Nov. 17, 1963. p. 6

Where did mad Dangerfield go and madder Mac Doon? What happened to Cocklan, Malarkey and O'Keefe, that fantastic host of *The Ginger Man?* . . . Where a Joycean prose was so richly befitting to Dangerfield . . . the same device when employed by George Smith [of *A Singular Man*] comes out in a voice flattened like a ventriloquist's. . . . Dangerfield, a tragic yet dangerous clown, asked questions worthy of a saint. . . . But Smith has no questions to ask. . . .

For such a falling-off only the author may account. Yet one wonders whether, in a civilization so affluent that it is no longer necessary to think, there may not be an indication here that, to be a writer, it has become equally inessential to write.

Nelson Algren. *Nation*. Dec. 14, 1963. pp. 422–3

Nihilism is given its full head in . . . J. P. Donleavy's *The Ginger Man*. . . . it comes as a momentous shock when we begin to realize that Dangerfield is not an endearing "Rabelaisian" rascal. Not only does he treat his wife with appalling cruelty, but we learn that because he has been stealing their baby's milk money, the infant has developed a case of rickets. This is no joke, and it jolts us right out of the realm of pleasant fantasy into the most sordid of realities—which, of course, is exactly what Donleavy wants it to do. Why, then, do we continue to feel the attraction of Dangerfield? What claim does he exert on our sympathies? The decisive factor, I think, is his honesty. Unlike almost everyone else in the book (and incidentally unlike Kerouac's heroes, with whom he has been foolishly compared), he never simulates feelings that he does not in fact feel, he refuses to make excuses, and he will not hide behind empty pieties. He is not a bum and a scoundrel out of ill will or malice or insensitivity. On the contrary, he strikes us as a man who has looked into himself and found nothing, and then looked about the world and found no set of values (neither "traditional" nor "liberal") in sufficiently robust condition to exert any pull over his soul. Dangerfield, in short, is not exacting a fantasy of release, he is living by the truth of his times. Nor is he a rebel, for there is nothing to rebel against, everything gives way before him.

Norman Podhoretz. *Doings and Undoings* (Farrar). 1964. pp. 168–9

Compared to *The Ginger Man, A Singular Man* is an extremely neat presentation of the hero consenting to the trap of his society. For all of its incidental invention, however, it is a repetitive and finally rather dull book. *The Ginger Man* shows some of the same tendencies, but, in it, the style has not yet become mannered. The rhetoric, hovering between bathos and mockery, is suitable to Sebastian. The stylistic device—and a very clever one—which allows sudden shifts from first to third person within a paragraph suggests that Sebastian speaks as himself and then steps back to see himself, that he is always both sufferer and observer. The interplay between Sebastian's reality and his fantasies give a richness to the novel which is diluted only by the recognition that, in fact or in fancy, he is a somewhat tiresome man to spend much time with.

Gerald Weales in *Contemporary American Novelists,* edited by Harry T. Moore (Southern Illinois). 1964. p. 153

See *The Ginger Man, A Singular Man, The Saddest Summer of Samuel S.* (novels).


# DOOLITTLE, HILDA (H.D.) (1886–1961)

The word *temperamental* qualifies the whole manner and substance of her verse, and the degree of the reader's appreciation will depend on the amount of natural sympathy with which he temperamentally can approach it. . . . The affinity of her art to the radical characteristics of her own time is to be found . . . not in choice of subject but in the following characteristics: She has rejected the traditional forms of English poetry in favour of a more personal rhythm which derives its impulse from such rules as her own temperament may dictate. Poetry is to her an art to be cultivated, not an inspired message to be conveyed. Bulk of production is of no importance to her as compared with excellence of finish.

Harold Monro. *Some Contemporary Poets* (Parsons). 1920. pp. 103–4

The poems of H.D. do not lend themselves to convenient classification, as Poems of Passion and Emotion, Poems of Reflection, Poems of the Imagination, and Poems Descriptive, and so on. In all of them, passion, emotion, reflection, and the image, the sharp, vivid image that does the work of description, are fused together in the burning unity of beauty. . . . H.D. invariably presents her subtlest, most metaphysical idea under some living sensuous image solid enough to carry the emotion. The air we are given to breathe may be rarefied to the last degree, yet we are moving always in a world of clear colours and clear forms.

May Sinclair. *Dial.* Feb., 1922. p. 203

It has been said of H.D.'s earlier poetry that it was perfectly wrought but cold and passionless, and that it was concerned rather with the loveliness of a perished age than with the modern world of everyday emotions. . . . Perfectly wrought the poems are: the rhythms swoop in and out of the head as birds perch and flutter in and out of apple-branches. Lines haunt the ears as the sound of rain in the South. The use of some simple but unexpected syllable brings all the fragrance into a mood that Ionian roses suddenly awaken after some swift storm. But they are not cold, they are not passionless; and apart from the color of some Attic names how are these songs anything but the expression of the emotions and desires of an extremely present age?

Winifred Bryher. *Poetry.* March, 1922. pp. 334–5

It had better be said that H.D.'s scope (at least, her characteristic scope) is narrow. At the same time it may be retorted that her poetry is of a kind to which scope has uniquely slight application. With other poets of modern life, we are compelled to go on asking for a wider apprehension, a broader spiritual awareness more fundamentally expressed. But H.D. implies what the others do not, that she is asserting no spiritual attitude of her own; but building upon traditional assumptions. She assumes that what may be called the moral factor in our reception will demand of beauty what the Greeks were content to demand.

H. P. Collins. *Modern Poetry* (Cape). 1925. p. 157

To one who is as extreme a classicist as H.D., a knowledge of the machinery of verse is of as much moment as the material selected, and as regards her early work one might say both discreetly and truthfully that it is not so much the matter as the manner that is important. The emotion resulting from such a synthesis is one that H.D. calls "intellectual ecstasy"; a curious condition in which intensity of emotion is quite dependent upon the perfection and definiteness of the artificial form: the passion of a seagull in a bright steel cage.

Frank A. Doggett. *SwR.* Jan., 1929. p. 1

H.D.'s thoughts were not often concerned with the world she lived in; another one, to her far more desirable, filled her mental vision almost completely. . . . She often sat with us, chatting of everyday things, when I am sure her spirit was somewhere near the shores of the Aegean. . . . I think a large part of her peculiar charm lay in the fact that she was always coming back to us; and she never came back reluctantly. . . . We had . . . the idea that she found us satisfying in our way and that her pre-occupation with an ancient world only made her the more pleased with her own when she was in it. Her sudden entries into our talk and her effortless domination of it filled us with elation because she brought with her such disarming enthusiasms and delivered herself with such amazing speed and clarity on any subject that might be uppermost.

James Whitall. *English Years* (Harcourt). 1935.

pp. 55–6

There was about her that which is found in wild animals at times, a breathless impatience, almost a silly unwillingness to come to the point. She had a young girl's giggle and shrug which somehow in one so tall and angular seemed a little absurd. She fascinated me, not for her beauty, which was unquestioned if bizarre to my sense, but for a provocative in-difference to rule and order which I liked. She dressed indifferently, al-most sloppily and looked to a young man, not inviting—she had nothing of that—but irritating, with a smile.

William Carlos Williams. *Autobiography* (Random).

1951. pp. 67–8

Her special form of the mode of Imagism—cold, "Greek," fast, and en-closed—has become one of the ordinary resources of the poetic language; it is a regular means of putting down words so that they will keep; and readers are mistaken who confuse familiarity with flatness or who think facile imitation of the form emulates the perception that goes with the mode. She has herself made sharply varied use of her mode, but she has not exhausted it; she has only—for present changing purposes of a chang-ing mind—partly broken it down into the older, perhaps primary mode of the distich. The relatively long uncoiling of a single spring of image, unpredictable in its completeness, now receives a regular series of im-pulses and arrests, of alternations and couplings.

R. P. Blackmur. *Language as Gesture* (Harcourt).

1952. p. 352

H.D. has herself abandoned the "Imagist" effects of her early poems, the best of which suggest the clean line of Greek vase-paintings and, for all the passion they assert, have a lapidary quality about them. In her later work the old vehemence, if subdued, is present, and the phrasing recalls the familiar cadences. Yet it differs from what went before in carrying a far heavier weight of symbolic meaning and in being overtly subjective. ... Again and again, turning the pages of this quondam Imagist, the reader hears a melody not only in the lines themselves but suggested by them, as it were, hovering just beyond the expressed sounds for some musician, not a maker of verse, to capture and realize.

Babette Deutsch. NYT. Sept. 22, 1957. p. 37

"Invisible," "most proud," in love: these are the strength of the poet throughout the work of H.D. Ardent and clear, her lyrics show us that an everpresent devotion to the art of the poem sustains passion. The strength of the poem lies in her command of words so that they call up sensual immediacies (as images) and are themselves sensual immediacies (as elements of a most skilled tonal structure), and, increasingly in the later work, in her knowledge of words, their roots and histories, their lore and powers. Her trilogy written during the Second World War *(The Walls Do Not Fall, Tribute to Angels,* and *The Flowering of the Rod)* stands with Ezra Pound's *Cantos,* Eliot's *Four Quartets,* and William Carlos Williams' *Paterson* as a major work of the Imagist genius in its full.

Robert Duncan. Poetry. Jan., 1958. p. 256

She gives us the best glimpse we have today of classic poetry, an English poetry so nearly Greek in concept and execution as to be remarkable. She gives us that stasis in the poem which keeps a perfect tension between emotion and reason, between fact and idea, between sensitized perception and elegant restraint, between the brute world and art. . . . She gives us, in rare poems, the early poems, a glimpse and capture of an ideal world of eternal poetic values, crystal-bright, hard and pure, clean and fine. H.D. has the impersonal height from which streams a radiant purity.

Richard Eberhart. Poetry. Jan., 1958. p. 265

H.D. in her perceptions of timelessness, and in her search for the "real," has always seemed to be writing in advance of her times. In that respect the present generation might well regard her as "a poets' poet."

To be "a poets' poet" has few tangible rewards, for this means that the poet who holds that title must often wait upon the future for true recognition. Yet the poems of H.D. have acquired a life, a being of their own; at this date one need not argue that they should be read. Of contemporary poets H.D. is among the few whose writings are likely to endure.

Horace Gregory. Com. April 18, 1958. p. 83

See *Selected Poems* (1957 edition).

# DOS PASSOS, JOHN (1896–      )

Dos Passos *may* be, more than Dreiser, Cather, Hergesheimer, Cabell, or Anderson the father of humanized and living fiction . . . not merely for America but for the world.

Just to rub it in, I regard *Manhattan Transfer* as more important in every way than anything by Gertrude Stein or Marcel Proust or even the great white boar, Mr. Joyce's *Ulysses*. For Mr. Dos Passos can use and deftly does use, all their experimental psychology and style, all their revolt against the molds of classic fiction. But the difference! Dos Passos is *interesting!*

Sinclair Lewis. SR. Dec. 5, 1925. p. 361

If we compare Dos Passos with other of our leading novelists, we find no one who is his superior in range of awareness of American life. In his tone, he most nearly approaches Hemingway. He can be as "hard-boiled" as the latter, particularly when he is dealing with hard-boiled characters; his freedom of language is, if anything, greater; his viewpoint, also, is nearly as external and behavioristic. But he has a greater range of sympathy. . . . And his social sympathies, one might almost say his class passions, give a drive to his work that Hemingway's, with its comparatively sterile point of view lacks. In its social implications Dos Passos' work is more nearly akin to that of Dreiser and Sinclair Lewis, and still more to that of Upton Sinclair. But where Sinclair's people are wax dummies, Dos Passos' are alive and convincing.

Henry Hazlitt. Nation. March 23, 1932. p. 344

We can say now that the Harvard aesthete in Dos Passos is almost dead. The spiritual malady of tourism no longer drains his powers. He has entered the real world. He has definitely broken with capitalism and knows it is but a walking corpse. He wars upon it, and records its degeneration. But he has not yet found the faith of Walt Whitman in the American masses. He cannot believe that they have within them the creative force for a new world. This is still his dilemma; a hangover from his aristocratic past; yet this man grows like corn in the Iowa sun; his education proceeds; the future will find his vast talents, his gift of epic poetry, his observation, his daring experimentalism, and personal courage enlisted completely in the service of co-operative society.

Michael Gold. EJ. Feb. 1933. p. 97

Dos Passos will perhaps be remembered more as the inventor or at least the early practitioner of a technique in fiction than for the lasting significance of his novels. . . . Dos Passos attempts to catch in fiction the inventions of the day, the camera eye, the movie, the newspaper headline. He conveys dates and the background by flashes of contemporary events. The effect on the unity of the novels is confusing but the representation of confusion is evidently one of the author's chief aims. The "hero" of the novels is the contemporary scene rather than any individual. He attempts to crowd an era, a whole cross-section of a city or a period of economic development into a novel.

Halford E. Luccock. *Contemporary American Literature and Religion* (Willett). 1934. p. 148
Courtesy of Harper and Brothers

Dos Passos owes to Joyce the conception of a novel devoted to the life of a city (for *Ulysses* is more concerned with Dublin than Mr. Bloom), to Proust the use of significant detail and careful documentation, to Stein (of the *Three Lives* period) the notions of the importance of the simple lives of obscure people and the effectiveness of bald narration. But he added to his borrowing a great deal of his own: a feeling for the common man which led him to picture all the strata of life, a knowledge of life on the great majority of these levels, a sense of the universality of the evils that he found, a lyrical spirit, and some technical devices which are remarkable for their success—and for their failure, in the main, to put off the traditional reader.

Mason Wade. *NAR*. Winter, 1937. p. 356

He has again and again hazarded bold and enlightening solutions to problems of both content and structure that few traditional novelists have even recognized and fewer still have dealt with. Paramount has been his attempt to get a sense of the whole complex social panorama, and, as corollary, a sense of the flux, of the simultaneity of lives and events, and the passage of time in terms of the entire culture as well as individuals. Equally significant have been his attempts to integrate the individual with the period, to leave us everywhere conscious of how the age has moulded the man, made him one of its peculiar products.

Milton Rugoff. *SwR*. Oct. 1941. pp. 467–8

Certainly he is not a Tolstoy or even a Zola, to mention two masters of the panoramic form. In America today he ranks below Hemingway and Faulkner for many reasons, but principally because he seldom feels his way deeply into his characters. As a novelist—and in life, too—he is always moving, always hurrying off to catch a taxi, a bus, a train, a plane or a transatlantic steamer; and he tells us as much about people as a sensitive and observing man can learn in a short visit. That leads to his writing a special type of novel, broad and wind-scarred into intricate patterns like the Aral Sea, not deep like Lake Baikal, that gash in the mountains which is said to contain more water than all the Great Lakes together.

There is, however, a converse to this statement. To achieve breadth in a novel is a difficult art in itself and it is one in which no other American writer—not even Frank Norris—has ever approached Dos Passos.

Malcolm Cowley. NR. Feb. 28, 1949. p. 21

Nothing is deeper in the man than his fear of power. To begin with, he feared the power of the military, as he had experienced it in the first World War, and the power of men of wealth. The hatred of war and exploitation grew so acute that he accepted for a time the tempting radical doctrine that only power can destroy power. But what he saw of communism in Russia, in Spain, and at home convinced him that the destroying power could be more dangerous than the power it overcame. . . . His sympathies are wholly with the people who get pushed around, whether it is Big Business or Big Government that does the pushing. His trouble is simply that he has not found the "better than that," the alternative to both bignesses, and hence his growing fear of government can only be accompanied by a growing toleration of business. . . . He has allowed himself to be forced into choosing one horn of the dilemma, and he is nicely impaled.

Granville Hicks. AnR. Spring, 1950. pp. 95–8

Dos Passos' libertarianism is generally anarchist in character. That is to say, Dos Passos believes in absolute or primitive liberty, the supreme good of the anarchist creed. With Lord Acton, he believes that power always corrupts because by its very nature it exercises restraints. All social wrongs are therefore rooted in family, government or state authority; and the remedy lies in the curbing of this oppressive power. Each individual must live as he wishes and must not permit anyone to rule over his fellows, for each is a sovereign power.

Martin Kallich. AnR. Spring, 1950. p. 100

Chronic remorse, most moralists agree, is an unsalutary sentiment—the sinner who has genuinely repented does not become any the cleaner by rolling interminably in the mud; and chronic remorse is peculiarly disastrous where novelists are concerned. The novelist obsessed with the errors of the past—John Dos Passos is a case in point, since his political switch from far left to far right—is irresistibly drawn to revenge himself on his past by rewriting it, by showing that what he found good was disgusting. And the literary results of such an enterprise are apt to resemble a dredging operation: the principal yield is mud.

Charles J. Rolo. At. Oct. 1954. p. 98

Dos Passos' hate, despair and lofty contempt are real. But that is precisely why his world is not real; it is a created object. I know of none—not even Faulkner's or Kafka's—in which the art is greater or better hidden. I know of none that is more precious, more touching or closer to us. This is because he takes his material from our world. And yet, there is no stranger or more distant world. Dos Passos has invented only one thing, an art of story-telling. But that is enough to create a universe. . . . Dos Passos' world—like those of Faulkner, Kafka, and Stendhal—is impossible because it is contradictory. But therein lies its beauty. Beauty is a veiled contradiction. I regard Dos Passos as the greatest writer of our time.

Jean-Paul Sartre. Literary and Philosophical Essays<br>(Criterion). 1955. pp. 89, 96

In retrospect, the work of Dos Passos falls into three periods. There is first the expression of the lonely dissident, the esthetic recluse. . . . Almost alone among the high individualists of the 1920's, those gifted expatriates and exiles, Dos Passos had, by the end of the decade, found a cultural base for his literary work.

This base was a theoretical rather than strictly political Marxism. The product of the second period included *Manhattan Transfer* in 1925 and the major trilogy, *U.S.A.,* published from 1930 to 1936. These are still the core of Dos Passos' fiction; they are persuasive and penetrating novels; and their description of American civilization, which hardly applied in the 1930's, may seem all too prophetic in the 1950's. But the crux of the Dos Passos problem is right here, too. The collapse of his belief in the Russian Revolution, the disillusionment with the methods of the Communist Party, led not only to a major revision of his thinking, but, apparently, to a complete cessation of his creative energy and his human emotions. There was a psychic wound that has never stopped bleeding.

Maxwell Geismar. Nation. April 14, 1956. p. 305

John Dos Passos writes with great ease and he is technically inventive. He has conceived various means to write the story of his times as he sees it. *The Great Days* is a well and even an ingeniously constructed book. It is remarkable to think of how much it takes in, because the novel is only of normal length. Dos Passos has always been best at establishing scenes, rather than in portraying characters with depth and strong individuality. The characters reflect a world that is constantly changing, bringing failure and defeat. . . . The broken hopes of youth and of the days when this century was young have never been repaired. The expectations of the Wilsonian period have never been recovered. The later disappointments of the New Deal and the Second World War and the post-war era arouse less anger and, in the end, there is resignation. This is the sense of Dos

Passos' writing as I can gauge it. He has honestly recorded the play of hope and disappointment over four decades. He has done this with dignity and seriousness.

(K)                                    James T. Farrell. *NR*. April 28, 1958. p. 18

With the change in emphasis since *U.S.A.* from the novel to history, there has been a corresponding change in the content and stimulus of Dos Passos' writing: from the imaginative toward the intellectual, from the need to create toward the need to understand and to preserve, from synthesis toward analysis. Dos Passos has not lost sight of his original twin goals of life, art and thought, "the desire to create" and "the desire to fathom"; and the writing of history is still *an art*. But it is not art (no great historian has been accused of artistic genius), and Dos Passos has simply moved nearer one guidepost than the other. He has been less concerned to produce lasting works of the imagination—art—and more concerned to devote his efforts to maintaining a civilization in which art is possible. . . . In his recent novels and reportorial commentaries, Dos Passos is too oppressed by the immediate and also too conscious of the writer's duty to inform and to teach before it is too late. Only in the histories, in which he is looking back a century and more, does the reader feel the aesthetic distance of the artist from his materials: the possibility of a view broad enough to be comprehensive and meaningful, and of a serenity permitting him to be wise and undidactic.

(K)                                    John H. Wrenn. *John Dos Passos* (Twayne).
1961. pp. 170, 175

Dos Passos' external devices are so obtrusive as to make us suspect that they are a mechanical attempt to establish a unique style and language not otherwise forthcoming. Clearly Dos Passos has *wanted* to discover a language which would be *internal,* in the sense of being an organic quality of his fiction, informing the whole with its tonality and structure. This quest for a language is suggested in the prologue to *U.S.A.* Here we have the familiar theme of the homeless young man on the road, and after a Whitmanesque catalogue of the places he has been to, the young man muses "it was the speech that clung to the ears, the link that tingled in the blood; U.S.A. . . . mostly U.S.A. is the speech of the people." This may remind us of other writers who are in the Whitman tradition: Thomas Wolfe—"Remembering speechlessly we seek the great forgotten language"—and William Carlos Williams—"What common language to unravel?" And it reminds us of Whitman himself, the Whitman of *Democratic Vistas,* who says that it is the duty of American writers to find a language which is at once a personal style and an archetypal expression of the culture. Lacking the thaumaturgic power to turn this difficult trick, Dos Passos has manufactured over the years a style that is energetic, efficient, and mostly anonymous.

(K)                                    Richard Chase. *Cmty*. May, 1961. pp. 398–9

Dos Passos' theme might be described as the capture of the nation by "strangers" who have penetrated the American Eden as insidiously as the tribe of the Snopeses infiltrated into William Faulkner's Yoknapatawpha County. To the Puritan "Saints" of the seventeenth century, the "strangers" were merely the unsanctified or unregenerate portion of the community. To Dos Passos, who ferociously memorialized them in a famous passage in *U.S.A.*, the "strangers" are the subverters of the American dream, spiritual parricides of the Founding Fathers. They might be old-stock Americans—college presidents, judges, statesmen, clergymen, labor czars —anyone in short who, as Dos Passos once wrote, "turned our language inside out" and "took the clean words our fathers spoke and made them slimy and foul." They scored terribly in 1927 when they electrocuted two Italian anarchists, but during the intervening years, according to Dos Passos' novelistic history of the Republic, they have infected the entire body politic, corrupted the labor movement, corrupted the values of the nation, and reduced the "Saints" to a tiny embattled minority of libertarians.

(K)                                    Daniel Aaron. *Harper*. March, 1962. p. 55

By the calendar, the period from 1921 to 1962 comes to forty-one years. But the distance between *Three Soldiers* and *Mr. Wilson's War* in the life and writing of John Dos Passos measures from here to eternity.

To end the suspense, let me say right now that the difference created by the years is wholly to my taste. *Three Soldiers* was called intensely realistic by the critics, as invariably happens when any story of men in war is slanted toward morbidity. To my mind, it was grotesque in the same way that *All Quiet on the Western Front* was a travesty: it did not mirror life as the troops know it.

Dos Passos has never written with a lighter, more whimsical touch than in *Mr. Wilson's War*. Chatty, gossipy, frivolous—such adjectives may seem to have a nasty ring when applied to a historical work; but one must take that chance and hope for understanding. There is something in this book for everyone, including AEF vets whose memories are fast fading, historians digging for obscure items, embryo politicians who would know how the game is played, soldiers who dote on tactics and the moral forces, and housewives who believe that love conquers all.

(K)                                    S. L. A. Marshall. *SR*. Dec. 29, 1962. p. 42

Although *Midcentury* is a contemporary chronicle of corruption, the novel does not reflect any fundamental shift in the author's social philosophy. In light of what has been examined, there emerges a consistent conviction based on the idea that work is a source of virtue and salvation. Dos Passos must war against all those forces in society which prevent man from engaging in meaningful work, whether these forces are rooted in finance capitalism, government regulation, or union bossism. As for the characters themselves, those who adhere to their craft and try to live in and through their work can be saved; those who forsake their craftsmanship destroy themselves in a meaningless search for conspicuous wealth. I believe this gospel of work is a central principle in the social thought of John Dos Passos.

(K)                    John P. Diggins. *AnR*. Winter, 1963–64. p. 496

. . . Dos Passos has always been a negative function of power; that is, one finds him always at the opposite pole of where he conceives power to be. In this sense, he is more an anarchist, and always was, than a socialist or a conservative.

What Dos Passos achieved in *U.S.A.* was the creation of a form appropriate to the theme of the overwhelming, impersonal force of society, a structure which would carry the meaning of the primacy of society and make the anonymous processes of society the very stuff of a fictional world. . . .

The ultimate despair we confront in *U.S.A.* relates closely to what happens to language in the book. From the preface where the voice of the Camera Eye sections first identifies the meaning of America with American speech and the meaning of words, there is a constant concern, dramatically as well as explicitly, with the corruption of language. As we have seen, the betrayal of the promise of America is that words have grown slimy in the mouths of the ruling classes who have perverted old ideals. . . . Power superpower finally overwhelms even the language which creates the identity of America and if Dos Passos could say "we stand defeated," the defeat was particularly keen for the writer, the man who depends on words and his belief in the efficacy of language to sustain his personal identity. I would even speculate wildly and suggest that the vision of society Dos Passos presents in *U.S.A.* was a defeat for him personally and that is perhaps why he seems, to me at least, less estimable a writer after *U.S.A.* than before it. He had ceased to believe in the power of words.

(K)                    John William Ward. *Carleton Miscellany*.
                                        Summer, 1965. pp. 26–7

Critics who have written about Dos Passos's journey to Spain during the Civil War, and who point to his shocking discovery while there of how ruthlessly the Communists were undercutting their supposed allies within the Popular Front as the operative cause of his disillusionment with radicalism, miss the point; the central experience in Dos Passos's political education in the early 1930's was the titanic labor of creating *U.S.A.* The trilogy changed the man who wrote it, inducing in him a new respect for "the ground we stand on," a new awareness of historical continuity, a new appreciation of the complexities of human motivation. History was not escapable, after all, nor was it as simple as it had seemed. . . . The battle-cry of *U.S.A.*—"all right we are two nations"—evokes the certainty of the younger author's mind, while the title Dos Passos gives to his Midcentury sketch of J. Robert Oppenheimer—"The Uncertainty Principle"—indicates the older writer's state of mind.

(K)                     Kenneth S. Lynn. Introduction to *World in a Glass*
                        by John Dos Passos (Houghton). 1966. p. xv

The heroines, lost girls all, as well as the heroes of *U.S.A.* rest on 19th century types and naturalistic techniques which culminate in our standard cinematic images. Inadequately individualized and lacking complex and subtle development, the stereotypes nonetheless merge into a revealing vision of this country. The sordid patterns of defeat and the harsh cadences of the style, with their hypervisuality of place, poeticize the U.S.A., providing us with an America as recognizable and painfully endearing as an old movie. The experience of reading *U.S.A.* represents just this poetic and cinematic image of America, and in this Don Passos does not fail.

(K)                     Eleanor Widmer in *The Thirties,* edited by Warren
                        French (Everett Edwards). 1967. p. 19

## U.S.A.

In Dos Passos . . . there is a beautiful imaginative sympathy which permits him to get under the skin of his characters, but there is no imagination, and no Don Quixote. Dos Passos testifies to all this by his use of newsreels, just as he seeks the full sensibility in the impressions of the camera eye and the heroic character in the biographies; but in his central narrative the standpoint is always narrowed to what the character himself knows as the quality of his existence, life as it appears to him. And this leveling drags with it and tends to make rather crude and sometimes commonplace the sensibility shown in the other panels. . . . The whole truth of experience (if past literature is not wholly nonsense) is more than the quality of most lives. One is sure that Dos Passos knows this, since it is the reason for his four forms and his discontinuity. His novel is perhaps the greatest monument of naturalism because it betrays so fully the poverty and disintegration inherent in that method. Dos Passos is the gifted victim of his own extraordinary grasp of the truth. He is a victim of the truth and the whole truth.

                        Delmore Schwartz. *SoR*. Autumn, 1938. pp. 364–7

*U.S.A.* demonstrates Dos Passos' extraordinary capacity for observation; his "scholarship" in this respect is amazing; the sheer bulk and variety of his reading as reflected in both the biographies and the fictional sections have been tremendous. The work as a whole is one of the most impressive performances in contemporary writing. Yet one cannot say, "Here is the essence of American life." One can say rather that here in parallel columns is a pretty complete report of the human and social elements of American life from which the essence might be distilled. Eventually, however, the reading of parallel columns becomes monotonous.

Margaret Marshall. *Nation.* Jan. 6, 1940. p. 17

The philosophy of *U.S.A.* was taut, as the book itself was taut. Everything in it echoed its mass rumble, and the far-reaching tactile success of the book came out of that massed power, the heaping together of so many lives in symmetrical patterns of disaster. Dos Passos' effects have always depended on a violence of pace, on the quick flickering of the reel, the sudden climaxes where every fresh word drives the wedge in. No scene can be held too long; no voice can be heard too clearly. Everything must come at us from a distance and bear its short ironic wail; the machine must get going again; nothing can wait.

Alfred Kazin. *NR.* March 15, 1943. p. 353

In his trilogy Dos Passos looked backward to the optimistic American faith of 1900 from the vantage point of the collapse of prosperity in 1929 and drew a savage indictment of those forces in our society which had frustrated its immense promise. Could that promise be reinstated with some chance of fulfillment? The poet in Dos Passos reached beyond indictment and social criticism into prophecy and the first two volumes of his trilogy implied the answer to this question. Nothing less than an overturn of the existing order would restore the promise of American life, he surmised; and he pledged his faith to a future social revolution. But before the third volume of his trilogy appeared, this faith had deserted him. The work that had begun as an epic closed as an elegy, and on a note of despair.

Lloyd Morris. *NYHT.* Jan. 2, 1949. p. 3

Dos Passos . . . knows the everyday world of the ordinary apprehension—in which the essential Dos Passos appears to be so self-consciously not at home—as the movement of whole groups and classes and the clash of group prejudices. He is so preoccupied with representing these movements by newspaper headlines, historical figures, and, above all, by type characters that he reduces the movement of awareness in his characters to the simplified pattern we ascribe to the imaginary average man. You do not know his people except as you know the journalist's average businessman,

Vassar girl, or labor leader; nor can you believe that the drama of their lives represents Dos Passos' full awareness of experience; the stifling personal and sensory awareness of the "Camera Eye," so completely isolated from any larger context, is the Dos Passos who is omitted from the narrative: it is his Mallarmé, as the narrative is his Lenin.

Arthur Mizener. *KR.* Winter, 1950. pp. 16–7

See *Three Soldiers, Manhattan Transfer, U.S.A., District of Columbia, The Great Days, Midcentury* (novels); *The Best Times* (memoir); *Occasions and Protests* (essays); *The Men Who Made the Nation, The Shackles of Power, Mr. Wilson's War* (history).

# DREISER, THEODORE (1871–1945)

In his muddled way, held back by the manacles of his race and time, and his steps made uncertain by a guiding theory which too often eludes his own comprehension, he yet manages to produce works of art of unquestionable beauty and authority, and to interpret life in a manner that is poignant and illuminating. There is vastly more intuition in him than intellectualism; his talent is essentially feminine, as Conrad's is masculine; his ideas always seem to be deduced from his feelings. . . . He gets his effects, one might almost say, not by designing them, but by living them.

But whatever the process, the power of the image evoked is not to be gainsaid. It is not only brilliant on the surface, but mysterious and appealing in its depths. One swiftly forgets his intolerable writing, his mirthless, sedulous, repellent manner, in the face of the Athenian tragedy he instills in his seduced and soul-sick servant girls, his barbaric pirates of finance, his conquered and hamstrung supermen, his wives who sit and wait.

H. L. Mencken. *A Book of Prefaces* (Knopf). 1917.
pp. 95–6

Theodore Dreiser is one of those who are utterly incapable of swallowing the world as a young cuckoo swallows the grub that its wagtail mother has brought to it. He must look under every leaf, turn over every stone. His great, lumbering imagination, full of a divine curiosity, goes roaring through the prairie-lands of the Cosmos with the restless heavy-shouldered force of an old bull *wildebeest.* Whenever I am with him and can watch his cumbersome intellect at work upon any one of the manifold subjects like "the trickiness of women," the breeding of pigeons, the reasoning power of a spider he studied once in his bed-chamber, or the electronic basis of the Universe, I never fail to feel awe at the struggles of this ungainly giant, whose limbs are still half-buried in clay.

Llewelyn Powys. *The Verdict of Bridlegoose* (Harcourt). 1926. p. 64

It must not be supposed, of course, as has now and then been done, that the writings of a man of his stature can be without artistic virtue. Far from it. He possesses the central artistic virtues, though he lacks the peripheral ones. . . . Dreiser has the root of the matter in him, which is detachment and transcendence during the creative process. He can keep his eye on the object, only and solely and entirely on the object. . . . He can take the clay and mold men; he can create the relations between them. . . . What counts against him is . . . the heavy, amorphous verbiage, which will seem duller as time goes on, the unrestrained meticulousness in the delineation of the trivial, the increasing grittiness of his texture.

Ludwig Lewisohn. *Expression in America* (Harper). 1932. pp. 481–2

It is a prime refreshment in the works of Theodore Dreiser that he is free of the mysterious sense of degradation, of filth and discomfort into which most Americans and many Europeans have translated one of the three elements of desire. Life then in his books is free to assert its own volume, where the huge desire to live, the wild desire to love, the insane desire to excel, variously mingled, produce various actions. And they disclose the special chasms that have come about because in some hidden way we have sacrificed the second to the first and third of these angles. But without dogma: "They can't put me down as a liberal or free thinker," he insists. "I don't know, I wouldn't say I know. I know nothing."

Dorothy Dudley. *Forgotten Frontiers* (H. Smith). 1932. p. 481

I admired the things which he could do in writing which nobody else could do—the simple and poignant truths of life; and I thought his philosophic notions bosh and his historical truths mere uneducated ignorance. I found that he did not agree with those critics who praised him for the immense amount of bricks and mortar that were visible in his towering structure of fiction—the multiplicity of details which such critics called "realism." He was not especially interested in the details, but was using them, and perhaps over-using them, earnestly in trying to achieve beauty. He once told me with honest tears in his eyes that a novel had no excuse for existence unless it was beautiful. And by beautiful I knew that he meant true to the deep emotions of the human heart, not to the mere visible surface aspects of life.

Floyd Dell. *Homecoming* (Farrar and Rinehart).

1933. p. 268

It is because he has spoken for Americans with an emotion equivalent to their own emotion, in a speech as broken and blindingly searching as common speech, that we have responded to him with the dawning realization that he is stronger than all the others of his time, and at the same time more poignant; greater than the world he has described, but as significant as the people in it. To have accepted America as he has accepted it, to immerse oneself in something one can neither escape nor relinquish, to yield to what has been true and to yearn over what has seemed inexorable, has been Dreiser's fate and the secret of his victory.

Alfred Kazin. *On Native Grounds* (Reynal). 1942.

pp. 89–90

Theodore Dreiser . . . suggested to me some large creature of the prime wandering on the marshy plains of a human foreworld. A prognathous man with an eye askew and a paleolithic face, he put me in mind of Polyhemus . . . a Rodinesque figure only half out from the block; and yet a remark that someone made caused him to blush even up to the roots of his thin grey hair. Dreiser was hypersensitive, strangely as one might have thought,—he was a living paradox in more than one way; but a lonelier man there never was.

Van Wyck Brooks. *Days of the Phoenix* (Dutton).

1957. p. 20

Dreiser's true form has revealed itself with time, and has nothing to do with our relative sympathy for the characters or any conventional suavity of construction, but a great deal to do with the intensity of the process and the "representation" resulting from it. . . . In the kind of organic plotting for which Dreiser . . . deserve(s) to be famous, intuition and intelligence work together to supersede the type of novel in which action flows more directly from character and character is more opaque and compact. . . . Dreiser uses such conventional devices as the trial, often quite ineptly, for terminal suspense; but the common refusal to grant him tragic status comes from a failure to see the *emotional* unity of his plot. . . . Dreiser's success made him *the* great American novelist of his time and place (no competition with James implied), the one in whom we feel the most sustaining and exhilarating press of life.

R. W. Flint. *Nation.* April 27, 1957. p. 372

There is little question that Theodore Dreiser is the most distinguished member of the whole group of modern American novelists. . . . He was a realist. . . . Yes, he, partly through his own innocence, perhaps, and early origins, told the truth about life when he could discover it. Probably no one else in our literature has had such a direct and intimate feeling for the common forms of experience, pleasant or disgraceful. But he was also, like Balzac, who is the closest European counterpart, one of the high romantics of literature.

What gave his work its remarkable texture, its glamour, really, was his simple sense of the variety and mystery of life on all its levels.

Maxwell Geismar. *American Moderns* (Hill and
Wang). 1958. p. 50

He was not, by and large, an attractive figure, and the letters present his unattractive qualities more relentlessly than the books that have been written about him have done. One notes, for instance, his dependence on other persons, particularly women, and his offhand acceptance of their services to him. One notes his arrogance and his greed. But at the same time one feels in the letters, as in the novels, that this was a man who was utterly faithful to his own vision of life.

As he wrote Mencken, he was born with a bias, a bias not so much in favor of the common man as a bias in favor of men and women as victims —of the economic system, of their own impulses, of life itself. This bias led him into ridiculous contradictions, but it also gave him insights that have made his novels, with all their many faults, a permanent part of our literature.

Granville Hicks. *SR*. April 4, 1959. p. 16

Dreiser was willing to risk being wrong; and he had great wrong-looking juts to his character. He was a stiff-armer, an elbower who never gave ground outside his novels or in them. And though outside the books he could be so obtuse and unjust, inside them his passion for justice rang true. At the height of his success, when he had settled old scores and could easily have become the smiling public man, he chose instead to rip the whole fabric of American civilization straight down the middle, from its economy to its morality. It was the country that had to give ground.

Nelson Algren. *Nation*. May 16, 1959. p. 459

Dreiser's novels have an important aim, significant because he was a keen, if often naïve observer of the social and political realities of his day. He saw America as being at middle age, and he was concerned with a culture which, by creating and encouraging artificial goals, was perverting its worthwhile institutions and, more important, was robbing the individual of his chance to live up to a full, meaningful potential. Each of Dreiser's novels illustrates a different aspect of what he felt was a crucial misdirection of American energy. Often his insights were vague and muddied: in *The "Genius"* (1915), for example, Dreiser attempts to explain the forces harmful to the creative artist, and by placing the blame on a curious mixture of capitalism and eroticism his novel rests on a faulty base. Which is to say that Dreiser is usually a bad writer at the point he leaps past his immediate feelings and his own past. In his first two books, *Sister Carrie* (1900) and *Jennie Gerhardt* (1911), Dreiser studies the failure of the American as an individual and of Americans as a family group, and his theme provides a valid and compassionate foundation for the novels. He was writing out of the misery and passion of his own experiences.

Dreiser's works, while exploring many sides to a problem, would adhere to a single point of view, and the focus, often shifting, from book to book, in various economic and philosophical directions, would originate in what he believed at the moment to be the deepest roots of American unhappiness.

(K)                    Charles Shapiro. *Theodore Dreiser* (Southern
                                    Illinois). 1962. p. 4


Randolph Bourne once said that Dreiser had the "artist's vision without the sureness of the artist's technique." This is true of most of Dreiser's books, and in a limited sense may be true of *An American Tragedy*. I have used the phrase "Dreiser's art" in full awareness that most critics, even critics as dangerous to disagree with as Lionel Trilling, will find it absurd; and in full awareness that even those who admire Dreiser will, with few exceptions, concede a point on "art," or apologetically explain that Dreiser's ineptitudes somehow have the value of stylistic decorum and can be taken as a manifestation of his groping honesty, and will then push on to stake their case on his "power" and "compassion."

But ultimately how do we know the "power" or the "compassion"— know them differently, that is, from the power or compassion we may read into a news story—except by Dreiser's control? Except, in other words, by his grasp of the human materials and his rhythmic organization of them, the vibrance which is the life of fictional illusion, that mutual interpenetration in meaning of part and whole which gives us the sense of preternatural fulfilment? Except, in short, by art?

(K)                    Robert Penn Warren. *YR*. Autumn, 1962. pp. 8–9


Dreiser's characters are low in the sense of being stupid. Carrie and Jennie and Clyde would probably rank well below the norm in any verbal intelligence test. Neither sentimentality nor disgust mars Dreiser's handling of inarticulate people—although both these patronizing attitudes repeatedly disfigured the "naturalist" tradition to which he is supposed to belong. That Dreiser loved his helpless, unconscious people has often been said, but he did so with the very special love of a sibling, carrying with it acceptance, identification, shame, detachment and an honesty related to the contempt that is bred by familiarity. In the most literal sense, as his letters and autobiographical writings show clearly, Dreiser wrote as a brother. This is the central fact about his work, far more important than the clichés thrown at him in the 1930's and '40's: that he was a peasant, a linguistic immigrant, a naturalist, a People's realist, an American and so on. . . . Without much in the line of theory, using only family materials, Dreiser could easily work out a view of life somewhat at variance with the conventional homilies of his day. More important, from the contrast between day-by-day life as it was lived by his brothers and sisters, and life as it was played out in popular melodrama, he devised a literary style that gave form, and even heroism, to the inarticulate.

(K)                    Ellen Moers. *AS*. Winter, 1963–64. pp. 109–10

Dreiser was the first American to portray with truth and power our modern world of commerce and mechanization, the first to portray the dismal depersonalization of the individual which results from urbanization and intensifying societal pressure to conform, the first to draw us frankly and grimly as a nation of status-seekers. . . . *Sister Carrie* of 1900 and *The Bulwark* of forty-five years later, aside from particulars, tell the same story about America. Man is a mechanism, his pitiful existence determined by factors of biology and social environment which Dreiser, for want of a better term, labels "chemisms." The cosmos operating in his stories is uncaring, unfeeling; at bottom it is an unfair universe, controlled by gods who disdain involvement in their creation. We can nod in agreement with the writer or cavil at the darkness of his pessimism, but we are forced above all to stop, to consider, to think. . . . Probably because of his philosophy—we are all companions in the same sinking ship—Dreiser feels keenly the plight of each individual human soul at the mercy of chance and of forces beyond his control. It is significant that, though failures abound in his novels, there are no villains, only human beings who are more or less fortunate than their neighbors. In the Dreiser world, each life is necessarily a tragedy.

(K)                    Philip L. Gerber. *Theodore Dreiser* (Twayne).
                                          1964. pp. 173–5

Dreiser's genius is for feeling, feeling uncontrolled by, unaided by thought. It is characteristic of his peculiar confusion that when he wished to tell a tale of American youth destroyed by the inequalities of a corrupt, money-mad class system he should have declined to do anything more than sketch the system so that he could devote all his effort to recreating a banal and wordless triangle between a weakly good-looking, utterly uninteresting man, and two women—one of whom is merely pathetic and the other of whom is capable not of conveying "the pain of wanting and not having" but only pain.

Dreiser lacked more than art; he lacked a sense of what he lacked.

(K)                    Charles Thomas Samuels. *YR*. Summer, 1964. p. 637

No newspaper could catch the prodigious drama of this strange life— the sensitive, shoeless Indiana boy with hurts that never healed, the anguish over the stillborn *Sister Carrie,* the interval of dress-pattern splendor, then the long, bitter struggle for freedom and acceptance that would be his greatest glory and that ended with *An American Tragedy* in 1925. That the work he had done in those years made a bridge between Howells and Hemingway that no one else could have built was achievement enough of itself. It was not the final achievement. Bridge or no bridge, the work was colossal in its own right. . . . The original creative artist had languished after 1925, if he had not quite died, and the personality that persisted was something different: the crusading zealot, the bullheaded, uninformed visionary. The great realist had lost his way, abandoned realism, when he turned his enormous compassion solely on the squid and began to hate all lobsters. The intuition and sympathy that had created Carrie, Jennie and Clyde were poor weapons when they grappled with the hard world of politics. Hatred could grow tiresome.

(K)                    W. A. Swanberg. *Dreiser* (Scribner). 1965. pp. 523–4

His inability to achieve literary effects except through the amassing of details worked hand in hand with his ignorance of the common axioms, and his ponderous rediscovery of some, and his innocent though radical replacement of others. A geometer of genius who had never heard of Euclid would have to gather together his own set of assumptions and begin the confinement of space anew; the result would not be the world familiar to Euclid's followers. So Dreiser begins the confinement of life anew. He is a literary radical in the basic sense of the word, for he plants new roots, not as an act of rebellion, for this argues an understanding of the bases of society, but as an act of creation, as if the society which he portrays had never been portrayed before. And indeed, as *Sister Carrie* demonstrates, it had not. . . .

The whole that results from Dreiser's remarkably detailed manner is a world in which nothing stands between the individual and the whirl of life. Dreiser looks and looks, wrings his hands, and looks again, but for all his details does not see families, friendships, or other forms of community which act as protective screens between the individual and the onslaught of his environment. To look at matters conventionally and to say that such protections exist is, for Dreiser, to look at a wilderness and say it is a botanical garden.

(K)                    Larzer Ziff. *The American 1890s* (Viking). 1966
pp. 338–9

## An American Tragedy

In its larger features the construction of *An American Tragedy* is as solid as a bank building. It is very long, to be sure, but there is little in it which is not functional, not a part of Mr. Dreiser's ponderous design. I was very nervous for fear that the roof would fall during a couple of sagging chapters early in the second volume; but, no, he slowly swung his heavy timbers into place, restored his tension and retained it to the end. The structure of a novel he has mastered. It is the structure of a sentence which has remained a mystery to him. Often he plunges into a sentence head foremost, "trusting to God Almighty to get him out of it"; and is vouchsafed no divine aid. And yet the work as a whole is massively impressive. I do not know where else in American fiction one can find the situation here presented dealt with so fearlessly, so intelligently, so exhaustively, and *therefore* with such unexceptionable moral effect.

Stuart Sherman. *The Main Stream* (Scribner). 1927.
p. 144

His difficulty is that his mechanistic naturalism compels him so to select and manipulate facts of experience as to deny, through his narrative, that human life has any meaning or value. The attempt is suicidal, and the more consistently it is carried out the more completely is Mr. Dreiser forced to divest his creatures and their actions of any distinctively human quality and meaning. The more successful he is the more insignificant his work becomes. *An American Tragedy* . . . is more skilfully, faithfully, and consistently executed on the naturalistic level than any of its author's earlier novels, and precisely for this reason it contains no single element of tragedy in any legitimate sense of the word, and it impresses thoughtful readers as a mere sensational newspaper story long drawn out.

Robert Shafer in *Humanism and America,* edited
by Norman Foerster (Farrar and Rinehart). 1930.
pp. 165–6

The best of Theodore Dreiser is in this book. It is an epic of one important aspect of American life, its crass materialism, its indifference to all that is not glitter and show, its irresponsibility for the youth, its condemnations instead of understanding, its thirst for punishment instead of prevention, its hypocrisy, its ruthless savagery, and the ferocity of its mobs and courts of prosecution. There is less naturalistic detachment and more of the fire and brooding pity for men who live with such impoverished ideals. It is an indictment without malice.

> Harlan Hatcher. *Creating the Modern American Novel* (Farrar and Rinehart). 1935. p. 55

The great advantage of *An American Tragedy* (over Dreiser's other novels) was that it was dramatized rather than reported in events. For the first time and the only time in Dreiser's career he had a subject that could be presented dramatically for at least three-fourths of its length. As a result, this novel, despite its tremendous size (840 closely printed pages), has much the best integrated dramatic structure of any Dreiser novel. . . . Basically the story is without novelty; in fact, at first glance it even appears unpromising. But in the hands of a writer of Dreiser's sympathies and tragic sense, it becomes a great one. He explored every possible mutation of his theme; he probed more deeply and developed greater significance from the simple human story than had been done by any American who handled a similar theme before him.

> George Snell. *The Shapers of American Fiction* (Dutton). 1947. pp. 244–5

See *Sister Carrie, Jennie Gerhardt, The Financier, The Titan, The Genius, An American Tragedy,* and *The Bulwark* (novels); also *A Book about Myself* and *Dawn* (autobiographies).

# DUGAN, ALAN (1923–    )

This is not a young poetry, though it appears in a Series dedicated to young poets. It is as old as Granicus, and older. Neither is it an elaborately wrought poetry, though there are moments when the anti-rhetoric becomes rhetorical in its own dissent. Others will find other pleasures or hesitations; I am moved chiefly by the plainness of Mr. Dugan's themes and by his nuances of imagery, phrasing, run, and rhythm. The cast of mind is hard, yet the detail is often wonderfully ingenuous and tender.

> Dudley Fitts. Foreword to *Poems* by Alan Dugan (Yale). 1961. p. x

. . . it is through mockery, invective, sudden reversal and exposure that he gains some of his strongest effects. . . . Yet his ironic revelations have not the satirist's frequent impulse to reform so much as the desire to identify something for what it is, understand it and elude it. . . . By modified roughness of tone and rhythm, realism of language, occasional obscenities, and a dark, harsh humor, Mr. Dugan ekes out a protective spiritual margin in which to exist. He is seldom given to lyricism; when he does employ it, as in "On an East Wind from the Wars," it is tempered with the theme of death and destruction.

Ralph J. Mills. *Poetry*. July, 1961. pp. 245–6

Alan Dugan in his *Poems* . . . takes the role of a soldier, an infantryman, the dogface of Bill Mauldin's cartoons. So many of the controlling images in Dugan's first book emerge from the knowledge of the squalor and confusion of war, from the self-absorption of the captive, from the inner suffering of the tortured prisoner, that it is not, perhaps, surprising that the poems dealing with other themes often lapse into wordiness and contrivance. When Dugan is at work in his favorite role, the language simplifies itself, the verse takes on a crestfallen irony, and the lines speak in a straightforward earthy rhythm.

Peter Davison. *At.* Nov., 1961. p. 172

It is as if the shade of Lucretius had been reincarnated, secular and skeptical, speaking a plain stodgy no-nonsense American prose, like that of your nearest bartender. Dugan, by the way, has a sharp eye for the sights and sounds of New York, its winos and beggars. Perhaps it is his role as businessman, tenant of "offices away from weather," that enables him to see an urban landscape with a bitter accuracy uncommon to bards who subsist either in coffeehouses or on campuses. Like the trees he celebrates in one fine anti-Kilmer piece, his poems "take liberties in spreading out." And they put forth good green leaves.

X. J. Kennedy. *NYT*. Dec. 22, 1963. p. 5

It isn't that you have to really throw away the usual poetic flap when discussing Alan Dugan's work, but it helps. Nothing is here "in the old combinations," and this second book of his isn't going to make him any more friends in some centers of literary orthodoxy south of the Ohio River. But then, he is a great gambler: he takes chances on variations of tone, on in-and-out relationships in his imagery, on rhetorical effects that double back on the structure of what he has written, on bald profanity and ludicrous irony. . . .

I think the most exciting aspect of Alan Dugan's work is that all the gambles arise from his predisposition, his insistence, on portraying what he sees from a bluntly personal point of view, and Dugan has a sensibility a hemisphere removed from the involutions of American Calvinism: his is the immediacy and heat of a Celtic temperament, and some of his best poems are those in which he takes a classical subject and ignites it with his own acid diction. . . . [H]e is a riverboat gambler, a weather-cock, a gadfly, and a painfully honest moralist. What can one say? He is exactly what we need, but I am not sure we know what he is. He is good for us; I hope in the long run we will be good for him.

Bruce Cutler. Poetry. March, 1964. pp. 390–1

He is complex, cantankerous, and middle-aged. Also very American. Yet he seems to possess that true weather-beaten eye, that bardic appetite that looks for nothing, accepts nothing without a fissure in it, the "lewd scratches" which "mar design." Dugan has few themes and few variations, but all of his poems have a grudging pathos or jaunty comic eloquence, and all run true to form or character. His is the truth that there is nothing so tragic that someone somewhere will not think of as comic. What he has seen he gets down, and what he has experienced he lets you know about. . . . What is striking in the poetry of Alan Dugan—the rancorous insights, the self-mocking wit—is paramount in the literature of today, a literature of limitations, an all encompassing grinding down, one that knows you test the strength of a man's character less by what he denies himself, than by what he's been denied. " 'Be alive,' they say, when I/ am so alive I ache with it. . ." But the ache is energy struggling with emptiness.

Robert Mazzocco. NYR. Nov. 23, 1967. pp. 20, 22

See *Poems, Poems 2, Poems 3.*


# DUNCAN, ROBERT (1919–    )

What the themes are is hard to say, and not because the poetry has completely absorbed them. Instead, it suggests—suggests with much clang and glitter of banners, helmets, swans, and tapestries, and with some good steady writing. . . . But the clarity is deceptive, and in the end one concludes either that Mr. Duncan's symbols are the elements of an esoteric rite, or that he has little of importance to say, for all the shining surface. . . . Mr. Duncan seems to combine a kind of primitivism in ideas with sophistication of manner; this is as close as I can come to indicating his peculiar tone.

Isabel Gamble. Poetry. Nov., 1950. p. 118

His poems are illustrations, objectifications of the interchange between order and disorder, accompanied by appropriate emotions, which are more nearly suggested than realized, of amazement and love at the sight of perfect order, awe and fear at the possibilities of new forms (sometimes monstrous) arising from disorder, and grief at the processes of decay, disintegration, and return. Art—specifically, poetry—is a part of this large concern, and references to poetry or to the poet occur in nearly every poem. Duncan's relationship to poetry, to the creation of form, becomes the symbol of order and change operating in all aspects of reality. . . .

Every *possibility* of the outstanding poet exists in this work: development of the poem's total form (as opposed to a few flashy lines), excellent sonant quality and movement, conservation of statement, and intensity of rendered image, and a commanding point of view. It is because Mr. Duncan is already an accomplished poet that I ask more of him: more immediate experience, less comment and explanation.

A. R. Ammons. *Poetry*. April, 1960. pp. 53–5

Robert Duncan is another excellent poet whose work is measured and spare, although many of his poems are long. The diction is uncluttered, like that of Mr. Creeley; but whereas the sound of the latter's verse is like that of a human voice speaking, Mr. Duncan's considerable talent most often assumes the form and measure of a human voice singing. He is a lyrical poet in the most traditional sense: that is, he is a musician. I do not mean that his poems, as such, need to be set to music. And I do not mean that they drip like Swinburne. At his best, he is a master of rhetoric in the Elizabethan sense of the word. Employing the simplest diction and rhythm, he can lead the reader to expect a certain pattern of sound, and then he varies it, so that the music of his verse produces a fusion of fulfillment and  surprise which is one of the chief delights created by such a great lyric poet as, say, Thomas Campion.

James Wright. *MinnR*. Winter, 1961. p. 251

Robert Duncan has that special quality of temper which he shares with Edmund Wilson or Pandit Nehru, he is a Good European. Although Duncan has been singularly open to all the influences of all times and places, and has learned from all the Old Masters of Modernism, from Reubén Darío to Yves Bonnefoy, his distinguishing characteristic is not the breadth of his influences, but the depth and humanness of his heart. Now that he is approaching early middle age he has begun to take on something of the forgotten grandeur of the great nineteenth-century "men of the world" of letters—Monckton Milnes or Walter Bagehot. I can think of no other poet of my time of which anything like this could be said— with most, the very idea is ridiculous. As mentor and example, Duncan's influence on the younger men of the new New Poetry has been incalculable.

The now widely publicized San Francisco Renaissance owes more to Duncan than to any other one person.

Kenneth Rexroth. *Assays* (New Directions).
1961. p. 192

*The Opening of the Field,* Robert Duncan's latest book, shows what the Dionysian genie can do if granted his freedom; Duncan's visionary power is as undeniable as Blake's was, and his plea for open as against closed form, on the strength of Pound's and Williams' example, is far from empty.

Glauco Cambon. Recent American Poetry (Minnesota).<br>1962. p. 43

All of this power has come to him only gradually. Reading his *Selected Poems* of 1942–1950, one felt at times that Duncan, though entitled to experiment, didn't have to print so many tentative jottings from his laboratory. As the fifties went on, his work grew firmer and more sure, resulting in the very good collection, *The Opening of the Field,* which the present book *Roots and Branches* surpasses. Containing his work of the past four years, it is a hefty book with little chaff in it.

In approaching Duncan's poems, the reader may find a bit of blind faith useful. With it, he may surmount a few private allusions, mysterious gaps in syntax and quirky spellings (meant to distinguish the sounds of -ed endings: *calld, many-brancht*). . . .

Duncan's themes are the changes that take place in the self, the search for love, the decline of faith in the supernatural. . . . One of that large clan of poets who emerged in the fifties from Black Mountain College and the cafes of San Francisco, Duncan in this book stands as the most serious of them all, the most capable.

X. J. Kennedy. NYT. Dec. 20, 1964. pp. 4–5

Only Duncan will ever know why the words are arranged and spaced as they are or how precisely one can or should read an image like "stars flew out into the deserted souls." No amount of sympathetic reading can dispel the overwhelming sense of arbitrariness. But after a while it is reassuring to discover that Duncan does not care how good his poems are. They follow the patterns of his mind, nothing else, and anyone who writes this way is cheerfully oblivious of all who are not kindred spirits. Nothing is more serious than a Duncan poem, yet little asks so completely to be read as a kind of sport. Every reader will probably be able to follow along his curious paths for a passage or even a whole poem, and then the shout becomes a kind of song. To read Duncan in bulk is to become oneself an action painter, and for that process to work, nothing can be very clear. To believe in him, I should think, is to be quite mad.

Roger Sale. HdR. Summer, 1965. pp. 302–3

We return, a third time, to find both first and second impressions valid. To find Duncan both master and mountebank; or perhaps poetic master because poetic mountebank. His mystique, down to typography, being finely fitted to the sense of purity and conquest which his poems instill. His craft giving character—even dignity—to his pose as guru; his need to teach acceding, so fully, to his skill, that we are only later aware of the skill. His skill hewn so densely into argument that we have nothing left, after all, except a book in hand. Which we begin again. Ready to be cozened into an (unmistakable) catharsis.

Frederic Will. Poetry. Sept., 1965. p. 428

The orphic element in Duncan's poetry presupposes a belief in the kind of communication that, related to a mystical life force, transcends conventional language in the same way that music "transcends" words. One recalls Hart Crane's intention for the second part of "For the Marriage of Faustus and Helen": to "invent an idiom for the proper transposition of jazz into words," or, conversely, to find an idiom that had the musical qualities appropriate to a Dionysian experience. Important here is the assumption of an elemental sound or rhythm, prior to the language of significance, and quintessential to what is taken to be true poetry.

L. S. Dembo. Conceptions of Reality in Modern American Poetry (California). 1966. p. 217

. . . Robert Duncan is probably the figure with the richest natural genius among the Black Mountain poets. His work lacks [Robert] Creeley's consistent surface simplicity and [Charles] Olson's familiar cluster of localist and radically critical attitudes, and is consequently less well known than their writings. Also, it is cluttered by certain 'interferences,' partly stylistic and willful, partly related to his mystical and private attitudinal assumptions. . . . Though it seems clear now that Duncan's art is to some degree selfdefeating, one has only to leaf through these books to find poems and passages that mark him as a modern romantic whose best work is instantly engaging by the standards of the purest lyrical traditions.

M. L. Rosenthal. The New Poets (Oxford). 1967. p. 174

See Selected Poems (1942–1950), The Opening of the Field, Roots and Branches.

# EBERHART, RICHARD (1904–     )

Richard Eberhart insists on the immaculate Ego. He allows himself contaminating identification with no system of ideas, while his tradition is that of the traditionless. Writing under the more primitive compulsions of the heart, he makes his way through an emotional and intellectual labyrinth whose relation to the real world is, at best, a verbal accident. . . . His finest poems . . . express with economy and intellectual beauty the sovereign individual. Convention drops away and the reader feels the immediate record of free sensibility. . . . Such exaltation, however, illuminates but the barest handful of his poems. For the most part, it appears in disassociated examples momentarily, like vistas opened by lightning.

John Malcolm Brinnin. *Poetry*. Dec., 1942. pp. 508–9

Mr. Eberhart, either because his ear is defective or because he is over-anxious to avoid the merely smooth, makes the not uncommon mistake of establishing violence and perversity as his norm, with the inevitable result that where everything shrieks and clashes, the uproar at last cancels itself out, and it is as if nothing had been heard at all. This is a great pity, for he has a wonderful energy of vision, together with a fine gusto in phrase and an enviable muscular capacity for compressed statement: if he could only be severe with himself, and canalize his gifts, instead of simply going hell-for-leather at his Idea, with capitals, he could be one of the very best of contemporary poets, as he is already one of the most exciting.

Conrad Aiken. *NR*. Apr. 2, 1945. p. 452

In the manufacture of malt whiskey the barley is soaked, then dried, and then the malt thus obtained is brewed into a beer-like liquid. This liquid, when distilled, produces the raw whiskey. It has to lie mellowing a long time in sherry casks. Mr. Eberhart is always a good brewer but he does not always bother with the further processes of distilling and maturing—or rather, he often matures without distilling. Let him distil his poetry more often: the finer, subtler, stronger and more profound flavor of pot-stilled malt whiskey (now almost unobtainable, alas) is more exciting to the discriminating palate than the pleasantest of beers.

David Daiches. *Poetry*. May, 1945. p. 95

His trouble has always been that his faults are very obvious and easy to feel superior to, because they are as unmodish as it is possible for faults to be; they are Victorian faults. That Mr. Eberhart has also the Victorian virtues is easy to overlook. . . . When Mr. Eberhart succeeds, he achieves a kind of direct rightness of feeling towards central experiences which is about the rarest thing there is in contemporary verse; and he does it in a language as simple and perfect for its purpose as you could ask.

Arthur Mizener. *Poetry*. Jan., 1949. pp. 226–7

To be a poet, he has taken greater risks than most of his contemporaries. That is there is rather little intellectual content in his verse. . . . But the open mind or heart is just as hobbled as the closed one. It is not enough for a man simply to keep his head clear or his nose clean. He needs to dance between these opposites like the angels. And Mr. Eberhart's great quality is that he can put up a show of violence behind the heartfeltness and the vision—just as Blake could, of course. All the same he is a man with a definite and tragic sense of the small use of his kind of experience in the world of busyness, with a feeling (not especially contemporary) of having been cornered; a man much given to backward-looking. He is obsessed with childhood and death and union with earth; he has a hatred of fuss and affairs, and a liking for subtlety, harmony, oddness, and the natural.

Peter Duvall Smith. *NSN*. July 21, 1951. p. 78

What . . . must be said for him . . . is the compassion, the sad and gentle and terribly exact understanding he has of his own and of all human experience. This is his "bias toward the spiritual," and it comes near greatness. It was in "The Groundhog," the war poems, and the many contemplations of death, and in the short unforgettable "The Full of Joy" and "Cover Me Over." Wisdom and compassion permeate the poetry.

John Holmes. *NYT*. Aug. 19, 1951. p. 14

Oddly, though he has a very recognizable poetic personality, Mr. Eberhart has never acquired a distinctive "style" of his own. . . . Perhaps a "style" is sometimes a mere crystallizing of stereotyped responses. Though the unevenness and imperfection of much of his work is a heavy price to pay for this, Mr. Eberhart has a quality which is very rare indeed in contemporary poets. He does not feel himself bound by what the last stanza of a poem is going to be like while he is grappling with the first stanza. There is nothing preconceived or ready-made in his work.

G. S. Fraser. *NSN*. Nov. 21, 1953. p. 647

Richard Eberhart without ever raising his voice, using for the most part the forms that are supposed to be worn out, is a natural poet, and, happily, one who just keeps getting better and better. . . . For all his intellectual preoccupation with death, there is a sunny disposition, an even temper, a healthy optimism, a muscular goodwill in Eberhart that stamps his writing as peculiarly American.

Selden Rodman. NYT. Nov. 22, 1953. p. 5

In the romantic mode, Eberhart's individualism is naked and unashamed; and in contrast to the tormented, metamorphic victims of our age, it rings adventurous and cheerful. It is almost as if the great age of the individual were beginning all over again, instead of fighting for its life. . . . Because his style is governed so much by the extreme individualism of the unconscious, Eberhart's use of reckless imagery sometimes involves him (and his reader) in blind-alley surrealism. . . . More often, he achieves an opaque magnificence, however arbitrary the tropes.

Gerard Previn Meyer. SR. May 22, 1954. p. 22

Eberhart's lyric gives us almost always the diction of a single speaker who is arguing a relation between appearance and reality. The language differs from the seventeenth-century poet chiefly in its determination to avoid the elaborate or extended figure of speech, or conceit. During his career, Eberhart has developed through, and out of, some aspects of this influence partly through a progression of subjects—from an early concern with mortality, through an intermediate concern with the problem of human knowledge, into a later concern with God and nature. . . . His direction has been from the sharply lyrical toward the more free-handed narrative and satiric forms and from them, by a leap, into verse dialogue and drama.

Reuel Denney. Poetry. Nov., 1954. p. 103

His mysticism is self-aware and a little humorous. He writes in a good grainy language that puts him squarely in the most attractive tradition of American verse, and he reveals, in some of his poems at least, a marvelous control of stress and pitch, the play of the spoken language within poetic forms. Moreover, like Emily Dickinson, he possesses the ability to hit sometimes upon the absolutely perfect image, startling and simple, lustrous against the setting of the poems.

Hayden Carruth. Poetry. Oct., 1957. pp. 55–6

Whatever it is that makes a "true" poet, in the old Platonic or the new subliminal sense, Richard Eberhart has it. When the god's hand is on him, the language pours forth, powerfully channeled, alive without bombast, rhetorically true. . . . Too many of his poems do begin in brilliant fashion, then fade into some forced paradoxical turn, or into the thick, guttered out language of a conventional and semi-mystical piety, or even into tautology.

. . . But though we should not quite forgive him his failures of self-criticism, it is quite likely that Eberhart needs to work as he does; that if he allowed himself certain kinds of "doubts," the greater successes, those poems in which we sense the god's presence at every moment would be impossible.

M. L. Rosenthal. *Nation*. Dec. 21, 1957. p. 480

Eberhart is a romantic poet in the old style. I don't mean that he imitates particular poets or poems, but that his ideas of poetical structure, and of effective combinations of words resemble the ideas of poets in the early years of the last century. Often he tells an anecdote and follows it with an ecstatic moral. But where Wordsworth moved toward speech and away from poetic diction, Eberhart's direction is characteristically the reverse. Wordsworth's capitalized abstractions are involuntary survivals of the old style; but Eberhart's predecessor was T. S. Eliot, and when Eberhart uses grammatical inversion he is in effect renovating poetic diction. His language is a rhetoric which constantly approaches rhapsody.

(K)                          Donald Hall. *SR*. Feb. 11, 1961. p. 65

However much his poems share common themes with other Romantic poets, Eberhart's style and idiom are nevertheless always his own. His lines are short, his rhymes oblique or infrequent, and his rhythms intentionally irregular, but within these limits he shows a quite extraordinary range. Some of his lyrics are fluent, with simple unaffected diction, and in almost regular metric stanzas. The beauty of these poems, I think, as is the case with many of Blake's short stanzas or with Wordsworth's "Lucy" poems, lies in the reader's appreciation of restraint, of the tension between the apparently artless simplicity of the verse and the intensity of the controlled emotion.

(K)                 Peter L. Thorslev in *Poets in Progress,* edited by
                    Edward B. Hungerford (Northwestern). 1962. p. 88

Richard Eberhart's poetry is excellent only when it is religious in theme and tone, and not always then. In an interview with Denis Donoghue (*Shenandoah,* Summer 1964) Eberhart says that over the years many of his most successful poems have been god-given. I believe him, for those poems have an elevation and intensity quite incommensurate with most of those he has published. When the god speaks through him, the words come out right; sometimes when he meditates on religious subjects, he entrances himself, as it were, and the words come out mostly right; but a lot of the time, when he is being occasional or playful, everything goes wrong. No highly self-critical craftsman would write, much less publish, poems as embarrassing as "Father and Son" and "Father and Daughter"; but then, highly self-critical craftsmen are much less likely to be seized

by the god, whose taste is not always impeccable; and what a poet gives the world importantly is his good poems, not the average of his good and fair and bad. None of the poems in *The Quarry* are of the high, inspired kind. The three best ones are meditative: a very long parable called "The Kite," and the two long concluding Meditations. In these the poet talks himself up to a pitch such that the big abstract nouns and ideas which are a source of gas in his bad poems here become sources of elevation.
(K)                             George P. Elliott. *HdR*. Autumn, 1964. p. 459

Poetry as knowledge, poetry as power—between these two tendencies Eberhart has divided his art. The poems that capture in all their suddenness and gratuitousness moments of illumination do not in any way contradict those moral essays that call to account human motives and actions. Each aspect of his verse complements and enriches the other. What counts in both is the instantaneous, sharp, and piercing vision, and its expression: the words which create an experience because they are of its essence and are not an afterthought.
(K)                             Ralph J. Mills. *Contemporary American Poetry*
(Random). 1965. p. 29

What we are captivated by in his work is the paradox of his unsophisticated attitude: the sense of spontaneous reaction communicated without primitive catalogues of detail, the civilized voice of innocence.

From "This Fevers Me" to "Meditation One" what is memorable is a voice in awe of life and death, appearance and idea, the dead flesh of the groundhog alive with maggots, the lamb whose putrescence feeds the daisies, the anti-aircraft battery's deadly tracers illustrating in the dark "the beautiful disrelation of the spiritual."
(K)                             Robert Huff. *Poetry*. Oct., 1966. p. 44

See *Collected Poems 1930–1960, The Quarry*.

# EDMONDS, WALTER (1903–    )

*Rome Haul* would be a notable book in any season. As the first novel of a man born in 1903 it is extraordinary. There are men and women here, of course. But not one of them bulks so large, in the completed tapestry, as the Erie Canal on which they live. . . . Mr. Edmonds undoubtedly set forth to make this a chronicle of the Erie Canal. In this he has succeeded most admirably. . . . Great deeds were done and great lives lived along the canal. *Rome Haul* is a fitting, if somewhat belated, monument.
William Vogt. *NYHT*. Feb. 17, 1929. p. 5

One need hardly say more than that *Erie Water* is as good an historical novel as was Mr. Edmonds's first, *Rome Haul*. It is full of accurate detail and incidents recreated with all the stress and drama of the moment. The conversations, the expletives, in fact, the complete scene of that period and region are utilized with a mastery which points to the author's special study and love of his subject. The romance with which he flavours his story has not the virtue of originality, but its sincere emotion and suspense adequately serve the purpose of narrative interest.

Archer Winsten. *Bkm*. March, 1933. pp. 295–6

Whether the mood is light or dark, you will find in these stories (*Mostly Canallers*) a freshness of characterization which goes far to explain their eminent readableness, and which itself calls for some explanation. It seems to be founded not merely on quick imagination and the shrewd sense of where one man differs from another but in the author's solid admiration for these rough people of his, on the humor and sympathy with which he draws them out. . . . He has . . . given them an idiom and a relation to environment which give them individuality as a group. When they are lounging or storming about in their own peculiar attitudes they are honest-to-God, and very satisfying to know.

Otis C. Ferguson. *NYHT*. Feb. 25, 1934. p. 2

*Drums Along the Mohawk* is crowded with people and with incidents. And they all . . . are convincing. Mr. Edmonds is obviously not a born novelist. He cannot create clearly individualized characters who dominate a book and walk away with the reader's emotions. But he can do very well in painting a society, a countryside full of people. He did it expertly enough in his stories of the building of the Erie Canal; he has done it still more expertly and vigorously in this full book of the Valley in the days of Tories and hostile armies.

Allan Nevins. *SR*. Aug. 1, 1936. p. 5

Because he is primarily an artist, the work of Walter D. Edmonds goes beyond a local realism. Beneath his faithful use of local color he attempts to express the essential truths of human experience. His novels and stories have been compared to the folk literature of a region, for he treats innocence, courage, the home, as the ancestral virtues of our national birthright. . . . In style as a device for literary experiment he is not at all interested; he holds firmly to the story-telling tradition of the Anglo-Saxon novel. He has a story to tell as well as characters to present, and from characters against a definite background come the outlines of plot.

Dayton Kohler. *EJ*. Jan., 1938. pp. 10–1

Mr. Edmonds does not content himself with going up into the attic and fetching down a beaver hat and a hoop skirt. He fetches in a whole lost age and makes it so natural that soon one is living in it. He is almost as much at home in Northern New York in the Eighteen Thirties as Mark Twain was with life on the Mississippi. He catches the incidental things. . . . The reader need not look for social significance (in *Chad Hanna*), for this is a yarn of local color, romance, and adventure. . . . This book is a vacation. It is an escape book. It pictures a land and time in which one would like to be for a change, and experiences not too painful to live through—and certainly not too dull!

R. L. Duffus. NYT. April 7, 1940. p. 1

His outlook is almost exclusively masculine; his best portraits of women are those of women who might as well have been men, and he shows little delicacy of insight regarding the other sex. Against this objection if it is one, we may set the fact that he has great delicacy of perception regarding natural beauty, animals of all sorts, and children. He has not yet exhibited the highest type of constructive imagination, and his invention is in general short-breathed. But on the other hand few writers can excel him in straight story-telling or in the brilliancy with which he can flash a scene. His historical perspective has seldom achieved grandeur and his portrayal of the past lacks both latitude and altitude. He has, however, chosen to cultivate a restricted field intensively and he may have no ambition to extend it.

Robert M. Gay. At. May, 1940. p. 658

Mr. Edmonds is a romantic realist, he enjoys spinning a yarn for the yarn's sake, but he likes people for themselves rather than—as is the way of so many yarn-spinners—for the function they may be made to perform in the unfolding of the story. So his characters, whom one gets to know slowly, and likes better and better as one knows them, are a refreshingly genuine collection of characters from an America that is gone.

The words that Mr. Edwards puts into their mouths are particularly admirable. This, one says to oneself, is the way Americans must have talked in those days.

Robert Littell. YR. Summer, 1940. pp. vi–viii

Like all Mr. Edmond's historical novels, *In the Hands of the Senecas* plays tricks with your calendar. It projects a more dangerous, headier age plump in your living room, and for a few hours you find yourself battling flames and hostile savages with no aid available from fire department or police; none, either, from your immediate neighbors, for in all likelihood you have none. You have become a rugged individualist, not from choice but

in order to survive. . . . Mr. Edmonds takes advantage of every opportunity offered by his material and often creates breathless suspense by
such devices as escapes, pursuits, and the like. But a different, more
organic type of suspense also pervades the story, one's natural anxiety to
know what will happen next to a group of always believable characters.

                              Jennings Rice. *NYHT*. Jan. 26, 1947. p. 8

See *Rome Haul, Erie Water, Chad Hanna*, and *In the Hands of the Senecas*
(novels); also *Mostly Canallers* (short stories).


# ELIOT, T. S. (1888–1965)

Eliot's own opinions are not merely related to his poetry. They qualify his
whole critical attitude, and they make him to some extent a preacher.
His aim as a writer has been to be a traditionalist: the tradition which
he has adopted, being derived from the Church, has also sociological and
educative implications. It is his object to show that the application of
these principles in social life is as just as it is correct to apply them to
literature. He seems to feel that unless he can prove this, he is, in his
work, an individualist: not a traditionalist radically connected with the
historic process: but isolated, original, personal, in the sense that he is
writing about his own beliefs which are "home-made," and so make him
eccentric and different from the people around him.

                              Stephen Spender. *The Destructive Element*
                              (Houghton). 1936. pp. 164–5


If there is a metaphysical distinction between the poetry and the prose of
T. S. Eliot, it is this: that in the former he is sceptical of his own knowledge of truth, and in the latter he is indicating the path along which he
hopes to find it. In the poetry he sees things through a glass darkly; in
the prose he is proclaiming the truth that will make us free. Both these
activities, however, are offshoots of a unified intelligence, of a man who is
singularly whole in his conception of the dignity and importance of his
art. There is no real divergence between his theory and practice, no matter
how lucid he may contrive to make his criticism, or how obscure his poetry.

                              A. C. Partridge. *T. S. Eliot* (Pretoria). 1937. p. 3


It is to him, together with Ezra Pound, that we can trace the awareness
of the urban scene, the employment of anti-poetic imagery, conversational
rhythms, cinematic transitions and close-ups, which make contemporary
verse deserve the adjective. And even the most vigorous and provocative
of the younger men have not shown an "auditory imagination" equal to

Eliot's. . . . What his "feeling for syllable and rhythm" has brought back, in its curious workings, has been chiefly a sense of disorder, of frustration and waste, an intimate and horrifying vision of death.

Babette Deutsch. *AS*. Winter, 1939. p. 30

Eliot, in brief, has surrendered to the acedia which Baudelaire was able to judge; Eliot suffers from the delusion that he is judging it when he is merely exhibiting it. He has loosely thrown together a collection of disparate and fragmentary principles which fall roughly into two contradictory groups, the romantic on the one hand and on the other the classical and Christian; and being unaware of his own contradictions, he is able to make a virtue of what appears to be private spiritual laziness; he is able to enjoy at one and the same time the pleasure of indulgence and the dignity of disapproval.

Yvor Winters. *KR*. Spring, 1941. p. 238

Eliot seldom involves himself steadily with the world about him. Instead he makes brief and startling sallies into the world and hence his poetry sometimes strikes us either as a discontinuous anthology of images or as an imitation of involuted psychological or biological processes which remain purely verbal. . . . Another result of this nervous intermittence is that Eliot's criticism of other poets—such as Donne, Marvell, or Dryden —makes the excellence of their poetry depend too much on their surprising success in image-making and too little on their steady sense of life. Eliot tends to give us what is occasional and spasmodic in a poet, rather than the poet's normal excellence.

Richard Chase. *KR*. Spring, 1945. pp. 220–1

The reconciliation of opposites is as fundamental to Eliot as it was to Heraclitus. Only thus can he envisage a resolution of man's whole being. The "heart of light" that he glimpsed in the opening movement of "Burnt Norton" is at the opposite pole from the *Heart of Darkness* from which he took the epigraph for "The Hollow Men." Essential evil still constitutes more of Eliot's subject matter than essential good, but the magnificent orchestration of his themes has prepared for that paradisal glimpse at the close, and thereby makes it no decorative allusion, but an integrated climax to the content no less than to the form. Such spiritual release and reconciliation are the chief reality for which he strives in a world that has seemed to him increasingly threatened with new dark ages.

F. O. Matthiessen. *The Achievement of T. S. Eliot*
(Oxford). 1947. p. 195

Eliot's mind, let us say, is a mind of contrasts which sharpen rather than soften the longer they are weighed. It is the last mind which, in this century, one would have expected to enter the Church in a lay capacity. The worldliness of its prose weapons, its security of posture, its wit, its ability for penetrating doubt and destructive definition, its eye for startling fact and talent for nailing it down in flight, hardly go with what we think of today as English or American religious feeling. . . . However that may be, within the Church or not, Mr. Eliot's mind has preserved its worldly qualities. His prose reflections remain elegant, hard (and in a sense easy —as in manners), controlled, urbane (without the dissimulation associated with ecclesiastical urbanity), and fool-proof.

R. P. Blackmur. *Language as Gesture* (Harcourt). 1952. pp. 176–7

[F. H.] Bradley, of course, didn't solve Eliot's initial poetic problem; there is no evidence that Eliot paid him any attention until after he had written *Prufrock* and *Portrait of a Lady*. (He did not buy his own copy of *Appearance and Reality* until mid-1913.) The study of Bradley, however, may be said to have done three things for a poet who might otherwise not have passed beyond the phase of imitating Laforgue. It solved his *critical* problem, providing him with a point of view towards history and so with the scenario for his most comprehensive essay, "Tradition and the Individual Talent"; it freed him from the Laforguian posture of the ironist with his back to a wall, by affirming the artificiality of *all* personality including the one we intimately suppose to be our true one; not only the faces we prepare but the "we" that prepares; and it released him from any notion that the art his temperament bade him practice was an eccentric art, evading for personal and temporary reasons a more orderly, more "normal" unfolding from statement to statement.

(K)                                    Hugh Kenner. *The Invisible Poet* (McDowell, Obolensky). 1959. p. 55

Sir Herbert Read tells me that the English poet for whom Eliot felt a conscious affinity, and upon whom he perhaps in some degree modelled himself, was Johnson. All the same it seems to me that the more we see of the hidden side of Eliot the more he seems to resemble Milton, though he thought of Milton as a polar opposite. As we look at all the contraries reconciled in Eliot—his schismatic traditionalism, his romantic classicism, his highly personal impersonality—we are prepared for the surprise (which Eliot himself seems in some measure to have experienced) of finding in the dissenting Whig regicide a hazy mirror-image of the Anglo-Catholic royalist. Each, having prepared himself carefully for poetry, saw that he must also, living in such times, explore prose, the cooler element. From a consciously archaic standpoint each must characterize the activities of the sons of Belial. Each saw that fidelity to tradition is ensured by revolutionary action. (Eliot would hardly have dissented from the proposition that "a man may be a heretic in the truth".) Each knew the difficulty of finding "answerable style" in an age too late. With the Commonwealth an evident failure, Milton wrote one last book to restore it, and as the élites crumbled and reformed Eliot wrote his *Notes [toward the Definition of a Culture]*. If Milton killed a king, Eliot attacked vulgar democracy and shared with the "men of 1914" and with Yeats some extreme authoritarian opinions.

(K)                    Frank Kermode. *SwR*. Jan.-March, 1966. pp. 228–9

In between his visits we used to call upon him in London—once on Good Friday, when his precision occupied itself much with the exactly right temperature at which hot cross buns should be served. What was peculiar to TSE in this sort was the delicately perceptible trace, the ghostly flavor of irony which hung about his manner as though he were preparing a parody. For example, when we went to Peking in 1929, we wrote pressing him to come to stay with us in that enchanting scene. His reply: "I do not care to visit any country which has no native cheese." Not too much, I think, should be made of these "deliberate disguises", but he did have a repertory of more or less confessed poses which his friends were not debarred from seeing through.

(K)                         I. A. Richards. *SwR*. Jan.-March, 1966. p. 26

Eliot is a two-way phenomenon of the sort he himself treated in "Tradition and the Individual Talent", a man who is influenced by what went before him and whose work in turn, by introducing something radically new into the tradition, forces a revaluation of what the tradition previously possessed. All poets and critics are products of their age, but all do not interact with their age so vigorously or so publicly as did Eliot. The force of the interaction can be gauged by the fact that Eliot has been claimed both by a revolution and by an establishment. . . . In these late essays [*To Criticize the Critic*] one senses a lacuna which was not so evident when Eliot was still considered the young Turk but which became increasingly noteworthy after World War II. He appears to lack to some degree a spirit of extreme *Angst,* the existentialist agony which, according to some, marks all the "authentic" thought of our age. In his sphinx-like but essentially good-humored (Old Possum) calm, Eliot was relatively unperturbed by such *Angst,* not because he did not know it but seemingly because he knew it so well that he was immunized to it.

(K)                       Walter J. Ong. *Poetry*. July, 1966. pp. 266–7

It won't be easy to reclaim his work from the conceptual and scholarly currency already invested in it. It will mean forcing ourselves to forget most of what exegesis has burdened us with, and it will mean returning for help to those very few difficult critics I've mentioned [Leavis, Blackmur, Kenner], all of whom have insisted, to almost no effect, on Eliot's deliberate irrationality. In trying to release Eliot from schematizations contrived mostly for the clarification and boredom of undergraduates, these, and a few others, direct us away from the seductions of neatness and into the wonderful mystery at the center of Eliot's poetry and criticism. What we find there, if we stay long enough, is that for Eliot ideas have no more organizational power than do literary allusions and that neither is as preoccupying as are the furtive memories and hallucinations, the sensuous images that stimulate a poem like "Preludes" but which remain at the end as unassimilated to any design as they were at the beginning.

(K)                    Richard Poirier. *NR*. May 20, 1967. pp. 19–20

### Poetry

By technique we . . . mean one thing: the alert hatred of normality which, through the lips of a tactile and cohesive adventure, asserts that nobody in general and some one in particular is incorrigibly and actually alive. This some one is, it would seem, the extremely great artist: or, he who prefers above everything the unique dimension of intensity, which it amuses him to substitute in us for the comforting and comfortable furniture of reality. If we examine the means through which this substitution is allowed by Mr. Eliot to happen in his reader, we find that they include: a vocabulary almost brutally tuned to attain distinction; an extraordinary tight orchestration of the shapes of sound; the delicate and careful murderings —almost invariably interpreted, internally as well as terminally, through near-rhyme and rhyme—of established tempos by oral rhythms.

E. E. Cummings. *Dial*. June, 1920. p. 783

It is true his poems seem the products of a constricted emotional experience and that he appears to have drawn rather heavily on books for the heat he could not derive from life. There is a certain grudging margin, to be sure, about all that Mr. Eliot writes—as if he were compensating himself for his limitations by a peevish assumption of superiority. But it is the very acuteness of his suffering from this starvation which gives such poignancy to his art. And, as I say, Mr. Eliot is a poet—that is, he feels intensely and with distinction and speaks naturally in beautiful verse— so that, no matter within what walls he lives, he belongs to the divine company. . . . These drops, though they be wrung from flint, are none the less authentic crystals.

Edmund Wilson. *Dial*. Dec., 1922. p. 615

The writer of "The Waste Land" and the other poems of that period appeals to us as one struck to the heart by the confusion and purposelessness and wastefulness of the world about him. . . . And to that world his verse will be held up as a ruthlessly faithful mirror. The confusion of life will be reflected in the disorganized flux of images; its lack of clear meaning in the obscurity of language. . . . And now against this lyric prophet of chaos must be set the critic who will judge the world from the creed of the classicist, the royalist, and the Anglo-Catholic. . . . I think . . . that a sensitive mind cannot read "Ash Wednesday" without an uneasy perception of something fundamentally amiss in employing for an experience born of Anglo-Catholic faith a metrical form and a freakishness of punctuation suitable for the presentation of life regarded as without form and void. . . . He is a leader and a very influential leader. Our difficulty is that he seems to be leading us in two directions at once.

Paul Elmer More. SR. Nov. 12, 1932. p. 235

When Eliot stood isolated and dispossessed amid the ruins of a familiar universe, every nerve and sensation quivered with its own life. The antennae of his intelligence were alive with nervous vitality. This resulted in images and allegories of great focal sharpness. In more recent years, approaching a stranger territory, this grip on identity is no longer held, and with its relaxation the nervous sensibility of his diction and cadence has lessened. He writes either a more relaxed and speculative verse, or a sort of argument which attempts to extend his intellectual problems beyond their own limits. He has become a poet of more public qualities, of religious responsibilities, and even (in *The Rock*) of social concerns. These have entailed a change from a style of cryptic historical reference and erudition to one of dialectic lucidity, or even of popular simplification.

Morton Dauwen Zabel. SoR. Summer, 1936. p. 170

The rich store of childhood treasure which is contained within Eliot's poetry, and more particularly, within his imagery, is obvious to any reader. The repetition of the same small group of images in poem after poem, from the early Jamesian ironies to the time of the later "Quartets," the recurrence of the curling smoke of evening, of stairs and windows and doors, of the hidden bird and the pool, the children's voices and the garden, the music and the thunder: these things by themselves argue that such images have a personal origin and a deep personal significance. It is this habitual use of optical "constants," of material which could be described as in a sense "obsessive," that imparts to Eliot's work its characteristic quality of seeming to be less a collection of single pieces than one continuing poem in permanent process of revision.

S. Musgrove. T. S. Eliot and Walt Whitman (New<br>Zealand). 1952. p. 11

More than one critic has remarked that in Eliot the over-all organization
of the poem as a whole is not lyrical in any recognizable and traditional
way; nor is the poem organized in terms of narrative; nor is it dramatic in
the literal theatrical sense; and it is certainly not logical, argumentative,
or expository. . . . Where poets in the past would have used a logical, emotional, dramatic, or narrative basis for the transition from part to part,
Eliot uses some one of these kinds of transition freely and alternatively
and without committing himself to any one of them or to any systematic
succession of them; or he omits the connection between one passage and
the next, one part and the part which succeeds it. . . . The characteristic
over-all organization of the poem—of which "The Waste Land" is the
vividest example—can be called, for the lack of a better phrase, that of
sibylline (or subliminal) listening.

Delmore Schwartz. Poetry. Jan., 1955. pp. 236–7

Eliot's poetic craftsmanship has been praised by very diverse critics, who
agree that everything that he has to say, he says extremely well. We never
get the feeling that he cannot quite say what he means, or that the felt
significance is too big for the poem which has been used to express it
(a feeling we experience with some of Dylan Thomas's poetry). The limitation of Eliot's poetry is in the subject matter. Only a narrow range of
human experience seems to be subjected to the poetic process, a range
which deals almost entirely with states of mind and soul, and which looks
over a lonely territory where the poetic protagonist stands isolated from
other beings. To adopt an expression of Eliot's, which he uses to describe
Dante's poetic power, this is a poetry which comprehends the height and
the depth of experience but is limited in breadth. This leads in Eliot's
poetry to that unity of development of which we have spoken, but it also
leads to a very *personal* poetry, for the states of mind and soul which he
deals with are *his own:* he is his own subject matter.

(K)                    Sean Lucy. *T. S. Eliot and the Idea of Tradition*
(Barnes and Noble). 1960. p. 160

In poetic form and imagery Eliot avoids all kinds of overloading, unless
he is out for very special effects. Generally he finds a middle way between
intellectualism and lyricism, or he balances the two in alternate lines and
stanzas. The difficult and involved is continually set off by the simple and
translucent, a fact which immediately emerges if his poetry is compared
with the far opaquer medium of W. H. Auden. And Eliot's symbolism is
supported and made accessible by naturalistic imagery, as a comparison
with Yeats will bring out.

Eliot is not the arch-intellectualist in poetry that many people think.
But, of course, his intellectual habits are mirrored in his poetry, so that

the latter presents the attitudes of one accustomed to reflection. He may have had good reasons for the anti-emotionalism expressed in "Tradition and the Individual Talent", but it is impossible to refine emotion out of poetry altogether; and this Eliot has recognized, for he has told us repeatedly that his poetry expresses what it *feels* like to believe in something.

(K)                    Kristian Smidt. *Poetry and Belief in the Work of*
*T. S. Eliot* (Humanities Press). 1961. p. 233

Eliot wrote the work [*The Waste Land*] under the stress of illness. Six years of strenuous double-living—wage-earning faithfully and efficiently pursued, intellectual conquests pursued at the same time—had exhausted him. But a poet's breakdown is often the moment of creation. To let slip his hold on the day is to slip free of the day's hold on him; he gathers all that he has experienced into an innovative act. . . .

*The Waste Land* is a work in which the poet, like some of his predecessors, writes simultaneously about his own illness and the world's illness, of which his own is a reflection. He records and condemns his own "despairing" state and prescribes a discipline for his cure and for the healing of the city civilization of which he is the representative.

(K)                    Herbert Howarth. *Notes on Some Figures Behind*
*T. S. Eliot* (Houghton). 1964. pp. 234, 237

The image of structural unity pervades Eliot's social and literary criticism. What of his own poetry? Is he able to reach his goal of organic unity and write poems which live because they share the life of the European mind?

Most of Eliot's poems depend on the assumption that the poet can enlarge his private consciousness to coincide with a collective consciousness. This assumption is so easily and persuasively sustained that it is easy to forget what an extraordinary arrogation of power it is. Only a few early poems, such as "Prufrock" or "Portrait of a Lady," are limited to the perspective of a single ego. In most poems the reader is placed within everybody's mind at once. An act of self-surrender has expanded the private mind of the poet into the universal sphere of the mind of Europe.

(K)                    J. Hillis Miller. *Poets of Reality* (Harvard). 1965.
p. 172

### Drama

He will soon make ordinary drama look cheap because of its lack of metaphysical interest, just as he had part in making the ordinary shallow poetry of twenty years ago look the same way, and for the same reason. . . . On the realistic level Mr. Eliot is superb in his mastery of characterization (both the satiric and the sympathetic), handling of plot sequence, exposition of background through dialogue, and, I imagine, such other techniques as belong to an oral form like drama. It is comforting to think that an intellectualist, so strict and unconceding that he has been accused of living in a tower, has picked up without any fuss the knack for the close structural effects of drama.

John Crowe Ransom. *Poetry*. Aug., 1939. pp. 264–6

What is it that marks these plays off from the commercial drama, and from previous plays in verse or even in prose, and forces us to classify them as poetic drama? There is, first, their mixture of high seriousness in poetry and human colloquial speech, both in prose and verse. There is the tone of liveliness and intensity. There is the action on more than one level, the perpetual parable or allegory, and there is, finally, the startling variety of elements derived from every conceivable theatrical activity past and present. In short, there is a wider theatrical equipment harnessed to a deeper poetical purpose.

J. Isaacs. *An Assessment of Twentieth-Century Literature* (Secker). 1951. pp. 142–3

What most critics of Mr. Eliot's plays seem to ignore is that he is writing a new kind of drama. Whereas most plays appeal to the passions—pity, terror, the glamor of love—or to the intellect, or would stir our zeal for political reform, his plays are based on an appeal to the conscience, or the consciousness of self. Here is this person, he says in effect, guilty of this or that; how far are you, dear spectator, in the like case? Our response comes from a different center. That is why some people do not applaud his plays; nobody likes to be made to think about his weakness, his failures, or his sins. Not that many of us have committed crimes: but then crimes, as we are told in this play (*The Elder Statesman*) are in relation to the law, sins in relation to the sinner. . . . In all the plays about conscience, from Sophocles to Ibsen, we are detached spectators. . . . Here, however, we are forced to ask ourselves: "Have I never run away from myself? Have I never tried to blot out incidents from my past?"

Bonamy Dobrée. *SwR*. Winter, 1959. pp. 109–10

The origin of his attempt to develop a new theater is to be seen in his view that, just as man's nature needs to be guided by discipline and order, so dramatic art needs to be given a form which can draw a circle of abstraction around experience in order to make drama conform to the standard of all art—the ordered relationship of the parts to the whole. Believing that of all literary forms drama has the greatest capacity for recreating a complete and ordered world, Eliot developed a dramatic structure which was intended to lead the audience to a sense of religious awareness by demonstrating the presence of the supernatural order in the natural world. His dramatic theme is also the product of his religious concern to integrate the real and the ideal. In each of his plays he has portrayed the plight of the individual who perceives the order of God but, forced to exist in the natural world, must somehow come to terms with both realms.

(K)                               Carol H. Smith. *T. S. Eliot's Dramatic Theory and*
                                        *Practice* (Princeton). 1963. p. 31

## Criticism

Eliot not only follows the classical dogma because he cherishes classicism; he follows it also because he cherishes dogma. . . . He loses much by being fastidious. He loses much by having no humor whatever, but he is capable of something else by having splendid wit. And the presence of wit and the absence of humor in Eliot argue his possession of great intellect and egoism, his lack of humanity, his lack of modesty and unselfconsciousness. He rests with those men who have chosen to see life distantly, from a single vantage-point; and had he, in the absence of warmth and sinew, a great intensity, he might possess permanent value for us. . . . But he is not intense, he is merely correct.

                                Louis Kronenberger. *Nation*. Apr. 17, 1935. p. 453

In spite of everything, Eliot *has,* in his critical essays, said many of the things that most needed to be said in our time. He has documented with appropriate *dicta* the final ebb of the romantic movement, the reversal of the trend which saw poetry as the expression of the poet's unique personality, the rediscovery of the glories of the metaphysical poets, and the parallel reintroduction into English and American poetry of wit *and* passion. In some of his best essays—those on Dante, for example—he is often rearranging (as Mario Praz has shown) the ideas of Ezra Pound or others; in some of his worst, he is merely perverse or pigheaded or exhibitionistic. But his critical ideas are in themselves full of interest and excitement, and have become part of the intellectual atmosphere of our time.

                                David Daiches. *YR*. Spring, 1949. pp. 466–7

To my notion T. S. Eliot is the greatest of all literary critics. . . . Eliot's merit lies almost equally in his ability to raise the pertinent problems and in the fineness of his taste. He gave himself a rule of cogency early on and has had the strength of mind to obey it without evasion. This is the first critic of whom we can feel sure that the most important question will always be answered—namely, how successful *as art* is the work of art in hand? Eliot is no philosopher of aesthetics or criticism; he is both more and less than that: his critical practice demonstrates the right principles in action and we recognize them by their fruits rather than their definition.

Clement Greenberg. *Nation.* Dec. 9, 1950. p. 531

See *Complete Poems and Plays* and *Selected Essays;* also *The Elder Statesman* (play).

# ELLIOTT, GEORGE P. (1918–    )

Mr. Elliott has published short stories that I greatly admire, and in his novel [*Parktilden Village*] there is much firm, perceptive writing of the kind I anticipated, but I feel I have been let down by the book as a whole. . . .

The situation suggests that this is to be a comedy of manners; so does the title; so, most emphatically, does the style. . . . His whole air is that of a man who hopes the reader will be as amused by what he is writing about as he himself is. . . . People are behaving rather badly, to be sure, but they are behaving no worse than people the reader knows, and he can afford to be amused by them.

Suddenly, however, . . . the tone changes. . . . One could say that there are precedents for so great an alteration of tone. T. S. Eliot's *The Cocktail Party,* for instance, begins as comedy but develops the most serious religious implications. The play, however, moves gradually from the trivial to the serious, and the comic framework is retained. *Parktilden Village,* on the other hand, promising one thing and delivering another, leaves a bad taste in the mouth.

Granville Hicks. *SR.* May 31, 1958. pp. 10, 26

Now the subject of *Parktilden Village* is a genuine one: surely there can be few more interesting matters these days than the terrifying distance between the generation born after 1940 and the rest of us. Mr. Elliott is a naturally gifted writer who keeps things moving nicely, cleverly. But in the end one feels cheated. The material has been set up to serve a case: it all seems too neat, everything bends too conveniently to the writer's preconceptions, and what should have been an imitation of life comes to read like a fictional gloss on an essay in *Sewanee Review.*

Irving Howe. *NR.* Nov. 10, 1958. p. 17

Within the confused contemporary American literary scene, in which many writers seem to strive for attention as the classical starlet strives for parts —by pan-fried personal lives immediately translated into the negotiable currency of the news item—George P. Elliott has managed to make his reputation in a curious way. As poet, critic, essayist, short-story writer, and novelist . . . he has quietly assumed the burden of the old-fashioned man of letters. The odd and effective method by which he has sent his name into the busy world is this one: Beneath all the demand for brilliance in a "young writer," he has kept his gaze upon the need for truth.

*Among the Dangs,* a collection of ten of his stories, shows a thickly questing imagination at work. Many of the stories have that density of feeling and character, and complexity of event, which only a generous mind dares to employ in the story form. . . . Increasingly, especially in the later stories, Elliott has learned to recognize the humor of his horrors, and with his wit, he has increased his powers.

Herbert Gold. NR. Jan. 16, 1961. p. 19

Elliott is a sophisticated satirist, and his subject is the tension between modernism, materialism, and scientism and man's continued need for faith, rituals, love, and esthetic satisfaction. His humor is not unlike that of J. F. Powers. Each of them enjoys, in a sympathetic way, the humor attendant upon dedicated men, frequently monks or priests, attempting to transcend their human limitations, and the ironical contrasts between monasteries and modern urban life. But the sympathy does not interfere with the disinterested and detached manner in which the situations are viewed. Elliott's stories at their best have something of what Henry James called the "sacred hardness of art."

William Van O'Connor. SR. Jan. 28, 1961. p. 15

*David Knudsen* purports to be an autobiographical account of the hero's quest for meaning. . . . Elliott is good at portraying the horror beneath the skin of modern society. . . . It is part of the virtue of this novel that it can make us think about metaphysical questions without being heavy or pretentious; every question is adequately embodied. Elliott is clearly to be one of the important writers of this decade, and this is an example of the quest-novel that one can be thankful for.

Wayne C. Booth. YR. Spring, 1962. pp. 635–6

He writes with that air of cool judicious detachment that is now universally recognized as one of the signatures of serious fiction in this period, but after reading a few pages of *Parktilden Village,* you become pleasantly aware of the absence of portentous solemnity in the tone, and you begin to see that for once the cool judiciousness is doing something more than calling your attention to the author's subtlety and good taste: it is working to define a critical attitude toward the main character.

Norman Podhoretz. Doings and Undoings (Farrar).<br>1964. p. 166

Mr. Elliott's anecdotes [in *A Piece of Lettuce*] are all of seemingly incon-
sequential sort. . . . He insists upon his provinciality, using it as a kind
of surprise weapon against those who would dictate what life and literature are supposed to be like. His hidden argument seems to run: if I can
be loyal to my ordinary background, if I can be spontaneous and frank
even when this entails saying nothing of importance, then I will mirror
the truth of things; I will be dealing with reality.

Deliberately rejecting what he calls "the miniature art of the conscious
essay," Mr. Elliott weaves together childhood impressions and miscellaneous current opinions, always stressing the way experience never quite
comes up to the level of poetry. Correspondingly, his literary taste runs to
unpretentious, imperfect, frankly minor works. . . .

Mr. Elliott's low-keyed style does have limitations. . . . I also suspect
that his distrust of mere logic serves in part to cover an ambiguous flirta-
tion with Christianity that runs through nearly all his fiction and retains
its coyness here. Mr. Elliott would evidently like to believe some things
he regards as factually untrue, and his non-rational style enables him to
avert a showdown. Nevertheless, the general impression I get from *A Piece
of Lettuce* is one of refreshing directness.

Frederick C. Crews. NYHT. March 15, 1964. p. 13

But if there are matters upon which one wants to take issue with Mr.
Elliott, it is chiefly for the sake of that greater portion of his work, as a
novelist, poet, and essayist, for which one is honestly grateful. Of the
fifteen essays in the present collection [*A Piece of Lettuce*], at least ten
strike me as first-rate—by which I don't mean to suggest that they are
unexceptionable, but rather that they are illuminating. Mr. Elliott's peculiar virtue is an inability to let anyone else do his thinking for him. The
defects of that pre-industrial bent are obvious. The advantage is that
mostly we get from Mr. Elliott his own opinions, and mostly they have
the quality of something made by hand, for a specific purpose, and in-
corporating the vital force of the man who made them. That is particularly
true of the autobiographical essays in this book, six of which figure in my
private list of the ten elect. They further persuade me of something suggested already by Mr. Elliott's verse and by his fiction, that he is less
interesting as a critic of literature than as the poet of his own experience.

Emile Capouya. SR. April 4, 1964. p. 26

[*A Piece of Lettuce*] is by no means an orthodox book of literary criticism
in any approved contemporary mode. Like Anatole France, Elliott recounts the adventures of his soul among masterpieces; but we don't live
among masterpieces alone, and Elliott doesn't isolate his experience of
them from the unanalyzable wholeness of his living. . . .

The best parts of the book, however, are the autobiographical parts: "The Sky and a Goat," "Getting Away from the Chickens," "A Brown Fountain Pen," "Coming of Age on the Carob Plantation," "Home Again," and "A Piece of Lettuce." That piece of lettuce illuminated *War and Peace* for Elliott, but *War and Peace* also illuminated the piece of lettuce. His special virtue as a critic is his willingness to talk about such illuminations. Our own lives are full of opportunities of this kind, but we don't permit ourselves to see them. Such prissiness damages us not only as critics but as people—a word that isn't quite O.K. nowadays, except for those who, like Elliott, let neither Madison Avenue nor Carl Sandburg dismay them.

J. Mitchell Morse. HdR. Autumn, 1964. pp. 479–80

. . . the novelistic virtues of George P. Elliott are precisely those which spring from a kind of equanimity. . . . His first novel, *Parktilden Village,* impressed some readers by the calmness with which it viewed the complexities of love and generation, and his second, *David Knudsen,* was not more objectionable. In these works, as in the essays of *A Piece of Lettuce* and the stories of *Among the Dangs,* one feels that Elliott needs to understand the changing values of our world, values by which he is puzzled and somewhat repelled. The need is honest, firm, consistent; its expression is often tactful if not elegant, and the resources of the moral and artistic imagination behind it are unpretentious.

The judgment, I think, is confirmed by his most ambitious work to date. . . . As for the theme, it's the Modern World. . . . Elliott's intention in this big book [*In the World*] is clear. He wants to portray the moribund world of liberal values and foreshadow another world which the young are still powerless to create. And he wants the portrait to include the jumble of private feeling and public action. How much does Elliott succeed?

Not very much. All the pressing issues are here: religion, marriage, money, eugenics, war, sex, social justice. Yet no issue is projected with the intensity that brings illumination; nothing obeys the original force of insight. . . . But if a kind of softness, a kind of banality really, cripples this work, one feels wonder and sympathy that it can still move so far, impelled by the spirit of human decency, by the conviction that somehow man matters.

Ihab Hassan. NYHT. Oct. 24, 1965. pp. 5, 30

It is difficult to pin down with any precision the reasons for Elliott's exceptional independence of spirit, but my own guess is that he enjoys a kind of inward harmony that comes of knowing one's own nature and powers and limitations. Something very much like inward harmony, it seems to me, is reflected in the calm suavity of his prose style, his gentle humor, and his easy authority. Writing out of the center of his own experience, Elliott has become one of America's most engaging essayists; and his criticism, which he frequently blends with autobiographical fragments, is consistently excellent and never dull.

Yet how useful the maxim "know thyself" is to the novelist is by no means certain. Although Elliott has now published three novels—in addition to the already-mentioned collection of short stories—his fiction remains the product of a mind most interesting in its analytical and critical, rather than dramatic, aspects.

Joseph Epstein. NR. Nov. 27, 1965. p. 40

His latest novel, *In the World* . . . is an interesting attempt to raise the novelist's ante by getting back to the nineteenth century. How refreshing it is to find a novelist who still has enough nerve and enough sense of past to take society for granted, to demand of life that it be meaningful. For ours is a time when hysteria and alienation have become as commonplace to novelists as brushing one's teeth. . . . *Who cares?* cries the existential chorus. *I do,* answers George P. Elliott. It is a very protestant refusal to take the world's chaos for granted, an insistence that people behave as if they are in this world by choice, not necessity. . . .

George P. Elliott is almost the novelist the WASP world has been crying for—almost, but not quite. His deficiency, finally, is the other side of his strength, for if he has enough nerve to take society for granted, he does not seem quite able to artistically come to grips with the destructive instincts in modern life. This is not to say that he is unaware of those instincts. . . . But when he is faced with the problem of integrating that aspect of life with the other, his talent seems confused and short of the mark.

Leonard Kriegel. Com. Dec. 3, 1965. p. 276

Even stranger is what happens in George P. Elliott's *In the World*. In its demeanor it is not different from his *Parktilden Village* and *David Knudsen,* novels which seemed to demonstrate that the flat heavy American style is even less valid than cool English intelligence. *In the World* is long, over two hundred thousand words. As befits Elliott's efforts to allow his characters all the room they need to make their decisions and to live with them, the book is in the usual sense plotless. It should have been a disaster, adequate reward for someone who really wants to be Tolstoi. But there is great strength in this novel, derived more from Thackeray, really, than from Tolstoi; Elliott is determined to make "the world" as resonant a metaphor as "Vanity Fair." Of course it does not work, for

Elliott is far less interestingly baffled by his overriding idea than Thackeray was by his.

Roger Sale. *HdR*. Spring, 1966. pp. 131–2

See *Parktilden Village, David Knudsen, In the World* (novels); *Among the Dangs* (stories); *A Piece of Lettuce* (essays).

# ELLISON, RALPH (1914–    )

Many Negro writers of real distinction have emerged in our century. . . . But none of them except, sometimes, Richard Wright has been able to transcend the bitter way of life they are still (though diminishingly) condemned to, or to master patiently the intricacies of craftsmanship so that they become the peers of the best white writers of our day. Mr. Ellison has achieved this difficult transcendence. *Invisible Man* is not a great Negro novel; it is a work of art any contemporary writer could point to with pride.

Harvey Curtis Webster. *SR*. April 12, 1952. p. 23

The reader who is familiar with the traumatic phase of the black man's rage in America, will find something more in Mr. Ellison's report. He will find the long anguished step toward its mastery. The author sells no phony forgiveness. He asks none himself. It is a resolutely honest, tormented, profoundly American book. . . . With this book the author maps a course from the underground world into the light. *Invisible Man* belongs on the shelf with the classical efforts man has made to chart the river Lethe from its mouth to its source.

Wright Morris. *NYT*. April 13, 1952. p. 5

Ellison has an abundance of that primary talent without which neither craft nor intelligence can save a novelist; he is richly, wildly inventive; his scenes rise and dip with tension, his people bleed, his language stings. No other writer has captured so much of the confusion and agony, the hidden gloom and surface gaiety of Negro life. His ear for Negro speech is magnificent. . . . The rhythm of the prose is harsh and tensed, like a beat of harried alertness. The observation is expert. . . . For all his self-involvement, he is capable of extending himself toward his people, of accepting them as they are, in their blindness and hope.

Irving Howe. *Nation*. May 10, 1952. p. 454.

Unquestionably, Ellison's book is a work of extraordinary intensity—powerfully imagined and written with a savage, wryly humorous gusto.

It contains many scenes which are brought off with great *brio* and a striking felicity of detail. To my mind, however, it has faults which cannot simply be shrugged off—occasional overwriting, stretches of fuzzy thinking, and a tendency to waver, confusingly, between realism and surrealism.

Charles J. Rolo. *At.* July, 1952. p. 84

Ralph Ellison's *Invisible Man* is a basically comic work in the picaresque tradition, influenced by the novels of Louis-Ferdinand Céline. The hero of *Invisible Man* just happens to be a Negro, and everything he is and does includes ultimately the experience of all modern men. But this is not accomplished by abstraction; Mr. Ellison has managed to realize the fact of his hero's being a Negro in exactly the same way as nineteenth-century novelists realized their characters being French or Russian or middle-class: by making it the chief fact of their lives, something they take for granted and would not think of denying. Mr. Ellison displays an unapologetic relish for the concrete richness of Negro living—the tremendous variety of its speech, its music, its food, even its perversities.

Steven Marcus. *Cmty.* Nov., 1953. p. 458

Many may find that *Invisible Man,* complex in its novelistic structure, many-sided in its interpretation of the race problem, is not fully satisfying either as narrative or as ideology. Unlike the novel which depends for its appeal chiefly on the staple elements of love or sex, suspense and the dynamics of action, *Invisible Man* dispenses with the individualized hero and his erotic involvements, the working out of his personal destiny. Here we have, subtly and sensitively presented, what amounts to an allegory of the pilgrimage of a people. . . . By means of the revealing master symbol of vision, Ralph Ellison has presented an aesthetically distanced and memorably vivid image of the life of the American Negro.

Charles I. Glicksberg. *SWR.* Summer, 1954. pp. 264–5

Ellison is a writer of the first magnitude—one of those original talents who has created a personal idiom to convey his personal vision. It is an idiom compounded of fantasy, distortion, and burlesque, highly imaginative and generally surrealistic in effect. It possesses at bottom a certain mythic quality. . . . He was striving, he recounts, for a prose medium "with all the bright magic of the fairy tale."

Though not in the narrow sense a political novel, *Invisible Man* is based on a cultivated political understanding of the modern world. The first half of the novel portrays the disillusionment of the protagonist with the shibboleths of American capitalism—a social system which he apprehends through the institutional structure of the Southern Negro college. The latter half treats of his disillusionment with Stalinism, which he encounters through a revolutionary organization known as the Brotherhood. By means of this carefully controlled parallel development, Ellison penetrates to the heart of the two great illusions of his time.

(K)                    Robert Bone. *The Negro Novel in America* (Yale).
                                                        1958. pp. 196–7

Ellison, who has the formal sense of a jazz musician and the instinct of a singer of blues, understands that anger or agony is transient without art. Turbulence, in private or political life, amounts to a denial of the dignity of man. To acknowledge the innate dignity of mankind is also to reconcile the idea of freedom prescribed in the founding political documents of America with the violence of a Harlem race riot. The act of reconciliation is an action of what Ellison calls Mind, a fact of *form*. The "Negro question" becomes a question of determining the essence of the human in a way that the questioning and tormented Mind can grasp. This, if any, is the artistic credo of Ellison. The credo is one that requires him to exploit the resources of irony. And it prompts him, as will become evident, to draw upon the healing powers of the American joke and Negro blues.

(K)                    Ihab Hassan. *Radical Innocence* (Princeton).
                                                        1961. p. 169

The novel's series of ironic negations is, after all, a series of negatives. It can and does reach its last possibility. Ellison will be left with only stale repetitions of the act of dying unless he can in fact assert social responsibility and mind and love—and, because the "Negro problem" is entirely an American problem, democracy. That is the only way he can keep possibility open.

That is to say that the end of *Invisible Man* is the beginning of another novel, one that will draw the complicated positive engagement of the hero in this life, specifically this American life. It is the huge achievement of *Invisible Man,* meanwhile, that it has got a vastness of experience as Negroes particularly must know it—there can be very little that it has left out—into a single meaning. The novel creates a negative metaphor, invisibility, that is fully analytic and fully inclusive, that does hold together for a moment the long experience of chaos that has met Ellison's vision.

(K)                    Marcus Klein. *After Alienation* (World). 1964.
                                                        pp. 145–6

In the course of these pages [of *Shadow and Act*], the portrait of a strong, reserved and honest man emerges. More, it is when he addresses his attention to his particular experience that what the writer says is of the greatest importance. It is not by means of conceptualizing and abstracting, as he tended to do in the essays written in the forties, that Mr. Ellison gets to the difficult statements; it is by reaching so far into himself that he reaches right through to the other side and fetches forth truths he could have got in no other way.

He accomplishes this by always remaining *a man who*. He refuses to be put into attributive categories, but subordinates the attributes to himself. He does not say, "I am a Negro, a writer, an American." He says, "I am a man who is a Negro, a writer, an American." He is not egotistical; he does not dump personal confession on you, assuming that what happened to him is worth your reading about because he is eminent. He always speaks of his own experience in order to make a larger point; reciprocally, the larger point is valid only as it is supported by evidence from his own experience.

(K)                                     George P. Elliott. *NYT*. Oct. 25, 1964. p. 4

*Invisible Man* . . . was published twelve years ago and Ellison's second novel has long since taken on that unreal quality that haunted the unpublished *Ship of Fools*. Ellison spent two years in Rome, attended writer's conferences, submitted to interviews, wrote journalism, taught at various universities, and almost inevitably admirers have felt that the second novel, when it did appear, would reflect damagingly the anguish that accrues to a brilliant writer who takes so long to publish a book that nothing less than a masterpiece will justify the years of work and waiting.

Now, perhaps in lieu of the novel, Ellison has published a collection of essays. Such books have a way of quietly announcing the temporary or permanent demise of a novelist's will to imagine, so when *Shadow and Act* was announced, it was hard not to fear the worst. But though it is certainly not a great book, it shows that the fears were groundless. Ellison is still with us—large, impressive, ironic, cumbersome in his own polished way—and he seems to have lost no more faith in himself than is natural in a proud and serious man who finds writing difficult.

(K)                                     Roger Sale. *HdR*. Spring, 1965. p. 124

To Ralph Ellison, the Blues or Blues Mood is a symbolic expression of the human condition. The meaning of the Blues is identical with the meaning of man's existence, and, in the end, is the meaning of Ellison's novel, *Invisible Man*. . . . The Blues express all the ambiguities, contradictions, possibilities, hopes and limitations that lie in the human circumstance. They offer the opportunity to soar free of tradition, of all ties, and they expose the limits of this freedom. They are a joke at the core, but a joke that mocks and transcends the very meaning of its lyrics. They are a human assertion and they sing of the flux and variety of the human soul; they cry despair, hope, joy, sorrow, love, loneliness, pride, and disappointment all in one glorious ambiguous voice. The Blues present challenge, success, hope, and defeat, and always promise possibility, and the possibility is there for the performer to seize.

The narrator of *Invisible Man* sings his own Blues in telling us his tale, and by singing the Blues he discovers the meaning of his own being and the nature of his reality; it is a tale that tells of the growth of an individual consciousness and the growth of perception.

(K)                                 Raymond M. Olderman. *WSCL*. Summer, 1966.
                                                                  pp. 142–3

See *Invisible Man* (novel); *Shadow and Act*. (essays).

# FARRELL, JAMES THOMAS (1904–      )

Like Proust, Farrell seems to have endured certain personal experiences for the sole purpose of recording them; but he also desired to avenge them, and he charged his works with so unflagging a hatred of the characters in them, and wrote at so shrill a pitch, that their ferocity seemed almost an incidental representation of his own. Like Caldwell, he wrote with his hands and feet and any bludgeon within reach; but where Caldwell's grossness seemed merely ingenuous or slick, Farrell wrote under the pressure of certain moral compulsives that were part of the very design of his work and gave it a kind of dreary grandeur.

> Alfred Kazin. *On Native Ground* (Reynal). 1942.
>
> p. 380

In Farrell's view, the people of his stories—whether of the exploiting or exploited class—were the natural products of a competitive social order in which material acquisition represented the highest good. Their human failure, to the degree that they were brutalized and rendered both spiritually and socially sterile, flowed inevitably from the culture which an acquisitive society had imposed on them. As a novelist, Farrell reported the mores of an economic jungle. . . . For him, the "dark realities" and the "pervasive spiritual poverty" of American society could not be eliminated within the present social order. For regeneration, for restoration of genuine social function, only the Marxian revolution would suffice.

> Lloyd Morris. *Postscript to Yesterday* (Random).
>
> 1947. p. 166

Farrell has exploited the documentary novel very ably. He should be judged as a documentary novelist. It is quite true that even when viewed in this light he does not loom as large as a Dos Passos or a Wolfe, but neither does he look the blithering incompetent that some of his reviewers have represented him to be. . . . The importance of Faulkner is his private vision, whereas the importance of the documentary, and of the novel of James Farrell to the extent that it succeeds in achieving documentary status, is that the vision is completely public.

> W. M. Frohock. *The Novel of Violence in America*
>
> (Southern Methodist). 1950. pp. 69, 71

The accurate ear and the retentive memory of such a writer as James T. Farrell constitutes a kind of literary field-telephone, a two-party line possessing the double advantage of getting a message down straight without getting smacked in the teeth with a hatful of slops. A method based on the judicious non-com's understanding that if you can keep from getting hit by anything long enough you'll still be around when the war is won.

Where the field-telephone school, of which Farrell is the most prolific protagonist, succeeds is in its photographic fidelity. Where it fails is in affording that convulsive sense of life we discover in a Conrad, a Poe, a Stephen Crane, or a Scott Fitzgerald.

Nelson Algren. SR. Nov. 14, 1953. p. 29

Farrell the moralist is all-of-a-piece with Farrell the fiction writer. The one reflects upon the experience the other records. The fiction writer composes canvases depicting frustrated petty hopes and mean defeats, prolix obituaries of the spiritually impoverished, of greenhorns and other outsiders, the anonymous integers that go only to swell the population figures, the devalued people of his time whose fruitless dignity and courage (when these they have) are eternally betrayed by what Thomas Hardy called "circumstances." . . . The writer of fiction may leave us with the impression that his vision is of the drabness and tawdriness of life; and Farrell has indeed been beaten over the head innumerable times for precisely that crime, but the moralist takes a different tack and from the same data draws the conclusion that these things need not be.

C. Hartley Grattan. Harper. Oct., 1954. p. 93

Anderson and Dreiser taught him integrity; they took him aside and patted him on the head and told him always to speak the truth, my son, and no harm will ever come to you. They helped to develop in him the one quality for which today we rightly do him honor. But then Farrell stopped learning. . . . The integrity that became an obsession, the integrity that made him an honest writer, has held fast to its truth, and the truth now holds Farrell fast, blocking his ascent into the greatness that might have been his. It has forced him, instead, deeper and deeper into his pedantry, his thick, almost scholastic preoccupation with every last physical detail of his world.

John W. Aldridge. Nation. April 2, 1955. p. 291

Mr. Farrell has always had two important qualities that make it impossible to dismiss him. He is relentlessly honest and in the face of a fact he is artistically humble. These very virtues, perhaps, are responsible for the stylistic deficiencies. . . . His limited vision is honestly passed along and, however limited, it is vision. He sees not deeply but he sees clearly and what he sees is a part of the American experience. While he is not to everyone's taste, it would be a shame to miss him because of fastidious feelings about syntax.

Frank Getlein. Com. Jan. 27, 1956. pp. 436–7

Twenty years ago a validating conjunction of the time and the circumstances enabled us to forgive the heedless ineptitudes of the Studs Lonigan and Danny O'Neill books, allowing us in fact to accept them with pride (others may have the style and the art, but what are those; these have the power and the truth). Much writing of the thirties got by because of a misunderstanding of what literature is, through a misconception of the term "naturalism." But now, when we are no longer confused by quasi-literary doctrine, we are no longer willing to forgive bad writing, or a vision which is never superior to that of the least of us.

Saul Maloff. Nation. Feb. 11, 1956. p. 124

Mr. Farrell's stories are painful, awful and wonderful.

How can he commute so easily between such extremes? I think the answer proceeds from the fact that Mr. Farrell dispenses with art as well as with artifice. . . . Mr. Farrell is innocent of all the invisible but complicated apparatus now fashionable with the short-story writer—the subtleties of form, the casual but cunning clues for motivation, the deployment of symbol and the planned ambiguities. His language is humble, but never studiedly so. He doesn't make an *outré* elegance out of plainness, as Hemingway sometimes does, or Steinbeck in his portraits of the primitive. Mr. Farrell's simplicity is helpless and genuine. . . . Yet who is better— the slide-rule fictioneer of our day, who frequently refines his short story into a weary and well-tailored void, or Jim Farrell, who reaches out with a rough hand and comes up, quite often, with an authentic fistful of human truth?

Frederic Morton. NYT. Feb. 10, 1957. p. 30

The critics are usually bored by his dogged, humorless methods, but they are also surprised by his quality. Farrell has not only gone on doing his chosen job as well as he did in his early years—they keep saying—but does it with deepened insight and humanity. *The Face of Time,* published in 1953, for instance, received the sort of respect which would have stirred general excitement about a new author. Yet even though living writers are being given intensive treatment in a steady stream of studies pouring from the academic presses, Farrell is virtually ignored. Inevitably, by the mysterious laws of literary favor, he will be rediscovered, though not perhaps until one or two books from now. . . .

Sooner or later Farrell will be given his place as a sort of William Dean Howells of Jackson Park in recognition of the scope and faithfulness with which he recorded the day-to-day, almost hour-by-hour suffering, sentimentality, dignity, coarseness and despair of an important part of the nation's population at a time of decisive change in its psyche.

(K)                    Robert Gorham Davis. *NYT*. May 12, 1963. pp. 1, 43

In the midst of a long-overdue assessment of his contribution to American fiction, it is not generally recognized that Farrell's critical writing forms in itself a body of searching and incisive judgments much richer and of wider range than those of his novelist contemporaries. To read this criticism is not only to probe in retrospect the dilemmas of the artist in American life over the past three decades; it is also to visualize Farrell's deliberate involvement in social and political agitation at the cost of precious time taken from his art. In this choice Farrell has nothing in common with Hemingway and Faulkner. Both as writer and social critic he has felt closer to Dreiser and Anderson than to writers born in this century. A refreshing thing about Farrell is that he rejects no vision as alien to his art or his thought. Thus he was profoundly influenced simultaneously by Joyce and Tolstoy, Dreiser and Dostoievsky, Trotsky and Pater. Such a catholic openness to the thought of his great predecessors has given Farrell's critical outlook a richness and perspective unique on the American scene of our generation.

(K)                    Don M. Wolfe. Introduction to *Selected Essays* by
                       James T. Farrell, edited by Luna Wolfe (McGraw).
                       1964. pp. ix–x

Studs is not Farrell, something that can hardly be said of the novelist's subsequent chief characters. Studs may indeed reflect much in the writer's life and experience: the sense of the neighborhood, the ambivalent attitude toward the church, memories of childhood sweethearts, aversions toward particular people. But Farrell succeeded in bringing to bear upon his character the passion for his task when it was at its highest, together with a degree of objectivity that has always given to Studs a certain authenticity and independent existence. The writer, in other words, controlled his character and thus gave him life. Ever since, the novelist has been somehow forced to adjust his Danny O'Neill, his Bernard Carr, his Eddie Ryan, to what changing memory and perspective suggest that the novelist himself was—or should have been. In the process the character has been denied a life of his own. The later characters become walking shadows, and after a while they don't even walk.

(K)                    Gerhard T. Alexis. *CE*. Dec., 1965. p. 225

If he would persist in his folly, it has been said, the fool would be wise. I am not saying James T. Farrell has been foolish in his persistent and repeated explorations of what is by now his own terrain. But persistent he certainly has been. And that in the face of continued critical and, in recent years, popular neglect. What is interesting in reading his new novel, *Lonely for the Future,* is to realize that with persistence has come distance. The magic of time has transformed Farrell into a historical novelist: his period, the Twenties and early Thirties; his place, Chicago. Now, as a profoundly probing recording angel of the social scene, as exemplified by the lower middle classes (Irish-Catholic variety), Farrell is not the American Balzac he would like to be. However, as a fairly accurate painter of the social and sexual agonies of the young of a more naïve time, he is quite good. . . .

. . . what prevents this book [*Lonely for the Future*], like most of Farrel's work, from having any great substance is that he is perhaps too closely identified with his characters. Their naïveté seems to be his; their awakenings to the possibilities of life that lie beyond the middle-class home seem to be his own awakening of many years ago, obsessively re-enacted over and over again. Just that—and no more.

(K)                                    Daniel Stern. *SR*. Jan. 22, 1966. pp. 43–4

## Studs Lonigan

This is not only Farrell's best book . . . it is also a distinguished and outstanding contemporary novel. To the American reader, who whether bored or amused, is not self-conscious about seeing in print the kind of talk that would be bandied about in the Greek's poolroom by the Fifty-eighth Street gang, who doesn't have to swallow his naturalism as though he were taking a dose of castor oil, who doesn't feel called upon to write or talk apologetically about it, *The Young Manhood of Studs Lonigan* is recommended as an absorbing novel, a book of significance, a great piece of American realism. One pushes through it with accelerating speed, unable to drop it. And it leaves one shaken.

Fred Marsh. *NR*. March 21, 1934. p. 166

A major problem Farrell faced in his attempt to create a sense of what life meant to Studs was how to convey simultaneously a consciousness of the larger world of mature action and emotion, that background of facts, tendencies and values largely outside Studs' circumscribed awareness. Farrell set out to present experience subject to severe limitations, yet had to show Studs in perspective if his readers were to feel the full import of the waste in Studs' life and its consequences. Such a perspective also would show that the city provided possible avenues for Studs' humane development. In short, Farrell could not afford to omit the ideal element in Studs' culture even though his narrative point of view imposed difficult restrictions. We have already noticed how Farrell's handling of characters and viewpoint gives depth and range to his writing.

In addition it should be observed that not all persons in the trilogy end as Studs does. Bit by bit Farrell builds up the life stories of many of Studs' contemporaries. . . . Chance may play a part in the success or failure of all these characters, but determination and intelligent planning are usually important for those who succeed.

Farrell presents the ideal in life through ironic implication. If it is true that man's sorrow is the inverted image of his nobility, most readers of *Studs Lonigan* should be constantly aware of the levels Studs never reaches. The ignorance portrayed is so profound, many of the actions so shameful, that they vibrate with a sense of their opposite.

(K)                    Edgar M. Branch. *UKCR*. Winter, 1962. pp. 110–11

See *Studs Lonigan, The Face of Time, Bernard Carr, The Silence of History, What Time Collects, Lonely for the Future* (novels); *Selected Essays*.

# FAST, HOWARD (1914–      )

*Place in the City* is an astonishing novel for a boy of twenty three to have written; but it is astonishing not because it is so good, for most of it is not good at all, but because it is so exasperatingly soft. . . . Despite the superficial toughness the book is really a study in innocence, full of garlands and tears and sighs, and there are passages, in fact, where it reads like a cross between Fannie Hurst and Sherwood Anderson. . . . Mr. Fast has talent and that talent bubbles in this book; but he has not learned that second-hand pathos is the easy refuge of second-hand thoughts.

Alfred Kazin. *NYT*. Aug. 8, 1937. p. 7

Mr. Fast . . . has a certain pretentiousness in his asides and betrays his immaturity in many of his Causes and Reasons, but he tells his tale so swiftly and glibly that it doesn't make much difference whether the Causes fit or not. He writes easily, probably too easily.

Paul Love. *Nation*. Aug. 14, 1937. p. 177

Mr. Fast writes with a catch in his breath and sometimes brings tears to his own eyes instead of the readers'. Sometimes his words are less an echo of history than they are of Hemingway. . . . Sometimes he takes his characters from the same casting agencies that are used by other historical novelists. . . . If his book does not belong to the history of American literature, at least it will be important in the history of the popular mind.

Malcolm Cowley. *NR*. Aug. 17, 1942. p. 203

Once again Howard Fast has taken a figure out of American history and by the intensity of his emotional sympathy and intellectual respect had made him into a living man. Just as in *The Unvanquished* George Washington became under Mr. Fast's austerely glowing art an individual of flesh and blood, beset by doubts and fears of personal inadequacy in the role he had to play, so does Thomas Paine in the novel *Citizen Tom Paine* become a creature known and knowable in his moments of grandeur and his moments of degradation. . . . Mr. Fast's story of this unique character in history is a brilliant piece of fictional biography.

Rose Feld. *NYHT*. April 25, 1943. p. 3

When a writer of historical fiction is in top form he somehow can suggest that he does not merely re-create the past but rather that he lives there and is reporting on the life around him. Sometimes the author of *Citizen Tom Paine* and *Freedom Road* does this . . . when he is writing well and effectively, in a minor key, and you follow along with him and belong to the world he evokes. . . . His gift in his best work is for a certain reticence— and this is no negative virtue in the historical school, many of whose practitioners would dazzle you by piling up of theatrical "props" and are concerned with character only secondarily, if at all.

John K. Hutchens. *NYT*. Apr. 8, 1945. p. 6

In half a dozen novels this popular author has dealt with various critical periods in the American past and the last three of his books—*Citizen Tom Paine, Freedom Road,* and now *The American*—fit the same pattern. A society full of class tyranny, economic exploitation and political corruption; a proletariat, dumb, yearning, struggling, that plainly waits for a great leader; a hero who rises to struggle against the entrenched forces of Mammon and the dead weight of middle-class complacency; a defeat that gloriously points the way to future victories—this is the general scheme that Mr. Fast uses.

Allan Nevins. *NYT*. July 21, 1946. p. 4

In the writing career of Howard Fast we trace the unusually rapid decline of a pleasant fictional talent into dull political servitude. . . . His eye (has) been ever more tightly shutting itself to the kind of truth with which fiction is properly concerned, his heart increasingly hardening under the strain of pumping such a steady stream of practical benevolences until now . . . all that remains of any original creative gift is some kind of crude energy of intention, a shallow but complex urge to pedagogic power. Mr. Fast has come of literary age in a period in which to be a radical or even a liberal is to feel no need to smile when one says patriotism.

Diana Trilling. *Nation*. Aug. 3, 1946. p. 134

Howard Fast is a historical novelist with a difference. He has always shunned the standard ingredients of that art—sex, saber, and swash-buckling—and he has never permitted the drama on the stage to be obscured by the opulence of the setting. Nor has he tried to retell our history or ancient legends with our modern vision, pouring in (as Thomas Mann has done in the Joseph cycle) the intellectual resources of the twentieth century. Rather has he always been fascinated by the spectacle of those who either singly or in groups gave their powers and their lives for a cause, for the extension of human dignity and for what is perhaps the greatest of all rights, the right to be let alone.

Thomas Lask. NYT. Oct. 10, 1948. p. 4

Fast was long considered to be a diabolical Communist, hardly even human; now, as he presents himself as a disillusioned idealist, he seems sincere and very human. If we trust his motive and listen to what he has to say, we must grant his idealism and humanity even while a Communist. . . . It is far better when a man like Fast leaves his party for the reasons he did than because of fear or other opportunistic reasons.

Paul Knopf. NYT mag. June 30, 1957. p. 2

See *The Last Frontier, The Unvanquished,* and *Citizen Tom Paine* (novels).

# FAULKNER, WILLIAM (1897–1962)

Faulkner seems to me to be melodramatic, distinctly. All the skies are inky black. He deals in horror as in a cherished material. Coincidence, what he would call "fate," does not stand on ceremony, or seek to cover itself in any fussy "realistic" plausibility, with him. . . . A man like William Faulkner discovers fatalism, or whatever you like to call it: it at once gives his characters something to live for—namely a great deal of undeserved tribulation culminating in *a violent death*. That simplifies the plot enormously—it is, in fact, the great "classical" simplification, banishing expectation.

Wyndham Lewis. Men Without Art (Cassell). 1934.<br>pp. 54–5

Not since Swift's conclusion to *Gulliver's Travels* (with the possible exception of some of the pages of Aldous Huxley) has humanity in all walks of life been pictured as such contemptible vermin. Nor has anyone probed with greater power into the volcanic fury, the corruption, the depravity in the black hearts of men who are only incidentally dwellers in the South, or written of such matters in more brilliant prose, or with finer control of mood and suggestion and careful spacing of atrocities. . . . It is the natural and ultimate extension of the materials and the moods clearly to be discerned in the literature of the contemporary period.

Harlan Hatcher. *Creating the Modern American Novel* (Farrar and Rinehart). 1935. p. 240

As a thinker, as a participant in the communal myth of the South's tradition and decline, Faulkner was curiously dull, furiously commonplace, and often meaningless, suggesting some ambiguous irresponsibility and exasperated sullenness of mind, some distant atrophy of indifference. Technically he soon proved himself almost inordinately subtle and ambitious, the one modern American novelist whose devotion to form has earned him a place among the great experimentalists in modern poetry. Yet this remarkable imaginative energy, so lividly and almost painfully impressed upon all his work, did not spring from a conscious and procreative criticism of society or conduct or tradition, from some absolute knowledge; it was the expression of that psychic tension in Faulkner . . . which, as his almost monstrous overwriting proves, was a psychological tic, a need to invest everything he wrote with a wild, exhilarated, and disproportionate intensity—an intensity that was brilliant and devastatingly inconclusive in its energy, but seemed to come from nowhere.

Alfred Kazin. *On Native Grounds* (Reynal). 1942.
pp. 456–7

Certain features of Faulkner's work suggested that it originated in a profound need to account, to himself, for the retarded condition of culture and civilization in the South. To some extent, therefore, his books recorded an exploration, a sustained and consistent effort to arrive at a coherent explanation of the nature of his environment in his own time. His exploration was imaginative rather than purely historical. His purpose was to understand events in terms of the human experiences which had produced them; the ambitions, the needs, the attitudes of mind and heart that had shaped destiny. The result was a series of volumes which, collectively, formed a single saga.

Lloyd Morris. *Postscripts to Yesterday* (Random).
1947. pp. 160–1

Inside this amazing, convolute and inimitable saga is everything that Poe was able to suggest in his macabre tales, much that Brown and Melville and Hawthorne foreshadowed, plus not only Faulkner's own incredibly fecund conjurations of the terrible and phantasmal, but also a very definite and real world of social significances and broad slapstick humor, which is outside the domain of any apocalyptic writer, any Gothic novelist of any time or place.

George Snell. *The Shapers of American Fiction*
(Dutton). 1947. p. 88

In addition to being a fatalist, Faulkner is also an idealist, more strongly so than any other American writer of our time. The idealist disguises itself as its own opposite, but that is because he is deeply impressed by and tends to exaggerate the contrast between the life around him and the ideal picture in his mind . . . of how the land and the people should be—a picture of painted, many-windowed houses, fenced fields, overflowing barns, eyes lighting up with recognition. . . . And both pictures are not only physical but moral; for always in the background of his novels is a sense of moral standards and a feeling of outrage at their being violated or simply brushed aside. Seeing little hope in the future, he turns to the past, where he hopes to discover a legendary and recurrent pattern that will illuminate and lend dignity to the world about him.

Malcolm Cowley in *A Southern Vanguard,* edited by
Allen Tate (Prentice). 1947. pp. 26–7

The quality of Faulkner's vision, his fundamental way of seeing people, seems to me to approach the Euripidean. . . . If we read him as though he were a tragic poet, many difficulties disappear. It becomes natural now that he should withhold much that the reader wants immediately to know, in order to prepare the recognition scene; that he should abandon the traditional time manipulation of the novel for one which turns the fullest, whitest light possible upon the moment of crisis . . . that personal relations among the characters should be determined by their sense of the inevitability of the evil yet to come upon them; and that Faulkner's effort should go into showing how the world looks to his characters rather than how it should look to them.

W. H. Frohock. *The Novel of Violence in America*
(Harvard). 1950. pp. 123–4

Faulkner believes that individual responsibility is the most important goal for man. Here is his positive answer to his own negative despair. . . . Thoreau based his personal individualism upon his tremendous love of nature. In Faulkner the love of nature is replaced by the love of the land. How much one would want to distinguish between land and nature I don't know. Basically the only difference is . . . the transcendental ideas in Thoreau's concept of nature. . . . Instead of having Thoreau's leaven of transcendentalism, he has Hawthorne's leaven of the brotherhood of man. Man must love the land that God has supplied to him for his well-being.

Through the intimate association with the land, man acquires a sense of loyalty to his family, his immediate social environment, and the all-encompassing land itself. Loyalties, as with so much of man's activities, are governed by what is inherited from the past. By accepting these loyalties and the force of the past, man develops his individuality—the end for which all the other things of man's existence are means.

Ward L. Miner. *The World of William Faulkner*
(Duke). 1952. pp. 153–4

Faulkner's style and content have been the subject of endless scholarly analysis. The best as well as the shortest analysis may well be that contained in an interchange between him and his cousin Sallie Murray Williams. She asked, "Bill, when you write those things, are you drinkin'?" and he answered, "Not always."

Robert Coughlan. *The Private World of William
Faulkner* (Harper). 1954. p. 125

Faulkner's post of observation usually lies with some individual who, out of his need for self-knowledge, even salvation from those complications of the human scene which "outrage," tells the story and, in telling it, resolves it, not solves it which only God can do. But in the resolution there is usually a fuller knowledge which rescues the protagonist from the accidents of his own situation, or allows him to see it in a larger context of meaning, by means of which he can "endure"; or his plight in the end illumines by its shock some disaster of epical proportions implicit in the enveloping action. Or else the point of view roves from individual to individual, each of whom discloses differing insights and revelations of the complication. But whatever, the point of view is essentially bardic, with the difference that the bard himself is crucially involved.

Andrew Lytle. *SwR.* Summer, 1957. p. 475

Faulkner had what (giving up the attempt to define it more closely) we call genius. It is what Herman Melville had when he wrote *Moby Dick* and rarely manifested thereafter. We know that genius seldom lasts, but we are always saddened when it goes.

On the other hand, if something has been lost (in *The Mansion*), something has been gained. In his note Faulkner says that "the author has learned, he believes, more about the human heart and its dilemma than he knew thirty-four years ago." Indeed he has. He has learned, for one thing, to respect deeply the human capacity for sheer endurance. He has also acquired compassion. . . . The Snopeses, it turns out, are not personifications of greed or anything of the sort; they are poor sons of bitches like the rest of us.

Granville Hicks. *SR.* Nov. 14, 1959. p. 21

Faulkner is right in assuming that the hope in man's will to endure and prevail has been the subject of his fiction all along; but this will is variously represented, and the degree and quality of context in which we see it vary considerably from the beginning of his career to the present. He moves from what is almost a total lack of awareness to a vague and fleeting insight into human beings—to the point where the meaning of existence is not only seen but overtly defined. Throughout this progress, however, there are many uncertainties which upset the calculation, and his characters are frequently seen missing their chances and blundering badly despite their sense of dedication. This is one among many reasons for the value of Faulkner's work; it appears an endless variety of new experiments in the means to express not only man's worth but the elaborate stratagems he is guilty of using to conceal it.

Frederick J. Hoffman. William Faulkner (Twayne).<br>1961. pp. 117–8

Evil for Faulkner involves the violation of the natural and the denial of the human. . . . Yet Faulkner is no disciple of Jean-Jacques Rousseau. He has no illusions that man is naturally good or that he can trust to his instincts and emotions. Man is capable of evil, and this means that goodness has to be achieved by struggle and discipline and effort. Like T. S. Eliot, Faulkner has small faith in social arrangements so perfectly organized that nobody has to take the trouble to be good. Finally Faulkner's noblest characters are willing to face the fact that most men can learn the deepest truths about themselves and about reality only through suffering. Hurt and pain and loss are not mere accidents to which the human being is subject; nor are they mere punishment incurred by human error; they can be the means to deeper knowledge and to the more abundant life.

Cleanth Brooks. MR. Summer, 1962. p. 712

The European reader finds something uniquely American in Faulkner, and obviously no European could have written his books; the few European commentators that I have read seem to me to glorify William Faulkner in a provincial American (or Southern) vacuum. I believe that as his personality fades from view he will be recognized as one of the great craftsmen of the art of fiction which Ford Madox Ford called the Impressionistic Novel. From Stendhal through Flaubert and Joyce there is a direct line to Faulkner, and it is not a mere question of influence. Faulkner's great subject, as it was Flaubert's and Proust's, is passive suffering, the victim being destroyed either by society or by dark forces within himself. Faulkner is one of the great exemplars of the international school of fiction which for more than a century has reversed the Aristotelian doctrine that tragedy is an action, not a quality.

Allen Tate. SwR. Winter, 1963. p. 162

To the neophyte Faulkner reader, the prose may seem a continual flow of words that obscures the story action rather than developing it. The difficulties should not be minimized. The diction, the syntax, seem designed to obfuscate, not communicate. Faulkner sometimes deliberately withholds important details, and the narrators frequently refer to people or events that the reader will not learn about until much later, making the style seem even more opaque than it actually is. And the long sentences are difficult to follow, with clauses that proliferate, developing not from the main subject or verb of the sentence, but growing out of preceding clauses. As a result, the main thought is often lost in the mass of amplifying or qualifying ideas. Antecedents of personal pronouns are frequently not clear. Faulkner's style does not provide relaxing reading, but forces the reader to participate in the search for understanding and truth. . . . Had Faulkner been a U. S. senator, his speeches would have been squarely in the tradition of Southern oratory. Some of his sentences sound almost like selected passages from a filibuster. Rather than run the risk of interruption and lose the floor, he does not pause; he rolls on, using all the rhetorical devices of the speechmaker: colorful, grandiloquent and emotive words, repetition, parallel structure, a series of negative clauses preceding a positive, delayed climax.

(K)                              Edmund L. Volpe. *A Reader's Guide to William
                                 Faulkner* (Farrar, Straus). 1963. pp. 38–9


In the past fifteen years Faulkner has been approached from almost every direction. And this is, in part, as it should be; for contemporary psychology, literary history, philosophy, and sociology illuminate and help explain some aspects of Faulkner's work. Yet the authority, the prestige of this same "outside" criticism, stands in the way of full assessment. And even more of an obstacle is the apparent hostility of many American critics to what Mr. Faulkner has to say. He has yet to be approached on his own terms; and until he is, not only his themes but also the art with which he develops them will be misunderstood. Faulkner's ambiguities must be faced as ambiguities; the fundamental conservatism of his outlook must be, not simply recognized, but built upon; the relationship of his use of the over-voice to the oral roots of his narrative art must be established; his habit of giving comic treatment more often to characters he admires than to those he would reject must be explained; the special way in which he uses certain words (such as "endure") that play a major role in his thinking must be examined; and [Peter] Swiggart's discussion of the effect of self-consciousness and public inquisition on the work of the mature Faulkner must be carried further.

(K)                              M. E. Bradford. *SwR*. Winter, 1964. p. 150

If Faulkner is indeed concerned not only to explore the range of possibility in character but to probe for its essential humanity, no matter how shrivelled, he must have complete freedom to proceed in any order, in any temporal or spatial direction, and to recall and re-examine any action, situation, or character from a new perspective. Consequently, Faulkner experiments endlessly not because, like Henry James, he is interested in form and technique as values in themselves but because no single method can accomplish his purpose of rendering the unique figure of his carpet. The difference between the two is clear. James is the most conscious and consummately skilful craftsman America has ever produced; Faulkner is the dedicated student of human nature driven by the demon of compassionate curiosity to literary experimentation.

(K)                                   Olga W. Vickery. *SAQ*. Summer, 1964. p. 322

. . . although Faulkner seems to find the Christian description of man's condition true, it is not at all clear that he is willing to accept the end of the Christian story as true. That man is fallen in some sense is certain; that he lives in a moral universe in which evil has real effect, in which he becomes the victim of himself, is also sure; but that God acts to redeem man is less sure. That man must work out his own salvation is probable, but that he has within him the resources which can save him is problematic.

(K)                                   John W. Hunt. *William Faulkner: Art in Theological Tension* (Syracuse). 1965. p. 22

Inversion indeed is often at the very heart of his work: in the Faulknerian beatitude which says, blessed be the Lena Groves, for they shall inherit the earth; in the admiration that tenders a rose for Emily, a murderess whom the townspeople consider a crazy old party; in the tenderness that transmutes a death-watch for a . . . baby-killer into a requiem for a nun. And then there is the supreme inversion: Faulkner's idiots. Although Mr. Faulkner may not have thought much of the Church Militant, he most firmly ascribed to belief in the Idiot Triumphant.

(K)                                   Victor Strandberg. *SwR*. Spring, 1965. p. 182

If Faulkner feels the past as the repository of great images of human effort and integrity, he also sees it as the source of a dynamic evil. If he is aware of the romantic pull of the past, he is also aware that submission to romance of the past is a form of death. If he finds in modernity a violation of the dream of the "communal anonymity of brotherhood," of nature, and of honor, he does not see it as the barred end of history; it is also the instant in which action is possible, with a choice between action as "doom" from the past and action as affirmation. If the Flems and the Jasons drive hard to define a dehumanized future, there are the Dilseys and the Ratliffs who see the future as part of the vital human continuity. In other words, Faulkner's dialectic of time is inclusive, dynamic—and painful.

(K)                                    Robert Penn Warren. *SoR*. Summer, 1965. p. 526

The vice of Snopesism is that its practitioners ape human traits without being fully human. They give man no reason to believe that he can be better than he is; rather they seek to destroy his distinguishing traits of compassion and spontaneity by exploiting them. . . . The automatism of Faulkner's characters results not, however, from the dehumanizing forces of mechanization that many critics have decried, but from the peculiar political atmosphere in a state in which any true assertion of one's feelings might ruin one's prospects. Certainly the life in Frenchman's Bend is as primitive and unmechanized as life in an organized culture can be. Faulkner's novel sardonically points out that man cannot regain his spontaneity simply by fleeing the city and the machine.

(K)                                    Warren French. *The Social Novel at the End of an Era* (Southern Illinois). 1966. pp. 38–9

Faulkner's rural world is one of small men, small planters, small business-men; but he has invested these men with an intense response, with a search for meaning, with a cataclysmic energy so that they loom larger than life and become overwhelmingly representative of ideas and of regions, and some of that energy is borrowed from the present day historical context. . . .

At the heart of what Faulkner does is the historical myth which is most plainly told in Thomas Sutpen's story. None of the characters that tell it know quite what it means, and different aspects of it fascinate each of them. And this is, I think, true for the reader, as, I suspect, it must have been for Mr. Faulkner himself. Sutpen in *Absalom, Absalom!* meant something about the history of the South. Just what, none of us know; but that the history of the South is a microcosm of the whole macrocosmic nature of human experience Faulkner feels certain. I share his certainty and will be surprised if this cosmic meaning does not transcend the passing of the emotions inherent in the events he uses.

(K)                                    C. Hugh Holman. *Three Modes of Modern Southern Fiction* (Georgia). 1966. pp. 46–7

And Faulkner himself: did he find the right answers to his problems in life and in the continued production of his works? There are no completely right answers. It had better be said that his later books, in general, had not the freshness and power of the early ones. That is the common fate of imaginative writers (except for a few poets); some original force goes out of them. The books they write after the age of fifty most often lose in genius what they may possibly gain in talent.

Faulkner lost substantially less than others. Though none of his later books was on a level with *The Sound and the Fury* or *Go Down, Moses,* none of them made concessions to other people's tastes. One hears a person speaking in each of them, not an institution, and a person with reserves of power who may surprise us on any page. Some of Faulkner's best writing is in passages of *Requiem for a Nun,* and *Intruder in the Dust,* and especially—almost at the end—in the Mink Snopes chapters of *The Mansion.* In retrospect I should judge that he solved the problem of keeping alive his genius better than any other American novelist of our century.

(K)                      Malcolm Cowley. *SR.* June 11, 1966. p. 26

### The Sound and the Fury

It is as merciless as anything I know which has come out of Russia. I find myself wishing for someone with whom to compare William Faulkner, but to compare this writer from Mississippi with James Joyce or Marcel Proust or Chekov or Dostoevsky gets one nowhere, for Faulkner is definitely American. . . . If Faulkner is mad, then James Joyce is equally so; if Faulkner is obsessed with futility and insanity, so is Fyodor Dostoevsky. It is true that *The Sound and the Fury* is insane and monstrous and terrible, but so is the life that it mirrors. . . . I believe simply and sincerely that this is a great book.

Lyle Saxon. *NYHT.* Oct. 13, 1929. p. 3

Certainly the craft of *The Sound and the Fury* is brilliantly planned. Once the central structure is arrived at, every detail falls into its place with a sort of astounding precision. Like the opening of a safe, given the combination, we can hear all the bolts clicking into place; and we may suspect that Faulkner has added a few extra bolts just for the satisfaction of making them click. . . . Very often the use of these details at once so mathematical and dramatic is justified. . . . For in *The Sound and the Fury* the technique of the novel, and its pyrotechnics, are after all subordinated to a meaning —to the history of the degenerating Compsons.

Maxwell Geismar. *Writers in Crisis* (Houghton).
1942. pp. 157–8

To speak of greatness with regard to one's contemporaries is dangerous. But if there are any American novels of the present century which may be called great, which bear comparison—serious if not favorable—with the achievements of twentieth-century European literature, then surely *The Sound and the Fury* is among them. It is one of the three or four American works of prose fiction written since the turn of the century in which the impact of tragedy is felt and sustained. Seized by his materials,

Faulkner keeps, for once, within his esthetic means, rarely trying to say more than he can or needs to. *The Sound and the Fury* is the one novel in which his vision and technique are almost in complete harmony, and the vision itself whole and major. Whether taken as a study of the potential for human self-destruction, or as a rendering of the social disorder particular to our time, the novel projects a radical image of man against the wall. Embodied and justified, this is an image of great writing.

Irving Howe. *William Faulkner* (Random). 1952.
pp. 126–7

It is the mark of Faulkner's mind that at the end of *The Sound and the Fury,* after all the decay and catastrophe, three widely different characters remain: on the one hand Benjy, the weakest and most vulnerable, and on the other side Jason and Dilsey, respectively the morally worst and best of all the figures. Dilsey "endured"; the word is used of her kind in the 1945 "Appendix" to *The Sound and the Fury,* almost all of which is written in the exultant style, in contrast to the novel itself. As often observed, the word is one of Faulkner's favorites, and is related to his love of strong assertion, the radical trait; simple existence is looked on as the great gift, and the measure of victory is the power to maintain it in the face of what Faulkner sees as life's great difficulties. To search out one's identity, whether through the unconscious processes of nature or the deliberate cultivation of the will, to maintain this firm definition against all those forces in life which move toward weakness and decay—this capacity is something to which Faulkner gives his highest respect, and which his language celebrates.

(K)                                     Carl F. Hovde. *SAQ.* Autumn, 1964. p. 537

See *Sartoris, The Sound and the Fury, As I Lay Dying, Sanctuary, Light in August, Pylon, Absalom, Absalom!, The Unvanquished, The Hamlet, Intruder in the Dust, Requiem for a Nun, A Fable, The Town, The Mansion, The Reivers* (novels); *Go Down, Moses* (includes short novel, "The Bear," and related stories).

# FEARING, KENNETH (1902–1961)

The world of Fearing is nothing if not metropolitan. He is as involved in, and fascinated by, metropolitan existence (with its "touch of vomitgas in the evening air") as Frost with his New England landscape, decorated with commonplaces, and Jeffers with his prop boulders and gulls. . . . Held by this life in futile ambivalence that has persisted for fifteen years, Fearing's mood appears to have changed little . . . although the tone has become increasingly harsh. In the ticker tape, the radio, the tabloid, the pulp magazine and the advertisement he has found an objective correlative that has never deserted him.

Weldon Kees. *Poetry*. Jan., 1941. p. 265

He wants as many people as possible to react with immediate horror or delight; consequently he has dramatized the most ordinary sights and happenings of everyday living. What, then, is added to make it poetry and not mere reporting? Principally, it is Fearing's imaginative viewpoint. He has the double vision of the poet who sees the object we all see and sees at the same time its universal shadow.

Ruth Stephan. *Poetry*. Dec., 1943. p. 164

Mr. Fearing is a poet who can compete in excitement with the journalists and surpass them in that his words have a speed equal to his impressions. He at times seems too closely in competition with them, so rapidly does he pass from a personal anguish to a cold impersonal dismay. What saves him is that, in his approach to what he sees, "hatred and pity are exactly mixed." He is a product of the depression and somewhat limited to its mood. In his America is more despair than hope, and even hope is ominous. But it is a country in which, while he disclaims his ability to bring miracles to pass, he knows that miracles still occur.

John Peale Bishop. *Collected Essays* (Scribner).
1948. pp. 319–20

Kenneth Fearing has sought and found his permanent level in the range of modern verse, and . . . it lies somewhere between Auden and Ogden Nash, with something of the former's surrealist imagination and a good deal of the latter's urban ability to pillory suburban mediocrity. Fearing does not, of course, derive his style from either. His style (it is a very good one, and by this time wholly his own) originated in Walt Whitman's long and casual line.

Selden Rodman. *NYT*. Oct. 24, 1948. p. 18

Kenneth Fearing's poems are less prosy, more formal, than their appearance on the page would indicate. The long line, the irregular, or not particularly anything stanza pattern invite the risk of sagging; Mr. Fearing is a master of not letting the line down, and he can, with a very slight and deft touch indeed, point up his ironic effects with a brief parenthesis, an apparent afterthought, a single adverb or adjective. . . . Mr. Fearing does what he does so very well that it is all a little exasperating; you wish that he would be a bit more venturesome, inventive, experimental.

Rolfe Humphries. *Nation*. Nov. 13, 1948. p. 557

As a practiced writer, Mr. Fearing can do a great deal with repeated words that would sound like material for nursery rhymes were it not for the grown-up ideas of change and decay that accompany them. It is readable, often brilliant writing of innuendo, of things seen out of the corner of his eye, of fears and doubts and strange characters in the background.

Eugene Davidson, *YR. Summer*, 1949. pp. 725–6

I don't think a poet can be much more American, in the psychological if not the Fourth-of-July sense, than Kenneth Fearing. He talks the lingo straight, simple, and sardonic and knows the native panic at being lost in the shuffle which has created it. . . . In Fearing's writing, the "enemy" gradually becomes the Mob, official and unofficial, that thrives on the regimentation of individual thought and feeling through ever-greater control of the avenues of communication. . . . Fearing is an original, a canny Quixote and—more to the point—a kind of melancholy Jacques of the age, whose writing has often a topical surface that belies its depth of wry compassion and its stylistic purity. Edward Dahlberg once compared him with Corbière, and the comparison was apt. But there are also American comparisons: He is one of the harder-bitten sons of Walt Whitman, a more mordant Masters or Sandburg, a poetic Lardner of wider scope.

M. L. Rosenthal. *Nation*. Jan. 19, 1957. pp. 64–5

It is a fighting poetry, thank God, a poetry of angry conviction, few manners and no winsome graces. It is stubborn in its Old Guard attitude, stubborn in its technique: so unfashionable, indeed, in its resistance to the prevalent obsession with metrical vacuity, that a well-bred young neo-classicist might regard it as almost theatrically conservative.

Dudley Fitts. *NYT*. Feb. 17, 1957. p. 4

His tone, for the most part, remains ironic. If he is a revolutionary poet, out of the proletarian tradition of the Thirties, and the best survivor of that tradition, he is one without a revolution to propose. . . . His art of brilliant surfaces and quick contemporaneity seemed more daring once, as a poetic configuration, than it does today, though the best poems keep their early lustre.

Stanley Kunitz. *SR*. June 29, 1957. pp. 25–6

The irony sometimes seems dated and callow, despite its honesty and technically accomplished presentation. It is as if Fearing's habitual irony only permitted him to see things by the gross or in generalities (as conventional as the "finny tribes" of earlier mannerists). Often, the consequence is too insufficient a discrimination to see a world behind the old stereotypes. For thirty years Fearing has fought the dragons of commercialism and conformity; the effects of the struggle on his poetry have not been altogether good. But there are those poems like "Five A. M.," "Continuous Performance," and "The Face in the Bar Room Mirror" that transcend the struggle and comment on it with the ominous and witty power Fearing can achieve at his best.

Leonard Nathan. *Poetry*. Aug., 1957. p. 328

The sense of the ominous is a dominant feature in all of Fearing's books of poems, though the face and shape of the threatening spectres shift. In the 20s his men and women are spooked by the fear that the affluence of the decade, the quick fortunes built on inflated stocks, merely gilded a life that had no moral center or stability. When the great bull market died in 1929, and the era of depression began, the characters of Fearing's poems not only still shake from the reverberations of the economic collapse that toppled both fortunes and the dream of eternal security but also they quake because in some subterranean way they sense the shaping of a new disaster, some second coming of a world war. For those who survived the 1929 crash, as well as the decade of the great depression and World War II, there are still new spectres to threaten them. In the poems of the 40s Fearing makes us aware of brutal and coercive forces and devices: the secret police, the informers and intriguers, the listening devices that monitor the individual man and the society with the purpose of rendering each man faceless and efficient. Any eccentricity of the human mind and heart are corrected or erased in order to make the person smoothly fit and remain faithful to a new totalitarian social order; if the customer proves too tough, he can be eliminated altogether. There is little relief for the Fearing man, haunted by the old disasters of the past and threatened by a new conspiracy of ruthless forces dedicated to the principles of subservience and conformity to the will of the state. For the Fearing man, as the books of poetry define his cosmos, every horizon is ominous, and the big clock strikes the hour of doom twenty-four times a day.

(K)                       Sy Kahn in *The Thirties*, edited by Warren French
                          (Everett Edwards). 1967. pp. 134–5

See *New and Selected Poems*.

# FERBER, EDNA (1887–1968)

. . . although [*Dawn O'Hara*] deals in tragedy, it is a fabric woven from threads of sheer light heartedness, unquenchable courage, warm-hearted understanding of the things which go to make the essential joy of living. There are, for instance, certain chapters in the book picturing a delightful, unique, inimitable German boarding-house in Milwaukee that makes one sigh while reading them, partly from a vague nostalgia for happy bygone days in German pensions, partly also from sheer envy of the subtle touch that penned them. And then, too, there is one portrait of a broken-down sporting editor, a man whose days are numbered, a man vulgar in speech and with many sins upon his conscience, but who, nevertheless, is rich in some of the rarest gifts that human nature knows and whose final tragedy leaves a vacant spot in the heart akin to that of a personal bereavement. For these reasons it seems the part of wisdom to inscribe the name of Edna Ferber in some easily accessible part of our memory whereby there shall be no danger in the future of missing anything that may come from her pen.

F. T. Cooper. *Bkm.* July, 1911. p. 534

Any reader who has hoped that sometime he might have the opportunity to make the *amende honorable* to Edna Ferber has it now. If you have found yourself led along protestingly, however divertingly, through Miss Ferber's previous writings; if you have had an uncomfortable feeling that perhaps your author did not quite respect her reader, her art, or herself, here comes the chance to change your mind, to alter your attitude toward one of the most up-and-coming of our present-day fictionists. *Fanny Herself . . .* is the most serious, extended, and dignified of Miss Ferber's books. *. . . Fanny Herself* is a vivid, vital, full-blooded book; dealing with "big business" and the ascent of a forceful and persistent race, it is more successful than some of its kind in avoiding offences to ideality and taste.

*Dial.* Nov. 8, 1917. p. 463

The stiff plan of her story is forgotten once she begins to let her characters shift for themselves without regard to arriving at any definite point at a given time. There is emotion in *The Girls* and with it a persuasive clear-headedness. It is eloquent in its appeal for the right which the new generation seems to insist upon before all others—the right to be wrong. The book follows the development of a female line from its place in the home out to sunlight. Before we are done we know the chief figures of the novel intimately. Some of the minor sketches are meagre. Miss Ferber has not quite forgotten that she is a writer of short stories and she is inclined to be satisfied at times with fast blocking in of two-dimensional folk. She tries occasionally to make a sentence or so do the work of a paragraph.

Heywood Broun. *Bkm.* Dec., 1921. p. 393

At a time when realism is all but monopolizing literature, one experiences a sensation of delighted relief in encountering *Show Boat*. It is gorgeously romantic . . . romantic because it is too alive to be what the realists call real; because it bears within itself a spirit of life which we seek rather than have; because it makes a period and mode of existence live again, not actually different from what they were, but more alluring than they could have been. *Show Boat* is romantic not because its people and events violate any principle of possibility, but because they express a principle of selection. Miss Ferber has chosen the brightest colors and let the dull ones go. . . . With *Show Boat* Miss Ferber establishes herself not as one of those who are inaugurating first-rate literature, but as one of those who are reviving first-rate story telling. This is little else but an irresistible story; but that, surely, is enough.

Louis Kronenberger. *NYT*. Aug. 22, 1926. p. 5

Miss Ferber's talent, this reviewer is irrevocably convinced, does not lie in the way of the novel at all. She writes a novel as a modern athletic girl might wear a crinoline and a bustle. She manages the trick, but she is self-conscious and filled with secret amusement over the masquerade. Why so many words? Why such a portentous enclosure for a mere story? So I imagine Miss Ferber secretly regarding the novel form. Her forte, I humbly submit, is the short story. She has the gift, and it is my belief she has the predilection, for that form of literary art. But editors and publishers demand novels spun out to serial length and Miss Ferber, who can do it, supplies the demand. That does not vitiate the argument that her short stories are remarkably good stories, while her novels are only remarkably good short stories spun out to novel length and thereby largely spoiled.

William McFee. *NR*. Sept. 15, 1926. pp. 101–2

With this background, Miss Ferber, practiced writer that she is, could not fail to make a tale [*Cimarron*] that would fire the imagination of a great many thousand readers. But she has done more than draw a brilliant picture of Oklahoma. She has created men and women who go there to live— and in a measure do live there in the pages of her book. I say in a measure because I think Sabra and Yancey Cravat, and certainly Sol Levy and Dixie Lee and Cim and Donna and Felice, have a tendency to be gorgeous painted figures on the back drop of the West. . . . It turns out to be a fairy story. No matter if it really happened. It is the Fairy Story of the Pioneer and the Indian. It delights my eye but, like most fairy stories, it does nothing to my heart.

Dorothy Van Doren. *Nation*. April 23, 1930. p. 494

Warm, alive, observant, her short stories skim the cream from the surface of modern life and preserve it in all its richness. That is all they do. Depth, subtlety, intensity are beyond Miss Ferber and with the possible exception of *The Girls,* that is as true of her novels as of her short stories.

Edith H. Walton. *NYT*. May 14, 1933. p. 7

Reading one of her books gives you the pleasant sense of toil vicariously accomplished. And her novels are always success stories, in spite of the threatening implications she turns up and pats neatly back into place—which makes her popular reading. She squares off at her job in workmanlike fashion and turns out a nationally advertised product that looks as sound as this year's model always does, until next year's model comes along.

T. S. Matthews. *NR*. March 6, 1935. p. 107

The public will rush toward the book [*A Peculiar Treasure*] from many directions. Fiction writers will read it like gospel—and well they may for the frank story of developing craftsmanship, for authentic description of ways of writing, moods of writing, rewards of writing, fatigues of writing. They will find that, for all her frankness, she can no more put down the complete reason for her own success than she could give them a recipe for success of their own. Dramatists will read the book. Jews will read it, to uphold their faith and pride in their race, to revive memories of Jewish life in America, to share the exciting courage and warmth and devotion to family and race and work which is so true and apparent. It will be a very tonic book in that respect alone, and its title, with the verse from which it comes, will be quoted widely. The title is a little too heavy, a fine Scriptural phrase which is somehow not quite suited to the modern story of this successful, non-churchgoing writer.

Margaret Culkin Banning. *SR*. Feb. 4, 1939. p. 5

In *Show Boat* (from which, with the help of Jerome Kern, came the most appealing American opera in existence), in *So Big,* and in *Cimarron,* Miss Ferber has stressed with genuine feeling the exuberance, the fearlessness, and the roving instinct which make us what we are. . . .

The theme [of *Saratoga Trunk*]—as Colonel Maroon, now a millionaire, proclaims it in his opening interview with the press—is honestly American. For he has no false pride about how he got his millions and doesn't forget the scars his kind left on this country. But it is the development of this story that troubles me: in it I miss Edna Ferber's homely knowledge of city and country; I think she lost the chance to play up our special brand of integrity, and at the end I am left wondering if the author really cares deeply for any of the people in this book.

Edward Weeks. *At*. Dec., 1941. n.p.

. . . Miss Ferber is at her best when she stays closest to the milieu of her formative years—when she was carving out the raw material of her art as a reporter in the Middle West. Her back-street Chicago is more convincing than her Riviera romances; her prairie mornings will stay in your memory long after you've forgotten her station-wagon repartee. But even the most severely hand-tailored of her stories is much more than merely entertaining: if her matriarchs are terrifying and completely real, her star-crossed women executives, faded ingenues, and freshly lacquered adolescents are no less human under their patter. Sometimes, as in her novels, Miss Ferber's sheer, exuberant talent, her flair for the theatrical, outruns her material—with a consequent loss of realism. But even here, the emotion is honest. Her effective range is much narrower than these titles would indicate—yet every story is written from her heart.

James MacBride. NYT. Feb. 16, 1947. p. 3

Miss Ferber makes it very clear that she doesn't like the Texas she writes about, and it's a cinch that when Texans read what she has written about them they won't like Miss Ferber either. Almost everyone else is going to revel in these pages. . . . *Giant* makes marvelous reading—wealth piled on wealth, wonder on wonder in a stunning splendiferous pyramid of ostentation. . . . This is the Texas Miss Ferber has put into her bitter, brilliant, corrosive, excoriating novel. . . . It requires courage to take all this apart as scathingly as Miss Ferber has done; and in the process of so doing she paints a memorable portrait of that new American, *Texicanus vulgaris,* which is all warts and wampum. . . . For all the slickness of its writing (and Miss Ferber is a past mistress of best seller style), *Giant* carries the kind of message that seldom finds expression in such chromium-plated prose. What's more, Miss Ferber states it with a conviction that carries the ring of sincerity. All this may make it impossible for her to revisit the great Commonwealth without the law at her hip, but at least she has written a book that sets the seal on her career.

John Barkham. NYT. Sept. 28, 1952. pp. 4–5

It was inevitable that Edna Ferber should write a novel about Alaska. The magnetic northern land has all the qualities that draw her to a scene—robustness, magnitude, epic tradition, the clash of strong-willed men and their stubborn duel with Nature. In her novel *Ice Palace* she has put more of Alaska between covers than any other writer in its short and crowded history. . . . Here is the difference between Miss Ferber and the "modern" novelists, and a reason for the multitude of her readers. She still sees people in large dimensions, strong enough to be actors rather than to be acted upon. This novel contains a whole gallery of them, with Christine Storm in the center. Frankly heightened and exaggerated, they are men and women to match the seas and skies and mountains of the big North Country.

Walter Havighurst. SR. March 29, 1958. p. 26

. . . her accounts [in *A Kind of Magic*] of the slave laborer's crematories at Nordhausen, of her visit to Buchenwald, and of VJ Day in New York City are first-class reportage.

A seasoned, hard-working, and dedicated writer, Edna Ferber is similarly interesting when she tells of the trials and delights of her trade. Moreover, apart from a tendency to overvalue her own fiction, she is worth listening to.

William Peden. *SR*. Oct. 19, 1963. p. 38

See *Dawn O'Hara, Fanny Herself, The Girls, So Big, Show Boat, Cimarron, Saratoga Trunk, Giant, Ice Palace* (novels); *One Basket* (stories); *A Peculiar Treasure, A Kind of Magic* (autobiographies); *Stage Door* (play, with George S. Kaufman).


# FERLINGHETTI, LAWRENCE (1919–    )

Owner of the City Lights bookshop (headquarters for the San Francisco literary movement) and publisher of the Pocket Poets Series (most notable entry, Allen Ginsberg's *Howl*), Lawrence Ferlinghetti has been a leader in all that Jazz about poetry on the West Coast. He now appears with some verse [*A Coney Island of the Mind*] of his own, which I find highly readable and often very funny. . . . like many writers who keep pointing to their bare feet, Ferlinghetti is a very bookish boy: his hipster verse frequently hangs on a literary reference. His book is a grab bag of undergraduate musings about love and art, much hackneyed satire of American life and some real and wry perceptions of it.

Harvey Shapiro. *NYT*. Sept. 7, 1958. p. 10


Lawrence Ferlinghetti is certainly one of those advocates of universal nakedness, etc. . . . but he differs from most of the others in his high-flying joyousness of spirit and in his stylistic sophistication. He knows he is not the first man to take a peek at Darien and he has learned some useful things, and gladly, from various European and American experimenters. The religion of sex-and-anarchy, like other religions and creeds, starts off with certain simplicities but does not require its communicants to reiterate them monotonously and mechanically. Ferlinghetti can preach a little tiresomely; he proves he can in the seven "Oral Messages," written "specifically for jazz accompaniment," in which he tries to rival the worst of Ginsberg, Corso, et al. . . . Apart from the "Oral Messages," however, and from a few other preachy pieces, Ferlinghetti is a deft, rapid-paced, whirling performer.

M. L. Rosenthal. *Nation*. Oct. 11, 1958. p. 215

This regional activity had been going full swing for many years when suddenly it received a number of spectacular recruits. First was Lawrence Ferlinghetti. He is a successful book dealer, secretly the possessor of three degrees, one from the Sorbonne, a most imaginative editor and publisher, whose "Pocket Poets" series has sold hundreds of thousands of copies, and a genuinely popular poet. His own *A Coney Island of the Mind* nudges *Howl* for first place as the most popular poetry book of the decade, and without the latter's somewhat dubious publicity. Resident for many years in France, he "thinks in French"; his verse bears strong resemblance to that of Raymond Queneau, Jacques Prévert and Paul Éluard. Its nearest American analogues are the work of e. e. cummings and James Laughlin.

Kenneth Rexroth. Assays (New Directions). 1961. p. 193

Reality in this novel [*Her*] is all a fluid jumble and has no center other than the mind of the male protagonist as he searches for his completion, for his Sunday wife, for his Jungian "anima." Paradoxically, the very fact that the censor of this mind has been removed seems to produce a monotonously repetitive sequence of babbling rhyme associations which invariably lead to the hero's affirmation of self through protest and erection. As the protagonist blunders along "looking for the main character of my life," the sustaining image becomes that of the darkened movie house in which the "celluloid sequence" seems to be coiling and recoiling both image and existence, and this vision of reality may in part explain the technique with its flowing sentences, its merging of objects and its fuddling of time and space.

Daniel Leary. MinnR. Summer, 1961. p. 505

. . . there seems to be nothing in Ferlinghetti's new narrative method that James Joyce didn't discover some time ago, while there is obviously a great deal that Joyce found out and which Ferlinghetti has evidently not yet discovered, such as the use of humor and understatement and irony. What is it that *Her* has to tell us? I have only read it twice, so I am not sure, but it seems to be that the short, fat man wishes he could be like Leda and couple with the godhead, except that the swan would have to be Hera and not Zeus because he, the short, fat man, is obviously not himself divine.

Louis D. Rubin. SwR. Summer, 1962. p. 505

Mr. Ferlinghetti documents his claim to being an oral poet by including, flipped in the back cover of his new book [*Starting from San Francisco*], a 7″ LP record of himself reading his own poems. . . . Mr. Ferlinghetti's verse is perfectly suited to his style of delivery, and his style of delivery is effective and engaging. Free verse such as his needs plenty of room for its organizational necessities: repetition, listings, a long looping flow that goes back to its beginnings so as to make a rounded form. . . . He has the usual American obsession, asking, "What is going on in America and how does one survive it?" His answer might be: By being half a committed outsider and half an innocent fool. He makes jokes and chants seriously with equal gusto and surreal inventiveness, using spoken American in a romantic, flamboyant manner.

Alan Dugan. Poetry. Aug., 1962. pp. 314–15

The Beats made a great mistake in permitting a label to be glued on them, especially after they started believing what it said. Every moment Ferlinghetti expends on the hairs of Fidel's "beat beard" is snatched from the service of an underdeveloped gift. He is, or could be, a *comic* writer with a curiously neutral idiom. . . . On the predictable themes—Castro, Euphoria, Pot dreams, Journeys across the continent, Nausea, Negative sanctity . . . he is portentously dull. But no stereotyped Beat has the wit for "The Great Chinese Dragon," exalting it into the type of the orgiastic apocalypse, but not failing to note that the feet walking beneath it wear Keds.

Hugh Kenner. National Review. Aug. 14, 1962. p. 110

Neither Ferlinghetti's plays [*Unfair Arguments with Existence*] nor the hypothetical theater for which he intends them are new. In techniques and the themes of isolation and absurdity, he identifies himself with obvious antecedents: Sartre, Albee, Beckett, Genet, Camus. Most of the time he sounds as though he were giving back to his mentors, in a different idiom, what they have given him.

They would be pleased. Generally, these plays turn back upon and within themselves in miniature labyrinths of irony and pun, at the ends of which squats the same patient, grinning Minotaur. The paraphernalia of waste, the perplexing similarity between waking and dreaming, the potential dead-end of men's use of atomic energy, the tricks and masks of desire are the stuff the inhabitants of Ferlinghetti's insidious sewers grovel through.

Dabney Stuart. Poetry. July, 1964. p. 260

*Routines* comprises twelve "plays" which are closer to formalized "happenings," a genre which was given the hipster's kiss of death. I don't know what to make of them. They are not enough. Most of them deal with the miasmal condition of the current culture, but at the same time, they avoid coming to grips with that culture. They are against war, fascism, the bomb, witch hunts, and so forth—Ferlinghetti's heart is in the right place. But again, it's not enough. . . . It is a book which tells the truth, but which skates over the well-springs of that truth.

Gilbert Sorrentino. NYHT. Aug. 8, 1965. p. 15

At the end of "The Sleeper," one of twelve brief plays making up *Routines,* Ferlinghetti quotes the etymology of the word, *jazz:* "jas: jass: jasm: gism." Jazz carried back to gism is a lovely analogy for a way of writing plays that wants to get behind established drama, to re-see the beginning, radically, as form, exactly as that etymology lets us re-see jazz. . . . Though Ferlinghetti writes at a secondary intensity, he is, after all, professionally oriented, always with his ear to the ground, listening, smart and talented. He is, I think, clearly a good playwright. The form is proper to him. Additionally, for whatever it's worth, I cannot help feeling—after reading the last piece, "Bore"—how extraordinarily effective a politician he could be. Whatever he does it is always with, or from, the whole man. And that man is smart.

Richard Duerden. Poetry. May, 1966. pp. 125–6

See *A Coney Island of the Mind, Starting from San Francisco* (poems); *Her* (novel); *Unfair Arguments with Existence, Routines* (plays).

# FIEDLER, LESLIE (1917–    )

Mr. Fiedler is a very clever writer; he has an engaging gift of candor. and he learned long ago not merely to accept himself as a Jew, an intellectual, a writer passionately interested in political events and a political critic essentially dedicated to literature, but, wherever possible, to throw his "tragic" knowledge at people in such a way as to embarrass them. He tells us that his essay on *Huckleberry Finn* has outraged the homosexuals, and adds—"This, I suspect, is success." This may be success, but I'm afraid that it is the only kind of success that can come from such deliberate provocativeness—this air of talking, talking brightly, brashly, penetratingly, all the time, no matter what the subject or whom he embarrasses.

Alfred Kazin. NR. Aug. 29, 1955. p. 20

A great deal of American fiction, Fiedler says, has been an escape from a society under female domination into an imagined world of male companionship. Much of it has revealed a fear of darker races, which represent wild Nature; and the hero of the novel is often involved in some close relation with an Indian, a Polynesian or a Negro (Chingachgook in *The Last of the Mohicans,* Queequeg in *Moby Dick,* Nigger Jim in *Huckleberry Finn* and Sam Fathers in *The Bear*). Fiedler wants us to believe that this

relation is "a homoerotic fable," and he adduces a great deal of evidence—
sometimes persuasive, sometimes based on a misreading of the text—in
favor of his special interpretation. . . . It works pretty well with some of
our best authors, including Hawthorne, Melville and Faulkner, but not
necessarily with their best novels; for example, Fiedler has fresher things
to say about Melville's deplorable nightmare, *Pierre,* than about *Moby
Dick*; nightmares are more Freudian. It doesn't work at all with a whole
galaxy of novelists whom Fiedler dismisses as "middlebrow": William
Dean Howells, Edith Wharton, Willa Cather, Sinclair Lewis, James Gould
Cozzens, or anyone else who tries to present normal Americans.

Malcolm Cowley. NYT. March 27, 1960. p. 1

It is an occasion for very considerble, if wary, satisfaction to have those
ideas and countless more like them, jostling one another with a kind of
cheery, subversive vigor within the covers of a single text. *Love and Death
in the American Novel* is, at the least, an immensely valuable corrective
to what, despite everything that has been said, is a continuing misappre-
hension about our literature and ourselves. But it is a good deal more
than that, too. . . .

But the perspective *is* fresh, and what Mr. Fiedler says by means of it is
memorable. He is one of the very few literary critics of his generation whose
ideas one can actually remember from one day to the next. And if so, it is
because his deliberately disturbing habit of seizing literature from the side
or from below has not simply wrenched the works he studies into unnatural
shapes. It is because, by yanking and pulling, he has also forced some of
them back toward their proper shape. It is because this fresh viewpoint has
managed to take hold of a serious portion of the truth about the motivations
that inform the American novel. "Truth" is a strong word, and it is here
intended as such.

R. W. B. Lewis. YR. June, 1960. pp. 611, 614

One side of Fiedler's mind seems honestly drawn to Melville's commitment
to "No! in thunder." The other side is satisfied only when he can show
he's the sharpest and wittiest guy in class. "I'm Oliver Cool, the cleverest
boy in school." Fiedler has a good eye for pretense, he can worry an idea
like a cat toying with a mouse, but he has a terrible need to be a show-off.

The various Fiedlers appear to write in different tones. The treatment
of Warren is quite deferential until near the end, that of Faulkner is patronizing, and the article on Kingsley Amis and his contemporaries is fairly
sober and well considered. One is never sure what the tone is going to be.
But one is never surprised to see Fiedler sitting astride his subject, pressing
its nose in the dirt, and saying grimly and gleefully, "Say Uncle!"

William Van O'Connor. SR. Nov. 19, 1960. p. 46

Leslie Fiedler, a man of learning and intelligence, has composed another of those fascinating catastrophes with which our literary scholarship is strewn. *Love and Death in the American Novel* seems to me destined to become a classical instance of sophisticated crankiness; it rides a one-track thesis about American literature through 600 pages of assertion, never relenting into doubt or qualification, and simply ignoring those writers and books that might call the thesis into question. . . . Most American fiction, suggests Fiedler, falls either into the gothic or sentimental category, neither of which allows a confrontation with the needs of maturity. . . .

In such essays [*No! In Thunder*] the appearance of Fiedler's writing is all energy and verve, but what lies beneath it is a corrosive knowingness, a void of nihilism. Opinion, the clash of interest, the confrontations of belief—all give way under the pressure of his need to dazzle and display, to thrust his ego between the reader and his ostensible subject, to remain— all else failing—brilliant, brilliant, brilliant to the last bitter and anxious word.

Irving Howe. NR. Dec. 5, 1960. pp. 17–19

Leslie Fiedler's most famous book, *Love and Death in the American Novel,* aroused all its readers, if sometimes only to exasperation. The stories in *Pull Down Vanity* express his commitment to life more satisfyingly than his erratic criticism. The viewpoint is that of alienation: the youth, the Jew, the Negro, the artist—all who face a hostile or pathetic society. . . .

Again and again the Baudelairean impulse toward evil and outrage appears in these stories both as a means of asserting personality and of negating the vast complacencies of modern life. . . . People—life itself— move to negate that impulse; but in the conflict, often comic but always serious, he reveals what we know but rarely admit about the weakness, the fear, the vanity and nobility of man.

Peter Buitenhuis. NYT. May 6, 1962. p. 4

Fiedler is by far the most flamboyant example of the new "liberal" critic in all his excesses. In a way, he seems an artistic creation (as Jay Gatsby was an imaginative rendering of James Gatz), a brilliant caricature of the All-American *Partisan Review* critic: the New York-Disillusioned-Intellectual-Alienated-Jewish-Polemical-Sophisticated Provincial. . . . What I am questioning is not the use of Freudian interpretation but Fiedler's abuse of it. His frantic search for a homosexual *mythos*—with its methods of distortion, assertion, and innuendo—smacks of a bizarre parody of the McCarthy witch hunts: a sad, ironic note considering his essay on the late Senator.

Paul Levine. HdR. Spring, 1962. pp. 97–8, 101

Some of the verbal horseplay is funny, and some of the ideas being mocked deserve Menippean or Huxleyan satire. But the satirist has no position of his own, the exaggerated phrases cancel each other out, and all meaning or possibility of it soon disappears down a particular and often invoked drain. . . . Only four or five paragraphs in the whole novel [*The Second Stone*], one of them on Michelangelo's *Pieta*, suggest how much has been omitted in the way of beauty, history, magnanimity, myth and a dozen other elements one might name.

Robert Gorham Davis. *HdR*. Summer, 1963. pp. 284–5

In the good old days, Jewish sons faced their fathers and verbally slapped them in order to be men. In these post-D. H. Lawrence times the hero smirks in his Buddha-like shell till he shrieks at the woman beside him he both needs and despises. Fiedler, who as a critic can comment so brilliantly on the psychological inadequacies of American writers, reads here [*Back to China*] like one of his targets in *Love and Death in the American Novel*.

The reaction to *Back to China* is likely to be intense, if only because one justly expects a great deal from Fiedler. Like Mailer, however, Fiedler is so immersed in his associations that he has not created a whole world, but has presented the undigested world of his vital imagination. Like Bellow, he has not created a structure, or at least a structure that is compelling enough to make the reader forget the constant appearances of literary gratuitousness and autobiographical reminiscences. . . .

Having said all these things, it may seem odd that I also want to praise the book. *Back to China* attempts a large view of society and it is not afraid to reveal its author's feelings. Fiedler grasps for the heavens and stumbles; but the space travelled has been through meaningful places.

Martin Tucker. *Com*. June 11, 1965. p. 388

. . . *Love and Death in the American Novel* is to my mind probably the best single book on American fiction ever written, and it is surely unsurpassed in its definition of Gothicism as a characteristic of that fiction. The book has been most resented for its purported emphasis on sexual perversity in American literature and in its use of this as an index to certain historical and cultural tensions. Actually Fiedler is altogether less daring and less insistent on this aspect of our literature than was Lawrence in his much earlier study, and he is in no sense as moralistic about sex as a literary component. . . . Fiedler's methods are not essentially different from those of other commentators who are concerned with recurrences of literary motifs and with the elaboration of these into archetypes or myths. It may be more provocative but it is not more or less valid to reduce American literature to certain versions of sexual dislocation than to reduce it to versions of Eden, Christ or the Frontier.

Richard Poirier. *PR*. Fall, 1966. pp. 636–7

Leslie Fiedler's greatest talent as a critic is his ability to offend almost everyone except Granville Hicks, but despite the sustained hostility of his reviewers he is coming to have an increasing reputation as a major critic, perhaps partly because the volume of his writings now looms up over America like the Rockies. As Fiedler shifts from a shocking young tiger to a middle-aged cultural heavyweight, it is time to stop reacting to his excess of style, time to begin taking him seriously. And it is relatively easy to judge Fiedler philosophically, for his writings are dominated by a single theme: a rage at the loss of a patriarchal system of values and the consequent condemnation of modern American culture.

Grant Webster. *Denver Quarterly*. Winter, 1967. p. 44

See *An End to Innocence, Love and Death in the American Novel, No! In Thunder, Waiting for the End* (essays); *The Second Stone, Back to China* (novels); *Pull Down Vanity, The Last Jew in America* (stories).


# FISHER, DOROTHY CANFIELD (1879–1958)

Miss Canfield wants the whole of the psychic life to be carried on under the spot-light of the attention. It follows that she is opposed to the creation of instinct; that she desires, in fact, that the psyche should be like a country that refers all its business to a central government. That is a system that leads in the end to a tyrannous and inefficient bureaucracy and the decay of provincial life. . . . The fact is that Miss Canfield's mind is a stranger to the idea of "the thing in itself"; and that makes her very little of a poet and rather less of a moralist.

Rebecca West. *NSN*. July 28, 1921. p. 444


To satisfy . . . worried, but conscientious souls, and perhaps to satisfy herself, Dorothy Canfield has written an earnest and serious vindication of marriage. . . . She has evidently tried to be honest. . . . Dorothy Canfield makes marriage a real thing—a thing of substance and color—but she makes its alternative weak and pitiful. . . . If Dorothy Canfield would face the intensity of love and the lure of freedom as willingly as she faces the reality and depths of family life, she could make a memorable contribution to current thought.

Freda Kirchwey. *Nation*. Dec. 7, 1921. pp. 676–7


Mrs. Fisher has taken issue with the indictment of the American scene which has colored the writing of many of our most significant contemporary novelists. Her loyalties are the old ones of the New England school; she finds neither malice nor stagnation nor dulless in the village. Her New

Hampshire landscape glows with the veritable color of the hills; her village folk are kindly and simple and human; for her rural life still has the atmosphere of contentment and of a large peace. These contacts are notable because, in a sense, they place her definitely among the conservative in her outlook on life.

Lloyd Morris. *NYT*. Oct. 15, 1922. p. 25

Dorothy Canfield's sense of humor is keen but she has not wit. Neither does she indulge in epigram. She has done very effective scenes but she is not a quotable novelist. It comes back, I should say, to the fact that with her the story is the thing. Very earnest people are seldom witty. . . . Dorothy Canfield is concerned with ideas and with people. She has chapters of passion and beauty, but you must take them as a whole.

Dorothea Lawrence Mann. *Bkm*. Aug., 1927. p. 700

Her stories seem to be verifiably true, because they are never written with scorn or with the endeavor to prove anything; unless it be to prove that ordinary day-by-day life may be filled with excitement, that love may grow in the intimacy of marriage stronger instead of weaker; that there are just as many Main Streets in Europe as in America; that the society of one's own children is more diverting than the average crowd at a Night Club. . . . I sometimes think that Dorothy Canfield, who has a deservedly international reputation, would be even a greater novelist if she did not possess so much common sense. She knows actual life so well, her ideas are so rational, so sound, and so sensible that her love of truth and reality may actually stand in the way of her reaching the highest altitudes.

William Lyon Phelps. *SR*. Oct. 11, 1930. p. 199

Despite an imperfect mastery of the art of compression and terseness, Dorothy Canfield is foremost today among those novelists who stand for sane perspective rather than sensationalism, for verity rather than realism, for selection of facts focused upon an indwelling universal law rather than a chaos of facts-for-facts'-sake, for limited free will rather than complete determinism. Thus, amidst the stultifying and stale conventions of naturalism, Dorothy Canfield is radiantly and dynamically unconventional.

H. H. Clark. *Bkm*. Nov., 1930. p. 300

Because she has been popular from the beginning of her career, because her shrewd common sense and understanding of the conditions of everyday life, even more than her emotional power, make her the "favourite author" of enormous numbers of unanalytical women who find in every story some illumination for their own lives, she has never had the recognition which her work deserves. She is journalistic to the extent that she produces constantly. She is unliterary partly because she is completely unself-conscious. If she achieves a beautiful passage it is because the words and sentences express what she has to say, and not because she is interested in beautiful writing except as a tool.

Elizabeth Wyckoff. Bkm. Sept., 1931. p. 44

Like Miss Cather, her wide knowledge at first hand of many sections of the United States and of some of Europe, prevented her from making those superficial generalizations which weaken the work of the satirists like Lewis, Dreiser, and Sinclair, and her knowledge of adolescence gained through her experience as a teacher, spared her from the errors of those novelists like Anderson who picture youth as a quagmire of evil. If her material seems at times to overwhelm her power of artistic assimilation and expression, her best fiction has an acuteness of insight which will keep her place secure.

Arthur Hobson Quinn. American Fiction (Appleton-<br>Century) 1936. p. 714

It's always illuminating to see Dorothy in process of stabilizing all she writes by her constant re-pinning it fast to the common lot, to generic human experience. Her greatest achievement, to my way of thinking, lies in her power to stand firmly on this realistic ground, while at the same time she pulls a possible future through the present. It's a thing teachers sometimes do, but they seldom know how they do it, and I'm fairly sure Dorothy doesn't know how she does it. Teachers do it for individual children, whom they know fairly well; Dorothy does it for an unknown multitude. . . . Nobody could single out the influences strongly affecting American life for the first quarter of this century without including Dorothy's novels. They seize the reader by an intimate hand and take him at once on an incursion and an excursion.

Sarah N. Cleghorn. Threescore (H. Smith). 1936.<br>pp. 132–3

Miss Canfield has had an accumulated mass of experience and anecdote from which to build her tales, and a birthright understanding of the persons of whom she writes. . . . Miss Canfield writes from the inside, looking out. . . . It is the ageless and universal striving of the human spirit of which she writes, and the material she has chosen is less noteworthy than the way she uses it.

All of us who are still learning to write should mark and envy the transparent simplicity, the quiet fluency of these tales. . . . Even more than these inestimables, warm tenderness that doesn't grow mawkish and sentiment that never sugars-off into sentimentality make the pretty every-day raw substances of Miss Canfield's tales beautiful and memorable.

Frederic F. Van de Water. *NYT*. Oct. 23, 1949. p. 4

See *The Bent Twig, The Brimming Cup, The Deepening Stream,* and *Seasoned Timber* (novels).

## FISHER, VARDIS (1895–1968)

Mr. Fisher has written strikingly of a great subject, of the appalling and beautiful Wilderness and of the men and women who conquered it. He has remembered them, the way they talked and moved, the loneliness in their faces as winter came on, their astonishing adaptability in difficulty, the grim laconic quality of their heroism, their coarseness and lewdness and wildness. . . . *In Tragic Life* . . . ranks with the best work of our young writers. It is strong and vital and holds forth great promise for its sequels.

John Bronson. *Bkm.* Jan., 1933. p. 91

The novels of Vardis Fisher, emerging from the last stronghold of the American frontier tradition, the Rocky Mountain West, belong in the main stream of American letters. These are not mere regional novels. In their courage and rigorous honesty they are kin to the great works of confessional literature which know no national boundaries. But just as surely they grow out of the heroic, tragic, building and destroying conquests and aspirations of the pioneers—the fruits of which are now visited on the sons unto the third and fourth generation. . . . Vardis Fisher, single-handed, as he sees it, is conducting a revolution against the pioneer tradition. . . . Like Rousseau, he is intent on showing, without modesty, his hero's courage and nobility; and, without shame, his hero's sins and silliness, ineptitudes and secret mortifications.

Fred T. Marsh. *NYT*. Jan. 20, 1935. p. 4

A tetralogy concerned with present-day life in the United States, which remains to the end a puzzling combination of obvious talent for fiction, extreme egocentricity, an honest search for the meaning of life and loose thinking, comes to an end with Vardis Fisher's *No Villain Need Be*. Like its three predecessors, *In Tragic Life, Passions Spin the Plot,* and *We are Betrayed,* it takes its title from a poem of George Meredith's. . . . There is no justification whatever for the loose and scattered ending of the work. . . . Nothing could be more fatal to an author's attempt to communicate his meaning to others than this deliberate failure to take into account the obligation to give his work as much coherence as possible, to use form as a means of communication, and not to deceive himself into thinking that he is being more honest than anybody else merely by discarding the conventions of the novel.

Herschel Brickell. *NAR*. June, 1936. pp. 358–9

With all its faults—its sprawling formlessness, its monotony of tone, its occasional pomposity, and the didacticism and loss of story interest consequent upon the eventual absorption of Vridar Hunter in Mr. Fisher himself—the tetralogy had moments of power and passion. The naked spectacle of the awful secret agonies of childhood and adolescence dominated by terror and shame compelled emotional response; and there was conviction and trenchancy in the unsparing portrayal of the pettiness and pusillaminity of certain aspects of academic life.

Lucy Ingram Morgan. *CF*. April, 1937. p. 30

A novelist can make no more serious demand on his art than that it tell us this: Granted such and such circumstances—and they will probably be those which the unsought experience of his own life has led him to consider—how shall a man conduct himself so that his soul may not sicken and die? It is because Vardis Fisher makes this demand that he commends himself to our interest. His resources as an artist are limited, his taste is uncertain, and his sense of form is not strong enough to allow him with impunity to discard the common conventions of the novel. But no one could doubt the earnestness of his moral purpose. His effort has been extreme to set down his conclusions honestly.

John Peale Bishop. *SoR*. Oct., 1937. p. 350

Placing Vardis Fisher is one of the sharpest problems offered by recent American fiction. Fisher's sincerity is so marked and his refusal to be beaten down is so gamely stubborn that he may seem at times to be a more significant novelist than he really is. . . . It is not a pleasant duty to list the faults of an author with so much talent and honesty and sense of human justice. . . . Perhaps Fisher could probe deeper into the current evasions if he also had a social scalpel, and his work might be given a logic and balance it now lacks. But the whole situation isn't so simple. Because Fisher has fallen into the trap of writing novelese, part of the answer to his problem would have to be technical.

Harry T. Moore. *NR*. July 27, 1938. p. 342

Vardis Fisher has chosen for his very considerable literary talents a very considerable fictional task. He has decided to write a family saga encompassing the history of man, beginning with prehistoric nomads and ending with whatever is left of contemporary humanity after the present military engagement. . . . It is his contention that the great discoveries which modern science has made concerning the origin and early experiences of man are locked away from the average citizen in text books and technical studies. Pondering this, he concluded that if such knowledge were put into the most popular form of literature, i.e., the novel, it would reach a general audience, and be absorbed into the national consciousness, where it might do some good by giving the voters in a democracy better knowledge of themselves and their problems.

Thomas Sugrue. *S. R.* March 27, 1943. p. 22

(He) is, in part, fascinating, in part tedious and, throughout, plethoric. . . . No one can quarrel with (him) for being a novelist and wanting to be an anthropologist. One can only wish that he would keep his ambivalences to himself and be one or the other, for what emerges from his efforts is certainly not a novel and even less a reliable source-book. It is, rather, a kind of cross-pollination of the two and the resulting hybrid, defying classification, tends unpleasantly to baffle the reader.

R. J. Bender. *CS.* Aug. 10, 1947. p. 6

In Fisher's case (as opposed to that of Erskine Caldwell) we have none of (the) sense of removal; he insists that we identify ourselves with his people. His characters' ignoble patterns of thought and pretenses of superiority are presented as the norm for humanity. Our self-love is affronted, and we read insults into these books. That is exactly the trouble: we feel that this is precisely how Fisher wants us to react. It is as if he has a perverse wish to outrage us, as if in his desire to publish discoveries of our common fraility he stands in the position of prosecutor and accuses us of crimes.

George Snell. *Shapers of American Fiction* (Dutton).
1947. p. 278

In each of the first four volumes (of the *Testament of Man* series) he has examined the deep motives and the major contrivings of early men and women, adroitly deployed in the various fateful circumstances of the misty dawn of humanity. Each book is self-sufficient, an engrossing story of male and female, of man and the gods he dreamed, of the pains of man's writhing emergence from all that he once was. . . . Touching as it does the most tender sensitivities of our self-consciousness, it will enlighten, disturb and delight its readers in all the ways that their own age-old symbolic conditionings will allow and necessitate.

Wendell Johnson. *NYT.* Sept. 19, 1948. p. 21

Mr. Fisher's interpretations of man's development are naturally personal and conjectural. It is easy to see that there is more of modern psychology

than anthropology in his approach, and it is possible to feel that his ancient men and women, only just out of the caves, have a strangely modern
quality of subtlety in their thinking. Nevertheless, Mr. Fisher is creating
his continuous fabric of man's mental history with considerable success
and is bringing to bear upon it a powerful poetic imagination.

Nathan L. Rothman. *SR*. Oct. 2, 1948. p. 30

See *In Tragic Life, Children of God, Darkness and the Deep,* and *The Valley
of Vision* (novels).

# FITCH, CLYDE (1865–1909)

In his early original plays such as *A Modern Match, The Moth and the
Flame* and *Love's Lane,* Fitch used many old-fashioned dramatic conventions, but there is already a well-defined promise of finer work. He
abandoned hackneyed stage phrases, filled his work with technical in-
novations and touches of realism, gave evidences of keen insight into
human motives and emotions, and of a remarkable instinct to chronicle
the minutest detail and circumstances of the life he saw around him. . . .

In his latest work, however, Fitch has . . . made an advance on anything he has yet done. His powers are becoming more symmetrical, and
[*The Truth*] is a fine example of his ability to invest a play with an air of
sincerity. He has learned that sound logic and straightforwardness are not
incompatible with effective threatrical situations. The fact is that the level
of his recent original work is unquestionably high. . . .

Martin Birnbaum. *Independent*. July 15, 1909. pp. 125–7

In all apparent ways his career was a success; he made more money and
achieved a wider reputation than any other American playwright, past or
present; his work was popular and well rewarded with critical esteem, not
only in his own country but in England, Germany, and Italy as well; and
yet, looked at largely, this same career appears to be a failure, because
Fitch has left behind him no single drama that seems destined to
endure. . . .

His very best and most important characters, if we examine them
critically, are seen to be amplifications of what, in essence, are "bit" parts.
In the girl with the green eyes, Fitch achieved a very searching study of a
young woman afflicted with ineradicable jealousy; and in the heroine of
*The Truth* he rendered with very wonderful insight the character of a
woman constitutionally doomed to telling fibs. Fitch's truest people are
women rather than men; and they are nearly always women who are
weakened by a flaw in character. They are, in any real sense, *little* people.

Thus, even at his best, Fitch achieves his effect by amplifying the little instead of by imagining the large.

> Clayton Hamilton. *Bkm.* Oct., 1909. pp. 135–6

Great interest naturally attaches to Clyde Fitch's last play, and his posthumous triumph with *The City* adds a pathetic touch to the history of his career. The workmanship of this play is so fine that it would seem that he had reached the perfection of his artistic growth. The philosophical meaning of *The City* is less definite than its effective passages of tragedy. The scenes are abhorrent and appalling, but this laying bare of a vicious soul in such a way that its absolute truth is felt is an achievement. . . . The play is as abhorrent . . . as Ibsen's *Ghosts*—perhaps because it has as much of a lesson.

> *The Theatre Magazine.* Feb., 1910. p. 34

His letters reveal that he never outgrew his depressing reaction to unfavorable criticism of his plays; not that he resented being told wherein he had failed, but so often the spirit behind the public comment was heedless and personal. . . . A review of the attitude of the press toward him would indicate that there was a stereotyped approach toward everything he did; that is why he liked to read to his friends the foreign estimates of him, which approached his plays on their individual merits, and placed him high as a man of letters in the theatre. At home the papers praised his dexterity, his clever use of familiar detail, his feminism, which they put into a formula until answered by *The City,* his unerring choice of casts. They pigeonholed him without weighing his literary worth, which, at the time, was a rare exception in the American theater. But Italy, Germany, and France were more ready to place him high for such a play as *The Truth.*

> Montrose J. Moses. *Clyde Fitch and His Letters*
> (Little). 1924. p. ix

His public career covered exactly twenty years, from 1889 to 1909. When he began to write, American drama scarcely existed; when he died, it was a reality. He did more for the American stage than any other man in our history; when the chronicles of our original plays come to be written, he will fill a large space. He made a permanent impression on the modern theatre; for he was essentially a man of the theatre.

> William Lyon Phelps. *Essays on Modern Dramatists*
> (Macmillan). 1929. p. 152

Fitch's position in American dramatic literature has never been fairly settled. Among critics old enough to have seen his plays in their original production, and what is more important, with the surrounding atmosphere of American society of that day, they hold, undoubtedly, a higher value than they deserve. . . . They reveal, it is true, a fidelity to detail, and an occasional sharp commentary on social manners and customs, but it is obvious that they are more concerned with personality than with character and that the comment goes no deeper than a smartly superficial humor.

John Anderson. *The American Theatre* (Dial). 1938.
pp. 63–4

The early work of Clyde Fitch was tentative, but when he produced *The Climbers* . . . he entered upon a more definite period of workmanship, and showed himself a master in delineation of the actions and motives of people moving in social relations. This social consciousness had been in his work from the first. . . . Fitch, however, did not limit himself to social satire; his greatest plays have in them a central idea, which unifies the drama and gives it body.

Arthur Hobson Quinn. *Representative American Plays*
(Appleton). 1938. p. 639

There was, in Fitch, a *grand couturier* of genius. He could, with equal success, either invent a mode or perfect an established one; the result was always certain to become the actress for whom he designed it. When historical romances and costume plays were in vogue, he produced the best. When taste shifted to drawing-room drama, he was quick to excel in that fashion also. . . . In some ways, Fitch understood women better than they understood themselves. This insight accounted for much of his success.

His best comedies framed a series of portraits of the American woman of fashion at the opening of the twentieth century. . . . Fitch's most memorable heroines, for all their presumptive elegance and fastidiousness, were apt to be deeply tainted. . . . The flower of native "good society," they were, fundamentally, what a later generation would describe as vulgar bitches.

All this the moralist in Fitch perceived and implied. The artist in him . . . sought to disguise it by sheer bravura, so that the "mist of shams" might seem to represent the solid substance of life. . . . For forty years afterwards, Fitch could still be reckoned a master of scenic illusion whose drawing rooms were peopled by women idly chattering, displaying their vacuous souls and their delightful gowns, whose "society" resembled a wilderness of apes and wantons. . . . This was as close as Fitch dared come to expressing his sober verdict on his social environment.

Lloyd Morris. *Postscript to Yesterday* (Random). 1947.
pp. 175–7

. . . the untimely death of Clyde Fitch was commonly said to have cut off the one writer who might have produced the "Great American Drama." Fitch had, it is true, worked zealously in many styles in his few years in the theater and scarcely a season passed in the early years of the century without at least two of his plays competing vigorously for the entertainment dollars of New Yorkers. He was acclaimed for the power of his characterization, the freshness of his themes, and the frankness of his dialogue. Indeed for the last he was not infrequently reproached. . . . The scene in *The Girl with the Green Eyes* attests Fitch's close observation of human behavior and only increases the regret that he could not shake off the collar of theatricalism in connection with his major characters and their problems.

> Alan S. Downer. *Fifty Years of American Drama:*
> *1900–1950* (Henry Regnery). 1951. pp. 8, 12

Clyde Fitch . . . began to write under the spell of the romantic theater, but ended his short career with a number of realistic character-problem plays. . . . Yet even the romantic social comedies, melodramas, and period plays which gave Fitch an international eminence during his first decade were decidedly in advance of their times. . . . Fitch surpassed his mid-century predecessors in such romantic or even melodramatic situations by his wit, and by the appeal of the characters whom he has projected upon scenes so obviously idealized or exotic. . . . The character-problem plays of his last decade no doubt constitute Fitch's more lasting contribution to the literature of the stage.

> Sculley Bradley in *Literary History of the United*
> *States,* edited by Robert E. Spiller *et al* (Macmillan).
> 1953. p. 1012

See *The Girl with the Green Eyes, The Truth, The City* (plays).


# FITTS, DUDLEY (1903–1968)

Mr. Dudley Fitts has a subtle mind, sensitivity to beauty, an esoteric sense of humor . . . , and a most elliptical manner. He is already known as a translator of the *Alcestis,* and another of his translations from the Greek will be forthcoming this fall. . . . Mr. Fitts seems to me, more than most, to possess authentically the kind of mind and temper that have contributed to the achievement of T. S. Eliot. . . . I admire the deftness of Mr. Fitts, but he does not recapture that first fine careless robustness. This is not meant to imply that he has not his own originality.

> William Rose Benet. *SR.* July 3, 1937. p. 18

Like these men [Pound and Eliot], many of whose stylistic traits he has taken over (as witness his falling cadences, esoteric allusions, and juxtaposition of classicism and slang), he voices an attitude of disillusionment and despair tempered by irony and wit. But because he is writing at a later point in time, that is, at a time when these sentiments have lost their *raison d'être,* he is unable to bring to them the same vigor and conviction. Whereas Pound was disgusted and Eliot agonized by contemporary brutality and anarchy, Fitts tends to exhibit boredom and polite cynicism. . . .

Mr. Fitts is least successful when his disillusionment is self-conscious rather than lyrically spontaneous, when it seems the result of an attitude rather than of assimilated experience. In most of the longer poems . . . the sentiment is offered as a quasi-philosophical commentary, is conveyed through abstract rather than sensory terms. In the short lyrics, however— and Mr. Fitts's talent is essentially a lyric one—the emotion is objectified; there is unity of sentiment and form. Here the poet contents himself with the presentation of conventional moods such as nostalgia and melancholy and achieves a coherent and convincing poetic statement. The poetic personality is not diffused through any contradiction between approach and expression.

T. C. Wilson. Poetry. Nov., 1937. pp. 108–9

The poet in Fitts was more often than not concealed behind his adaptations into English from the Greek and Latin, which he seemed to carry before him as a shield—to protect, perhaps, and to keep alive the sensibility and wit which never failed to delight the sensitive reader of poetry. Fitts's sensibility in poetry was not one of possessing a "melodic ear" but rather one of tonal propriety and grace; his verse . . . moved with formal elegance within the traditions that inspired it. . . . The clean diction, the sense of classical restraint, the finely balanced periods and rhythms place Fitts's adaptations of the Greek anthology in a world far removed from the far more clumsy, thickly worded, unrhymed verses of Edgar Lee Masters' *Spoon River Anthology.*

Horace Gregory and Marya Zaturenska. A History of<br/>American Poetry, 1900–1940 (Harcourt). 1946.<br/>pp. 356–8

Dudley Fitts . . . has gone for "faithfulness" rather than "strictness," with the result that his *Lysistrata* comes through as a powerful experience in English. As a non-reader of Greek I had previously known the *Lysistrata* only in two feeble translations that may have caught the words but certainly missed the force, the tragedy, and the great roaring bawdiness of Aristophanes. With this rendering by Fitts I have found the play for the first time, an experience in delight. . . . Aristophanes, after all, went for what *Variety* calls the "boff." He wrote for the theater. And what would his audience—holding its side at a good raucous piece of bladder-flailing —care for the derivation of the gag? What it wanted was a gag it could respond to. And Fitts delivers it with an assurance that would certainly have delighted the old goat himself.

John Ciardi. *Nation.* June 14, 1954. p. 525

Spontaneous as his gaiety seems it is frequently also remarkably faithful, . . . and where his raciness seems labored, Aristophanes too seems to limp. The issues of the play [*The Frogs*] (poetry and politics, and not, as the jacket says, the nether world) and the jokes stemming from the incongruities of the situation, Mr. Fitts reproduces with admirable sharpness; where he (and every modern reading of Aristophanes) must fall short is in the mercurial play of literary wit and in lyrics. . . . Vitality is not Mr. Fitts' only merit. His divisions of the text clarify the articulation of what usually appears as a jumbled mass. His Introduction and Notes present essential information succinctly and with spirit.

Moses Hadas. *NYT.* Sept. 11, 1955. p. 10

For Dudley Fitts, as for Aristophanes, *The Birds* is fun. This modern, colloquial translation is, of course, aimed at introducing the comic literary and dramatic genius of Aristophanes to the general reader, but the apparatus of scholarly and critical notes and the index of proper names have a fresh exuberance that Aristophanes would surely have enjoyed. Fitts, moreover, has the imaginative insight to meet the Greek dramatist on his own literary grounds. . . . These literary games are not precocious mannerisms, for Fitts makes them an integral part of Aristophanes's dramatic and thematic structure. Instead of finding a unifying base in some dubiously allegorical Utopia, Fitts molds a play, not of ideas, but of dramatic voices— human and not so human, bird-like, and divine. The beauty and excitement of this version arise out of his ability to counterpoint a wide variety of voices—gentle, buoyant, crude, arrogant.

Paul H. Cubeta. *SR.* June 22, 1957. p. 30

Until very recently we were unhappily dependent upon the dated Aristophanes of B. B. Rogers or the clumsy prose of the Anonymous translation as debowdlerized by O'Neill. But with the gradual appearance of Fitts' versions . . . and the complete Greek Comedy forthcoming from Michigan, the gap should be filled. At the moment Fitts stands alone, and he is very good indeed. His virtues are fine wit, style, readability and a keen sense of comic motion, marred only by occasional lapses into an owlish coyness and archness.

William Arrowsmith in *The Craft and Context of Translation,* edited by William Arrowsmith and Roger Shattuck (Texas). 1961. p. 180

Some 40 years ago, it was Ezra Pound who advised young poets to revitalize the classics; and if they enjoyed the work of an ancient writer, to "make it new." In this country, Pound's immediate successor was Dudley Fitts, who converted the chore of translating Greek and Latin verse into one of the liveliest of modern arts. The brilliance of his new versions of the Greek Anthology is now well known, and in the effort to revive Aristophanes, no one has equalled Fitts's *Lysistrata* and *The Frogs*. What he has done has been to breathe new life into the comic spirit of Athens and of Rome. . . .

Some kind of critical moral may be drawn from the success of [his] new version of Martial's epigrams: throughout the course of his career as a maker of ancient verse into something new, Dudley Fitts has never compromised his wit, his taste, or his well-assured affinity with the work that inspired him to write. His version of *Sixty Poems of Martial* is a supreme example of light verse in the 20th-century manner.

Horace Gregory. *NYT*. Oct. 29, 1967. p. 12

See *Poems 1929–1936; Anthologia Graeca, Lysistrata, The Frogs, The Birds, Ladies' Day, Sixty Poems of Martial* (translations).


# FITZGERALD, F. SCOTT (1896–1940)

The world of his subject matter is still too much within Fitzgerald himself for him to see it sustainedly against the universe. Its values obtain too strongly over him, and for that reason he cannot set them against those of high civilization and calmly judge them so. Hence, wanting philosophy, and a little overeager like the rest of America to arrive without having fully sweated, he falls victim to the favorite delusions of the society of which he is a part, tends to indulge it in its dreams of grandeur, and misses the fine flower of pathos. He seems to set out writing under the compulsion of vague feelings, and when his wonderfully revelatory passages appear, they come rather like volcanic islands thrown to the surface of a sea of fantasy. . . . He has seen his material from its own point of view, and he has seen it completely from without. But he has never done what the artist does: seen it simultaneously from within and without; and loved it and judged it too.

Paul Rosenfeld. *Men Seen* (Dail). 1925. pp. 222–3

I think of all you did
And all you might have done, before undone
By death, but for the undoing of despair. . . .
None had such promise then, and none
Your scapegrace wit or your disarming grace; . . .

And there was none when you were young, not one,
So prompt in the reflecting shield to trace
The glittering aspect of a Gorgon age.

John Peale Bishop. NR. March 3, 1941. p. 313

And now it seems almost too contrived that Scott should have chosen this year in which to die. For it is altogether fitting that Scott's career should begin where one world war ends and end where another begins. He spoke for a new generation that was shell-shocked without ever going to the front. He was one of our better historians of the no-man's-time between wars. He was not meant, temperamentally, to be a cynic, in the same way that beggars who must wander through the cold night were not born to freeze. But Scott made cynicism beautiful, poetic, almost an ideal.

Budd Schulberg. NR. March 3, 1941. p. 312

His style keeps reminding you, particularly in his earlier stuff, of his own sense of the enormous beauty of which life, suitably ornamented, is capable; and at the same time of his judgment as to the worthlessness of the ornament and the corruptibility of the beauty. The irony of regret lies deep in the individual contour of phrase and assortment of words; if the felicity of its expression is no doubt not to be explained, it is still, it seems to me, the key to the consistency of the peculiar Fitzgerald tone.

Andrew Wanning. PR. Sept., 1943. pp. 547–8

Fitzgerald, as writer, wanted above all, he said, to achieve a wise and tragic sense of life. There are places enough in his books where he seems to do this beautifully and so it does not sound funny or whimsical when he jots down: "My sometimes reading my own books for advice. How much I know sometimes—how little at others." But the conclusion which forces itself out is that he was finally less wise than tragic. It is probably not possible for a writer to be as wise as he was tragic. Only saints come that size.

J. F. Powers. Com. Aug. 10, 1945. p. 410

There are novelists who find their material almost entirely outside themselves, and there are others who find it almost entirely within themselves. Scott Fitzgerald's talent lay in an unusual combination of these two modes. The basis of his work was self-scrutiny, but the actual product was an eloquent comment on the world. He was that rare kind of writer, a genuine microcosm with a real gift of objectivity. The combination explains his success. It is the reason that the force of his best work always transcends its subject matter.

Mark Schorer. YR. Autumn, 1945. p. 187

Fitzgerald's great accomplishment is to have realized in completely American terms the developed romantic attitude, in the end at least in the most responsible form in which all the romantic's sensuous and emotional responses are disciplined by his awareness of the goodness and evilness of human experience. He had a kind of instinct for the tragic view of life. . . . He had, moreover, with all its weakness and strength and in a time when the undivided understanding was rare, an almost exclusively creative kind of intelligence, the kind that understands things, not abstractly, but only concretely, in terms of people and situations and events.

Arthur Mizener. SwR. Jan., 1946. pp. 66–7

Horror and compassion were what Fitzgerald quickly came to feel for the segments of American society he chose to explore. These segments were as narrow as those claimed by Henry James and Mrs. Wharton, but they were equally representative. They exhibited the way of life deliberately adopted by those who were absolutely free to choose. And, while they represented the reality of only a very few, they also represented the aspiration of many. Almost from the first, Fitzgerald had been pretty aware that living wasn't the reckless, careless business these people thought. And, in even his earliest tales, unnoticed by most readers, there was always a touch of disaster.

Lloyd Morris. Postscript to Yesterday (Random).<br>1947. p. 151

The root of Fitzgerald's heroism is to be found, as it sometimes is in tragic heroes, in his power to love. Fitzgerald wrote much about love, he was preoccupied with it as between man and woman, but it is not merely where he is being explicit about it that his power appears. It is to be seen where eventually all a writer's qualities have their truest existence, in his style. Even in Fitzgerald's early, cruder books, or even in his commercial stories, and even when his style is careless, there is a tone and pitch to the sentences which suggest his warmth and tenderness, and, what is rare nowadays and not likely to be admired, his gentleness without softness.

Lionel Trilling. The Liberal Imagination (Viking).<br>1950. p. 244

The odd, the haunting thing about F. Scott Fitzgerald himself is how close he always was to being a "fringe writer." Or a marginal writer, perhaps, always treading the edge of the abyss, following a narrow ledge between achievement and disaster. And perhaps it was this artist's original confusion about fame (or popularity or cash) and art which led him so swiftly to catastrophe. In any case Fitzgerald's work is split down the middle, between the "objective" novels like The Great Gatsby, which lacked somewhere a solid center, and the "confessional" novels like *The Beautiful and the Damned* which lacked a solid form.

Maxwell Geismar. *SR*. April 26, 1958. p. 17

More important than the nature of Fitzgerald's moralism, of course, is its quality. The most serious charge that must be leveled against him is that he never made a really searching inquiry into the sources of his moral ideas or of the reasons behind the situations that moved him to render moral judgment. His own specific references to his tendency to moralize were always oblique, as though he felt he should either get rid of this predilection or make light of it. Instead of trying to understand it, he tried to direct his reader's attention to something else. When this was no longer possible, he found himself in the midst of a tangle of sometimes adolescent, sometimes senile ways of coping with the moral issues raised in his fiction and in his life.

The absence of a mature, well-defined position of moral perception in a writer is important only if it damages the effectiveness of his writing. In Fitzgerald's case it is clear that his work was damaged, and seriously so. This deficiency kept him from realizing the brilliant potentialities of some of the characters he created. It meant that even the best of them must be only pathetic creatures lost in a world they never made, a world that was hopelessly bewildering.

(K)    Kent and Gretchen Kreuter. *MFS*. Spring, 1961.

p. 80

With success Hemingway's slight early diffidence was vanishing into the restrained bravado of a champ. Comparing him to Fitzgerald at this time would be like comparing a butterfly and a bull; the butterfly has beautiful colors on its wings, but the bull is *there*. Hemingway was a force. His personality overpowered you, making you do the things he wanted to do, making you enthusiastic about the things he was enthusiastic about. The world revolved around *him,* while Fitzgerald—off to one side—was subtler, more insidious, more sympathetic, more like light playing through clouds. Fitzgerald had the dangerous Athenian qualities of facility and grace as against Hemingway's Spartan virtues of ruggedness and perseverance. Both were accomplished artists, but perhaps the ultimate choice lay between Fitzgerald's more sensitive penetration of human lives and Hemingway's harder, more burnished style.

(K)    Andrew Turnbull. *Scott Fitzgerald* (Scribner).

1962. p. 188

The legend of Fitzgerald's disorderly romantic life answers, and with a better writer, the intense American need for a mythical artistic hero like

Poe. An interest in Fitzgerald's work can scarcely escape entanglement in the Fitzgerald legend. Nevertheless, his work today seems to enjoy great favor, perhaps because he seems less mannered than Hemingway, less tortuous than Faulkner, and less clumsy than any of a dozen novelists in the naturalistic tradition. The excellence of his style tends to hold his reputation high while other reputations tumble. But at least two other matters operate in his favor. The first is the hard core of morality which makes him one with those writers of greatest strength in American fiction: Melville, Hawthorne, and James. Second, unlike a majority of modern American writers, he offers a fiction which is hard to imitate but from which much can be learned.

(K)                    Kenneth Eble. *F. Scott Fitzgerald* (Twayne). 1963.
p. 153

Fitzgerald accomplished more than a chronicle of Jazz Age belles and playboys, with whom he has been consistently associated. His repeated emphasis on the theme of corruptive wealth—present even in the notes for the unfinished parts of *The Last Tycoon*—and his depiction of the melancholy implications in the dream of the social aspirer—these represent the core of his commentary on our experience. His contribution was twofold: he distilled in beautiful prose the spirit of an age, and he urged a penetrating criticism of the values that formed its foundation.

(K)                    William Goldhurst. *F. Scott Fitzgerald and His
Contemporaries* (World). 1963. p. 228

In these "crack-up" pieces one becomes gradually aware that Fitzgerald is referring not to a brief period of only two or even five years, but to the span of his whole career. The moral sickness was always there, and in 1936 it erupts like an ugly boil for all to see; although painful, perhaps the discharge will aid the cure—or at least relieve the inflammation. Like Melville's Bartleby the scrivener, Fitzgerald seems ready to face the blank wall and stare in profound silence for the remainder of his life, for he seems to have withdrawn completely from the human scene, and to have lost even the sense of his own identity. . . . The only element throughout these terrible revelations which suggests that Fitzgerald is not doomed by self-revulsion is his acute sense of time. . . . Only a man haunted by possible achievement could possess such an obsessive awareness of time.

(K)                    James E. Miller. *F. Scott Fitzgerald* (NYU).
1964. p. 129

Humility, generosity, loyalty—"goodness" is the word Malcolm Cowley has used to describe his sense of the man in the letters—these are some of the virtues that grow out of the rich soil at Fitzgerald's disillusion and failure. And intelligence—not a virtue exactly, but an important power that must be accorded Fitzgerald, and that went a long way toward compensating for his very real ignorance—a delicate, intuitive intelligence about life and art whose enrichment, over the years, into understanding is recorded directly in these letters. And eloquence, finally, the gift of articulating his own touching humanity, and through that the humanity of others. (K)                              Richard Foster. *HdR*. Spring, 1964. p. 135

Artistically, however, it was a long step from a sense of the tragic complexities that emerged in him about 1923 to the embodiment of that sense in a viable work of art. As a novelist he had yet to create a hero who was indeed tragic, who could command the reader's admiration as well as his compassion. To this pursuit, from about 1923 onward, he devoted the rest of his life.

We can watch him struggling in this direction in the surviving drafts that we have of *The Great Gatsby*. But because the book has two half-heroes—Nick the thinker and Gatsby the doer—instead of a single tragic hero, its artistic power is divided and diffused and it fails as formal tragedy. *Tender Is the Night* was also intended to be tragedy and Dick Diver possessed the attributes of a truly tragic hero: a keen intellect and a fine sensibility. He was to be the modern middle-class American raised to heroic stature and then destroyed by an excess of virtue, by his fatal gift of charm. But Fitzgerald could not maintain the necessary aesthetic distance, and halfway through, Dick lost his heroic attributes. As a result this novel also fails to sustain the tragic vision.

In the fragmentary *Last Tycoon,* Fitzgerald most fully realized his desire to write a modern tragedy that would fit the traditional design. Monroe Stahr is the classic hero who compels our respect and admiration as neither Gatsby nor Dick Diver could. Stahr is one of the archetypal heroes of American society—the self-made man doomed to fulfill his tragic destiny as a successful man of affairs. (K)                          Henry Dan Piper. *F. Scott Fitzgerald* (Holt). 1965. p. 295

The thing to be emphasized about *Paradise,* after the apologies, is that it sincerely wished to grapple with the ominous sense of fate which obsessed Fitzgerald's youthful "philosophers." Today's critics usually point out that this fatalism was a period melancholy, neither authentic nor universal. It was, admittedly, subject to egregious sentimentalisms, as in *Paradise,* but the malaise running through post-war fiction was anything but unauthentic, and more than a simple historical emotion. The novel's search for meaning through art, for order and purpose and self-identity, tells us something about the age and Fitzgerald's central role in it—his early awareness that the gift of imagination was at once the American's fall and his possible redemption, that the self was the imagination and the imagination the self, to be used upon life's exchange as the medium of a very precarious purchase. Unfortunately for Fitzgerald, and for a great many of his contemporaries, there were no absolute economic laws governing the expenditure of self, only ones made up as you went along.

(K)                    Joseph N. Riddel. *MFS*. Winter, 1965–66. p. 339

Yet to recognize the lapses of form in *Tender Is the Night* should not detract from the novel's extraordinary achievements. In a way Fitzgerald fulfilled the ambitions with which he had begun his new novel back in 1925. *The Great Gatsby* had placed him among the leaders of the modern movement in the arts, and yet he had wanted to move beyond, to write a novel that would be "the model for the age that Joyce and Stein are searching for, that Conrad didn't find." With *Tender Is the Night* he did move beyond the modern movement, moved away from universal myths and toward the pathos of history. This novel is a vision in art of an era in American history, of the failure of a society and of an individual who embodied its graces and its weaknesses. In *Tender Is the Night* Fitzgerald created a work of fiction rare in American literature, a novel uniting romantic beauty and also historical and social depth; and he proved by his creation that his art, and his identity as an artist, could survive the death of the society which had nurtured and sustained him.

(K)                    Robert Sklar. *F. Scott Fitzgerald: The Last Laocoon*
                    (Oxford). 1967. pp. 291–2

### The Great Gatsby

The novel is one that refuses to be ignored. I finished it in an evening and had to. Its spirited tempo, the motley of its figures, the suppressed undersurface tension of its dramatic movements, held me to the page. It is not a book which might, under any interpretation, fall into the category of those doomed to investigation by a vice commission, and yet it is a shocking book—one that reveals incredible grossness, thoughtlessness, polite corruption, without leaving the reader with a sense of depression, without being insidiously provocative.

Walter Yust. *LR*. May 2, 1925. p. 3

Let us mean by (a masterpiece) a work of the literary imagination which is consistent, engaging, and dramatic, in exceptional degrees; which exhibits largely mastered a human subject of the first importance; and which seems in retrospect to illuminate the whole physical and spiritual situation of which it was, by the strange paturition of art, an accidental product.

One easy test will be the rapidity with which, in the imagination of the good judge, other works of the period and kind will faint away under any suggested comparison with it. Now a small work may satisfy these demands as readily as a large one, and *The Great Gatsby* satisfies them, I believe, better than any other American work of fiction since *The Golden Bowl*.

> John Berryman. *KR*. Winter, 1946. pp. 103–4

In contrast to the grace of Daisy's world Gatsby's fantastic mansion, his incredible car, his absurd clothes . . . all appear ludicrous. But in contrast to the corruption which underlies Daisy's world, Gatsby's essential incorruptibility is heroic. Because of the skilful construction of *The Great Gatsby* the eloquence and invention with which Fitzgerald gradually reveals this heroism are given a concentration and therefore a power he was never able to achieve again. The art of this book is nearly perfect.

> Arthur Mizener. *The Far Side of Paradise* (Houghton). 1951. p. 177

He is so familiar with the characters and their background, so absorbed in their fate, that the book has an admirable unity of texture; we can open it to any page and find another of the touches that illuminate the story. We end by feeling that *Gatsby* has a double virtue. Except for *The Sun Also Rises* it is the best picture we possess of the age in which it was written and it also achieves a sort of moral permanence. Fitzgerald's story of the innocent murdered suitor for wealth is a compendious fable of the 1920's that will survive as a legend for other times.

> Malcolm Cowley. Introduction to *The Great Gatsby* (Scribner). 1953. p. xx

Into the figure of Gatsby he put much of what he admired in America. . . . There is something in Gatsby's generous, ideal aspirations which transcends their sordid base and survives their squalid destiny. His hopes are visionary, even though his end is coldly actual. . . . Fitzgerald is remarkable because he never blinks the gaudiness and sentimentality, indeed the almost majestic vulgarity of Gatsby's imagination, yet he can catch what is truly lyrical and valuable and rare in the spirit behind it. He never fell into cynical disillusion even though he went on to show how inwardly fallible and outwardly foredoomed the wondering idealist was.

(K)    Tony Tanner. *The Reign of Wonder* (Cambridge). 1965. p. 360

See *This Side of Paradise, The Beautiful and the Damned, The Great Gatsby, Tender Is the Night, The Last Tycoon* (novels); *Collected Stories; Letters; The Crack-Up* (articles).

# FITZGERALD, ROBERT (1910–     )

Robert Fitzgerald is one of the many young poets who have learned a great deal from the school of Eliot. His poetry is obviously influenced in technique and in philosophy by those figures in poetry who since 1925 have dominated the scene. This is both good and bad. He writes exceedingly well, with a fine command of form, of phrase and with a careful selection of imagery. He understands the use of the heightened statement. But he has not, as yet, a great deal to say that has not already been said.

Eda Lou Walton. NYHT. Jan. 26, 1936. p. 4

"Craftsman" is by a shade too earthy a word for Mr. Fitzgerald; "artificer," which suggests the silver-smith, the lace-maker, and the illusionist, is better. His first volume reveals a technique that is not equaled in subtlety and polish by any other of our younger poets. The magic of these poems springs from precision in the descriptive use of language, brilliance and intricacy of metaphor, and a mastery of elaborate patterns of sound. . . . This poetry has both the merits and the limitations of a mind that seems to be an isolated and a highly introspective one.

Philip Blair Rice. Nation. Feb. 19, 1936. pp. 227–8

A follower of Eliot and Pound, Mr. Fitzgerald is at present notable chiefly for the intelligent use he has made of his models and for his scrupulous craftsmanship. There is here little of the uncertainty or crudity of statement common to first books of verse—even when most derivative, these poems evince a skillful manipulation of cadence and phrasing that must command our respect.

In absorbing the stylistic virtues of his masters, however, this poet seems to have been obliged also to accept their philosophic and emotional attitudes. Loneliness, nostalgia, despair and bitter resignation are ghosts Mr. Fitzgerald seems unable to rout from his pages.

T. C. Wilson. NR. June 10, 1936. p. 138

At every turn Fitzgerald gives the impression of knowing what he is doing and where he is going. He has devoted himself to a definite method with an admirable but perhaps needlessly exclusive single-mindedness. . . . Here is none of the nibbling at many uncongenial stylistic foods, none of the purblind groping that goes so far to damage most initial efforts. Here, instead, is the work of a man who is sensitively aware of his method and of his own temperament and who speaks with the tone of authority that is characteristic of the practiced.

C. A. Millspaugh. Poetry. June, 1936. p. 166

How good it is to read a book of poems not frantic with a message, not fancy with frilly fashions, using words gravely, for music's sake, or brightly, for that of image; literate without pedantry or affectation; sensitive without being neurotic or too full of nostalgia; moved but not excited; if not quite up to a pitch of high and joyous serenity, yet contemplative and calm, without complacence! How good, how rare; but these blessings are vouchsafed to us in Robert Fitzgerald's collection of poems, entitled *A Wreath for the Sea.*

Rolfe Humphries. NR. March 6, 1944. p. 324

Today we are more ready (than in 1936) to appreciate his remarkable modulation and poise. The absence of trickiness, fever and "drama" is a relief. The poems have color and vigor, a spry, confident intelligence constantly at work fusing picture, metaphor, emotion, reflection into deeply satisfying utterance. At times there is a touch of artificiality or super-refinement, but not often.

Kerker Quinn. NYHT. April 30, 1944. p. 10

Beyond any poet of my own generation, Fitzgerald seems to me to command the magic of evocative poetry; now in a phrase or line, now in a stanza, sometimes in an entire poem, scene and emotion are called up with a swiftness, an exactness, a poignancy so sharp and lovely and strong, that one is lifted past response to participation. . . . Fitzgerald seems to me a descendent of imagism, yet almost unrecognizably so since remarkably crossed with classicism. . . . It is the balance of emotion and intellect which so distinguishes these poems.

Winfield Townley Scott. Poetry. May, 1944. pp. 111–2

The poetry, the lyric gift of Robert Fitzgerald are probably best known in the fine translations, with Dudley Fitts as his collaborator, of *Oedipus Rex* and *The Antigone* of Sophocles. As reinterpreters of Greek drama in terms of twentieth-century poetry and wit, Fitts and Fitzgerald made a rare, an almost priceless combination. The wit of Dudley Fitts counterbalanced Fitzgerald's lyricism—and the brilliance of their collaboration has already withstood the test of time. . . . It would seem that for some undiscovered cause behind the poems Fitzgerald is at his best in his translations from the Greek. There is no question of his seriousness, or his fine temper; yet a paradox remains: he is most at liberty, and most profoundly his "own man" behind the mask of Sophocles.

Horace Gregory. NYT. Feb. 17, 1957. p. 5

Fitzgerald's material ranges through graceful lyrics to long, autobiographical recitatives, taking in translations from the Latin on the way. Among

the most amiable qualities of Fitzgerald's writing are calm and lucidity.
. . . Fitzgerald's lines are clean; and despite their often personal character,
cooly objective. . . . Here is none of the pseudo-elegance of dependence
on superficialities of form, like wearing borrowed clothes, but an authentic
grace implicit in the nature of the poems. It is a genuine poetry developing
from an inner organic need which, after all, is the hallmark of good things
at all times. Its classic qualities geometrically balance form and content,
the realities of existence with poetic imagination.

Byron Vazakis. *SR*. April 13, 1957. p. 20

While he has been little favored by the popular anthologists and curiously
neglected by the critics, the new volume of selected poems by Robert
Fitzgerald makes it clear that he has never belonged anywhere but in the
first rank of contemporary poetry. There is so much to commend in his
book, that, in fear of shading work that deserves only praise, one hesitates to make a preference or lay an emphasis. Here is a poet, rare in the
era of the one-shot chance and the jazzy push to "make it," who begins in
a spirit of apprenticeship to form, and to a twenty-five hundred year old
heritage which, in his case, is assumed as lightly as though it were a
personal endowment. Under hard taskmasters—the Greek and Latin poets
and the English poets of the seventeenth century—he proceeds at his own
pace toward refinement of technique and attitude the outcome of which
must either be self-determination or self-exemption.

John Malcolm Brinnin. *YR*. Spring, 1957. p. 455

See *In the Rose of Time* (poetry); also translations of Sophocles' *Oedipus Rex*
and *The Antigone* (with Dudley Fitts).

# FLETCHER, JOHN GOULD (1886–1950)

In the idea of a series of symphonies in which the sole unity was to be a
harmony of color, in which form and emotional tone could follow the
lead of coloristic word-associations no matter how far afield, Mr. Fletcher
discovered an "Open Sesame!" so ideal to his nature, and so powerful as
to not merely open the door, but at one stroke to lay bare his treasure
entire. . . . The result was, naturally, the most brilliant and powerful work
which Mr. Fletcher has yet given us—a poetry of detached waver and
brilliance, a beautiful flowering of language alone, a parthenogenesis, as
if language were fertilized by itself rather than by thought or feeling.

Conrad Aiken. *Dial*. Feb. 22, 1919. p. 190

He has yet to learn the restraint of the Greeks, whose exuberance was
always proportioned and controlled. But since the first naïve blossoming

of Imagism he has grown steadily. He has thought and felt deeply and sincerely. . . . Even when Mr. Fletcher describes what is dead or dying, he keeps his own vitality; even when he presents the grotesque, he sees it in relation to beauty. . . . He has not accepted the doom of an echoing discipleship. He realizes that to go alone is to arrive.

Marguerite Wilkinson. NYT. March 13, 1921. p. 6

What Mr. Fletcher has not is patent enough; he has no instinct for telling a story, he employs neither wit nor satire, he is dramatic only in the large. What he has are his own unique perceptions and impressions, great knowledge, love of colour, form, and significance, and understanding to interpret the forces behind the actions of men.

Amy Lowell. LR. April 16, 1921. p. 1

It is a question how far deliberation is creative. One rarely feels in Mr. Fletcher's art the true lyric rapture, the emotion that seizes the singer and carries him away. But one does feel something only a little less impassioned—the absorption of the contemplative spirit in its object, the self uplifted, and transcended into ecstasy. This latter mood or method, while more conscious than the other, while invoked rather than inspired, is but a little less authoritative in all the arts. It implies an imagination sensitive and worshipful, keen to accept and reflect all of this world's varied manifestations of beauty.

Harriet Monroe. Poetry. Jan., 1926. p. 206

His work would be important, if for no other reason, on account of the extension of rhythmical possibilities of the language and the peculiar care bestowed upon the richness and variety of verse texture. In the verse of both Swinburne and Hopkins there is a great intricacy and richness of texture, but a certain monotony. In his "highly-orchestrated and colored words" Fletcher has exploited surprise and resolution in a fashion not dissimilar to the verse of "Ash Wednesday". . . . And Fletcher was the first, or one of the first, to develop in English a type of imagery which Edith Sitwell has since erected into something like an oblique technique of vision.

Robert Penn Warren. Poetry. May, 1932. pp. 106–7

His imagery, curiously delicate, pale-tinted, often vague, is now accompanied by an echo of formal music, as though it were something made precious by distance and imperfect hearing. Like Shelley, like Whitman, his verse contains air-pockets: there is a frequent decline into soft, blurred phrasing, but at this point we must recall again that Fletcher's work also retains the imprint of the lesser Symbolists, whose poetry reveals the flaws as well as the sensibilities of their master, Paul Verlaine.

Horace Gregory. NYHT. Dec. 29, 1935. p. 6

There is nothing to burrow in to find and feel the meaning out. There is more meaning immediately, at first glance, than can ever be found on subsequent intimacy; that is because the general intent, not the specific datum, is viable. You do not anywhere weigh these poems: you run through them. If you run through a lot of them, you will get quite a lot of Mr. Fletcher himself, a generous, brilliant, prodigal lot. . . . Mr. Fletcher is a personal poet in that it is the prevalent sense of his personality that animates his poems and alone gives them form.

R. P. Blackmur. Poetry. March, 1936. pp. 346–7

I think it is fair to say that Mr. Fletcher's noticeable defects as a poet have been these: his sense of humor sometimes fails to come to his rescue, he often seems to lack a real centre, whether geographical or emotional or both, he has diffused his effort into much experimentation, and his disillusionment, though understandable, is tiresome because it seems to have no beginning, no middle and no end. But these faults are occasional, and even if he had not outgrown them he would still be one of the three or four greatest living American poets.

Baucum Fulkerson. SwR. July, 1938. pp. 286–7

The early work of John Gould Fletcher illustrates the weaknesses intrinsic in a strict application of the Imagist creed. The most memorable parts of his early poetry are the eleven color-symphonies in Goblins and Pagodas. These remarkable sequences of beautiful images are a practical demonstration of the inability of the human mind to live by images alone. It is not enough to string bright images on the thread of a single color; the reader demands the dynamic allurements of emotion or thought or action. But Imagism was merely a stage in Fletcher's complex development; in succeeding volumes, emotion and thought were not absent.

Fred B. Millett. Contemporary American Authors<br>(Harcourt). 1940. p. 142

Although he shared in many group enterprises, he was never truly of any group or coterie, never had the support of any claque or organization, cultural, commercial, or political, never was the darling of any publisher, never enjoyed a real popular success. He is an extraordinary, almost unique example of the isolated artist. Independent to the last degree, outspoken and frank, uncompromising where his principles were involved, yet wholly without guile, he won all that he won by the test of merit alone.

. . . He gave his strength to the cause of art and to those who were enlisted in that cause. To Fletcher, this was a chivalric pursuit, the only
chivalric pursuit left to modern man to cherish. For this, and for much
more, he will be remembered and honored.

Donald Davidson. *Poetry*. Dec., 1950. pp. 160–1

When he is compared with his contemporaries, his stature is not lessened.
His range is greater than that of Frost; he takes into account nations and
not alone individuals. His literary background is as rich as that of Amy
Lowell, and his sympathies are broader. He is as philosophic as Robinson,
and though he lacks the Maine poet's sense of narrative, his verse has
greater clarity and equal lyric dexterity. . . . Through his residence abroad,
his Americanism was thrown into sharper relief. Because of his prolific
output, his technical abilities, his breadth of sympathy and experience, he
may eventually come to be considered the poet most representative of
his generation.

Norreys Jephson O'Conor. *SWR*. Summer, 1953.
p. 243

See *Selected Poems* and *Burning Mountain* (poems).

# FOWLIE, WALLACE (1908–    )

There is something lofty, elegant and austere in the style Wallace Fowlie
has made his own. Capable of tremendous absorption, condensation, sift-
ing and synthesis, he imparts his profound erudition lightly. He is at home
amidst the most antagonistic elements, directing his frail bark with the
skill of a born mariner. . . . His certitude is never arrogant or pedantic.
Woven into his skill, his grace, his dexterity there is always the element
of risk, of daring, known alike by the acrobat and the poet. His moments
of suspense are those same moments known to the performer and the man
of solitude—when he takes flight with his whole being and emerges from
the experience a new man, a man dedicated to still greater flights of daring,
whether in the air or in the mind.

Henry Miller. *Chimera*. Autumn, 1944. pp. 47–8

Repeatedly he insists that "all great poetry is knowledge of the occult."
But Dante's poem, to which greatness cannot be denied, offers the knowledge that comes of a journey through the moral universe, which is not
quite the same thing as "knowledge of the occult," and Homer's epics,
even when they take us in the realms of the dead, are wonderfully lacking
in mystery, except that mystery to which all being is inescapably knit.

There are more kinds of poetry than the kind that Rimbaud wrote, and to take cognizance of their value is not to destroy or impair his greatness. One wishes that Mr. Fowlie had shown his appreciation of this fact. . . . His hierophantic air detracts from his most acceptable pronouncements.

Babette Deutsch. NYHT. Oct. 27, 1946. p. 30

Two outstanding gifts distinguish Wallace Fowlie as a critic. First, in the Bergsonian sense he understands "duration," the curve which is both art and philosophy and which marks a configuration in time. . . . His second gift is his reduction of multiple details to key symbols and categories. Fowlie's successors will be his debtors. They will borrow and debate his key signs. . . . Maritain characterizes Thomas Aquinas as a theocentric humanist. Fowlie extends the terms to Maritain. It is also applicable to Fowlie himself. His range of vision saves him many stumbles.

Jeremy Ingals. SR. Sept. 20, 1947. p. 34

The author fell in love with the French language at school. He mastered the language as well as any American ever has, wrote several books of criticism . . . and became one of the most inspired teachers in the country. . . . Some of the sketches (in <i>Pantomime</i>) . . . are drawn with a delicate pen and reveal a sensibility which rarely coexists with scholarly knowledge or survives an academic career. . . . Behind the delicate and discreet touch of the author one gradually perceives a tragic obsession with the problem of the artist in the world and especially in America.

Henri Peyre. NYT. June 3, 1951. p. 5

He considers himself a spectator, a person playing different parts throughout life. He feels himself strongly attracted to the clown, "unashamedly awkward, exalted by the noblest dreams, and always tricked in some way before touching his dream."

And his reminiscences, like his interpretation of the clown, completely lack irresponsible spontaneity, a healthy sense of malice, and a reassuring arrogance: traits indispensable to the true clown. If Mr. Fowlie were the least bit fairer or more poised and gentle, he would be dull.

Serge Hughes. Com. July 13, 1951. p. 338

Fowlie can write with equal ease about people and places and ideas, he can be intimate and general, poetic and grave: and yet one has the feeling that it is all of a piece. It might be added, too, that this writing is in the French tradition of the journal; and this is not at all surprising coming from one who has so thoroughly adopted his beloved country that his work has sometimes been more generally appreciated abroad than at home. . . . Fowlie—in making his own the great French tradition—has brought to his prose-writing something of the penetration and sweep which he had found in his French masters.

Robert Heywood. *Ren.* Autumn, 1951. p. 110

Before visiting a foreign city or foreign country, we often avoid dull Baedekers and consult friends who have been there. . . . In dealing with the foreign domain of contemporary French letters, Wallace Fowlie offers just such informal advice to the prospective traveler. His *causeries* are lively, personal, and stimulating. . . . If Mr. Fowlie frequently remains superficial and spends space in anecdotes, this in inherent in his conversational manner which is at the opposite extreme from the academic monograph.

Justin O'Brien. *NYT.* Nov. 17, 1957. p. 56

See *Clowns and Angels, Rimbaud, Age of Surrealism,* and *Mallarmé* (criticism); also *Pantomime* (autobiography).

# FRANK, WALDO (1889–1967)

Waldo Frank's book [*Our America*] IS a pessimistic analysis! The worst of it is, he has hit on the truth so many times. I am glad to see such justice done to Sherwood Anderson, but this extreme national consciousness troubles me. I cannot make myself think that these men like Dreiser, Anderson, Frost, etc., could have gone so far creatively had they read this book in their early days. After all, has not their success been achieved more through natural unconsciousness combined with great sensitiveness than with a mind so thoroughly propagandistic (is the word right?) as Frank's? But Frank has done a wonderful thing to limn the characters of Lincoln and Mark Twain as he has,—the first satisfactory words I have heard about either of them. The book will never be allowed to get dusty on the library shelves unless he has failed to give us the darkest shadows in his book,—and I don't think he has.

Hart Crane. Letter to Gorham Munson, Dec. 13, 1919, in *The Letters of Hart Crane,* edited by Brom Weber (Hermitage House). 1952. pp. 26–7

Both the novels of Waldo Frank, *The Dark Mother* as well as the earlier *The Unwelcome Man,* are large and remarkable conflagrations. But they are conflagrations which pour forth less clear orange flame than choking black smoke. The presence of a literary force, a force potentially richer and more abundant than that of perhaps any other of the young American prosemen, is most indubitably announced in them. The traits of the man who could cast up the many deposits of bulky, energetic, and hot-blooded prose to be found in both, who could agglutinate words into the arresting forms scattered through them, entertain such piercingly personal visions, and construct, even theoretically, a complicated pattern of human relationships like that in *The Dark Mother,* must appear well-nigh grandiose to any clear-sighted person. In his most confused, most jejune moments one knows, always, that Frank is a passionate and powerful and living creature, a man who has something to express, and who is driven by a veritable need of expression. But, unfortunately, the immense narrative power of Frank is still intimated rather than revealed. His force is still a force tangled and uneducated.

Paul Rosenfeld. Dial. Jan., 1921. p. 95

*Rahab* . . . is a good deal more confused than profound. . . . the doctrine seems to be that what the vulgar call salvation comes through what the vulgar call sin. Both story and doctrine call for careful statement, but both instead are clapperclawed and mauled and dragged through keyholes and kept in the cellar until only God and Waldo Frank can guess what the row is all about. It is a pity, for Mr. Frank has at times a quite uncanny perception and a quite arresting candor. Where in fiction has the leaping flame of a man's jealousy been hinted at with a more fiery accuracy than on page 64 of this novel? And there is a vividness in a method which, eschewing narrative, darts from mood to mood, seen always from within the consciousness. But the total effect is not that of clear light; it is that of lights tangled and blinding; it is that of several films projected all at once upon the same sheet, and all flickering.

Carl Van Doren. Nation. April 26, 1922. p. 497

One goes into a park and sits down, and immediately, if one is an artist, the park becomes a problem. It lies there. The individual feels his edges knocking improperly against it. He is sitting in somebody else's park. Then, if he is Waldo Frank, he starts remaking that park. Exorbitant characters appear, the skyline begins to churn, mad speeches are ground out. And we have "John the Baptist," one of the most interesting stories of *City Block.* But such a park is a personal creation, and is statistically false; it is true as a reflection of Waldo Frank's temperament, true in a sense that Mallarmé's fauns are true, but completely erroneous as a gauge of our environment.

My reason for pointing this out is a somewhat complicated one. But first of all, I feel that it provides us with a criterion for approaching Mr Frank. Thus, we have the two possibilities: a book must be statistically true, a whole and proper valuation of life; or it must be true in the sense that Mallarmé's fauns are true, must be a beautiful possibility created in the mind of the artist. I have consistently objected that Mr Frank does not qualify on condition one; life as he presents it is assiduously culled, the volitional element of the artist is over-emphasized. Or, to borrow from a colleague, M. Cowley, I should say that he has stacked the cards. However, if we admit this cheating, take it as a basis of our calculations, we must next inquire as to whether Mr Frank cheats dextrously; we shall not ask if he is false, but if he is *superbly* false. On the whole, I think he is not, for the two books under consideration are not *finally* beautiful. They lack just that element of cold carving, that bloodless autopsy of the emotions, which allows Mallarmé so near an approach to perfection.

Kenneth Burke. *Dial*. Oct. 22, 1922. pp. 450–1

It is about time that the truth was told about this kind of thing. Critics for the most part, while they are eager to stop real progress and the development of literature, are afraid to tell the truth when they are brought face to face with anything as noisy as this book, for fear "there should be something in it." Any one who foams at the mouth may be gifted with prophecy. They need not be afraid in this case. Mr Frank is not a writer of genius. He has, however, talent and is interested in things, and if he would stop thinking about genius, and would try to exercise restraint and develop his talent, he would give us writing as admirable as the chapter from "The Will of Saint and Sinner." In this chapter [in *Virgin Spain*] he discards all his faults and develops all his virtues. . . . It is a great pity that Mr Frank is not content to restrain himself and give us writing like this more often. He would deepen and widen his talent and develop his powers, which are real. His admirers are doing this writer the worst disservice in bolstering him up to works of noisy bombast. No amount of shouting will bring fire down from heaven; but a beautiful household fire is within the reach of this writer of talent, if he cares to work for it.

Sacheverell Sitwell. *Dial*. Jan. 27, 1926. pp. 64–5

. . . Frank wishes passionately to communicate his world view, his sense of the Whole, his religious vision, to an audience. Yet his paradox is that he writes in such a way that most of his readers cannot see his form for the style, cannot, this is to say, grasp his message, that of a human being valiantly striving to solve the meaning and aim of existence, because of the intrusion of his personality. He does not wish to be simply a writer's writer nor a self-communer who happens to please a coterie: yet he does not pay the price of consciously manipulating the reader's psychology and so conducting him *through* his ordinary impressions, associations, and prejudices to a new insight. . . . Frank has a less naive view of man in relation to the cosmos than the majority of his contemporaries, and he strives to formulate this view, to become aware of it. As an artist, he is distinguished in his conceptions of form: all his books have an astutely planned unity of larger organization. The two are related. Equally related are one's personality (a product mainly of education, taking that word in its widest sense) and style. And Frank's style shows so markedly the effects of artistic theories current to-day that it defeats his more profound intentions.

Gorham B. Munson. *Style and Form in American Prose*
(Doubleday). 1929. pp. 184–5

Waldo David Frank's chosen method of writing, expressionism, is, after all is said, a way natural to him, at least in his rhapsodic moods—and they are frequent. It is failure to recognize this fact that is at the bottom of the frequent misunderstanding of the man and his purposes by the critics whose dislike for the mode prevents their getting at the matter of his work. It is a pity that this is so, because Frank's basic philosophy and ideas are good for all of us, especially now when any self-hood worth the keeping is in danger of being lost in the leveling process of standardization of thinking as well as of living.

John Jocelyn. *SwR*. Oct., 1932. p. 405

The strange career of Waldo Frank offers an instructive symbol of the intellectual fog through which America has blundered during the last two decades. A brilliant and ambitious critic, he has not been content merely to appraise books and literary forms; he has been driven by a nostalgia for the absolute to seek cosmic and abiding values, to frame a philosophy of life so comprehensive and organic that it would serve both as a religion and a *Weltanschauung*. What he sought in culture was not knowledge, but light and faith. He became a God-seeker, a passionate mystic who turned from the quest for a personal deity to embrace Humanity as God. Whatever he writes is permeated by the peculiar character of the man; everything that comes from his pen, be it impressions of travel, literary criticism, discussions of the drama or dance, is stamped with the same personal quality. No American writer today, not even Gertrude Stein, has a more individualized style and manner of thought. He is the most metaphysical of native critics—a strange mixture of mysticism rooted in the culture of the west, science employed against the pretensions of science, Marxism combined with a romantic conception of cosmic mystery. He is a visionary gifted with a turbid style which occasionally emits prophetic flashes of insight.

Charles I. Glicksberg. *SAQ*. Jan., 1936. p. 13

Mr. Frank is one of those writers who tries to say more than he can. But no one can afford to dismiss the body of his thought smugly because the whole of it has been an attack on American smugness.

Max Lerner. *SR*. May 25, 1940. p. 3

. . . it is not only that Frank's poetic world—in which virtue and "wholeness" are achieved through naivety and "darkness," through philosophical sexual raptures, metaphysical breasts and teleological wombs—is poetically inadmissible; practically and politically it is even to be feared. If Frank criticizes the Marxian determinism as but a niggardly conception of man and the world, what he offers for its enrichment is a Marxian Rosicrucianism. His creation of "higher" realities leaves no reality whatsoever; he can play with radical politics, for example, until it ceases to be politics and becomes a kind of activistic Nirvana in which all spiritual burdens are laid down. . . . In short, Frank makes the familiar leap from the frying-pan of rationalistic determinism into the fire of mystic authoritarianism; it is a feat that will, I think, be emulated with increasing frequency in our time of political irrationalism, easy feeling and undisciplined moral fervor.

Lionel Trilling. *KR*. Winter, 1940. pp. 96–7

Before passing from Frank's fiction to his cultural studies, one should note that Frank's experiments with form in the novel make him one of the important innovators of the American Renaissance. The studied imitation of the rhythms of Whitman and of the Song of Solomon in *Rahab,* which become free verse in *Holiday* and *Chalk Face,* have undeniably affected the prose of several novelists, notably Sherwood Anderson in *Many Marriages* and *Dark Laughter.* The expressionism of Frank, best exemplified in *City Block,* is alleged to have exerted an influence on O'Neill and Dos Passos, while it is apparent the pattern of the book has a genetic relationship to Elmer Rice's *Street Scene.* Frank's influence will keep him alive long after any legitimate interest in his ideas is dead. He has been a fountain of power—for others—in our time.

Oscar Cargill. *Intellectual America* (Macmillan). 1941.
p. 674

Indeed, many of the now mature and middle-aged literary men of the present day were as profoundly impressed with *Our America* as [Hart] Crane confessed himself to be. There was one important exception, however. Frank stressed the importance of spiritual components in the new pioneering. When he called for realism in literature, it was a realism controlled by spiritual realities and inner searching and not by material factors. Only upon Crane of all his contemporaries did this spiritual necessity postulated by Frank exert a compelling force of its own, and only in his work do we see its flowering to any considerable degree.

Brom Weber. Hart Crane (Bodley). 1948. pp. 166–7

In Frank's early novels one observes the materials of the artist, scarcely integrated, just as they appear in his early critical evaluations of American culture. One discovers that Frank is, after all, going beyond his materials, imposing a philosophy of his own upon his ideal hero, a fictional archetype whom he has sought for in vain in his studies of historical and contemporary characters. This ideal man is in some way or other a rebel against the world of statistics and profits. . . . Waldo Frank's debt to Freud is extensive. We discover it at first in the early works, which, though sincere in intention, are immature in form. Their mass of inadequately assimilated facts are the raw materials which he is to use later in subtler form. In the course of his development several clues suggest that he has not thrown off the influence of Freud: his preoccupation with the unconscious life of his later characters is not merely a deeper study of motivation; for the unconscious of his central character is always the point to which events are referred. What-Frank *does* furnish is the creative means of victory over death—the "mystic x" which Freud hesitates to allow.

Frederick J. Hoffman. Freudianism and the Literary<br>Mind (Louisiana State). 1957. pp. 257, 263

The basis of all of Frank's writing is his sense of the unity of all things: this unifying force in the multiverse he calls God; not a being or an object, but an action, expressing itself through its parts, among which are persons, peoples, and the total dynamics of creation. Philosophically, he fits in with Emerson, Thoreau, and Whitman. He continues Emerson's concept of the Whole Man and Whitman's "I" who is both Walt Whitman and mankind. To Frank, achievement of the self, becoming a Person, conscious of oneself as a part of the Whole, involves recognition of being partial—existing only in relation to all other persons and all other things —and at the same time involves recognition of God—not fragmented, but entire—within oneself. The Person aware of God within him does not live "in terms of the part as if it were the whole," but "in terms of the Whole expressed through its parts." If God is within the Person, God can be within the People, and achievement of harmony in a society—harmony within itself and harmony with other societies—involves the same awareness on the part of a people. . . . In his later fiction, Frank has been en-

gaged in demonstrating the analogy between a healthy society—a People
—and a whole Person. In this too, he has been unconventional.

William Bittner. *The Novels of Waldo Frank*
(Pennsylvania). 1958. pp. 16–17

See *Our America, Salvos, Virgin Spain, The Rediscovery of America, In the
American Jungle, The Jew in our Day* (essays); *City Block* (stories); *The
Dark Mother, Rahab, The Death and Birth of David Markand* (novels).


# FREDERIC, HAROLD (1856–1898)

Mr. Harold Frederic's sketch [*The Copperhead*] of a farmland township
in northern New York is written in his usual clear and defined style with
his usual desire to do the Copperhead justice. . . . It is a fresh and interesting contribution to the history of all that went to make the war. Mr.
Frederic has done his task well, and has set the little drama felicitously
in the region where his muse wanders with the freedom born of intimate
knowledge.

*Nation*. April 12, 1894. p. 277


The force and interest of Mr. Frederic's book [*The Damnation of Theron
Ware*] (and though painful it has both) lie in the presentation of the
seamy side of creed and dogma. We have not only the Methodist preacher
who comes to grief, but the Methodist debt-raisers—a man and woman
whose past has been full of alarming variety, and who are delighted to
settle down into the "chance and change" of being "good frauds." There
is the Catholic priest who talks about the "Christ-myth," yet remains an
active and devoted priest, and whose hope for the American church is
that the Irish shall take to lager beer and become in time a new type of
American. There is the Catholic girl who is avowedly "Greek." There is
also the man of science who declares all art to be decay, pointing to the
perishing of nations in "artistic riot," and proclaiming the end of the Jews
because they begin to produce painters and sculptors. The trenchant talk
of all these persons is brilliantly set down, and there are curious pictures
of the mechanism of Methodist worship and organization which we should
think might stir up ire in high places. The story, however, leads nowhither,
and the reader is advised to make the most of the panorama as it passes.

*Nation*. Sept. 3, 1896. pp. 180–1


It is now evident, however, even to the untrained mind, that the probation-
ary stage of his evolution has ended; and in the book that he has just
completed no one can fail to see that a master of fiction has come into the

reward that he has so richly earned. *The Damnation of Theron Ware* is distinctly a great novel. It has all the originality of theme and treatment that distinguish *The Lawton Girl* and *The Copperhead;* and it has also a sureness of touch and a conscious power that are lacking in all of the author's earlier books. In them he always left one with the impression of a *coup manqué;* in this he forces an irresistible conviction of success upon the most unfriendly reader.

H. T. Peck. *Bkm.* June, 1896. p. 351

Frederic's understanding of racial and theological ideas is at times penetrating; for example, his analysis of the conflicting elements in the Irish character and his contrast of the Greek and the Hebrew ideal of life in Christianity. Frederic's picture of the Catholic Church is very interesting, but he is drawing with sympathy only one element in it, that of the man who loves its artistic side and is not concerned with dogma. . . . The general effect of this book [*The Damnation of Theron Ware*] is to paint religions as necessary concessions to human weakness. But, being an artist, he does this without descending into crude caricature as Sinclair Lewis does in *Elmer Gantry.* His people are real, and he never allows them to become shrill or disgusting, however he may be turning their souls inside out. His satire is therefore all the more effective.

Arthur Hobson Quinn. *American Fiction* (Appleton).
1936. p. 452

In one of his most passionate novels, *Seth's Brother's Wife,* Frederic commented on the fact that American humor grew out of "the grim, fatalist habit of seizing upon the grotesque side," and his bitterness made the most of it. His most famous novel, *The Damnation of Theron Ware,* is a mischievously written museum piece, persistently overrated because it was among the first American novels to portray an unfrocked clergyman and to suggest the disintegration of religious orthodoxy. But the unfrocked clergyman was to become as useful a symbol of the new era as the businessman. . . .

Alfred Kazin. *On Native Grounds* (Reynal). 1942.
pp. 35–6

Frederic could agree with the age of Howells that the application of reason to passion could save; and *Seth's Brother's Wife* has a happy ending. When he came to investigate the growing complexities of other realms of the human mind, however, Frederic wrote not a comedy, but a tragedy: the story of the fall of a man, rather than his salvation, through illumination and knowledge: *The Damnation of Theron Ware.* . . . The really extraordinary objectivity of the author—the story was told strictly from the minister's point of view—involved the reader completely with the protagonist, so that he was unaware that the education of Theron Ware was anything but good; he was shown "expanding, growing in all directions," and only gradually was it realized that what seemed improvement was, instead, moral degeneration.

Everett Carter. *Howells and the Age of Realism*
(Lippincott). 1954. pp. 243–4

Many elements of the American Dream appear in this strong novel [*The Damnation of Theron Ware*] and participate in its vitality. There is the flouting of mere conventional morality, the belief in a scientific or rationalistic view of man and his relations, and the earnest faith in intelligence, human dignity, and freedom. There is also, initially, a firmly monistic sense of the interdependency of nature and spirit: both the rasping piety of the community and the personal inadequacy of Theron are introduced as functions of the environment. But, just as in *Seth's Brother's Wife,* the stream of moral earnestness separates from the stream of scientific analysis, and presently it appears that Frederic has slipped back into the simple formula of orthodoxy which says that a person who displays moral weakness is one of the damned. . . . What appears in the novel as the indignant condemnation of Theron for his moral deterioration began as Frederic's moral indignation with the small town. Because he did not have the technique to lay out the whole spiritual landscape, he funneled his passion into the study of Theron—and there it appears, transformed but still providing the novel's vitality and interest.

Charles C. Walcutt. *American Literary Naturalism,
a Divided Stream* (Minnesota). 1956. p. 52

*The Damnation of Theron Ware* is such an interesting novel and so neglected a minor classic that one hardly knows how to begin talking about it. Those who have read it sympathetically can only nod in wise agreement about the intricacies of its narration and its wry ironies, its humor and its ultimate terror. There is a Theron Ware in all of us, a capacity for pride and its consequence, damnation. . . . Yet we do not stand outside this process and look down at the hero, always knowing more than he does; we are involved to a degree in Theron's own lack of perception. . . . For what happens to Theron is also an illumination that casts relentless and searching light on the illiberal fanaticism of his religion and on the paltriness and inflexibility of his upper New York State rural background.

John Henry Raleigh. *AL*. May, 1958. pp. 210–11

In any case, he wrote a prodigious amount of fiction and nonfiction and he was read (even if not popularly) by a large group of discriminating people who understood and appreciated his efforts. Yet it would be something of an oversimplification to fit him snugly into a school of realists and fail to recognize those other aspects of his career and of his multifaceted personality that formed Harold Frederic, the artist. Had he lived a longer life, had he been free from the deadlines of his paper, and had he been less driven by the needs of two households, the patterns of his literary output might have become more clearly defined. Nevertheless, it must be admitted that many of his major works are strongly realistic, no matter what the impulses from which they derived, and that they push out of the drawingroom realism of Howells and James to deal with the more moving and vital forces at work in a less polite and sequestered world of men and women. Not the Back Bay in Boston nor the tea tables of England and the Continent, but the hardier farm and town along the Mohawk became the milieu for Frederic's bestknown fiction.

> Thomas F. O'Donnell and Hoyt C. Franchere. *Harold Frederic* (Twayne). 1961. p. 145

Satirical humor of a broader sort is the main virtue of . . . *The Damnation of Theron Ware.* . . . This interesting but recently overrated novel is at once an effort of critical realism—dealing as had Frederic's first novel, *Seth's Brother's Wife* . . . , with the decadence of village life and faith— and a problem novel. . . . Frederic is justly remembered as a forerunner in provincial satire of Sinclair Lewis.

> Warner Berthoff. *The Ferment of Realism: American Literature, 1884–1919* (Free). 1965. pp. 131–2

Possessed of an imaginative knowledge of his home county, in which character was inseparable from ethnic, religious, historical, political, and social conditions, he was able to follow Howells' lead in producing a fiction of the commonplace, yet to surpass the dean in rendering a sense of communal density. Not until Faulkner's Yoknapatawpha County did American literature have a region so fully and intimately explored as Frederic's fictionalization of his native area—the land around the invented cities of Tyre, Tecumseh, and Thessaly. In *Seth's Brother's Wife* (1887); *The Lawton Girl* (1890); *In the Valley* (1890), a historical romance about the region in colonial times; *The Damnation of Theron Ware* (1896); and several collections of short stories, Harold Frederic, sitting in London, detached from the immediate political maneuverings of upstate New York, brought into existence a fully articulated human community. The peculiar quality of rural brutality as well as rural speech, the way the political boss Beekman rules the countryside as well as the town, the relation of the best families to the processes of making public policy, the aldermanic view of responsibility, the contrasting social roles played by the Methodist and the

Episcopal Churches, the Dutch resentment of the English settlers who had migrated from Massachusetts, and the code of the masculine small-town world as opposed to the public code of sexual morality, all emerge dynamically; they are, in Frederic's pages, so rich a context of action that the American would appear to be comprehensible only in terms of his dwelling place and the multifold allegiances and enmities that he has inherited with it.

Larzer Ziff. *The American 1890s* (Viking). 1966. p. 209

See *Seth's Brother's Wife, In the Valley, The Lawton Girl, The Copperhead, The Damnation of Theron Ware* (novels).


# FRIEDMAN, BRUCE JAY (1930–    )

The peculiar pressure that inflates this book [*Stern*] to the bursting point is created by the author's relentless juxtaposition of the inadequacy of the common notion of manliness with the unavoidable compulsion of the hero to judge himself by it. The texture of the book is essentially poetic; it is the poetry of the feminine, accepting, creative personality challenged from without and within by the necessity to be a man and defend one's home and family against forces which are probably insuperable. . . . The terrible thing about Stern's fantasies—the quality which makes them grip and hurt—is that they have a large foundation in fact. Could Stern use the history of this century to soothe away his nightmares? The fact of the pogrom shadows every page of the book. But of course Stern's Jewishness is just a special instance of a general fear and trembling. . . . Friedman is nervously alive to every bit of brutality that men grab to get through their lives untouched; he is wide open to the comedy and sadness that attend a man who will be touched.

Jeremy Larner. *Nation*. Dec. 1, 1962. pp. 380–1


Last year, Bruce Jay Friedman won critical acclaim with his first novel, *Stern*. His wit, his surrealist imagination, his hard, trenchant prose stamped him as a writer eminently worth watching. At his best, he is a very funny man with a knack, not unlike Nathanael West's, for seeing the sad, grotesque hilarity of the commonplace. . . . the author seems to be at his best as a novelist, not as a short-story writer. His weakness—and it is peculiar to the short story—is that he is addicted to gimmicks, vaudeville turns and switcheroos. There is also occasionally a coarseness of sensibility, a random cruelty, that suggests he is trying a little too hard to make it in the hipster league.

David Boroff. *NYT*. Oct. 6, 1963. p. 38

The American Jew's conflicting attitude toward his Jewishness is a familiar enough subject in recent American fiction. The thing that makes this first novel [*Stern*] a surprise—and a pleasant one—is that the author has managed to convey a deep sense of the psychological validity of that ambivalence by means of something almost like surrealist fantasy. Most of the book has to do with what goes on in Stern's head. To escape a momentarily distasteful situation, Stern invents a world, born of group fears and bad movies, in which he is a victim or a hero in a fantasy that is always either sexual or violent. These scenes—which range from a single sentence to pages in length—are frequently very funny; I laughed out loud at some of them. Friedman's best achievement is that he is able to play happily with so sensitive a subject matter without losing either the seriousness or the horrible comedy of it.

Gerald Weales. KR. Winter, 1963. p. 187

*Stern* was a small but brilliant book, kept from an absolute triumph only by a late flagging of impulse and decisiveness, but wonderfully consistent and revelatory for most of its length. Friedman's second novel is brilliant, too, largely in ways that its predecessor broke ground for. It confirms the feeling that his comic gifts are almost unique among writers of his generation, since they do not depend, as nearly everyone else's do, on contrivance or exaggeration; they do not press reality to yield up arbitrary and exotic charades but release it, through purely verbal agencies, into its inherent sense of displacement and sad, domestic absurdity.

Yet something is wrong with *A Mother's Kisses*—on a very high level, but wrong. It is a much less imagined and considered work than *Stern*, having clearly been appropriated from what one assumes is Friedman's own past. And this results in a failure of *transformation*, a failure to metamorphosize personal history into present vision.

Richard Gilman. NYHT. Aug. 23, 1964. p. 5

Friedman has nothing of the cleverness of [Philip] Roth; he lacks Bellow's intellectualism altogether. Unlike Malamud, his people don't even have connections to a life of the past. . . . Friedman uses no props: his people simply lead ash-can lives. . . . What makes Friedman more interesting than most of Malamud, Roth and Bellow is the sense he affords of possibilities larger than the doings and undoings of the Jewish urban bourgeois, which, after all, comprises but an infinitesimal aspect of American life. What makes him more important is that he writes out of the viscera instead of the cerebrum. What makes him more dangerous is that while they distribute prose designed by careful planning for careful living, Friedman really doesn't know what he's doing. . . . Bruce Jay Friedman is that rarity, a compulsive writer whose innocence makes his flaws of greater value, ultimately, than the perfections of skilled mechanics.

Nelson Algren. *Nation.* Sept. 21, 1964. pp. 142–3

*Stern,* it seemed to me, was nothing more than promising because its situation and tone were so totally conventional. It was good because intelligent and unpretentious, but I think his second book [*A Mother's Kisses*] shows more encouraging signs. Here mama dominates, primarily her son Joseph, who wants to go to college and ends up at Kansas Land, and though mama is drawn strictly within the confines of the type, any book that ends up at Kansas Land cannot be accused of having been written before, not even by Malamud. Besides, Friedman is trying to whoop up his style, not in itself a good thing, but it shows he is aiming at more than simple jokes and tears.

Roger Sale. *HdR.* Winter, 1964–1965. p. 615

No young writer is more frightened than Bruce Jay Friedman. From the first pages of his first novel, *Stern,* he has been using fiction as juju—to control or appease or amuse the pressing uglinesses of modern life. Superfluously, I note that his work is such good art that it also functions for us or else he would be a mere autistic diarist. . . . *Stern,* movingly and bitterly, fixes—one may say, immobilizes—the ridiculousness of anti-Semitism and the way it can make Jews ridiculous. In his first book of stories, *Far from the City of Class,* assorted fears and fallacies are tickled into momentary lulls. In his second novel, *A Mother's Kisses,* he depicts the possessiveness of motherhood as a hilarious horror, with the Bosch-like image of a young man tied by an umbilical cord to a gaping womb that he drags after him as he flees it.

Now Friedman publishes a book of stories, *Black Angels,* in which he pushes, or is pushed, past black humor into black fantasy. In the past, like other black humorists, he has had fantastic visions of reality; most of these new stories are realistic visions of fantasy.

Stanley Kauffmann. *NR.* Oct. 8, 1966. p. 20

Friedman is a cynical pro. His idiom is a contemptuous wise-cracking patter. He snows the marks, who don't realize that the contempt includes them. He is slick, slick, slick. . . . Reading these stories [*Black Angels*], we can easily see why he is in what *Esquire* some time ago called "the hot center" of literary importance. All but one of them have previously appeared in such magazines as *Esquire, Playboy, Cavalier, The Gentlemen's Quarterly* and *The Saturday Evening Post.*

J. Mitchell Morse. *HdR.* Winter, 1966–1967. p. 677

See *Stern, A Mother's Kisses* (novels); *Far From the City of Class, Black Angels* (stories).

# FROST, ROBERT (1875–1963)

Mr. Frost's book (*A Boy's Will*) is a little raw, and has in it a number of infelicities; underneath them it has the tang of the New Hampshire woods, and it has just this utter sincerity. It is not post-Miltonic or post-Swinburnian or post-Kiplonian. This man has the good sense to speak naturally and to paint the thing, the thing as he sees it. And to do this is a very different matter from gunning about for the circumplectious polysyllable. . . . One reads the book for the "tone," which is homely, by intent, and pleasing, never doubting that it comes direct from his own life, and that no two lives are the same.

Ezra Pound. *Poetry*. May, 1913. pp. 72–4

"Yankees is what they always were," sings Mr. Frost. His New England is the same old New England of the pilgrim fathers—a harsh, austere, velvet-coated-granite earth. . . . To present this earth, these people, the poet employs usually a blank verse as massive as they, as stript of all apologies and adornments. His poetry is sparing, austere, even a bit crabbed at times; but now and then it lights up with a sudden and intimate beauty; a beauty springing from life-long love and intuition.

Harriet Monroe. *Poetry*. Jan. 1917. pp. 203–4

The Frostian humour is peculiarly important for America. No other of our poets has shown a mood at once so individual and so neighborly. Moreover, the comparative thinness of American literature, its lack of full social body and flavor, is due to the extraordinary interval between our artistry and our national life. Our nation is widespreading and unformed, tangled in raw freedom and archaic conventionalities. Our poetry, now responding to and now reacting from our national life, tends to be rather banal, or rather esoteric—in either case, thin. Mr. Frost's work is notably free from that double and wasting tendency. His own ambiguity is vital: it comes from artistic integrity in rare union with fluent sympathy. His poetic humour is on the highway toward the richer American poetry of the future, if that is to be.

G. R. Elliott. *VQR*. July, 1925. pp. 214–5

He is a poet of the customary in man and nature, not the exploiter of the remarkably arresting and wonderful. Nor does his feeling for decorous proportion require argument beyond saying that he does not commit the mistake of the neo-classicists who have been properly accused by Professor Babbitt of confusing the language of the nobility with the nobility of language. Frost's people are humble, but they speak a language and utter feelings appropriate to them: they are restrained by conventions which are inherently worthy of respect, and the result is decorum in the true sense.

Gorham B. Munson. *Robert Frost* (Doran). 1927.
pp. 108–9

Robert Frost is as near English "as makes no difference." So English is he, in fact, that if one had to name the poet whose work is most like his, one would inevitably instance that most English of all English poets, the late Edward Thomas. The likeness between their poetry is quite extraordinary; and it is no wonder that Frost counted Thomas among his best friends and dedicated to his memory the *Selected Poems* which appeared in America some two years ago. Both loved the same things in life; and (by one of those miracles that unite men over seas and centuries) both found much the same way of expressing in poetry their delight.

C. Henry Warren. *BkmL.* Jan., 1931. p. 242

Upon the eve of Robinson's fame, some spoke of Frost in the same breath; and now Robinson is dead, Frost is our leading poet. His fame shall rest upon a firmer basis. Robinson, like MacLeish, can be judged not so much by his work as by why people like it, whereas with Frost the audience counts less than the good work. He has never been able to be as boring as Robinson's most boring; his best is beyond Robinson's best.

John Wheelwright. *Poetry.* Oct., 1936. pp. 45–6

Mr. Frost's poetry was first awarded critical approval because it was thought to be in revolt against something at a time when poetry must be in revolt. . . . Poetry must now not be anything like Imagism and must not even revolt, but must be the kind of poetry that Mr. Pound or, more purely and quintessentially, Mr. Eliot wrote. . . . It is quite true that Frost does not write like Eliot, Pound, Auden, or Spender. Fools may conclude that he is therefore a bad or an unimportant poet, but intelligent people look at the poetry he has written. When you do that, unless your nerves are sealed with wax, you immediately and overwhelmingly perceive that it is the work of an individual and integrated poet, a poet who is like no one else, a major poet not only in regard to this age but in regard to our whole literature, a great American poet.

Bernard DeVoto. *SR.* Jan. 1, 1938. pp. 4, 14

If he does not strike far inward, neither does he follow the great American tradition (extending from Whitman through Dos Passos) of standing on a height to observe the panorama of nature and society. Let us say that he is a poet neither of the mountains nor of the woods, although he lives among both, but rather of the hill pastures, the intervales, the dooryard in autumn with the leaves swirling, the closed house shaking in the winter storms (and who else has described these scenes more accurately, in more lasting colors?). In the same way, he is not the poet of New England in its great days, or in its late-nineteenth-century decline (except in some of his earlier poems); he is rather a poet who celebrates the diminished but prosperous and self-respecting New England of the tourist home and the antique shop in the abandoned gristmill. And the praise heaped on Frost in recent years is somehow connected in one's mind with the search for ancestors and authentic old furniture.

Malcolm Cowley. *NR*. Sept. 18, 1944. pp. 346–7

Frost . . . may be described as a good poet in so far as he may be said to exist, but a dangerous influence in so far as his existence is incomplete. He is in no sense a great poet, but he is at times a distinguished and valuable poet. . . . He is the nearest thing we have to a poet laureate, a national poet; and this fact is evidence of the community of thought and feeling between Frost and a very large part of the American literary public. . . . The principles which have hampered Frost's development, the principles of Emersonian and Thoreauistic Romanticism, are the principles which he has openly espoused, and they are widespread in our culture. Until we abandon them in favor of better, we are unlikely to produce many poets greater than Frost.

Yvor Winters. *SwR*. Autumn, 1948. p. 596

Creatively, there are at least three Frosts—the actual artist, the legendary public character, posed and professed, and the latent, potential poet that might have been. . . . Frost himself all through his work, more or less, offers clues as to the kind of thing he might have done, the line of a frightful and fascinating interest that he almost dared to follow. The road not taken. . . . One wishes he had been a little less fearful of evil tidings, less scared of his own desert places. One wishes he had wasted less time being sane and wholesome, and gone really all out, farther than he did beyond the boundaries of New England's quaintness into its areas of violence, madness, murder, rape, and incest. . . . It is this night side of life and nature that Frost's art has, I think, scamped reporting, and not because he did not know it; no American poet, nor Poe in his stories, has come closer to Baudelaire.

Rolfe Humphries. *Nation*. July 23, 1949. pp. 92–3

The controlled development of his talent, and the finality and grace of statement in his best poems, are of moral no less than artistic value, exemplary for all who practice this art. . . . His vein of romantic triviality and perversity is not hard to distinguish, and it may be indulged.

That stern critic, Yvor Winters, considers Frost an Emersonian and therefore untrustworthy sage; but he would probably concede that on occasion Frost has had a harder edge and eye than Emerson, more humor, and more of the fear of God. It would be going too far to think of him as a religious poet, but his work tends towards wholeness, and thus towards a catholicism of the heart.

Robert Fitzgerald. *NR*. Aug. 8, 1949. p. 18

His cheerfulness is the direct opposite of Mr. Babbitt's or even of Mr. Pickwick's. It is a Greek cheerfulness. And the apparent blandness of the Greeks was, as Nietzsche showed in his *Birth of Tragedy* the result of their having looked so deeply into life's tragic meaning that they had to protect themselves by cultivating a deliberately superficial jolliness in order to bear the unbearable. Frost's benign calm, the comic mask of a whittling rustic, is designed for gazing—without dizziness—into a tragic abyss of desperation. . . . In the case of this great New England tragic poet, the desperation is no less real for being a quiet one, as befits a master of overwhelming understatements.

Peter Viereck. *At*. Oct., 1949. p. 68

Frost is that rare thing, a complete or representative poet, and not one of the brilliant partial poets who do justice, far more than justice, to a portion of reality, and leave the rest of things forlorn. When you know Frost's poems you know surprisingly well how the world seemed to one man, and what it was to seem that way: the great Gestalt that each of us makes from himself and all that isn't himself is very clear, very complicated, very contradictory in the poetry. The grimness and awfulness and untouchable sadness of things, both in the world and in the self, have justice done to them in the poems, but no more justice than is done to the tenderness and love and delight; and everything in between is represented somewhere too, some things willingly and often and other things only as much—in Marianne Moore's delicate phrase—"as one's natural reticence will allow."

Randall Jarrell. *KR*. Autumn, 1952. pp. 560–1

Mirth has always been attendant on his moral. He will not, for earnest half-truths, stay completely reverent. He has to keep the door ajar for the other half of the truth. Even in his caperings that irk the solemn and embarrass the earnest, wisdom is usually implicit. Trifling is pertinent, though often it seems pesky, when dealing with inflated trifles. And even with God, the fear of not pleasing whom is the beginning of wisdom,

Robert Frost sets his soft hat on one side of his head and looks Him in the eye.

Sidney Cox. *A Swinger of Birches* (NYU). 1957.
pp. 2–3

I think of Robert Frost as a terrifying poet. Call him, if it makes things any easier, a tragic poet, but it might be useful every now and then to come out from under the shelter of that literary word. The universe that he conceives is a terrifying universe. . . . But the *people,* it will be objected, the *people* who inhabit this possibly terrifying universe! About them there is nothing that can terrify; surely the people in Mr. Frost's poems can only reassure us by their integrity and solidity. . . . They affirm *this* of themselves: that they are what they are, that this is their truth, and that if the truth be bare, as truth often is, it is far better than a lie. For me the process by which they arrive at that truth is always terrifying. The manifest America of Mr. Frost's poems may be pastoral; the actual America is tragic.

Lionel Trilling. *PR*. Summer, 1959. pp. 451–2

The conditions which circumscribe Frost's poems are those of a world not yet dominated by urban, industrialized, bureaucratized culture—the very world which, seeing its inevitable coming, Emerson and his kind strove to confront and save for man before it would be too late. Frost glances at this world, only to turn to a one he knows better. In that world the proper life style—which in turn generates the literary style—is that of Frost's characteristic protagonists: individuals who again and again are made to face up to the fact of their individualism as such; who can believe that a community is no more than the sum of the individuals who make it up; who are situated so as to have only a dim sense, even that resisted mightily, of the transformations which the individual might have to undergo if he is to live fully in the modern world and still retain his identity as an individual. But, of course, Frost's protagonists refuse to live fully in the modern world and will have little or nothing to do with such transformations. Frost's work is in the end a series of expressions of that refusal and assessments of its cost.

Roy Harvey Pearce. *KR*. Spring, 1961. pp. 261–2

Let the School System make a whited saint of Mr. Frost if it must; and as, alas, it will. The man himself remains an *hombre*. If he is half radiance he is also half brimstone, and praise be. His best poems will endure precisely because they are terrible—and holy. All primal fire is terrible—and holy. Mr. Frost could climb to heaven and hear the angels call him brother—*frater*, they would probably say—but he could as well climb

Vesuvius and equally hear every rumble under his feet call out to him. The darkness in his poems is as profound as the light in them is long. They are terrible because they are from life at a depth into which we cannot look unshaken.

John Ciardi. *SR*. March 24, 1962. pp. 15–6

A question arises from Frost's *Collected Poems* . . . : what are the possibilities for a poetry based upon nothing more than a shared sense of human fact? Is this enough? Will it serve instead of those other "certainties" which are, for many readers, insecure?

Frost would seem to answer "Yes." Yeats relied on nervous improvisations or religious patterns hired for the occasion of the poem. . . . Frost committed himself to the common ground he *knew* existed between himself and his putative reader. He knew that if he were to tell a pathetic story in a few common words whose weightings were part of our blood, we would respond feelingly. And that was something. Frost has spent a lifetime seeing how much he could say on those terms. He is the poet most devoted to bare human gesture.

Denis Donoghue. *YR*. Winter, 1963. p. 216

Both poets [Frost and Wallace Stevens] accept the physical world of positive, scientific, fact; both put aside comforting myths that deny the evidence of the senses, and for both truth is many observable truths. But both have experienced transforming moments in which the imagination creates undeniable reality of another sort. Both Frost and Stevens have given up Romantic metaphysics, but they are engaged in a sophisticated balancing act of enjoying the Romantic dream while 'having just escaped from the truth,' from 'the doctrine of this landscape.' (Stevens: 'The Latest Freed Man.') The poems also offer a clear index to the difference between the two writers, in that Frost concludes with 'parts of a world' as 'measured by eye'; Stevens, with a 'supreme fiction.' Stevens being closer to the Romantics leaves us in the 'strange world' of illusion (though we know from the start that it is one), and Frost takes us out of it (though we know what the illusion is like).

(K)                          Reuben Brower. *The Poetry of Robert Frost*
(Oxford). 1963. pp. 94–5

And here, in the abrasive play among the poems, there emerges, at least as a personal solution, a rather whimsical figure, the "literate farmer." (I take the term from the poem "The Literate Farmer and the Planet Venus.") This figure reveals himself at times as the clown, at times as the grotesque sage ("the tramp astrologer"), but eventually we see him as the fallible yet fulfilled man in "West Running Brook." His essential quality is that of a kinetic mind always in motion: the humorist yielding to fantasist in turn yielding to thinker. He is always in part the bright schoolboy—some patient soul ought to count Frost's references to school-boys, college boys—the mercurial tease, the enquirer. The most notable facet of the personality, however, is the erudition, all the outdoor table talk, which seems at first glance at odds with probability. . . . when the literate farmer sends out his thought like a sonic signal and awaits the echo, he waits for the abstract to touch the enduring surface of nature—and to return; to return transformed. And this transformation buys a lyric intensity which perhaps diminishes the claims of realism or appropriate-ness. But the literate farmer has a stronger claim for acceptability. There is, after all, a tradition of the thoughtful country man in New England.

(K)                      Radcliffe Squires. *The Major Themes of Robert Frost*
(Michigan). 1963. pp. 67–8

Even in meter his departures from strict iambic pentameter go as far as Shakespeare's latest experiments and anticipate the relaxed verse-approximations of Eliot's plays. Though he believed that formal meter was the discipline most essential to poetry, he knew that language keeps breaking out of all attempts to order it, and he wanted to preserve this freedom even as he brought it to form. His characteristic rhythms are produced by a tug-of-war between the absolute demands of meter and the flexible patterns of speech, with an edge of victory to the latter.

(K)                      Charles R. Anderson. *SR*. Feb. 23, 1963. p. 19

In some quarters, even his acknowledged masterpieces have been tried and found wanting, at least in the light of his apparent self-indulgence in the role of national cultural hero. Yet the facts, the poetic facts, speak for themselves; the poems must be left to survive the spate of memoirs, com-mentary, letters, juvenilia, and appreciations, that has already swelled to something more than a spring freshet. Much of this material will prove valuable in the long run; but it will take a scholar of extraordinary gifts—one who is an acute reader of the poetry as well as a disinterested observer of the 20th century literary scene—to separate the trivia from the essen-tials, the useless from the useful. And because the trivial is sometimes use-ful, his task will be all the more difficult.

(K)                      Samuel French Morse. *Poetry*. July, 1964. p. 254

If these letters are used initially to clarify discrepancies between the mythic and actual Robert Frost, as is hoped, certain warnings are in order lest the general public jump from one false extreme of assumption to another. Those who knew the poet largely from his poetry and his public appearances—and who take pleasure in remembering the evidence of his affirmations, encouragements, cherishings, tenderness, humor, wit, playfulness, and joviality—may not be prepared to see how often his private correspondence reveals periods of gloom, jealousies, obsessive resentments, sulking, displays of temper, nervous rages, and vindictive retaliations. Partly because he lacked confidence in himself, he suspected the presence of enemies everywhere, and he frequently indulged his passion for hurting even those he loved. "I'm a mere selfish artist most of the time," he admitted to one correspondent.

All of his self-deprecations complicate rather than simplify the problem of understanding Robert Frost. They suggest, through a mingling of frankness and guilt, his own constant awareness of the tension between his commitments as an artist and as a human being. If the artist in him demanded priority, as it almost always did, he never forgot that he had made two different kinds of promises and that he wanted to keep them both.

(K)                    Lawrance Thompson. Introduction to *The Selected Letters of Robert Frost* (Holt). 1965. pp. viii–ix

The aim in Frost's poetry is to develop a human act which has meaning in terms of the world man really lives in. The first step is to find out what kind of world it really is. The world Frost discovers, and he depicts the making of this discovery in many nature lyrics, is not friendly to man's great hopes, dreams and needs. But to despair in it is *not* the human answer to the grim world discovered. . . .

On the other hand, grandiose, sustained or programmatic actions are not the answer either, for this is a world in which such actions can be initiated only through blindness or willful self-deception, neither of which states accords with Frost's picture of "mind." What is possible is the small gesture, which, however, must be unremittingly repeated. The human life is not heroic in an epic sense. It is a life of staying.

This solution is certainly not transcendental. This is not a life in conformity with nature, nor a life striving to be merged into nature. On the contrary, it is rather an endless battle against the decaying flux which nature, lacking mind, is continually victim to and therefore continually illustrates. Because the flux endures as long as existence endures, the battle against it is endless.

(K)                    Nina Baym. *AmQ*. Winter, 1965. pp. 722–3

Frost's innate Emersonianism never showed as plainly as when he observed Emerson's directive to "feel all confidence in himself, and never to defer to the popular cry." When some act of government, or fashion, or personality was being cried up by half the populace and cried down by the rest, and the impression was left that all history depended upon the moment, the resultant crisis provided the test of the self-reliant individual. "Let him not quit his belief," advised Emerson, "That a popgun is a popgun, though the ancient and honorable of the earth affirm it to be the crack of doom." Thus it was for Frost with the Imagism of the World War I years, the art-for-art's sake of the 1920's, the social consciousness of the 1930's, the superpatriotism of the forties. In none of these seductive pools did Frost more than wet his toes.

(K)                    Philip L. Gerber. *Robert Frost* (Twayne). 1966.

p. 69

See *Complete Poems, In the Clearing; Selected Letters; Selected Prose.*


# FUCHS, DANIEL (1909–    )

Though he never quite succeeds, it is impossible to read *Summer in Williamsburg* without being aware of its sincerity, its vitality and—in a way—its importance. . . . No comment on *Summer in Williamsburg* would be complete without mention of Mr. Fuchs's style, which is extremely competent and incisive. . . . His talent lies chiefly in the direction of dialogue. . . . He has captured the very cadence, the accent and inflection, of a local idiom.

Margaret Wallace. *NYT*. Nov. 18, 1934. p. 6


With this second novel [*Homage to Blenholt*] Mr. Fuchs performs a rare feat in switching from the naturalistic approach of his first book *(Summer in Williamsburg)* to a racy, caricaturing manner, appealing strongly to the sense of humor. What is still more unusual, he does not direct his satire against Babbitts or intellectuals—the customary targets for satire in America—but sticks to the locale he knows best, that drab Jewish section in Brooklyn known as Williamsburg. . . . His manner is fundamentally his own. Its main features may be traced to a keen ear for picking up the rich idiomatic language of his characters, an intense dislike (which sometimes gets out of hand) for the social system that smothers them, and an almost morbid sensitiveness to the folly of human beings influenced by a tabloid-movies atmosphere.

Jerre Mangione. *NR*. April 1, 1936. pp. 229–30


His novels, of which *Low Company* is the third, are as inclusive as they are terse and clever. Their humor is inimitably Jewish, but few other novelists have conveyed it so unobtrusively, and for the same purpose. It is a humor that consists largely of the homely metaphors that abound in Yiddish, but which sound uproarious only when heard in literal translation. Too many Jewish writers have stopped at that, and as a result their work reads like mimicry. In Mr. Fuchs' hands the humor retains its extravagance and its crude vitality, but it is a humor that is pointed to indicate the desperation that so often lies behind it.

Writing in that spirit, Mr. Fuchs has proved again and again that the ghetto was never destroyed; it was merely moved, piece by piece, from the East Side to Williamsburg and Brownsville and the Bronx.

Alfred Kazin. *NYHT*. Feb. 14, 1937. p. 8

*Low Company* is the story of petty lives, of petty tragedies. Fuchs hates all his characters. When he writes with pity, it is a merciless, steely, stiletto kind of pity. A few times we are appalled at what happens to the characters and are just about to lavish our sympathy, when the author pours his icy water over every living thing in Neptune Beach. And here we come to the debit side of Fuchs' artistry. Fuchs, at this stage of his writing, has found no place to lay down his burden. His hate is a slow, burning, consuming hate, and he vents it ruthlessly. The superb humor, the comical situations magnificently described in *Low Company*, are actually merciless jabs at his characters. There have been comments that Fuchs, because of his penchant for grotesquerie, stems from Charles Dickens. Nothing, however, could be further from the truth. While Dickens hated many of his characters, he had a great love and compassion for his heroes and heroines. Dickens was a confirmed believer in the happy ending. Fuchs is a child of sorrow.

Albert Halper. *NR*. Feb. 24, 1937. p. 90

Sympathy is a dominant note in Fuchs' writing. He has a keen eye, an excellent ear for the speech of his characters, a quick perception of the grotesque, the whimsical, the pathetic, the tragic in crowded urban life. And underlying these capacities is a genuine respect for his characters, for the human animal. . . .

The present novel [*Low Company*], like its predecessors, is constructed almost like a drama. There is considerable dependence on dialogue, there is a fairly strict effort to obtain objectivity, and an ingenious sense of plot and construction is displayed. In fact, the author's gift for construction threatens to become a defect. The concluding pages of *Low Company* unite and complete the novel's many stories in such a fashion that one almost sees the seams and stitchings. Yet I know of few novelists in America today of Fuchs's age who possess his natural talent and energy or his sense of life.

James T. Farrell. *Nation*. Feb. 27, 1937. p. 244

The first of Daniel Fuchs' novels opens with a "hard mad" summer storm which sends the inhabitants of Williamsburg scurrying for shelter. The last one ends in a steamy heat that promises to bring business at last to the desperate concessionaires of Neptune Beach. In between is a richly knowing account of sudden changes in psychic weather, destructive twisters, brief, illusory periods of sunlight, in the lives of some yearning, trapped, angry, wrong-headed, immensely vocal individuals. They are mostly from Brooklyn, mostly Jews. Mr. Fuchs treats them with satiric relish and yet with a deep sense of identification. . . . Except for the movies and radio programs they name, these novels are not dated in the least. The author deals with the conditions of bad housing, corruption, widespread dishonesty and racketeering that preoccupy New Yorkers today and he deals with them—though his novels are a quarter of a century old—in a way that is fresh and revealing as literature.

Robert Gorham Davis. NYT. Sept. 10, 1961. p. 5

Very few writers are able to evoke anything out of the environment that depressed them as they grew. Fuchs has been compared to James T. Farrell, but it is clear now that he had greater gifts than Farrell, and did much more than transcribe. His dialogue, from the very beginning, had a flavor of its own; while seemingly realistic it is as artful as Hemingway's or O'Hara's, and read aloud it usually makes one laugh. In this book, as in the others, there are the sensitive and the brutal; they encounter and are astonished by each other, and Fuchs judges not, for they are all human.

Reading the novels again, I was fearful that they might not hold up, but time has neither dimmed nor darkened them, and I suspect they are more readable and compelling today, if only because the problems are different now, and we can meet all of the author's wonderful people simply as people and not as representatives of a condition. They are fixed now, the nice ones, the evil ones, the old, the young, as a wonderful tapestry of "low life" captured with unsentimental warmth.

Hollis Alpert. SR. Sept. 23, 1961. p. 18

See <i>Three Novels</i>.

# BIBLIOGRAPHIES

The bibliographies list the major books and plays of the authors included in this work; the dates are of first publication or, in the case of plays, usually of first production. Pamphlets, one-act plays, juveniles, contributions to multi-authored collections, and other minor publications are included only selectively. Stories and articles in periodicals are not included.

## GENRE ABBREVIATIONS

| | | | |
|---|---|---|---|
| a | autobiography | n | novel |
| b | biography | p | poetry |
| c | criticism | pd | poetic drama |
| d | drama | r | reminiscence |
| e | essay | rd | radio drama |
| h | history | s | short stories |
| j | journalism | sk | sketches |
| m | memoir | t | travel or topography |
| misc | miscellany | tr | translation |

## HENRY ADAMS
1838–1918

(with Charles F. Adams) *Chapters of Erie and Other Essays*, 1871; *The Administration—A Radical Indictment!* 1872 (e); *Syllabus. History II, Political History of Europe from the Tenth to the Fifteenth Century,* 1874; (editor and contributor) *Essays in Anglo-Saxon Law,* 1876; *The Life of Albert Gallatin,* 1879 (b); *Democracy,* 1880 (n); *John Randolph,* 1882 (b); *Esther* [pseud. Frances Snow Compton], 1884 (n); *History of the United States of America During the First Administration of Thomas Jefferson,* 1884; *History of the United States of America During the Second Administration of Thomas Jefferson,* 1885; *History of the United States of America During the First Administration of James Madison,* 1888; *History of the United States of America During the First Administration of Thomas Jefferson,* 1888 (first trade edition, corrected and revised); *History of the United States of America During the Second Administration of Thomas Jefferson,* 1890 (first trade edition, corrected and revised); *History of the United States of America During the First Administration of James Madison,* 1890 (corrected and revised); *History of the United States of America During the Second Administration of James Madison,* 1891; *Historical Essays,* 1891; *History of the United States of America,* 1891-92 (English edition); *Memoirs of Maran Taaroa Last Queen of Tahiti,* 1893; *Memoirs of Arii Taimai E Marama of Eimeo Terürere of Tooraai Terünui of Tahiti,* 1901 (by Tauraatua I Amo, Tahitian adoptive name of Henry Adams); *Mont-Saint-Michel and Chartres,* 1904 (h) (slightly revised, 1912); *The Education of Henry Adams,* 1907 (a) (slightly revised, 1918); *A Letter to American Teachers of History,* 1910 (e); *The Life of George Cabot Lodge,* 1911 (b); *The Degradation of the Democratic Dogma,* 1919 (e); *Letters to a Niece and Prayer to the Virgin of Chartres,* 1920; *A Cycle of Adams Letters, 1861–1865,* 1920; *Letters of Henry Adams, 1858–1891,* 1930; *Henry Adams and His Friends,* 1947 (letters); *Great Secession Winter of 1860–61, and Other Essays,* 1958; *A Henry Adams Reader,* 1960 (misc)


## LEONIE ADAMS
1899–

*Those Not Elect,* 1925 (p); *High Falcon and Other Poems,* 1929; *This Measure,* 1933 (p); (with others) *Lyrics of Francois Villon,* 1933 (tr); *Poems: A Selection,* 1954

## JAMES AGEE
### 1909–1955

*Permit Me Voyage*, 1934 (p); *Let Us Now Praise Famous Men*, 1941 (t); *The Morning Watch*, 1954 (n); *A Death in the Family*, 1957 (n); *Agee on Film*, Vol. One, 1958 (c); *Agee on Film*, Vol. Two, 1960 (d); *Letters of James Agee to Father Flye*, 1962; *The Collected Poems*, 1968


## CONRAD AIKEN
### 1889–

*Earth Triumphant and Other Tales in Verse*, 1914; *The Jig of Forslin*, 1916 (p); *Turns and Monies and Other Tales in Verse*, 1916; *Nocturne of Remembered Spring*, 1917 (p); *The Charnel Rose, Senlin: A Biography, and Other Poems*, 1918; *Scepticisms*, 1919 (c); *The House of Dust*, 1920 (p); *Punch: The Immortal Liar*, 1921 (p); *Priapus and the Pool*, 1922 (p); *The Pilgrimage of Festus*, 1923 (p); *Priapus and the Pool and Other Poems*, 1925; *Senlin: A Biography*, 1925 (p); *Bring! Bring!* 1925 (s); *Blue Voyage*, 1927 (n); *Costumes by Eros*, 1928 (s) *Prelude*, 1929 (p); *Selected Poems*, 1929; *John Deth, A Metaphysical Legend, and Other Poems*, 1930; *Gehenna*, 1930 (e); *The Coming Forth by Day of Osiris Jones*, 1931 (p); *Preludes for Memnon*, 1931 (p); *And in the Hanging Gardens . . .* , 1933 (p); *Great Circle*, 1933 (n); *Landscape West of Eden*, 1934 (p); *Among the Lost People*, 1934 (s); *King Coffin*, 1935 (n); *Time in the Rock*, 1936 (p); *A Heart for the Gods of Mexico*, 1939 (n); *And in the Human Heart*, 1940 (p); *Conversation: or, Pilgrims' Progress*, 1940 (n); *Brownstone Eclogues*, 1942 (p); *The Soldier*, 1944 (p); *The Kid*, 1947 (p); *The Divine Pilgrim*, 1949 (p); *Skylight One*, 1950 (p); *Short Stories*, 1950; *Wake 11*, 1952 (p); *Ushant*, 1952 (a); *Collected Poems*, 1953; *A Letter from Li Po*, 1955 (p); *The Fluteplayer*, 1956 (p); *Mr. Arcularis*, 1957 (d); *A Reviewer's ABC*, 1958 (c) (published as *Collected Essays*, 1968); *Sheepfold Hill*, 1958 (p); *Collected Short Stories*, 1960; *Selected Poems*, 1961; *The Morning Song of Lord Zero; Poems Old and New*, 1963; *Collected Novels*, 1964; *A Seizure of Limericks*, 1964; *Cats and Bats and Things with Wings*, 1965 (p)


## EDWARD ALBEE
### 1928–

*The Zoo Story*, 1958 (d); *The Death of Bessie Smith*, 1959 (d); *The Sandbox*, 1959 (d); *The American Dream*, 1960 (d); (with James Hinton, Jr.) *Bartleby*, 1961 (d); *Who's Afraid of Virginia Woolf?*, 1962 (d); *The Ballad of the Sad Cafe,* 1963 (d); *Tiny Alice,* 1964 (d); *Malcolm,* 1965 (d); *A Delicate Balance,* 1966 (d); *Everything in the Garden,* 1967 (d); *Box,* 1968 (d); *Quotations from Chairman Mao Tse-tung,* 1968 (d)

## WILLIAM ALFRED
1923–

*Agamemnon,* 1954 (pd); *Hogan's Goat,* 1965 (d)

## NELSON ALGREN
1909–

*Somebody in Boots,* 1935 (n); *Never Come Morning,* 1942 (n); *The Neon Wilderness,* 1947 (s); *The Man with the Golden Arm,* 1949 (n); *Chicago: City on the Make,* 1951 (t) (new edition, 1968); *A Walk on the Wild Side,* 1956 (n); *Who Lost an American?* 1963 (t); *Conversations,* 1964; *Notes from a Sea Diary,* 1965 (m)

## MAXWELL ANDERSON
1888–1959

*White Desert,* 1923 (d); (with Laurence Stallings) *What Price Glory,* 1924 (d); *You Who Have Dreams,* 1925 (p); (with Laurence Stallings) *First Flight,* 1925 (d); *Outside Looking In,* 1925 (d); *The Buccaneer,* 1925 (d); *Three American Plays (What Price Glory, First Flight, The Buccaneer),* 1926; *Sea-Wife,* 1926 (d); *Saturday's Children,* 1927 (d); (with Harold Hickerson) *Gods of the Lightning,* 1928 (d); *Gypsy,* 1929 (d); *Elizabeth the Queen,* 1930 (pd); *Night Over Taos,* 1932 (pd); *Both Your Houses,* 1933 (d); *Mary of Scotland,* 1933 (pd); *Valley Forge,* 1934 (pd); *Winterset,* 1935 (pd); *The Masque of Kings,* 1936 (pd); *The Wingless Victory,* 1936 (pd); *High Tor,* 1937 (pd); *The Star-Wagon,* 1937 (d); *The Feast of Ortolans,* 1938 (pd); *Knickerbocker Holiday,* 1938 (d, lyrics); *The Essence of Tragedy,* 1939 (e); *Key Largo,* 1939 (pd); *Eleven Verse Plays,* 1940; *Journey to Jerusalem,* 1940 (pd); *Candle in the Wind,* 1941 (d); *The Eve of St. Mark,* 1942 (d); *Storm Operation,* 1944 (d); *Truckline Cafe,* 1946 (d); *Joan of Lorraine,* 1947 (d) (also published as *Joan of Arc,* 1948); *Anne of the Thousand Days,* 1948 (pd); *Lost in the Stars,* 1950 (d, lyrics); *Barefoot in Athens,* 1951 (d); *The Bad Seed,* 1955 (d)

## ROBERT ANDERSON
1917–

*Come Marching Home,* 1945 (d); *Dark Horses,* 1951 (d); *The Eden Rose,* 1952 (d); *Love Revisited,* 1952 (d); *All Summer Long,* 1952 (d);

*Tea and Sympathy*, 1953 (d); *Silent Night, Lonely Night*, 1959 (d); *The Days Between*, 1965 (d); *You Know I Can't Hear You When The Water's Running*, 1967 (d); *I Never Sang for My Father*, 1968 (d)

## SHERWOOD ANDERSON
### 1876–1941

*Windy McPherson's Son*, 1916 (n); *Marching Men*, 1917 (n); *Mid-American Chants*, 1918 (p); *Winesburg, Ohio*, 1919 (s); *Poor White*, 1920 (n); *The Triumph of the Egg*, 1921 (s); *Many Marriages*, 1923 (n); *Horses and Men*, 1923 (s); *A Story Teller's Story*, 1924 (a); *Dark Laughter*, 1925 (n); *The Modern Writer*, 1925 (c); *Sherwood Anderson's Notebook*, 1926 (misc); *Tar, A Midwest Childhood*, 1926 (n); *A New Testament*, 1927 (p); *Hello Towns!* 1929 (e); *Nearer The Grass Roots*, 1929 (t); *The American County Fair*, 1930 (e); *Perhaps Women*, 1931 (e); *Beyond Desire*, 1932 (n); *Death in the Woods*, 1933 (s); *No Swank*, 1934 (e); *Puzzled America*, 1935 (e); *Kit Brandon*, 1936 (n); *Plays, Winesburg and Others*, 1937; *Home Town*, 1940 (t); *Memoirs*, 1942; *The Sherwood Anderson Reader*, 1948; *The Portable Sherwood Anderson*, 1949; *Letters of Sherwood Anderson*, 1953; *Return to Winesburg*, 1967 (misc, j)

## LOUIS AUCHINCLOSS
### 1917–

*The Indifferent Children* (pseud. Andrew Lee), 1947 (n); *The Injustice Collectors*, 1950 (s); *Sybil*, 1952 (n); *A Law for the Lion*, 1953 (n); *The Romantic Egoists*, 1954 (s); *The Great World and Timothy Colt*, 1956 (n); *Venus in Sparta*, 1958 (n); *Pursuit of the Prodigal*, 1959 (n); *The House of Five Talents*, 1960 (n); *Reflections of a Jacobite*, 1961 (c); *Portrait in Brownstone*, 1962 (n); *Powers of Attorney*, 1963 (s); *The Rector of Justin*, 1964 (n); *Pioneers and Caretakers*, 1965 (c); *The Embezzler*, 1966 (n); *Tales of Manhattan*, 1967 (s); *A World of Profit*, 1968 (n)

## W. H. AUDEN
### 1907–

*Poems*, 1930 (revised 1932); *The Orators*, 1932 (e, p); *The Dance of Death*, 1933 (p); (with Christopher Isherwood) *The Dog Beneath the Skin*, 1935 (d); *Look, Stranger!* 1936 (p); (with Louis MacNeice) *Letter from Iceland*, 1937 (p, e); *Spain*, 1937 (p); (with Christopher Isherwood) *On the Frontier*, 1938 (d); *Selected Poems*, 1938; *Ballad* of Heroes (words for Benjamin Britten's music), 1939; (with Christopher Isherwood) *Journey to a War*, 1939 (p, e); *Some Poems*, 1940; *Another Time*, 1940 (p); *New Year Letter*, 1941 (p) (American edition, *The Double Man*); *Hymn to St. Cecilia* (words for Benjamin Britten's music), 1942; *For the Time Being* (including *The Sea and the Mirror*), 1945 (p); *Collected Poems*, 1945; *The Dyer's Hand*, 1948 (e); *The Age of Anxiety*, 1948 (p); *Collected Shorter Poems, 1930–1944*, 1950; *The Enchaféd Flood*, 1951 (c); (with Chester Kallman) *The Rake's Progress*, 1951 (libretto); *Nones*, 1951 (p); *Delia*, 1953 (libretto); *Mountains*, 1954 (p); *The Shield of Achilles*, 1955 (p); *The Old Man's Road*, 1956 (p); *Making, Knowing and Judging*, 1956 (e); (with Chester Kallman) *The Magic Flute*, 1957 (libretto, tr); *Selected Poetry*, 1958; *Daniel* (verse narrative for the 13th century play), 1958; *W. H. Auden: A Selection by the Author*, 1958 (p); *Homage to Clio*, 1960 (p, c); *Five Poems for Music*, 1960; *Elegy for Young Lovers*, 1961 (libretto); *The Dyer's Hand*, revised edition, 1963 (e); *About the House*, 1965 (p); *Selected Shorter Poems, 1927–1957*, 1968

## GEORGE AXELROD
1922–

Beggar's Choice, 1947 (n) (published in 1951 as *Hobson's Choice*); (with others) *Small Wonder*, 1948 (sk); *Blackmailer*, 1952 (n); *The Seven Year Itch*, 1952 (d); *Will Success Spoil Rock Hunter?* 1955 (d); *Goodbye Charlie*, 1959 (d)

## IRVING BABBITT
1865–1933

Literature and the American College, 1908 (e); *The New Laokoon*, 1910 (e); *The Masters of Modern French Criticism*, 1912 (e); *Rousseau and Romanticism*, 1919 (e); *Democracy and Leadership*, 1924 (e); *French Literature*, 1928 (e); *On Being Creative and Other Essays*, 1932; *The Dhammapada*, 1936 (tr); *Spanish Character and Other Essays*, 1940

## JAMES BALDWIN
1924–

Go Tell It on the Mountain, 1953 (n); *Notes of a Native Son*, 1955 (e); *Giovanni's Room*, 1956 (n); *Nobody Knows My Name*, 1961 (e); *Another Country*, 1962 (n); *The Fire Next Time*, 1963 (e); *Blues for Mister Charley*, 1964 (d); *Going to Meet the Man*, 1965 (s); *Tell Me How Long the Train's Been Gone*, 1968 (n); *The Amen Corner*, 1968 (d)

## DJUNA BARNES
1900–

A Book, 1924 (misc); Ryder, 1928 (n); Nightwood, 1936 (n); The Antiphon, 1958 (pd); Selected Works, 1962

## PHILIP BARRY
1896–1949

A Punch for Judy, 1921 (d); You and I, 1923 (d); The Youngest, 1924 (d); In a Garden, 1925 (d); White Wings, 1926 (d); John, 1927 (d); Paris Bound, 1927 (d); (with Elmer Rice) Cock Robin, 1928 (d); Holiday, 1928 (d); Hotel Universe, 1930 (d); Tomorrow and Tomorrow, 1931 (d); The Animal Kingdom, 1932 (d); The Joyous Season, 1934 (d); Bright Star, 1935 (d); Spring Dance, 1936 (d); War In Heaven, 1938 (n); The Philadelphia Story, 1939 (d); Liberty Jones, 1940 (d); Without Love, 1942 (d); Foolish Notion, 1944 (d); Second Threshold, 1951 (d)

## JOHN BARTH
1930–

The Floating Opera, 1956 (n) (revised edition, 1967); The End of the Road, 1958 (n); The Sot-Weed Factor, 1960 (n) (revised edition, 1967); Giles Goat-Boy, 1966 (n); Lost in the Funhouse, 1968 (s)

## S. N. BEHRMAN
1893–

(with Kenyon Nicholson) Bedside Manners, 1924 (d); (with Kenyon Nicholson) A Night's Work, 1926 (d); The Second Man, 1927 (d); Meteor, 1930 (d); Brief Moment, 1931 (d); Biography, 1933 (d); Three Plays (Serena Blandish, Meteor, The Second Man), 1934; Rain from Heaven, 1935 (d); End of Summer, 1936 (d); Wine of Choice, 1938 (d); Amphitryon 38, 1938 (d, tr); No Time for Comedy, 1939 (d); The Talley Method, 1941 (d); The Mechanical Heart, 1941 (d); The Pirate, 1943 (d); Jacobowsky and the Colonel, 1944 (d, tr); Dunnigan's Daughter, 1946 (d); I Know My Love, 1952 (d, tr); Jane, 1952 (d); Duveen, 1952 (b); The Worcester Account, 1954 (a); Fanny, 1955 (d, tr); The Cold Wind and the Warm, 1959 (d); Portrait of Max, 1960 (b); Lord Pengo, 1963 (d); But for Whom Charlie, 1964 (d); The Suspended Drawing Room, 1965 (t); The Burning Glass, 1968 (n)

## DAVID BELASCO
1859–1931

*The Creole,* 1876 (d); *Olivia,* 1878 (d); (with James A. Herne) *Within an Inch of His Life,* 1879 (d); *Drink,* 1879 (d); (with James A. Herne) *Hearts of Oak,* 1879 (d); *Paul Arniff, or, The Love of a Serf,* 1880 (d); *The Eviction,* 1881 (d); *La Belle Russe,* 1881 (d); *The Stranglers of Paris,* 1881 (d); *The Lone Pine,* 1881? (d); (with Peter Robinson) *The Curse of Cain,* 1882 (d); *American Born,* 1882 (d); *May Blossom,* 1882 (d); *Valerie,* 1886 (d); *The Highest Bidder,* 1887 (d); (with Clay M. Greene) *Pawn Ticket No. 210,* 1887 (d); (with Henry C. DeMille) *The Wife,* 1887 (d); (with Henry C. DeMille) *Lord Chumley,* 1888 (d); (with Henry C. DeMille) *The Charity Ball,* 1889 (d); (with Henry C. DeMille) *Men and Women,* 1890 (d); *Miss Helyett,* 1891 (d); (with Franklyn Fyles) *The Girl I Left Behind Me,* 1893 (d); *The Younger Son,* 1893 (d); *The Heart of Maryland,* 1895 (d); (with Clay M. Greene) *Under the Polar Star,* 1896 (d); *Zaza,* 1898 (d, tr); *Naughty Anthony,* 1899 (d); (with John Luther Long) *Madame Butterfly,* 1900 (d); *DuBarry,* 1901 (d); (with John Luther Long) *The Darling of the Gods,* 1902 (d); *Sweet Kitty Bellairs,* 1903 (d); (with John Luther Long) *Adrea,* 1904 (d); *The Girl of the Golden West,* 1905 (d); (with Richard Walton Tully) *The Rose of the Rancho,* 1906 (d); (with Pauline Phelps and Marion Short) *A Grand Army Man,* 1907 (d); *The Lily,* 1909 (d, tr); *The Return of Peter Grimm,* 1911 (d); (with Alice Brady) *The Governor's Lady,* 1911 (d); *The Secret,* 1913 (d, tr); *My Life Story,* 1914 (a); (with George Scarborough) *The Son Daughter,* 1919 (d); *The Theatre Through the Stage Door,* 1919 (r); *Kiki,* 1921 (d, tr); *A Souvenir of Shakespeare's The Merchant of Venice,* as presented by David Belasco, at the Lyceum Theatre, Dec. 21, 1922, 1923; *The Comedian,* 1923 (d, tr); *Laugh, Clown, Laugh,* 1923 (d, tr); *Plays Produced under the Stage Direction of David Belasco,* 1925 (c); (with Willard Mack) *Fanny,* 1926 (d, tr); *Mimi,* 1928 (d); *Six Plays* (*Madame Butterfly, DuBarry, The Darling of the Gods, The Girl of the Golden West, The Return of Peter Grimm*), 1928; *The Heart of Maryland, and Other Plays,* 1941

## SAUL BELLOW
1915–

*Dangling Man,* 1944 (n); *The Victim,* 1947 (n); *The Adventures of Augie March,* 1953 (n); *Seize the Day,* 1956 (n, s, d); *Henderson the Rain King,* 1959 (n); *Herzog,* 1964 (n); *The Last Analysis,* 1964 (d); *Mosby's Memoirs,* 1968 (s)

## ROBERT BENCHLEY
### 1889–1945

Of All Things, 1921 (e); Love Conquers All, 1922 (e); Pluck and Luck, 1925 (e); The Early Worm, 1927 (e); 20,000 Leagues Under the Sea, or, David Copperfield, 1928 (e); The Treasurer's Report and Other Aspects of Community Singing, 1930 (e); No Poems, or, Around the World Backwards and Sideways, 1932 (e); From Bed to Worse, or Comforting Thoughts about the Bison, 1934 (e); Why Does Nobody Collect Me? 1935 (e); My Ten Years in a Quandary and How They Grew, 1936 (e); After 1903—What? 1938 (e); Inside Benchley, 1942 (e); Benchley Beside Himself, 1943 (e); Benchley—Or Else! 1947 (e); Chips Off the Old Benchley, 1949 (e); The Benchley Roundup, 1954 (e)

## STEPHEN VINCENT BENÉT
### 1898–1943

Five Men and Pompey, 1915 (p); The Drug Shop, 1917 (p); Young Adventure, 1918 (p); Heavens and Earth, 1920 (p); The Beginning of Wisdom, 1921 (n); Young People's Pride, 1922 (n); The Ballad of William Sycamore, 1923 (p); King David, 1923 (p); Jean Huguenot, 1923 (n); Tiger Joy, 1925 (p); Spanish Bayonet, 1926 (n); John Brown's Body, 1928 (p); The Barefoot Saint, 1929 (s); Ballads and Poems, 1915–1930, 1931; (with Rosemary Benét) A Book of Americans, 1933 (p); The Story of the United Press, 1933 (j); James Shore's Daughter, 1934 (n); Burning City, 1936 (p); The Magic of Poetry and the Poet's Art, 1936 (e); The Devil and Daniel Webster, 1937 (s); Thirteen O'Clock, 1937 (s); Johnny Pye and the Fool-Killer, 1938 (s); The Ballad of the Duke's Mercy, 1939 (p); Tales Before Midnight, 1939 (s); The Devil and Daniel Webster, 1939 (d); The Devil and Daniel Webster, 1939 (libretto); Nightmare at Noon, 1940 (p); Dear Adolf, 1942 (sk); A Child Is Born, 1942 (d); Selected Works, 1942; Selected Poetry and Prose, 1942; Twenty-five Short Stories, 1943; Western Star, 1943 (p); America, 1944 (h); We Stand United and Other Radio Scripts, 1945; The Last Circle, 1946 (s, p); Selected Letters, 1960

## JOHN BERRYMAN
### 1914–

Poems, 1942; The Dispossessed, 1948 (p); Stephen Crane, 1950 (b); Homage to Mistress Bradstreet, 1956 (p); 77 Dream Songs, 1964 (p); Berryman's Sonnets, 1967 (p); Short Poems, 1967 (p); His Toy, His Dream, His Rest, 1968 (p)

## AMBROSE BIERCE
### 1842–1914?

*The Fiend's Delight,* 1872 (fables and aphorisms); *Nuggets and Dust,* 1872 (fables and aphorisms); *Cobwebs from an Empty Skull,* 1874 (fables) (printed in 1893 as *Cobwebs*); *The Dance of Death,* 1877 (e); *Tales of Soldiers and Civilians,* 1891 (s); *The Monk and the Hangman's Daughter,* 1892 (n); *Black Beetles in Amber,* 1892 (p); *In the Midst of Life,* 1892 (s); *Can Such Things Be?* 1893 (s); *Fantastic Fables,* 1899 (fables); *Shapes of Clay,* 1903 (p); *The Cynic's Word Book,* 1906 (printed in 1909 as *The Devil's Dictionary*); *A Son of the Gods,* 1907 (s); *The Shadow on the Dial,* 1909 (e); *Write It Right,* 1909 (c); *Collected Works,* 1909: I *Ashes of the Beacon—The Land Beyond the Blow —For the Ahkoond—John Smith, Liberator, Bits of Autobiography;* II *In the Midst of Life;* III *Can Such Things Be?;* IV *Shapes of Clay;* V *Black Beetles in Amber;* VI *The Monk and the Hangman's Daughter— Fantastic Fables;* VII *The Devil's Dictionary;* VIII *Negligible Tales—On With the Dance—Epigrams;* IX *Tangential Views* (e); X *The Opinionator* (c); XI *Antepenultimata* (e); XII *In Motley—King of Beasts— Two Administrations—Miscellaneous; My Favorite Murder,* 1916 (s); *A Horseman in the Sky,* 1920 (s); *The Letters of Ambrose Bierce,* 1922; *Ten Tales,* 1925 (s)

## ELIZABETH BISHOP
### 1911–

*North and South,* 1946 (p); *Poems: North and South & A Cold Spring,* 1955 (p); (with the editors of Life) *Brazil,* 1962 (t); *Questions of Travel,* 1966 (p); *The Ballad of the Burglar of Babylon,* 1968 (juvenile)

## JOHN PEALE BISHOP
### 1892–1944

*Green Fruit,* 1917 (p); (with Edmund Wilson) *The Undertaker's Garland,* 1922 (s, p); *Many Thousands Gone,* 1931 (s); *Now With His Love,* 1933 (p); *Act of Darkness,* 1935 (n); *Minute Particulars,* 1935 (p); *Selected Poems,* 1941; *Collected Poems,* 1948; *Collected Essays,* 1948; *Selected Poems,* 1960

## R. P. BLACKMUR
### 1904–1965

*The Double Agent,* 1935 (e); *From Jordan's Delight,* 1937 (p); *The Expense of Greatness,* 1940 (c); *The Second World,* 1942 (p); *The Good*

*European, and Other Poems,* 1947; (with others) *Lectures in Criticism,* 1949; *Language as Gesture,* 1952 (c); *The Lion and the Honeycomb,* 1955 (e); *Anni Mirabiles, 1921–25,* 1956 (e); *Form and Value in Modern Poetry,* 1957 (c); *New Criticism in the United States,* 1959 (e); *Eleven Essays in the European Novel,* 1964; *A Primer of Ignorance* 1966 (e)

## MAXWELL BODENHEIM
### 1893–1954

*Minna and Myself,* 1918 (p); *Advice,* 1920 (p); *Introducing Irony,* 1922 (p); *Blackguard,* 1923 (n); *The Sardonic Arm,* 1923 (p); *Crazy Man,* 1924 (n); *The King of Spain,* 1924 (p); *Replenishing Jessica,* 1925 (n); *Against This Age,* 1925 (p); *Ninth Avenue,* 1926 (n); *Returning to Emotion,* 1926 (p); *Georgie May,* 1927 (n); *Sixty Seconds,* 1929 (n); *Bringing Jazz,* 1930 (p); *A Virtuous Girl,* 1930 (n); *Naked on Roller Skates,* 1931 (n); *Duke Herring,* 1931 (n); *Run, Sheep, Run,* 1932 (n); *Six A.M.,* 1932 (n); *New York Madness,* 1933 (n); *Slow Vision,* 1934 (n); *Lights in the Valley,* 1942 (n); *Selected Poems,* 1946; *My Life and Loves in Greenwich Village,* 1954 (a)

## LOUISE BOGAN
### 1897–

*Body of This Death,* 1923 (p); *Dark Summer,* 1929 (p); *The Sleeping Fury,* 1937 (p); *Poems and New Poems,* 1941; *Achievement in American Poetry, 1900–1950,* 1951 (c); *Collected Poems,* 1954; *Selected Criticism,* 1955; (with Elizabeth Roget) *The Journal of Jules Renard,* 1964 (tr); *The Blue Estuaries,* 1968 (p)

## VANCE BOURJAILY
### 1922–

*The End of My Life,* 1947 (n); *The Hound of Earth,* 1955 (n); *The Violated,* 1958 (n); *Confessions of a Spent Youth,* 1960 (n); *The Unnatural Enemy,* 1963 (e); *The Man Who Knew Kennedy,* 1967 (n)

## RANDOLPH BOURNE
### 1886–1918

*Arbitration and International Politics,* 1913 (e); *Youth and Life,* 1913 (e); *The Tradition of War,* 1914 (e); *The Gary Schools,* 1916 (j); (with others) *Towards an Enduring Peace,* 1916 (e); *Education and Living,* 1917 (e); *Untimely Papers,* 1919 (e); *The History of a Literary Radical and Other Papers,* 1920 (e); *War and the Intellectuals,* 1964 (e); *The World of Randolph Bourne,* 1965

## JANE BOWLES
1917–

*Two Serious Ladies,* 1943 (n); *In the Summer House,* 1954 (d); *Collected Works,* 1966 (n, d, s)

## PAUL BOWLES
1910–

*The Sheltering Sky,* 1949 (n); *The Delicate Prey,* 1950 (s); *Let It Come Down,* 1952 (n); *The Spider's House,* 1955 (n); *Yallah,* 1958 (t); *The Hours After Noon,* 1959 (s); *Their Heads Are Green and Their Hands Are Blue,* 1963 (t); *Up Above the World,* 1966 (n); *The Time of Friendship,* 1967 (s); *Love with a Few Hairs* (by Mohammed Mrabet), 1968 (tr); *Scenes,* 1968 (p)

## KAY BOYLE
1903–

*Wedding Day,* 1930 (s); *Plagued by the Nightingale,* 1931 (n); *Year Before Last,* 1932 (n); *Devil in the Flesh,* 1932 (tr); *The First Lover,* 1933 (s); *Gentlemen, I Address You Privately,* 1934 (n); *My Next Bride,* 1934 (n); *Death of a Man,* 1936 (n); *The White Horses of Vienna,* 1937 (s); *Glad Day,* 1938 (p); *Monday Night,* 1938 (n); *The Crazy Hunter* (with *The Bridegroom's Body* and *Big Fiddle*), 1940 (n); *Primer for Combat,* 1942 (n); *Avalanche,* 1944 (n); *Thirty Stories,* 1946; *A Frenchman Must Die,* 1946 (n); *1939,* 1948 (n); *His Human Majesty,* 1949 (n); *The Smoking Mountain,* 1951 (s); *The Seagull on the Step,* 1955 (n); *Three Short Novels* (*The Crazy Hunter, The Bridegroom's Body, Decision*), 1958; *Generation Without Farewell,* 1960 (n); *Collected Poems,* 1962; *Nothing Ever Breaks Except the Heart,* 1966 (s); Supplementary chapters to revised edition of *Being Geniuses Together, 1920–1930* (by Robert McAlmon), 1968 (r)

## CLEANTH BROOKS
1906–

(with Robert Penn Warren) *Understanding Poetry,* 1938 (c); *Modern Poetry and the Tradition,* 1939 (c); *The Well-Wrought Urn,* 1947 (c); (with Robert Penn Warren) *Modern Rhetoric,* 1950 (c); (with W. K. Wimsatt) *Literary Criticism: A Short History,* 1957 (c); *The Hidden*

*God,* 1963 (c); *William Faulkner: The Yoknapatawpha Country,* 1963 (c)


## GWENDOLYN BROOKS
### 1917–

*A Street in Bronzeville,* 1945 (p); *Annie Allen,* 1949 (p); *Maud Martha,* 1953 (n); *Bronzeville Boys and Girls,* 1956 (p); *The Bean Eaters,* 1960 (p); *Selected Poems,* 1963; *In the Mecca,* 1968 (p)


## VAN WYCK BROOKS
### 1886–1963

(with John Hall Wheelock) *Verses by Two Undergraduates,* 1905; *The Wine of the Puritans,* 1908 (e); *The Malady of the Ideal: Obermann, Maurice de Guérin and Amiel,* 1913 (e); *John Addington Symonds,* 1914 (b); *America's Coming-of-Age,* 1915 (e); *The World of H. G. Wells,* 1915 (b); *Letters and Leadership,* 1918 (e); *The Ordeal of Mark Twain,* 1920 (b); *Paul Gaugin's Intimate Journals,* 1921 (tr); *Jean Jacques Rousseau* (by Henri-Frederic Amiel) 1922, (tr); (with Eleanor Stimson Brooks) *Some Aspects of the Life of Jesus from the Psychological and Psycho-analytic Point of View* (by Georges Bergner), 1923 (tr); *Henry Thoreau, Bachelor of Nature* (by Léon Bazalgette), 1924 (tr); (with Eleanor Stimson Brooks) *Summer* (vol. II of *The Soul Enchanted,* by Romain Rolland) 1925 (tr); *The Pilgrimage of Henry James,* 1925 (b); *Emerson and Others,* 1927 (e); *Mother and Son* (by Romain Rolland) 1927 (tr); *The Road* (by André Chamson), 1929 (tr); *Roux the Bandit* (by André Chamson) 1929 (tr); *The Crime of the Just* (by André Chamson) 1930 (tr); *Sketches in Criticism,* 1932 (c); *The Life of Emerson,* 1932 (b); *Three Essays on America* (*America's Coming-of-Age, Letters and Leadership, The Literary Life in America*), 1934 (e); *The Flowering of New England, 1815–1865,* 1936 (h) (revised edition, 1946); *New England Indian Summer, 1865–1915,* 1940 (h); *Our Literature Today,* 1941 (c);*The Opinions of Oliver Allston,* 1941 (n); *The World of Washington Irving,* 1944 (h); *The Times of Melville and Whitman,* 1947 (h) (second edition, 1953); *A Chilmark Miscellany,* 1948; *The Confident Years, 1885–1915,* 1952 (h); *The Writer in America,* 1953 (c); *Scenes and Portraits,* 1954 (r); *From a Writer's Notebook,* 1955 (e); *Makers and Finders* (*The Flowering of New England, New England Indian Summer, The World of Washington Irving, The Times of Melville and Whitman, The Confident Years*), 1955 (h); *John Sloan: A Painter's Life,* 1955 (b); *Helen Keller,* 1956 (b); *Days of the Phoenix,* 1957 (r); *The Dream of Arcadia,* 1958 (h); *Howells: His Life and World,* 1959 (b); *From the Shadow of the Mountain,* 1961 (r); *Fenellosa and His*

*Circle*, 1962 (b); *An Autobiography* (*Scenes and Portraits, Days of the Phoenix, From the Shadow of the Mountain*), 1965

## PEARL S. BUCK
1892–

*East Wind: West Wind*, 1930 (n); *The Good Earth*, 1931 (n); *Sons*, 1932 (n); *The Young Revolutionist*, 1932 (n); *The First Wife and Other Stories*, 1933 (s); *All Men Are Brothers*, 1933 (tr); *The Mother*, 1934 (n); *A House Divided*, 1935 (n); *House of Earth* (*The Good Earth, Sons, A House Divided*), 1935 (n); *The Exile*, 1936 (b); *Fighting Angel*, 1936 (b); *This Proud Heart*, 1938 (n); *The Chinese Novel*, 1939 (c); *The Patriot*, 1939 (n); *Other Gods*, 1940 (n); *Today and Forever*, 1941 (s); *China Sky*, 1941 (n); *Dragon Seed*, 1942 (n); *The Promise*, 1943 (n); *Twenty-Seven Stories*, 1943 (s); *The Exile, Fighting Angel*, 1944 (b); *Portrait of a Marriage*, 1945 (n); *Pavilion of Women*, 1946 (n); *Far and Near: Stories of Japan, China and America*, 1947 (s); *Peony*, 1948 (n); (with Eslanda Goode Robeson) *American Argument*, 1949 (conversations); *Kinfolk*, 1949 (n); *The Child Who Never Grew*, 1950 (e); *God's Men*, 1951 (n); *The Hidden Flower*, 1952 (n); *Come, My Beloved*, 1953 (n); *My Several Worlds*, 1954 (a); *Imperial Woman*, 1956 (n); *Letter from Peking*, 1957 (n); *Long Love*, 1959 (n); *Command the Morning*, 1959 (n); *Fourteen Stories*, 1961 (s); *Hearts Come Home*, 1962 (s); *A Bridge for Passing*, 1962 (m); *Satan Never Sleeps*, 1962 (n); *The Living Reed*, 1963 (n); *Stories of China*, 1964; *Death in the Castle*, 1965 (n); *Children for Adoption*, 1965 (e); *People of Japan*, 1966 (t); *The Time Is Noon*, 1967 (n); *To My Daughters With Love*, 1967 (e); *The New Year*, 1968 (n)

## FREDERICK BUECHNER
1926–

*A Long Day's Dying*, 1950 (n); *The Season's Difference*, 1952 (n); *The Return of Ansel Gibbs*, 1958 (n); *The Final Beast*, 1965 (n); *The Magnificent Defeat*, 1966 (e)

## KENNETH BURKE
1897–

*The White Oxen and Other Stories*, 1924; *Death in Venice*, 1925 (tr); *Genius and Character* (by Emil Ludwig), 1927 (tr); *Saint Paul* (by Emile Baumann), 1929 (tr); *Counterstatement*, 1931 (c); *Towards a Better Life*, 1932 (n); *Permanence and Change*, 1935 (e); *Attitudes towards History*, 1937 (e); *The Philosophy of Literary Form*, 1941 (c);

*A Grammar of Motives,* 1945 (e); *A Rhetoric of Motives,* 1950 (e); *Book of Moments,* 1955 (p); *Poems 1915–1954,* 1955; *Attitudes towards History* (revised edition), 1959; *The Rhetoric of Religion,* 1961 (e); *Perspectives by Incongruity,* 1963 (e); *Collected Poems, 1915–1967,* 1967; *Language as Symbolic Action,* 1967 (c); *The Complete White Oxen,* 1968 (s); *Counterstatement* (second edition), 1968 (e); *Towards a Better Life* (second edition), 1968 (n)

## JOHN HORNE BURNS
### 1916–1953

*The Gallery,* 1947 (n); *Lucifer with a Book,* 1949 (n); *A Cry of Children,* 1952 (n)

## WILLIAM BURROUGHS
### 1914–

*Junky* (pseud. William Lee), 1953 (n); *The Naked Lunch,* 1959 (n) (American edition, *Naked Lunch,* 1962); *The Exterminator,* 1960 (n); *Minutes To Go,* 1960 (n); *The Soft Machine,* 1961 (n); *The Ticket That Exploded,* 1962 (n); *Dead Fingers Talk,* 1963 (n); *The Yage Letters* (to Allen Ginsberg), 1963; *Nova Express,* 1964 (n)

## JAMES BRANCH CABELL
### 1879–1958

*The Eagle's Shadow,* 1904 (revised edition, 1923); *The Line of Love,* 1905 (s) (revised edition, 1921); *Gallantry,* 1907 (s) (revised edition, 1922); *Branchiana,* 1907 (h); *The Cords of Vanity,* 1909 (n) (revised edition, 1920); *Chivalry,* 1909 (s) (revised edition, 1921); *Branch of Abingdon,* 1911 (h); *The Soul of Melicent,* 1913 (n) (revised edition, titled *Domnei,* 1920); *The Rivet in Grandfather's Neck,* 1915 (n); *The Majors and Their Marriages,* 1915 (h); *The Certain Hour,* 1916 (s); *From the Hidden Way,* 1916 (p) (revised edition, 1924); *The Cream of the Jest,* 1917 (n) (revised edition, 1922); *Jurgen,* 1919 (n); *Beyond Life,* 1919 (e); *The Judging of Jurgen,* 1920 (c); *Joseph Hergesheimer,* 1921 (c); *Figures of Earth,* 1921 (n); *The Jewel Merchants,* 1921 (d); *Taboo,* 1921 (sk); *The Lineage of Lichfield,* 1922 (c); *The High Place,* 1923 (n); *Straws and Prayer-Books,* 1924 (e); *The Silver Stallion,* 1926 (n); *The Music from Behind the Moon,* 1926 (s); *Something About Eve,* 1927 (n); *Works,* 1927–1930; *The White Robe,* 1928 (s); *Ballades from the Hidden Way,* 1928 (p); *The Way of Ecben,* 1929 (n); *Sonnets from Antan,* 1929 (p); *Some of Us,* 1930 (e); *Townsend of Lichfield,* 1930 (c); *Between Dawn and Sunrise* (selections), 1930; *These Restless*

*Heads*, 1932 (e); *Special Delivery*, 1933 (e); *Smirt*, 1934 (n); *Ladies and Gentlemen*, 1934 (e); *Smith*, 1935 (n); *Preface to the Past*, 1936 (c); *Smire*, 1937 (n); *The King Was in His Counting House*, 1938 (n); *Of Ellen Glasgow*, 1938 (e); *Hamlet Had an Uncle*, 1940 (n); *The First Gentleman of Virginia*, 1942 (n); (with A. J. Hanna) *The St. Johns*, 1943 (h); *There Were Two Pirates*, 1947 (n); *Let Me Lie*, 1947 (e); *The Devil's Own Dear Son*, 1949 (n); *The Witch Woman (The Music from Behind the Moon, The Way of Ecben, The White Robe)*, 1949 (n); *Quiet, Please*, 1952 (e); *As I Remember It*, 1955 (r); *Between Friends*, 1962 (letters)

## ABRAHAM CAHAN
1860–1951

*Yekl: A Tale of the New York Ghetto*, 1896 (n); *The Imported Bridegroom and Other Stories of the New York Ghetto*, 1898 (s); *The White Terror and the Red*, 1905 (n); *Raphael Naarizoch*, 1907 (n) (in Yiddish); *The Rise of David Levinsky*, 1917 (n); *Bletter von Mein Leben*, 1926–31 (a) (5 volumes, in Yiddish); (with others) *Socialism, Fascism, Communism*, 1934 (e); *Scholum Asch's Neier Veg*, 1941 (c) (in Yiddish)

## JAMES M. CAIN
1892–

*Our Government*, 1930 (sk); *The Postman Always Rings Twice*, 1934 (n); *Serenade*, 1937 (n); *Mildred Pierce*, 1941 (n); *Love's Lovely Counterfeit*, 1942 (n); *Three of a Kind (Career in C Major, The Embezzler, Double Indemnity)*, 1943 (n); *Past All Dishonor*, 1946 (n); *Butterfly*, 1947 (n); *The Moth*, 1948 (n); *Galatea*, 1953 (n); *Mignon*, 1962 (n); *The Magician's Wife*, 1965 (n)

## ERSKINE CALDWELL
1903–

*The Bastard*, 1930 (n); *Poor Fool*, 1930 (n); *In Defense of Myself*, 1930 (e); *American Earth*, 1931 (s); *Tobacco Road*, 1932 (n); *Mama's Little Girl*, 1932 (s); *God's Little Acre*, 1933 (n); *We Are The Living*, 1933 (s); *A Message for Genevieve*, 1933 (s); *Journeyman*, 1935 (n); *Kneel to the Rising Sun*, 1935 (s); *Some American People*, 1935 (e); *Tenant Farmer*, 1935 (e); *The Sacrilege of Alan Kent*, 1936 (s); (with Margaret Bourke-White) *You Have Seen Their Faces*, 1937 (e); *Southways*, 1938 (s); (with Margaret Bourke-White) *North of the Danube*, 1939 (t); *Trouble in July*, 1940 (n); *Jackpot*, 1940 (s); *Say! Is This the U.S.A.?*

1941 (t); *All-Out on the Road to Smolensk,* 1942 (j); *All Night Long,*
1942 (n); *Georgia Boy,* 1943 (n); *Tragic Ground,* 1944 (n); *Stories,*
1944; *A House in the Uplands,* 1946 (n); *The Sure Hand of God,* 1947
(n); *This Very Earth,* 1948 (n); *Place Called Estherville,* 1949 (n);
*Episode in Palmetto,* 1950 (n); *Call It Experience,* 1951 (a); *The
Humorous Side of Erskine Caldwell* (selections), 1951; *The Courting of
Susie Brown,* 1952 (s); *A Lamp for Nightfall,* 1952 (n); *Complete
Stories,* 1953; *Love and Money,* 1954 (n); *Claudelle,* 1955 (n) (American edition, *Claudelle Inglish,* 1957); *Gretta,* 1956 (n); *Gulf Coast
Stories,* 1956 (s); *Certain Women,* 1957 (n); *When You Think of Me,*
1959 (s); *Jenny By Nature,* 1961 (n); *Men and Women* (selected
stories), 1961; *Close to Home,* 1962 (n); *The Last Night of Summer,*
1963 (n); *Around About America,* 1964 (t); *In Search of Bisco,* 1965
(e); *The Deer at Our House,* 1966; *In the Shadow of the Steeple,* 1967
(n); *Miss Mamma Aimee,* 1967 (n); *Summertime Island,* 1968 (n);
*Deep South,* 1968 (m)

## TRUMAN CAPOTE
### 1924–

*Other Voices, Other Rooms,* 1948 (n); *A Tree of Night,* 1949 (s); *Local
Color,* 1950 (t); *The Grass Harp,* 1951 (n); *The Grass Harp,* 1952 (d);
*House of Flowers,* 1954 (d); *The Muses Are Heard,* 1957 (t); *Breakfast
at Tiffany's,* 1958 (n); *Observations,* 1959 (commentary on photographs
by Richard Avedon); *Selected Writings,* 1963; *A Christmas Memory,*
1966 (m); *In Cold Blood,* 1966 (j); *The Thanksgiving Visitor,* 1968 (m)

## WILLA CATHER
### 1876–1947

*April Twilights,* 1903 (p); *The Troll Garden,* 1905 (s); *Alexander's
Bridge,* 1912 (n); *O Pioneers!* 1913 (n); *The Song of the Lark,* 1915
(n); *My Ántonia,* 1918 (n); *Youth and the Bright Medusa,* 1920 (s);
*One of Ours,* 1922 (n); *April Twilights and other Poems,* 1923; *A Lost
Lady,* 1923 (n); *The Professor's House,* 1925 (n); *My Mortal Enemy,*
1926 (n); *Death Comes for the Archbishop,* 1927 (n); *The Fear That
Walks by Noonday,* 1931 (misc); *Shadows on the Rock,* 1931 (n);
*Obscure Destinies,* 1932 (s); *Lucy Gayheart,* 1935 (n); *Not Under
Forty,* 1936 (e); *The Novels and Stories of Willa Cather,* 1937–8;
*Sapphira and the Slave Girl,* 1940 (n); *The Old Beauty,* 1948 (s);
*Writings from Willa Cather's Campus Years,* 1950; *Willa Cather in
Europe: Her Own Story of the First Journey,* 1956 (t, newsletters of
1902); *Collected Short Fiction,* 1965; *April Twilights* (newly edited),
1968 (p)

## RAYMOND CHANDLER
### 1888–1959

The Big Sleep, 1939 (n); Farewell, My Lovely, 1940 (n); The High Window, 1942 (n); The Lady in the Lake, 1943 (n); Five Murderers, 1944 (s); Five Sinister Characters, 1945 (s); Finger Man and Other Stories, 1946 (s); Red Wind, 1946 (s); Spanish Blood, 1946 (s); The Little Sister, 1949 (n); The Simple Art of Murder, 1950 (e, s); The Raymond Chandler Omnibus (The Big Sleep, Farewell, My Lovely, The High Window, The Lady in the Lake), 1953 (n) (England); The Long Goodbye, 1954 (n); Playback, 1958 (n); Smart-aleck Kill (from The Simple Art of Murder), 1958 (s); Pearls Are a Nuisance (from The Simple Art of Murder), 1958 (s); The Second Chandler Omnibus (The Simple Art of Murder, The Little Sister, The Long Goodbye, Playback), 1962 (n) (England); Raymond Chandler Speaking, 1962 (Letters and previously unpublished fiction)

## JOHN CHEEVER
### 1912–

The Way Some People Live, 1943 (s); The Enormous Radio, 1953 (s); The Wapshot Chronicle, 1957 (n); The Housebreaker of Shady Hill, 1958 (s); Some People, Places and Things That Will Not Appear in My Next Novel, 1961 (s); The Wapshot Scandal, 1964 (n); The Brigadier and the Golf Widow, 1964 (s)

## KATE CHOPIN
### 1851–1904

At Fault, 1890 (n); Bayou Folk, 1894 (s); A Night in Acadie, 1897 (s); The Awakening, 1899 (n)

## JOHN CIARDI
### 1916–

Homeward to America, 1940 (p); Other Skies, 1947 (p); Live Another Day, 1949 (p); From Time to Time, 1951 (p); The Inferno, 1954 (tr); As If, 1955 (p); I Marry You, 1958 (p); 39 Poems, 1959; How Does a Poem Mean? 1960 (c); The Purgatorio, 1961 (tr); In the Stoneworks, 1961 (p); In Fact, 1962 (p); Dialogue with an Audience, 1963 (j); Person to Person, 1964 (p); This Strangest Everything, 1966 (p); An Alphabestiary, 1967 (p)

## WALTER VAN TILBURG CLARK
### 1909–

*The Ox-Bow Incident*, 1940 (n); *The City of Trembling Leaves*, 1945 (n); *The Track of the Cat*, 1949 (n); *The Watchful Gods*, 1950 (s)

## RICHARD CONDON
### 1915–

*Men of Distinction*, 1953 (d); *The Oldest Confession*, 1958 (n); *The Manchurian Candidate*, 1959 (n); *Some Angry Angel*, 1960 (n); *A Talent for Loving*, 1961 (n); *An Infinity of Mirrors*, 1964 (n); *Any God Will Do*, 1966 (n); *The Two-Headed Reader* (*The Oldest Confession* and *The Manchurian Candidate*), 1966 (n); *The Ecstasy Business*, 1967 (n)

## MARC CONNELLY
### 1890–

(with George S. Kaufman) *Dulcy*, 1921 (d); (with George S. Kaufman) *To the Ladies*, 1923 (d); (with George S. Kaufman) *The Deep Tangled Wildwood*, 1923 (d); (with George S. Kaufman) *Beggar on Horseback*, 1924 (d); (with George S. Kaufman) *Merton of the Movies*, 1925 (d); *The Wisdom Tooth*, 1927 (d); (with Herman J. Mankiewicz) *The Wild Man of Borneo*, 1927 (d); *The Green Pastures*, 1930 (d); (with Frank B. Elser) *The Farmer Takes a Wife*, 1934 (d); (with Arnold Sundgaard) *Everywhere I Roam*, 1938 (d); *The Traveler*, 1939 (d); *The Flowers of Virtue*, 1942 (d); *Story for Strangers*, 1948 (d); *Hunter's Moon*, 1958 (d); *A Souvenir from Qam*, 1965 (n); *Voices Offstage*, 1968 (m)

## MALCOLM COWLEY
### 1898–

(with others) *Eight More Harvard Poets*, 1923 (p); *Racine*, 1923 (c); *On Board the Morning Star* (by Pierre Mac Orlan), 1924 (tr); *Joan of Arc* (by Joseph Delteil), 1926 (tr); *Variety* (by Paul Valéry), 1927 (tr); *Catherine-Paris* (by Marthe Bibesco), 1928 (tr); *Blue Juniata*, 1929 (p); *The Count's Ball* (by Raymond Radiguet), 1929 (tr); *The Green Parrot* (by Marthe Bibesco), 1929 (tr); *The Sacred Hill* (by Maurice Barrés), 1929 (tr); *Exile's Return*, 1934 (r); (with Bernard Smith and others) *Books That Changed Our Minds*, 1939 (e); *The Dry Season*, 1941 (p); *Imaginary Interviews* (by Andre Gide), 1942 (tr); (editor) *The Portable Hemingway*, 1944; (editor) *The Portable Faulk-*

*ner*, 1946; *Exile's Return* (revised edition), 1951 (r); *The Literary Situation*, 1954 (c); (with Daniel Pratt Mannix) *Black Cargoes: A History of the Atlantic Slave Trade*, 1962 (h); *Letters and Memories* (of William Faulkner), 1966 (r); *Think Back on Us*, 1967 (h); *Blue Juniata* (enlarged edition), 1968 (p)

## JAMES GOULD COZZENS
1903–

*Confusion*, 1924 (n); *Michael Scarlett*, 1925 (n); *Cockpit*, 1928 (n); *The Son of Perdition*, 1929 (n); *S. S. San Pedro*, 1931 (n); *The Last Adam*, 1933 (n) (English edition, *A Cure of Flesh*, 1933); *Castaway*, 1934 (n); *Men and Brethren*, 1936 (n); *Ask Me Tomorrow*, 1940 (n); *The Just and the Unjust*, 1942 (n); *Guard of Honor*, 1948 (n); *By Love Possessed*, 1957 (n); *Children and Others*, 1964 (s); *Morning, Noon and Night*, 1968 (n)

## HART CRANE
1899–1932

*White Buildings*, 1926 (p); *The Bridge*, 1930 (p); *Collected Poems*, 1933; *Letters*, 1952; *Complete Poems and Selected Letters and Prose*, 1966

## STEPHEN CRANE
1871–1900

*Maggie: A Girl of the Streets*, 1893 (n); *The Black Riders*, 1895 (p); *The Red Badge of Courage*, 1895 (n); *George's Mother*, 1896 (n); *The Little Regiment and Other Episodes of the American Civil War*, 1896 (s); *The Third Violet*, 1897 (n); *The Open Boat and Other Tales of Adventure*, 1898 (s); *War Is Kind*, 1899 (p); *Active Service*, 1899 (n); *The Monster and Other Stories*, 1899 (enlarged edition, 1901); *Whilomville Stories*, 1900; *Wounds in the Rain*, 1900 (s); *Great Battles of the World*, 1901 (h); (with Robert Barr) *The O'Ruddy: A Romance*, 1903 (n); *The Work of Stephen Crane*, 1925–27; *The Collected Poems*, 1930; *The Blood of the Martyr*, 1940 (d); *The Sullivan County Sketches*, 1949 (s); *Stephen Crane: An Omnibus*, 1952; *Letters*, 1960; *Complete Short Stories and Sketches*, 1963; *The War Dispatches of Stephen Crane*, 1964 (j); *The New York City Sketches*, 1966; *The Poems of Stephen Crane: A Critical Edition*, 1968

## ROBERT CREELEY
1926–

*Le Fou*, 1952 (p); *The Immoral Proposition*, 1953 (p); *The Kind of Act*, 1953 (p); *The Gold Diggers*, 1954 (s); *All That Is Lovely in Men*,

1955 (p); *If You,* 1956 (p); *The Whip,* 1957 (p); *A Form of Women,* 1959 (p); *For Love: Poems, 1950–1960,* 1962; *The Island,* 1963 (n); *The Gold Diggers* (revised edition), 1965 (s); *Poems: 1950–1965,* 1966; *Words,* 1967 (p)

## COUNTEE CULLEN
### 1903–1946

*Color,* 1925 (p); *The Ballad of the Brown Girl,* 1927 (p); *Copper Sun,* 1927 (p); *The Black Christ,* 1929 (p); *One Way to Heaven,* 1932 (n); *The Medea,* 1935 (p); *The Lost Zoo,* 1940 (s, p); *My Lives and How I Lost Them,* 1942 (s); *St. Louis Woman,* 1946 (d); *On These I Stand* (selected poems), 1947

## E. E. CUMMINGS
### 1894–1962

*The Enormous Room,* 1922 (n, m); *Tulips and Chimneys,* 1923 (p); *& (And),* 1925 (p); *XLI Poems,* 1925 (p); *Is 5,* 1926 (p); *Him,* 1927 (d); *VV (ViVa),* 1931 (p); *Eimi,* 1933 (t); *No Thanks,* 1935 (p); *Collected Poems,* 1938; *1 x 1,* 1944 (p); *Anthropos: The Future of Art,* 1944 (e); *Santa Claus,* 1946 (d); *XAIPE,* 1950 (p); *i: Six Nonlectures,* 1953 (a); *Poems 1923–1954,* 1954; *E. E. Cummings: A Miscellany,* 1958 (revised edition, 1965); *95 Poems,* 1958; *73 Poems,* 1963

## EDWARD DAHLBERG
### 1900–

*Bottom Dogs,* 1930 (n); *From Flushing to Calvary,* 1932 (n); *Those Who Perish,* 1934 (n); *Do These Bones Live,* 1941 (e) (republished in 1960 as *Can These Bones Live*); *Sing, O Barren,* 1947 (e); *The Flea of Sodom,* 1950 (e); *The Sorrows of Priapus,* 1957 (e); (with Herbert Read) *Truth Is More Sacred,* 1961 (c); *Because I Was Flesh,* 1964 (a); *Alms for Oblivion,* 1964 (e); *Reasons of the Heart,* 1965 (maxims); *The Leafless American,* 1967 (e); *Epitaphs of Our Times,* 1967 (letters); *The Edward Dahlberg Reader,* 1967; *The Carnal Myth,* 1968 (e)

## FLOYD DELL
### 1887–

*Moon-Calf,* 1920 (n); *The Briary-Bush,* 1921 (n); *King Arthur's Socks and Other Village Plays,* 1922 (d); *Janet March,* 1923 (n); *Looking at Life,* 1924 (e); *This Mad Ideal,* 1925 (n); *Runaway,* 1925 (n); *Intellectual Vagabondage,* 1926 (e); *Love in Greenwich Village,* 1926 (s, p);

*An Old Man's Folly*, 1926 (n); *An Unmarried Father*, 1927 (n); *Souvenir*, 1929 (n); *Love in the Machine Age*, 1930 (e); *Love Without Money*, 1931 (n); *Homecoming*, 1933 (a)

## BERNARD DeVOTO
### 1897–1955

*The Crooked Mile*, 1924 (n); (with others) *The Taming of the Frontier*, 1925 (e); *The Chariot of Fire*, 1926 (n); (with W. F. Bryan and Arthur H. Nethercot) *The Writer's Handbook*, 1927; *The House of Sun-Goes-Down*, 1928 (n); *Mark Twain's America*, 1932 (c); *We Accept with Pleasure*, 1934 (n); *Forays and Rebuttals*, 1936 (e); (with others) *Approaches to American Social History*, 1937 (h); *Troubled Star* [pseud. John August], 1939 (n); *Minority Report*, 1940 (e); *Essays on Mark Twain*, 1940 (c); (editor) *Mark Twain in Eruption*, 1940; *Advance Agent* [pseud. John August], 1941 (n); *Mark Twain at Work*, 1942 (c); *Rain Before Seven* [pseud. John August], 1942 (n); *The Year of Decision: 1846*, 1943 (h); *The Literary Fallacy*, 1944 (c); *The Woman in the Picture* [pseud. John August], 1944 (n); *Across the Wide Missouri*, 1947 (h); *Mountain Time*, 1947 (n); *The World of Fiction*, 1950 (c); *The Hour*, 1951 (e); *The Course of Empire*, 1952 (h); *The Easy Chair*, 1955 (e); *Women and Children First* [pseud. Cady Hewes], 1956 (e)

## PETER De VRIES
### 1910–

*The Handsome Heart*, 1943 (n); *No, But I Saw the Movie*, 1953 (s); *The Tunnel of Love*, 1954 (n); *Comfort Me with Apples*, 1956 (n); *The Mackerel Plaza*, 1958 (n); *The Tents of Wickedness*, 1959 (n); *Through the Fields of Clover*, 1961 (n); *The Blood of the Lamb*, 1962 (n); *Reuben, Reuben*, 1964 (n); *Let Me Count the Ways*, 1965 (n); *The Vale of Laughter*, 1967 (n); *The Cat's Pajamas* and *Witch's Milk*, 1968 (n)

## JAMES DICKEY
### 1923–

*Into the Stone*, 1957 (p); *Drowning with Others*, 1962 (p); *Interpreter's House*, 1963 (p); *Helmets*, 1964 (p); *The Suspect in Poetry*, 1964 (c); *Buckdancer's Choice*, 1965 (p); *Poems 1957–1967*, 1967; *Babel to Byzantium*, 1968 (c)

## EMILY DICKINSON
### 1830–1886

*Poems*, 1890; *Poems, Second Series*, 1891; *Letters*, 1894; *Poems, Third Series*, 1896; *The Single Hound*, 1914 (p); *Complete Poems*, 1924;

*Further Poems*, 1929; *Letters*, 1931; *The Poems of Emily Dickinson*, 1937; *Bolts of Melody*, 1945 (p); *Emily Dickinson's Letters to Dr. and Mrs. Josiah Gilbert Holland*, 1951; *Emily Dickinson: A Revelation*, 1954 (letters); *The Poems of Emily Dickinson, Including Variant Readings Critically Compared with All Known Manuscripts*, 1955; *Emily Dickinson's Home: Letters of Edward Dickinson and His Family*, 1955; *The Letters of Emily Dickinson*, 1958; *The Complete Poems* (based on Variant Edition), 1960; *Final Harvest* (selected poems, based on Variant Edition), 1961; *The Lyman Letters: New Light on Emily Dickinson and Her Family*, 1965

## J. P. DONLEAVY
### 1926–

*The Ginger Man*, 1958 (n); *The Ginger Man*, 1961 (d); *A Singular Man*, 1963 (n); *Meet My Maker the Mad Molecule*, 1964 (s); *The Saddest Summer of Samuel S.*, 1966 (n); *The Beastly Beatitudes of Balthazar B.*, 1968 (n)

## HILDA DOOLITTLE
### 1886–1961

*Sea Garden*, 1916 (p); *Choruses from* Iphigeneia in Aulis, 1916 (tr); *The Tribute and Circe*, 1917 (p); *Choruses from* Iphigeneia in Aulis *and* Hippolytus, 1919 (tr); *Hymen*, 1921 (p); *Heliodora*, 1924 (p); *Collected Poems*, 1925; *Palimpsest*, 1926 (s); *Hippolytus Temporizes*, 1927 (pd); *Hedylus*, 1928 (s); *Red Roses for Bronze*, 1931 (p); *The Hedgehog*, 1936 (s); *Ion*, 1937 (tr); *The Walls Do Not Fall*, 1944 (p); *Tribute to the Angels*, 1945 (p); *The Flowering of the Rod*, 1946 (p); *By Avon River*, 1949 (p); *Tribute to Freud*, 1956 (e); *Selected Poems*, 1957; *Bid Me To Live*, 1960 (n); *Helen in Egypt*, 1961 (p)

## JOHN DOS PASSOS
### 1896–

*One Man's Initiation: 1917*, 1920 (n) (republished as *First Encounter*, 1945); *Three Soldiers*, 1921 (n); *Rosinante to the Road Again*, 1922 (n); *A Pushcart at the Curb*, 1922 (n); *Streets of Night*, 1923 (n); *Manhattan Transfer*, 1925 (n); *The Garbage Man*, 1926 (d); *Orient Express*, 1927 (n); *Airways, Inc.*, 1928 (d); *42nd Parallel*, 1930 (n); *1919*, 1932 (n); *In All Countries*, 1934 (j); *Three Plays* (*The Garbage Man, Airways, Inc., Fortune Heights*), 1934; *The Big Money*, 1936 (n); *U.S.A.* (*42nd Parallel, 1919, The Big Money*), 1937: *The Villages Are the Heart of Spain*, 1937 (t); *Journeys Between Wars*, 1938 (t); *Adventures of a Young Man,* 1939 (n); *The Ground We Stand On,* 1941 (h); *Number One,* 1943 (n); *State of the Nation,* 1944 (j); *Tour of Duty,* 1946 (j); *The Grand Design,* 1949 (n); *The Prospect Before Us,* 1950 (e); *Chosen Country,* 1951 (n); *District of Columbia (Adventures of a Young Man, Number One, The Grand Design),* 1952 (n); *The Head and Heart of Thomas Jefferson,* 1954 (b); *Most Likely to Succeed,* 1954 (n); *The Theme Is Freedom,* 1956 (e); *The Men Who Made the Nation,* 1957 (h); (with others) *Essays on Individuality,* 1958 (e); *The Great Days,* 1958 (n); *Prospects of a Golden Age,* 1959 (h); *Midcentury,* 1961 (n); *Mr. Wilson's War,* 1962 (h); *Brazil on the Move,* 1963 (t); *Occasions and Protests,* 1964 (e); *The Shackles of Power,* 1966 (h); *The Best Times,* 1966 (a); *World in a Glass: A View of Our Century Selected from the Novels of John Dos Passos,* 1966

## THEODORE DREISER
1871–1945

*Sister Carrie,* 1900 (n); *Jennie Gerhardt,* 1911 (n); *The Financier,* 1912 (n) (revised edition, 1927); *A Traveler at Forty,* 1913 (a); *The Titan,* 1914 (n); *The Genius,* 1915 (n); *A Hoosier Holiday,* 1916 (a); *Plays of the Natural and the Supernatural,* 1916; *Free, and Other Stories,* 1918; *The Hand of the Potter,* 1918 (d); *Twelve Men,* 1919 (b); *Hey, Rub-A-Dub-Dub!* 1920 (e); *A Book About Myself,* 1922 (a); *The Color of a Great City,* 1923 (t); *An American Tragedy,* 1925 (n); *Chains,* 1927 (s); *Moods,* 1928 (p) (revised edition, 1935); *Dreiser Looks at Russia,* 1928 (e); *A Gallery of Women,* 1929 (b); *My City,* 1929 (t); *The Aspirant,* 1929 (p); *Epitaph,* 1929 (p); *Fine Furniture,* 1930 (s); *Dawn,* 1931 (a); *Tragic America,* 1931 (e); *America Is Worth Saving,* 1941 (e); *The Bulwark,* 1946 (n); *The Stoic,* 1947 (n); *The Best Short Stories* (ed. Howard Fast), 1947; *The Best Short Stories* (ed. James T. Farrell), 1956; *Letters,* 1959

## ALAN DUGAN
1923–

*Poems,* 1961; *Poems 2,* 1963; *Poems 3,* 1967

## ROBERT DUNCAN
1919–

*Heavenly City, Heavenly Earth,* 1945 (p); *Medieval Scenes,* 1947 (p); *Poems 1948–49,* 1950 (p); *Song of the Borderguard,* 1951 (p); *The Artist's View,* 1952; *Medea at Kolchis,* 1956 (pd); *Caesar's Gate,* 1956 (p); *Letters,* 1958 (p); *Selected Poems (1942–1950),* 1959; *The Opening of the Field,* 1960 (p); *Roots and Branches,* 1964 (p); *Writing Writ-*

*ing*, 1964 (p, e); *As Testimony: The Poem and The Scene*, 1964 (e); *Wine*, 1964 (e); *The Years as Catches: First Poems (1939–1946)*, 1966; *The Sweetness and Greatness of Dante's Divine Comedy*, 1968 (c); *Bending the Bow*, 1968 (p); *Of the War: Passages 22–27*, 1968 (p); *Medea at Kolchis, The Maiden Head*, 1968 (pd); *Names of People*, 1968 (p); *The Truth & Life of Myth in Poetry*, 1968 (e)

## RICHARD EBERHART
### 1904–

*A Bravery of Earth*, 1930 (p); *Reading the Spirit*, 1937 (p); *Song and Idea*, 1942 (p); *Poems, New and Selected*, 1944; *Burr Oaks*, 1947 (p); *Selected Poems*, 1951; *Undercliff: Poems 1946–1953*, 1953; *Great Praises*, 1957 (p); *Collected Poems, 1930–1960*, 1961; *Collected Verse Plays*, 1962; *The Quarry*, 1964 (p); *Selected Poems, 1930–1965*, 1966; *Thirty-One Sonnets*, 1967 (p); *Shifts of Being*, 1968 (p)

## WALTER EDMONDS
### 1903–

*Rome Haul*, 1929 (n); *The Big Barn*, 1930 (n); *Erie Water*, 1933 (n); *Mostly Canallers*, 1934 (s); *Drums Along the Mohawk*, 1936 (n); *Chad Hanna*, 1940 (n); *The Matchlock Gun*, 1941 (juvenile); *Young Ames*, 1942 (n); *Tom Whipple*, 1942 (juvenile); *Two Logs Crossing*, 1943 (juvenile); *Wilderness Clearing*, 1944 (n); *In the Hands of the Senecas*, 1947 (n); *The Wedding Journey*, 1947 (n); *The First Hundred Years*, 1948 (h); *They Fought With What They Had*, 1951 (h); *The Boyds of Black River*, 1953 (n); *Hound Dog Moses and the Promised Land*, 1954 (juvenile); *Uncle Ben's Whale*, 1955 (juvenile); *Three Stalwarts (Drums Along the Mohawk, Rome Haul and Erie Water)*, 1961 (n); *They Had a Horse*, 1962 (juvenile); *The Musket and the Cross*, 1968 (h)

## T. S. ELIOT
### 1888–1965

*Prufrock and Other Observations*, 1917 (p); *Ezra Pound, His Metric and Poetry*, 1917 (c); *Poems*, 1919; *Ara Vos Prec*, 1920 (p); *The Sacred Wood*, 1920 (e); *The Waste Land*, 1922 (p); *Homage to John Dryden*, 1924 (e); *Poems, 1909–1925*, 1925; *Journey of the Magi*, 1927 (p); *Shakespeare and the Stoicism of Seneca*, 1927 (e); *A Song for Simeon*, 1928 (p); *For Lancelot Andrewes*, 1928 (e); *Animula*, 1929 (p); *Dante*, 1929 (e); *Ash-Wednesday*, 1930 (p); *Anabasis*, 1930 (tr) (revised edition, 1949); *Marina*, 1931 (p); *Thoughts After Lambeth*, 1931 (e); *Charles Whibley: A Memoir*, 1931; *Triumphal March*, 1931 (p);

*Sweeney Agonistes*, 1932 (pd); *Selected Essays, 1917–1932*, 1932; *John Dryden*, 1932 (e); *The Use of Poetry and the Use of Criticism*, 1933 (e); *The Rock*, 1934 (pd); *After Strange Gods*, 1934 (e); *Elizabethan Essays*, 1934 (e); *Words for Music*, 1935 (p); *Two Poems*, 1935; *Murder in the Cathedral*, 1935 (pd); *Collected Poems, 1909–1935*, 1936; *Essays Ancient and Modern*, 1936; *Old Possum's Book of Practical Cats*, 1939 (p); *The Family Reunion*, 1939 (pd); *The Idea of a Christian Society*, 1939 (e); *East Coker*, 1940 (p); *Burnt Norton*, 1941 (p); *The Dry Salvages*, 1941 (p); *Points of View*, 1941 (e); *The Music of Poetry*, 1942 (e); *The Classics and the Man of Letters*, 1942 (e); *Little Gidding*, 1942 (p); *Reunion by Destruction*, 1943 (e); *Four Quartets*, 1943 (p); *What Is a Classic*, 1945 (e); *On Poetry*, 1947 (e); *Milton*, 1947 (e); *A Sermon*, 1948; *Notes Towards the Definition of Culture*, 1948 (e); *From Poe to Valéry*, 1948 (c); *The Cocktail Party*, 1949 (pd); *The Undergraduate Poems*, 1949; *The Aims of Poetic Drama*, 1949 (e); *Selected Essays* (new edition), 1950; *Poems Written in Early Youth*, 1950; *Poetry and Drama*, 1951 (e); *The Confidential Clerk*, 1954 (pd); *On Poetry and Poets*, 1957 (e); *The Elder Statesman*, 1959 (pd); *Collected Plays*, 1962; *Collected Poems, 1909–1962*, 1963; *Knowledge and Experience in the Philosophy of F. H. Bradley*, 1964 (e); *To Criticize the Critic*, 1965 (e)

## GEORGE P. ELLIOTT
### 1918–

*Parktilden Village*, 1958 (n); *Among the Dangs*, 1961 (s); *Fever and Chills*, 1961 (p); *David Knudsen*, 1962 (n); *Fourteen Poems*, 1964; *A Piece of Lettuce*, 1964 (e); *In the World*, 1965 (n); *An Hour of Last Things*, 1968 (s)

## RALPH ELLISON
### 1914–

*Invisible Man*, 1952 (n); *Shadow and Act*, 1964 (e)

## JAMES T. FARRELL
### 1907–

*Young Lonigan*, 1932 (n); *Gas-House McGinty*, 1933 (n); *The Young Manhood of Studs Lonigan*, 1934 (n); *Calico Shoes*, 1934 (s); *Judgment Day*, 1935 (n); *Studs Lonigan* (*Young Lonigan, The Young Manhood of Studs Lonigan, Judgment Day*), 1935 (n); *Guillotine Party*, 1935 (s); *A World I Never Made*, 1936 (n); *Can All This Grandeur Perish?* 1937 (s); *The Short Stories of James T. Farrell*, 1937; *No Star Is Lost*, 1938 (n); *Tommy Gallagher's Crusade*, 1939 (n); *Father and*

*Son,* 1940 (n); *Ellen Rogers,* 1941 (n); *$1000 a Week,* 1942 (s); *My Days of Anger,* 1943 (n); *Fifteen Selected Short Stories,* 1943; *To Whom It May Concern,* 1944 (s); *The League of Frightened Philistines,* 1945 (c); *Bernard Clare,* 1946 (n) (republished as *Bernard Carr*); *When Boyhood Dreams Come True,* 1946 (s); *Literature and Morality,* 1947 (c); *The Life Adventurous,* 1947 (s); *The Road Between,* 1949 (n); *An American Dream Girl,* 1950 (s); *This Man and This Woman,* 1951 (n); *Yet Other Waters,* 1952 (n); *The Face of Time,* 1953 (n); *Reflections at Fifty,* 1954 (e); *French Girls Are Vicious,* 1955 (s); *An Omnibus of Short Stories,* 1956; *My Baseball Diary,* 1957 (e); *A Dangerous Woman,* 1957 (s); *Saturday Night,* 1958 (s); *It Has Come To Pass,* 1958 (t); *Short Stories* (collected), 1961; *The Silence of History,* 1963 (n); *What Time Collects,* 1964 (n); *Selected Essays,* 1964; *Collected Poems,* 1965; *Lonely for the Future,* 1966 (n); *When Time Was Born,* 1966 (p); *A Brand New Life,* 1968 (n)

## HOWARD FAST
### 1914–

*Two Valleys,* 1933 (n); *Strange Yesterday,* 1934 (n); *Place in the City,* 1937 (n); *Conceived in Liberty,* 1939 (n); *The Last Frontier,* 1941 (n); *Haym Solomon,* 1941 (juvenile); *The Unvanquished,* 1942 (n); *Goethals and the Panama Canal,* 1942 (juvenile); *Citizen Tom Paine,* 1943 (n); *Freedom Road,* 1944 (n); *Patrick Henry and the Frigate's Keel,* 1945 (s); *The American,* 1946 (n); *Clarkton,* 1947 (n); *The Children,* 1947 (n); *My Glorious Brothers,* 1948 (n); *Departure,* 1949 (s); *The Proud and the Free,* 1950 (n); *Literature and Reality,* 1950 (c); *Spartacus,* 1951 (n); *Peekskill, USA,* 1951 (j); *The Passion of Sacco and Vanzetti,* 1953 (n); *Silas Timberman,* 1954 (n); *The Last Supper,* 1955 (s); *The Story of Lola Gregg,* 1956 (n); *The Naked God,* 1957 (e); *Moses, Prince of Egypt,* 1958 (n); *The Winston Affair,* 1959 (n); *The Howard Fast Reader,* 1960 (n, s); *Sylvia* [E. V. Cunningham, pseud.], 1960 (n); *April Morning,* 1961 (n); *The Edge of Tomorrow,* 1961 (s); *Power,* 1962 (n); *Phyllis* [E. V. Cunningham, pseud.], 1962 (n); *Alice* [E. V. Cunningham, pseud.], 1963 (n); *Shirley* [E. V. Cunningham, pseud.], 1963 (n); *Agrippa's Daughter,* 1964 (n); *The Hill,* 1964 (screenplay); *Lydia* [E. V. Cunningham, pseud.], 1964 (n); *Penelope* [E. V. Cunningham, pseud.], 1965 (n); *Helen* [E. V. Cunningham, pseud.], 1966; *Torquemada,* 1966 (n); *Margie* [E. V. Cunningham, pseud.], 1966 (n); *Sally* [E. V. Cunningham, pseud.], 1967 (n); *The Hunter and the Trap,* 1967 (n); *The Jews,* 1968 (h)

## WILLIAM FAULKNER
### 1897–1962

*The Marble Faun,* 1924 (p); *Soldiers' Pay,* 1926 (n); *Mosquitos,* 1927 (n); *Sartoris,* 1929 (n); *The Sound and the Fury,* 1929 (n); *As I Lay*

*Dying*, 1930 (n); *Sanctuary*, 1931 (n); *These Thirteen*, 1931 (s); *Salmagundi*, 1932 (e, p); *Light in August*, 1932 (n); *A Green Bough*, 1933 (p); *Doctor Martino and Other Stories*, 1934; *Pylon*, 1935 (n); *Absalom, Absalom!* 1936 (n); *The Unvanquished*, 1938 (n); *The Wild Palms*, 1939 (n); *The Hamlet*, 1940 (n); *Go Down, Moses and Other Stories*, 1942 (s, also *The Bear*, n); *The Portable Faulkner*, 1946; *Intruder in the Dust*, 1948 (n); *Knight's Gambit*, 1949 (n); *Collected Stories*, 1950; *Requiem for a Nun*, 1951 (n); *Requiem for a Nun*, 1951 (d); *A Fable*, 1954 (n); *The Faulkner Reader*, 1954; *Big Woods*, 1955 (s); *Faulkner at Nagano*, 1956 (interviews); *The Town*, 1957 (n); *New Orleans Sketches*, 1958 (sk); *The Mansion*, 1959 (n); *Faulkner in the University*, 1959 (interviews); *The Reivers*, 1962 (n); *Early Prose and Poetry*, 1962; *Essays, Speeches and Public Letters*, 1966; *Lion in the Garden*, 1968 (interviews)

## KENNETH FEARING
### 1902–1961

*Angel Arms*, 1929 (p); *Poems*, 1935; *Dead Reckoning*, 1938 (n); *The Hospital*, 1939 (n); *Collected Poems*, 1940; *The Dagger in the Mind*, 1941 (n); *Clark Gifford's Body*, 1942 (n); *Afternoon of a Pawnbroker*, 1943 (p); *The Big Clock*, 1946 (n); (as Donald F. Bedford, with D. Friede and H. Bedford-Jones) *John Barry*, 1947 (n); *Stranger at Coney Island*, 1948 (p); *The Loneliest Girl in the World*, 1951 (n); *The Generous Heart*, 1954 (n); *New and Selected Poems*, 1956; *The Crozart Story*, 1960 (n)

## EDNA FERBER
### 1887–1968

*Dawn O'Hara*, 1911 (n); *Buttered Side Down*, 1912 (s); *Roast Beef, Medium*, 1913 (s); *Personality Plus*, 1914 (s); *Emma McChesney and Co.*, 1915 (s); *Our Mrs. McChesney*, 1916 (d); *Fanny Herself*, 1917 (n); *Cheerful—By Request*, 1918 (s); (with Newman Levy) *$1200 a Year*, 1920 (d); *Half Portions*, 1920 (s); *The Girls*, 1921 (n); *Gigolo*, 1922 (s); (with George S. Kaufman) *Minick*, 1924 (d); *So Big*, 1924 (n); *Show Boat*, 1926 (n); *Mother Knows Best*, 1927 (s); (with George S. Kaufman) *The Royal Family*, 1928 (d); *Cimarron*, 1930 (n); *American Beauty*, 1931 (n); (with George S. Kaufman) *Dinner at Eight*, 1932 (d); *They Brought Their Women*, 1933 (n); *A Peculiar Treasure*, 1933 (a) (revised edition, 1960); *Come and Get It*, 1935 (n); (with George S. Kaufman) *Stage Door*, 1938 (d); *Nobody's in Town*, 1938 (n); (with George S. Kaufman) *The Land Is Bright*, 1941 (d); *Saratoga Trunk*, 1941 (n); *Great Son*, 1945 (n); *One Basket*, 1947 (collected stories); *Giant*, 1952 (n); *Ice Palace*, 1958 (n); *A Kind of Magic*, 1963 (a)

## LAWRENCE FERLINGHETTI
1919–

A Coney Island of the Mind, 1958 (p); Her, 1960 (n); One Thousand
Fearful Words for Fidel Castro, 1961 (p); Starting from San Francisco,
1961 (p); Unfair Arguments with Existence, 1963 (pd); Routines,
1965 (d)


## LESLIE FIEDLER
1917–

An End to Innocence, 1955 (e); Love and Death in the American Novel,
1960 (c) (revised edition, 1967); No! In Thunder, 1960 (e); Pull Down
Vanity, 1962 (s); The Second Stone, 1963 (n); Waiting for the End,
1964 (e); Back to China, 1965 (n); The Last Jew in America, 1966 (n);
The Return of the Vanishing American, 1968 (e)


## DOROTHY CANFIELD FISHER
1879–1958

Corneille and Racine in England, 1904 (c); Gunhild, 1907 (n); What
Shall We Do Now? 1907 (e); The Squirrel Cage, 1912 (n); A Montessori Mother, 1912 (e) (published as Montessori for Parents, 1940);
The Montessori Manual, 1913 (e); Mothers and Children, 1914 (e);
The Bent Twig, 1915 (n); Self-Reliance, 1916 (e); (with Sarah N. Cleghorn) Fellow Captains, 1916 (e); The Real Motive, 1916 (misc);
Understood Betsy, 1917 (n); Home Fires in France, 1918 (s); The Day
of Glory, 1919 (s); The Brimming Cup, 1921 (n); Raw Material, 1921
(s); The Life of Christ (by Giovanni Papini), 1921 (tr); Rough Hewn,
1922 (n); What Grandmother Did Not Know, 1922 (e); The French
School at Middlebury, 1923 (e); The Home-Maker, 1924 (n); Made-
to-Order Stories, 1925 (s); Her Son's Wife, 1926 (n); Why Stop Learning? 1927 (e); Learn or Perish, 1930 (e); The Deepening Stream, 1930
(n); Basque People, 1931 (s); Bonfire, 1933 (n); Tourists Accom-
modated, 1934 (sk); Fables for Parents, 1937 (s); Seasoned Timber,
1939 (n); Tell Me a Story, 1940 (juvenile); (with Sarah N. Cleghorn)
Nothing Ever Happens and How It Does, 1940 (s); The Knot Hole,
1943 (n); Our Young Folks, 1943 (e); American Portraits, 1946 (b);
Four-Square, 1949 (s); Something Old, Something New, 1949 (juvenile); A Fair World for All, 1952 (e); Vermont Tradition, 1953 (e); A
Harvest of Stories, 1956; Memories of Arlington, Vermont, 1957 (m);
And Long Remember, 1959 (m)

## VARDIS FISHER
1895–

*Sonnets to an Imaginary Madonna*, 1927 (p); *Toilers of the Hills*, 1928 (n); *Dark Bridwell*, 1931 (n); *In Tragic Life*, 1932 (n); *Passions Spin the Plot*, 1934 (n); *We Are Betrayed*, 1935 (n); *The Neurotic Nightingale*, 1935 (e); *No Villain Need Be*, 1936 (n); *In April*, 1937 (n); *Forgive Us Our Virtues*, 1938 (n); *Children of God*, 1939 (n); *City of Illusion*, 1941 (n); *The Mothers*, 1943 (n); *Darkness and the Deep*, 1943 (n); *The Golden Rooms*, 1944 (n); *The Caxton Printers in Idaho*, 1944 (h); *Intimations of Eve*, 1946 (n); *Adam and the Serpent*, 1947 (n); *The Divine Passion*, 1948 (n); *The Valley of Vision*, 1951 (n); *The Island of the Innocent*, 1952 (n); *God or Caesar?* 1953 (e); *A Goat for Azazel*, 1956 (n); *Jesus Came Again: A Parable*, 1956; *Pemmican*, 1956 (n); *Peace Like a River*, 1957 (n); *My Holy Satan*, 1958 (n); *Tale of Valor*, 1958 (n); *Love and Death*, 1959 (s); *Orphans in Gethsemane*, 1960 (n); *Suicide or Murder?* 1962 (h); *Thomas Wolfe as I Knew Him*, 1963 (m); *Mountain Man*, 1965 (n)

## CLYDE FITCH
1865–1909

*Beau Brummell*, 1890 (d); *Frédérick LeMaître*, 1890 (d); *Betty's Finish*, 1890 (d); *Pamela's Prodigy*, 1891 (d); *A Modern Match*, 1892 (d) (produced in London as *Marriage 1892*); *The Masked Ball*, 1892 (d, tr); *The Social Swim*, 1893 (d, tr); *The Harvest*, 1893 (d) (revised as *The Moth and the Flame*, 1898); *April Weather*, 1893 (d); *A Shattered Idol*, 1893 (d); *An American Duchess*, 1893 (d, tr); *His Grace de Grammont*, 1894 (d); (with Leo Ditrichstein) *Gossip*, 1895 (d, tr); *Mistress Betty*, 1895 (d) (produced in 1905 as *The Toast of the Town*); *Bohemia*, 1896 (d); *The Liar*, 1896 (d, tr); (with Leo Ditrichstein) *The Superfluous Husband*, 1897 (d, tr); *Nathan Hale*, 1899 (d); (with Leo Ditrichstein) *The Head of the Family*, 1899 (d, tr); *The Cowboy and the Lady*, 1899 (d); *Barbara Frietchie*, 1899 (d); *Sapho*, 1899 (d, tr); *Captain Jinks of the Horse Marines*, 1901 (d); *The Climbers*, 1901 (d); *Lovers' Lane*, 1901 (d); *The Last of the Dandies*, 1901 (d); *The Marriage Game*, 1901 (d); *The Way of the World*, 1901 (d); *The Girl and the Judge*, 1901 (d); *The Stubbornness of Geraldine*, 1902 (d); *The Girl with the Green Eyes*, 1902 (d); *The Bird in the Cage*, 1903 (d, tr); *The Frisky Mrs. Johnson*, 1903 (d); *Her Own Way*, 1903 (d); *Major André*, 1903 (d); *Glad of It*, 1903 (d); *The Coronet of a Duchess*, 1904 (d); *Granny*, 1904 (d, tr); *Cousin Billy*, 1905 (d, tr); *The Woman in the Case*, 1905 (d); *Her Great Match*, 1905 (d); (with Willis Steell) *Wolfville*, 1905 (d); *The Girl Who Has Everything*, 1906 (d); *Toddles*, 1906 (d, tr);

(with Edith Wharton) *The House of Mirth*, 1906 (d); *The Truth*, 1906 (d); *The Straight Road*, 1906 (d); (with Cosmo Gordon Lennox) *Her Sister*, 1907 (d); *The Honor of the Family*, 1908 (d, tr); *Girls*, 1908 (d, tr); *The Blue Mouse*, 1908 (d, tr); *A Happy Marriage*, 1909 (d); *The Bachelor*, 1909 (d); *The City*, 1909 (d); *Plays*, 1915

## DUDLEY FITTS
### 1903–1968

*Two Poems*, 1932 (p); (with Genevieve Taggard) *Ten Introductions*, 1935 (c); (with Robert Fitzgerald) *Alcestis*, 1935 (tr); *Poems, 1929–1936*, 1937; *One Hundred Poems from the Palatine Anthology*, 1938 (tr); (with Robert Fitzgerald) *Antigone*, 1939 (tr); *More Poems from the Palatine Anthology*, 1941 (tr); (with Robert Fitzgerald) *King Oedipus*, 1949 (tr); (with Robert Fitzgerald) *The Oedipus Cycle*, 1949 (tr); *Lysistrata*, 1954 (tr); *The Frogs*, 1955 (tr); *The Birds*, 1956 (tr); *Poems from the Greek Anthology*, 1956 (tr); *Thesmophoriazusae*, 1958 (tr); *Ladies' Day*, 1959 (tr); *Sixty Poems of Martial*, 1967 (tr)

## F. SCOTT FITZGERALD
### 1896–1940

*The Evil Eye*, 1915 (lyrics for Triangle Club show); *Safety First*, 1916 (lyrics for Triangle Club show); *This Side of Paradise*, 1920 (n); *Flappers and Philosophers*, 1920 (s); *The Beautiful and the Damned*, 1922 (n); *Tales of the Jazz Age*, 1922 (s); *The Vegetable*, 1923 (d); *The Great Gatsby*, 1925 (n); *All the Sad Young Men*, 1926 (s); *Tender Is the Night*, 1934 (n); *Taps at Reveille*, 1935 (s); *The Last Tycoon*, 1941 (n); *The Crack-Up*, 1945 (e, m); *The Stories of F. Scott Fitzgerald*, 1951; *Three Novels of F. Scott Fitzgerald (The Great Gatsby, Tender Is the Night* (revised version), *The Last Tycoon)*, 1951; *Afternoon of an Author*, 1958 (s, e); *The Pat Hobby Stories*, 1962; *The Fitzgerald Reader*, 1963; *Letters*, 1963; *The Apprentice Fiction of F. Scott Fitzgerald, 1909–1917*, 1965; *Letters to His Daughter*, 1965

## ROBERT FITZGERALD
### 1910–

*Poems*, 1935; (with Dudley Fitts) *Alcestis*, 1936 (tr); (with Dudley Fitts) *Antigone*, 1939 (tr); *Oedipus at Colonus*, 1941 (tr); *A Wreath for the Sea*, 1943 (p); (with Dudley Fitts) *Oedipus Rex*, 1949 (tr); *In the Rose of Time*, 1956 (p); *Chronique* (by St. John Perse), 1960 (tr); *The Odyssey*, 1961 (tr); *Birds* (by St. John Perse), 1966 (tr)

## JOHN GOULD FLETCHER
### 1886–1950

*The Book of Nature*, 1913 (p); *The Dominant City*, 1913 (p); *Fire and Wine*, 1913 (p); *Fool's Gold*, 1913 (p); *Visions of the Evening*, 1913 (p); *Irradiations, Sand and Spray*, 1915 (p); *Goblins and Pagodas*, 1916 (p); *Japanese Prints*, 1918 (p); *The Tree of Life*, 1918 (p); *Some Contemporary American Poets*, 1920 (c); *Breakers and Granite*, 1921 (p); *Paul Gauguin*, 1921 (b); *Preludes and Symphonies*, 1922 (p); *Parables*, 1925 (p); *Branches of Adam*, 1926 (p); *The Dance over Fire and Water* (by Elie Faure), 1926 (tr); *The Reveries of a Solitary* (by Jean Jacques Rousseau), 1927 (tr); *The Black Rock*, 1928 (p); *John Smith—Also Pocohantas*, 1928 (b); *The Crisis of the Film*, 1929 (e); (with others) *I'll Take My Stand*, 1930 (e); *The Two Frontiers*, 1930 (e) (English edition, *Europe's Two Frontiers*); *XXIV Elegies*, 1935 (p); *The Epic of Arkansas*, 1936 (p); *Life Is My Song*, 1937 (a); *Selected Poems*, 1938; *South Star*, 1941 (p); *Burning Mountain*, 1946 (p); *Arkansas*, 1947 (t)

## WALLACE FOWLIE
### 1908–

*Matines et Vers*, 1937 (p); *From Chartered Land*, 1938 (p); *Ernst Psichari*, 1939 (c); *Intervalles*, 1939 (p); *La Pureté dans l'art*, 1941 (c); *Clowns and Angels*, 1943 (c); *De Villon á Péguy*, 1944 (c); *Rimbaud*, 1946 (c) (revised edition, 1966); *Jacob's Night*, 1947 (c); *The Clown's Grail*, 1948 (c); *Sleep of the Pigeon*, 1948 (n); *Sixty Poems of Sceve*, 1949 (tr); *The Age of Surrealism*, 1950 (c); *Pantomime*, 1951 (a); *Mallarmé*, 1953 (c); *Rimbaud's Illuminations*, 1953 (c); *Mid-Century French Poets*, 1955 (tr); *The Journals of Jean Cocteau*, 1956 (tr); *Seamarks* (by St. John Perse), 1957 (tr); *Studies in Modern Literature and Thought*, 1957 (c); *A Poet Before the Cross* (by Paul Claudel), 1958 (tr); *French Stories*, 1960 (tr); *Dionysus in Paris*, 1960 (c); *Break of Noon* (by Paul Claudel), 1960 (tr); *Tidings Brought to Mary* (by Paul Claudel), 1960 (tr); *A Reading of Proust*, 1964 (c); *André Gide*, 1965 (b); *Love in Literature*, 1965 (c); *Jean Cocteau*, 1966 (c); *Climate of Violence*, 1967 (c); *Works of Rimbaud*, 1968 (tr)

## WALDO FRANK
### 1889–1967

*The Unwelcome Man*, 1917 (n); *The Art of the Vieux Colombier*, 1918 (c); *Our America*, 1919 (e); *The Dark Mother*, 1920 (n); *City Block*, 1922 (n); *Rahab*, 1922 (n); *Holiday*, 1923 (n); *Salvos*, 1924 (e); *Chalk Face*, 1924 (n); *Virgin Spain*, 1926 (t) (revised edition, 1942); *Time*

*Exposures* [pseud. Search-Light], 1926 (b); *The Rediscovery of America*, 1929 (e); *New Year's Eve*, 1929 (d); *America Hispana*, 1931 (t); *Dawn in Russia*, 1932 (t); *The Death and Birth of David Markand*, 1934 (n); *In the American Jungle*, 1937 (e); *The Bridegroom Cometh*, 1938 (n); *Chart for Rough Water*, 1940 (e); *Summer Never Ends*, 1941 (n); *South American Journey*, 1943 (t); *The Jew in Our Day*, 1944 (e); *Island in the Atlantic*, 1946 (n); *The Invaders*, 1948 (n); *Birth of a World*, 1951 (b); *Not Heaven*, 1953 (n); *Bridgehead*, 1957 (j); *The Rediscovery of Man*, 1958 (m, e); *Cuba, Prophetic Island*, 1962 (t)

## HAROLD FREDERIC
### 1856–1898

*Seth's Brother's Wife*, 1887 (n); *In the Valley*, 1890 (n); *The Lawton Girl*, 1890 (n); *The Return of the O'Mahoney*, 1892 (n); *The Copperhead*, 1893 (n); *Marsena and Other Stories of the Wartime*, 1894; *The Damnation of Theron Ware*, 1896 (n); *March Hares*, 1896 (n); *Gloria Mundi*, 1898 (n); *The Market Place*, 1899 (n)

## BRUCE JAY FRIEDMAN
### 1930–

*Stern*, 1962 (n); *Far from the City of Class*, 1963 (s); *A Mother's Kisses*, 1964 (n); *Black Angels*, 1966 (s); *Scuba Duba*, 1967 (d)

## ROBERT FROST
### 1874–1963

*A Boy's Will*, 1913 (p); *North of Boston*, 1914 (p); *Mountain Interval*, 1916 (p); *New Hampshire*, 1923 (p); *Selected Poems*, 1923 (revised editions, 1928, 1934); *West-Running Brook*, 1928 (p); *Collected Poems*, 1930; *A Further Range*, 1936 (p); *Selected Poems*, 1936 (English edition); *A Witness Tree*, 1942 (p); *A Masque of Reason*, 1945 (p); *The Poems of Robert Frost*, 1946; *Steeple Bush*, 1947 (p); *A Masque of Mercy*, 1947 (p); *Complete Poems*, 1949; *In the Clearing*, 1962 (p); *The Letters of Robert Frost to Louis Untermeyer*, 1963; *Robert Frost and John Bartlett: The Record of a Friendship*, 1963 (letters); *Selected Letters*, 1964; *Robert Frost Speaks*, 1964 (e); *Selected Prose*, 1966 (e); *Interviews with Robert Frost*, 1966

## DANIEL FUCHS
### 1909–

*Summer in Williamsburg*, 1934 (n); *Homage to Blenholt*, 1936 (n); *Low Company*, 1937 (n); *Three Novels*, 1961